THE OXFORD HANDBOOK OF

SPORTS ECONOMICS

VOLUME 1

THE OXFORD HANDBOOK OF

SPORTS ECONOMICS

VOLUME 1: THE ECONOMICS OF SPORTS

Edited by

LEO H. KAHANE

and

STEPHEN SHMANSKE

OXFORD

UNIVERSITY PRESS

OXFORD
UNIVERSITY PRESS

Oxford University Press, Inc., publishes works that further
Oxford University's objective of excellence
in research, scholarship, and education.

Oxford   New York
Auckland   Cape Town   Dar es Salaam   Hong Kong   Karachi
Kuala Lumpur   Madrid   Melbourne   Mexico City   Nairobi
New Delhi   Shanghai   Taipei   Toronto

With offices in
Argentina   Austria   Brazil   Chile   Czech Republic   France   Greece
Guatemala   Hungary   Italy   Japan   Poland   Portugal   Singapore
South Korea   Switzerland   Thailand   Turkey   Ukraine   Vietnam

Published by Oxford University Press, Inc.
198 Madison Avenue, New York, New York 10016
www.oup.com

Oxford is a registered trademark of Oxford University Press

Library of Congress Cataloging-in-Publication Data
The Oxford handbook of sports economics / edited by Leo H. Kahane and
Stephen Shmanske.
p. cm.
Includes bibliographical references and index.
ISBN 978-0-19-538777-3 (cloth : alk. paper)   1. Sports—Economic aspects.
I. Kahane, Leo H.   II. Shmanske, Stephen, 1954–
GV716.O94 2011
796.06′91—dc22
2010036086

1 3 5 7 9 8 6 4 2
Printed in the United States of America
on acid-free paper

CONTENTS
·····················

VOLUME 1: THE ECONOMICS OF SPORTS

PART I   ECONOMICS OF LEAGUES
AND CONTEST DESIGN

PART II   ECONOMICS OF MAJOR LEAGUE SPORTS

PART III   ECONOMICS OF OTHER SPORTS

PART IV   ECONOMICS OF COLLEGE SPORTS

PART V   ECONOMICS OF MEGA EVENTS

PART VI   ECONOMICS OF REFEREEING

Contributors

Andrew Abere, Princeton Economics Group, Inc.

Jason Abrevaya, Department of Economics, The University of Texas at Austin

Roger D. Blair, Department of Economics, University of Florida

Peter Bronsteen, Princeton Economics Group, Inc.

Dennis Coates, Department of Economics, University of Maryland, Baltimore County

Peter Dawson, Department of Economics, University of Bath

Craig A. Depken, II, Department of Economics, University of North Carolina, Charlotte

Christian Deutscher, Department of Organizational and Media Economics, University of Paderborn

Kenneth G. Elzinga, Robert C. Taylor Professor of Economics, University of Virginia

Aju J. Fenn, John L. Knight Chair of Free Enterprise, Department of Economics and Business, The Colorado College

Bernd Frick, Department of Organizational and Media Economics, University of Paderborn

Bill Gerrard, Leeds University Business School, Leeds University

Malcolm Getz, Department of Economics, Vanderbilt University

John Goddard, Professor of Financial Economics, Bangor University

Jessica S. Haynes, Department of Economics, University of Florida

Matthew Hood, Department of Finance, University of Southern Mississippi

Ira Horowitz, Information Systems and Operations Management, University of Florida and Information and Decision Systems, San Diego State University

Brad R. Humphreys, Department of Economics, University of Alberta

Stefan Kesenne, Department of Economics, University of Antwerp

Victor A. Matheson, Department of Economics, College of the Holy Cross

Evan Osborne, Department of Economics, Wright State University

Kevin G. Quinn, Department of Economics, St. Norbert College

Duane W. Rockerbie, Department of Economics, University of Lethbridge

John Siegfried, American Economic Association, Vanderbilt University, and University of Adelaide

Rob Simmons, Department of Economics, Lancaster University

Peter J. Sloane, School of Business and Economics, Swansea University

Paul D. Staudohar, Department of Management, California State University, East Bay

Stefan Szymanski, Professor of Economics and Director of Sports, Cass Business School, City University London

Robert D. Tollison, Department of Economics, Clemson University

John Vrooman, Department of Economics, Vanderbilt University

Nicholas M. Watanabe, Department of Recreation, Sport, and Tourism, University of Illinois

G. E. Whittenburg, School of Accountancy, San Diego State University

John O. S. Wilson, Professor of Banking and Finance, University of St. Andrews

Andrew Zimbalist, Robert A. Woods Professor of Economics, Smith College

Preface to Volume One: The Economics of Sports

This is the first volume of a two-volume effort to capture the essence and variety of the quickly growing field of sports economics. In arranging these volumes, we have divided the field into two thematically separate but often overlapping parts called The Economics of Sports (this volume), and Economics Through Sports (in the companion volume). Specifically, in thinking about the field it struck us that many lines of inquiry were essentially economic analyses of certain institutions in sports, like league structure, salary caps, the NCAA, and international labor mobility. Meanwhile, the abundant, high-quality data about salary, performance, competition between teams, and expected and actual outcomes of specific games allows economists to test a variety of propositions that have larger social consequences such as discrimination, antitrust, efficient markets, and managerial efficiency. Admittedly, the separation is not always complete and many of the chapters in these volumes hit on both themes. Nevertheless, the two-volume approach has helped us to organize our thoughts on sports economics and helped us organize the chapters we have received from nearly every important author in the field of sports economics.

Volume 1 is divided into six parts. Part I, the Economics of Leagues and Contest Design, is composed of four chapters that introduce many of the topics that made the economic analysis of sports so fascinating to begin with. In the opening chapter, Stefan Szymanski introduces the idea of the economic design of a sporting contest, explaining how the analysis works in individual sports and in two different styles of league organization, namely, the open, promotion-and-relegation leagues in European football and the closed leagues, as in the North American major leagues in various sports. This one difference in league structure carries myriad implications for a variety of institutions in sports. Szymanski's characteristically clear prose explains how these two organizational structures affect things as varied as: the number of teams; entry into and exit from the league; financial stability; competitive balance; effort expended to win; effort expended to avoid losing; revenue sharing; restrictive labor policies; and public finance of stadiums, thus setting the stage for the remainder of the volume. In the second chapter, Brad Humphries and Nicholas Watanabe take the reader through the important issue of competitive balance in the economics of leagues. They start with Simon Rottenberg's uncertainty of outcome hypothesis, which essentially posits that the value of a game is positively related to the closeness in the playing strengths of the teams involved, that is, competitive balance at the level of the individual game. This hypothesis gets extended to uncertainty with respect to winning the season, making the playoffs, or winning the championship in any one given season. Even further, the analysis gets extended to the frequency with which a team wins multiple championships over a series of seasons. These different forms of uncertainty or balance, can be measured in a variety of ways, each capturing different aspects of the problem. The competitive-balance issue is extremely important in the economics of sports because a variety of league behaviors can be alternatively explained as anticompetitive abuses of monopoly and monopsony power or as benign, total-surplus-enhancing behaviors on the part of leagues attempting to maintain competitive balance in order to provide value to their customers. In the third chapter of this section, Stefan Kesenne furthers the analysis of the competitive balance in a formal model that focuses attention on the nature of the market for talent (that is, free agency versus a reserve system) and the nature of the club owner's objective function (that is win maximization versus profit maximization). The analysis again goes back to a seminal notion from Simon Rottenberg that has become known as the invariance proposition. The invariance proposition is essentially a prestatement of what is later published by Ronald Coase and becomes known as the Coase theorem, namely, that the ownership of productive assets is not relevant to their ultimate allocation because whoever owns an asset has the incentive to employ it in the way that maximizes its value. Thus, competitive balance may be unaffected by a change from a reserve-clause system to a system of free agency. However, if there is a system of revenue sharing that taxes success, or if the owners are not attempting to maximize profit, then subtle differences may exist in the equilibrium distribution of talent. Intuitively, one should expect any differences to be subtle because winning is correlated to increased revenue and because even win maximizers must purchase talent in markets and operate subject to a budget constraint. It takes Kesenne's careful manipulation of a formal model to sort out the variety of effects. In the final chapter of this section, John Vrooman throws a new wrench into the analysis of club objectives, competitive balance, and the invariance proposition. Vrooman considers the differences between competition in the regular season and competition in the playoffs. He argues that there is a closer connection between talent and outcome during the regular season because of the sheer number of contests and more randomness and uncertainty in the playoffs because of the shorter series. Because the rules for making and advancing in the postseason differ between leagues, Vrooman is able to develop testable implications about the movement of players from team to team as they posture for the regular-season-ending race for playoff position. Additionally, there are implications concerning the correlation between regular season success and post season success that can be teased out by reference to the playoff format. All four chapters of this opening section are stellar examples of how economic logic and reasoning can be fruitful in analyzing and understanding institutions and outcomes in the world of sport.

Part II, entitled the Economics of Major League Sports, is divided into five sections covering the sports of baseball, American football, basketball, hockey, and soccer. Two chapters make up the first section, entitled Baseball. Roger Blair and Jessica Haynes present an historical and legal analysis of Major League Baseball's antitrust exemption. Noting that the individual franchises in a league must cooperate off the field on such matters as rules and schedules in order to organize the competition on the field, they suggest that leagues might be granted some latitude that seems to run afoul of a strict interpretation of Section 1 of the Sherman Act. However, baseball has more than just some latitude, it has a blanket exemption due to an anomalous 1922 Supreme Court interpretation that a baseball game is not "commerce among the several States." Blair and Haynes briefly present the theory and background of antitrust law. They go on to describe how the system allowed club owners to exploit players in the labor market. Finally, they show how more recent rulings with respect to bargaining between baseball clubs and the players' union have introduced constraints on the clubs that render the antitrust exemption largely irrelevant. The second chapter in this section, by Paul Staudohar, combines economics, history, and law in an analysis of the baseball players' labor market. He explains how the reserve clause in labor contracts worked to limit the negotiating power of the players, allowing the teams to offer low salaries. Staudohar's analysis goes back as far as 1876, almost 50 years before baseball's antitrust exemption, describing how different leagues and players associations grappled with the issue. Later, through much of the twentieth century, the reserve clause was protected by baseball's antitrust exemption. Staudohar explains how the breakthrough on free agency came about in the 1970s when Andy Messersmith and Dave McNally each played for a year without signing a new contract leading to an arbitrator's binding ruling that the reserve clause became null and void after a year. Staudohar's ability to weave historical facts with descriptions of the personalities involved makes for a delightfully informing analysis of the reserve clause, free agency and their effects on labor mobility.

In the second section of Part II, entitled Basketball, economic analysis is used to explore the institutions of salary caps and luxury taxes and to examine international labor mobility, especially in the context of professional basketball. Dennis Coates and Bernd Frick look at the constraints that leagues impose on teams for payrolls and individual compensation. These issues are peculiar to the sports industry and appear in no other industrial setting. The form that salary caps take is explained. Furthermore, the motivations behind them, from monopsonistic exploitation on the one hand to attempts to equalize the playing strengths of the various teams on the other are critically considered. Evan Osborne examines the issue of international labor mobility. The NBA has seen a burgeoning of talent coming from throughout the world, essentially as would be predicted by economic analysis of trade, arbitrage, and global competition.

Hockey is taken up in the two chapters that make up the third section of Part II. Duane Rockerbie examines violence, specifically fighting, which seems to be condoned in hockey more than in any other sport. Although penalties are assessed for fighting, the expulsions, fines, and suspensions that are typical in other sports are mostly absent in hockey. Rockerbie examines new evidence on the effects of violence on NHL attendance and considers the extent to which fighting is a jointly produced output having its own value over and above its effect on the game outcome. Jason Abrevaya examines rules changes that the NHL has recently employed regarding overtime games. At issue is how aggressively or conservatively the opponents play near the end of tied games and in overtime. Under older rules regimes, teams had incentives to play conservatively, which was not as exciting for fans. Abrevaya uses a probability model to show how team incentives change toward more aggressive play when the rules change, and statistically documents the extent to which hockey players and coaches, the economic actors involved, respond to incentives.

The fourth section of Part II covers American football in three chapters. Kevin Quinn uses economics in the sense of decision making under scarcity and uncertainty to examine several aspects of the game. He looks at field position and strategy and describes how it is possible to put a statistical value, say, in terms of expected points, on field position, on the choice of whether to run or pass, and on what to do on fourth down. Quinn describes previous research and presents results based on the 2007 NFL season. The economics of play calling on fourth down is particularly interesting and presents somewhat of an economic puzzle. According to the statistics, coaches seem to be too conservative with respect to "going for it" on fourth down. One possible explanation is that a coach may err on the side of making the conventional or expected call, even if it is suboptimal, rather than sticking his neck out by going for it on fourth down and possibly putting his job tenure in jeopardy. In the second chapter in this section Ira Horowitz and G. E. Whittenburg explore the links between television revenue growth, television revenue sharing, and competitive balance in professional football. They describe how professional football grew from obscurity (at first teams paid to televise games as a promotional tool) to become the most popular team sport in the United States. Along the way they detail the issues surrounding the television contracts including network competition, blackout rules, and revenue sharing. The authors explain how the teams and the league have an interest in producing competitive games and how the league has implemented rules such as reverse order drafts, salary caps, and revenue sharing that might yield the desired effect. Interestingly, the statistics show that, although competitive balance has increased through time, the independent effect of revenue sharing, while controlling for an upward trend in balance, appears to be in the opposite direction. The final chapter in this section is by Aju Fenn. Fenn reviews the existing historical and economic literature on American football. He explains the origins of football leagues and their evolution into the modern mature National Football League. Beyond this literature describing mergers, expansions, and team relocation, Fenn also characterizes other areas of economic analysis of football, including, competitive balance, race of players and coaches, betting on NFL games, and the cost-benefit analysis of having a local franchise. As is clearly shown by the three chapters in this section and by the numerous citations to related literature, economics is very useful in the analysis of the institutions of American football.

The last section of Part II includes two chapters covering soccer (football). John Goddard, Peter Sloan, and John Wilson examine the Bosman ruling that overturned the retain-and-transfer system (the European equivalent of the American reserve clause) and established free agency for professional soccer players in the European Union. The authors first provide an overview of the development of soccer labor markets and detail how the Bosman ruling provides for player mobility within Europe and relaxes some restrictions on importing talent from outside Europe. Then the authors review the predicted effects of the landmark 1995 ruling and use economic analysis to develop testable implications that they pursue with data from before and after 1995. Among the implications that are tested are: (1) that the ruling will hurt the finances of small market clubs, with effects on player development; (2) that the ruling will lead to higher and more unequal player salaries; (3) that the ruling will lead to longer-term contracts; and (4) that the ruling will harm competitive balance particularly in the top-paying English leagues. The authors get answers to some of their questions and develop new issues to be analyzed in future work. In the second chapter, Bill Gerrard uses a variety of economic models to examine the success of teams in the Football Association (FA) Premier League in England. He argues that the coaching efficiency literature is only part of the story and that the development and mixture of talent in multiple dimensions must also be considered. The chapter gives a nice overview of the managerial efficiency literature and the human capital formation literature. In addition, Gerrard provides a richly detailed account of player development that contrasts the North American system in which player development is mostly left to high schools and colleges to the English system of team-sponsored academies that target youths as young as five years old. The academy system could be the efficient method of developing and maintaining team-specific human capital that some evidence shows leads to a competitive advantage for the team. For all the sports covered in Part II, economic analysis has been fruitful in explaining and describing the industry and in pointing the way to new research questions. These two chapters prove that soccer is no exception.

Part III of Volume 1, the Economics of Other Sports, picks up the analysis of two other professional sports that are not typically analyzed as league competitions, although they could be, namely, golf and automobile racing. Matthew Hood surveys the literature on the labor-supply decision of professional golfers and is able to replicate with new data three important results. Using economic and statistical analysis of ten years of European tour data, Hood shows how the incentives of prize money, the costs of travel, and a golfer's placement in rank-order lists all interact to influence the golfer's labor-supply decision in ways that are not necessarily apparent to observers until viewed through the lens of economics. Once again, Hood's chapter illustrates the theme of this volume, namely, the economic analysis of sports. Andrew Abere, Peter Bronsteen, and Kenneth Elzinga apply their efforts to analyzing NASCAR. Analysis of motor sports is relatively new on the block, even though attendance surpasses or rivals that of other sports. This valuable chapter explains both the history of the sport and the business model of the vertical relationship between the contesting teams, the oversight body, and the racetracks themselves. Additionally, the uncertainty of outcome hypothesis has a counterpart in motor sports that contributes to its growing popularity. The rich discussion of institutional detail will certainly encourage others to continue to economically analyze this popular sport.

Part IV, the Economics of College Sports, consists of four chapters that apply economic analysis to the NCAA and to college athletic departments. Robert Tollison lays the groundwork by describing alternative views of the NCAA, namely, as a benign administrator of rules and promoter of amateurism versus as a cartel. Tollison goes on to explain why economic theory indicates that many of the behaviors and rules of the NCAA are more consistent with the cartel view. In a nutshell, the NCAA helps college athletic departments exercise monopsony power by eliminating the avenue of paying college athletes and helps them exercise monopoly power by jointly negotiating media contracts and setting up revenue sharing formulas. Tollison also offers additional testable implications with respect to the discovery and punishing of potential cheaters on cartel arrangements that limit the competition for talent. In the second chapter, Malcolm Getz and John Siegfried discuss the peculiarly American phenomenon of colleges and universities sponsoring organized athletic competitions against each other. They examine an array of potential pecuniary and nonpecuniary reasons that college athletic departments are as important as they are. The reasons include: direct effects on revenues from staging competitions; indirect effects on revenues from state legislatures and from alumni contributions; and indirect effects on student recruiting costs, on the size of the application pool, and on student quality. A variety of empirical evidence on each of these avenues is presented and discussed. In the third chapter, Craig A. Depken II examines the most prominent NCAA event, namely, the annual "March Madness" NCAA Division I men's college basketball tournament. There are direct monetary benefits to schools and conferences based on success in the tournament. In addition to these, Depken documents the indirect benefits that come from future attendance increases for regular-season games that can be traced to previous success in the tournament. Particular attention is paid to a possible distinction between colleges that are members of the most prestigious conferences and those that are members of minor conferences. In the final chapter of this part, Andrew Zimbalist takes the analysis in a different direction by examining women's sports and gender equity. With rich institutional and historical detail, Zimbalist covers Title IX and its implementation. He shows how women's sports participation has made enormous gains due to Title IX but still has a little way to go. Zimbalist argues that the resources necessary to further expand women's sports programs would be available if there were less waste and fewer inefficiencies in men's sports programs. For example, he argues, theoretically and empirically, that coaches salaries in men's sports are artificially bloated and suggests a policy change to rectify the situation.

Part V of Volume 1, the Economics of Mega Events, covers the economics of special, large events, in particular, the Olympics, the World Cup, and the Super Bowl. When discussing such mega events, interest naturally turns to the resulting economic impact of staging the events, and the authors in this section do not disappoint. Discussions of the shortcomings of the multiplier approach and documentation of the inflated *ex ante* projections of economic growth or economic returns are common to all three chapters in this section. But as testimony to the innovative cleverness of economists working in the sports economics field, each of the chapters develops a different, tangential, inquiry of their targeted mega event. In particular, Peter Dawson, in discussing the Olympics, distinguishes between the tangible economic benefits and intangible benefits, such as increased participation of citizens in sports activities of all types. He challenges future analysts to explore the mechanism between a host country's sponsorship of the Olympics and future active involvement in sports. Alternatively, Rob Simmons and Christian Deutscher examine international-labor-supply issues in the context of World Cup competition, noting that playing in the World Cup boosts salaries of the players in their regular clubs. Finally, Victor Matheson highlights a time series of comparative advertising revenue and ticket prices in secondary markets for the preeminent event in American sports, the NFL's Super Bowl.

Finally, Part VI of this volume, The Economics of Refereeing, examines a necessary part of any sporting competition, namely, the referee. Bernd Frick brings considerable institutional knowledge of the top tier German professional soccer league, the Bundesliga, along with expertise in labor economics to study the careers of German soccer referees. Among other results, statistical evidence from 1960 forward shows how the German institutions reward the better officials with more income over longer careers, a result in line with theory and with the interests of the league. Because soccer leagues in other countries have different contractual relationships with respect to remuneration, this study sets the stage for future research that can compare subtle differences in selection and incentive effects in the markets for referees. The economics of refereeing is a relatively new area of concentration in the economics of sports, one that is sure to grow by leaps and bounds in the coming years.

PART I

ECONOMICS OF LEAGUES AND CONTEST DESIGN

CHAPTER 1

ECONOMICS OF LEAGUE DESIGN

OPEN VERSUS CLOSED SYSTEMS

STEFAN SZYMANSKI

1. INTRODUCTION

THE notion of a competition is central to our understanding of sport.[1] The essence of a sporting contest is the struggle to win. Professional sports involve a complex combination of both sporting competition and economic competition. Professional team sports have created a specific organizational structure that is both highly successful and unique in the field of economic organization.

The first professional sports league was the National Association of Professional Base Ball Clubs, founded in 1871. Although this folded in 1875, its successor, the National League founded in 1876, not only survives to the present day but created the template for all North American sports leagues. The National League is made up of club franchises, each of which owns an equal share in the league so that collectively the franchises control it. The Football League created in England in 1888 was based, in the view of some contemporaries, on the American format, but it came to adopt one critical difference in its structure—the system of promotion and relegation. From early on the Football League expanded its numbers aggressively, starting with twelve teams but admitting a further seventy-six teams by 1923.[2] To make competition manageable, teams were organized into a hierarchy of divisions, and the principle of promotion and relegation was established, whereby the worst performing teams in each division are automatically demoted to the next league down the hierarchy at the end of the season, being replaced by the best performing teams from that division. From an economic perspective the key implication is that in a promotion-and-relegation league hierarchy, entry and exit from the division is ever present, so the league may be called *open*. In the American franchise league model, entry is only permitted to franchises willing to pay a sizable fee and with the full agreement of the league members. Entry is rare compared to open league systems, and hence we call this model *closed*.

This chapter explores the implications of the closed and open league systems for economic performance. There are many other aspects in the design of a league format that organizers need to consider. Some of these issues may be seen as purely sporting in character, but in general all rules have implications for the economic performance of the league. In section 2, the distinction between sporting competition and economic competition is considered in more detail, the objectives of league organizers are discussed, and the general implications of open versus closed leagues in professional sport is analyzed. In section 3 the economic theory of contests is introduced and the insights of the theory for promotion and relegation are drawn out. Section 4 discusses some of the practical implications of open and closed leagues, and section 5 concludes.

2. The Sports Contest

Most sports leagues are initiated by the clubs themselves, the league format having a number of advantages for the clubs as organizations. A league format introduces an extra dimension of competition above and beyond the one of friendly, and creates a sense of structure and purpose to a season. A league provides stability to its members and to the consumers by providing a guaranteed sequence of games, even if not all these games are necessarily that interesting (e.g., a clash between midtable teams at the end of the season). A knock-out format, such as the Football Association (FA) Cup in England or NCAA basketball's March Madness is, in many ways, a more compelling form of competition, because every team faces the threat of elimination in every game, but it is hard to organize a professional team around such a structure. To remain solvent, for instance, investment in player wages would have to be kept at a level that allowed for the possibility that the team could be eliminated in the first round of competition. In a league structure, by contrast, teams can plan for a season ahead. There is also something more solid in the triumph of a league champion, who has typically had to play a lot more games against a much wider range of opponents than in a knockout competition.

In professional team sports, the club generates an income from charging fans for entrance to the game, from merchandising and sponsorship, and from the sale of TV and new media broadcast rights. The success of league structures is such that most clubs around the world are able to generate much more income by playing in a league format than any other, because fans tend to be more attached to league competition.[3]

In thinking about the design of a league, we have to consider the objectives of the organizers. In the North American case, the professional leagues are controlled by their member clubs, which are in turn typically controlled by businessmen or commercial organizations, and economists have tended to assume that these owners seek to maximize their profits, although the concept of the sportsman owner, who is willing to forgo some profit in order to improve performance in the league competition is also sometimes mentioned. The owners organize the team, pay the players, and receive any surplus that accrues from the various income sources. Almost everywhere else in the world, leagues are organized within a structure of national federations, which regulate the leagues so that team owners have to comply with the national rules, although the large professional clubs tend to possess a considerable degree of influence. The profit maximizing assumption is seldom deemed appropriate. There are clubs that are owned in the same way as they are in the United States. In England, for example, in recent years, a number of American sports entrepreneurs have acquired teams in the English Premier League. However, in other cases clubs may be membership organizations in which a club president is elected by the fans (e.g., Barcelona and Real Madrid) or have limited liability status but with regulatory controls over their commercial action (e.g., in France). Economists studying the behavior of clubs in these leagues (mostly in a European context) have assumed that the clubs themselves are win maximizers (see chapter 3 in this volume by Stefan Kesenne).

From an economic perspective, the key element in this formulation is the notion of *sporting competition* as distinct from *economic competition*. Thus, the first peculiarity of sport is that a sporting competition can only be produced if there are at least two rivals. This makes professional sport unique among commercial activities; no other business enterprise depends on joint production with one of its rivals.[4] At one extreme, this point has led some to conclude that sporting rivals, even if organized as formally independent undertakings, in reality form a single economic entity for the purposes of producing a contest or championship (this single-entity doctrine is discussed in more detail later, along with alternative interpretations). At a minimum, it is necessary for some agreement, explicit or tacit, to exist among competitors, if nothing more than an agreement to be bound by the rules of the sporting competition.

The first peculiarity can be said to relate to all sporting competition, whether it entails a commercial dimension or not. A second peculiarity is specific to the commercial exploitation of sporting events. The so-called *uncertainty-of-outcome* hypothesis contends that interest of spectators in a sporting contest will tend to increase the more uncertain the outcome of that contest. Unfortunately this hypothesis is not terribly precise. At one extreme, it can be acknowledged that, if the outcome is known with certainty, the appeal of the contest is limited, a fact demonstrated by the large difference in payments by broadcasters for the right to broadcast live events (whose outcome is unknown) compared to the willingness to pay for delayed broadcast rights (if a broadcaster is interested at all) where the viewer might know the outcome before watching the event. At the other extreme, it is not obvious that a race between two athletes where each has a 50 percent chance of winning will attract a larger viewing audience than a race in which one athlete has a slightly better chance of winning than the other (say 55 percent against 45 percent). This is more than just a *ceteris paribus* problem. In some cases consumers may prefer to see an uneven contest in which an established champion is pitted against a less successful challenger (e.g., *David v. Goliath*) than an evenly matched contest.

If it is accepted that uncertainty of outcome at some level is desirable, then organizers of sporting competitions may have an economic incentive to establish rules and regulations intended to achieve a particular degree of uncertainty of outcome so as to maximize spectator interest. In particular, organizers may seek to create a degree of *competitive balance* among competitors in order to ensure that results fall within a desired range of uncertainty of outcome. To analyze this more fully it is necessary to consider the economic theory of contests.

3. Economic Models of a Sporting Contest

A sporting contest is a zero sum game in which rivals compete for a share of a fixed quantity of success. Success can be measured in terms of ranks (first, second, third, etc.), championship points won (depending on the scoring rule— e.g., 2 points for a win and 1 point for a draw/tie) or percentage of games won. Analogous to the production function, a *contest success function* can be defined as "that which relates the contributions of the contestants (e.g., effort, ability, investment in playing talent, etc.) to the outcome of the contest." At one extreme, the player/team with the highest contribution wins with probability one (with some randomizing device if contributions are exactly equal) and so the contest can be described as an all-pay auction.[5] More plausibly, increasing effort simply increases the probability of success, but the outcome is always to some extent uncertain. A convenient formulation of this problem is provided by the Tullock contest-success function, which equates the probability of winning with the share of total effort contributed to the contest.[6] The key parameter in this contest success function is the discriminatory power of the contest. When this is high, small differences in effort contributions lead to large differences in success probabilities, while low discriminatory power means that success probabilities are largely unaffected by variations in effort.

Every contest has a *contest organizer,* whose interest lies in the attractiveness of competition as a whole, and *contestants,* whose objectives are to win and to obtain the maximum possible return from their participation in the contest. In many cases, the contest organizer and contestants are clear—for example if we consider the organization of athletic races (e.g., the New York marathon), horse races (e.g., the Epsom Derby), or cycling (e.g., the Tour de France). In these cases, the organizer sets the rules of the contest, invites entrants, offers prizes, and seeks to generate income to cover costs and generate a surplus. However, if we consider sports leagues such as Major League Baseball in the United States or the English premier league (football), the teams themselves own and control the league (even if, in the latter case, they are subject to the rules of the national federation). By and large, the separation of contest organizer and contestants tends to be observed in individualistic sports, whereas the functions tend to be integrated in team sports. However, there is no necessity about this, and there are some cases in which the team sports have a contest organizer (for example, Formula One and NASCAR motor racing are both sports in which the competitors are teams but the race organization is controlled independently, whereas the board of the ATP, which organizes international tennis tournaments, includes representatives of the senior players).

If we consider the demand function of spectators/fans, then it seems reasonable to suppose that it is increasing in:

1. the quality/effort of the contestants (better players make more attractive contests) and
2. outcome uncertainty
3. the probability that their preferred player/team wins

Point 3 tends to be more important in team sports, where clubs tend to be identified with a particular location (generally a city) and fans tend to identify with their local team. Note that points 2 and 3 are, to some extent, in conflict with each other. However, because most leagues operate on a "home-and-away" basis, with teams alternating between games played at their home stadium and the stadium of a rival, a league championship can appear balanced if teams always win their home games.

a. Design of an Individualistic Contest

Given a contest-success function, an organizational structure, and a demand function, we can now consider how a contest organizer would run a contest (e.g., a foot-race). The organizer needs first to take account of the incentives of the contestants. It is possible that contestants are motivated simply by the desire to compete and to win and will, thus, always supply maximum feasible effort. The organizer still has the problem of determining who to admit to the contest. Given the demand for uncertainty of outcome, the organizer wants to select entrants based on the distribution of talent. Talent is likely to be distributed according to a log normal or pareto distribution, with small numbers of highly talented individuals at the top end of the distribution. As a result, the organizer faces a trade-off between the quality of the race and outcome uncertainty. By including the most talented contestants the organizer might create a very unbalanced contest, whereas a group of contestants from the middle of the distribution might not offer the highest quality but produce a balanced contest.

The organizer's problem is more complex when the contestants respond to incentives. In practice, most entrants in professional contests are paid a fixed fee for participating and a prize, depending on their success in the contest. Often the prize structure can be quite complex, offering not only a prize to the winner but also a range of prizes depending on rank, and also possibly a prize based on absolute performance (e.g., a world-record-breaking time). Contestants are expected to supply more effort when prizes are larger, and so the greater the share of their reward that comes in the form of a fixed fee, the lower the incentive to supply effort. However, contestants can also generate income from their success through endorsements and sponsorships paid for by advertisers, providing additional incentives for the contestants to be successful. At the same time as responding to prize incentives, it can also be assumed that contestants dislike supplying effort. Although many sport stars seem highly motivated to win at all times, regardless of the effort required, in practice athletes need to train consistently and often deny themselves the opportunity to participate in pleasurable activities, which may be considered part of their effort.

In the simplest case, in which the contestants have identical abilities and dislike supplying effort, it is straightforward to show that the organizer can maximize demand by offering a single prize to the winner and the lowest feasible fixed fee.[7] If abilities are heterogeneous, then matters are more complex. First, if there is competition among contest organizers, then it may be optimal to increase the size of the fixed fee and reduce the prize so as to attract higher ability entrants.[8] Second, if outcome uncertainty is highly desirable, then the organizer could prefer to exclude the highest-ability contestants so as to have a more balanced contest. Third, if abilities are widely distributed, multiple prizes (e.g., by rank) may elicit more effort in total, because lower ability contestants with little chance of winning the first prize will invest more effort if there are lesser prizes.[9]

A difficult choice for the organizer when abilities are heterogeneous is whether to maximize winning effort (e.g., breaking the world record) or total effort (so that all contestants try their hardest). This clearly depends on the nature of demand function. Heterogeneity also raises the issue of handicapping. Handicapping is common in horse racing (where presumably the horses themselves do not respond to financial incentives and always run as fast as the jockey can make them), because the organizers want evenly balanced contests so as to provide an attractive range of betting options (viewing for its own sake is far less important from a commercial standpoint). Handicapping is much less common in individual sports, presumably because individuals would respond negatively: what would be the incentive to train hard to win if you knew that this effort would then be canceled out by a handicap? There is also a danger that handicapping leads to strategic behavior, misrepresenting ability in smaller contests in order to obtain a more favorable handicap in bigger contests.[10]

b. Design of a Team-Sport Contest and the Competitive Balance Defense

As mentioned earlier, in a team-sport contest, each team is usually organized as a club located in a city with its own stadium and plays home and away against other teams in the league. Professional clubs undertake commercial activities in the form of hiring players in the labor market while selling tickets, merchandising, sponsorship, and broadcast rights to consumers. The club provides an identity with which fans can associate and forms the basis of long-term support, and to many supporters the club is more important than the individual players. Although there is considerable attraction for individual sports in the creation of a single contest (such as a race or tournament staged over a few days at most), maintaining the interest and support of local fans is better achieved by providing a regular sequence of games over time, generally in the form of a league championship. Although a knock-out championship format such as the FIFA World Cup is the most exciting, because the result is all or nothing, a league format offers an extra dimension to competition by creating a narrative throughout the playing season. However, the league format extends the joint-production interdependence of contestants beyond a single event to an entire season. The capacity of teams to complete the entire sequence of scheduled games is essential to the financial stability of a league. Each away game that a club plays can be seen as a form of gift exchange with rival teams, where the rivals then gift in return a visit to the club's stadium. Each club faces a financial risk that one team may be unable to fulfill its undertakings to play at its stadium. There is a systemic risk not dissimilar to systemic risk in banking, in which the failure of one threatens the failure of all.

From the point of view of contest design and incentives, prizes would seem just as appropriate a mechanism for rewarding effort as they are in individual contests, but, in practice, the use of explicit financial prizes is almost unknown in team sports. Instead, the reward for success in team sports is typically an increase in attendance at games, the ability to raise ticket prices, increased advertising and merchandising opportunities, and increased value of broadcasting rights.

In team sports the significance of the uncertainty of outcome hypothesis is as great, if not greater, when it comes to league competition than it is in relation to an individual game. As stated earlier, if clubs have local fans, then they will be more interested in the home team winning with a probability, making an unbalanced contest. However, the league narrative will be more exciting if more teams stay in contention for the league title for a longer period of time. It has been argued that

the need to maintain a competitive balance among teams through the season neces-
sitates collective agreements between the teams to redistribute resources. This can
be called the competitive balance defense of cartel-like restraints in sports leagues.
The competitive balance defense can be said to have two legs:

1. Fans prefer a more competitively balanced league championship than the
   one that results from unrestricted competition among the clubs (market
   failure)
2. Restraints in the form of restrictions on the operation of the labor market
   or agreements to share income can achieve more attractive levels of
   competitive balance

The first leg of the competitive balance defense is a statement about the nature
of competitive equilibrium in a contest. There exists some distribution of success
within the league that will maximize the interest of the fans. The precise form of
this distribution will depend on the uncertainty-of-outcome hypothesis balance
and the distribution of fans in the league. If each club has equal potential to draw
fans from a given level of success, then the implication is that an equal distribution
of success will maximize fan interest. However, given that cities or fan bases for
teams tend to vary in size, the optimal degree of competitive balance is likely to
reflect the inequalities in their drawing powers.[11] Economic modeling of the equilibrium of league competition has produced ambiguous results, and remains an
area of active research. See chapter 2 in this volume.[12]

  The second leg of the competitive balance defense rests on the capacity of clubs
and leagues to design mechanisms that will achieve something closer to the ideal
competitive balance for the league. It is, in fact, typical for clubs and leagues to claim
that the unrestricted free market distribution will be too tilted in favor of large-
market teams at the expense of small-market teams, and that, therefore, redistribution is required from the big to the small. Mechanisms that can be employed include
measures to redistribute revenues, such as gate sharing, or measures to control the
allocation of playing talent (labor-market restraints). These types of mechanisms
are central to the analysis of professional sports and competition law. In order for
social welfare to be increased, not only is it necessary to show that a particular
restraint can achieve its stated aim of achieving a superior degree of competitive
balance, but also that the restraint is necessary to the achievement of this end and
does not, at the same time, generate new inefficiencies whose costs outweigh the
benefits attributable to the restriction.

c. Promotion and Relegation in the Model of a Sports Contest

One of the few formal models of the promotion-and-relegation system was
developed in Szymanski and Valletti (2005).[13] They illustrate the impact of a
promotion-and-relegation system. A simple starting point for thinking about the
problem is to imagine that there exists a fixed number of clubs willing to enter

sporting competition on an annual basis. These clubs can be organized within a single league or into two divisions with promotion and relegation, for example, the team ranked last in the top division is demoted at the end of each season to play in the second division while being replaced in the top division by the highest-ranked team in the second division. If we suppose that the only reward to teams is a prize for winning the top division and that all teams are identical and supply identical effort, then the only effect of promotion and relegation is to create inequality in the expected payoffs to teams. In the closed system each team has an equal probability of winning the prize but, in the open system, teams presently in the top division are the only ones that can win the prize in the current year and so have a higher expected return. However, since lower division teams have some probability of entering the top division in future years they still have a positive present value. This makes the basic point that a promotion-and-relegation system tends to promote inequality among teams. Moreover, an open system can admit a very large number of teams while maintaining divisional competition of a manageable size. By contrast, when closed systems have expanded, they have created divisions within the league to sustain a viable schedule, without adding a hierarchical element. This raises the question about how far such leagues could expand without creating such a fragmented divisional system that the competition would lose coherence. Within closed systems, the preference seems to have been to retain leagues of limited size and then establish a hierarchy of leagues without promotion and relegation, for example, Major League Baseball, triple A, double A, single A, and so on. Here players may move up and down the hierarchy but teams may not.

To extend the model further Szymanski and Valletti consider the implication of endogenizing the effort choice of the teams. To do this a model is required that can account, not only for the probability of winning the prize contingent on contributing effort (the conventional contest success function), but also for the probability of being relegated, which they call the "contest losing function." They contrast a closed league with a fixed number of teams with an open system consisting of two equally sized leagues with the promotion and relegation of a single team, played on an annual basis. Once again, each team competes for a prize (in the open system, this is available only to teams currently in the top division) and, given equal effort, each team has an equal probability of success or failure. The comparison of effort levels between these two systems depends on the discriminatory power of the contest (the sensitivity of winning to relative effort). When discriminatory power is high, then effort levels in general tend to be high. There will be little difference in effort levels of teams between the top division of the open system and the closed system, but, in the lower division, effort levels are lower because these teams do not currently have access to the prize. Total effort supplied is quite similar in the two systems. However, when the discriminatory power of the contest is low, total effort declines in both systems, but it falls by less in the open system because of the relevance of the relegation—teams not only have to consider the benefits of winning but also the penalty for losing.

In their final model Szymanski and Valletti contrast the open and closed systems when there is asymmetry between teams. Asymmetry is an important characteristic of leagues—some teams come from big cities and some from small ones, but the problem is deciding exactly what aspect of asymmetry to model, given the unlimited possibilities. They chose to look at the model with two large city teams and two small city teams, which could either play in a closed four-team league or in an open system of two divisions of two teams. The aim was to analyze the impact of the incentive to share revenues in order to promote competitive balance, which, in their model, they assume enhances the value of the prize. In particular, when would large teams be willing to surrender some of their dominance in order to enhance the value of the prize. They show that teams in open systems are less likely to be willing to share prizes because, when they share, they will also tend to be relegated more frequently.

These insights from contest theory can be used to think about the comparison of open and closed systems in practice.

4. THE PRACTICAL IMPLICATIONS OF OPEN AND CLOSED SYSTEMS

To any independent observer, the most striking difference between the closed systems of North American professional leagues and the open systems used elsewhere, most notably in European soccer, is inequality. For example, among the thirty-two teams of Major League Baseball the ratio of the highest earning team (the Yankees) to the lowest (the Marlins) was 2.7 to 1 in 2008 (Forbes data), whereas in the twenty-team English Premier League the ratio was almost 6 to 1 (Deloitte data). Moreover, Major League Baseball is not the most balanced of the major leagues and the English Premier League is not the least balanced of the European soccer leagues. This inequality has translated into the perpetual dominance of big teams in Europe (Manchester United and Liverpool in England, Real Madrid and Barcelona in Spain, Bayern Munich in Germany, etc.). Major League Baseball may have the Yankees, but, generally, dynasties in the majors do not last that long. This appears paradoxical. As Buzzacchi et al. (2003)[14] show statistically, over time an open system produces the opportunity for many more teams to become champions, but in reality many fewer teams succeed in open systems than in closed ones.

It is thus perhaps not unnatural to look for an explanation in the nature of the open and closed systems themselves. Closed systems are characterized by agreements between the clubs to equalize resources. This is done in one of two ways: explicitly sharing revenues (gate revenue, broadcasting income, merchandising income) or agreeing restraints on competition for players (salary caps, luxury taxes, roster limits, reverse-order-of-finish draft systems). These have a propensity to redistribute resources so that weaker teams get stronger and stronger teams get weaker. Few teams are perpetual winners and few remain in the basement forever. Such redistribution mechanisms are less commonly used in open systems. In European soccer (football) leagues there is limited sharing of TV revenues, no sharing of league gate money, no sharing of merchandising income. Maximum wage rules have existed in the past, but they were abolished about half a century ago; there is no draft system and few limits on squad sizes. In European soccer, rich teams stay rich and are able to buy their way to almost perpetual dominance.[15]

The essence of a promotion-and-relegation system is that teams at all levels right up to the highest are not only rewarded for sporting success but punished for sporting failure. In professional leagues this represents, not just a sporting punishment, but also an economic one. Relegated teams face a significant fall in income[16] and, therefore, teams will compete aggressively to avoid the drop. Indeed, it might almost seem that, although the open systems punish failure, the closed systems reward it. It would not be surprising, therefore, if open systems were characterized by a greater aversion to failure on the part of the clubs, which would then color their approach to league agreements. In a closed system, with redistribution, if you are currently successful there is little to fear about becoming unsuccessful. You may lose a few fans, but you will still remain at the top flight of competition and your income is to some degree hedged. Thus, your incentive to engage in redistributive agreements, if you perceive these to bring wider benefits to the league, is not constrained by a fear of consequences if your team's performance deteriorates. It should not be surprising, therefore, if teams in closed systems are less willing to engage in redistributive agreements. To be clear, it is not that the strong teams in an open system fear that they would be in imminent danger if they engaged in U.S.-style redistribution but rather that the long-term consequences of redistribution would lead to relegation *eventually*. Thus, although policymakers in Europe have called for more solidarity in European leagues, meaning more redistribution, the likelihood is that this could only be achieved in a meaningful way by introducing a closed system, which is seen as anathema to the European model of sport.

However, despite the tendency of teams at the top to dominate the league, there is a considerable degree of mobility in a promotion relegation system, a point made in an excellent study of the English system by Roger Noll (2002).[17] Thus, critics of promotion and relegation often question whether there is any point allowing weaker teams from lower divisions to enter the highest level of competition only to lose badly and get relegated. However, this is to underestimate the important role of the labor market. Promoted teams are able to buy players to compete at a higher level (and relegated teams can sell players to avoid bankruptcy). Noll shows that, although some teams are relegated immediately following promotion, in many cases teams may enter the higher level for an extended period. Although the strongest teams are rarely relegated, they are soon promoted again.

Much of what has been said so far concerns the positive analysis of league systems—the consideration of how the different systems work in practice. However, there is at least as much interest in the normative issues: Which kind of system brings the greatest benefit to consumers?

Advocates of promotion and relegation tend to focus on the following benefits:

1. Excitement for the fans.   Promotion and relegation adds an extra dimension to the interest in a season's play. Although the prospect of playing in a higher division may be important, far more so is the possibility of demotion. In a closed league, teams out of contention for the championship title have little incentive to win matches, and, indeed, the purpose of the play-off system is to keep as many teams in the race for as long as possible. The threat of relegation guarantees that there are few teams that do not have something at stake until the end of the season. Promotion also ensures turnover among the teams, adding to the variety of match-ups that fans can see.

2. Free entry.   The fact that any team can enter the league hierarchy and be promoted to the highest divisions means that a larger fraction of towns have the prospect of achieving major league status. Thus, in the North American closed leagues, teams have been able to extract significant financial concessions from local taxpayers faced with the threat of relocation, exploiting the limited scope for new teams to enter the market. In leagues with promotion and relegation such threats are unheard of, because any town can invest in its own team, which can then win promotion to the highest division.[18]

3. Inclusiveness.   Sports leagues with promotion and relegation tend to be governed by bodies that take an interest in the development of the sport at all levels, because their members cover all sections of society, from the elite to the grass roots. This means, in particular, that some of the wealth that is created at the highest level of the game can be used to invest in the development of the sport. This has been a notable feature of the governance structure in world soccer, where income from competitions, such as the World Cup, has been successfully invested to develop the game in Asia and Africa. Closed leagues tend to neglect this aspect of the game, and to invest little in the development of the sport.

Critics point to the following potential costs:

1. Financial instability.   The threat of relegation means that teams are less likely to be profitable, since the investment of teams trying to avoid relegation tends to lead to a rat-race, in which all invest to the financial limit. The dissipation of economic profit through competition of this kind need not be a bad thing, but there is a threat of financial instability if teams borrow against future earnings. This seems to have happened in European soccer in the 1990s, and the governing bodies are trying to introduce regulations that will limit financial profligacy.

2. Underinvestment. The incentive to invest in facilities and stadium capacity is reduced when teams face the threat of relegation. Even if the owners are willing to put up money, banks may be unwilling to lend when future revenues are risky and the cost of capital will be higher than in a closed league.

Although these arguments are frequently presented, there is limited empirical evidence to decide these issues one way or the other.

5. CONCLUSIONS

This chapter has contrasted the operation of open and closed sports-league systems from both a positive and a normative perspective. Although the author is, in fact, an advocate of open systems, there still remains relatively little research into the practical implications of the two systems, and there is scope for more work, both on the theory and the empirical side. It must be observed that in terms of their overall attractiveness to sports fans, both open and closed leagues have been hugely attractive to fans. Economic questions remain, however. Hoehn and Szymanski (1999)[19] questioned whether the open system in Europe would survive, given that owners might have incentives to create a more profitable closed league, even if this were not in the interest of the fans. This raises important policy questions.

As Rosen and Sanderson (2001) observed:

> All schemes used in the United States punish excellence in one way or another. The European football approach punishes failure by promoting excellent minor league teams to the majors and demoting (relegating) poor performing major league teams back down to the minors. The revenue loss from a potential demotion to a lower class of play is severe punishment for low quality—severe enough that salary treaties, league sharing arrangements, and unified player drafts are so far thought to be unnecessary, even though star salaries are enormous. It is an interesting economic question as to which system achieves better results.[20]

NOTES

1 It is good to bear in mind that this notion is not uncontroversial. Since the nineteenth-century advocates of alternative forms of physical exercise opposed the notion of sport precisely because of its competitive element. For example the gymnastic Turnen movement in Germany saw sport as unnecessarily divisive, and modern educationalists have often challenged appropriateness of the competitive sport in schools. See, for example, Guttmann (2004), pp. 273–280.

2 By contrast, the National League expanded to eleven franchises between 1892 and
   1899, but then reduced to eight again. With the recognition of the American League
   at the beginning of the twentieth century the number of major league franchises
   expanded to sixteen, but did not increase again until 1961.

3 In England the Football Association (FA) Cup, which is older than the Football
   League, was, for a long time, seen as a superior competition. League clubs participated
   in both competitions, but if two teams from the same division were drawn against
   each other in the Cup, the attendance at the Cup game would attract a far larger
   crowd than the same game played in the league. However, Szymanski (2001) showed
   that, since the end of the 1970s the appeal of the League relative to the Cup grew
   substantially, and by the late 1990s attendance at the former outstripped attendance at
   the latter.

4 See, e.g., Neale (1964). There may be other cases where joint production is feasible or
   even desirable, but none where it is *necessary*.

5 An all-pay auction differs from conventional auctions in which only the winning
   bidder pays (although other bidders may pay an entry fee), because the bidders
   incur expenses in trying to win, which cannot be recouped. See S. Szymanski, "The
   Economic Design of Sporting Contests," *Journal of Economic Literature*, XLI, 2003:
   1137–1187 for a review of the contest literature.

6 For example, in a two-person contest, the probability of winning for player 1 is
   simply $e_1{}^{\gamma}/(e_1{}^{\gamma}+e_2{}^{\gamma})$ where e_1 is the effort contribution of player 1 and e_2 is the effort
   contribution of player, and γ is the discriminatory power of the contest success
   function.

7 Contestants expend effort in order to win a valuable prize; both aggregate and
   individual effort are increasing and net returns are decreasing in the discriminatory
   power of the contest. If the discriminatory power is too high, a purely strategy
   equilibrium may not exist, although mixed strategy equilibria are possible.

8 For example, if entrants are risk averse and organizers are risk neutral then increasing
   the fixed fee provides insurance, even if it also reduces effort.

9 See, e.g., Szymanski, S. and Valletti, T. (2005) "Incentive effects of second prizes,"
   European Journal of Political Economy, 21(2), 2005: 467–481.

10 This might be considered analogous to bluffing in poker.

11 Suppose, for example, that attendance is an increasing concave function of success
    (i.e., there are some diminishing returns), then the maximum attendance at the league
    is achieved where the marginal returns from success are equalized. Typically, one
    would expect this to mean that the big-city teams should win more often than the
    small-city teams, but, strictly speaking, what matters is the marginal returns, and it
    is possible that the optimal distribution of wins could favor a small-city team, whose
    fans were highly sensitive to success, over a large-city team, whose fans remained loyal
    regardless of the level of success.

12 See, for example, Simon Rottenberg, "The baseball player's labor market," *Journal of
    Political Economy*, 64, 1956: 242–258. The conventional model used in the literature
    is based on Quirk, James, and Mohamed El Hodiri, 1974, "The economic theory
    of a professional sports league" in *Government and the Sports Business,* ed. Roger
    Noll (Washington, DC: Brookings Institution, 1956). An alternative way to view this
    problem was proposed in Stefan Szymanski and Stefan Késenne, "Competitive balance
    and gate revenue sharing in team sports" *Journal of Industrial Economics*, LII (1), 2004:
    165–177, and further analyzed in Stefan Szymanski, "Professional team sports are only

a game: the Walrasian fixed supply conjecture model, Contest-Nash equilibrium and the Invariance Principle" *Journal of Sports Economics*, 5(2), 2004: 111–126.

13 Stefan Szymanski, and Tommaso Valletti, "Promotion and relegation in sporting contests" *Rivista di Politica Economica*, (December 2005), 3–49.

14 Luigi Buzzachi, Stefan Szymanski and Tommaso Valletti, "Equality of opportunity and equality of outcome: open leagues, closed leagues and competitive balance," *Journal of Industry, Competition and Trade*, 3(3), 2003: 167–186.

15 Although in some cases wealthy owners have invested to turn midrank teams into dominant teams. Most notable in recent years has been the investment of Roman Abramovitch, estimated to be in the region of £1 billion, to turn Chelsea into a dominant club in the English Premier League. Obviously this is not an option open to many.

16 For example, when Derby County was relegated from the English Premier League in 2008, their income in the following season fell by £17.3 million to £31.3 million, a decline of more than one third.

17 Roger Noll, "The economics of promotion and relegation in sports leagues: The case of English football," *Journal of Sports Economics*, 3(2), 2002: 169–203.

18 The present author has collaborated over several years with the sports law professor Stephen F. Ross on the normative analysis of sports league structures and we have argued that a promotion-and-relegation system produces welfare benefits. See Ross and Szymanski, *Fans of the World Unite! A Capitalist Manifesto for Sports Consumers* (Stanford: Stanford University Press, 2008).

19 Thomas Hoehn and Stefan Szymanski, "The Americanization of European Football," *Economic Policy* 28, 1999: 205–240.

20 Sherwin Rosen and Allen Sanderson, "Labor Markets in Professional Sports" *Economic Journal*, 111(469) 2001: F47–F68.

CHAPTER 2

....

COMPETITIVE
BALANCE

....

BRAD R. HUMPHREYS AND
NICHOLAS M. WATANABE

INTRODUCTION

....

RESEARCH on competitive balance accounts for significant amount of the sports economics research published over the past fifty years. A Google Scholar search on the term *competitive balance* in January 2010 returned more than 6,400 citations. In the same month, three of the five most frequently cited articles ever published in the *Journal of Sports Economics* focused on competitive balance. Competitive balance occupies an important position in the sports economics literature because it addresses a fundamental economic issue: The distribution of a scarce resource—in this case wins—across competing agents. In addition, research on competitive balance focuses on measurement issues, primarily on how to best characterize observed distributional patterns.

The term *competitive balance* generally refers to research on the distribution of wins in sport. Most competitive balance research focuses on the distribution of wins among teams in a sports league, but the analytical tools of competitive balance research can also be applied to individual sports (del Corral, 2009). The balance part implies a positive element to research in this area. Economic theory suggests that some distributions of wins are superior to others. Why are some distributions of wins better than others? Because fan interest in sporting events depends, in part, on the perception that outcomes are uncertain. Economists call this the uncertainty-of-outcome hypothesis (UOH). The distribution of wins in a sports league reflects how uncertain outcomes are in that league, linking the UOH and competitive balance research.

The literature on competitive balance is large and contentious. The contentious nature stems from disagreements about how to properly measure competitive balance and disagreements about the proper focus of research in this area. In this chapter, we survey the competitive balance literature with an eye to explaining why the literature is so contentious, understanding how the literature has progressed, and discussing where it should go in the future. We first discuss the UOH and the seminal research of Simon Rottenberg (1956). We then discuss the way that competitive balance is measured, including a critical survey of the strengths and weaknesses of each measure. Next, we discuss the exchange between Zimbalist (2002, 2003) and Fort and Maxcy (2003) about the nature of research on competitive balance and document the effect of this exchange on subsequent literature. Finally, we survey research on competitive balance in promotion-and-relegation leagues, a common league arrangement outside of North America.

The Uncertainty-of-Outcome Hypothesis and Competitive Balance

Simon Rottenberg (1956) wrote the perhaps the first scholarly article in sports economics in which he first articulated the uncertainty of outcome hypothesis (UOH). Rottenberg wrote

> Attendance at baseball games, as a whole is a function of the general level of income, the price of admission to baseball games relative to the prices of recreational substitutes, and the goodness of substitutes. Attendance at the games of any team is a positive function of the size of the population of the territory in which the team has the monopoly right to play; the size and convenience of location of the ball park; and the average rank standing of the team during the season in the competition of its league. It is a negative function of the goodness of leisure-time substitutes for baseball in the area and of the dispersion of percentages of games won by the teams in the league. (Rottenberg, 1956, p. 246)

This is a thorough description of the demand function for sport and, in the last sentence, the heart of the UOH. Note the clear link to modern competitive balance research implied by "the dispersion of percentages of games won." More than five decades have passed since the publication of this article, yet it remains influential. Fort (2005) thoroughly analyzed this article, so it requires no detailed recapitulation here. However, we briefly document the legacy of this article, because it provides important context for understanding competitive balance research.

THE LEGACY OF ROTTENBERG'S UNCERTAINTY-OF-OUTCOME HYPOTHESIS

The influence of Rottenberg's seminal paper is so extensive that to discuss every article influenced by it would require a chapter in itself. However, it is important to consider a number of pieces that truly reflect the scope and importance of Rottenberg's research (1956). In introducing the first issue of the *Journal of Sports Economics,* Kahane, Idson, and Staudohar (2000) discuss the variety of research that exists in the realm of sports economics and point toward the importance of Rottenberg (1956) in influencing much of the research within the field. In this, they note that Rottenberg's work was the first economic article that was focused in to sports. To further highlight Rottenberg's importance, he was also invited to contribute the first article published in the journal's first issue.

Although Dr. Rottenberg passed away in 2004, his contributions were not forgotten and still play an important role in the sports economics literature. In 2005 and 2006, as the fiftieth anniversary of the publication of Rottenberg's article approached, there was renewed interest in the article among researchers around the world. Notable among this is Fort's (2005) article discussing the fiftieth anniversary of the piece and the widespread influence and implications it had. Furthermore, a book of essays was published, each of which was dedicated to the golden anniversary of the piece, and in a similar manner as Fort's (2005) work noted the various influences that have come about from Rottenberg's (1956) work. In a further testament to the reach that this seminal work has had, even to today, there is still research that is considering the implications of Rottenberg's ideas.

Krautmann (2008) focused on the invariance principle that Rottenberg (1956) also proposed, examining the principle from a theoretical standpoint, and exploring its relationship to the more famous, and later, Coase theorem. The invariance principle states that outcomes in a sports league (primarily the distribution of wins) will be invariant to any attempt to alter property rights (in the case of sports leagues, the rights to labor inputs by players through entry drafts, reserve clauses in contracts, and other player allocation policies). This paper provides further evidence of the importance of Rottenberg's (1956) work and documents the influence Rottenberg's paper in other areas of sports and economics. Clearly, Rottenberg's (1956) work has influenced much of the research in sports economics, and remains just as important today, as the day it was published. It is safe to say that Rottenberg's influence on sports economics is as great as that of any other economist to date, and knowledge of this seminal work is essential to understanding research in sports economics.

COMPETITIVE BALANCE MEASURES

Most of the commonly used measures of win distribution used in the competitive balance literature comes from other areas like industrial organization, information theory, or income distribution research, although variance-based measures also exist. Competitive balance measures contain two important elements: determining the temporal scale and defining wins. Competitive balance can be measured over the course of a single season, or over a number of seasons. Wins can be defined as games, postseason appearances, or regular season or postseason championships. Because only one championship gets awarded in a given season, measures of the distribution of postseason appearances or championship wins must be carried out over a number of seasons. Measures of the distribution of regular season wins can focus on a single season or on multiple seasons.

We focus only on measures of the distribution of regular season wins in the following discussion. In addition, we confine the discussion to research published in scholarly journals, and not in books or edited volumes. Quite a bit of the early research on competitive balance appeared in books and collected volumes, including Demmert (1973), Noll (1974), Scully (1989), Quirk and Fort (1992), and Zimbalist (1992). We recognize the importance of these publications in this literature, and do not intend to diminish their importance. We simply focus on research in peer-reviewed academic journals as a matter of convenience.

Variance based measures of competitive balance were the first to appear in the literature. Variance, or its square root, standard deviation, is an easy-to-calculate measure of dispersion of a variable. This makes variance a natural measure for the distribution of wins within a sports league. Fort and Quirk (1995) analyzed the variation in winning percentages in the four major North American leagues, including a detailed examination of the tails of the distribution of wins—team-season winning percentages more than 2 or 3 standard deviations from the mean—in these leagues, a competitive balance measure closely related to variance. Because of the computational simplicity of variance measures, the standard deviation of win percentage (SDWPCT)[1] has become one of the most popular metrics by which to measure competitive balance in empirical research (Soebbing, 2008).

Although the SDWPCT is a convenient and relatively simple metric to calculate, a number of issues arise when using this metric. One issue concerns SDWPCT-based comparisons of competitive balance across leagues and seasons. SDWPCT does not control for differences in the number of games played in a season. SDWPCT is sensitive to the number of games played by teams in a season, so leagues such as the NFL with only sixteen games will have a much different estimated variance of win percentage than a league such as the Major League Baseball, which plays 162 games in a season. To correct for this, economists have created an idealized measure of standard deviation that is essentially the expected value of the standard deviation given the number of teams, the number of games, and a probability of winning of .5 for each team in each game. Then, with any number of games or any size league, the ratio of the actual standard deviation to this idealized standard deviation is a measure of the excess standard deviation that is comparable across different leagues and different seasons. Although this metric would seem rather useful, Zimbalist (2002) argues that fan's preference may not be responsive to such a metric. The rationale behind this lies in the idea that fans will consider poor performance in a season to be poor, no matter how many games a team played. Thus, in some cases, SDWPCT could be preferred to the idealized version, depending on the goal of the research being conducted. Further issues arise because variance-based competitive balance measures do not reflect relative positions in standings from season to season (Humphreys, 2002).

Eckard (1998, 2001a, 2001b) developed an ANOVA based approach to measuring competitive balance, a variance decomposition, closely related to the methods discussed earlier. Eckard's (1998) impetus for the creation of this measure can be traced back to the inability of SDWPCT to capture changes in relative standings over seasons. To address this limitation, Eckard's (1998) ANOVA approach decomposes the variation in team-winning percents into a time component and a cumulative component. The time component reflects relative changes in order of finish over time. However, because the ANOVA approach contains two different measures of competitive balance, it cannot be easily applied to empirical UOH research, because both components reflect outcome uncertainty. Eckard (1998) applied this measure to competitive balance in NCAA football over fifty seasons.

Humphreys (2002) developed another variance based measure of competitive balance, the competitive-balance ratio (CBR), in order to address the relative standing problem using a single measure of competitive balance. The CBR is the ratio of the variation in a team's winning percentage over time to the variation in the league's winning percentages. Because the CBR is expressed as a single number, it can easily be used in empirical UOH research. Humphreys (2002) applied the CBR to Major League Baseball over the period 1900–1999 in a UOH study and determined that variation in the CBR explained observed variation in attendance better than the SDWPCT. Both the ANOVA measure of competitive balance and the CBR suffer from the limitation that, as dynamic measures of competitive balance, they must be calculated over some period of time, and the time period over which they are calculated must be determined by the researcher. This produces a certain level of arbitrariness in these measures of competitive balance.

The Herfindahl-Hirschman index (HHI) comes from the industrial-organization literature, where it is used to describe the distribution of revenues earned by companies within an industry. The HHI has been widely applied in industry studies, examination of antitrust issues, and many other applications, including the distribution of wins in sports leagues. The HHI for an industry with n firms can take any value from $10,000/n$ to $10,000$, where higher values indicate a more unequal distribution of wins. Eckard (1998) was the first to apply this metric to the measurement of competitive balance in a sporting context, in his examination of competitive balance in the National Collegiate Athletic Association (NCAA) cartel. In this article, Eckard (1998) used the HHI to measure the distribution of championships among teams in each of the major NCAA conferences. Although this specific measurement of the HHI reflects balance in terms of championship distribution over a 25-year period, the HHI can be used to assess the distribution of a variety of team performance measures within sports. For example, the HHI can be used to measure the distribution of playoff appearances, wins, or points. Therefore, the HHI can be considered to be quite a versatile measure of competitive balance. However, it is important in the use of the HHI, to note the specific performance measure it is being applied to.

The HHI, though useful for measuring competitive balance does have its drawbacks. The primary problem with the HHI is that, like SDWPCT, it is sensitive to the number of teams in the league. This makes HHI values difficult to compare across time in leagues that expand, as well as across leagues with different numbers of teams. Depken (1999) proposed a transformation of the HHI that accounts for variation in the number of teams in the league. In addition, the HHI does not capture changes in relative standings over time.

The Spearman rank correlation coefficient (SRCC), a competitive balance measure used to track reordering in rankings within an industry, was first used by Maxcy (2002). The SRCC reflects the reordering in standings in a league from one season to the next because it captures the correlation in relative standings across all teams in a sports league from one season to the next. The SRCC takes values between –1 and 1, with –1 indicating perfect reordering in relative standings and 1 an indication that no teams changed their place in league ranking relative to the previous season. The main benefit derived from using the SRCC is that it captures changes in relative standings across seasons in a league. Other measures of competitive balance reflect changes in the dispersion of wins, which, although useful, can vary greatly from one season to the next, without any change in relative standings. The primary drawback of the SRCC is that it does not reflect the magnitude of the dispersion of wins. A league could have no change in standings from one season to another and still have significant changes in the dispersion of wins. That is, the SRCC focuses on an ordinal ranking of teams, and does not consider how close or far teams are apart in terms of their performance in leagues.

Fort and Quirk (1995) introduced the Gini coefficient as a measure of competitive balance, a widely employed measure of inequality in income and wealth distributions in economies. In the sports literature, the Gini coefficient is calculated from observed win dispersion within a league, and, thus, it measures in inequality of win distribution. Using this coefficient, 0 is considered to be "perfect" parity within a league, as wins are equally distributed among teams when the Gini coefficient takes this value; 1 represents the highest possible level of imbalance within a league, because one team would have all the wins in the league when the Gini coefficient takes this (impossible) outcome. Fan attendance has been shown to be responsive to changes in the Gini coefficient in time frames longer than a single season (Schmidt & Berri, 2001). This observation suggests that competitive balance may only be perceived over a number of seasons, and not a single one (Borland & Macdonald, 2003). In other words, fans may not be responsive to measures of competitive balance that focus on single seasons, because it takes several seasons of observation for fans to gather enough information to assess the relative parity within a sports league. Like all competitive balance metrics, the Gini coefficient does have limitations, including the fact that a Gini coefficient of 1 represents a situation in which all the wins in a season have been captured by a single team, a situation that is impossible except in the uninteresting case of a two-team league. Therefore, although the Gini Coefficient may be a measure that shows response to fan attendance in UOH studies, its theoretical range does not match its effective range. In addition, the Gini coefficient does not capture changes in relative standings over multiple seasons.

Although the SDWPCT, HHI, the ANOVA measure, the CBR, and Gini coefficients have garnered much attention in competitive balance research, several other measures, such as relative entropy (Horowitz, 1997), concentration ratios (Kining, 2000), and Markov switching (Hadley, Ciecka, and Krautmann, 2005) have also been used to measure competitive balance in sports leagues. Relative entropy, first introduced in sports by Horowitz (1997), is one of the first proposed measures of competitive balance, but it has been rarely used in the literature. Relative entropy has been used as a measure of uncertainty in information theory. Relative entropy is the ratio of the percentage of league total wins accounted for by a single team to the percentage of league total wins that team would have accounted for if the probability of winning each game was 0.5. Relative entropy is bounded above by 1, and bounded below by a minimum value that depends on the number of teams in the league. Horowitz (1997) applied relative entropy to Major League Baseball over the period 1903–1978.

Koning (2000) introduced the concentration ratio (CR) as a measure of competitive balance in sports leagues. Like the HHI, concentration ratios are widely used in industrial organization to measure the concentration of economic activity in industries. The CR is calculated as the ratio of the number of points accumulated from wins and ties in soccer (football) leagues by the top N teams in a league to the total number of points that could have been earned by those N teams. If the CR is near one, the top N teams in that league did not lose many points to lower teams. Being one of the more recently developed measures of competitive balance, the C5-index has yet to receive much attention or further empirical testing. However, the metric itself may be problematic in its consideration of only the top five teams in a league and ignoring the rest of the league. In this manner, the standard for competitive balance falls solely on the performance of the top five teams in comparison to their idealized performance. This could, hypothetically, be problematic, because the performance of the top five may be consistent from one year to the next, but the distribution of points among other teams not considered in the metric could vary greatly. Furthermore, issues arise in the number of teams in a league, and the definition of a league. Although this measure is ideal for soccer leagues that often have close to twenty teams in a single league, it may be more problematic for smaller leagues or leagues that are subdivided into smaller divisions.

Hadley, Ciecka, and Krautmann (2005) developed a Markov switching method to examine competitive balance in sports leagues that reflects turnover in relative standings. This Markov switching method generates transitional probabilities that reflect how likely it is for a team in a league to transition from a losing state to a winning state from one season to the next. This competitive balance measure attempts to address the same problem as the ANOVA approach and the CBR discussed earlier. Hadley, Ciecka, and Krautmann (2005) applied this Markov switching method to Major League Baseball before and after the 1994 players strike. One limitation of this Markov switching method is that the researcher must define the winning and losing states. A second limitation is that this measure is difficult to incorporate into UOH research.

Clearly, many measures of competitive balance have been developed over the past twenty years. Each has relative strengths and weaknesses, and each captures a different element of competitive balance. In order to understand the development of this literature over time, we next turn to an important exchange between scholars in the competitive-balance literature that has had a lasting impact on the evolution of the literature.

THE FORT-ZIMBALIST EXCHANGE

One key point can be identified in the development of research on competitive balance. Andrew Zimbalist guest edited a special issue of the *Journal of Sports Economics* focused on competitive balance in 2002. In the guest editor's introduction, Zimbalist (2002) argued that, because fans' perceptions of competitive balance may differ from statistical estimates of competitive balance, competitive-balance research should focus on the link between competitive balance and fan interest in sports events. Zimbalist (2002) argued that UOH research should be the primary focus of the competitive-balance literature.

In a comment published the following year in the *Journal of Sports Economics*, Fort and Maxcy (2003) took issue with the claims made by Zimbalist (2002), asserting that Zimbalist (2002) took "an unfortunate stance" on competitive-balance research. In particular, Fort and Maxcy (2003) argue that both the UOH and research focused entirely on measuring and comparing competitive balance, called the "analysis of competitive balance" (ACB), are needed for a complete understanding of competitive balance in sports leagues.

Fort and Maxcy (2003) argue that, instead of identifying a "best" measure of competitive balance, a more general review of the literature would have been more appropriate for a special issue on competitive balance. Fort and Maxcy (2002) argue that a general literature review would have helped avoid making many of the "misguided" comments and statements made by Zimbalist (2002), which they believed were unnecessary. Also, they argue that a general review of research on competitive balance would have been helpful to readers not familiar with the subject, because there are a number of issues that they believe are central to the research on competitive balance that are not covered by Zimbalist (2002).

To frame their argument, Fort and Maxcy (2003) began with a literature review focused on both the theoretical underpinning of competitive balance and the relevant empirical research. Fort and Maxcy (2003) identified, not a single line of competitive-balance research, but instead two lines, UOH and ACB, and argued that Zimbalist (2002) focused only on UOH research and ignored the growing and important area of ACB research. Fort and Maxcy (2003) criticize Zimbalist (2002) for ignoring ACB research, which at the time contained at least a dozen studies. Although this pales in comparison to the studies done on UOH, Fort and Maxcy (2003) claim that neither line of research can be said to be more important than the other. The distinction between the UOH and ACB literature is quite important in this exchange and is mentioned on multiple occasions by Fort and Maxcy (2003) to highlight their disagreement with Zimbalist's statements.

Fort and Maxcy (2003) also disagree with the issues of measurement raised by Zimbalist (2002). Specifically, they focus on Zimbalist's (2002) observation that the best competitive- balance measures are the ones to which fan preferences are most sensitive. Fort and Maxcy (2003) point out that this statement reflects Zimbalist's too-narrow focus on the UOH, and ignores the ACB line of research. Fort and Maxcy (2003) state: "Both UOH and ACB contributions are important to our understanding of the relationship between league behavior, competitive balance, and fan welfare. And the standard deviation of winning percentages is a perfectly acceptable tool for ACB practitioners." (p. 155). To further highlight this point, empirical examples are give from prior research (Fort, 2001), which show that the ACB approach can be useful in understanding fluctuations in competitive balance, especially when fan attendance is shown to be stable over the periods of fluctuation in competitive balance. In this manner, Fort and Maxcy (2003) convincingly demonstrate the importance of ACB research, and the reason ACB needs to be considered along with UOH research in any complete analysis of competitive balance.

Fort and Maxcy (2003) point out several additional areas in which they disagree with Zimbalist (2002) about research on competitive balance. One given special attention is a claim that Zimbalist identifies as a prevailing attitude among researchers against the UOH line of research, noting that he makes this statement without any citations (Fort & Maxcy, 2003, p. 157). They conclude, "Although the issue of fan welfare is outside ACB analysis, it is not an issue that invalidates the ACB approach." (p. 157). Following this, Fort and Maxcy (2003) reiterate the importance of the ACB line of research, indicating that Zimbalist and others, should take into account both the UOH and ACB approaches when analyzing competitive balance.

Fort and Maxcy (2003) note that neither the ACB or UOH should be distinguished above the other, because, not only is such a distinction unnecessary, it also prevents the two lines of research from being beneficial to one another. Fort and Maxcy (2003) clearly believe that Zimbalist (2002) did the literature a disservice by arguing that UOH research take precedence, and they encourage future research on both the ACB and UOH, because only a two-pronged approach will lead to greater understanding of competitive balance.

Zimbalist (2003) replied to Fort and Maxcy (2003) in the same issue of the *Journal of Sports Economics,* seeking to clear up certain misunderstandings he thought others might have had about the content of his 2002 article. Zimbalist (2003) first clarifies his position, and asserts firmly that his positions were not necessarily misfortunate or incorrect. Zimbalist first tackles his treatment of the issue of measurement of competitive balance, which Fort and Maxcy (2003) claimed was inadequate. Zimbalist (2003) reiterated that his comments about fans not caring about the SDWPCT referred to the idealized SDWPCT and argued that his discussion of competitive balance reflects his belief that no single competitive balance measure will ever be better than the others, thus there will always be the need for multiple measures.

In addressing the division of the competitive balance literature into ACB and UOH lines, Zimbalist (2003) argues that this division, although possible to make, could lead to competitive- balance research unformed by theory, thereby increasing the risk of data mining and leading to what Zimbalist (2003) describes as "mindless empiricism." (p. 162). Zimbalist (2003) reiterated his position that the best measures of competitive balance are those to which fans are most responsive, noting that Fort and Maxcy (2003) themselves discuss the use of the SDWPCT as if it were the ideal competitive balance measurement, contradicting their own argument about the issues in Zimbalist's (2002) introduction. Zimbalist concludes by pointing out that research into competitive balance is not a simple thing, and if there is a best measure of competitive balance, it may not be a simple one. Furthermore, he notes that the best measure for one league may not be the best measure for another league, but, in either case, the appropriate approach is to begin with fan behavior.

Two main issues emerge from this interesting exchange. First, the consequences of the division of competitive balance research into strands, UOH and ACB. Second, how to measure competitive balance, whether an ideal measure of competitive balance exists, and how researchers might identify the best measure. In thinking about these issues, the question arises of how the field responded to

the exchange between Zimbalist (2002; 2003) and Fort and Maxcy (2003). A natural way to assess this controversy is to assess how the literature responded to the
competing positions articulated in this exchange.

Fort and Maxcy (2003) noted that only a few studies that could be catego-
rized as belonging to the ACB line of research existed when the paper was written.
Since then, a number of papers focused on the analysis of competitive balance,
changes in competitive balance within sports leagues, and the effect of institutional changes on competitive balance have been published. Sutter and Winkler
(2003) examined the effect of changes in scholarship limits on competitive balance
in NCAA Division I-A football using the margin of victory in games, the ratio
of actual to idealized standard deviation of winning percentages, and the HHI of
wins in conferences. Buzzacchi, Szymanski, and Valletti (2003) examined competitive balance in Major League Baseball, NFL, NHL, and three professional football
leagues in Europe using the ratio of actual to idealized standard deviation of winning percentages and a dynamic measure of competitive balance that reflects entry
into the top positions in each league, a new measure of competitive balance. Quirk
(2004) examined competitive balance in NCAA Division I-A football conferences
using Gini coefficients. Hadley, Ciecka, and Krautmann (2005) examined the effect
of the 1994 players strike of competitive balance in Major League Baseball using
Markov transition probabilities, a new measure of competitive balance. Booth
(2005) examined the effect of player drafts and salary caps on competitive balance
in three professional sports leagues in Australia, using the ratio of actual to idealized standard deviation of winning percentages. Berri, Brook, Frick, Fenn, and
Vicente-Mayoral (2005) examined the effect on changes in average height on competitive balance in the National Basketball Association (NBA) using the ratio of
actual to idealized standard deviation of winning percentages. Schmidt and Berri
(2005) examined the effect of an influx of foreign talent on competitive balance
in Major League Baseball using the HHI. Fenn, von Allmen, Brook and Pressing
(2005) examined the effect of an influx of international players on competitive balance in the National Hockey League (NHL), using the ratio of actual to idealized
standard deviation of winning percentages, the HHI, and the competitive-balance
ratio. Lee and Fort (2005) examined the time series properties of the ratio of actual
to idealized standard deviation of winning percentages and the excess tail frequencies of winning percentages in each season in Major League Baseball over the
period 1901–1999; Fort and Lee (2007) extended this analysis to the rest of the professional sports leagues in North America. Maxcy and Mondello (2006) examined
the effect of free agency on competitive balance in three professional sports leagues
in North America using the standard deviation of winning percentages, the ratio
of actual to idealized standard deviation of winning percentages, and a new measure of competitive balance—the Spearman rank correlation coefficient of standings. Larsen, Fenn, and Spenner (2006) examined the effect of free agency and
the salary cap on competitive balance in the NFL using Gini coefficients and the
HHI. Krautmann and Hadley (2006) used the ratio of actual to idealized standard

deviation of winning percentages and Markov switching probabilities to examine competitive balance and dynasties in Major League Baseball. Lee (2009) examined the effect of the 1993 collective bargaining agreement on competitive balance in the NFL using only winning percents as a measure of competitive balance. Del Corral (2009) examines competitive balance in grand slam tennis using a new metric that is based on how far players at various seeds advance in tournaments.

Clearly the ACB literature has grown significantly since the Fort-Zimbalist exchange. A number of new measures of competitive balance have been developed, and ACB research has been applied to a growing number of sports around the world. Much of the ACB research has focused on developing new measures of competitive balance, using these measures to examine the effect of changes in league policies on competitive balance—in effect testing the invariance principle first made by Rottenberg (1956)—and comparing the implications from different measures of competitive balance. These tests of the invariance principle before and after league policy changes implicitly treat these policy changes as "natural experiments" in competitive balance research.

The recent UOH literature contains two types of papers: those focused only on outcome uncertainty and those that examine both competitive balance and outcome uncertainty. Studies focused entirely on UOH research include Owen and Weatherston's (2004) examination of Super 12 Rugby attendance and outcome uncertainty; Meehan, Nelson, and Richardson's (2007) study of attendance outcome uncertainty in Major League Baseball; Rascher and Solmes' (2007) study of uncertainty of outcome and attendance in the NBA; Madalozzo and Villar's (2009) study of Brazilian football attendance and outcome uncertainty; Falter, Perignon, and Vercryusse's (2008) study of World Cup attendance and outcome uncertainty; Lemke, Leonard, and Tlhokwane's (2009) study of outcome uncertainty and attendance in Major League Baseball; and Benz, Brandes, and Franck's (2009) study of attendance and outcome uncertainty in the Bundesliga. Forrest, Simmons, and Buriamo (2005) examine the relationship between match uncertainty and television viewing audiences in the English Premier League, an interesting extension to the other live attendance studies mentioned earlier. Paul and Weinbach (2007) perform a similar analysis on the television-viewing audience for Monday Night Football in the United States.

All these papers use match or game level data to test uncertainty of outcome, so the common measures of competitive balance discussed earlier cannot be used. Instead, they employ variables like betting odds or standings of the teams prior to the game to proxy for outcome uncertainty. Dawson and Downward (2005) discuss some problems associated with both of these commonly used measures of outcome uncertainty at the match level. Forrest, Beaumont, Goddard, and Simmons (2005) make a similar point, and provide an interesting empirical illustration of one problem, namely, home advantage.

The second group of papers focuses on both UOH and competitive balance; they both document changes in competitive balance, using one or more measures, and also examine the relationship between these measures and fan interest empirically. Brandes and Franck (2006) undertook an impressive analysis of both competitive balance and UOH in European football leagues using sophisticated time series econometric techniques. This paper documents changes in competitive balance captured by different measures and assesses how each measure of competitive balance relates to attendance. Soebbing (2008) used both the ratio of actual to idealized SDWPCT and the number of games behind to examine competitive balance and attendance in Major League Baseball. Lee (2009) examined the effect of playoff uncertainty on attendance in Major League Baseball. This paper provides an excellent example of how the Fort-Zimbalist exchange has ultimately paid dividends in terms of moving the literature forward. Lee (2009) combines ACB and UOH research in a single measure, much as Fort and Maxcy (2003) suggested. The paper develops a new measure of competitive balance that reflects uncertainty about a team's chances to play in the postseason, and shows fans' behavior to be sensitive to this measure.

Uncertainty-of-outcome-hypothesis research also grew significantly following the Fort-Zimbalist debate. This strand of literature contains mixed results on the relationship between outcome uncertainty and fan behavior. Because much of the research uses game or match level data that are not suited for use with standard measures of competitive balance, research in this area diverged from mainstream ACB since the Fort-Zimbalist exchange. However, recent research in this area includes papers that incorporate both ACB and UOH elements, as Fort and Maxcy (2003) urged.

In general, research in both areas identified by Fort and Maxcy (2003), ACB and UOH, advanced in the past five years. Many, but not all, authors recognized the importance of this exchange, and framed their research in the context of this debate. ACB research saw a proliferation of new measures of competitive balance developed, and the effect on competitive balance of a number of interesting "natural experiments" in sports leagues, like collective-bargaining agreements, investigated. However, there has been little assessment of why these new measures of competitive balance matter, as well as a drift toward atheoretic research that focuses on the data-generating process instead of the underlying economic behavior. Two recent ACB papers focus mostly on the time series properties of various measures of competitive balance. In this sense, Zimbalist's (2003) warning about pitfalls associated with research not informed by theory appears justified. Much of the UOH research has focused on game- or match-level data and appears to be drifting away from ACB. In this sense, Fort and Maxcy (2003) appear to have been correct in arguing that two separate areas of inquiry exist in the literature. However, several recent papers have appeared that draw on both the UOH and ACB to provide important new insight into competitive balance. It took some time to happen, but it appears that the unified, "two-pronged approach" to competitive-balance research advocated by Fort and Maxcy (2003) may finally be emerging.

COMPETITIVE BALANCE IN PROMOTION AND RELEGATION LEAGUES

Although the discussion of the ACB-UOH debate explains some of the development of research on competitive balance, competitive balance research has another important dichotomy: competitive balance in closed, static leagues, like those in North America, and competitive balance in open leagues with promotion and relegation, like those in Europe. Open leagues, commonly found in Europe, use the process of promotion and relegation to determine which teams will constitute the league in the following season. Promotion-and-relegation leagues consist of interrelated, hierarchically organized leagues in which the teams that finish at the top of each league move up to the next higher league in the following season and the teams that finish at the bottom of the league move down to the next lower league in the following season. The composition of teams in each league changes from season to season. Closed leagues, found in North America, on the other hand, consist of a fixed group of teams, entry to which can only be gained through league expansion, which requires consent of all existing league members and large entry fees.

This fundamental difference in the structure of sports leagues in North America and Europe is quite intriguing, for it has direct implications for competitive balance. The use of promotion and relegation in European sports leagues serves the purpose of moving stronger teams into divisions with a relatively higher level of playing skill, and weaker teams into ones with lower skill level, ensuring a uniform level of competition in leagues. Because of the very nature of this system, teams at the top of a league compete for championships, as well as the possibility of moving into higher level competitions. What makes promotion and relegation more distinct from North American leagues is the incentives to win for the teams outside the top regions of the league standings. In promotion-and-relegation leagues, teams in the middle of the table, who are safe from the "drop-zone" of teams that will be relegated to a lower league will have very little incentive to win, but those teams at the bottom of the table face strong incentives to win matches at the end of the season, in the hopes of avoiding being relegated to a lower league.

Conversely, in North America, teams in the middle of the table may have the chance at reaching postseason play through the use of "wild-card" playoff berths, giving teams hopes at a potential championship. Furthermore, as North American professional sport leagues employ a reverse-order draft, in which teams at the bottom of the table have first choice at picking new players for the upcoming season, these teams are actually given incentive to not win matches at the end of a season, in order to improve their chances of getting a more highly talented player. Static North American leagues provide incentives for teams at the bottom of a league to lose games at the end of the season (Taylor and Trogden, 2002), whereas the promotion-and-relegation system does the opposite, providing incentives for teams in the lower regions of the standings to give more effort at the end of a season (Ross &

Szymanski, 2000). Thus, from a theoretical standpoint, it is posited that precisely because of the different incentives that teams at various parts of the table have in European and North American professional sport leagues, there will be better competitive balance within those leagues that use promotion and relegation.

Noll's (2002) examination of the competitive balance in promotion-and-relegation leagues, another piece from the *Journal of Sports Economics* special issue, empirically examines the effects of open leagues on competitive balance. Noll presents several interesting results; most interestingly, Noll (2002) finds an unclear effect of promotion and relegation on competitive balance. This ambiguity arises because many teams promoted to the top tier of soccer (football) in England (The Premier League) are placed in a situation in which they cannot reasonably afford to purchase the level of talent needed to compete in the Premier League. In situations such as this, Noll (2002) finds certain teams are caught between a vicious cycle of spending money to be promoted to the Premier League, and then cutting spending on player salaries once promoted, eventually leading to them being demoted to lower leagues again. Thus, Noll's (2002) empirical evidence suggests that the theoretical prediction that competitive balance should be "better" in open leagues because of promotion and relegation is not necessarily true.

Promotion and relegation also has an effect on measures of competitive balance. The promotion-and-relegation system changes the composition of the league each season. Over time, there will be many more possible championship winners in an open league than in a closed league. This requires special attention when assessing the distribution of championships over time. Buzzacchi, Szymanski, and Valletti (2003) developed a "dynamic" measure of competitive balance that accounts for this change in the composition of promotion-and-relegation leagues and applied this measure to three closed and three open leagues over a fifty-year period. This paper concluded that open leagues had more balance in championship distribution than closed leagues after accounting for the dynamic nature of open leagues.

Clearly, it is difficult to determine whether one league has better competitive balance than another, because of the sensitivity of many competitive-balance measures to league composition and structure. Consider, for example, the distribution of championships, that is, how often different teams within a league win championships. Some evidence suggests more parity in closed North American sport leagues compared to open European leagues, in terms of Gini coefficients and HHIs for championship distributions. This is not a surprising conclusion, as the premiership has been dominated by only a few teams since its creation, whereas leagues such as the NFL, NBA, Major League Baseball, and NHL have had a larger number of different teams win championships over time. If one approaches competitive balance by purely looking at championships using measures of competitive balance that do not account for league composition, it would thus appear that the major professional sports leagues of North America have better competitive balance.

However, championships alone are not the full picture, and, as Buzzachi et al. (2002) show, different measures of competitive balance suggest different patterns in relative parity. Also, moving beyond the distribution of championships, alternative measures of competitive balance can be used to examine the distribution of win percentage among teams in a league. This measure considers the entire season of play (but not the playoffs) and indicates how well balanced teams are within in a league during a season. Employing this measure of competitive balance presents a quite different point of view than the championship method. In considering the SDWPCT for teams in a season, the Premier League has a much better distribution of win percentage than the North American professional sport leagues. Based on the distribution of wins in a season, the Premier League appears to have better parity, but based on the distribution of championships over a number of seasons, and for certain measures of competitive balance, North American leagues have better competitive balance.

This example highlights the difficulties inherent in understanding the nature of competitive balance, especially when comparing one league to another. Thus, it is important to consider the type of variables used to capture competitive balance, what these variables measure, and the strengths and weaknesses of the measures of competitive balance used. Although theoretical evidence suggests that promotion-and-relegation leagues should have more parity, empirical evidence shows a more varied picture.

CONCLUSION

Competitive-balance research in economics has followed a twisting path over the past fifty years. Rottenberg (1956) identified the major research questions, the invariance principle, and the UOH, which have dominated the literature ever since. However, competitive balance has proved difficult to quantify, and the analysis of competitive balance emerged as an equally important component of research in this area in the past decade. Sanderson (2002) posited that the questions of identifying an optimum level of competitive balance and devising an appropriate measure of competitive balance to compare actual competitive balance to ideal are ultimately intractable problems that will not be solved, because competitive balance has too many features to be measured easily. Our examination of the path taken by competitive balance research over the past fifty years in part bears this out. UOH research contains a number of contradictory results about the effect of outcome uncertainty on fan behavior. ACB research continues to develop new measures of competitive balance without fully considering why these measures are needed. Furthermore, tests of the invariance principle based on league policy changes as "natural experiments" show little consistency. Although many studies find that free agency or the institution of an entry draft had no effect on competitive balance, others conclude that competitive balance was affected by these changes. UOH research, especially at the level of match or game uncertainty, appears to be drifting away from ACB research, despite the clear links between these two areas of study. ACB research appears to be increasingly focused on atheoretic examinations of the time series properties of various measures of competitive balance that do not appear to move the literature forward; we hope that this trend does not lead to a never ending battle of competing unit root tests and lag length criteria like that seen in modern applied macroeconomic research.

Despite these problems, some recent signs of unification and important new directions in the literature exist. Recent papers by Brandes and Franck (2006). Soebbing (2008) and Lee (2009) combine UOH and ACB research and provide new insight for both areas. Future research should expand on the themes in these papers. In addition, sports leagues continue to tinker with league policies about the assignment of property rights, providing researchers with new "natural experiments" to test the invariance principle, and competitive balance research has been extended to new settings. Finally, the tension identified earlier in research on the relative degree of competitive balance generated by open and closed sports leagues holds considerable promise for future research. The ability of various measures of competitive balance to account for differences in league structure more complex than simply differences in the number of teams in the league or games in the season presents a interesting and perhaps fruitful new avenue of inquiry in the literature, for both UOH and ACB research.

References

Benz, Men-Andri, Leif Brandes, and Franck, Egon. 2009. Do soccer associations really spend on a good thing? Empirical evidence on heterogeneity in the consumer response to match uncertainty of outcome. *Contemporary Economic Policy,* 27(2): 216–235.

Berri, David J., Stacey L. Brook, Bernd Frick, Aju J. Fenn, and Roberto Vicente-Mayoral. 2005. The short supply of tall people: Competitive imbalance and the National Basketball Association." *Journal of Economic Issues,* 39(4): 1029–1041.

Booth, D. Ross. 2005. Comparing competitive balance in Australian sports leagues: Does a salary cap and player draft measure up? *Sport Management Review,* 8(2): 119–143.

Brandes, Leif, and Egon Franck. 2006. How fans may improve competitive balance—An empirical analysis of the German Bundesliga. Working Paper No. 41: 1–26.

Buzzacchi, Luigi, Stefan Szymanski, and Tommaso M. Valletti. 2002. Equality of opportunity and equality of outcome: Open leagues, closed leagues, and competitive balance." *Journal of Industry, Competition, and Trade,* 3(3): 167–186.

Dawson, Alistair, and Paul Downward. 2005. Measuring short-run uncertainty of outcome in sporting league: A comment. *Journal of Sports Economics*, 6(3): 3030–3313.

del Corral, Julio. 2009. Competitive balance and match uncertainty in grand-slam tennis: Effects of seeding system, gender, and court surface." *Journal of Sports Economics*, 10(6): 563–581.

Demmert, Henry G. 1973. *The economics of professional team sports.* Lexington, MA: Lexington Books.

Eckard, E. Woodrow. 1998. The NCAA cartel and competitive balance in college football. *Review of Industrial Organization*, 13(3): 347–369.

Eckard, E. Woodrow. 2001a. Baseball's blue ribbon economic report: Solutions in search of a problem. *Journal of Sports Economics*, 2: 213–227.

Eckard, E.Woodrow. 2001b. Free agency, competitive balance, and diminishing returns to pennant contention." *Economic Inquiry*, 39: 430–443.

Falter, Jean-Marc, Christophe Perignon, and Olivier Vercryusse. 2008. "Impact of overwhelming joy on consumer demand: The case of a soccer World Cup victory." *Journal of Sports Economics*, 9: 20–42.

Fenn, Aju J., Peter von Allmen, Stacey Brook, and Thomas J. Pressing. 2005. The influence of structural changes and international players on competitive balance in the NHL. *Atlantic Economic Journal*, 33(2): 215–224.

Forrest, David, Robert Simmons, and Babatunde Buraimo. 2005. Outcome uncertainty and the couch potato audience. *Scottish Journal of Political Economcy*, 52(4): 641–661.

Forrest, David, James Beaumont, John Goddard, and Robert Simmons. 2005. Home advantage and the debate about competitive balance in professional sports leagues. *Journal of Sports Sciences*, 23(4): 439–445.

Fort, Rodney. 2001. "Revenue disparity and competitive balance in major league baseball." In *Baseball's revenue gap: Pennant for sale?* Hearing before the Subcommittee on Antitrust, Business Rights, and Competition of the Committee on the Judiciary (pp. 42–52), U.S. Senate, 106th Congress, 2nd Session, November 21, 2000.

Fort, Rodney. 2005. The golden anniversary of "The baseball players' labor market," *Journal of Sports Economics*, 6: 347–358.

Fort, Rodney, and Joel Maxcy. 2003. Comment: Competitive balance in sports leagues: An introduction, *Journal of Sports Economics*, 4(2): 154–160.

Fort, Rodney, and James Quirk. 1995. Cross-subsidization, incentives, and outcomes in professional team sports leagues. *Journal of Economic Literature*, 33(3): 1265–1299.

Hadley, Lawrence, Ciecka, James, and Anthony C. Krautmann. 2005. Competitive balance in the aftermath of the 1994 players' strike. *Journal of Sports Economics*, 6(4): 379–389.

Horowitz, Ira. 1997. The increasing competitive balance in major league baseball. *Review of Industrial Organization*, 12: 373–387.

Humphreys, Brad R. 2002. Alternative measures of competitive balance in sports leagues. *Journal of Sports Economics*, 3: 133–148.

Kahane, Leo H., Todd L. Idson, and Paul D. Staudohar. 2000. Introducing a new journal. *Journal of Sports Economics*, 1(1): 3–10.

Koning, Ruud H. 2000. Balance in competition in Dutch soccer. *The Statistician*, 49: 419–431.

Larsen, Andrew., Fenn, Aju J., & Spenner, Erin L. 2006. The impact of free agency and the salary cap on competitive balance in the National Football League. *Journal of Sports Economics,* 7(4): 374–390.

Lee, Young Hoon. 2009. The impact of postseason restructuring on the competitive balance and fan demand in major league baseball. *Journal of Sports Economics* 10: 219–235.

Lee, Young Hoon, and Rodney Fort. 2005. Structural change in baseball's competitive balance: The Great Depression, team location, and racial integration. *Economic Inquiry,* 43: 158–169.

Lee, Young Hoon, and Rodney Fort. 2007. Structural change, competitive balance, and the rest of the major leagues. *Economic Inquiry,* 45(3): 519–532.

Lemke, Robert J., Matthew Leonard, and Kelebogile Tlhokwane. 2009. Estimating attendance at major league baseball games for the 2007 season. *Journal of Sports Economics* (August, 2009).

Madalozzo, Regina, and Rodrigo B. Villar. (2009). Brazilian football: What brings fans to the game? *Journal of Sports Economics* (May 2009).

Maxcy, Joel G., and Mike Mondello. 2006. The impact of free agency on competitive balance in North American professional team sports leagues. *Journal of Sport Management,* 20(3): 345–365.

Meehan, James W. Jr., Randy A. Nelson, and Thomas V. Richardson. 2007. Competitive balance and game attendance in major league baseball,"*Journal of Sports Economics,* 8: 563–580.

Noll, Roger G. 1974. *Government and the sports business.* Washington, DC: Brookings Institution Press.

Owen, P. Dorian, and Clayton R. Weatherston. 2004. Uncertainty of outcome and Super 12 Rugby union attendance. *Journal of Sports Economics,* 5(4): 347–370.

Paul, Rodney J., and Andrew P. Weinbach. 2007. The uncertainty of outcome and scoring effects on Nielsen rating for Monday night football. *Journal of Economics and Business,* 59(3): 199–211.

Quirk, James P. 2004. College football conferences and competitive balance. *Managerial and Decision Economics,* 25(2): 63–75.

Quirk, James P., and Rodney Fort. 1992. *Pay dirt.* Princeton, NJ : Princeton University Press.

Rascher, Daniel A., and John P. Solmes. 2007. Do fans want close contests?: A test of the uncertainty of outcome hypothesis in the National Basketball Association. *International Journal of Sport Finance,* 3(2): 130–141.

Rodriguez, Placido, Stefan Kessene, and Jaume Garcia, Jaume, eds. 2006. *Sports economics after fifty years: Essays in honour of Simon Rottenberg.* Oviedo, Spain: University of Oviedo, 227 p.

Ross, Stephen F., and Stefan Szymanski. 2000. Open competition in sports leagues. Retrieved from http://papers.ssrn.com/paper.taf?abstract_id=243756

Rottenberg, Simon. 1956. The baseball players' labor market. *Journal of Political Economy,* 64: 242–258.

Rottenberg, Simon. 2000. Resource allocation and income distribution in professional team sports. *Journal of Sports Economics,* 1(1): 11–20.

Sanderson, Allen R. 2002. The many dimensions of competitive balance. *Journal of Sports Economics,* 3(2): 204–228.

Schmidt, Martin B., and David J. Berri. 2001. Competitive balance and attendance: The case of major league baseball. *Journal of Sports Economics,* 2: 145–167.

Schmidt, Martin B., and David J. Berri. 2005. Concentration of playing talent: Evolution in major league baseball. *Journal of Sports Economics,* 6: 412–419.

Scully, Gerald W. 1989. *The business of major league baseball,* Chicago, IL: University of Chicago Press.

Soebbing, Brian P. 2008. Competitive balance and attendance in major league baseball: An empirical test of the uncertainty of outcome hypothesis. *International Journal of Sport Finance,* 3(2): 119–126.

Sutter, Daniel, and Stephen Winkler. 2003. NCAA scholarship limits and competitive balance in college football. *Journal of Sports Economics,* 4(1): 3–18.

Szymanski, Stefan, and Tommaso M. Valletti. 2005. Promotion and relegation in sporting contests. *Revista DI Politica Economica,* 4–39.

Taylor, Beck A., and Justin D. Trogdon. 2002. Losing to win: Tournament incentives in the National Basketball Association. *Journal of Labor Economics,* 20(1): 23–41.

Zimbalist, Andrew S. 1992. *Baseball and billions.* New York: Basic Books.

Zimbalist, Andrew S. 2002. Competitive balance in sports leagues: An introduction. *Journal of Sports Economics,* 3: 111–121.

Zimbalist, Andrew S. 2003. Reply: Competitive balance conundrums. *Journal of Sports Economics,* 4(2): 161–163.

CHAPTER 3

CLUB OBJECTIVES, COMPETITIVE BALANCE, AND THE INVARIANCE PROPOSITION

STEFAN KESENNE

1. INTRODUCTION

THERE has been some controversy in the sports-economics literature regarding the differences in competitive balance between a league in which all teams are maximizing profits and a league in which the objective of the teams is to maximize their season winning percentage. Kesenne (1996, 2000), using a simple fixed-supply Walrasian model, has shown that the distribution of playing talents in a win-maximization league will be more unequal than in a profit-maximization league. However, Fort and Quirk (2004) have questioned the validity of this result, showing that nothing can be derived about the difference in competitive balance between a win- and a profit-maximization league, if no other assumptions are made on the club-revenue functions beyond concavity. In section 2 of this chapter, we will further investigate this issue by deriving the conditions that have led to these dissenting results about the competitive balance. In section 3, we try to derive the optimal competitive balance in a league theoretically, and whether a win- or profit-maximizing club, comes closest to the social optimum. Section 4 deals with the invariance proposition, analyzing the effects of restrictions on player mobility and revenue-sharing arrangements. Section 5 concludes.

2. COMPETITIVE BALANCE

The conclusion of Fort and Quirk (2004) that nothing can be derived regarding the competitive balance between a win- and a profit-maximization league if no further assumptions are made on the club-revenue function beyond concavity is, no doubt, correct. This can be illustrated graphically in Figure 3.1 for a simple two-team league with linear marginal- and average-revenue curves. The large-market team x is portrayed from left to right, and the small-market team y from right to left. The distance between the two origins is determined by the (constant) supply of playing talent. Under the profit-maximization assumption, both clubs' demand curves for talent are given by their marginal revenue curves with the competitive market equilibrium in point (T_p). Under the win maximization assumption, both clubs' demand curves for talent are given by the average-revenue curves, and the market equilibrium is found in point (T_w) (see Kesenne, 1996, 2000).

In this particular representation, which shows a very steep slope of the MR-curve of large-market team x and a very flat slope of the small-market team y, it can be seen that that the competitive balance under profit maximization (T_p) is more unequal than under win maximization (T_w). However, there might be good reasons to make further assumptions about a club-revenue function in team

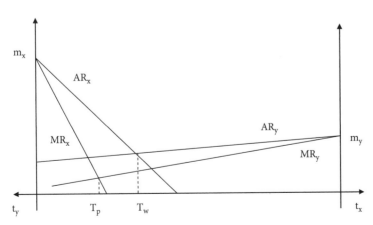

Figure 3.1 Profit and Win Maximization Equilibrium
with Ill-Behaved MR-Curves.

sports that will allow drawing some valuable conclusions on the competitive-balance issue. The slope of the *MR*-curve is affected by the preferences of the spectators regarding the win percentage of the team and the competitive balance in the league. We try to show here that there should be a relationship between the slope and the intercept of the *MR*-curves in order to become well-behaved revenue functions.

Most sports economists agree that five major variables should enter a club's revenue function:

1. The market size or drawing potential of the team
2. The winning percentage
3. The competitive balance in the league
4. The ticket price
5. The absolute quality of the league (see Scully, 1989; Noll, 1974; Zimbalist, 1992; Vrooman J., 1995; Downward and Dawson, 2000; Dobson and Goddard, 2001; Szymanski, 2003; Sandi, Sloane, and Rosentraub, 2004; Gerrard, 2006; Fort, 2006; Kesenne, 2007).

The absolute quality, however, is constant in a fixed-talent supply model. Because we want to concentrate on the player labor market, we also start from an exogenously given and constant ticket price. Based on the extensive empirical evidence (see Simmons, 1996; Forrest and Simmons, 2001; Garcia and Rodriguez, 2002), the positive impact of the market size is unquestioned, but there is some reasonable doubt about the relative importance of the winning percentage and the competitive balance. In particular, the importance of the uncertainty of outcome on attendances and public interest is doubtful (see Borland and Macdonald, 2003; Szymanski and Leach, 2006). This is a crucial issue regarding the competitive balance between win- and profit-maximization leagues.

In the following two-club model, we start from a specification of a club-revenue function that leaves open the relative importance of winning and competitive balance. As in Vrooman (2008), we assume that a linear combination of winning w and uncertainty of outcome (uo) positively affects club revenue, with unspecified weights β_i.

$$
\begin{aligned}
R_x &= m_x[(\beta_x w_x(1-w_x)+(1-\beta_x)w_x] \\
R_y &= m_y[(\beta_y w_y(1-w_y)+(1-\beta_y)w_y]
\end{aligned}
\quad \text{with} \quad m_x > m_y
\tag{1}
$$

In this specification, the uncertainty of outcome is approached by the product of the winning percentages of the two teams: $uo = w_x w_y = w_x(1-w_x)$. This variable reaches its maximum value for $w_x = 0.5$. If x is the large-market team and y the small-market team; $m_x > m_y$. We also allow the weights β_i to be different for the large- and the small-market teams, because it is possible that the supporters of small-market teams attach a different value to winning percentage and competitive balance than the supporters of large-market teams.

Rearranging the revenue functions from Eq. (1), they can be written as:

$$R_x = m_x w_x - m_x \beta_x w_x^2 \qquad \qquad MR_x = m_x - 2m_x \beta_x w_x$$
$$\qquad \qquad \qquad \text{with}$$
$$R_y = m_y w_y - m_y \beta_y w_y^2 \qquad \qquad MR_y = m_y - 2m_y \beta_y w_y \qquad (2)$$

What appears are the simple quadratic club-revenue functions and linear marginal-revenue functions that are often used in the sports economics literature (Fort and Quirk, 1995; Vrooman, 1995; Szymanski, 2004; Dietl, Lang, and Rathke, 2009). However, it is important the notice here that, based on specification (1), a positive relationship emerges between the absolute value of the slope and the intercept of the marginal revenue functions. This condition is necessary to get well-behaved quadratic club-revenue functions, meaning that, ceteris paribus (all else equal), the large-market team is at least as talented as the small-market team. Without this condition, the large-market team can turn out to be less talented than the small-market team in the market equilibrium. Without this condition, there is also no guarantee that a market equilibrium will be found with positive talent demands and a positive unit cost of talent. By only assuming concavity, club-revenue functions can be ill-suited, so that nothing can be derived regarding the competitive balance between a win- versus a profit-maximization league, as asserted by Fort and Quirk (2004). With well-suited revenue functions, one will always find more talents in the large-market club, all else equal, for whatever values of the market sizes, as can be shown later.

On the cost side, the total season cost of a team consists of the player labor cost (ct_i) and the capital cost (c_i^0). In the long term, one can assume that the capital cost is proportional to the number of talents in a team (with the same proportionality factor $v \geq 0$), because successful teams with top talents need a larger stadium, and well-paid top players are not content with poor stadium facilities. So, the cost function can be written as: $C_i = ct_i + c_i^0 = ct_i + vt_i = (c+v)t_i$.

The market equilibrium can be found by equalizing the marginal revenue function in Eq. (2):

$$m_x - 2\beta_x m_x w_x = m_y - 2\beta_y m_y (1 - w_x) \qquad (3)$$

All else equal $(\beta = \beta_1 = \beta_2)$, the winning percentages are:

$$w_x = \frac{m_x + (2\beta - 1)m_y}{2\beta(m_x + m_y)}$$

$$w_y = \frac{m_y + (2\beta - 1)m_x}{2\beta(m_x + m_y)} \qquad (4)$$

With $0<\beta\leq1$, it is clear from Eq. (4) that $w_x \geq w_y$. In the extreme case with $\beta=1$, meaning that supporters do not care at all about the winning percentage of their team but only value a balanced competition, we find that $w_x = w_y = 0.5$.

If the winning percentages are given by the ratio of the playing talents of a team and the total supply of talents in the league:

$$w_x = \frac{t_x}{t_x+t_y} \quad \text{and} \quad w_y = \frac{t_y}{t_x+t_y} \tag{5}$$

The *MP* of talent can then be derived as:

$$\frac{\partial w_x}{\partial t_x} = \frac{t_x+t_y-t_x\left(1+\dfrac{\partial t_y}{\partial t_x}\right)}{(t_x+t_y)^2} \tag{6}$$

Because the controversy in the literature about the competitive balance between a profit- and a win-maximization league refers to the fixed-supply Quirk/Fort model (1992) of the player labor market, we concentrate on that model in this paper. If the supply of talent is constant and normalized to equal unity, and the externalities of talent hiring are internalized—that is, club managers take into account, in calculating their marginal revenue, that if they hire an extra talent, the other team is losing a talent—it follows that $\partial t_y / \partial t_x = -1$, which is the so-called Walras fixed-supply conjecture. So, the *MP* of talent simplifies to:

$$\frac{\partial w_x}{\partial t_x} = \frac{t_x+t_y}{(t_x+t_y)^2} = \frac{1}{t_x+t_y} = 1 \tag{7}$$

Under these hypotheses, the winning percentage in the revenue functions of Eq. (2) can simply be replaced by the number of talents. A somewhat odd feature of this Walrasian fixed-supply conjecture model is that team managers have full control of their winning percentage, and also that one team has no choice of talents because $t_y =1-t_x$. See Szymanski and Kesenne (2004) and Szymanski (2004) for a critical discussion of this model. With the Nash conjecture $\partial t_y / \partial t_x = 0$, the *MP* of talent becomes:

$$\frac{\partial w_x}{\partial t_x} = \frac{t_y}{(t_x+t_y)^2} \tag{8}$$

If teams are profit maximizers, the non-cooperative Nash-Cournot equilibrium can be found by solving the two teams' reaction functions:

$$\frac{\partial R_x}{\partial w_x}\frac{\partial w_x}{\partial t_x} = (m_x - 2m_x\beta_x w_x)\frac{t_y}{(t_x + t_y)^2} = c + v$$

$$\frac{\partial R_y}{\partial w_y}\frac{\partial w_y}{\partial t_y} = (m_y - 2m_y\beta_y w_y)\frac{t_x}{(t_x + t_y)^2} = c + v \qquad (9)$$

However, if the number of teams in a league is large enough, the non-cooperative Nash equilibrium approaches the competitive equilibrium. It follows that with a large number of teams, the Walrasian competitive equilibrium model can be used to derive the competitive balance, also under the Nash conjecture. Given these hypotheses, the demand curves for talent of two profit maximizing teams can be written as:

$$\frac{\partial R_x}{\partial t_x} = m_x - 2m_x\beta_x t_x$$

$$\frac{\partial R_y}{\partial t_y} = m_y - 2m_y\beta_y t_y \qquad (10)$$

In order to derive the number of talents of the large-market team in the market equilibrium (talent demand equals talent supply) under profit maximization, we have to solve the following equation:

$$m_x - 2\beta_x m_x t_x = m_y - 2\beta_y m_y (1 - t_x) \qquad (11)$$

So that:

$$t_x^p = \frac{m_x - m_y + 2\beta_y m_y}{2(\beta_x m_x + \beta_y m_y)} \qquad (12)$$

The equilibrium number of talents of the large-market team in a win-maximization league, taking into account that the demand curves are now determined by the average revenue curves, can be found by solving the equation:

$$m_x - \beta_x m_x t_x = m_y - \beta_y m_y (1 - t_x) \qquad (13)$$

This results in the following number of talents in the large market team:

$$t_x^w = \frac{m_x - m_y + \beta_y m_y}{(\beta_x m_x + \beta_y m_y)} = \frac{2(m_x - m_y) + 2\beta_y m_y}{2(\beta_x m_x + \beta_y m_y)} \qquad (14)$$

Comparing Eq. (14) to Eq. (12), one can see that $t_x^w > t_x^p$, whatever the size of the weights β_i in the large and the small market club. It follows that, under the specified conditions above, *the distribution of talent will be more unequal under win maximization, whatever the differences in the spectators' preferences for winning and competitive balance.*

It is also possible that the teams in one league have different objectives. If we consider these mixed leagues and start from the scenario with a profit-maximizing large-market club and a win-maximizing small-market club, the solution is found by solving:

$$m_x - 2\beta_x m_x t_x = m_y - \beta_y m_y (1 - t_x) \tag{15}$$

So that:

$$t_x^{pw} = \frac{m_x - m_y + \beta_y m_y}{2\beta_x m_x + \beta_y m_y} \tag{16}$$

If the large-market club is a win maximizer and the small-market team is a profit maximizer, we have to solve the following equation:

$$m_x - \beta_x m_x t_x = m_y - 2\beta_y m_y (1 - t_x) \tag{17}$$

so that the number of talents in the large-market team is:

$$t_x^{wp} = \frac{m_x - m_y + 2\beta_y m_y}{\beta_x m_x + 2\beta_y m_y} \tag{18}$$

Comparing Eq. (18) to Eq. (16), we can see that $t_x^{wp} > t_x^{pw}$, meaning that a more unbalanced competition can be expected if the large-market club is a win maximizer and the small-market club is a profit maximizer.

On can also derive, by comparing Eq. (16) to Eq. (12) and Eq. (18) to Eq. (14) that $t_x^p > t_x^{pw}$ and that $t_x^{wp} \geq t_x^w$, as long as $t_x^w \leq 1$. In case $t_x^w > 1$ *and* $t_x^{wp} > 1$, which is impossible in reality, both are truncated to equal unity. Summarizing, the following proposition holds, whatever the spectators' preferences for winning and uncertainty of outcome:

$$t_x^{wp} \geq t_x^w > t_x^p > t_x^{pw} \tag{19}$$

In other words, the highest uncertainty of outcome will be reached in a league in which the large-market clubs are profit maximizers and the small-market clubs are win maximizers. The most unequal competitive balance can be expected in a league in which the large-market clubs are win maximizers and the small-market clubs are profit maximizers. The competitive balance will be more unequal in a pure-win-maximization league than in a pure-profit-maximization league.

These results are presented graphically in Figure 3.2.

3. OPTIMAL COMPETITIVE BALANCE

Another interesting question is which one of these four competitive balances from section 2 is optimal? One possible optimality criterion is the maximization of total league revenue. It is clear that, in a league in which all clubs are profit maximizers,

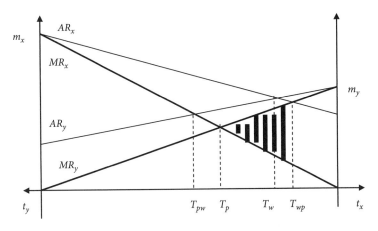

Figure 3.2 Comparing Competitive Balances with
Well-Behaved MR-Curves.

total league revenue will reach its highest possible level, because only in this market equilibrium is MR_x, = MR_y, so that the allocation of talents over the teams is optimal. That is, every talent is playing on the team in which its marginal productivity is highest. In the three other leagues, it is clear from Figure 3.2, that there is some misallocation of resources, causing a welfare loss in terms of total league revenue. This welfare loss can be measured by the size of the triangular area between the two MR-curves and between the profit-maximizing equilibrium and the actual market equilibrium. This loss is largest in a league in which the large-market club is a win maximizer and the small-market club is a profit maximizer (T_{wp}), as indicated by the shaded area in Figure 3.2.

However, this welfare criterion does not take into account the preferences of the public regarding the competitive balance. If the public prefers a perfectly balanced competition, which means that the win percent of every team is 0.50, it is clear from the foregoing analysis that the league in which the large-market clubs are profit maximizers and the small-market clubs are win maximizers comes closest. It is doubtful, however, from both theoretical and empirical research, that this is what spectators want (see Rasher and Solmes, 2007). Theoretically, starting from the uncertainty of outcome specification, $uo_i = w_i(1-w_i)$, maximizing the spectators' utility function over winning percentage and competitive balance, $U = w \cdot uo = w^2(1-w)$, it is clear that the optimal winning percentage can be found from $\partial U / \partial W = 2w - 3w^2 = 0$ so that $w^* = 2/3 = 0.67$ Also, graphically, it can be seen in Figure 3.3 that the point of tangency between the constraint given by the uo specification and the highest possible indifference curve will result in a winning percentage of their favorite team well above 0.5.

Obviously, given this specification of the spectators' utility function, the supporters of both teams will prefer a winning percentage of 0.67 for their favorite team, which is impossible. What we need is a social-welfare function that takes into account the preferences of the supporters of both teams. If the large-market

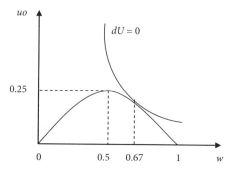

Figure 3.3 Optimal Winning Percentage.

team has more supporters, the supporters of the large-market team should get a
larger weight in the welfare function. The weight α could be set equal to the ratio
of the market sizes: $\alpha = m_x / m_y > 1$

If the social-welfare function is specified as:

$$W = U_x^\alpha U_y = w_x^{2\alpha+1} w_y^{\alpha+2} \tag{23}$$

The competitive balance, which maximizes welfare, can be found by solving
the first-order condition:

$$\frac{\partial w}{\partial w_x} = (2\alpha+1)w_y^{\alpha+2} w_x^{2\alpha} - (\alpha+2)w_x^{2\alpha+1} w_y^{\alpha+1} = 0$$

$$or: \; w_y^{\alpha+1} w_x^{2\alpha} \{(2\alpha+1)w_y - (\alpha+2)w_x\} = 0 \tag{24}$$

$$so \; that: \; \frac{w_x}{w_y} = \frac{2\alpha+1}{\alpha+2}$$

If the two markets are of the same size ($\alpha = 1$), it does not come as a surprise
that both teams should have the same winning percentage, equal to 0.50. However,
if the large market is 50 percent larger than the small market ($\alpha = m_x / m_y = 1.5$),
the ratio of the winning percentages should be $w_x / w_y = 4/3.5 = 1.14$, with
$w_x^* = 0.53$ and $w_y^* = 0.47$. The larger the difference in market size, the larger should
be the welfare optimal winning percentage of the large-market team. For whatever
difference in market size, the optimal winning percentage of the large team stays
between 0.5 and 0.67.

Which league comes closest to this welfare optimum? We try to find out using
a simple numerical example.

Assume that the market size of club x is 15,000 and the market size of club y
is 10,000, or $\alpha = m_x / m_y = 1.5$. It is reasonable to assume that a club's marginal
revenue approaches zero if its winning percentage approaches 100 percent. So

$MR_i = m_i - 2\beta_i m_i w_i = 0$ if $w_i = 1$; that is, if $m_i - 2\beta_i m_i = 0$ or $\beta_i = m_i/2m_i = 0.5$. So, a reasonable β_i-value for both clubs in this numerical example is $\beta_x = \beta_y = 0.5$.

With these values in mind, we can now calculate the competitive balance for the four leagues discussed in section 2, that is, Eqs. (12), (14), (16), and (18), respectively:

$$w_x^p = 0.60 \quad w_x^w = 0.80 \quad w_x^{pw} = 0.50 \quad w_x^{wp} = 085 \qquad (25)$$

Given the optimum under these conditions, $w_x^* = 0.53$, the mixed league with a profit- maximizing large-market club and a win-maximizing small-market club comes closest, followed by the league with all profit-maximizing clubs. The two other leagues are too unbalanced to reach the optimum. Based on this competitive equilibrium model, the competitive balance in a win-maximization league is too unbalanced to reach the optimum, so some revenue sharing among clubs would be preferable.

4. THE INVARIANCE PROPOSITION

The well-known invariance proposition, which goes back to Rottenberg's (1956) seminal article, and which was formally proven by Quirk and El-Hodiri (1974), states that the restrictions on player mobility, imposed by a reservation or a retain-and-transfer system, do not affect the competitive balance if clubs are profit maximizers. The distribution of talent remains unchanged because the marginal revenue of talent is not affected by paid or received transfer fees. With or without a transfer system, a player will end up on the team where his marginal revenue is highest. However, profit- maximizing team owners in a monopsonistic player market that is created by a transfer system will exploit players. Scully (1974, 1986) has observed a high rate of monopsonistic exploitation of baseball players in de United States before the abolition of the reserve clause in the mid-1970s. After the abolition, baseball players were paid according to their marginal revenue (see Scully, 1999). However, in a win-maximization league, things are different. Under a retain-and-transfer system, the small-market club, as a net-seller of talent in the transfer market, will use the received transfer fees to increase its demand for talent, which is now determined by the net average revenue of talent ($NAR_i = (R_i - c_i^0)/t_i = AR_i - v$). The large-market club will reduce its demand for talent so that a more equal distribution of talent will emerge. This positive effect on the competitive balance will be very limited, though, because a team in a small market will not be able to attract many talents that can be sold to the large-market team. Also, a win-maximizing club will not exploit its players, who would be rather overpaid, that is, above their marginal revenue, even in a monopsonistic player market (see Kesenne, 2002, 2007).

Later on, the invariance proposition has been extended to gate sharing. Also, gate-revenue sharing among clubs does not affect the competitive balance in a profit-maximization league, because both clubs, large and small, will reduce their demand for talent if the home club has to share its marginal revenue of talent with the visiting team. The only effects of revenue sharing will be lower salary levels (see Quirk and Fort, 1992), and higher profits in the small-budget clubs. The profits of the large-budget clubs can be reduced by sharing if the presharing profits of a club are larger than the average budget in the league (see Kesenne, 2007).

As distinct from a profit maximization league, in a win-maximization league, gate-revenue sharing among teams does improve the competitive balance because the small-market team will increase and the large-market club will reduce its demand for talent. Because the upward shift of the small-market club's demand for talent will also be stronger than the downward shift of large-market club's demand for talent, revenue sharing can have an increasing effect on player salaries (see Kesenne, 2007). Therefore, the invariance proposition does not hold in a league where teams are win maximizers.

In a mixed league where the large-market club is profit maximizer and the small-market club is a win maximizer, gate revenue sharing will slightly improve the distribution of talent, because the large team will reduce its demand for talent (MR) and the small team will increase its demand (AR). In the mixed league where the small-market club is a profit maximizer and the large-market club is a win maximizer, the impact of revenue sharing on the competitive balance is theoretically indeterminate, because both teams will reduce their demand for talent. Consequently, revenue sharing will now reduce the player salary level. *The invariance proposition no longer holds if one of the teams in a league is a win maximizer.*

Moreover, Szymanski and Kesenne (2004), criticizing the constant-supply Walrasian model, have shown that, in both the flexible supply model and the fixed-supply model under the Nash conjecture, revenue sharing worsens the competitive balance under profit maximization, because the negative external effects from hiring talents are larger for the high-revenue teams, so that they are better off if revenues are shared.

5. Conclusion

In this contribution, we have argued that, under some reasonable assumptions, such as well-behaved club-revenue functions, it can shown that the competitive balance in a win maximization league will be more unbalanced than in a profit maximization league. We have also compared the competitive balances in the so-called mixed leagues, in which some clubs are profit maximizers and others are win maximizers. In a first and simple welfare-economic exercise, we have shown that, in a league with profit-maximizing large-market clubs and win-maximizing small-market clubs, the expected competitive balance will be closest to the welfare optimum. Whereas little can be expected from a player reservation system to improve the competitive balance in both a profit- and a win-maximization league, revenue sharing will only affect the distribution of talent in a win maximization league.

REFERENCES

Andreff, W., and S. Szymanski. 2006. *Handbook of sports economics.* Cheltenham, UK, and Northampton, MA: Edward Elgar.

Borland, J., and R. MacDonald. 2003. Demand for sport. *Oxford Review of Economic Policy,* 19(4): 478–503.

Dobson, S., and J. Goddard. 2001. *The economics of football.* Cambridge: Cambridge University Press.

Downward, P., and A. Dawson. 2000. *The economics of professional team sports,* London and New York: Routledge.

Fort, R., and J. Quirk. 1995. Cross-subsidization, incentives and outcomes in professional team sports leagues. *Journal of Economic Literature* XXXIII: 1265–1299.

Fort, R., and J. Quirk. 2004. Owner objectives and competitive balance. *Journal of Sports Economics* 3(1).

Forrest, D., and R. Simmons. 2002. Outcome uncertainty and attendance demand in sport: The case of English soccer. *The Statistician,* 51(2): 229–241.

Garcia, J., and P. Rodriguez. 2002. The determinants of football match attendance revisited: Empirical evidence from the Spanish Football League. *Journal of Sports Economics,* 3(1): 18–38.

Gerrard, B., ed. 2006. *The economics of association football.* Cheltenham, UK, and Northampton, MA: Edward Elgar.

Jones, J. 1969. The economics of the national hockey league. *Canadian Journal of Economics,* 2(1): 1–20.

Kesenne, S. 1996. League management in professional team sports with win maximizing clubs. *European Journal for Sports Management,* 2(2).

Kesenne, S. 2000. Revenue sharing and competitive balance in professional team sports. *Journal of Sports Economics,* 1(1).

Kesenne, S. 2007. Revenue sharing and owner profits. *Journal of Sports Economics,* 8(5).

Kesenne, S. 2007. *The economic theory of professional team sports: An analytical treatment.* Northampton, MA: E. Elgar.

Noll, R., ed. 1974. *Government and the sport business.* Washington, DC: The Brookings Institution.

Quirk, J., and R. Fort. 1992. *Pay dirt, the business of professional team sports.* Princeton: Princeton University Press.

Rascher, D., and Solmes, John Paul G. 2007. Do fans want close contests? A test of the uncertainty of outcome hypothesis in the National Basketball Association. *International Journal of Sport Finance,* 1(4).

Sandy, R., P. Sloane, and M. Rosentraub. 2004. *The economics of sport: An international perspective.* New York: Palgrave Macmillan.

Scully, G. 1974. Pay and performance in Major League Baseball. *American Economic Review* 64(6).

Scully, G. 1989. *The business of Major League Baseball.* Chicago: University of Chicago Press.

Scully, G. 1999. "Free agency and the rate of monopsonistic exploitation in baseball." In *Competition policy in professional sports,* edited by C. Jeanrenaud and S. Kesenne. Antwerp: Standard Editions Ltd.

Simmons, R. 1996. The demand for English League Football: A club-level analysis. *Applied Economics,* 28: 139–155.

Szymanski, S. 2003. The economic design of sporting contests. *Journal of Economic Literature,* 41(4): 1137–1187.

Szymanski, S. 2004. Professional team sports are only a game: The Walrasian fixed-supply conjecture model, contest—Nash equilibrium and the invariance principle. *Journal of Sports Economics,* 5(2): 111–126.

Szymanski, S., and S. Kesenne. 2004. Competitive balance and gate revenue sharing in team sports. *Journal of Industrial Economics,* 51(4): 513–525.

Szymanski, S., and S. Leach. 2005. Tilting the playing field: Why a sports league planner choose less, not more, competitive balance? Working paper, Tanaka Business School, Imperial College, London.

Vrooman, J. 1995. A general theory of professional sports leagues. *Southern Economic Journal,* 61(4): 971–990.

Vrooman, J. 2008. Theory of the perfect game: Competitive balance in monopoly sports leagues. *Review of Industrial Organization* 31: 1–30.

Zimbalist, A. 1992. *Baseball and billions.* New York: Basic Books.

CHAPTER 4

THEORY OF THE BIG DANCE

THE PLAYOFF PAY-OFF IN PRO SPORTS LEAGUES

JOHN VROOMAN

The baseball season is structured to mock reason, because science doesn't work in the games that matter most.

—Michael Lewis, author of
Moneyball, a book about Billy Beane

My sh*t doesn't work in the playoffs. My job is to get us to the playoffs. What happens after that is f***ing luck.

—Billy Beane, General Manager of Oakland Athletics

INTRODUCTION

OVER the last decade there has been an academic revolution in professional sports leagues. The evaluation of talent has closely followed abstract notions that the worth of a player is equal to a magic metric of his marginal revenue product (*MRP*). The revolution began in Major League Baseball (MLB) with midmarket teams' need for efficient talent-evaluation techniques in leagues dominated by large-market clubs. The most celebrated practitioner of scientific evaluation technique is Billy Beane, the general manager of the mid-market Oakland Athletics since 1998. Every MLB team now uses a unique blend of new-school science with old-school intuition in finding the true economic measure of a ballplayer.

Recently, the revolution has faltered for two reasons. First, it seems that the new science can be effective over regular seasons because the number of games reduces uncertainty of the expected result, but it does not always translate to the post-season. The new science is less effective during playoffs because outcomes inherit the randomness of shorter series and knockout tournaments. In his first five years (1999–2003) as general manager of the Atheletics, Beane's record was 479–330, with a winning percentage of .592. The good news was that the Athletics made the playoffs in four straight seasons, 2000–2003; the bad news was that they lost all four first-round series in five games. The second problem is that if a mid-market club develops a successful evaluation technique, large-market clubs will soon improve it at a higher level.[1]

The peculiar economics of the playoffs in professional sports leagues has been largely neglected in sports economics (Whitney, 1988; Vrooman, 2007). This knowledge gap is surprising, given the emotional and financial importance of the post-season to fans, players, and teams. The purpose of this paper is to address the economic aspects of championship playoffs and the nexus of the regular season and the post-season (the two seasons) in the four major North American professional sports leagues and the English Premier League (EPL).

The argument begins with the basic Quirk, Fort, and Vrooman (QFV) model (Fort and Quirk 1995, and Vrooman 1995) of professional sports leagues. QFV is expanded to examine the feedback effect that the post-season prize from playoffs may have on competitive balance during the regular season. The *champion effect* is the hypothesis that post-season revenue complicates competitive balance for the regular season (Vrooman 2007). The strength of the *champion effect* depends on the relative size of the post-season prize and its certainty, which depends on the formats of the two seasons. The *champion effect* is strongest when the two seasons are both long and the playoffs are seeded from the regular season. In this case, the second season replicates the first. The connection is weakest when post-season results inherit the randomness of a short series. In this case "science doesn't work in the games that matter most." (Lewis, 2003)

After the theoretical propositions, the parameters of the *champion effect* are isolated, and the playoff structures and payoffs to the teams and players are compared for each of the sports leagues. The paper concludes with an examination of the internal contradiction of the post-season. The leagues receive disproportionate revenue for playoff tournaments and yet the participating teams and players are rewarded the least for the games that matter most.

OPEN AND CLOSED CASE

The *champion effect* is a variant of QFV theory that assumes a simplified two-team league with twin profit functions:

$$\pi_1 = R_1[m_1, w_1(t_1, t_2)] - ct_1 \qquad \pi_2 = R_2[m_2, w_2(t_2, t_1)] - ct_2 \qquad (1)$$

Team 1 revenue R_1 is a function of market size m_1 and win percent $w_1 = t_1/(t_1 + t_2)$, determined by its relative share t_1 of league talent T, where a zero-sum constraint requires $\partial w_2/\partial w_1 = -1$. Team 1 sets payroll ct_1 by acquiring talent until the marginal revenue product of talent MRP_1 is equal to the cost per unit of talent c, which is the same for both teams.

$$MRP_1 = MR_1 \, MP_1 = (\partial R_1/\partial w_1)(\partial w_1/\partial t_1) = c \qquad (2)$$

Simultaneous profit maximization (mutual best response) for both teams requires

$$MRP_1 = (\partial R_1/\partial w_1)(\partial w_1/\partial t_1) = c = MRP_2 \qquad (3)$$

The win function $w_1 = t_1/(t_1 + t_2)$ yields the marginal product of talent (MP_1) for each team:

$$MP_1 = \partial w_1/\partial t_1 = (t_2 - t_1 \, \partial t_2/\partial t_1)/(t_1 + t_2)^2 \qquad (4)$$

In equilibrium, the MRP of talent for both teams equals their mutual cost per unit of talent:

$$MRP_1 = MR_1 \, MP_1 = [\partial R_1/\partial w_1][(t_2 - t_1 \, \partial t_2/\partial t_1)/T^2] = c = MRP_2 \qquad (5)$$

In a *closed league,* an inelastic supply of skilled talent T is fixed, and one team's talent gain is another team's zero-sum loss, such that $\partial t_2/\partial t_1 = -1$. Substitution of $\partial t_2/\partial t_1 = -1$ into Eq. (5) yields the equilibrium condition for simultaneous profit maximization in a closed league:

$$MR_1 = cT = MR_2 \qquad (6)$$

By comparison, an *open league* faces an elastic supply of talent available at an exogenous wage rate c. In an open league, one team's talent acquisition has no effect on talent of its opponent, so $\partial t_1/\partial t_2 = 0$. Substituting $\partial t_1/\partial t_2 = 0$ into (5) yields the open league solution:

$$MR_1 \, w_2 = cT = MR_2 \, w_1 \qquad (7)$$

The Yankee paradox is the empirical proposition that fans want their teams to win closely matched games instead of blowing out the opposition. In a sports league, any team is only as strong as its weakest opponent. The Yankee paradox implies strictly concave revenue functions that dampen asymmetric revenue advantages of larger market clubs.

Asymmetric large market of Team 1 $m_1 > m_2$ can be captured with a parameter $\sigma > 1$ that reflects $R_1 = \sigma R_2$. The Yankee paradox implies a parameter $\phi \in \{0,1\}$ that measures fan preference for competitive balance $\phi < 1$. Interaction of large-market σ-advantage with the Yankee paradox can be shown for both open and closed profit-max leagues.

$$\pi_1 = \sigma[\phi\omega_1 + (1 - \phi)] \, w_1 \, w_2 - ct_1 \quad \pi_2 = [\phi\omega_2 + (1 - \phi\omega_2\,\omega_1)] - ct_2 \tag{8}$$

Consider the Yankee paradox where $\phi = .5$, and the restriction $\partial w_2 / \partial w_1 = -1$ simplifies (8):

$$\pi_1 = \sigma \, (w_1 - .5w_1{}^2) - ct_1 \quad \pi_2 = w_2 - .5w_2{}^2 - ct_2 \tag{9}$$

In a closed league of Eq. (6), simultaneous profit maximization yields:

$$MR_1 = \sigma \, w_2 = cT^* = w_1 = MR_2 \tag{10}$$

The *closed league* has a competitive solution $w_1/w_2 = \sigma$ with respective winning percentages $w_1 = \sigma / (1 + \sigma)$ and $w_2 = 1/(1 + \sigma)$. By comparison the open-league solution is:

$$MR_1 w_2 = \sigma w_2{}^2 = c^*T = w_1{}^2 = MR_2 \, w_1 \tag{11}$$

An open league is more balanced $w_1/w_2 = \sigma^2$; where $w_1 = \sigma^2/(1 + \sigma^2)$, and $w_2 = 1/(1 + \sigma^2)$. The asymmetric large market advantage has been dampened twice, on the revenue side by the Yankee paradox and on the cost side by the diminishing marginal product of talent. Compare the closed-market solution at A with the open market solution at B in Figure 4.1.

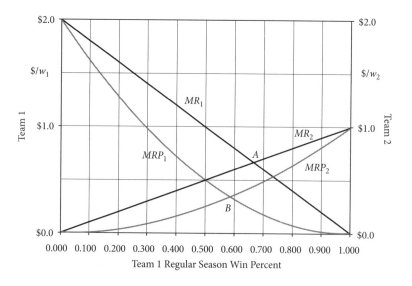

Figure 4.1 Open and Closed Case.

CHAMPION EFFECT

Post-season championship tournaments complicate the academic convenience of concave revenue functions, because the redoubled importance of winning counteracts the Yankee paradox. With an additional chance for post-season play, each team is built not only to win the regular season, but also to qualify for the post-season tournament. The champion effect is the polarizing feedback that the post-season may have on regular season competitive balance. The degree of revenue convexity caused by the champion effect depends on the size and certainty of the post-season prize compared to regular-season revenue.

The probability of team 1 making the post-season tournament θ_1 based on its regular-season performance w_1 is expressed as a logistic cumulative density function (CDF),

$$\theta_1 = 1 / [1 + \exp(\alpha + \beta w_1)] \tag{12}$$

where $\theta \in \{0,1\}$; $\alpha < \beta > 0$. The league mean $\mu = -\alpha/\beta$ is the regular season win threshold where teams have a 50 percent chance of making the post-season. If δ is the ratio of the playoff prize to regular season revenue and $\omega_1 = w_1/(w_1 + \mu)$ is the probability of playoff success against teams with an expected win percentage μ, then the combined two-season revenue function R_1^* becomes complicated by convexity:

$$R_1^* = \sigma [\, w_1 - 5w_1^2 + \delta\theta\,(\omega_1 - .5\omega_1^2)] \tag{13}$$

The *champion effect* on combined regular and post-season revenue R_1^* of team 1 is shown in Figure 4.2 hypothetically for $\sigma = 2$, $\mu = .550$ and $\delta = .5$.

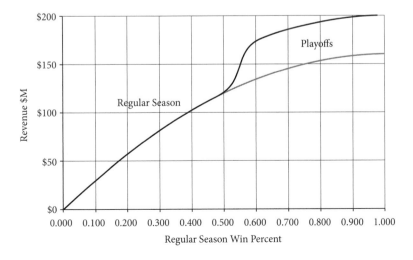

Figure 4.2 Champion Effect.

THE EDGE

An important complication of the champion *effect* is that post-season revenue convexity introduces instability and polarization into the regular season. Intuitively, the *MRPs* of both teams reflect the probability distribution function (*PDF*) derivatives of the respective *CDFs*. The instability of the *champion effect* on the league solution is shown in Figure 4.3 for an open league with a playoff threshold $\mu = .550$. As either team approaches the playoff threshold at $\mu = .55$ the marginal revenue of winning each additional qualifying game explodes and creates dual solutions at *A* and *B*. These twin equilibria explain observed threshold behavior during interseason and intraseason trade/transfer windows in North American and European sports leagues for teams on the edge of qualifying for the playoffs.[2]

It is clear that the *champion effect* in sports leagues not only depends on the relative size of the playoff payoff δ and the steepness of the threshold β but also the relative position of the threshold μ and the resulting quality of the teams in the post-season tournament. In the NBA and NHL, for example, sixteen of thirty teams in each league qualify for the playoffs. In this case, the higher seeded teams should be more assured of success in the early rounds of the tournament, but this mutes the *champion effect* because the marginal revenue of a win is simultaneously higher for all teams when their *MRPs* all peak around .500. There will be several potential talent buyers at the midseason trade window because the *MRP* of talent is higher for all teams around the .500 threshold, but there will be few talent sellers because the same is true for all teams, regardless of market size. If both curves simultaneously peak at the $w = .500$ threshold for the NBA and NHL in Figure 4.3,

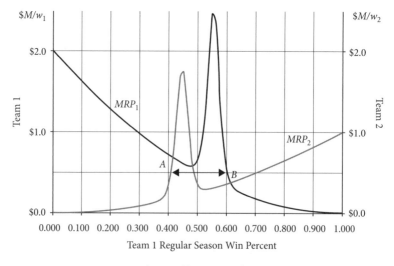

Figure 4.3 Trade Deadline/Transfer Window.

then the champion effect becomes irrelevant and the league solution returns to the dominance of the large revenue team.

Inactivity in midseason transfer windows could also occur in European leagues with multiple revenue convexities at lower winning percentages. Revenue convexities reflect the possibility of midlevel clubs qualifying for the Union of European Football Associations' (UEFA) consolation Europa League (UEFA Cup before 2009) and the threat of catastrophic relegation to a lower-revenue league. These revenue convexities imply multiple kinks along revenue functions and coincidental *MRP* thresholds for winning and losing clubs. Top clubs on the edge of qualifying for UEFA Champions' League (UCL) will find few transfer partners among lesser clubs on the edge of relegation to lower leagues.[3]

Logit regression estimates of the *champion effect* are compared in Table 4.1 and shown in Figure 4.4 for the four major North American Leagues during 1995–2008 and English Premier League (EPL) champion and relegation effects for 2003–2008. The strength of the *champion effect* is directly related to the link between the regular season performance and qualification for post-season β and the asymmetry of the playoff threshold μ among teams (deviation of playoff-qualifying mean μ from regular season mean $w = .500$).

Based on these preliminary findings, the best candidates for experiencing the *champion effect* are MLB and EPL. The β-qualifying effect still depends on the relation between regular-season and post-season success once a team has made the playoffs, and the μ-threshold effect still depends on the absence of additional revenue convexity kinks at lower levels of regular-season performance. In other words the *champion effect* could still be dampened in MLB by

Table 4.1 Playoff Probability Estimates

League	α	β	$\mu = -\alpha/\beta$	N	R^2
Major League Baseball	−41.89	76.21	.550	414	.681
	(5.19)	(9.49)			
National Football League	−19.66	34.94	.563	437	.738
	(2.36)	(4.21)			
National Basketball Association	−23.12	47.01	.492	407	.767
	(3.11)	(6.22)			
National Hockey League	−23.82	48.36	.493	369	.671
	(2.75)	(5.51)			
English Premier League	−26.28	42.15	.623	140	.808
UEFA Champions League	(7.04)	(11.54)			
English Premier League	−32.95	90.35	.365	140	.798
Relegation	(10.31)	(28.21)			

Standard errors in parentheses. All coefficients significant at .01.

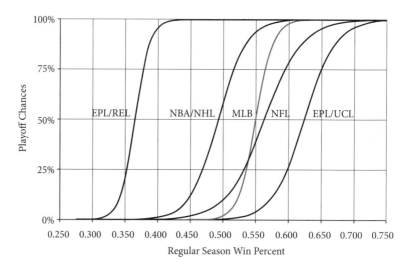

Figure 4.4 Playoff Probability CDF.

risk and uncertainty in playoff success and weakened in EPL by a *relegation effect* at $w_2 = .365$, which is symmetrical (around $w_1 = w_2 = .500$) with UEFA Champions League (UCL) threshold at $w_1 = .623$.

FINAL FOUR

The connection between regular-season and post-season performance is a function of various regular and post-season structures among the leagues. The strongest relationship between the two seasons would be long regular season and long seeded playoff among an inclusive pool of teams. In this case, the risk of an early upset is minimized and the second season replicates the first. The weakest connection would involve a short playoff series or a one-game knockout elimination series. A random playoff outcome reduces the *champion effect* because it introduces risk and uncertainty into pursuit of the playoff prize.

Playoff structures of the big-four North American leagues are shown in Table 4.2 and EPL/UCL in Table 4.3. Although all tournaments are seeded to ideally match the best teams in the finals, that prospect is diminished with fewer rounds (3) and shorter series (MLB's best-three-of-five-game series in round one) and the chances of a hot team knockout in the case of the NFL's one-game playoffs.[4] These playoff designs introduce randomness and upset into the post-seasons of MLB and NFL, whereas the stronger teams should prevail in the NBA, the NHL, and UCL. More than half of the teams qualify for the NBA and NHL playoffs, which extend

Table 4.2 Post-season Playoff Rules in North American Sports Leagues

League	MLB	NFL	NBA	NHL
Size/ Season	30 teams, 2 leagues, 6 divisions, 162 games	32 teams, 2 conferences, 8 divisions, 16 games	30 teams, 2 conferences, 6 divisions, 82 games	30 teams, 2 conferences, 6 divisions, 82 games
2007/08 Revenue	$6.08 billion league total	$6.54 billion league total	$3.57 billion league total	$2.6 billion league total
Midseason Deadline	$203 million team average	$204 million team average	$119 million team average	$87 million team average
	Straight non-waiver trades July 31, 4 P.M. EST; waiver trades August 31	Tuesday following week 6 of regular season, 4 P.M. EST	Second to last Thursday in February, 3 P.M. EST	40 days before end of regular season, 3 P.M. EST
Playoffs	3 rounds, 8 teams, 2 wild cards	4 rounds, 12 teams, 4 byes	4 rounds, 16 teams	4 rounds, 16 teams
Seeding	3 division winners get 3 top seeds by record in each league; best non-division winner is 4th wild card seed. Home field based on record. No home field for wild card.	4 division winners seeded 1–4 by record in each conference; best non-division winners 5–6 wild card seed. Home field based on seeding.	3 division winners best non-division winner seeded 1–4 by record in each conference; next best teams seed 5–8. Home court based on record.	3 division winners seeded 1–3 in each conference; best non-division winners seeded 4–8 in each conference. Home ice based on seeding.
Round 1	1 v. 4; 2 v. 3 in best 3 of 5 division series in each league. 2–2–1 format. Wild card cannot play v. own division.	Seeds 1 & 2 have byes in Round 1. 3 v. 8; 4 v. 5 in each conference. Reseeded after Round 1.	1 v. 8, 2 v. 7, 3 v. 6, 4 v. 5 in best of 7 series; 2–2–1–1–1 format. Not reseeded after Round 1.	1 v. 8, 2 v. 7, 3 v. 6, 4 v. 5 in best 4 of 7 series; 2–2–1–1–1 format. Reseeded after Round 1.
Round 2	Two winners in each league play in best of 7 League Championship Series; 2–3–2 format	#1 seed v lowest seed, #2 seed v other team in each conference in Division Playoffs	Winner #1 #8 v winner #4 v #5; winner #2 v #7 v winner #3 v #6 best of 7 series. 2–2–1–1–1 format	Top remaining seed v lowest seed, next seed v other team in each conference best of 7 series. 2–2–1–1–1 format
Round 3	World Series between League Champions, best of 7 games. 2–3–2 format. Home field to league all-star game winner.	Division Series winning teams play in American and National Football Conference Championship games.	Winning teams from each conference in best of 7 Championship series; 2–2–1–1–1 format.	Winning teams each conference in best of 7 Championship series 2–2–1–1–1 format.

(continued)

Table 4.2 (*Continued*)

League	MLB	NFL	NBA	NHL
Round 4	...	Super Bowl played between NFC AFC Champions on neutral site	Championship between Conference Champions in best of 7; 2–3–2 format; home court based on better record.	Stanley Cup between Conference Champions best of 7; 2–2–1–1–1 format; home ice based on better record.

Table 4.3 Playoff Rules in English Premier League/UEFA Champions League

EPL Size/Season	20 teams, 38-game season, bottom 3 teams relegated, replaced by 3 teams promoted from lower division.
2007/08 Revenue	$3.36 billion league total; $168 million team average
Transfer Windows	Winter transfer window: January 1–31, 17:00 GMT Summer transfer window; end of season through August 31, 17:00 BST
Group stage*	5 rounds, 32 teams
Seeding**	EPL Champion, runner-up and N3 (after 2009) are directly seeded in UCL group stage. N4 is seeded in final playoff round. N5 and N6 are seeded in consolation Europa League (UEFA Cup before 2009).
Round 1	Group Stage: 32 teams are split into 8 groups of 4 teams, seeded with country protection by UEFA coefficient. 6 home and away matches played within groups. Top 2 from each group enter Round 2, 3rd place enters consolation Europa League Round of 32, 4th place eliminated.
Round 2	16 team knock out-phase. Group winners play other group runners-up (other than teams from own pool or nation) home and away matches winner based on total goals.
Round 3	Quarter final draw is unseeded and open without country protection. Home and away legs with winner based on aggregate goals.
Round 4	Semifinals match 4 winners from quarter finals same unseeded open draw as round 3, home and away legs winner based on total goals.
Round 5	UEFA Champions League Finals is a single match at neutral site

*Starting in 2010, UCL has 3 qualifying rounds, a playoff round, a group stage, and 4 knockout rounds. 15 winners of qualifying rounds join automatic entrants from leagues 1–5 in 20-team playoff round. 10 winners of the playoff round face 22 (16 in 2009) automatic entrants in the 32-team group stage.
**Starting in 2010, the top three European leagues based on UEFA coefficients (England, Spain, Italy) each place 4 teams in UCL: 3 directly in 32-team group stage and 1 team in 20-team playoff round. The 4th–6th leagues (France, Germany and Russia in 2010) place 2 teams group stage and leagues 4–5 put 1 team in playoff round. Leagues 7–12 place1team in group stage. UCL Cup holder also placed in final 32.

well beyond the regular seasons. As UCL has evolved from an egalitarian knock-out tournament in 1993, the thirty-two-team-group stage has become a de facto Champions League. Beginning in 2010, twenty-two of thirty-two teams are directly preseeded from the elite European leagues to reduce the risk of their early knockout. UEFA loads Champions League in favor of dominant teams to maximize TV revenue and preempt a breakaway European superleague (Vrooman, 2007).

Based on these configurations, the playoffs in NBA, NHL, and UCL should replicate the regular season and the two seasons in MLB and NFL should be tenuously connected. In results not shown here, this is approximately true. Since 1995, the relation between the two seasons is the weakest in MLB and NFL and strongest in the NBA and NHL, but the connection weakens in all leagues after the final four teams have been decided in the quarterfinals. The major difference is that the regular season is irrelevant after round two in MLB; in round three in NFL, NBA, and NHL; and in round four in UCL.

Although these results increase the risk and lower the expected payoff of the champion effect particularly for MLB, they also suggest an optimum playoff strategy for profit-maximizing owners. It is very difficult to buy a championship in all leagues. Championship teams should be built optimally to make the final four, semifinal round. In the case of MLB, the magic number is $\mu = .550$ in the regular season. Beyond the MLB threshold of 90 regular-season wins, additional talent becomes redundant and the *MRP* of talent diminishes very rapidly. Beyond the final four in all leagues, the remainder of the post-season becomes a random walk.

THE PRIZE

The strength of the *champion effect* obviously depends on the relative size δ of the post-season prize. Post-season playoff revenue distributions for the participating teams are summarized in Table 4.4 for all five leagues. In the NFL, the playoffs and Super Bowl are a league-wide celebration of the regular season.[5] Media and gate revenue are divided evenly among the teams in the league whereas the home team keeps venue revenue. The NFL stipend paid to the playoff clubs barely covers traveling expenses for the games. The NFL playoffs are not a profitable proposition beyond the league championships in round 3.

The NBA commissioner's office captures 45 percent of playoff revenue compared to 6 percent during the regular season. (About 20 percent of the NBA commissioner proceeds are distributed as regular-season rewards and the remaining 80 percent is used for post-season player bonuses.) The home playoff team gets the remaining 55 percent, unless the series ends in an odd number of games, in which

Table 4.4 Team Post-Season-Playoff Revenue Distribution

Major League Baseball

Games 1–3 Division Series and 1–4 League and Championship Series: 60% to players (80% before division play began in 1995), 1.6% to umpires and 38.4% to home teams. Games 4–5 of Division Series and 5–7 of Championship Series: home team gets all gate revenue players get zero. MLB Commissioner gets 15% of World Series gate.

National Football League

Gate and Media revenue divided evenly among 32 teams in league. Home team keeps venue revenue. League pays flat expense fee:

Expense allowance	2004–2005
Wild card round	$500,000
Division round	$580,000
Championship round	$960,000
Super Bowl loser	$2,590,000
Super Bowl winner	$3,500,000

National Basketball Association

NBA Commissioner takes 45% (compared 6% in regular season). Home team gets 55% unless series ends in odd number of games. Then NBA Commissioner gets 30%, home team 45% and visiting team 25%

National Hockey League

NHL takes 50% of playoff revenue of top 10 revenue clubs, 40% of middle 3rd revenue clubs and 30% of bottom 3rd of revenue clubs, which is redistributed as revenue sharing.

English Premier League/UEFA Champions League 2008–2009

UCL Participation premium (32 clubs)	$4,200,000
Match fee ($560,000 per match)	$3,360,000
Match winning bonus per win	$840,000
1st knockout round bonus (16 clubs)	$3,080,000
Quarter finals bonus (8 clubs)	$3,500,000
Semi finals bonus (4 clubs)	$4,200,000
Runners-up bonus	$5,600,000
Winner bonus	$9,800,000

case the commissioner gets 30 percent, the home team gets 45 percent, and the visitor takes 25 percent. The share of the post-season revenue taken by the NHL commissioner depends on the regular season revenue of the clubs. The top third revenue clubs share 50 percent with the rest of the league as revenue sharing, the middle third shares 40 percent and the bottom third kicks in 30 percent of their respective home playoff revenue.[6] The proceeds are distributed as revenue sharing, and so a low-revenue club may have a cross-incentive not to make the playoffs.

The only significant direct championship revenue for the clubs occurs in MLB and UCL, where the post-season premium is significant. In MLB a mix of cross-incentives encourages players to end the playoff series with the minimum number of games, whereas the participating teams benefit if the series is extended to the maximum. Players receive 60 percent of the revenue from the minimum games required to win the series (games 1–3 in the division series and games 1–4 in the championship series) and the home team gets 38.4 percent (1.6 percent goes to the umpires). The team share is lower in the World Series when the MLB commissioner takes 15 percent of the gate off the top. Revenue from games 4–5 in the division series and games 5–7 in the championship series goes to the home teams, and the players get nothing. In 2006, the world champion St. Louis Cardinals and runner-up Detroit Tigers each received about $6.8 million, and the commissioner took $6.7 million, compared to the Cardinals players who received $20 million and Tigers players who got $13.3 million. In 2007 the MLB champion Boston Red Sox received $8.7 million, including $7.4 million from a seven-game series with the Cleveland Indians, and the runner-up Colorado Rockies received only $3.2 million, because they swept both division and league championship series in the minimum number of games. By comparison the Red Sox players received $18.9 million, and Rockies players were paid $12.6 million from the $52.46 million post-season players' pool.

The championship windfall is even greater for the EPL, where UCL TV rights fees are comparable to media rights fees in European domestic leagues. In 2008, UCL TV rights were $875 million per season—slightly more than French Ligue 1 ($840 million) and Italian Serie A ($784 million), and second only to $1.3 billion for EPL.[7] The merit allocation of UCL media rights fees is shown in Table 4.4 (excluding match-day revenues), and the direct impact of UCL bonuses on the EPL big-four clubs is summarized in Table 4.5.

In the 2008 UCL, three of the final four were EPL clubs. Liverpool ousted Arsenal in the quarterfinals, Chelsea defeated Liverpool in the semifinals, and Manchester United defeated Chelsea in an all-EPL final. In the UCL in 2009, all

Table 4.5 EPL Big-Four Revenues from UCL 2007–2008

EPL Club	UCL TV Pool	Total UCL	EPL & UCL
Manchester United	$27,270,600	$60,030,600	$454,720,000
Chelsea	$23,205,000	$50,925,000	$376,460,000
Liverpool	$16,261,000	$37,541,000	$370,160,000
Arsenal	$14,567,000	$32,487,000	$295,260,000
Total EPL Big Four	$81,303,600	$180,983,600	$1,496,600,000
Total UCL/ EPL	$387,800,000	$819,840,000	$3,360,000,000

UEFA also distributed $124 million in UCL solidarity payments in 2008.
$1 = € .714.

four again reached quarterfinals, where Chelsea defeated Liverpool to put three EPL clubs in the final four. In the last five seasons since 2004, the big-four have all been among the UCL thirty-two-team-group stage, and at least one of them has been in the final match. The big-four EPL teams enjoy almost certain expectations of $50 million bonus that boosts their revenue by at least 12 percent.

At the other end of the table, the threat of relegation creates a revenue convexity of greater relative magnitude. The cost of the drop is usually about $50 million in lost revenue. At the end of the 2009 season, Newcastle United was relegated from the Premiership where its revenues were $175.8 million, with a TV share of $69.3 million. Newcastle's TV money in the first division championship was about $20 million, including a TV half-share parachute of about $16 million. On the positive side, the Championship-EPL promotion playoff is considered the richest single game in Europe with a prize of about $56 million.[8] Multiple revenue convexities exist at both ends of the table throughout European football

THE RING

Perhaps the most intriguing aspect of the champion effect comes on the cost side. Post-season revenue convexities occur after players have completed their regular-season contract years. Therefore, unless players have post-season performance bonuses in their contracts, the marginal cost of playoff talent approaches zero. Post-season player compensation is paid in the form league merit bonuses previously specified by collective bargaining agreements (CBAs) in the respective leagues. As shown in Table 4.6 the most lucrative North American playoff bonuses are found in MLB where the size of the player pool is a straight 60 percent of the revenue received in the minimum number of games in each series. MLB team shares are predetermined and player shares are determined by player vote after the World Series.

All other player pools are arbitrarily determined. The NFL has specified the individual player bonuses for each game played in the playoffs through 2012. Although the NBA front office gets 45 percent of playoff revenue, the CBA has already specified the size of player pool through 2012, and team merit-shares are a fixed proportion for each round. Both NFL and NBA bonuses are paid per round/game played. The NHL has arbitrarily specified the same $6.5 million pool for each year of the current CBA through 2011. The absolute size of the team merit share is also predetermined and paid based on the highest round reached.

Estimates of the respective playoff pools and player bonuses for league champions and runners-up are compared to regular season per game average salaries in Table 4.7 for the four North American leagues.[9] MLB is the only sport in which the post-season bonus comes close to the regular-season per-game salary. World Series

Table 4.6 CBA Specified Player Playoff Shares

Major League Baseball	Shares	Season	Player Pool
World Series winning team	36.00%	2003	$41,363,446
World Series losing team	24.00%	2004	$42,198,640
LCS losing teams (2)	24.00%	2005	$40,788,566
Division Series losers (4)	12.00%	2006	$55,602,044
Division runners up (4)	4.00%	2007	$52,459,391

National Football League			
Player bonus per game	2007–2008	2009–2010	2011–2012
Wild card round (8)	$18,000	$19,000	$20,000
Division round (8)	$20,000	$21,000	$22,000
Championship round (4)	$37,500	$38,000	$40,000
Super Bowl loser	$40,000	$42,000	$44,000
Super Bowl winner	$78,000	$83,000	$88,000

National Basketball Association		Season	Player Pool
Regular season awards	20.73%	2002–2003	$8,750,000
1st round (16)	23.88%	2003–2004	$8,875,000
Conference semis (8)	14.20%	2004–2005	$9,500,000
Conference finals (4)	11.74%	2005–2007	$10,000,000
Losing team finals (1)	11.73%	2007–2009	$11,000,000
Winning team finals (1)	17.70%	2009–2012	$12,000,000

National Hockey League			Per Player
President's Trophy	3.85%	$250,000	$10,000
1st round losers (8)	15.38%	$1,000,000	$5,000
2nd round losers (4)	15.38%	$1,000,000	$10,000

winners and losers receive twice the bonus as Super Bowl winners and losers and ten times the stipend paid to NHL players. The MLB average per-game salary of $18,062 in 2008 lies between the $25,107 bonus received by the champion Philadelphia Phillies and the $13,962 paid to runner-up Tampa Bay Rays. The $45,000 per-game bonus for the NFL Super Bowl champion Steelers was less than half of the $109,000 per-game regular-season salary for the average NFL player. Playoff bonuses in the NBA and the NHL are insignificant compared to MLB and NFL, and they amount to only ten percent of the per-game average for their regular seasons.

The important point here is that, by their nature, playoffs are the joint production of monopsony leagues. If post-season bonuses are not directly paid by participating clubs, then the marginal cost of talent is zero and token bonuses suggest that the leagues are exploiting championship talent. The trophy ring

Table 4.7 Estimated Player Distributions in 2008 Playoff Finals

	MLB	NFL	NBA	NHL
Playoff pool	$51,159,328	$30,740,000	$11,000,000	$6,500,000
Finals winning team	$18,417,358	$7,181,500	$2,630,520	$1,875,000
Finals losing team	$12,278,239	$6,227,500	$1,972,710	$1,125,000
Finals winning player	$351,504	$135,500	$175,368	$75,000
Finals losing player	$223,390	$117,500	$131,514	$45,000
Average season salary	$2,926,000	$1,750,000	$5,356,000	$1,907,000
Winning player per game	$25,107	$45,167	$6,745	$3,409
Losing player per game	$13,962	$29,375	$6,263	$2,250
Season salary per game	$18,062	$109,375	$65,317	$23,256

Note: Games played in 2008 Finals: MLB Philadelphia 14, Tampa Bay 16; NFL Pittsburgh 3, Arizona 4; NBA Boston 26, Los Angeles 21; NHL Detroit 22, Pittsburgh 20. MLB player pool is actual and distributions are determined by team post-season vote. NFL player share is known and team share is estimated based on roster size of 53. NBA and NHL player share estimated from actual team share based on playoff roster sizes of NBA 15 and NHL 25.

awarded to league champions and runners-up (as conference champions) is a possible exception. In all leagues the design and cost of the ring are decided by individual clubs, but the NFL underwrites 150 rings at $5,000 each for the Super Bowl winner and 150 rings at $2,500 for the loser. The bad news is that players are paid the least for games that generate the most revenue. The good news is that reducing the playoffs to the "quest for the ring" may elevate post-season competition to its purest form.

Two Seasons

In spite of different variations in playoff formats, the role of dominant teams is remarkably similar in all leagues, including EPL. As shown in Table 4.8 all leagues have had one dominant dynasty with a second challenger over the last fourteen seasons. In MLB, the New York Yankees won four championships in six appearances, and the Atlanta Braves took one championship in three attempts. In the NHL, the Detroit Red Wings held four championships in six tries, and the New Jersey Devils won three of four Stanley Cup appearances. In the NBA, the Los Angeles Lakers mini-dynasty also took four of six championship tries, and the San Antonio Spurs were four for four. In the NFL, the New England Patriots have won four of five Super Bowls during the salary-cap era, and the Pittsburgh Steelers won two of three.

Table 4.8 North American Championship Distributions 1995–2009

Club	Champ	Finals	Club	Champ	Finals
Major League Baseball			*National Football League*		
New York Yankees	4	6	New England Patriots	3	5
Atlanta Braves	1	3	Pittsburgh Steelers	2	3
Boston Red Sox	2	2	Denver Broncos	2	2
Florida Marlins	2	2	New York Giants	1	2
St. Louis Cardinals	1	2	St. Louis Rams	1	2
Cleveland Indians	0	2	Green Bay Packers	1	2
Four Teams	1	1	Four Teams	1	1
Seven Teams	0	1	Eight Teams	0	1
Number of Different Clubs	9	17	Number of Clubs	10	18
National Basketball Association			*National Hockey League*		
Los Angeles Lakers	4	6	Detroit Red Wings	4	6
San Antonio Spurs	4	4	New Jersey Devils	3	4
Chicago Bulls	3	3	Colorado Avalanche	2	2
Detroit Pistons	1	2	Pittsburgh Penguins	1	2
Utah Jazz	0	2	Anaheim Ducks	1	2
New Jersey Nets	0	2	Carolina Hurricane	1	2
Boston Celtics	1	1	Dallas Stars	1	2
Miami Heat	1	1	Tampa Lightning	1	1
Seven Teams	0	1	Seven Teams	0	1
Number of Clubs	6	15	Number of Clubs	8	15

Note: MLB and NFL 1995–2008; NBA 1996–2009 and NHL 1995–2009 excluding lockout playoffs 2005.

The distribution of championships among other clubs is similar between MLB and NFL. Since MLB began division play in 1995, seventeen different teams have played in the World Series and nine different teams have won the MLB World Championship. Nine of the last twenty-eight participants and four of the fourteen winners have been wild-card teams. Eight of the last nine World Series have involved a wild card. During the salary-cap era in the NFL, eighteen different teams have played in the Super Bowl and ten different teams have won the Championship. Only four of the last twenty-eight teams and three of the fourteen winners have been wild-card teams. The NFL has engineered regular-season parity through the salary cap and revenue sharing, but seeding and first round byes have reduced added chaos of wild-card teams in the playoffs.

There are also similarities between the championship distributions of the NBA and NHL, where fewer teams have played and won the league championships than MLB and the NFL. The similarity is that fifteen different teams have played in the championship finals in each league. The difference is that the NBA has had only five different champions in fourteen seasons (including four non-division winners) whereas the NHL has had eight (including five non-division winners). The NBA has strategically engineered dynasties and team continuity through a soft salary cap that allows a team to exceed the cap to resign its own free agents.[10] This strategy has been followed throughout the playoff structure.[11] Only six different clubs have won the NBA championship during the twenty-six years of the soft salary cap.[12]

By comparison, in Table 4.9, UEFA Champions League final match has also had fifteen different participants over the fourteen-year period 1996–2009 and eight different champions. Real Madrid has won the championship match three times in three appearances; Manchester United and AC Milan are two for three; and Barcelona is two for two. The competitive imbalance of EPL is also shown in Table 4.9 where there have been only three champions over the last fourteen seasons. Manchester United has won nine championships, Arsenal has taken three and Chelsea has won twice. Liverpool has mastered the second season, but not the first by being one for two in UCL finals without winning the Premiership. Leeds United and Newcastle United, the only clubs to rival the big four, have since been relegated to the lower division championship.

Table 4.9 Championship Distributions EPL and UCL 1996–2009

UCL Club	League	Champ	Total	EPL Club	Champ	2nd	3rd
Real Madrid	ESP	3	3	Manchester United	9	2	3
Manchester United	ENG	2	3	Arsenal	3	5	2
AC Milan	ITA	2	3	Chelsea	2	3	2
Barcelona	ESP	2	2	Liverpool	0	2	5
Juventus	ITA	1	4	Newcastle United	0	2	1
Liverpool	ENG	1	2	Leeds United	0	0	1
Bayern München	GER	1	2	Different Clubs	3	5	6
Porto	POR	1	1				
Borussia Dortmund	GER	1	1				
Valencia	ESP	0	2				
Five Clubs	...	0	1				
Different Clubs		8	15				

Note: Chelsea bought by Russian Oil Man Roman Abramowich in 2003; Manchester United purchased by Malcolm Glazer owner of NFL Tampa Buccaneers in 2005; Liverpool bought by American Tom Hicks owner of MLB Texas Rangers and NHL Dallas Stars and George Gillett former owner of NHL Montreal Canadiens in 2007 and sold in 2010 to New England Sports Ventures (owners of MLB's Boston Red Sox). Leeds United was relegated in 2004; Newcastle United was relegated in 2009.

PRIME TIME

In sports-media rights contracts, broadcast networks are largely concerned with advertising revenue from more lucrative playoff seasons. As a result, regular-season games are being siphoned to cable regional sports networks (RSN) and league-owned networks. About 80 percent of advertising revenue from NFL broadcasts comes from the regular season compared to the other leagues, in which networks receive over 80 percent of ad revenues from the post-season. The contradiction is that leagues stand to make the most TV money from dominant teams in the playoffs, but they try to make outcomes the most balanced.

Siphoning of sports media rights is profitable because regular and post-season fan bases are not the same. Regionalization of the regular season isolates and price discriminates against the die-hard local fan on local cable or regional sports networks (RSNs), whereas post-season national broadcasts must appeal to the general-interest fan. The playoff structure for each league is an important factor in determining post-season TV ratings and size of the playoff prize. The question arises whether competitively balanced post-season finals are well received by the national fan base. Nielsen TV ratings for the championship finals are compared in Table 4.10 for MLB and NFL and Table 4.11 for NBA and NHL since 1995, when division play began in MLB.

Given media fragmentation and proliferation of cable and satellite platforms, it is difficult to compare diluted ratings numbers over time, but there are still a few observations that can be made. MLB ratings have fallen since play resumed after the 1994–1995 strike. The halving of ratings from 19.5 to 8.4, audience share from 33 percent to 14 percent, and number of viewers from 29 million to 13.6 million coincides with increased post-season competitive balance. The sharpest drop occurred in the 2005 World Series between the seldom-seen Chicago White Sox and Houston Astros. The New York Yankees are the missing ingredient from all lower-rated series. The Yankees were eliminated in the first round American League Division Series (ALDS) in 2005, 2006, 2007, and did not qualify for 2009 playoffs. The absence of the Bronx Bombers coincides precisely with the slide in World Series ratings of 2005–2009.

Ratings in the NFL Super Bowl are stronger than the other leagues partially because it is one final game played on its own weekend in an entertainment vacuum. Other league ratings are averages of all network and cable games often competing with other leagues.[13] Total viewership of MLB World Series (even in four games) is actually greater than the average NFL Super Bowl until the early exits of the Yankees after 2004.

Until the last two Super Bowls (2007–2008 seasons), the MLB World Series and NBA Championship Series have both run neck and neck with the NFL in terms of total advertising revenues. In 2006 for example, NFL total playoff ad revenues were $423 million compared to $424 million for the NBA and $382 million for MLB. The five-game 2006 World Series earned $160.8 million in advertising money for FOX, compared to Super Bowl XLI that took in $151.5 million

Table 4.10 Nielsen TV Ratings for Championship Finals

Year	Teams	Network	Games	Rating	Share	Viewers (K)
Major League Baseball						
2008	Philadelphia v. Tampa Bay*	FOX	5	8.4	14	13,635
2007	Boston v. Colorado*	FOX	4	10.6	18	17,123
2006	St. Louis v. Detroit*	FOX	5	10.1	17	15,812
2005	Chicago v. Houston*	FOX	4	11.1	19	17,162
2004	Boston* v. St. Louis	FOX	4	15.8	25	25,390
2003	Florida* v. New York (A)	FOX	6	13.9	25	20,142
2002	Anaheim* v. San Francisco	FOX	7	11.9	20	19,261
2001	Arizona v. New York (A)	FOX	7	15.7	25	24,528
2000	New York (A) v. New York (N)*	FOX	5	12.4	21	18,081
1999	New York (A) v. Atlanta	NBC	4	16.0	26	23,731
1998	New York (A) v. San Diego	FOX	4	14.1	24	20,340
1997	Florida* v. Cleveland	NBC	7	16.8	29	24,790
1996	New York (A) v. Atlanta	FOX	6	17.4	29	25,220
1995[†]	Atlanta v. Cleveland	ABC/NBC	6	19.5	33	28,970
National Football League						
2008	Pittsburgh v. Arizona	FOX	1	42.0	64	98,732
2007	New York (N)* v. New England	FOX	1	43.1	65	97,448
2006	Indianapolis v. Chicago	CBS	1	42.6	64	93,184
2005	Pittsburgh v. Seattle	ABC	1	41.6	62	90,745
2004	New England v. Philadelphia	FOX	1	41.1	62	86,072
2003	New England v. Carolina	CBS	1	41.4	63	89,795
2002[†]	Tampa Bay v. Oakland	ABC	1	40.7	61	88,637
2001	New England v. St. Louis	FOX	1	40.4	61	86,801
2000	Baltimore* v. New York (N)	CBS	1	40.4	61	84,335
1999	St. Louis v. Tennessee*	ABC	1	43.3	63	88,465
1998	Denver v. Atlanta	FOX	1	40.2	61	83,720
1997	Denver* v. Green Bay	NBC	1	44.5	67	90,000
1996	Green Bay v. New England	FOX	1	43.3	65	87,870
1995	Dallas v. Pittsburgh	NBC	1	46.0	68	94,080

* Wild-card teams or non-division winners.
† MLB went from 4 to 6 divisions in 1995 expansion to 28 teams and; NFL went from 6 to 8 divisions in 2002 expansion to 32 teams.

Source: Nielsen Media Research.

Table 4.11 Nielsen TV Ratings for Championship Finals

Year	Teams	Network	Games	Rating	Share	Viewers (K)
National Basketball Association						
2009	Los Angeles Lakers v. Orlando	ABC	5	8.4	15	14,347
2008	Boston v. Los Angeles Lakers	ABC	6	9.3	17	14,941
2007	San Antonio* v. Cleveland*	ABC	4	6.2	11	9,289
2006	Miami v. Dallas*	ABC	6	8.5	15	12,972
2005†	San Antonio v. Detroit	ABC	7	8.2	15	12,544
2004	Detroit* v. Los Angeles Lakers	ABC	5	11.5	20	17,942
2003	San Antonio v. New Jersey	ABC	6	6.5	12	9,864
2002	Los Angeles Lakers* v. New Jersey	NBC	4	10.2	19	15,678
2001	Los Angeles Lakers v. Philadelphia	NBC	5	12.1	23	18,996
2000	Los Angeles Lakers v. Indiana	NBC	6	11.6	21	17,402
1999	San Antonio* v. New York*	NBC	5	11.3	21	16,014
1998	Chicago v. Utah	NBC	6	18.7	33	29,040
1997	Chicago v. Utah	NBC	6	16.8	30	25,586
1996	Chicago v. Seattle	NBC	6	16.7	31	24,858
National Hockey League						
2009	Pittsburgh* v. Detroit	NBC/VS	7	2.7	5	4,780
2008	Detroit v. Pittsburgh	NBC/VS	6	2.6	5	4,479
2007	Anaheim v. Ottawa *	NBC/VS	5	1.2	2	1,764
2006	Carolina v. Edmonton*	NBC/OLN	7	1.8	3	2,834
2004	Tampa Bay v. Calgary*	ABC/ESPN	7	2.2	4	3,286
2003	New Jersey v. Anaheim*	ABC/ESPN	7	2.4	4	3,627
2002	Detroit v. Carolina	ABC	3/5	3.6	7	5,768
2001	Colorado v. New Jersey	ABC	5/7	3.3	6	5,058
2000	New Jersey* v. Dallas	ABC	4/6	3.7	8	5,511
1999†	Dallas v. Buffalo*	FOX	3/6	3.4	6	4,873
1998	Detroit* v. Washington	FOX	1/4	3.3	6	4,830
1997	Detroit* v. Philadelphia	FOX	1/4	4.0	8	6,370
1996	Colorado v. Florida*	FOX	2/4	3.6	7	5,090
1995	New Jersey* v. Detroit	FOX	2/4	3.4	8	5,210

* Wild-card teams or non-division winners.

† NBA went from 4 to 6 divisions in 2005 expansion to 30 teams and NHL from 4 to 6 divisions in 1999 expansion to 30 teams.

Source: Nielsen Media Research.

for CBS. This was in spite of the celebrated cost of Super Bowl ads. In 2006 a thirty-second Super Bowl spot ran about $2.4 million compared to $400,000 for MLB's World Series and $360,000 per spot for the NBA. In addition to its overall strength, Super Bowl shows significantly higher TV ratings for former dynasties in the Dallas Cowboys, Pittsburgh Steelers, and recently the New England Patriots. This translates into higher advertising rates and revenues. After the 2008 season, Super-Bowl XLIII advertising revenues topped $200 million with a rate of $3 million per thirty-second spot.

The NBA has strategically protected team continuity and marketed individual player matchups for national media appeal, since the imposition of the soft salary cap in 1984. Compare the ratings bonanza of Michael Jordan and Chicago Bulls dynasty against Karl Malone and the Utah Jazz with the low ratings for the midmarket San Antonio Spurs versus unfamiliar New Jersey Nets or Cleveland Cavaliers. NBA TV ratings were cut in half after the demise of Jordan's Bulls. The Los Angeles Lakers and Kobe Bryant have provided a significant boost, but not at the same level as former dynasties. A six- or seven-game Los Angeles Lakers series still has the same total number of viewers as an average Super Bowl.

Recent ratings for the NHL in 2009 have returned to prelockout (2004–2005) levels. Stanley Cup Game 7 was the most watched NHL game since 1973 with a 4.3 rating, 8 percent share, and 8 million viewers on NBC. The primary reason was the familiarity of hockey fans with the decade-dominant Detroit Red Wings rematched with the promising talent of the Pittsburgh Penguins. Competitive balance is not found or sought in European football (soccer), where imbalance and polarization are the accepted norm. The 2009 Champions League final match between England's Manchester United and Spain's Barcelona (each in its third appearance in fourteen years) drew a 37.1 percent share with 45.3 million viewers in the home countries of the big-five leagues.[14] If the Yankee paradox is an empirical question, the answer is that increased competitive balance is not ready for primetime television in Europe or North America.

Conclusion

The *champion effect* occurs when the post-season playoffs adversely affect regular season competitive balance. The *champion effect* depends on four factors: (1) size of playoff prize relative to regular-season revenue; (2) regular season length in games played sufficient to reduce randomness and increase the MRP of talent at playoff threshold; (3) playoff length and seeding sufficient to replicate regular season; and (4) playoff threshold asymmetry sufficient for talent buyers to find talent sellers at the threshold. As shown in Table 4.12, none of the five leagues satisfies all four conditions. The most likely candidates for the *champion effect* are MLB and EPL,

Table 4.12 Preconditions for Champion Effect

	MLB	NFL	NBA	NHL	EPL
Size of the playoff prize	■	□	□	□	■
Regular season length	■	□	■	■	■
Post-season playoff length	□	□	■	■	■
Playoff threshold asymmetry	■	■	□	□	□
Champion effect	■	□	□	□	■

with reservations about the uncertainty of MLB's short playoffs and the symmetry of EPL/UCL qualification and relegation.

Two contradictions emerge about the playoffs. Contradiction 1: Sports leagues receive the lion's share of national media revenue from the playoffs and yet they redistribute the least revenue to participating teams and players. Contradiction 2: National playoff fans prefer at least one dominant team in title games, and yet American leagues design series to make the quality of playoff survivors uncertain. Evidence suggests an optimum level of competitive imbalance and that the pursuit of absolute playoff parity is self-defeating.

In MLB, the short playoff system is designed to equalize playoff chances for midmarket clubs, but it also invites large-market teams spend to win in the regular season only to become ordinary in post-season chaos. Nine of the last fourteen World Series winners have had fewer regular-season wins than their opponents. The St. Louis Cardinals lost the World Series in 2004 with 105 wins but then won the World Series in 2006 with eighty-three regular-season wins, the fewest in World Series history. If the two seasons are disconnected, then evidence suggests that the optimum strategy in MLB is to aim for the playoff threshold of ninety wins (.556), and then suffer the slings and arrows of the outrageous playoffs.

In the end, *Moneyball* science is not new or revolutionary. Winning during the regular season is talent driven because good and bad luck usually even out. Winning in the post-season is riskier business because of random elements inherent in short series. All four of Billy Beane's Oakland Athletics post-season losses came in game 5 of American League Division Series to teams with lower regular-season records. Old-school manager Bobby Cox led the Atlanta Braves to fourteen consecutive division titles (1991–2005) based on the old saw that "offense sells tickets and defense wins championships." After the Braves won only one World Series (1995) in five appearances, Cox agreed that "the playoffs are a crapshoot."

Old-school intuition yields the same results as new-school science because defense has less variance and consistency is the key to surviving the playoffs. The old-school axiom that "good defense never sleeps" is true for each dynasty in all leagues. It is also true for wild-card teams that make unexpected runs through the playoff maze. In the 2005 "Miracle of Istanbul" Liverpool played through qualifying rounds to win Champions League based on defense, but the same club finished fifth in the EPL based on offensive mediocrity. Defense is also why the wild-card

New York Giants have "11 straight on the road" engraved on their 2008 Super Bowl Rings. During the regular season it is certainly better to be good than lucky, but in the playoffs it is probably better to be lucky than good.

Notes

1 In Beane's second five years, the Athletics record was 423–386 with a win percentage of .523. The good news was that the A's swept the Minnesota Twins in the 2006 first-round divisions series, the bad news was that they were then swept by the Detroit Tigers in the second round. They have since had two losing seasons 2007–2008.

2 Midseason player movement is also a function of team specificity of talent (Vrooman 1996). If talent is team specific, moves are made between seasons; if players are interchangeable parts, these moves are made midseason.

3 EPL clubs on either UCL or relegation threshold can transfer players from lower revenue leagues. This polarizes talent among European football leagues and alters UCL prospects of Euro-league champions (Vrooman, 2007).

4 Top seeds for division winners create seeding problems in the playoffs for all leagues, because teams with lower records can qualify and be seeded higher than teams with better regular seasons. This seeding format introduces additional risk into the post-season tournament. In NFL playoffs in 2008, the San Diego Chargers with an 8 out of 8 record were seeded fourth as AFC West Division winners, whereas the New England Patriots missed the playoff at 11 out of 5. This fueled proposals for NFL playoff expansion to fourteen teams. In MLB playoffs in 2006, St. Louis won the World Series with a regular season record of .519 (83 wins) that was lower than all other teams. As National League Central winner, the Cardinals entered the playoffs instead of the LA Dodgers with 88 wins (.543), who lost a regular season tie-breaker to the San Diego Padres for the National League West. Since 2005, the NBA seeds the top three division winners and best non-division winner 1–4. A prior rule that seeded division winners 1–3 created 2005 controversy when the best two teams in the Western Conference—the Dallas Mavericks and the San Antonio Spurs—were in the same division and prematurely matched in second round.

5 Participating Super Bowl teams split only 35 percent of Super Bowl tickets. The host team receives a 5 percent ticket share; the other twenty-nine teams each receive 1.2 percent, and 25.2 percent goes to the league office for sponsors, charities, and media.

6 The indirect playoff incentive is to boost regular-season gate and venue revenue. This is particularly true for teams that have been absent from the playoffs. After the Chicago White Sox 2005 Championship season ticket sales increased from 11,000 to 21,000; 2006 runner-up Detroit Tigers increased season ticket sales from 9,000 to 19,000, and 2008 Champion Philadelphia Phillies from 20,400 season tickets to 24,200.

7 Other annual rights fees: NFL $3.735 billion, NBA $930 million, MLB $803 million, NHL $300 million. In Spain, La Liga, Barcelona, and Real Madrid each paid annual rights fees over $210 million. This compares to the NFL team average of $116.7 million and New York Yankee implicit fees from YES network of about $145 million.

8 The top two teams in the lower division are promoted to EPL. Third promotion spot is decided by a playoff among teams 3–6. The playoff final is considered "the richest game

in the Europe." After winning the playoff in 2004, Crystal Palace increased revenue from $21 million to $73 million in 2005.

9 UCL bonuses are paid by EPL teams. In the 2008 season, EPL and UCL champion Manchester United players each received about $425,000 for winning the double. Chelsea player bonuses could have been $1 million for the double. Players for Hull City each received a bonus of about $125,000 for avoiding relegation by one point in 2009.

10 In an attempt to keep star players with their original clubs, the NBA granted the "Larry Bird" exception in 1984–1985 for clubs to exceed the soft cap to resign their own free agents. Now there are nine exceptions to the soft cap.

11 Based on autoregressive measures of season-to-season continuity, the EPL is the most deterministic league followed by the NBA (after soft cap 1984) and the NHL (before hard cap 2005). The NFL is the most random league (since hard cap 1994), and MLB has shown moderate competitive balance since the 1994–1995 strike. (Vrooman 2007, 2009)

12 NBA champions in salary cap era: Los Angeles Lakers, 7; Chicago Bulls, 6; San Antonio Spurs, 4; Boston Celtics, 3; Detroit Pistons, 3; Houston Rockets, 2; and Miami Heat, 1.

13 Nielsen ratings for the NCAA D1 football championship game have also been consistent from 17.4 for Tennessee–Florida State in 1999 to 17.4 for LSU–Ohio State in 2008, whereas the ratings for the NCAA Basketball Final have fallen from a recent high of 22.7 in 1992 for Duke–Michigan to 10.8 for North Carolina–Michigan State in 2009.

14 In the 2009 final match, Spain had a 62 percent share with 11.3 million viewers on Antena3; England had a 39 percent share with 9.6 million viewers on ITV1; Italy had 36 percent share with 9.63 viewers on RAI; Germany had 23 percent rating with 6.55 million viewers on Sat-1; and France had a 34 percent share with 8.25 million viewers on TF1.

REFERENCES

Fort, R. and J. Quirk. 1995. Cross-subsidization, incentives, and outcomes in professional team sports leagues. *Journal of Economic Literature*, September 1995: 1265–1299.

Lewis, M. 2003. *Moneyball: The art of winning an unfair game.* New York: Norton.

Vrooman, J. 1995. General theory of professional sports leagues. *Southern Economic Journal*, 61(4): 971–990.

Vrooman, J. 1996. *Baseball Player's Labor Market Reconsidered, Southern Economic Journal*, 63(2): 339–360.

Vrooman, J. 2007. Theory of the beautiful game: The unification of European football. *Scottish Journal of Political Economy*, 54(3): 314–354.

Vrooman, J. 2009. Theory of the perfect game: Competitive balance in monopoly sports leagues. *Review of Industrial Organization*, 34(1): 5–44.

Whitney, J. 1988. Winning games versus winning championships: The economics of fan interest and team performance. *Economic Inquiry*, 26(4): 703–724.

PART II

....

ECONOMICS OF MAJOR LEAGUE SPORTS

....

SECTION 1

BASEBALL

CHAPTER 5

BASEBALL'S ANTITRUST EXEMPTION

HISTORY AND CURRENT RELEVANCE

ROGER D. BLAIR AND
JESSICA S. HAYNES

1. INTRODUCTION

SPORTS leagues are associations of independently owned businesses that sell a variety of goods and services: tickets for admission, parking, food and drinks, programs, broadcast rights, logoed merchandise, and naming rights. These sales are made possible by the games. Collectively, the league members produce championship athletic competition on the field or in the arena. Some of the rivalries can be intense, to say the least. In Major League Baseball (MLB), the Dodgers–Giants and the Yankees–Red Sox rivalries immediately come to mind. For all the on-field competition, however, there is a lot more cooperation than competition off the field. Some of that cooperation is both necessary and beneficial to the fans. For example, cooperation on the rules of play, schedules, playoffs, and championships is necessary to the production of what the fan consumes—the games. Cooperation on these dimensions is clearly beneficial to the fans. Revenue sharing among league members is less obviously beneficial to the fans. It does, however, contribute to the financial stability of the league members and thereby assures continuing operation of some small-market franchises. Ordinarily, coordination among competitors raises antitrust issues. Sports leagues, however, are granted latitude that other industries would not enjoy because they must cooperate off the field to produce competition on the field. Nonetheless, there are limits to the permissible collaboration for most sports leagues. Some cooperation—on free agency, player drafts, expansion/contraction, and location/relocation—merely enhances the profits of the league's members. These higher profits come at someone's expense—the fans, the sponsors, the broadcasters, the venue owners. In most leagues, the antitrust laws protect these interests from monopoly and anticompetitive collaboration. Unique among the major sports leagues in North America, MLB is largely exempt from the antitrust laws. Many observers have noted that MLB's exemption is an anomaly that can be traced to a judicial blunder committed nearly ninety years ago.

In this chapter, we examine MLB's antitrust exemption and its current relevance. First, we begin with a brief overview of the antitrust laws in the United States. Next, we trace MLB's anomalous antitrust exemption and its vulnerability to Congressional action. The balance of the chapter analyzes the current significance of MLB's specific antitrust exemption. We will argue that the antitrust exemption is largely irrelevant today. Nearly all the labor issues are subject to collective bargaining and, therefore, exempt under the nonstatutory labor exemption. The anticompetitive pooling of broadcast rights is covered by the Sports Broadcasting Act, which shields such pooling from the antitrust laws. Many other issues, such as entry restrictions and equipment standards, have been resolved in other sports litigation. To the extent that some conduct would otherwise be subject to antitrust scrutiny, we explore those arguments.

2. ANTITRUST POLICY: LAW AND ECONOMIC RATIONALE

In the aftermath of the Civil War, a convincing case was made that the country was beset with problems of monopoly and cartel behavior (Thorelli, 1954: 54–164). As a result of this widely held view, the Sherman Act was passed in 1890. This brief statute, along with its judicial interpretation, are the cornerstones of modern antitrust policy. The statute deals with both collaborative behavior and unilateral conduct. If a sports league is considered to be a collection of independent economic entities, then they are legally capable of conspiring with one another, and the league's members will be subject to §1 of the Sherman Act:

> Every contract, combination ..., or conspiracy, in restraint of trade or commerce among the several States ... is hereby declared to be illegal.

Through judicial decisions over the past 120 years, this sweeping prohibition has gained specificity.[1] We now know that only *unreasonable,* that is to say *anticompetitive,* restraints are condemned, whereas those that are procompetitive or competitively neutral are not condemned under §1 (Blair and Kaserman, 2009). Consequently, agreements among the league's members on rules of play, schedules, playoff structure, and the like would not be unlawful because they are not unreasonable. In fact, they have little to do with restraining trade in any meaningful sense. In contrast, agreements among competitors to fix prices, rig bids, restrict output, divide markets, and exclude new entrants are anticompetitive and, therefore, are generally unlawful.

If a sports league is deemed to be a single entity and, therefore, is legally incapable of conspiring with itself, then §2 of the Sherman Act comes into play:

> Every person who shall monopolize [or] attempt to monopolize … any part of the trade or commerce among the several States … shall be deemed guilty of a felony. …

Despite the economists' objections to monopoly, the Sherman Act does not address the structural condition of monopoly; instead, it only deals with monopolizing conduct. Through 120 years of judicial experience, we now understand that §2 is confined to exclusionary or predatory conduct aimed at preventing competition.[2] These practices include predatory pricing, bundled discounts, loyalty discounts, refusals to deal, and some vertical restraints (exclusive dealing and tying). Interestingly, the mere exercise of monopoly power to raise price above the competitive level is not unlawful.

In the past, many goals have been advanced for antitrust policy, but a consensus has emerged. Modern antitrust policy is grounded on the belief that competition and competitive markets will maximize social welfare through the efficient allocation of scarce resources. The Sherman Act's prohibitions of monopolizing and collusive conduct are arguably aimed at behavior that will result in allocative inefficiency and losses in social welfare. The Supreme Court has recently emphasized that the focus is on consumer welfare rather than social welfare. In most instances, this will lead to the same outcome, but there could be room for mischief here.

Based on this economic goal, one would think that there would be precious few exemptions from antitrust. There are many industries, however, that are exempt to one extent or another from the antitrust laws. Exemptions can be found in agriculture, communications, energy, finance, health care, insurance, and transportation.[3] In nearly every case, there is a specific statute that substitutes some form of regulatory oversight for the discipline of the competitive market. Ordinarily, there is a unique set of industry characteristics that renders competition inappropriate and, therefore, demands an exemption, but this is not so for baseball. The antitrust exemption enjoyed by MLB was conferred not by Congress but by the Supreme Court, and, therefore, is unaccompanied by any regulation. This would seem to make MLB's exemption particularly valuable to its members.

3. Baseball's Antitrust Exemption

The antitrust exemption for baseball dates back to the Supreme Court's decision in *Federal Baseball,* which was decided in 1922. This decision may have made some sense in 1922, but even then its reasoning was of doubtful validity.[4] Today, however, the antitrust exemption makes no sense at all. As we will see, the practical significance of the exemption is now fairly limited. The exemption had an enormous financial impact for over fifty years as it protected and preserved MLB's monopsonistic reserve system, which meant that the club owners obtained nearly the entire surplus generated by the business of baseball.

The Reserve System

The reserve system in professional baseball came into existence in the late 1800s even before the Sherman Act was passed in 1890. Under that system, the standard player contract bound a player to the team that initially signed him.[5] The player's options were severely limited: he could play for that team or retire—those were the only options. All teams agreed to use the same contract and to refuse to sign any player who breached his contract with another team. Since the contract rights to a player's services could be sold or traded to another team, players could be compelled to uproot their families and relocate to another city at the pleasure of the team. Most importantly, the player was completely unprotected by the market because there were no reasonable alternatives to playing for the team that owned the contract.

The clubs agreed among themselves to adopt the uniform contract and to avoid competing in the market for players' services. In essence, they behaved like a collusive monopsony (Blair and Harrison, 2010, Chapter 3). In so doing, the clubs could pay their players little more than their reservation wages, which were normally far below the player's marginal revenue product in baseball. The clubs enjoyed all (or nearly all) of the surplus created by the baseball skills of the players. From the club's perspective, therefore, this was a system well worth defending and preserving.[6]

An Antitrust Trilogy

In *Federal Baseball Club of Baltimore, Inc. v. National League of Professional Baseball Clubs,* a 1922 case, the plaintiff objected to a number of exclusionary practices including the reserve system. The Supreme Court never reached the substantive question of whether the uniform adoption of the reserve system that eliminated competition in the labor market for Major League Baseball players was unlawful under §1 of the Sherman Act. Instead, the Court disposed of the matter on jurisdiction grounds. No matter how anticompetitive an agreement among ostensible competitors may actually be, if the agreement does not restrain *interstate* commerce, it cannot run afoul of the Sherman Act, which is a *federal* statute.

The business of baseball, according to Oliver Wendell Holmes, who was writing for the Court, was providing exhibitions of professional baseball that were local affairs. The Court held that professional baseball did not involve *interstate* commerce and, therefore, did not fall within the scope of the federal antitrust laws. Holmes, of course, knew that the teams necessarily traveled across state lines, but he characterized the travel as "incidental." This decision provided shelter for the reserve system, which was plainly anticompetitive because it choked off nearly all competition in the labor market.

Some thirty years later, the Supreme Court had an opportunity to reconsider *Federal Baseball* and correct what most observers believed was a mistake.[7] Instead, in *Toolson v. New York Yankees, Inc.,* the Supreme Court reaffirmed Holmes's error. Again, the plaintiff argued that the reserve system violated §1 of the Sherman Act. The Court pointed to the *Federal Baseball* precedent and pointed out that Congress knew about the earlier ruling. For thirty years, Congress had done nothing to bring baseball under the antitrust laws. Consequently, the Court inferred that "Congress had no intention of including the business of baseball within the scope of the federal antitrust laws."[8] It left *Federal Baseball* standing and left the players to the mercy of the club owners.

In 1972, the Supreme Court decided *Flood v. Kuhn,* which once again challenged the reserve system. Curt Flood had been a centerfielder for the St. Louis Cardinals from 1958 through 1969 and performed with considerable distinction. Following the 1969 season, Flood was traded to the Philadelphia Phillies, but he objected strenuously to the move. He asked Bowie Kuhn, the commissioner of MLB, to release him from his contract and declare him to be a free agent. When Kuhn refused, Flood filed his antitrust suit.

In its *Flood* opinion, the Court reviewed the legal history of antitrust challenges in baseball and elsewhere, the nature of the business, the widespread recognition that the foundation for the ruling in *Federal Baseball* was of "dubious validity,"[9] and other matters. In the end, however, it was persuaded that Congress had been fully and continuously aware of *Federal Baseball* for fifty years and had not seen fit to act. It determined that, at that late date, a change in antitrust exposure should be legislative rather than judicial. Accordingly, the Court ruled in favor of Kuhn and MLB. This left baseball's antitrust exemption intact, which, of course, included the enormously profitable reserve system. In *Toolson* and again in *Flood,* the Supreme Court was moved by Congressional inaction. Content to follow Congress's lead, the Court did not suggest that the business of baseball did not warrant antitrust scrutiny. Thus, Congress could kill the reserve system with a simple amendment to the Sherman Act that made it clear that it did intend to include the business of baseball within the scope of the Sherman Act.

At the time, there is little doubt that the MLB owners would have done a lot to protect the reserve system. The reserve system did not have much life left because of the gains made by the Major League Baseball Players Association (MLBPA). Three years after *Flood,* the reserve system was dead.

4. THE DEMISE OF THE RESERVE SYSTEM

The reserve system had begun in the 1880s. From the beginning, the players knew that they had no individual bargaining power and tried to form a players' union, but without much success. The early efforts at unionization all failed. Finally, with the aid of Marvin Miller, the modern MLBPA was organized in 1965. In 1970, the MLBPA negotiated the right to have a players' grievances heard by an independent arbitrator. As it turned out, this was a crucial concession. In 1975, Dave McNally and Andy Messersmith challenged the reserve system through the grievance process. The independent arbitrator ruled that the standard player's contract could not be extended involuntarily indefinitely, which was what the owners had been claiming. Instead, the arbitrator held that the contract could be extended involuntarily for only one additional year. After that year, the unsigned player would become a free agent. And just like that the reserve system was dead.[10]

With the demise of the reserve system, free agency was governed by the terms of the Collective Bargaining Agreement (CBA) between MLB and the MLBPA. Even if MLB's more general antitrust exemption were removed by Congressional action, the labor negotiations between MLB and the MLBPA would be shielded from antitrust prosecution by the nonstatutory labor exemption.

The CBA currently provides some limitations on free agency. These limitations were the product of collective bargaining and, therefore, were agreed to by the players. For a player's first three years in MLB, he is bound to the team that has him under contract. For the next three years, a player is not free to go elsewhere, but he receives some market protection because of final-offer arbitration. After six years of MLB service, an unsigned player is an unrestricted free agent and can go anywhere he can strike a deal. The value of free agency can be seen in the empirical work of Scully (1974) and Krautmann (1999).

Gerald Scully produced the first, truly pioneering, work on the dramatic disparity between pay and performance in MLB prior to the advent of free agency. Scully started from the proposition that team revenues increase when the team's winning percentage rises. This makes sense because fans do not get too enthusiastic about their favorite team when it is constantly losing. Players contribute to their teams' winning percentages through their performance on the field. As a result, Scully proceeded by estimating the impact of player performance on a team's winning percentage, which is akin to the player's marginal product. He then estimated the effect of an improved winning percentage on the team's revenue. In this way, he estimated the marginal revenue product of a player's performance.

Using data from the 1968 and 1969 seasons, Scully estimated marginal revenue products and compared them to the actual salaries paid. He found that the star players fared the worst as they received salaries that were about 15 percent of their marginal revenue product (MRP). Average players did somewhat better, but they still received salaries that were only about 20 percent of their MRP.[11] In sum, Scully concluded that monopsonistic exploitation was significant in MLB under the reserve system.

Things changed considerably when MLB players were set free. With free agency, one should expect that those players who were free agents would be paid their market value, that is, their MRP, or something very close to it.[12] This is the approach taken by Krautmann, who assumed that free agents received salaries equal to their MRPs. Using data on players eligible for free agency, he then estimated a wage equation in which the salary received by a free agent was a function of his performance. He then used that equation to estimate what the salary of those players subject to reserve restrictions would have been had they been free agents. Krautmann then compared the estimated salaries to the actual salaries paid to measure the extent of any monopsonistic exploitation that remained.

For the free agents, there was presumably no difference between their salary and their MRP, that is, no exploitation. Veterans with at least three seasons in MLB, but less than six seasons were not free agents, but they were protected to some extent by final-offer arbitration. When a player and his club reach an impasse on a new contract, the player can file for arbitration and have a third party choose between the player's final demand and the club's final offer. The independent arbitrators are looking at pay and performance of other players to aid their decision. As a result, the players should get pretty close to market value. Indeed, Krautmann estimated that these players received about 85 percent of their MRP. This, of course, is much better than the 15–20 percent of MRP that players received prior to free agency. Final-offer arbitration, therefore, introduced some market forces and improved those players' fortunes even though it did not completely eliminate monopsonistic exploitation. For those players with less than three seasons in MLB, there was no market mechanism to protect them. As one would expect, the clubs were somewhat less than generous. Those players who were wholly restricted were paid about 27 percent of their MRP. This is somewhat better than Scully's earlier estimates, but a far cry from fair market value.[13]

Collusion in the Free Agent Market

Of course, the teams have an incentive to collude in the free agent market rather than compete.[14] In that event, the CBA provided protection that looks very much like antitrust protection, but the players use the arbitration process rather than the judicial process.

Competition in the free agent market is currently dictated by the terms of the Collective Bargaining Agreement (CBA) between MLB and the MLBPA.[15] With respect to competition in the free-agent market, Article XX (E) of the CBA specifically forbids collusion among clubs or among players. Paragraph (E) (1) provides that:

> [t]he utilization or nonutilization of rights ... is an individual matter to be determined solely by each Player and each Club for his or its own benefit. Players shall not act in concert with other Players and Clubs shall not act in concert with other Clubs.

The CBA could hardly be clearer: collusion in the free-agent market is impermissible under Article XX of the CBA. Two or more free agents cannot put together a package deal.[16] Nor can two or more teams agree on how they will pursue players in the free-agent market.

Collusion in the free agent market constitutes a breach of contract, which would be resolved through the grievance procedure outlined in Article XI of the CBA. There are three arbitrators on the panel: one representing the MLBPA, one representing the MLB, and an independent arbitrator.

The arbitration panel considers the evidence put forward by the MLBPA and by MLB. It then decides whether collusion has occurred or not. In the event of collusion, the sanctions involve a damage award that looks very much like antitrust damages.

In the event that the arbitration panel concluded that two or more clubs colluded in the free-agent market, each affected player is entitled to recover treble damages.[17] These damages are limited to the "lost baseball income" that each player suffered as a result of the collusion. The lost baseball income is defined as "lost salary and other lost contractual terms, including lost additional contract years, lost signing bonuses, lost trade-restriction provisions, lost option buyout provisions, and lost incentive bonuses.[18] Thus, properly estimated damages will be equal to the economic value of the contract that each player would have signed "but for" the collusion minus the economic value of each contract that the players actually signed. This sum is then trebled automatically. Each affected player is also entitled to recover fees and interest.

5. AGREEMENTS ON OTHER LABOR ISSUES

There are a host of labor issues on which the MLB clubs agree. The uniformity among the clubs is, in many instances, the product of collective bargaining and is protected from antitrust prosecution by the nonstatutory labor exemption.[19] Financial terms, such as minimum salary, health benefits, pension benefits, and travel per diem, are uniform across all teams, but that is the necessary outcome of collective bargaining. Somewhat more controversial are reverse-order player drafts, the minimum age restriction, and maximum roster sizes. The nonstatutory labor exemption shields such practices when they are a necessary outcome of collective bargaining, such as wages, hours, and working conditions.[20]

Player Drafts

A player draft is the way that MLB teams select and allocate entry-level players. There is a rotation in the selection process that starts with the weakest teams going first. Ostensibly, the rationale for the player draft is competitive balance. By permitting the weakest teams to go first, they can select the best of the new crop of professionals. Consequently, the weakest teams should be able to improve relative to the stronger teams. This, in turn, is supposed to result in more even competition on the field, that is, competitive balance, which is good for the fans. This is a ruse. Competitive *imbalance* is the natural result of market forces (Quirk and Fort, 1992: 240–293). This occurs because, when a player is worth more to one team than he is to another, the player tends to wind up where he is most valuable. As long as draft picks can be traded or player contracts can be sold or traded, competitive imbalance will result.

Although player drafts may have some positive effects on competition on the field, they eliminate competition off the field. Each entry-level player is stuck with the team that drafts him. The player can accept that team's offer or sit out a year and enter the draft again—those are the only options. Obviously, when competition is eliminated, the team's offer need not be much above the player's reservation wage. Thus, player drafts have anticompetitive effects in the labor market.

In *Smith v. Pro Football, Inc.,* the courts correctly asserted that the "procompetitive" on-field effect of a draft is not relevant with regard to antitrust concerns. Instead, the anticompetitive effect of these restraints on the market for players' services is the correct focus.[21] Regardless of this reasoning, components of player drafts are exempt from antitrust scrutiny if they are essential to collective bargaining over wages, hours, or work conditions.[22] All four major sports leagues in North America have player drafts.

Age Restrictions

The major sports leagues, including MLB, all have age restrictions. Players may not be less than a certain age to be eligible to play professionally. The reasons for the age restriction are somewhat murky. The most charitable explanation involves paternalism. The leagues are trying to protect young athletes from the rigors of professional athletics until they are physically and emotionally mature enough to handle them.

There is some competitive significance to age restrictions. Some young players are ready to compete on the field but are not permitted to do so. This protects some older players who would otherwise be replaced. Thus, the restriction prevents some players from entering the sports labor market. In MLB, the minimum age requirement is sixteen years of age.[23] This minimum age generally applies to those players who enter through minor-league tryouts.[24] Players who enter through the draft are eligible in the year they graduate from high school. If they choose to attend college, then the player is not eligible until after his junior year.[25]

Because age requirements essentially foreclose the market to groups of potential players, there have been several antitrust challenges to this practice.[26] On the whole, these cases contend that the nonstatutory labor exemption guards minimum age requirements from antitrust consideration. None of the cases, however, have directly involved MLB or its minor-league affiliates.[27] Given MLB's overall antitrust exemption, any such challenge would have been futile.

One case that received a lot of media attention is *Clarett v. NFL*. The plaintiff challenged the NFL's "Special Eligibility" rule that required the player to be three seasons removed from high school graduation to be draft eligible. The Second Circuit Court of Appeals ultimately found that draft eligibility was subject to collective bargaining and, therefore, removed from antitrust scrutiny by the nonstatutory labor exemption.[28] This case clarifies the interaction of the antitrust laws and the nonstatutory labor exemption. In particular, the exemption applies to restraints of trade that produce effects predominantly in the labor market.[29] In other words, if the labor market is characterized by collective bargaining, and the practice does not result in anticompetitive effects in the product market, it should not be exposed to antitrust inquiry.

Roster Size

All the major sports leagues, including MLB, have limits on the size of the team roster. This rule seems innocent enough, but its effects are economic. When the teams agree not to compete on this dimension, fewer players are hired, which means lower payroll costs, lower travel expenses, and so on. This is another issue that is subject to collective bargaining and is presumably safe under the nonstatutory labor exemption.

6. RESTRICTIONS ON ENTRY

In most instances, the exercise of monopoly power leads to excess profits, which naturally attracts entry. When a sports league appears to be profitable, new teams will want to enter the league and garner a share of the monopoly profit enjoyed by the current members. League expansion, however, could result in lower average profits for league members. When that is the case, the league will reject the potential entrant's application. The incumbent teams will simply refuse to schedule any games with the would-be entrant. This raises an antitrust question: Can league members deny access to league membership? In short, the answer is yes. This issue was tried in football and the logic of the court's reasoning there extends to MLB as well as other leagues. Once again, MLB's antitrust exemption is unnecessary—the practice is not anticompetitive and, therefore, not unlawful under either §1 or §2 of the Sherman Act.

The World Football League (WFL) tried to compete with the NFL. It fought the good fight, but failed after only a season and a half. One of the teams, the Memphis Southmen, had been financially successful in the WFL. Following the demise of the WFL, Memphis changed its name to the Grizzlies and applied for membership in the NFL. The NFL rejected the Grizzlies' application for several reasons: (1) it had recently expanded into Seattle and Tampa and did not think that further expansion was desirable at that time, (2) sensible scheduling required an even number of teams, and (3) there was some unsettled labor litigation. The Grizzlies sued.[30]

For antitrust purposes, the NFL was considered a single entity and, therefore, the issue was whether the NFL was an unlawful monopoly. The antitrust analysis in a §2 case necessarily must begin with the relevant market definition. Here, the relevant market was defined as major league professional football in the United States. The NFL clearly had a monopoly in that market. Thus, the first prong of the *Grinnell* test for unlawful monopoly was satisfied. The question then was whether the NFL had acquired or maintained that monopoly through exclusionary or predatory practices. The court observed that Congress had permitted the merger of the NFL and the American Football League well before the WFL was formed. As a result, the original formation was not objectionable on antitrust grounds. As for maintaining its monopoly, the court found that excluding the Grizzlies was actually pro-competitive because the Grizzlies and the Memphis areas provided an organization and a site that could be part of a rival league. Merely joining the NFL and sharing in its pot of gold is not the same as providing legitimate competition with a rival league. The Grizzlies were unable to convince the Court that their exclusion from the NFL reduced competition in any relevant market.

Precisely the same logic would apply to MLB. This does not mean that a disgruntled, would-be entrant could not file suit, but it does mean that such a suit would probably fail even if MLB did not have an antitrust exemption.[31]

Contraction

There was a time when MLB considered contraction. Alarmed that MLB might eliminate one of the Florida teams, the Florida Attorney General began an antitrust investigation. This effort was quashed by the federal district court on the basis of

MLB's antitrust exemption. This early resolution saved a lot of resources, but the Grizzlies' logic suggests that the suit would have been unsuccessful. Eliminating two clubs would have been procompetitive—at least potentially—because those clubs could be the nucleus for a rival league.

7. COLLUSION IN THE SALE OF BROADCAST RIGHTS

There are thirty teams in MLB. This is a large enough number to assure competition in the sale of national and perhaps regional broadcast rights. The teams, however, do not compete among themselves in the sale of their broadcast rights. Instead, they pool their broadcast rights and exploit whatever monopoly power they collectively possess in this market.[32] If MLB were considered to be a single entity, there would be no antitrust issue associated with a simple sale of a package of broadcast rights. Problems could arise if MLB practiced price discrimination in violation of the Robinson-Patman Act, which forbids price discrimination that substantially reduces competition or tends to create a monopoly. Simple package deals—no matter how high the price—would not violate §2 of the Sherman Act.

Antitrust problems surface if MLB is not a single entity, but a collection of independent business firms. In that event, pooling broadcast rights is the sort of collusive behavior that would seem to violate §1 of the Sherman Act. Thus, baseball's antitrust exemption would appear to be quite useful. That exemption, however, is unnecessary in this particular market because of the Sports Broadcasting Act.

Sports Broadcasting Act

The National Football League (NFL) pooled the broadcast rights of its members and sold them as a package to CBS. In 1961, the NFL asked a federal district court to rule that the practice was permissible; but the court went in the opposite direction.[33] When the federal district court held that this pooling impermissibly eliminated competition among the teams and, therefore, was unlawful, the NFL did not appeal the ruling in court. Instead, it appealed to Congress for an exemption. At the NFL's urging, Congress passed the Sports Broadcasting Act of 1961 (SBA). The SBA allowed the professional sports leagues in football, baseball, basketball, and hockey to pool their TV broadcast rights for sale to a network. By doing so, it removed the threat of antitrust prosecution under §1 of the Sherman Act. The major professional sports leagues were not granted blanket antitrust immunity by the SBA. There were several limitations. First, the broadcast agreements could not impose territorial limitations on the purchasers of the broadcast rights. The only exception applied to blackouts to protect a team that had not sold out a home game. If, for example, the Detroit Lion's home game with the Green Bay Packers were not sold out, the television broadcast of that game could be blacked out in the Detroit area. Second, agreements were not exempt if they permitted broadcasts on days traditionally reserved for high school and college football games—Friday nights and Saturdays, respectably. Finally, the SBA specifically provided that it applied only to the specified agreements. It did not have anything to do with the applicability or nonapplicability of the antitrust laws to any other aspect of the sports business.

As a result of the SBA, the NFL's members could jointly market their broadcast rights without fear of antitrust prosecution. The same was true for the NBA, the NHL, and MLB. This, of course, gave each league a measure of market power in dealing with broadcasters. The structure of the market was no longer competitive. The economic results were predictable: the sports league became the sole seller and, therefore, could maximize its profits on the sale of broadcast rights just as any monopolist would. All members of the league would share the revenues. By making the networks and cable operators bid against one another, the league can extract a good deal of the profit that is generated by selling ad slots to advertisers.

The value of competitive bidding can be illustrated by MLB's experience in Europe. Prior to the entry of two new bidders for MLB's cable rights in Europe, the price was about $10 million over five years. When the North American Sports Network (NASN) entered the bidding, the rights fee jumped. Then along came ESPN. To avoid losing the MLB deal, NASN increased its offer by several million dollars. MLB finally got nearly $20 million over five years for its European cable rights.

8. CONCLUDING REMARKS

There is little doubt that MLB's antitrust exemption is an accident of history. Over the years, great deference has been paid to the national pastime and the courts have expressed great reluctance to change the business environment for fear that it could ruin the game for the fans. This time has long passed. We have argued that the antitrust exemption is now largely irrelevant. Competition in the labor market is dictated by collective bargaining. The conduct of the league with respect to entry, expansion, and pooling broadcast rights have either been found pro-competitive or otherwise exempt. Very few potential antitrust issues remain unresolved.[34]

There is still an extremely good reason for MLB to jealously guard its antitrust exemption. With the exemption, some antitrust suits never get filed and others are dismissed or terminated at a very early stage. In a world of extremely expensive litigation, this saves considerable sums of money. It also avoids having MLB's business executives distracted from their real jobs. It is difficult to overstate the significance of this benefit.

NOTES

1 For an economic analysis of this judicial development, see Blair and Kaserman (2009).
2 In *United States v. Grinnell Corp.*, 384 U.S. 563 (1966), the Supreme Court set out a two-prong test for unlawful monopolization:

> The offense of monopoly under §2 of the Sherman Act has two elements: (1) the possession of monopoly power in the relevant market and (2) the willful acquisition or maintenance of that power as distinguished from growth or development as a consequence of a superior product, business acumen, or historic accident. (*Ibid.* at 570–571).

The "willful acquisition or maintenance" term refers to anticompetitive exclusion or predation. ABA Section of Antitrust Law (2007) provides an excellent summary of exclusionary practices at pp. 240–301.
3 For a compact survey of those industries in which regulation has displaced reliance on competitive market forces, see chapter 15 in ABA Section of Antitrust Law (2007).
4 This decision has been described as not one of Justice Holmes's happiest days. *Flood v. Kuhn*, 92 S.Ct. 2099, FN 9 (1972).
5 A fairly complete description of the reserve system's essential elements is provided in the Supreme Court's *Flood* decision.
6 Gerald Scully's pathbreaking work provides some estimates of just how valuable the reserve system was (Scully, 1974). He found that MLB salaries were about 15–20 percent of the player's marginal revenue product. This, of course means that the bulk of any surplus went to the owners.
7 The dissenting opinion in *Toolson* makes it pretty clear that any assertion that MLB was not engaged in interstate commerce was fanciful if not disingenuous.
8 *Toolson v. NY Yankees, Inc.* 346 U.S. 356, 357 (1953)
9 This is a reference to Justice Clark's opinion in Radovich v. National Football League, 352 U.S. at 450.
10 The results showed the value of the system to the owners. Because a player could be lost to free agency after only one year of additional service, the clubs began offering multiyear contracts at much higher salaries. Free agency became a collective bargaining issue.
11 Scully, p. 929, (1974).
12 This inference depends on there being no collusion among the teams. Collusion, of course, could lead to exploitation of free agents, which would then lead to underestimates of the marginal revenue products.
13 These estimates, of course, are not directly comparable.
14 There is a history of collusion in MLB's free agent market. Following substantial salary gains in the 1975–1985 period, the owners stopped bidding on free agents. This

collusion resulted in arbitration that all went in the players' favor. For an account, see Weiler and Roberts (1998; 228).

15 The Collective Bargaining Agreement is available at http://www.MLBPA.com.

16 Prior to free agency, Don Drysdale and Sandy Koufax tried to join forces in negotiating their contracts with the Dodgers. This effort failed then and would be a violation of the CBA now. For a popular account, see Leavy (2002; 201).

17 See Article XX, Section E(2) of the CBA: "Upon any finding of a violation of Section E(1) of this Article XX by two or more Clubs, any injured Player (or Players) shall be entitled to recover in monetary damages three (3) times the lost baseball income he (or they) would have had but for the violation."

18 CBA, Article XX, Section E(2).

19 *Brown v. Pro Football, Inc.* 518 U.S. 231, 236 (1996).

20 This clarification is asserted in *Brown v. Pro Football.*

21 This argument was repeated in *Brown v. Pro Football, Inc.* 518 U.S. 231, 236 (1996), where the issue was fixed rookie salaries; see also Smith, 593 F.2d at 1186 (citing *National Society of Professional Engineers v. United States,* 435 U.S. 679 (1978)).

22 *Brown v. Pro Football, Inc.* was eventually decided in favor of the NFL because salary restraints are subject to collective bargaining and therefore fall under the nonstatutory labor exemption.

23 www.milb.com.

24 Some players recruited from outside the United States enter this way.

25 www.milb.com.

26 See *Haywood v. National Basketball Association*, 401 U.S. 1204 (1971), *Linsenman v. World Hockey Association*, 439 F.Supp 1315, *Boris v. United States Football League* 1984 WL 894 (C.D.Cal.1984).

27 In 1992, the MLBPA, however, did represent minor-league players in a grievance filed against changes to the eligibility rules. The arbitrator ultimately decided that these rules had to be decided through collective bargaining with the MLBPA. See Paul Staudohar, Franklin Lowenthal, and Anthony Lima. The evolution of baseball's amateur draft, *NINE: A Journal of Baseball History and Culture* 15(1), 2006, pp. 27–44 for a discussion of this arbitration.

28 The eligibility rules were not in the text of the collective bargaining agreement. They were located in the NFL Constitution and Bylaws. In the collective bargaining agreement, however, the Bylaws were discussed and provisions for negotiating changes to them were outlined.

29 *Brown v. Pro Football, Inc.*, 50 F.3d 1041,1056 (D.C.Cir.1995).

30 *Mid-South Grizzlies v. National football League*, 720 F.2 772 (3d Cir.1983).

31 The major benefit of MLB's antitrust exemption is the likelihood that an antitrust suit would be dismissed by the court at the pleading stage, which would save a considerable amount of money.

32 Even collectively, MLB may not possess much market power since this programming must compete with all other programming for broadcasters' attention.

33 *United States v. NFL*, 196 F.Supp. 455 (E.D. Pa. 1961).

34 Two issues remain: pooling intellectual property rights and relocation decisions. The Supreme Court will soon decide whether the NFL is a single entity. (See *American Needle Inc. v. NFL*, 129 S.Ct. 2859 (2009)). If sports leagues are found to be single entities, then §1 challenges in these two areas will be impossible. If not, then there will be some exposure.

REFERENCES

ABA Section of Antitrust Law. 2007. *Antitrust law developments,* 6th ed. Chicago: American Bar Association.

Blair, Roger D., and David L. Kaserman. 2009. *Antitrust economics,* 2nd ed. New York: Oxford University Press.

Blair, Roger D., and Jeffery L. Harrison. 2010. *Monopsony in law & economics.* New York: Cambridge University Press.

Blair, Roger D., and Jessica S. Haynes. 2009. Collusion in Major League Baseball's free agent market: The Barry Bonds case, *Antitrust Bulletin,* 54: 883–906.

Bradbury, J. C. 2007. *The baseball economist.* New York: Penguin Group.

Curtis C. Flood v. Bowie K. Kuhn, 407 U.S. 258 (1972).

Federal Baseball Club of Baltimore, Inc. v. National League of Professional Baseball Clubs, 259 U.S. 200 (1922).

Kahn, Lawrence M. 2009. Sports, antitrust enforcement, and collective bargaining. *Antitrust Bulletin,* 54: 857–882.

Kintner, Earl W., and Joseph P. Bauer. 1994. *Federal antitrust law* §§74.1–74.11. Newark, NJ: LEXIS/NEXIS.

Krautmann, Anthony. 1999. What's Wrong with Scully—Estimates of a Player's Marginal Revenue Product? *Economic Inquiry,* 37: 369–381.

Leavy, Jane. 2002. *Sandy Kaufax.* New York: Harper Collins Publishers.

Lopatka, John. 2009. Antitrust and equipment standards: Winners and whiners. *Antitrust Bulletin,* 54: 751–801.

Quirk, James, and Rodney D. Fort. 1992. *Pay dirt: The business of professional team sports.* Princeton: Princeton University Press.

Scully, Gerald W. 1974, Pay and performance in Major League Baseball. *American Economic Review,* 64: 915–930.

Thorelli, Hans B. 1954. *The federal antitrust policy: Origination of an American tradition.* London: George Allen & Unwin.

Toolson v. New York Yankees, Inc., 346 U.S. 356 (1953).

Weiler, Paul C. and Gary R. Roberts. 1998. *Sports and the law.* St. Paul, MN: West Publishing.

Zimbaltist, Andrew. 2003. *May the best team win.* Washington, DC: Brookings Institution.

CHAPTER 6

THE RESERVE CLAUSE AND LABOR MOBILITY

PAUL D. STAUDOHAR

ECONOMICS is the primary force driving decision-making by owners, players, agents, government, and other participants in the sports business. "Show me the money" is the catch-phrase that best describes the animating spirit of professional sports. Although economics is important, other academic disciplines—history and law—are also taken into account in examining the topic of this paper. Taking a multidisciplinary approach helps to provide a well-rounded perspective on the principal issues at stake and their impact on the baseball labor market.

This essay fits in with the overall theme of the volume on *Economics of Sports*, because it examines sports institutions, particularly players' unions, leagues, and the role of government. Six subsections are presented here: (1) origins of the reserve clause, (2) union opposition, (3) antitrust law, (4) breakthrough on free agency, (5) labor-market theories, and (6) impact of free agency.

ORIGINS OF THE RESERVE CLAUSE

In the early days of professional baseball, bidding for players led to a practice called "revolving." Some players who were under contract to a club would move to another club that made a better offer. Revolving was in full flower by 1869 and, despite efforts to prevent it, would remain a problem for years to come.[1] Revolving coincided with the rise of professionalism in baseball.

A. G. Mills, who is considered the father of the reserve clause (or reserve rule), stated the problem as follows:

> This condition was greatly aggravated by the general practice on the part of the richer clubs of stripping the weaker ones of their best playing talent. Then would follow the collapse of a number of these clubs in mid-season, leaving their players unpaid, while the winning clubs, owing to the disbandment of the weaker ones, would also frequently fall from inability to arrange a paying number of games.[2]

The Cincinnati Red Stockings was the first all-professional club in America and, in 1869, had an undefeated season, winning fifty-six games and tying one. The success of the Red Stockings induced other cities to establish professional clubs as well. As a result, the National Association of Base Ball Players (NABBP), which had been formed in 1858 as an amateur organization, evolved into a group of professional teams. It was the first professional league in any sport. Although it was the dominant organization in baseball, the NABBP was seriously compromised by revolving, as well as by widespread gambling, which created an impression that the games were rigged by crooked players.

As a result, fan interest in games flagged and several clubs in the NABBP went bankrupt. The void was filled by the creation of the National League of Professional Baseball Clubs in 1876. The main force behind the creation of the National League was William Hulbert, a Chicago businessman. Hulbert realized the damaging effects of inflated player salaries caused by revolving and overbidding.[3] However, much as he deplored the practice of inducing players by paying them more, he resorted to this tactic himself. Several players who were under contract to their teams were pirated away to Chicago's club, notably Albert Spalding and Adrian "Cap" Anson, who were among the greatest players in baseball and are enshrined in the Baseball Hall of Fame.

Despite efforts to control player salaries, club owners came to the realization that the high salaries were their own doing, caused by the competition among themselves for players. As we look at the modern era, nothing has changed much in this regard, even though the rules themselves have changed.

The solution the owners worked out was the reserve clause. Former player turned owner, Al Spalding, stated the objective of the reserve clause as "to prevent competition for the best players in each of the other clubs, and to keep those clubs together."[4]

The National League established the original reserve clause in 1879. At first, only five players were reserved by each club, ostensibly to preserve the stability of the game in the face of player salary inflation.[5] Over the years, the number of players so restricted was increased to include the entire 40-man roster of major league clubs. Another reason offered for the reserve clause was to keep the Chicago club, the league's only regular moneymaker, from corralling the best talent.[6]

Although the owners attempted to shield themselves from criticism that they were trying to enrich themselves at the players' expense, this stance is shown to be disingenuous by W. Woodward Eckard. Analyzing the relevant data, he found that the owners' apparent motive for the reserve rule was monopsonistic collusion rather than protecting the public interest.[7]

The reserve clause, as originally conceived, gave clubs a continuing option on player services. Once a player signed an initial uniform contract, he agreed to perform for the club for a specified period of time, say one year. The contract, however, allowed the club to "reserve" the player for the subsequent season. The only way a player could escape his obligation to remain with the club that originally signed him was to be traded or sold or to retire. Thus, by signing the first contract, the player gave up any right to sell his services to other teams. The only bidder for a player's services was the single monopsonistic club. In the absence of a rival league to which players might jump for more money, the club was in the driver's seat in salary determination. Players could hold out on signing contracts. Some did not play for the entire season, but, in the end, the player had no real option because he could make much more money playing baseball than at any other endeavor.

Under this system, player salaries were relatively low compared to their marginal revenue product. The clubs captured the rent from the difference. Some truly outstanding players like Babe Ruth and Ty Cobb made high salaries because there were no substitutes for them and they were worth far more to their teams than other players. However, even Ruth and Cobb were probably underpaid.

Besides the contractual obligation, which was enforceable in court, clubs maintained a blacklist. The league's constitution required that clubs could not employ any player who violated playing rules or who had been dismissed from another club.[8]

Several arguments for and against the reserve clause have been raised. The main ones are presented here:

For

1. Without the reserve clause wealthy clubs would garner all the best players, seriously compromising the desired objective of competitive balance in a league.
2. In the absence of the clause salaries would rise to inflated levels, thus jeopardizing the viability of poorer clubs.
3. Clubs would be reluctant to pay large bonuses or to assume training expenses for young ballplayers if they knew they might lose these players to a rival team later on.

Against

1. The reserve clause is an intolerable restraint on the freedom of players to move from one team to another in the labor market.
2. Without the reserve clause players might gravitate to the wealthy clubs, but under the clause the richer clubs wind up with the best talent anyway.
3. Outstanding players can get stuck on perennially second-rate clubs, with no chance of getting the higher pay associated with winning clubs.

UNION OPPOSITION

In 1885 the Brotherhood of Professional Base Ball Players was formed, with popular player John Montgomery Ward as president. The reserve clause was denounced by the union in the belief that it created a system of serfdom in baseball and interfered with the operation of supply and demand to regulate salaries. Although the Brotherhood negotiated with the owners, little was accomplished. In 1890 Ward, along with several star players, formed the Players League in direct competition with the National League. Although the new league discarded the strict reserve rules, players remained tied to their clubs, albeit for a limited time.

The National League mounted a trade war against the Players League with the focus of the struggle on gaining control of as many players as possible. This interleague competition caused player salaries to rise sharply. The reserve clause became a focal point as National League owners sought court injunctions preventing their players from jumping to the new league. The courts raised questions about the legal enforceability of reserve clauses, and players won two important rulings.

Buck Ewing, a National League star, had become player/manager of the New York club in the Players League. A federal court determined that the reserve clause in Ewing's contract was unenforceable because of lack of mutuality in the contract. In a similar case, involving John Montgomery Ward, a state court refused his National League club's request for an injunction on the grounds that the terms of the reserve clause were indefinite.[9] Although Ewing and Ward, both later inducted into the Hall of Fame, won their cases, their victories were limited by the collapse of the Players League after just one year of operation.

A second union in baseball, the Protective Association of Professional Baseball Players, was established in 1900, following a decade of perceived abuses in the wake of the Players League collapse. The timing was good because the rival American League came into existence in 1900 to challenge the hegemony of the National League, and salaries were expected to rise as a result of interleague rivalry.

Harry Taylor, a Buffalo attorney and former player, provided leadership for the union, whose president was Charley "Chief" Zimmer, an active player. Prominent players and eventual Hall of Famers Clark Griffith and Hugh Jennings also had leadership roles. Samuel Gompers, president of the American Federation of Labor, offered membership in the organization to the fledgling union but it was refused for fear of alienating club owners.

The union's constitution sought to limit but not abolish the reserve clause. The bylaws stated that every effort would be made to "prevent any member from being ... traded or sold to any baseball club without his consent."[10] Taylor also proposed a new form of contract, which contained a clause guaranteeing a player the right to his release upon giving ten days notice if the owner violated its terms.[11] The National League was willing to accept these proposals but only on condition that the union suspend any of its members who jumped to the American League.

The American League honored the National League's contracts except for the reserve clause. Similar to the Players League a decade earlier, the new league raided the old league of its players and was quite successful in doing so. Also, as occurred before, the National League tried to prevent player movement by taking action for enforceability of contracts in the courts.

Another future Hall of Famer, Napoleon Lajoie, wanted to jump from the National League Philadelphia Phillies club to the new Philadelphia Athletics of the American League. The National League club sued to prevent losing the player, who was under contract. In protracted litigation, finally decided by the supreme court of Pennsylvania, the National League prevailed. Meanwhile, however, Lajoie played the 1901 season in the American League, batting .422, a record that still stands. He was later traded to Cleveland because Ohio courts refused to follow the Pennsylvania court ruling.[12]

Shortly after the peace treaty between the National and American Leagues in 1903, the Protective Association passed from the scene. Because the leagues agreed to respect each others' contracts and reserve rights over players, the union was unable to effect any change in monopsony control.

The Base Ball Players Fraternity was created in 1912. A former ballplayer turned attorney, David Fultz, founded this union and was its first president. One of the Fraternity's objectives was to ensure that contracts were honored by both parties, although it did not propose elimination of the reserve clause. The union was bolstered by the formation of the rival Federal League in 1913. Initially the new league did not attempt to lure players from the established leagues. Nonetheless, the Federal League was highly competitive because it had clubs in several major league and top minor league cities such as Chicago, St. Louis, and Cleveland. It was also backed by some very successful businessmen.

The Federal League's policy on the reserve clause muted its force somewhat. The club owners had an option on the players' services for the upcoming season, provided that it was exercised before September 15. Clubs were also required to increase player salaries by five percent over the previous year's salary and ten-year veterans could become free agents.[13] Federal League team owners did not honor reserve clauses in the National and American League contracts.

As in the case of earlier rival leagues, a prominent player wound up in court. Bill Killefer, catcher for the Philadelphia Phillies, flirted with the Federal League's Chicago club, inducing the Phillies to promise a salary increase. Although Killefer gave an oral promise to the Phillies, he signed a three-year deal with the Chicago Federal League club. He was then induced to sign a three-year contract with the Phillies. As a result, the Chicago owner sought an injunction to prevent Killefer from playing for the Phillies. The injunction was denied because Chicago came to the court with "unclean hands." Although the Phillies won the case on moral grounds, the court found the uniform contract to be, "lacking in the necessary qualities of definiteness, certainty, and mutuality."[14]

The Killefer matter broke the good will and tacit understanding between the rival leagues, and the Federal League began pirating away more players. Player salaries shot upward while the parties continued to wrangle in the courts. Although the Federal League was well capitalized, it was difficult to compete with the entrenched major leagues. It also failed to pirate a sufficiently large number of players, and hardly any stars, from the established leagues, causing fans to wonder if the Federal League was second-rate.

Although the Fraternity was on the sidelines for most of the main events, the interleague competition strengthened its position. The union petitioned organized baseball on several grievances, many of which were accepted, including written notification to players who are released or transferred, and that ten-year veterans who were waived on by other clubs in the league were free agents. These changes gave players slightly more rights in the labor market but were small potatoes compared to the reserve clause.

When it became clear that the Federal League could not operate profitably in competition with the majors, it was paid $600,000 by organized baseball. Two Federal League clubs were merged with the major leagues. The Baltimore club rejected a settlement offer, and so a committee was appointed to decide its fate at a later time. This rejection would later lead to landmark litigation on the reserve clause.

Although the Federal League was finished, the Fraternity continued to function, but its strength was sapped by elimination of the rival league. Most of its efforts were redirected toward improving the lot of minor league players. The union passed from the scene in 1917.

The American Baseball Guild was formed in 1946 as a result of low salaries. World War II had siphoned off star players like Bob Feller, Ted Williams, and Joe DiMaggio, which had a dampening effect on overall salaries. At this time, the Mexican League was a thriving operation that attracted major leaguers by offering bonuses and higher salaries. One of these so-called Mexican jumping beans was Danny Gardella from the New York Giants. Because he signed with a Mexican League team, Gardella was suspended for five years by Major League Baseball for violating the reserve clause. As a result, he brought suit against Commissioner Albert "Happy" Chandler and Major League Baseball for a conspiracy to deny him his livelihood.

Although Gardella lost his case at the federal district court level, a federal appellate court in New York voted 2–1 to grant him a trial.[15] The judges were convinced that income from radio and television broadcasts brought Major League Baseball under the purview of interstate commerce.[16] Because it looked as though there was a good chance the courts would find the reserve clause illegal under the Sherman Act, the owners settled Gardella's case out of court in 1949.

Robert Murphy, a lawyer and former National Labor Relations Board trial examiner, used the Mexican League incident and salary dissatisfaction among players to organize the fourth players' union and the first since 1917. One of the objectives of the American Baseball Guild was replacement of the reserve clause with a system of long-term contracts. Murphy also proposed that players receive half their selling price and, if traded, were to be compensated with hefty salary increases.[17] The union did win a minimum player salary of $5,000, as well as agreement on a pension plan funded out of revenues from sale of national television and radio rights. This pension plan has turned out to be phenomenally successful.

However, like its predecessors, the union was overshadowed by the owners and could not sustain any real power at the bargaining table.

The fifth and last baseball players' union was formed in 1952. For several years the Major League Baseball Players Association (MLBPA) was relatively ineffective and dominated by owners. In 1953, for instance, when players Ralph Kiner and Allie Reynolds tried to bolster the MLBPA's effectiveness by acting more like a union, there was little inclination on the part of present or former players to embrace this idea.[18]

All this changed in 1966 when Marvin Miller was hired to run the union. The idea of setting up a permanent office and hiring a full-time director came from player Robin Roberts. He also proposed the name of Marvin Miller to fill this position.[19] Miller had been recommended to Roberts by George Taylor, an eminent professor at the Wharton School of the University of Pennsylvania. Other prominent players who were instrumental in turning the MLBPA into a union were Bob Friend, Harvey Kuenn, and Jim Bunning. Miller, an economist by training, was well versed in labor relations, collective bargaining, and labor law, as a result of serving for many years as an executive of the United Steelworkers Union.

A common misconception is the belief that Miller single-handedly accounted for the union's success, that he was the ventriloquist to the players' dummie. This notion is debunked by the leading authority on the players' union, historian Charles Korr. Korr points out that while Miller played a pivotal role in transforming the union, it was really the players who determined the objectives and what they were willing to risk to achieve them.[20]

ANTITRUST

Unlike football, basketball, and hockey, baseball is considered exempt from the application of federal antitrust law. The Sherman Antitrust Act of 1890 is the principal American law prohibiting monopolistic practices that stifle business competition. The key language of the law is, "Every contract, combination in the form of trust or otherwise on conspiracy in restraint of trade or commerce among several states ... is hereby declared illegal." The Sherman Act provides for treble damages for violation of the law.

Baseball's exemption from the antitrust law stems from a 1922 decision by the United States Supreme Court. The case is an outgrowth of the demise of the Federal League. When that league ceased operations, the remaining National League and American League teams bought out or otherwise brought closure to all of its teams except the Baltimore club. That club sued the existing leagues, contending that they conspired to put the Federal League out of business and that all teams were aided except Baltimore.

The federal district court, hearing the *Federal Baseball Club* case at the trial level, found a violation of the Sherman Act and awarded the Baltimore club damages of $80,000, which was tripled to $240,000 under the provisions of the law. On appeal, however, the U.S. Court of Appeals reversed the trial court on the grounds that baseball was not interstate commerce and was, therefore, not subject to antitrust law.

The U.S. Supreme Court agreed with the appellate court.[21] Famed Justice Oliver Wendell Holmes wrote the opinion for a unanimous court. He said: "The business is giving exhibitions of baseball, which are purely state affairs." Although players and clubs crossed state lines to play games, this was considered merely incidental to what is essentially a local game. Moreover, Holmes did not regard the baseball exhibition as trade of commerce because "personal effort, not related to production, is not a subject of commerce." Holmes' decision, when viewed in a contemporary context, is plainly wrong. As a multibillion-dollar business, baseball is clearly involved in interstate commerce. The sport can hardly be considered local as leagues today extend from coast to coast. There is also no doubt that baseball constitutes a monopoly that significantly restrains trade, because its franchises give sole power to a club to operate in a particular geographical area.

Despite the incongruity of the *Federal Baseball Club* case with modern economic reality, the decision of the U.S Supreme Court continues to govern antitrust policy in the sport. Over the years, the court has reaffirmed its position. The most significant of these cases involved player Curt Flood.[22]

Flood was an outstanding twelve-year centerfielder for the St. Louis Cardinals who was traded to the Philadelphia Phillies in 1969. He refused to report to Philadelphia and brought suit against Commissioner Bowie Kuhn, contending that the reserve clause restrained trade in violation of the Sherman Act. The U.S. Supreme Court's majority opinion, written by Justice Harry Blackmun, acknowledged that baseball was engaged in interstate commerce.[23] Nonetheless, the decision went against Flood because the court emphasized the doctrine of precedent or *stare decisis*, in upholding the *Federal Baseball Club* decision. The court also thought that it would be more appropriate for Congress to act to modify or remove the exemption. The court based its decision on its recognition and acceptance of baseball's unique characteristics and needs.

Since the *Flood* decision, Congress has brought the exemption under close scrutiny. For instance, in 1977 a joint Senate-House Committee on Professional Sports stated that there is no justification for baseball's antitrust immunity and recommended removal of the exemption. In 1988 a Senate task force threatened to repeal the exemption, arguing that the commissioner was not doing enough to expand the sport into new cities. As a result of the 1994–1995 baseball strike, Congress introduced legislation to apply antitrust law to baseball.[24] None of these Congressional initiatives bore fruit.

However, the exemption was modified somewhat in the Curt Flood Act of 1998. This law places Major League Baseball in the same position as other team sports with regard to the application of antitrust law to labor relations. In football and basketball, for example, individual players can bring an antitrust suit but the union cannot. This partial removal of the exemption in baseball is an anachronism, however, because, in order to bring an antitrust suit against the leagues, the MLBPA would have to decertify itself as the representative of the players. This process could take some time, and meanwhile a work stoppage could damage the sport, regardless of the Flood Act.[25]

FREE AGENCY BREAKTHROUGH

One of the most important, yet least publicized, accomplishments of Marvin Miller was negotiating a provision for grievance arbitration in the 1972 collective bargaining agreement. Although widespread in American industry, arbitration of matters involving the interpretation or application of contract terms was nonexistent in sports until Miller made the breakthrough. Also important was that the arbitration provision applied to players' contract disputes, including the reserve clause. The whole concept of arbitration was crucial to the MLBPA, because instead of having the team owner, league president, or commissioner make the final decision on disputes, the grievance could now be submitted to an outside neutral third party who was empowered to make a final and binding decision.

Arbitration was used to resolve an important dispute that arose in 1974. Jim "Catfish" Hunter was arguably the finest pitcher of his day. His team, the Oakland Athletics, won the World Series in 1972, 1973, and 1974, and he was the pitcher the team wanted on the mound in big games. The owner of the Athletics was Charles O. Finley, an innovative tight-fisted showman. Finley made his fortune in the insurance business. In order to capture a tax advantage for both himself and Hunter, Finley agreed to place half of Hunter's total salary of $100,000 into an insurance trust or annuity, which would be paid out as income in the future.

The deferral of taxes was a good idea for Hunter, but Finley soon realized that the arrangement did not save him any taxes. Therefore, Finley did not make a timely payment of the $50,000 into the trust on Hunters' behalf. Hunter notified the MLBPA of Finley's inaction and the union filed a grievance. When the parties were unable to resolve the grievance to their mutual satisfaction, the dispute was submitted to arbitrator Peter Seitz.

Seitz, from New York City, was baseball's "permanent" arbitrator, meaning that all grievances were submitted to him. He examined the facts of the case and determined that there was a breach of contract as a result of Finley's failure to make prompt payment into the insurance trust on Hunter's behalf, which Finley was contractually obligated to do. The remedy for the violation was to invalidate Hunter's entire contract, which made him a free agent. Because of Hunter's pitching prowess, many teams wanted to sign him to play for them. The winner of the bidding competition was the New York Yankees, who agreed to pay Hunter $3.75 million over five years.

The Hunter case is significant for three reasons: (1) it was the first time in the modern era that a top player was able to take advantage of free agency, (2) Hunter's salary rocketed upward by about 750 percent, which demonstrated dramatically the power that a high-quality player had in a free labor market, and (3) the Hunter case stimulated an attempt to extend free agency to other players as well.

Although the Hunter case was *sui generis* and did not apply to other players, it showed that, if the right set of circumstances could be brought before an arbitrator, additional significant change might occur. Two players decided to mount a challenge to the reserve clause. Andy Messersmith, a pitcher for the Los Angeles Dodgers, and Dave McNally, a pitcher for the Baltimore Orioles who had recently been traded to the Montreal Expos, each played a year for their teams without signing a contract. Under existing rules, if a player refused to sign a contract, the club had the option of utilizing the player's services by paying a salary slightly higher than the year before.

Messersmith and McNally contended that the language of their prior contracts allowed their clubs to extend these contracts only for a year. Because the players had played out this one-year option, they claimed that they were free agents. Their clubs argued that the reserve clause bound the players to the team forever. Arbitrator Seitz read the language to mean that the option was only for a year. He, therefore, declared Messersmith and McNally to be free agents. McNally retired from the game and Messersmith signed a multiyear deal with the Atlanta Braves, estimated at $1.75 million. Seitz's decisions in both the Hunter and Messersmith/McNally cases were unsuccessfully appealed by the club owners to the courts. Seitz was unceremoniously fired by the owners.

The second Seitz decision was a major event in the history of professional team sports because it opened the door to free agency for the first time. Within a few years, perpetual reserve clauses in football, basketball, and hockey were invalidated by court decisions.

Following the declaration of free agency for baseball players whose contracts had expired, the owners and the MLBPA decided on future rules for free agency. Although neither party felt that it was in the interests of the game to have unfettered free agency, the owners wanted to delay free agency as long as possible. Although it might be supposed that the union would want free agency upon contract expiration, it did not want too many free agents flooding the market in a given year. The compromise the parties agreed to was to allow free agency after six years of major league service, a rule that stands to the present day. Until a player achieves six years of service, he is subject to the reserve clause. After three years of service, a player becomes eligible for salary arbitration, which eases the impact of the reserve clause by allowing an outside neutral to decide on a one-year salary in the event of a dispute.

The effect of free agency on player salaries was immediate. Table 6.1 shows the sharp increase in average player salaries in the first ten years of free agency. Moreover, salaries have continued to rise as a result of free agency, with the average climbing to $3.26 million in 2009. The game itself has prospered, with about $7 billion in total revenue in 2010. Team competition on the playing field has never been keener. Attendance fell off slightly in 2008, but increased to record highs in each of the previous six years.[26]

Table 6.1 Average Player Salaries in the First Ten Years after Free Agency

Year	Average Salary	Percent Change
1976	$51,501	—
1977	$76,066	47.7
1978	$99,876	31.3
1979	$113,558	13.7
1980	$143,756	26.6
1981	$185,651	29.1
1982	$241,497	30.1
1983	$289,194	19.8
1984	$329,408	14.1
1985	$371,157	12.7

Source: Major League Baseball Players Association.

LABOR MARKET THEORIES

According to Simon Rottenberg, the reserve rule is the heart of the limitation on freedom in the baseball labor market. He states:

The defense most commonly heard is that the reserve rule is necessary to assure an equal distribution of playing talent among opposing teams; that a more or less equal distribution of talent is necessary if there is to be uncertainty of outcome; and that uncertainty of outcome is necessary if the consumer is to be willing to pay admission to the game. This defense is founded on the premise that there are rich baseball clubs and poor ones and that, if the players' market were free, the rich clubs would outbid the poor for talent, taking all the competent players for themselves and leaving only the incompetent for the other teams.[27]

Although this argument seems compelling on the surface, it is shown to be false by Rottenberg. He presents empirical evidence on the number of times each team in the major leagues won the pennant, and he found a significantly unequal distribution of talent among teams. Therefore, he concluded, a market in which freedom of player movement is limited by the reserve rule "cannot be expected to equalize the distribution of players among teams more than a market in which there is perfect freedom."[28]

The reason for this conclusion is that no team can be successful unless the other teams in the league also prosper, so that differences in quality of play are not too extreme. In short, a reasonable semblance of competitive balance is necessary for a league to be successful. There are also limitations of diminishing returns to signing top players, as well as diseconomies of scale when wealthy teams too-far outstrip their competitors. The conclusion is that a market characterized by a reserve rule, with severe restrictions on player movement, does not distribute players among teams any differently than that which would occur in a free labor market. Player exploitation would be reduced, but competitive balance would remain unaffected. The difference that occurs is that, under the reserve clause, the club captures the economic rent, whereas, in a free market, the player receives his full value if he moves to another team as a free agent.

Rottenberg's theory is closely connected with that of his University of Chicago colleague Ronald Coase. A few years after Rottenberg's article was published, Coase came up with a generalized theorem to the effect that ownership of a resource has no effect on the allocation of resources. Instead, changes in rules only affect the distribution of wealth.[29]

This theory, known as the invariance principle, holds that, under the reserve clause (where teams control the property rights), trades and sale of players ensure that a player will wind up on the team for which he generates the highest marginal revenue product. An example is that Alex Rodriguez, arguably baseball's greatest player, wound up playing for the New York Yankees where he has a higher MRP than he did with Seattle and Texas, his previous teams.

With the elimination of the reserve clause (after six years of major league experience) and the advent of free agency, players own the rights to their talent. A player is expected to sign with the team for which he generates the greatest value. The same distribution of talent will occur under free agency as under the reserve clause.[30]

The prevailing view is that the reserve clause affects the distribution of wealth (rents) between owners and players but has no effect on the allocation of playing talent among teams.[31] An alternative view is expressed by Daly and Moore.[32] Noting the major change that took place in the reserve clause in 1976, the authors inquire, based on empirical data, whether this change had an impact on the distribution of playing talent.

Daly and Moore challenge the prevailing view on two points. One is that the traditional economic model of a sports league contemplates the systematic sale of players from poor teams to rich teams by way of cash transactions. Therefore, the effect of the reserve clause is undone by cash sales of players. This traditional model, however, does not conform well to reality. Cash transactions were rarely made except for marginal players. Three frequently cited exceptions are Connie Mack's sale of star players for the Philadelphia Athletics in 1915 (e.g., Eddie Collins), Boston Red Sox owner Harry Frazee's sale of Babe Ruth to the New York Yankees in 1919, and Oakland Athletics owner Charles Finley's attempted sale of star players in 1976 (Vida Blue, Joe Rudi, and Rollie Fingers) to the Boston Red Sox, which was nullified by Commissioner Bowie Kuhn for not being in the best interests of baseball. These examples point up the rarity of sale of star players and seem to contradict a principal underpinning of the traditional model.

The second challenge to the prevailing view, according to Daly and Moore, is their finding, based on statistical evidence, of a clear trend for free-agent players to gravitate toward larger cities, so as to strengthen teams there.[33] This is reinforced in another study in which John Vrooman found that free agency in baseball has had the effect of lowering the year-to-year correlation in winning percentage by breaking up winning teams.[34] The Oakland Athletics appear to be an example of this point. The team won three World Series titles in the early 1970s but, as a result of free agency, lost most of its star players and became a mediocre team.

IMPACT OF FREE AGENCY

The pioneering research on individual performance measures is from Gerald W. Scully.[35] He estimates the MRP of players before free agency and finds generally that their MRP is much greater than what they were paid. On the other hand, studies vary on the ratios of player salaries to MRP after free agency. Most of the studies show that typically free agents are overpaid. Free agents in large markets ordinarily have higher MRPs, and large market teams sign more free agent talent than other teams.[36] Andrew Zimbalist found that in the years 1986–1989, players with six years or more of major league service were consistently paid about 30 percent more than their MRPs.[37] The longer the terms of the free-agent contract the greater the risk that he will under perform.

Why do teams pay free agents more than they are worth? Zimbalist offers several reasons, foremost among which is that owners misgauge a player's worth. A player's worth may be greater if the player is kept from performing for competing teams. Also, star players may lift the performance of teammates.[38]

Another study compared the postcontract performance of free agents with the postcontract performance of players who were eligible for free agency but elected to sign contracts with the clubs for which they had been playing. Kenneth Lehn found that the free agency market features an asymmetric distribution of information among clubs.[39] That is, the players' old clubs have more information with which to estimate players' future performance than do clubs who have not had the players on their teams. Granting that this asymmetry exists, the free agents are expected to have lower performance than that of eligible players who do not sign as free agents with other clubs. Lehn also found that free agents, especially pitchers, spent more time on the disabled list than non-free agents.

What is the impact of free agency on players' compensation and contract duration? Lawrence M. Kahn examined these variables in a longitudinal study of major league players.[40] He found that non-pitchers' free agency eligibility increased annual salaries by about 35–50 percent, with pitchers gaining a lesser increment.[41] Free agency was also found to increase contract duration, because eligibility is based on experience, and better players are kept longer. However, factoring out experience, the difference was slight, at about one year, and was not statistically different between pitchers and non-pitchers.[42]

Research on the impact of free agency has also focused on inefficiencies in the auction market for free agents. Cassing and Douglas, for instance, conclude that free agents are overpaid, because the teams acquiring these players are subject to a "winner's curse."[43] Information asymmetries and uncertainty exist among clubs, but the club that correctly estimates the value of a player has little chance of signing that player because another club (or clubs) overestimates the player's value and will prevail at the auction. The difference between the correct estimate of the player's value and the inflated bid that wins the player's services is the winner's curse. When Alex Rodriguez became a free agent while playing for the Seattle Mariners, several teams were interested in him. The Texas Rangers won the bidding, but it was widely reported that the $252 million for ten years that the Rangers paid, then the richest in team sports, was tens of millions of dollars more than they needed to pay in order to obtain Rodriguez's services.

An interesting area of inquiry is whether the assignment of property rights affects the incentive of baseball players to shirk (avoid performing work). Daniel Marburger examined this issue, posing the hypothesis that the conversion from the reserve clause to free agency should increase player effort because the rents from increased effort accrue to the player rather than the club.[44] Marburger found confirmation on this hypothesis, but with the qualification that in cases of multiyear contracts signed by free agents, their performance does not differ from that of reserve era players under the same circumstances.

Concluding Remarks

Baseball's labor unions had a long, hard struggle to shed the yoke of the reserve clause. The MLBPA went on to become the strongest union in professional sports and one of the most effective in the nation. Once the breakthrough on free agency occurred, as a result of the 1975 arbitration decision, players reaped unimagined gains. That average salaries of ball players in 1976 were about $50,000 and in 2008 averaged about $3 million is one of the greatest success stories in the history of American labor. Moreover, Major League Baseball continues to operate as a monopoly, in the exalted status of being mostly exempt from the antitrust laws. It is, therefore, not surprising that the sport is enjoying a modern golden age of prosperity.

The topic of the reserve clause and labor mobility is concerned with the operation of the labor market. Simon Rottenberg's 1956 article was the first on the labor market as well as being the first on sports economics. His examination of the players' labor market is so insightful that it continues to be a standard reference work. In Europe, Peter J. Sloane is the main sports economics pioneer, and he too dealt extensively with the labor market for players. From a baseball history perspective, Harold Seymour's books have extensive coverage on the labor market, because it is crucial to players' economic freedom and welfare.

Finally, Roger Noll's book, *Government and the Sports Business* (1974) is notable because it covers a diversity of topics on which little if anything was previously written. Precursors to the labor market theme of this essay are articles in Noll's book on labor relations, league operation, public policy on sports, and application of the antitrust law. The potential of the sports economics field became apparent from this book, and a critical mass of scholars began to emerge that eventually thrust sports economics into a leading position in contemporary social science.

NOTES

1 Harold Seymour, *Baseball: The Early Years* (New York: Oxford University Press, 1960), 52.
2 Quotation from U.S. Congress, *Organized Baseball: Report of the Subcommittee on Study of Monopoly Power of the Committee on the Judiciary* (Washington, DC: Government Printing Office, 1952). This study, commonly called the "Cellar Report" after Congressman Emanuel Cellar, is also cited in Simon Rottenberg, "The Baseball Players' Labor Market," *Journal of Political Economy* 64(3), June 1956: 247.
3 Seymour, *Baseball: The Early Years*, 77.
4 Ibid., 106.
5 E. Woodrow Eckard, "The Origin of the Reserve Clause: Owner Collusion Versus 'Public Interest,'" *Journal of Sports Economics*, 2(2), May 2001: 114.
6 Charles C. Alexander, *Our Game: An American Baseball History* (New York: Henry Holt and Company, 1991), 31.
7 Eckard, "The Origin of the Reserve Clause," 127.
8 Seymour, *Baseball: The Early Years*, 127.
9 For further discussion of these cases, see Robert C. Berry, William B. Gould, and Paul D. Staudohar, *Labor Relations in Professional Sports* (Dover, MA: Auburn House Publishing Company, 1986), 24–25.
10 Seymour, *Baseball: The Early Years*, 310.
11 Ibid., 311.

12 For more on this case, see Berry, Gould, and Staudohar, *Labor Relations in Professional Sports*, 26–27.

13 Harold Seymour, *Baseball: The Golden Age*, (New York: Oxford University Press, 1971), 201.

14 Ibid., 204.

15 *Gardella v. Chandler*, 172 F.2d 402 (Second Circuit, 1949).

16 David Q. Voigt, "Serfs versus Magnates: A Century of Labor Strife in Major League Baseball," in *The Business of Professional Sports*, eds. Paul D. Staudohar and James A. Mangan (Urbana, IL: University of Illinois Press, 1991), 112.

17 Ibid., 113.

18 Charles P. Korr, "Marvin Miller and the New Unionism," in *The Business of Professional Sports,* 116.

19 Ibid., 118.

20 Charles P. Korr, *The End of Baseball as We Knew It: The Players Union, 1960–1981* (Urbana, IL: University of Illinois Press, 2002), 11.

21 *Federal Baseball Club of Baltimore v. National League of Professional Baseball Clubs,* 259 U.S. 200 (1922).

22 For discussion of other court decisions on baseball's antitrust exemption, see Larry G. Bumgardner, "Baseball's Antitrust Exemption," in *Diamond Mines: Baseball and Labor,* ed. by Paul D. Staudohar (Syracuse, NY: Syracuse University Press, 2000), 84–88. See also Steven R. Rivkin, "Sports Leagues and the Federal Antitrust Laws," in *Government and the Sports Business,* ed. Roger G. Noll (Washington, DC: The Brookings Institution, 1974), 387–390.

23 *Flood v. Kuhn*, 407 U.S. 258 (1972).

24 Paul D. Staudohar, *Playing for Dollars: Labor Relations and the Sports Business* (Ithaca, NY: Cornell University Press, 1996), p. 22.

25 Paul D. Staudohar, "Introduction," in *Diamond Mines: Baseball and Labor,* xxii.

26 Tom Verducci, "Why They Deserved Better," *Sports Illustrated,* November 19, 2008:

27 Rottenberg, "The Baseball Players' Labor Market," 246.

28 Ibid., 248.

29 Ronald Coase, "The Problem of Social Cost," *Journal of Law and Economics,* 3, 1960: 1–44.

30 For an analysis of how Rottenberg's idea has evolved over the years, see Rodney Fort, "The Golden Anniversary of 'The Baseball Players' Labor Market,'" *Journal of Sports Economics,* 6 (4), November 2005: 347–358; and Placido Rodriguez, Stefan Kesenne, and Jaume Garcia, eds., *Sports Economics after Fifty Years: Essays in Honour of Simon Rottenberg* (Oviedo, Spain: University of Oviedo Press, 2006).

31 Rottenberg, "The Baseball Players' Labor Market," 255; Henry G. Demmert, The *Economics of Professional Team Sports* (Lexington, MA: Lexington-Heath, 1973), 36; Mohamed El-Hodiri and James Quirk, "An Economic Model of a Professional Sports League," *Journal of Political Economy,* 79 (6), November/December 1971: 1313.

32 George Daly and William J. Moore, "Externalities, Property Rights and the Allocation of Resources in Major League Baseball," *Economic Inquiry,* 19 January 1981: 77–95.

33 Ibid., 93.

34 John Vrooman, "The Baseball Players' Labor Market Reconsidered," *Southern Economic Journal,*. 63 (2), 1996: 340.

35 Gerald W. Scully, "Pay and Performance in Major League Baseball," *American Economic Review,* 64(6), December 1974: 915–930; *The Business of Major League*

Baseball (Chicago: University of Chicago Press, 1989); and *The Market Structure of Sports* (Chicago: University of Chicago Press, 1995).

36 Paul M. Sommers and Noel Quinton, "Pay and Performance in Baseball: The Case of the First Family of Free Agents," *Journal of Human Resources,* Summer 1982: 426–436; Andrew Zimbalist, "Salaries and Performance: Beyond the Scully Model," in Paul M. Sommers, ed., *Diamonds Are Forever: The Business of Baseball* (Washington, D.C.: The Brookings Institution, 1992), 109–133; Andrew Zimbalist, *Baseball and Billions: A Probing Look Inside the Big Business of Our National Pastime* (New York: Basic Books, 1992).

37 Zimbalist, *Baseball and Billions,* 92.

38 Ibid., 93–94.

39 Kenneth Lehn, "Information Asymmetries in Baseball's Free Agency Market," *Economic Inquiry,* 22, January 1984: 37–44.

40 Lawrence M. Kahn, "Free Agency, Long-Term Contracts and Compensation in Major League Baseball: Estimates From Panel Data," *Review of Economics and Statistics,* 75(1): 157–164.

41 Ibid., 163.

42 Ibid.

43 James Cassing and Richard Douglas, "Implications of the Auction Mechanism in Baseball's Free Agent Draft," *Southern Economic Journal,* July 1980: 112.

44 Daniel R. Marburger, "Does the Assignment of Property Rights Encourage or Discourage Shirking?" *Journal of Sports Economics,* 4(1), February 2003: 19–34.

SECTION 2

BASKETBALL

CHAPTER 7

SALARY CAPS AND LUXURY TAXES

DENNIS COATES AND
BERND FRICK

1. INTRODUCTION

SIMON Rottenberg's (1956) "The Baseball Players' Labor Market" is considered the first article in sports economics. His opening line notes, "Since its inception in the 1870's, organized baseball has developed a market for baseball players and their services in which there is less than perfect freedom to buy and sell." His focus in making that observation was on the reserve system under which a player who signed a contract with a team was bound to that team indefinitely, entirely at the discretion of the team. Several chapters in this volume have discussed the reserve clause, restrictions on player mobility, and their consequences for compensation, team success, and team profitability. Rottenberg also discussed these same issues, and many others that are staples of modern sports economics. Indeed, Rod Fort (2005) stated, "Only a few readers would trace the roots of the questions they address to any other source." The topic of this chapter is a direct descendant of Rottenberg's analysis.

Rottenberg (1956) refers to caps on salaries in two places. In the first, he notes that no major or minor league has a rule on the maximum salary of an individual player. However, he states that the American and National Leagues and the Pacific Coast League are the only professional baseball leagues without team maximum salary limits (Rottenberg, 1956, p. 250). Rottenberg's second mention of salary limits comes on pages 256 and 257. He analyzes the impact of ceilings on individual player salaries. His analysis is similar to that of any binding price ceiling in the market, concluding that competition for the players will switch to non-monetary compensation, and the team most willing and able to pay for a player's services will acquire that player. In other words, the limit on player salaries will have no effect on the distribution of players. If rules are passed and successfully enforced, players will choose to accept offers from teams with better players, which will raise the probability of their participating in and winning a World Series, outcomes from which they will earn additional income.

Rottenberg's analysis of limits on individual player salaries is clear and insightful. There is little with which to take issue. The interesting thing is that he mentions the existence of limits on team salaries, but doesn't explicitly analyze their impacts. Additionally, in all the major American sports leagues where salary limits exist, they are imposed predominantly on team salaries rather than on the individual player's salary. The main exceptions to this are Major League Soccer, where the single-entity league places a limit on how much it will pay any player, though individual clubs may supplement this amount; the rookie salary scale; and other restrictions in the National Basketball Association, and rookie and entry level player restrictions in the National Football League and National Hockey League. All of these are discussed in more detail later.

A team salary cap is much like something Rottenberg did discuss at some length, namely, pooled revenue sharing. Indeed, Fort and Quirk (1995) refer to the NBA salary cap plan as a "sharing-cap" plan, where the owners agree to share a fixed percentage of the revenues with the players in exchange for a salary cap, and proceed to analyze it as though every team paid the same salary bill in equilibrium. Sharing of gate revenues between the home and visiting team was the common practice in professional sports at the time Rottenberg was writing.[1] Obviously, under such an arrangement, each club has the same resources to spend, so there is implicitly a cap on salaries. Rottenberg noted that, under the pooled sharing arrangement, no team will have any particular reason to win or to try to improve. Win or lose, each team gets the same share of the total revenue. Rottenberg notes that teams taken as a whole have reason to perform well enough so that total revenues do not fall faster than total costs, but no individual team has incentive to spend to improve, and hence raise total revenues for the league, unless it can "be assured that others will also do so." His prediction was that all teams would hire mediocre players, interest in the game would fall, and consumers would find other "recreational substitutes."

Rottenberg did not explicitly or directly discuss luxury taxes. Major League Baseball has developed a system by which those teams whose payrolls exceed some limit will pay to the league a proportion of every dollar over the limit. In other words, if the limit is set at $162 million, as it was for the 2009 season, and the team pays $172 million in salaries, then the team must also pay to the league the luxury tax rate t times $10 million. Put differently, every dollar of salary over the limit costs the club $(1+t)$. Under the Major League Baseball collective bargaining agreement (CBA), the tax rate t has a basic rate of 22.5 percent, but it rises to 30 percent for a second violation and to 40 percent for a third or more violations of the threshold. The NBA tax rate is 100 percent, as teams pay in tax one dollar for every dollar by which they exceed a specified spending level (which is itself substantially above the salary cap level). Of course, any league imposing a luxury tax may redistribute the revenue generated by the tax to some or all of the other clubs or it may keep the funds to support league initiatives, such as extending the market for the sport worldwide, player development, or financing new stadium and arena construction for league members.

Discussions of salary caps and luxury taxes exist in the literature (see section 2). The theoretical analysis of each is an extension of the discussion and examination of the invariance proposition, revenue sharing, and competitive balance, all of which have been discussed in other chapters. With regard to salary caps, Szymanski (2003) perhaps overstates the consensus view that, "It is clear in theory that a salary cap should improve competitive balance." We will see why not everyone agrees.

Justifications for caps and luxury taxes are similar to justifications for other interferences in the operation of sports labor markets: Without caps or restraints on team spending, rich teams will buy the best players, win too much, damaging the demand for viewership or attendance, and hurt the sport. Weak-drawing teams or those from small markets will be unable to compete on the field and this will put them at financial risk. Salary caps and luxury taxes will resolve these issues by restraining the rich, big-market clubs. The available empirical evidence, however, is mixed at best (see later section 4). Before turning to the empirical evidence, however, a careful description of the institutions is warranted (see section 3).

2. SALARY CAPS AND LUXURY TAXES IN THE (ECONOMICS) LITERATURE

The literature on salary caps and luxury taxes has its beginning with Rottenberg (1956), as has already been described. It is largely an extension of the literature on the invariance proposition and the impact of revenue sharing on competitive balance. These topics have been covered in detail elsewhere in this volume. Here we focus on those issues that are distinct to salary caps and luxury taxes, especially on how each affects the distribution of playing talent, winning, and profits, and we provide only brief explanations where issues have been covered in depth in other chapters.

We discuss the salary cap first, then turn to the literature on the luxury tax. It is important to note that one can think of salary caps and luxury taxes as special cases of a more general policy on player compensation and club spending. Both the cap and the luxury tax identify a spending level for clubs beyond which a penalty becomes operative. The nature and severity of the penalty differs, of course. In the case of a hard salary cap, spending over the cap brings on heavy—even punitive—penalties; the luxury tax, on the other hand, involves penalties that are simply meant to raise the cost of spending at the margin, but carry little punitive value. Under either approach, the policy may or may not provide incentives or means for low spending clubs to raise their spending.

Rottenberg (1956) described the limits on individual player salaries and discussed equal revenue sharing, but he did not discuss the sort of caps that exist today on team salaries. Moreover, there was no formal modeling, which would allow exploration of the assumptions and sensitivity of the results to alternative assumptions. Fort and Quirk (1995) and Quirk and Fort (1997) provide analysis of a sports league with a team salary cap inspired by the introduction of the salary cap in the NBA in the early 1980s.[2] Vrooman (1995) also addresses these issues, though his model differs from the Fort and Quirk model by assuming explicit functional forms for the costs and revenues of team ownership. Rascher (1997) introduces an explicit comparison of models in which club owners maximize utility, which is a linear combination of profits and winning percentage. Kesenne (2000) and Rascher (1997) explicitly allow some teams to be at and other teams below the salary cap. Kesenne (2000) also analyzes a cap on individual salaries.

The insights from the Quirk and Fort model are clear and intuitive, though they are not robust to alternative, quite reasonable assumptions, as we shall see. Suppose each team has a total salary limited to a clearly specified level and that all teams spend that limit. Then, ignoring any randomness in outcomes of games, all teams will win half of their games. Unless the cap is set below the salary level of the lowest spending team, some teams will have to reduce spending and others raise it for all to spend the same amount. Of course, a players' organization will not agree to a reduction in payroll by every team in the league, except under very unusual circumstances.[3] Consequently, any team whose spending on salaries falls as a result of the cap is willing and able to spend more on talent than the cap allows; there is a wedge between desired spending and actual spending. That is, some teams must hire a less-than-profit-maximizing quantity of talent. On the other hand, some teams may be forced to hire a greater-than-free-agency-market profit-maximizing level of talent, so their spending must rise to the level of the cap.[4] The result is that competitive balance, here thought of simply as the disparity in playing abilities of the two teams, will improve because of the decreasing difference in talent levels.

Note also that league-wide revenues must fall. Simply put, the salary cap forces the league to reallocate talent away from teams whose marginal revenue of talent is high to teams whose marginal revenue of talent is low.[5] At the same time, the sharing percentage acceptable to the clubs must make leaguewide profits as high or higher than without the cap. Quirk and Fort (1995) provide a condition on the percentage of leaguewide revenues set aside for player salaries and bonuses such that total league profits rise under the salary cap; specifically, leaguewide revenues net of player salaries and bonuses under free agency as a proportion of leaguewide revenues under the salary cap must be less than the owners' share of revenues under the cap. The larger the players' share, the less likely this is to be true. As the players' share goes to zero, the implication is that total revenues under the cap must only exceed revenues net of salaries and bonuses under free agency.

To get a more intuitive understanding of this result, consider the two-team model. Suppose that both franchises spend exactly at the cap level. The greater the disparity in the marginal revenue functions, the smaller leaguewide revenues will be under the cap (the greater the fall relative to without a cap) for any given share going to the players, and the larger the ratio of net revenues in free agency to total revenues under the cap. The greater the disparity in marginal revenues, then, the smaller the share going to players that will result in higher total league profits. By contrast, the more alike marginal revenues are across clubs, the larger the share going to players that can lead to higher total profits.

The distribution of these profits is a more difficult issue; the question is whether all clubs *must* or all clubs *may* see an increase in their profits. Revenues for some clubs rise as they attract more fans due to winning a larger share of their games. Total revenues of some clubs fall, however, because they win a smaller percentage of their games. Moreover, the salary cap lowers the payrolls of teams, regardless of what happens to their revenues. For the clubs whose revenues fall, which of these reductions is greater (revenues or salaries) determines whether they see increasing or decreasing profits from the salary cap and, by extension, whether they will favor or oppose the cap.[6] Any clubs whose hiring of talent is forced away from the profit-maximizing level will have an incentive to evade the rules. As Quirk and Fort (1997) say, "by introducing a salary cap, the league has also introduced a nontrivial enforcement problem for itself" (the complexity and detail of the CBA with regard to measuring and defining revenues and salaries confirms the existence of the difficult enforcement problem—see later).

There are numerous assumptions in the model presented by Fort and Quirk (1995) and Quirk and Fort (1997), many of which have come under scrutiny as researchers have worked to understand the importance of revenue sharing, salary caps, luxury taxes, and other league institutions for the balance of competition between clubs. For our purposes in understanding the salary cap, the key assumptions are that (1) owners are profit maximizers, (2) home and visiting team quality are equally important in the determination of home game revenues, (3) marginal costs of winning are constant, and (4) all teams spend at the cap level. Relaxing any of these has the effect of weakening and possibly overturning the results that the cap improves competitive balance. If one also considers the luxury tax, the key assumptions include those just listed, and (5) whether the tax applies to all teams or only those beyond a certain spending threshold, and (6) how the tax revenues are allocated to the clubs, if they are in fact redistributed.

The specification in Fort and Quirk imposes an equal but opposite impact of home and visiting-team winning percentages on home-team revenues, as revenues depend upon the difference in the winning percentage of the two clubs. Marburger (1997) notes that this means that revenues from a game pitting the first-place team against the last-place team will exceed those from a game between the first- and second-place teams. He extends the model to allow the impact of winning percentage of each team to have a different impact on revenues of the home team, though his focus is on the luxury tax rather than the salary cap. Vrooman's (1995) model imposes the condition that visiting-team quality is irrelevant for revenues of the home team. Of course, Vrooman's specification is a special case of Marburger's. Vrooman does not analyze the luxury tax. Both Vrooman (1995) and Marburger (1997) conclude that the impact of sharing of revenues will depend on how the sharing is done, and how clubs respond to the incentives in the sharing plan.

Vrooman (1995) argues that the salary cap makes the marginal cost of winning zero for all teams, because all teams share equally in the added costs associated with higher leaguewide revenues. In this case, the league will operate like a joint profit maximizer, and the maximum profits will occur where league revenues are maximized. This is precisely the original, or non-cap, equilibrium when there are no diseconomies of market size raising costs to the club from the larger city. If there are diseconomies of market size, in an unfettered player market, balance will be better than in one with a salary cap. Vrooman's argument is that the salary cap makes the diseconomies irrelevant and, therefore, concludes that the cap promotes competitive *im*balance. He contends that Fort and Quirk (1995) assume the salary cap is about improving competitive balance when it may, instead, be about reducing or controlling player costs, enabling the league to maximize total leaguewide profits.

However, if Vrooman's analysis is correct, that is, that the cap promotes imbalance and increases leaguewide revenues, then it must also be the case that players support, even call for, a cap on salaries. Because players are granted a specific share of revenues, it is in their best interests for those revenues to be maximized. Although player unions have accepted salary caps through negotiations, there is little evidence of them lobbying for the imposition of a cap.

Much of the research assumes that clubs seek to maximize profit.[7] This may seem an innocuous assumption for professional sport franchises in the United States, but it was of doubtful validity for soccer clubs in Europe, where the assumption of win or utility maximization seemed more plausible (Sloane, 1971). Profit maximization seems a more reasonable assumption for many European soccer clubs now than it did just a few years ago. Rascher (1997) analyzed the impact of salary caps in a model in which the league engages in joint profit maximization whereas the owners maximize their utility under the constraints imposed by the league's decision. Owner utility is a function of winning and of profits from the club. Rascher's analysis suggests that the effects of a salary cap depend upon the distribution of owner preferences for winning versus profits and on how restrictive the cap is.

Rascher (1997) emphasized that there are three circumstances relevant to the analysis of salary caps: a cap may be binding on no team, it may be binding on some teams, or it may be binding on all teams. The specific results of the cap will depend on which of these circumstances applies (and upon the owner preferences for winning). Kesenne (2000) argues that Quirk and Fort (1995) analyze a combination of a salary cap and redistribution to the low-spending clubs because they assume that all clubs "actually spend the salary cap level" (Quirk and Fort, 1995, p. 1277). Kesenne models a "pure" salary cap, one that does not involve redistribution to bring low-spending clubs up to the cap. In other words, some clubs are under the cap, so their demand for talent is unaffected by the cap.

Kesenne (2000) also models two types of talent.[8] One advantage of this modeling assumption is that he is able to draw inferences about the distribution of pay between star players and regular players. The regulars may be hired at a constant price, because supply of regulars is infinitely elastic, but the cost of acquiring a star changes with demand because the supply of stars is completely inelastic. The gap between compensation of regular players and stars adjusts to changes in the demand for stars. The salary cap reduces demand for stars, lowering their pay relative to that of regular players. Kesenne (2000) concludes that balance is improved, but that all clubs' profits increase.

A second advantage of the modeling assumption that there are two types of players is that it allows Kesenne to analyze the impact of a cap on the salary of an individual player. The outcome of such analysis is ambiguous with regard to the impact on competitive balance, but Kesenne states his belief that the likely outcome is for balance to be worsened. His rationale is straight out of Rottenberg (1956). Clubs from big markets will be able to offer more and better non-salary inducements than clubs from small markets. Consequently, the former will attract more of the top players, and competitive balance will deteriorate.

Marburger (1997) and Gustafson and Hadley (1996) are explicit about the luxury tax. Gustafson and Hadley (1996) focus their attention on the luxury tax proposals that were under discussion by MLB and the MLB Players Association in 1995. The sides differed in the level of payroll beyond which the tax would bite and on the rate of taxation. Gustafson and Hadley's model assumed that there was a fixed supply of star players and an infinitely elastic supply of regular players. The impact of the luxury tax would be to reduce the relative demand for star players, driving down the premium such players received over the salary of regular players. They estimate that, under the owners' proposal of a 40 percent luxury tax rate, the star player premium would have fallen by over $412,000. The players' proposal of a 25 percent tax rate would only cost the star players about $58,000. In addition, as the star-player premium falls, there is a reallocation of such players away from the teams subject to the tax and toward the teams not subject to the tax, which improves competitive balance.

Marburger (1997) examines the luxury tax in a model in which club revenues depend upon the quality of both the home and the visiting teams. He shows that the impact of the luxury tax depends significantly on how the revenues from the tax are utilized and whether or not the tax rate is constant. Allocation to the clubs in a lump sum fashion, that is, one independent of the club's decisions, will have no impact on competitive balance. Additionally, allocation that is a constant proportion of total tax revenues will have no impact on competitive balance, as it shifts all marginal revenues equally. It will, of course, reduce demand for playing talent and, therefore, player compensation. Moreover, if the luxury tax rate or the sharing rate vary with the spending decisions of the club, then the marginal revenue curves of the clubs both shift and rotate, and competitive balance is affected.

Given these sometimes conflicting and sometimes incompatible positions, theory offers no definitive guidance about the likely effects of a salary cap and/ or a luxury tax. The (beneficial as well as the detrimental) effects of each of these instruments must, therefore, be demonstrated empirically.

3. SALARY CAP AND LUXURY TAX INSTITUTIONS

3.1 Setting the Cap

This chapter is in a section on basketball, which is fitting because imposition of a salary cap at the major league level first occurred in the National Basketball Association (NBA), under an agreement reached in 1983. The National Football League (NFL) and the National Football League Players Association (NFLPA) reached agreement on a salary cap in 1993, and the National Hockey League (NHL) and National Hockey League Players Association (NHLPA) produced a salary cap in 2005. The NHL had a salary cap on rookies beginning in 1995 as a result of a lockout in 1994–1995.

The basic structure of the salary cap is the same in each league. Players, through their players association, and owners, through the league office, agree to two basic but closely related points. First, the two sides must agree on the composition of the funds to be split between them. To do this, in each league the teams and the players agree to a definition of revenues or income.[9] The NFL calls this Total Revenues in the 2006 CBA,[10] the NBA refers to it as Basketball Related Income, and the NHL names it Hockey Related Revenue. In each case, the CBA between league and players goes to great lengths to explicitly state which revenues are included in this amount. The NFL and NBA agreements then subtract from this revenue an amount called Benefits, which includes team payments for retirement plans, medical insurance, educational programs, and other similar expenses to arrive at the fund to be divided. In the NHL, all of Hockey Related Revenue is subject to the sharing percentage, and then the value of player benefits is subtracted out.

The second point the two sides must agree to is the proportion of that fund that will be paid out to players. Clearly, players want a very inclusive definition of the fund with a large percentage going to salaries, whereas owners want many sources of revenues omitted from the fund and a small proportion of the defined fund to be paid to players. The NBA CBA expressly selects 51 percent for each year after the 2005–2006 season through the 2011–2012 season. For the NFL, the players' share of Total Revenues was set to be 57.7 percent in 2009, and 58 percent in 2010 and 2011. Of course, the owners have opted out of the CBA, meaning that there may be a season or more without a salary cap. The NHL has a sliding scale by which the players' share adjusts depending on the size of Hockey Related Revenue for a given season. The highest share the players could get is 57 percent; the lowest is 54 percent.

Once the proportion and the fund definition are agreed to and a forecast of the value of the fund and player benefits for a year are set, then each team in the league is allowed to spend the same amount of money for salaries. For example, if the agreement is for 55 percent of the agreed upon fund to be paid in salaries, the forecasted value of the fund net of player benefits is $1 billion, and there are 30 teams in the league, then the salary cap amount for each team is $18,333,333.33 (.55*1 billion/30).[11] For the NFL and NBA, these figures are the maximum team salaries, whereas the NHL adds $8 million to the previous result, which it calls the Midpoint, to determine an Upper Limit on team salaries. Each agreement also sets a minimum team salary; the NHL subtracts $8 million from the Midpoint, but the NBA and NFL make the Minimum Team Salary a percentage of the Salary Cap. In the NBA, it is 75 percent of the Salary Cap, but in the NFL the Minimum team Salary is 87.6 percent of the Salary Cap for the 2009 season, rising by 1.2 percent each year to a maximum of 90 percent of the Salary Cap amount in 2011. Each CBA also has provisions for enforcement of the cap, including penalties for violations, means of resolving discrepancies between forecasts of the fund and benefits values and their actual values, and exceptions to the rule such as specific spending guidelines for expansion teams and their exclusion from the denominator in dividing the players' share among teams. The CBA of each league has dozens of pages laying out the operation, enforcement, and verification of the salary cap. Every salary cap begins with the definition of revenues to be shared, and we now turn to a discussion of these revenues.

Table 7.1 shows some basic revenue streams that are incorporated into the balance of funds that are subject to the players' salary share. Some categories are largely self-explanatory, like regular-season and playoff gate receipts and broadcast-rights fees. The different CBAs vary in how explicit they are in mentioning different sorts of revenues, however. For example, the three CBAs address complimentary tickets in totaling gate receipts in different ways. Differences also exist in the way some specific sources of revenues enter the agreement between the league and players.[12]

The details of Hockey Related Revenues, Basketball Related Income, and Total Revenues are extensive. Players want to make sure that every bit of revenue that can be linked to their efforts be tabulated in determining the aggregate sum to be paid in salaries. Owners want to be sure nothing is captured in salaries that should not be attributed to players' efforts. Just as important as determining how much must be paid to the players is correctly counting as player compensation any expenditures or

Table 7.1 Defining Revenues to Be Shared

Revenue Type	League		
	NBA	NFL	NHL
Gate receipts			
Regular season	yes	yes	yes
Playoff	yes	yes	yes
Broadcast rights			
Regular season and playoff games	yes	yes	yes
Internet	yes	yes	yes
Exhibition game proceeds	yes	yes	yes
Novelties and concessions			
Novelties	yes	yes	yes
Parking and concessions	yes	yes	yes
Team sponsorships	yes	yes	yes
Advertising			
In arena or stadium			
Temporary	yes	yes	yes
Fixed	40% of gross	yes	conditional
Outside arena or stadium		yes	yes
Premium seat licenses	yes	yes	yes
Luxury suite lease or licensing	40% of gross	yes	yes
Stadium or arena naming rights	50%	yes	yes
Proceeds from properties	yes	yes	yes
Third-party usage of arena or stadium		conditional	

NBA—2005 CBA
NHL—2005 CBA
NFL—2006 CBA

transfers of things of value from owners to players. In this case, players want to be sure that they are getting their due, but owners want to be sure that the other owners have not found a way to pay a player that eludes the cap value. Recall that Rottenberg (1956) described what might happen in the event of a salary cap on cash payments, namely, that clubs will find non-cash inducements to the best players. Club owners do not want to get a salary cap and find that the other clubs get the better players by offering some alternative compensation. Therefore, defining salaries is as complex a process as defining revenues, and it is to that task that we now turn.

3.2 Toting Up Player Salaries

Calculating player salaries sounds like it should be straightforward and relatively easy. Although the NFL, NHL, and NBA have to determine player compensation so the Salary Cap and minimum salary levels are met, Major League Baseball has to determine Actual Club Payroll, an excess of which obligates the club to pay a Competitive-Balance Tax. This is what is commonly referred to as the luxury tax. Table 7.2 shows the basic items considered in adding up the player salaries to determine if the salary cap (or Competitive- Balance Tax in the case of Major League Baseball) requirements have been satisfied. Player salaries are, of course, counted by all leagues as part of compensation toward the salary cap. Major League Baseball and NHL contracts have explicit provision for players whose contracts are split between a major league club and a minor league club. Neither the NBA nor the NFL has such provisions. However, all contracts have provisions for signing players midseason, either because they replace injured players or those players are acquired via trade, waivers, or from available free agents. All the CBAs contain provisions accounting for signing bonuses, deferred compensation, and options clauses.

Table 7.2 Player Compensation Counted toward Sharing or Luxury Tax

	League			
Expenditure Type	NBA	NFL	NHL	MLB
Player salary	yes	yes	yes	yes
Benefits (insurance, retirement, education)	no	no	no	yes
Signing bonus	yes	yes	yes	yes
Incentive bonuses	yes	yes	yes	yes
Option year payments	yes	yes	yes	yes

NBA—2005 CBA
NHL—2005 CBA
NFL—2006 CBA
MLB—2007

Incentive clauses, signing bonuses, compensation of players signed midseason, and other issues all add great complexity to the CBA of each league, which must cover in detail how to allocate these expenses. The NHL includes performance bonuses in determining Actual Club Salary. However, the use of such bonuses is limited to "Players with Entry Level SPCs [Standard Player Contract]," "Players aged 35 or older … signed to a one-year SPC," or players who, for the purposes of the pension system, are "400-plus game Players" who in the last year of their most recent contract were on injured reserve for 100 days or more and who have signed a one-year contract for the next or current season. In describing player salary in computing

Actual Club Payroll for purposes of the Competitive-Balance Tax, the MLB CBA includes those amounts actually earned from performance bonuses. Article VII, Section 3 of the NBA CBA is called "Determination of Salary" and is over eight pages long. A page-and-a-half cover deferred compensation, two pages cover signing bonuses, incentive contracts take up more than a page, and loans to players cover almost a full page. The NFL CBA has a two-page section on computing team salary and a twenty-nine-page section on "Valuation of Player Contracts." Included in this section are twenty-one pages on incentive clauses, including exhibits on "Likely to be met" incentives, team and individual incentives, incentives by position, and "Rookie" incentives.

The CBAs also have restrictions on the pay of entering players. The NBA imposes a Rookie Scale (Article VIII) on salaries. With respect to determining Team Salary, the rookie pay scale for first-round picks is explicitly built into the Determination of Salary (Article VII, Section 3 (b)). Indeed, "A First Round Pick, immediately upon selection in the Draft, shall be included in the Team Salary of the Team that holds his draft rights at 100% of his applicable Rookie Scale Amount." Article 9 of the NHL CBA defines entry-level compensation, which sets duration of coverage under the entry-level system, based on a player's age at signing his first contract, and makes explicit limits on the total salary, signing bonus, and games-played bonuses for each year of the CBA. The NFL agreement sets a dollar value for the Entering-Player Pool, and each club gets a share of this amount based on the number of draft picks, the round in which the picks fall, and the positions played by the players the club drafts. The Entering-Player Pool for a year is at least the same as it was for the previous season and can rise by up to 5 percent over that season's value based on the projected revenues for the season. Article XVII, Section (4)(j) is explicit that nothing in the agreement predetermines a rookie's salary. Nonetheless, veteran players have been critical of the contracts signed by rookies who have never played a down in the NFL.[13]

4. The Effects of Salary Caps and Luxury Taxes

The NBA experience after the introduction of the salary cap for the 1984–1985 season seems to be evidence in favor of the arguments developed by its proponents. Between the 1984–1985 and the 1993–1994 seasons, the NBA experienced unprecedented growth. Quirk (1997) notes that franchise values increased from an average of $12 million in 1983–1984 to an average of $114 million during the 1993–1994 season. Over that same period, average player salaries rose from $400,000 to $1.3 million. He points out that many people, judges, sportswriters, and others

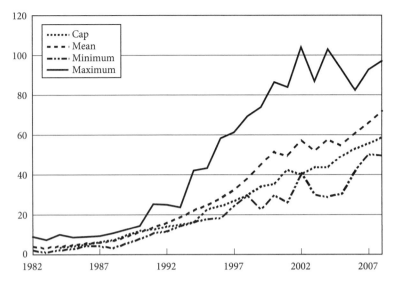

Figure 7.1 Salary Cap and Team Wage Bills in the National
Basketball Association.

attribute these changes to the salary cap. Quirk says, "the facts argue differently—
that the salary cap had next to nothing to do with the NBA's success between 1983
and 1995." Moreover, Quirk notes that there was neither an equalization of salary
expenditures among teams nor an improvement in competitive balance.

Indeed, despite changes in the basic agreement in 1995, 1999, and 2005, the
trend in average salaries is largely unchanged. Figure 7.1 shows the maximum,
minimum, average, and cap on team payrolls in the NBA. The maximum and the
average are always above the cap. More importantly, the disparity in salaries across
clubs has grown (the only evidence of impact of a CBA on salary disparity comes
at the very end of the time series). The gap between the maximum and the minimum grew over time. Thus, if the NBA salary cap had any impact on average
salaries or the disparity in salaries between rich/big-market franchises and poor/
small-market franchises, it is not evident in this data. Moreover, the salary cap has
apparently failed to increase competitive balance in the NBA because there is no
evident reduction in the standard deviation of winning percentages (multiplied by
100) over time (Figure 7.2).

Knowledgeable observers might argue the problem is that the NBA cap has
always been a soft cap, with numerous exceptions including the Larry Bird exception designed to allow clubs to resign their superstar players. The NFL is said to
have a much harder cap. Figure 7.3 shows the time path of average team salary and
standard deviation of team salary for the NFL. It is hard to look at Figure 7.3 and
infer that the salary cap has either slowed the growth in salaries or reduced the
disparity in spending across teams. Perhaps, despite doing little to alter spending
or the distribution of spending, the cap has improved competitive balance.

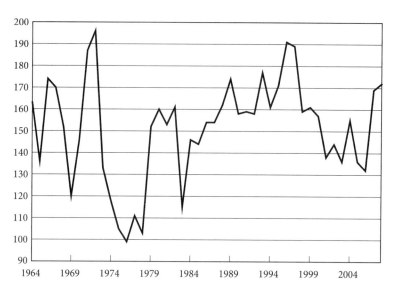

Figure 7.2 Salary Cap and Standard Deviation of Wins in the National Basketball Association.

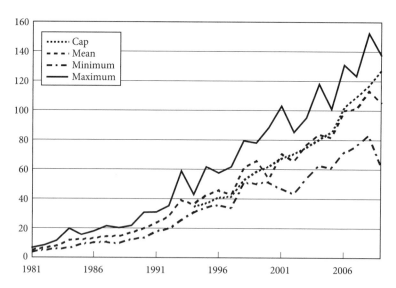

Figure 7.3 Salary Cap and Team Wage Bills in the National Football League.

Figure 7.4 shows the time path of the standard deviation of winning percentage for the NFL. The figure does not convey any clear or obvious improvement in competitive balance in the NFL after the introduction of the salary cap (this is similar to the situation in the NBA). However, the NBA does suggest distinct periods. From about 1983 until about 1996, the standard deviation of winning percentage seems to trend up in the NBA, but after that, until 2005, the standard deviation

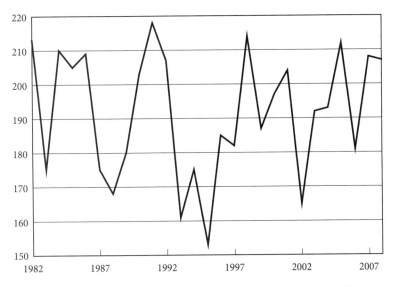

Figure 7.4 Salary Cap and Standard Deviation of Wins in the
National Football League.

trends downward. For the NFL, the standard deviation of winning percentage has
no trend but appears more like a random walk.

The NHL introduced a salary cap prior to the 2005–2006 season and has, therefore, only a quite-short experience with that instrument. Although it is clearly too
early to draw any definitive conclusions, it appears that the cap has led to a (minor)
reduction in wage bill disparities in the first two seasons and that this development
has already come to a stop—that is, the disparities have been rising again in the last
two seasons for which the data is available.

Similar to the development in the NBA and the NFL, the cap has virtually no
effect on the standard deviation of the winning percentage; that is, the cap seems
to have no effect on competitive balance. There is a possibility of a longer trend
toward greater balance in the NHL, from the peak imbalance of the 1992–1993 season through the end of the period. However, omitting that large spike in imbalance, the appearance of a long-term improvement is far less clear.

Fort and Quirk (1995) pointed out the enforcement problems associated with
the salary cap. Syzmanski (2003) agreed, stating that it is "equally clear that making an effective cap has proved elusive." Consider that in 2008–2009, only two of
the NBA's thirty teams were under the salary cap of $58.68 million. In every year
since 2005–2006, no fewer than twenty-four teams have exceeded the cap. During
the 2009–2010 season twenty-eight of the thirty teams exceeded the salary cap
of $57.70 million. Moreover, Larry Coon's NBA FAQ indicates that seven teams
exceeded the cap sufficiently that they had to pay the league's luxury tax. This is
not an aberration. Since the 2005–2006 season, at least five teams each year have
had to pay the luxury tax. The 2009–2010 season saw eleven of the thirty teams

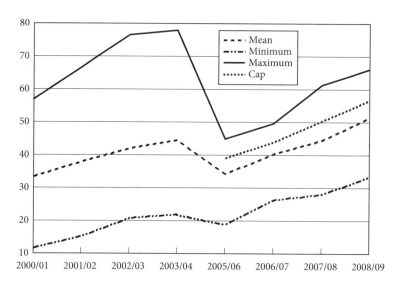

Figure 7.5 Salary Cap and Team Wage Bills in the
National Hockey League.

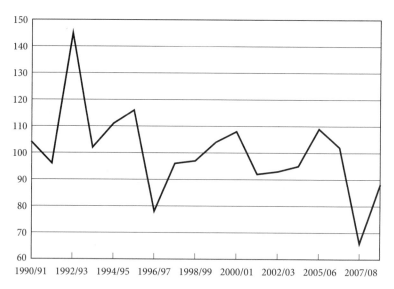

Figure 7.6 Salary Cap and Standard Deviation of Wins in the
National Hockey League.

paying a luxury tax, led by the Los Angeles Lakers whose tax was $21.40 million.
For the 2008–2009 season, for an NBA franchise to have a luxury tax obligation,
these teams had to pay salaries over $71.15 million, which is nearly $12 million above
the cap. These teams then paid a 100 percent tax on the salaries over $71.15 million.
The New York Knicks paid a tax of $23.7 million, meaning they exceeded the cap

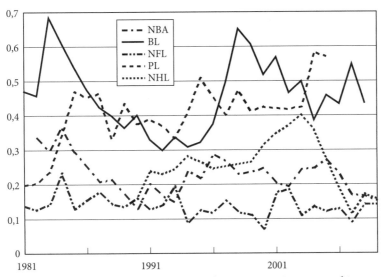

Figure 7.7 Wage Bill Disparities in the US Major Leagues and in English and German Football.

by over $35 million. The Knicks and Dallas Mavericks were the only teams to pay a luxury tax in all five years, and except for 2009–2010 when the Lakers moved into the top spot, they always had the two largest tax bills.

Comparing wage-bill disparities (standard deviation of wage bills, but not multiplied by 100) in American basketball, football, and hockey with wage-bill disparities in two of the big-five European soccer leagues—that is, the English Premier League and the German Bundesliga—yields interesting insights, because the latter leagues never had a salary cap (and are unlikely to introduce one in the near future).

It is certainly not surprising that wage disparities are significantly higher in the two European soccer leagues. This, however, is neither due to the absence of a salary cap nor to fewer redistributive efforts in the two European leagues. Because access to the respective first division in either of the two countries is mainly granted on the basis of sporting success (i.e., a particularly good performance in the second division), the clubs in the two countries differ much more with respect to their market potential than the clubs in either of the U.S. leagues. What is perhaps surprising to an American audience is that irrespective of the considerable wage-bill disparities and the low degree of revenue redistribution, the European soccer leagues are more balanced than the U.S. leagues. This is most likely due to the promotion-and-relegation system that rewards good performance (by granting access to European cup competitions) and simultaneously punishes poor performance (by relegating the respective clubs to a lower division; see Frick, Lehmann, and Weigand 1999 as well as Maennig and Feddersen 2004).

5. Summary and Implications

To summarize, we quote from Richard Sheehan (1996) writing more than a decade ago: "The bottom line is that there is no solid economic argument for a salary cap and there are lots of solid economic arguments against one. Most important: The salary cap distorts incentives. In addition, ... there is no evidence that a salary cap actually works" (Sheehan 1996, p. 197).

Nearly fifteen years later, despite lots of research and many changes in the institutions, Sheehan's statement remains an accurate conclusion for a discussion of salary caps and luxury taxes.

Notes

1 Of course, pooling all of the revenues and sharing them equally was not and is not used today, though it is something Rottenberg explicitly discussed.
2 Fort (2006) provides a good discussion of the luxury tax and salary cap based in the diagrammatic representation of the Quirk and Fort (1997) model.
3 The NHL players accepted a total salary reduction as part of the agreement that came out of the 2005 lost season.
4 Some of these latter clubs may require financial assistance from the other clubs to be capable of raising their spending to the required level. If this is true, then the salary cap also is a revenue sharing program (Kesenne, 2000).
5 Players, of course, having bargained for a set percentage of revenues, want to see those revenues large and growing, not falling.
6 Kesenne (2000) argues that a "pure" salary cap, one that does not impose redistribution of revenues to bring low-spending clubs up to the level of the cap, will raise the profits of all clubs.
7 Quirk and El-Hodiri (1974) briefly discuss a range of motives for owners but do not relate this to either the salary cap or the luxury tax.
8 Gustafson and Hadley (1996) modeled stars and regular players in their analysis of the luxury tax. Their model is discussed in more detail later.
9 Major League Baseball also defines revenues, but the purpose is not to delimit what is split with the players, but to determine sharing among the franchises. The revenue-sharing plan identifies net local revenues, which are all revenues from baseball operations net of revenues generated centrally by Major League Baseball and net of actual stadium expenses. Revenues from baseball operations are quite extensive, including revenues from any "activity that could be conducted by a non-Club entity but which [are] conducted by a Club because its affiliation or connection with Major League Baseball increases the activity's appeal."
10 The NFL took advantage of an escape clause in the CBA, opting out of it after the 2009 season. Unless a new agreement is reached, the NFL will be without a salary cap for the 2010 season and without a CBA at the end of the 2010 season.
11 For the NFL and NBA, the proportion is applied to the revenues net of benefits, which is then divided by the number of teams; for the NHL, the proportion is applied to the Hockey Related Revenue, then a forecast of player benefit spending is subtracted, and the result is divided by the number of NHL franchises.

12 The primary differences in revenues included come from the different nature of the facilities across sports. NBA and NHL teams frequently share an arena, whereas NFL teams are more likely to be the sole tenant of their stadium. Consequently, the NBA and NHL CBAs are more constrained in the way some revenues can be allocated. Also because they share facilities, NBA and NHL clubs have less control over third-party revenues generated in the arena than do NFL teams over third-party revenues from their stadiums.

13 Major league soccer is unlike any of the other leagues in one very important respect. The league is a single entity rather than a collection of clubs. In practice, what this means is that the league owners are more able to maximize joint profits and, indeed, are more explicitly doing so than in the other professional sports leagues. Moreover, Major League Soccer has both team and individual salary caps. Major league soccer is far more restrictive in its dealings with players than are the other professional sports leagues in other ways as well. These restrictions take a variety of forms, including a limit on the roster size, on the composition of the roster between foreign and domestic players, on the composition of the roster between senior and developmental players, and the qualifications to be a developmental player. Major League Soccer clubs are assigned a salary budget by the league. Neither the CBA nor the league rules available from the Internet explain how this budget is determined. The published rules indicate that developmental players' salaries do not count toward this budget; the CBA specifies the minimum value of player compensation by each team. The minimum for 2009 is $599,500 over whatever the team paid in salaries in 2004, though this amount is adjusted in the event of expansion of the league. As of 2007, each team is allowed one individual as a designated player, for whom the league salary restrictions are relaxed. In other words, Major League Soccer softened its hard salary cap with the introduction of the designated player. The maximum the league will contribute toward the salary of a single player varies over time, but currently it is about $450,000. The club can pay the designated player as much as it feels prudent beyond that amount, but anything over the explicit league contribution is entirely the obligation of the club. The designated-player rule is the mechanism by which the LA Galaxy club was able to offer David Beckham $6.5 million a year.

REFERENCES

Collective Bargaining Agreement Between the National Hockey League and the National Hockey League Players' Association, July 2005. http://www.nhlpa.com/CBA/index.asp.

Coon, Larry. 2009. "Larry Coon's NBA Salary Cap FAQ." http://www.cbafaq.com. Last accessed 2/12/11.

El-Hodiri, Mohamed, and James Quirk. 1972. An economic model of a professional sports league. *Journal of Political Economy*: 1302–1319.

Fort, Rodney D. 2005. The golden anniversary of "The baseball players' labor market." *Journal of Sports Economics,* 6(4): 347–358.

Fort, Rodney. 2006. *Sports Economics,* 2nd ed. Upper Saddle River, NJ: Pearson Prentice Hall.

Fort, Rodney D., and James Quirk. 1995. Cross-subsidization, incentives, and outcomes in professional team sports leagues, *Journal of Economic Literature,* 33(3): 1265–1299.

Frick, Bernd, Erik Lehmann, and J. Weigand. 1999. Kooperationserfordernisse
   und Wettbewerbsintensitaet im professionellen Team-Sport. In *Kooperation im
   Wettbewerb,* edited by Johann Engelhard and Elmar J. Sinz. Wiesbaden: Gabler.

Gustafson, Elizabeth, and Lawrence Hadley. 1996. The luxury tax proposal for Major
   League Baseball: A partial equilibrium analysis, in *Baseball Economics: Current
   Research,* eds. John Fizel, Elizabeth Gustafson, and Lawrence Hadley. Westport,
   CT: Praeger.

Meannig, Wolfgang, and Arne Feddersen. 2004. Determinanten der
   Wettbewerbsintensität in Sportligen unter besonderer Beruecksichtigung der
   Ligenstruktur. In *Kooperenz im Sportmanagement,* eds. Klaus Zieschang, Herbert
   Woratschek, and Klaus Beier, Hofmann: Schorndorf.

Marburger, Daniel R. 1997. Gate revenue sharing and luxury taxes in professional
   sports. *Contemporary Economic Policy,* 15(April):114–123.

NBAPA Collective Bargaining Agreement, http://www.nbpa.com/cba_articles.php.

NFL Collective Bargaining Agreement, March 2006. http://nflplayers.com/images/
   fck/NFL. Collective Bargaining Agreement 2006–2012.pdf

Quirk, James. 1997. The salary cap and the luxury tax: Affirmative action programs
   for weak-drawing franchises. In *Stee-rike four!: What's wrong with the business of
   baseball?* ed. Daniel R. Marburger. Westport, CT: Praeger.

Quirk, James, and Mohamed El-Hodiri. 1974. The economic theory of a professional
   sports league. In *Government and the sports business,* ed. Roger G. Noll.
   Washington, DC: Brookings Institution Press.

Quirk, James, and Rodney D. Fort (1997). *Pay dirt.* Princeton, NJ: Princeton
   University Press.

Rascher, D. A. 1997. A model of a professional sports league. In Advances in the
   economics of sport (Vol. 2), ed. W. Hendricks. Greenwich, CT: JAI Press, 27–76.

Rottenberg, Simon. 1956. The baseball players' labor market," *Journal of Political
   Economy,* 64(3): 242–258.

Sheehan, Richard G. 1996. *Keeping score: The economics of big-time sports.* South
   Bend, IN: Diamond Communications.

Sloane, Peter J. 1971. The economics of professional football: The football club as
   utility maximize. *Scottish Journal of Political Economy,* 17:121–146.

Staudohar, Paul D. 1997. *Playing for dollars: Labor relations and the sports business.*
   Ithaca, NY: Cornell University Press.

Staudohar, Paul D. 1999. Salary caps in professional team sports. In *Competition
   policy in professional sports: Europe after the Bosman case,* eds. Stefan Kesenne and
   Claude Jeanrenaud. Antwerp, Belgium: Standard Editions, Ltd.

Szymanski, Stefan 2003. The economic design of sporting contests. *Journal of
   Economic Literature,* 41(4): 1137–1187.

Vrooman, John. 2000. The economics of American sports leagues. *Scottish Journal of
   Political Economy,* 47(4): 364–398.

Vrooman, John. 1995. A general theory of professional sports leagues. *Southern
   Economic Journal,* 61(4): 971–990.

··

CHAPTER 8

INTERNATIONAL LABOR MOBILITY AND THE NATIONAL BASKETBALL ASSOCIATION

··

EVAN OSBORNE

WHAT has come to be known as globalization—the dispersal of economic activity across greater and greater distances, in response to lower transport costs—has been greeted with mixed reactions around the world. The globalization of labor markets, which has been expanding for years (Castles and Miller, 2009), has been greeted with particular skepticism in the developed countries that are the recipients of many migrants. The primary economic objection involves the impact of such migration on the wages of native workers. Migration's effects on consumer welfare have been little studied. When they have been, they are often judged to be small (Simon, 1996). Perhaps partly for that reason, significant negative effects of global labor mobility on domestic workers in recipient countries may make public opinion hostile to unfettered immigration.

However, one arena of labor mobility in which both the relevant economic models, and thus perhaps the public reaction, are frequently quite different is mobility in the market for athletes in professional team sports. Public policy, through such measures as the European Court of Justice's *Bosman* decision[1] and its judicial progeny has encouraged such mobility, as has pressure from consumers. In a manner notably absent from other industries, globalization has encouraged reluctant Japanese baseball and Chinese basketball owners to let their players move more freely to America, the explicit development of extensive labor search networks (in the form of scouting in Africa for college and high-school basketball recruits, the opening by North American Major League Baseball teams of training academies in impoverished Latin American countries, etc.) by team and league owners in wealthy countries to encourage the athletic equivalent of brain drain, and other signs that are often driven by consumer sovereignty (in the sense of teams trying to procure more wins at lower cost). Not only is athletic mobility across borders not generally seen as problematic, it is highly desirable to fans.

One sports league in which global labor mobility is very much in evidence is the U.S. NBA. This chapter uses data from the NBA to test several propositions from the literature on international migration and trade. This literature has some relevance, but only some, because of the vast advantage in both wealth and prestige (both of which might motivate players in other societies to ply their trade there) the NBA has over professional leagues in other countries. This dominance, like that of North America's Major League Baseball, means that the U.S. market for professional basketball generally attracts the most talented players from all over the globe. Given the small size of the NBA labor market relative to those of other industries and its entrenched first-mover advantages, its essentially free labor mobility makes it a complete substitute for goods trade; its product is in some sense a non-traded good, albeit one with mobile labor. To explore the impact of the globalization of labor supply in such a market, section 1 explores the unique properties of free mobility in such highly selective labor markets as high-level sports leagues, section 2 summarizes the relevant theory and empirical findings from the immigration literature, section 3 explores what we know so far from empirical work on wages in the NBA, section 4 explores whether global basketball is governed by comparative advantage, section 5 presents some further investigation of the effects of foreign players on the NBA labor market, and section 6 suggests directions for further research.

1. PROFESSIONAL TEAM SPORTS IN A GLOBAL LABOR MARKET

Global labor mobility has exploded across many industries in recent years because of the aforementioned lower transport costs. However, the market for professional team athletes is different from the markets for other kinds of labor, both of the casual and high-skill types. In those markets, there are large numbers of firms, found in a wide variety of wealthy countries, and so the adjustment to mobility across borders is best thought of in terms of equilibrium at the market level, in a more or less competitive market for labor. Mundell (1957) notes that labor mobility, if it is perfect, makes goods trade unnecessary.

However, in at least three sports—baseball, ice hockey, and basketball—one employer (Major League Baseball, the NHL, and the NBA, respectively) dominates the global market, in that it pays much higher wages based on much higher revenues, and is generally judged to have the highest quality of play by a significant margin. It is true that, in all of these sports, other countries have professional leagues, but these leagues (among other functions) perform the functions of minor leagues or lower divisions in baseball and the less lucrative national soccer leagues, respectively, allowing some younger players of lesser skill to invest in human capital as preparation for a potential role at the highest level. The NBA is, for the most skilled players, the destination of choice, and transport costs are irrelevant.

The model is not exact. For example, the vast majority of Japan's best baseball players are playing for fans in Japan, but, in recent years, more and more of the highest-skilled Japanese players have sought to ply their trade in North America, both for financial reasons and for the utility that players derive from performing on the greatest stage. Whereas a computer programmer or a day laborer may see his migration decision driven as much by geographic proximity as by major differences in compensation, and more than by differences in market prestige among countries, these differences loom very large in professional sports leagues. The one exception to this principle in a sense proves the rule. Elite soccer players are found in leagues throughout European countries, but that is only because soccer itself is so widely enjoyed by fans across wealthy countries that it is able to generate demand sufficiently high to generate high wages in many of them. Baseball, hockey, and basketball, by contrast, have their strongest roots in the United States and Canada and it is in those nations where demand is overwhelmingly the highest.

In addition, intrinsic to North American sports leagues is the monopoly/monopsony property—the fact that many leagues have been able to largely insulate themselves from competition from at least within the same sport (if not necessarily from other sources of entertainment) by dividing up national geographic jurisdictions, spacing teams in the manner of the Hotelling (1929) model of store location, and locking up the best athletic facilities, often, in the North American case, with substantial taxpayer assistance. The term *monopsony* is used with some caution, because leagues often allow teams significant latitude to compete for players, but clearly wage bargaining is restrained by collective bargaining agreements (CBA) and the lack of meaningful competition from other leagues. It is reasonable to expect that, *ceteris paribus,* a league in a jurisdiction in which product demand and, hence, the marginal revenue product of labor is higher should generate, not just higher monopsony profits, but higher wages, too. So it is not surprising in a globalized era that, when a single league dominates globally in demand and prestige terms, it is easily able to attract talent from all over the world.

The NBA has some features that some other sports markets do not. In particular, although limits on foreign players were long a feature of European soccer prior to the *Bosman* decision and are still found in some national soccer and basketball leagues (notably China) as well as Japanese baseball, such quotas have never existed in the NBA. Foreign entry into the NBA is considerably easier than into many other sports

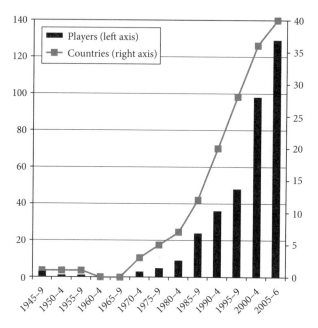

Figure 8.1 The Globalization of the NBA.

leagues around the world. (Discrimination against U.S. black players was, however, common at one time. The first black player to appear in an NBA game, Earl Lloyd, did so in 1950, only four years after the league's founding, but informal team ceilings on black players still suppressed their participation for years after.) Rents to domestic players from such explicit quotas (as opposed to discrimination in favor of domestic players based on consumer preferences) are thus presumably nonexistent.

Figure 8.1 demonstrates the growth in foreign players who played at least one regular-season game and in countries with such players in the NBA over five-year intervals from 1945–1949 (the league was founded in 1946) to 2005–2009. It is obvious that the last twenty years have seen a dramatic rise in the breadth and depth of foreign participation in the world's most important basketball league. This growth has been accompanied by a major effort by the NBA to expand its fan base worldwide. Globalization of labor markets, in general, being predicted to bring significant change to such markets, what effects has this change had? Investigation of the relevant theory is the first step to answering this question.

2. LABOR MARKETS IN A GLOBAL ERA

Global labor flows are now routine. Evaluating policy from the point of view of overall global welfare, theory generally recommends lowering legal barriers to labor mobility, as might be expected. In this work, migration is driven by both supply and demand. On the supply side, labor can change locations because it has unusual human-capital characteristics, not just ordinary work-place skills but ease of adaptation to new environments and a willingness to take risks (Kuznets and Thomas, 1958). On the other hand, demand can drive migration when labor is relatively scarce in one jurisdiction in a model of fixed domestic endowments (Ethier, 1985). Migration may, thus, partially sub-stitute for trade.

Absent the effect of tax-financed transfer payments that might flow dispro-portionately to immigrants and thus increase the tax burden on domestic resi-dents (not an issue in this instance), free movement of labor should function like free movement of goods in enhancing overall welfare. The early models posit that labor migrates until there is equalization of marginal products across jurisdictions (MacDougall, 1960). In such a situation, depicted in the top portion of Figure 8.2, the migration of workers to the destination country increases supply, thus transfer-ring (b) from domestic workers to labor purchasers (or, if passed on, to consumers), while the former retain (e). Newly created gains for domestic labor purchasers/consumers are (c) and (d), and (f), (g), and (h) accrue to foreign workers, who pre-sumably earn less in their home markets. $L_0 - L_1$ workers are replaced by $L_2 - L_0$ foreign ones, with the elasticities of domestic and foreign supply determining the exact division.

The empirical literature on wage and employment effects of immigration leans toward the position that immigration has few negative effects on either. The most influential papers include Grossman (1982) and LaLonde and Topel (1991), who find few wage effects. (LaLonde and Topel find no wage effects on domestic workers of immigrant flows into a particular U.S. jurisdiction, although they do find that greater flows have small negative wage effects on immigrants already working in the jurisdiction.) Evidence to the contrary pri-marily concerns wages. Aydemir and Borjas (2007) and Borjas (2003) find that the elasticity of wages with respect to immigration penetration in the labor mar-ket is −0.3 to −0.4 for overall employment, and Borjas (2005) reports a similar elasticity for skilled workers.

However, as with so many thick-market models, this framework is only mod-estly helpful for the NBA. In some suitably short run, the NBA is a market of fixed quantity. Although franchises can be added, it is relatively uncommon. Only one has been created in the last ten years, a time of vast growth in the foreign-player presence in the league. A fixed supply of jobs means that foreign-born players displace American-born players one for one. In the lower part of Figure 8.2, the quantity constraint of L_0 total jobs means that there is no expansion of employ-ment in response to the entry of lower-opportunity-cost workers. The equilibrium wage is indeterminate, a function of the relative bargaining power of owners and players. However, if would-be NBA players compete wages down vigorously, then much of (b) and (c) is redistributed from domestic players to team/league owners and consumers. Even here, however, there is a strong presumption that overall wel-fare increases relative to a market without labor mobility, not least because foreign

players may also increase the quality of the product. Note the similarity between
the quantity constraint in the bottom of Figure 8.2 and such controlled-immigration
programs as the U.S. H1-B visa program, which matches workers to specific firm
offers and is capped at a particular number of visas each year. Zavodny (2003)
finds that the program has detectable employment effects on domestic informa-
tion-technology workers in the U.S., although she does not find wage effects,
which may be harder to detect because the program requires that employers pay
the prevailing wage.

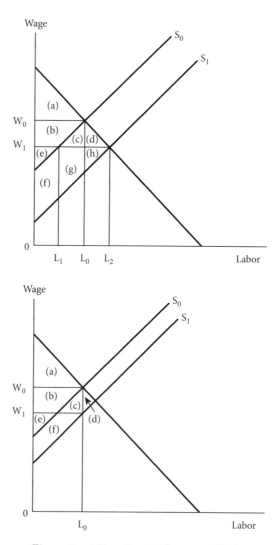

Figure 8.2 Migration Without and With
Quantity Restrictions.

3. THE NBA LABOR MARKET

3.1 Wages

The peculiarities of the NBA labor market have generated substantial research on the setting of wages. Perhaps its most distinctive characteristic is that the NBA relies on people of great height to perform many of the most important functions on the court. Such sharply constrained supply changes the distribution of marginal productivity among individual athletes, so that acquiring a single player in the far right tail of the skill/height distribution has considerably greater effects on team performance. Berri et al. (2005) find that "the short supply of tall people" generates greater competitive imbalance—the uneven distribution of on-court success among teams—than in other North American team sports. This feature, which also derives from basketball being a game in which comparatively few players (five) are on the field for a team at any moment, makes drafting players unusually fraught with danger. One star, particularly if he is a center, can make a huge difference in a team's long-term prospects. This may require a substantial amount of searching for small amounts of gold amid large amounts of dross in unusually tall foreign players.

Moral hazard has also been studied, with surprisingly weak results. Stiroh (2007) finds that players in the last year of their current contract perform at higher than expected levels, but that performance declines after a new (and generally more lucrative) contract is signed. However, Berri and Krautmann (2006) find that these findings are dependent on what is being measured, on-field performance or marginal revenue product. Similar ambiguity is found in baseball, with Scoggins (1993) and Lehn (1982) finding evidence for shirking, and Krautmann and Donley (2009) finding that such results are not robust to empirical functional form when on-field performance is used as the measure of shirking.

3.2 Particular Elements of Demand

The historical assumption in sports economics is that firm demand for players is best expressed in terms of individual teams rather than by the entire league, collectively. The earliest and still most common assumption is that sports fans' demand depends on ticket prices and on the team's success. However, within each sport there may be particular factors other than winning percentage or championships that, along with price, influence demand. Berri et al. (2004) report some, far from decisive, evidence that the presence of star players on a team influences NBA demand functions independently of their contribution to team success. Morse et al. (2008) also get this result but fail to find evidence that instability in team rosters affects demand.

3.3 Discrimination

The use of sports data to investigate the existence of ethnoracial discrimination is now widespread, with the NBA a particularly lucrative source of such data. The implications for labor mobility are unusually compelling because of the links between the ethnoracial composition of a team's fan base and the attractiveness of it for players of various ethnicities, and the ability of black players in particular to be judged by the same criteria as other players, both with regard to on-field performance and compensation. It is useful to distinguish between constricting discrimination—active taste-based discrimination by team owners—and matching discrimination—passive discrimination by owners in response to different fan preferences in different markets, resulting from the fact that markets demographically differ and fans prefer to watch athletes from their own ethnoracial group. The former implies actual damage to players of any race in theory but in practice primarily black ones because of different levels of opportunity. The latter merely implies taste-based matching of fans to players on racial grounds, which, in principle, is harmless and even valuable if it generates higher consumer and producer surplus.

With regard to constricting discrimination, Price and Wolfers (2007) have found evidence that there is opposite-race bias in the way referees call personal fouls in NBA games. Teams of black referees favor black players, and white-referee teams favor white players. Pay discrimination has also been extensively studied. In a widely cited paper, Hoang and Rascher (1999) find that discrimination manifests itself not just through lower salary but through shorter career length. After estimating a hazard function for the probability that a player's career will end in a particular year, and after standardizing for the player's statistical productivity, they find that black players have careers that are approximately two years shorter than white players. The monetary effect of this form of discrimination is considerably larger than differences in play while players are in the league. Groothuis and Hill (2004) argue that this effect vanished in the 1990s.

Earlier literature sometimes did find substantial racial discrimination in pay. Employing both direct measures of player productivity and indirect measures, such as All-Star performance and draft position from the 1980s, Kahn and Sherer (1988), Koch and Vander Hill (1988), and Brown, Spiro, and Keenan (1991) find that blacks suffer a pay penalty on racial grounds of between 10 and 25 percent. Kahn and Shah (2005) find racial effects on pay for players whose contract did not allow them to take advantage of NBA rules on rookie compensation and free agency, an effect absent for those with such protections. They interpret this result as discrimination, but confined to "marginal non-white players." However, much of the other literature finds little evidence for discrimination. Employing much the same approach but using newer data from the 1990s, Dey (1997) finds that such penalties have vanished. Hill (2004) criticizes earlier work that found discrimination either for relying only on OLS or for being confined to a single season, and uses 1990–2000 data to find that salaries exhibit no pattern of discrimination. Bodvarsson and Brastow (1999) specifically argue that prior wage discrimination vanished in the 1990s due to changes in collective-bargaining agreements and league expansion. With regard to searching for discrimination in contexts other than salaries, Coleman et al. (2008) find that journalists exhibit no racial bias in most-valued-player voting.

As for matching discrimination, the literature general agrees that it exists. The racial composition of a metropolitan area and of the team have been found to be positively associated by Kahn and Sherer (1988), Bodvarsson and Partridge (2001), Brown, Spiro, and Keenan (1991), and Burdekin and Idson (1991). A smaller number of papers (Dey, 1997; McCormick and Tollison, 2001) fail to find such a match. Burdekin, Hossfield, and Smith (2005) find some more recent evidence of the relation between team and market racial match and attendance and, the newly striking finding that such a match predicts the likelihood that a white player is traded. Hoang and Rascher (1999), Koch and Vander Hill (1988), and Kanazawa and Funk (2001) take a different approach and investigate television ratings rather than attendance. They argue that local ratings can be predicted by the racial composition of the teams compared to that of the metropolitan area, and that the preference of white viewers for white players is responsible for much of the discrimination gap.

If own-group preferences are purely based on race (rather than on nationality and race)—in other words, a preference for white or black players instead of white American or black American players—it may be optimal for team owners to actively recruit foreign players in ways that facilitate roster-to-market matching. Black African or white European players with lower opportunity costs than, respectively, American-born black or white players, for example, might be recruited as low-cost substitutes for the latter. (Recall that in the U.S. labor market generally there is only modest evidence that immigrants generate downward pressure on domestic wages.)

4. SPECIALIZATION

As noted earlier, the market for global basketball is highly segmented, with the NBA being the dominant market, and protectionism, whether league- or state-directed, operating as much to prevent domestic players from leaving for greener pastures rather than protecting them from foreign competition.[2] A question raised in Osborne (2006) is the extent of positional specialization among players from particular jurisdictions when there is open entry in a dominant league. Just as comparative-advantage theory predicts that countries specialize in producing specific kinds of goods, might their basketball leagues also produce specific kinds of players? Among the reasons to suggest they might are differences in physical characteristics and sustained differences in human capital resulting from particular features of player-development systems. For example, coaches who specialize only in rebounding instruction, or a series of initial players who make it to the NBA as

specialists in passing, may induce future players from that jurisdiction to specialize in these particular skills.

   To explore this question, Table 8.1 shows the distribution of players by five
positions throughout league history: guard (shooting and point combined), forward (small and power combined), and center, as well as combination guard/for-
wards and forward/centers. (Ideally one would wish to compare changes over time
in the distribution of players among positions, as in the case of baseball in Osborne
[2006], but the number of international players is too small in most time periods.)
The regions that are assumed to be the basis of specialization, analogous to countries in international-trade models, are Africa, Canada, the Caribbean, Eastern
Europe (including former Soviet states but not including countries formerly part of
Yugoslavia), Western Europe, and the former Yugoslavia. The distribution of players among these categories is tested against the multinomial distribution, where
the U.S. proportions in 2008–9 are the standard of comparison. The test statistic
for whether the distribution among categories is the same in the United States and
in a particular region across all player categories is distributed χ^2 with $n-1$ degrees
of freedom, where n is the number of categories. The test statistic for whether the
proportion of players in a *particular* category differs from the U.S. baseline is subject to the binomial distribution.

   Only for the Caribbean does the null that the positional distribution for talent
is different from that for U.S.-born players fail to be rejected at even the 0.1 percent
level of significance. Africa substantially underproduces both guards and guard/
forwards, as does Eastern Europe. Perhaps the most vivid result is that every region
except Latin America and Canada overproduces centers, often substantially. This
suggests that foreign centers may be contracted on a highly speculative basis—a
very tall player may or may not have a substantial amount of latent human capital
that may be brought out by team investments. As noted earlier, a peculiar feature
of the NBA is that it relies heavily on men at the extreme right of the distribution
of height. This effect is most dramatic at the center position, which means that a
single dominant center can have an outsized impact on a team's success.

   Note in this regard that the average career length is significantly shorter for
foreign-born NBA players. By position, foreign centers have an average career
length of 233 games, forward-centers of 311, guard-forwards of 353, and guards of
171. All these figures are considerably lower than the average length of 469 games
reported (as 5.72 years) for all players in Groothuis and Hill (2004).

   Thus, NBA teams may essentially treat foreign players as lottery tickets, men
whose potential is not well understood at the time of signing, because the estimates of their human capital are not as precise as those for American players whose
development has been observed for a long time. This effect may be particularly
pronounced for centers. It is possible that language difficulties may pose problems
for the degree of complementarity with American-born players, lowering both
wages and career lengths for foreign-born players, but the evidence in Section 5
suggest that this is unlikely.

Table 8.1 The Global Distribution of Position

	Guard	G/Forward	F	F/Center	C	Total
U.S. players, 2008–2009	111/360 (0.308)	88/360 (0.244)	65/360 (0.181)	79/360 (0.219)	17/360 (0.047)	
Foreign-born players, NBA history						
Africa	0/23 (0.000)	0/23 (0.000)	7/23 (0.304)	1/23 (0.043)	15/23 (0.652)	
	6.693***	5.405***	1.41	3.169	124.325***	141.002***
Canada	4/17 (0.235)	2/17 (0.118)	1/17 (0.059)	1/17 (0.059)	9/17 (0.529)	
	0.181	0.996	1.617	1.944*	57.537***	62.275***
Caribbean	6/20 (0.300)	1/20 (0.050)	5/20 (0.250)	4/20 (0.200)	4/20 (0.200)	
	.000	1.551**	0.310	0.024	0.064	7.665
Eastern Europe	3/31 (0.097)	0/31 (0.000)	1/31 (0.032)	14/31 (0.452)	13/31 (0.419)	
	4.019***	7.285***		4.845***	61.165***	87.782***
Latin America	7/25 (0.280)	1/25 (0.040)	12/25 (0.480)	3/25 (0.120)	2/25 (0.080)	
	0.038	4.045**	10.413***	1.067	0.100	15.662***
Western Europe	13/48 (0.271)	1/48 (0.021)	15/48 (0.313)	4/48 (0.083)	15/48 (0.313)	
	0.067	9.369***	3.348**	3.911**	46.314***	63.054***
Yugoslavia	11/43 (0.256)	4/43 (0.093)	6/43 (0.140)	3/43 (0.070)	14/43 (0.326)	
	0.183	3.688**	1.206	4.257***	45.973***	55.307***

Note: *** denotes statistical significance at 0.1% level.
** denotes statistical significance at 1% level.
* denotes statistical significance at 10% level.

5. WAGES FOR FOREIGN PLAYERS

Without question, one of the most controversial aspects of global migration is the competition it creates for domestic workers. An NBA example naturally suggests itself: Are foreign players increasingly relied upon in an attempt to drive down wages for domestic NBA players?

One of the few papers to explore this question is Eschker et al. (2004), who investigated NBA data by season from 1996–1997 to 2001–2002, which, as noted earlier, was a time of rising foreign participation in the NBA. They find that, for the first two years of their sample, foreign players were compensated at a higher rate, in the sense that being born in a foreign country and not having played college basketball in the United States was a statistically significant predictor of salary in those two years. After that time, foreign birth had no effect on salary after standardizing for statistical productivity.

This proposition can be tested using more recent data fairly straightforwardly. Following the standard convention in the sports-economics literature, Table 8.2 depicts results of a regression of salary (using the logarithm of salary hardly affects the results) in 2008–2009 on various measures of on-court productivity in the prior year, 2007–2008. These measures are two-point field goals made, three-point field goals made, free throws made, combined offensive and defensive rebounds, assists, personal fouls, and blocked shots. (Steals were initially included but dropped for consistently lacking statistical significance.) In addition, foreign status is used as a dummy variable. The criteria, both of which must be satisfied, for being classified as foreign are being born in a foreign country and not having attended an American high school.

All of the on-court performance measures are statistically significant in the expected direction. Players with more two-point field goals, three-point field goals, free throws, rebounds, assists, and blocked shots make more money. Players who commit more personal fouls earn less. Foreign nationality of a player, in contrast, makes no difference.

An alternative way to explore this question is to see whether it is justified to split the sample by foreign/domestic status. The information resulting from this test is contained in Table 8.3. The first column depicts results for foreign players and the second depicts results for domestic players. The general results are similar to the unified sample. Chow tests are conducted both for the null hypotheses that collectively the coefficients for the two subsamples are the same and that each individual coefficient is different. In neither case can these nulls be rejected, in the latter case, not even for a single coefficient—the p values for each coefficient are listed in the third column of Table 8.3. (The p value for rejecting the null of joint equality of all coefficients is 0.72.)

These findings indicate that in 2008–2009 foreign and domestic players were similarly compensated. In isolation, they are consistent with an equilibrium following the introduction of large numbers of low-cost players that has already seen

Table 8.2 Foreign Status and Salary (Dependent Variable: 2008–2009 Salary)

Variable	Coefficient
Three-point shots made	10623.25**
	(2.99)
Two-point shots made	9911.334***
	(3.34)
Free throws made	5609.111*
	(1.75)
Total rebounds	8216.018***
	(4.13)
Assists	5239.879**
	(3.00)
Personal fouls	−23097.99***
	(−4.89)
Blocked shots	13806.71*
	(−1.83)
Foreign-player dummy	525182.3
	(1.10)
Constant	1828078***
	(4.67)
F	47.50***
Adjusted R^2	0.5191
N	361

Note: *** denotes statistical significance at 0.1% level.
** denotes statistical significance at 1% level.
* denotes statistical significance at 10% level.

wages decline, although not with one in which low-cost foreigners are currently in the process of being substituted for high-cost domestic players. However, given that the average NBA salary increased 34.4 percent from 2002–2003 to 2008–2009, at a time when the U.S. urban consumer price index increased only 20.9 percent, so that average real wages were rising throughout the period, any interpretation of the increasing stock of foreign players as a source of significant downward pressure on wages during this six-year interval is seemingly difficult to justify. To investigate this possibility further, Table 8.4 repeats the regression of Table 8.3 with 2002–2003 salary as the left-hand variable and 2001–2002 player statistics as the right-hand variables. With only twenty-eight foreign players available, some of their statistics lack statistical significance, but those that do possess it tell an interesting story. For rebounds and assists the coefficients for foreign players are *larger* at a statistically significant level. This is consistent with the previous speculation that foreign players, in particular tall ones, were the subject of speculative investments, so that teams may have suspected that foreign players would be more productive as rebounders (and dispensers of assists) than they turned out to be. Still, by 2008–2009 this

Table 8.3 Sample Split (Dependent Variable: 2008–2009 Salary)

Variable	Coefficient (Foreign)	Coefficient (Domestic)	p-value (Equal-coefficient null)
Three-point shots made	19074.56* (2.38)	10072.57* (2.56)	(0.58)
Two-point shots made	13434.000* (2.26)	9190.143** (2.82)	(0.63)
Free throws made	6148.074 (0.88)	5482.237 (1.53)	(0.95)
Total rebounds	8275.942* (1.77)	8271.42*** (3.73)	(0.99)
Assists	3319.036 (1.15)	5417.061** (2.64)	(0.22)
Personal fouls	−32885.52*** (−3.88)	−21231.29*** (−3.81)	(0.37)
Blocked shots	32882.37* (2.34)	8954.714 (1.03)	(0.26)
Constant	2036915** (3.05)	1865449*** (4.21)	
F	24.35***	38.28***	
Adjusted R²	0.7283	0.4669	
N	62	299	

Note: ***denotes statistical significance at 0.1% level.
**denotes statistical significance at 1% level.
*denotes statistical significance at 10% level.

disparity had vanished. Thus, the argument that foreign players have significantly driven down wages of domestic players finds little support, similar to the majority of the results in Eschker et al. (2004).

6. UNEXPLORED TERRITORY

Other questions remain. One that is increasingly important in the theoretical labor literature but largely unexplored in the empirical sports-economics literature in particular is whether team diversity makes a difference on the field. The theoretical problem of managing a diverse workforce has been depicted by Lazear (1999) as a trade-off between the productive benefits of combining people from different nationalities or cultures, who tend to have different and perhaps complementary

Table 8.4 Sample Split (Dependent Variable: 2002–2003 Salary)

Variable	Coefficient (Foreign)	Coefficient (Domestic)	p-value (Equal-coefficient null)
Three-point shots made	446.7613 (−0.02)	−7625.559 (−1.37)	(0.1845)
Two-point shots made	−20176.52 (−1.01)	8430.174** (3.06)	(0.1107)
Free throws made	−22106.58 (−1.14)	3538.588 (1.17)	(0.1795)
Total rebounds	37494.73* (2.56)	3799.555* (1.92)	(0.0183)*
Assists	27443.08* (2.50)	3110.104* (1.77)	(0.0172)*
Personal fouls	−43186.94* (−2.38)	−3970.684*** (−3.86)	(0.1559)
Blocked shots	−3404.31 (−0.09)	6677.48* (2.20)	(0.6791)
Constant	2738238* (2.73)	1944271*** (5.63)	
F	3.31*	27.94***	
Adjusted R^2	0.5369	0.3830	
N	28	323	

Note: ***denotes statistical significance at 0.1% level.
**denotes statistical significance at 1% level.
*denotes statistical significance at 10% level.

skills, and communication costs among workers from different groups. Prat (2002) extends this analysis by thinking about different kinds of tasks. For tasks that are standardized and stable, the communication-cost effect is more likely to dominate. If the team's task is driven more by creativity, then diversity is more likely on balance to be an asset.

However, the empirical literature to this point is still sparse. Brandes et al. (2009) find little evidence that team diversity in German soccer has any effect on one clear measure of team-performance success, that is, winning percentage. However, the remainder of the literature on the relation between nationality or ethnoracial diversity and on-field performance has focused either on the separation of productivity skills across group boundaries (Osborne, 2006) or on the negative relation between the expanded universe of groups or jurisdictions from which to choose players (e.g., the desegregation of North American Major League Baseball or the expansion of the source of its players into other countries in Latin America and East Asia) and variability in player and team performance (Schmidt and Berri, 2005, Gould 1986). If diversity is not per se productive to team success in the NBA, it might indicate that communication costs in production of such success are sufficiently low and the competition among NBA owners sufficiently high to approximate a competitive market for player talent, so that ethnoracial identity would be irrelevant to on-court success, absent customer discrimination. However, it is ultimately still an unexamined question.

The dynamics of foreign participation in the NBA is also an area ripe for more research. Chau and Stark (1998) present a general hypothesis of migration dynamics in which employers in the destination country are poorly informed about migrant skill, and so the earliest migrants tend to be the highest-skilled, followed later by those of lesser skill. Very casual empiricism suggests such a pattern in the NBA, where several of the earliest African players, for example Hakeem Olajuwon and Dikembe Mutombo, ultimately had extremely successful careers, whereas many African players now (like players from every jurisdiction) do not. Because of the straightforward data on worker productivity found in the NBA, they would allow a useful test of such a model.

The final primary unexplored area concerns the global structure of basketball leagues. Although all the literature to this point investigates the NBA, even while the global presence of that league, particularly in China, is rising, other national leagues are becoming economically important actors. Recently, American high-school graduates, kept out of the NBA by that league's prevention of players from participating unless they are at least 19 years old and one year removed from high school, have contemplated playing in European leagues, both to earn income and to improve their human capital as preparation for the NBA. In addition, European and Chinese teams provide opportunities for American players whose skill levels have already been convincingly demonstrated to fall short of NBA levels, even as domestic players in those leagues might use the opportunity to play with players with NBA experience to augment their human capital, with an eye to jumping into the NBA themselves. If a Chinese player playing with second-tier American talent is able to increase his human capital substantially, such circumstances may resemble the classic problem of learning by doing, the study of which was pioneered by Arrow (1962). Whether non-American leagues can function in equilibrium as an unofficial minor league for the NBA is still a question worthy of theoretical study, as is the question about the conditions under which a non-American league might dislodge the NBA as the magnet for the best talent.

NOTES

1 *Belgian FA v Bosman* [1996] All ER [EC] 97.
2 Although in most countries the restriction of freedom of movement for players to foreign leagues is purely a private-sector collective-bargaining matter (e.g., in Japanese baseball), in the case of China the government, too, is involved in negotiating the terms of players' exit from their Chinese contracts through its state sports bureaucracy.

REFERENCES

Arrow, Kenneth. 1962. The economic implications of learning by doing. *The Review of Economic Studies*, 29 (3): 155–173.

Aydemir, Abdurrahman, and George J. Borjas. 2007. Cross-country variation in the impact of international migration: Canada, Mexico, and the United States. *Journal of the European Economic Association*, 5: 663–708.

Berri, David J., Stacey L. Brook, Bernd Frick, Aju J. Fenn, and Roberto Vicente-Mayoral. 2005. The short supply of tall people: Competitive imbalance and the National Basketball Association. *Journal of Economic Issues*, 39: 1029–1041.

Berri, David J., and Anthony C. Krautmann. 2006. Shirking on the court: Testing for the incentive effects of guaranteed pay. *Economic Inquiry* 44: 536–546.

Berri, David J., Martin B. Schmidt, and Stacey L. Brook. 2004. Stars at the gate: The impact of star power on NBA gate revenues. *Journal of Sports Economics* 5: 33–50.

Bodvarsson, Örn B., and Raymond T. Brastow. 1999. A test of employer discrimination in the NBA. *Contemporary Economic Policy*, 17: 243–255.

Bodvarsson, Örn B., and Mark D. Partridge. 2001. A supply and demand model of co-worker, employer and customer discrimination. *Labour Economics*, 8: 389–416.

Borjas, George J. 2005. The labor-market impact of high-skill immigration. *The American Economic Review*, 95: 56–60.

Borjas, George J. 2003. The labor demand curve is downward sloping: Reexamining the impact of immigration on the labor market. *The Quarterly Journal of Economics*, 118: 1335–1574.

Brandes, Leif, Egon P. Franck, and Philipp Theiler. 2009. The effect from national diversity on team production—Empirical evidence from the sports industry. *Schmalenbach Business Review*, 61: 225–246.

Brown, E., R. Spiro, and D. Keenan. 1991. Wage and non-wage discrimination in professional basketball: Do fans affect it? *American Journal of Economics and Sociology*, 50: 333–345.

Burdekin, Richard C. K., Richard T. Hossfeld, and Janet Kiholm Smith. 2005. Are NBA fans becoming indifferent to race? Evidence from the 1990s. *Journal of Sports Economics*, 6: 144–159.

Burdekin, Richard C. K., and Todd L. Idson. 1991. Customer preferences, Attendance and the racial structure of professional basketball teams. *Applied Economics*, 23: 179–186.

Castles, Stephen, and Mark J. Miller. 2009. *The age of migration*, 4th ed. (New York: Guilford Press).

Chau, Nancy H., and Oded Stark. 1999. Migration under asymmetric information and human capital formation. *Review of International Economics*, 7:455–483.

Coleman, B. Jay, J. Michael Dumond, and Allen K. Lynch. 2008. An examination of NBA MVP voting behavior: Does race matter? *Journal of Sports Economics*, 9: 606–627.

Dey, Matthew S. 1997. Racial differences in National Basketball Association players' salaries: A new look. *American Economist*, 41: 84–90.

Eschker, Erick, Stephen J. Perez, and Mark V. Siegler. 2004. The NBA and the influx of international basketball players. *Applied Economics*, 36: 1009–1020.

Ethier, Wilfred J. 1985. International Ttade and labor migration. *American Economic Review*, 75: 691–707.

Gould, Steven Jay. 1986. Entropic homogeneity isn't why no one hits .400 anymore. Discover, 7: 60–66.

Groothuis, Peter A., and J. Richard Hill. 2004. Exit discrimination in the NBA: A duration analysis of career length. *Economic Inquiry*, 42: 341–349.

Grossman, Jean B. 1982. *The substitutability of natives and immigrants in production.* *Review of Economics and Statistics*, 64: 596–603.

Hanson, Gordon H. 2009. The economic consequences of the international migration of labor. *Annual Review of Economics* 1: 7:1–7:29.

Hill, James Richard. 2004. Pay discrimination in the NBA revisited. *Quarterly Journal of Business and Economics*, 43: 81–92.

Hoang, Ha, and Dan Rascher. 1999. The NBA, exit discrimination, and career earnings. *Industrial Relations*, 38: 69–91.

Hotelling, Harold. 1929. Stability in competition. *Economic Journal*, 39: 41–57.

Kahn, Lawrence M., and Malav Shah. 2005. Race, compensation and contract length in the NBA: 2001–2002. *Industrial Relations*, 44: 444–462.

Kahn, Lawrence M., and Peter D. Sherer. 1988. Racial differences in professional basketball players' compensation. *Journal of Labor Economics*, 6: 40–61.

Kanazawa, Mark T., and Jonas P. Funk. 2001. Racial discrimination in professional basketball: Evidence from Nielsen ratings. *Economic Inquiry*, 39: 599–608.

Koch, James V., and C. Warren Vander Hill. 1988. Is there discrimination in the "black man's game"? *Social Science Quarterly*, 69: 83–94.

Krautmann, Anthony C., and Thomas D. Donley. 2009. Shirking in Major League Baseball: Revisited. *Journal of Sports Economics*, 10: 292–304.

Lazear, Edward P. 1999. Globalisation and the market for team-mates. *Economic Journal*, 109: C15–C40.

Lehn, K. 1982. Property rights, risk sharing, and player disability in Major League Baseball. *Journal of Law and Economics*, 25: 343–366.

Kuznets, S., and D.S. Thomas. 1958. Internal migration and economic growth. In Selected studies in migration since World War II: Proceedings of the 34th annual conference of the Milbank Memorial Fund. (New York: Milbank Memorial Fund).

LaLonde, Robert J., and Robert H. Topel. 1991. Labor market adjustments to increased immigration. In *Immigration, trade, and the labor market, A National Bureau of Economic Research project report*. (Chicago and London: University of Chicago Press).

MacDougall, G.D. A. 1960. *The benefits and costs of private investment from* abroad: A theoretical approach. *Economic Record*, 36: 13–35.

McCormick, Robert E., and Robert D. Tollison. 2001. Why do black basketball players work more for less money? *Journal of Economic Behavior and Organization*, 44: 201–219.

Morse, Alan L., Stephen L. Shapiro, Chad D. McEvoy, and Daniel A. Rascher. 2008. The Effects of Roster Turnover on Demand in the National Basketball Association. *International Journal of Sport Finance*, 3: 8–18.

Mundell, Robert A. 1957. International trade and factor mobility. *American Economic Review*, 47: 321–335.

Osborne, Evan 2006. Baseball's international division of labor. *Journal of Sports Economics*, 7: 150–167.

Prat, Andrea (2002). Should a team be homogeneous? *European Economic Review*, 46: 1187–1207.

Price, Joseph, and Justin Wolfers. 2007. Racial discrimination among NBA referees. National Bureau of Economic Research, Inc, NBER Working Papers: 13206.

Schmidt, Martin B., and David J. Berri. 2005. Concentration of playing talent: Evolution in Major League Baseball. *Journal of Sports Economics*, 6: 412–419.

Scoggins, J. 1993. Shirking or stochastic productivity in Major League Baseball: Comment. *Southern Economic Journal*, 60: 239–240.

Simon, Julian L. 1996. *The ultimate resource 2*. (Princeton, NJ: Princeton University Press).

Stiroh, Kevin J. 2007. Playing for keeps: Pay and performance in the NBA. *Economic Inquiry*, 45: 145–161.

Zavodny, Madeline 2003. The H-1 program and its effects on information technology workers. *Federal Reserve Bank of Atlanta Economic Review*, 88: 33–43.

SECTION 3

HOCKEY

CHAPTER 9

THE DEMAND FOR VIOLENCE IN HOCKEY

DUANE W. ROCKERBIE

INTRODUCTION

HOCKEY has always been a violent game in comparison to the three other major professional sports in North America (basketball, football, and baseball). The speed of the game combined with the limited ice surface results in frequent contact of the players and violations of the rules. Most of the time, these rule violations are not what society would deem violent acts. Interference, hooking, holding, and other minor penalties are often just the result of physical play that is deemed acceptable in certain game situations, justifying the small cost to the player and the team (a two-minute penalty). The National Hockey League (NHL) appears to tolerate more violent offences that are deemed major penalties, particularly fighting, than the other professional leagues (NFL, NBA, and MLB). Players who choose to fight each other are expelled from the game and often face stiff suspensions and fines in the other professional leagues. NHL players who fight receive five-minute fighting penalties, sometimes accompanied by 10-minute misconduct penalties, but rarely expulsion from the game. Suspensions and fines are at the discretion of the NHL commissioner and are typically small or nonexistent for pure fighting penalties, but they can be onerous for penalties involving a deliberate intent to injure. In European football (soccer), fighting is rare on the pitch, and the penalty is expulsion from the game and a reduction to nine players on the field. Curiously, fighting is more common among fans in the arena in Europe than it is in North America.

The purpose of this paper is to provide some revealing statistics about violence in the NHL, to review the economic literature on why violence is tolerated in the

NHL, and to provide some new evidence on the effects of violence on NHL attendance. The theme of this first volume of papers on sports economics is the unique aspects of the professional sports industry that distinguish it from other industries. Although many industries produce products and services that condone and profit from violence in indirect ways (weapons, video games, movies, etc.), the NHL condones and, perhaps, uses violence as a direct output in the production of its on-ice product. Therefore, it is important to understand the effects of violence on NHL attendance, and ultimately, profitability of the industry.

A HISTORICAL EXPLORATION OF VIOLENCE IN THE NHL

The NHL was established in 1917 from the ashes of the National Hockey Association with only three clubs: the Montreal Canadiens, the Toronto Arenas, and the Ottawa Senators. The game was rough and fights were frequent, often resulting in serious injuries. In 1922, the NHL adopted Rule 56 that established a five-minute penalty for fighting, rather than expulsion from the game. Making a controlled form of fighting semilegal was viewed as a better alternative to frequent expulsions of players from the game. The new system encouraged each club to carry a few players that would act as enforcers on the ice, expected to deal with the other club's enforcers in a controlled battle of fisticuffs. This established a long-standing code of conduct in the NHL that still exists today. Skilled players are not expected or encouraged to fight in their own defense when rules are ignored, instead, an enforcer comes to the aid of the stricken skilled player, with the expectation of being met by the other club's enforcer. This system of on-ice détente worked well. Fighting was less frequent through the 1960s, but particularly violent acts that went beyond fighting still occurred (Bernstein (2006)). Rule 46 (which replaced Rule 56) now even specifies the allowable behavior during a fight: The players must first drop their gloves and fight bare-knuckled; third men are not allowed into a fight between two players (immediate expulsion from the game); kicking with skates is strictly forbidden and severely punished; players must end the fight at the instruction of the referee if they separate; and pulling the opponent's sweater over his head is not permitted.

Since the 1960s, the incidence of fighting has displayed significant irregularity. Figure 9.1 displays the average number of fights per game over the 1975–1976 to 2008–2009 NHL seasons. The average number of fights peaked during the 1983–1984 season at 1.17 fights per game, and then began a steady decline to the 2008–2009 season at 0.53 fights per game, which is around the historical average prior to the 1975–1976 season. Figure 9.1 also displays the standard deviation of the number of fights per game among all NHL clubs for a given season. As the average

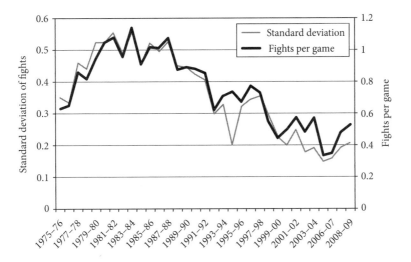

Figure 9.1 Fights per game in the National Hockey League, 1975–2008. (*Source*: http://www.dropyourgloves.com/).

number of fights climbed during the late 1970s and early 1980s, so did the standard deviation. In fact, the historical pattern between the two is remarkably similar up to the 1996–1997 season when the standard deviation began to climb again, but it never approached its historical high in the 1979–1980 season. The distribution of fights per game shifted to the right up to the 1983–1984 season and became more widely dispersed, shifting back to the left after the 1983–1984 season. The reduction in the average number of fights since then up to the 2008–2009 season has also been accompanied by a movement toward parity in the dispersion of fights per game among NHL clubs. In general, most NHL clubs today are equally violent with a low overall level of violence.

The 1980s was clearly a decade of increased violence in the NHL. What could have caused this? The NHL was in a state of flux and uncertainty in 1979 with the merger with four clubs who were members of the defunct World Hockey Association (WHA). This merger, combined with the rapid expansion of the number of clubs in the NHL during the 1970s, resulted in a dilution of talent in the league that may have contributed to more physical play and fighting in the 1980s. Fighting players are employed to protect more skilled players and with the average skill falling in the league, the more elite players needed more protection. The decade of the 1990s saw a dramatic drop in fighting as NHL and minor-league clubs adjusted to the greater demand for skilled players, partly by importing an increasing number of players from Europe.[1] Since that time, rule changes that enforce minor penalties to a greater degree have sped up the game and reduced the demand for the traditional enforcer player.

Casual observation provides mixed evidence about the effects of fighting on attendance in the NHL. Figure 9.2 displays average attendance per game in the NHL over the 1975–1976 to 2008–2009 seasons. Average attendance rose steadily during the 1980s, then fell from the 1989–1990 to 1993–1994 seasons. This coincides

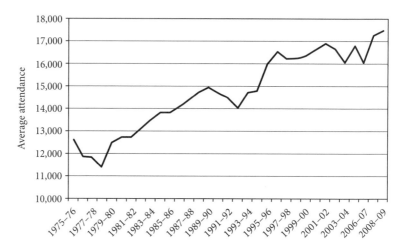

Figure 9.2 Average attendance per game in the National
Hockey League, 1975–2008.
(*Source*: http://www.rodneyfort.com/).

pro-cyclically with the pattern of fights per game displayed in Figure 9.1. After the
1993–1994 season, there is no clear association between fights per game and average attendance per game. If there was an association between fighting and attendance, it seems to have broken down over the last fifteen years, perhaps due to rule
changes and increases in the average skill level of players, or just the preferences
of fans for violence. Looking at violence and attendance at the league level can be
deceiving because, even though the average number of fights per game may not
change over many seasons, how the individual clubs move around in the distribution of fighting can change, and this might affect attendance at the club level.

THE EXISTING LITERATURE ON
VIOLENCE IN HOCKEY

The existing literature on violence in the NHL can be conveniently split into two
streams. The first stream investigates whether greater violence in NHL contests
contributes to greater attendance and higher salaries for players who exhibit violent
behavior. Economics suggests that violence can lead to a higher demand for tickets
for hockey games in two ways. First, violent behavior could intimidate the players
on competing clubs and result in greater success on the ice, usually expressed as a
better winning percentage. This improvement in the quality of the club can shift
the demand curve for tickets to the right if fans are responsive to the club's success.
Second, fans may just have a desire to watch violence, regardless of the quality of

the club—a sort of "blood lust" that will also shift the demand curve for tickets to the right. The two effects of violence must be disentangled and identified using econometric methods to estimate their separate effects on ticket demand.

The second stream of the hockey violence literature considers whether greater enforcement of the rules that are meant to deter violent behavior actually do so. Borrowing models from the economics of crime literature, these papers test whether more referees on the ice reduce the incidence and severity of violent behavior by players. Crime statistics from violent crimes off the ice (murders, robberies, and so on) typically do not include specific data about the offender. The NHL offers a natural laboratory to test crime models because data about the offenders are easily obtained, particularly, their past incidence of violent behavior.

VIOLENCE AND HOCKEY ATTENDANCE

The first paper that investigated the effects of violent behavior on hockey attendance is Jones (1984). This is the first of a series of excellent papers by the same author that considers some aspect of the demand for the NHL's product. Jones (1984) does not address the issue of hockey violence on demand in much detail; instead, it considers whether NHL attendance is determined by either "outcome uncertainty" or "winning." Outcome uncertainty is the idea that the demand for tickets will be greater the closer the two opposing clubs are in quality and winning percentage. Leagues can impose policies on club owners that promote outcome uncertainty, such as revenue sharing and salary caps, to ensure that an optimal level of competitive balance is reached to maximize league revenues.[2] The league objective is to maximize league profit by encouraging outcome uncertainty. Individual club owners maximize profit by winning, given some degree of outcome uncertainty. However, winning too much reduces outcome uncertainty, so there is a conflict between the objective of the league and the objective of the individual club owner. Neither is a viable goal by itself, so an optimal blend of the two must be found, but determining which objective has a stronger effect on attendance is an empirical issue.

Jones (1984) chooses average game attendance as the dependent variable in a least squares regression model that includes a large number of independent variables that reflect winning and uncertainty (winning percentage, rank finish in the league, and so on), specific team characteristics (playoff team, fighting team, skating team) and club market characteristics (per capita income, population, number of other professional sports clubs in the area and arena capacity). Although attendance is assumedly determined by the interaction of demand and supply, there is no discussion of simultaneity; in fact, the ticket price (usually measured by an average ticket price across all seats in an arena) is not included as an independent variable. Most likely, the regression equation was intended to be a reduced form, although, in that case, the price elasticity of demand is not recoverable from a single equation. Ticket price data was not easily available for each club in the NHL at that time, although it is readily available today beginning from the 1990 season.[3]

For our purposes, the most relevant results from Jones (1984) are the estimated coefficients for the independent variables that measure violent behavior. The regression model was estimated using individual game data for the 1977–1978 season. The results suggest that a fighting team can increase ticket demand, regardless of whether its opponent is also a fighting team or a skating team. The estimated coefficient suggests that attendance increases by about 2,500 fans if both clubs are fighting clubs; an increase in attendance of about 1,200 fans if only one of the clubs is a fighting club. The designation of whether a club is a fighting team is determined by penalty minutes for the previous season. This included penalty minutes for violent offenses (fighting, spearing, boarding, etc.) and nonviolent offenses (hooking, tripping, interference, etc.), so it is not clear if the designation of a fighting team is appropriate or not. What we can conclude from Jones (1984) is that a team that was penalized more often in the previous season attracted greater attendance in the current season, ceteris paribus.

Some of the methodological problems in Jones (1984) were addressed in Stewart et al. (1992) where the analysis was refocused to consider the effects of violence on ticket demand more closely than other factors. The paper constructs a model of a profit-maximizing club owner who considers violence to be an important input into the production of wins on the ice. The authors argue convincingly that violence shifts ticket demand through greater on-ice success and through the "blood lust" of the fans. This is an important paper since it builds a model of how hockey violence affects attendance through these two channels. Attendance is specified as a linear function of violence (v), winning percentage (w), the average ticket price (p), and a vector of other club and market variables ($\mathbf{y}$) for club i in season t.

$$A_{it} = \beta v_{it} + bw_{it} + cy_{it} - dp_{it} \tag{1}$$

The determination of the winning percentage is specified by an early form of the logistic contest function that is now popular in sport economics.

$$w_{it} = \frac{Q_{it}}{\sum_{\tau=1}^{T} Q_\tau \dfrac{n_{i\tau}}{n_t}} \tag{2}$$

In (2), $n_t = 80$ for each team (total number of games played in a season), and $n_{i\tau}$ is the total number of games played by team i against team τ, Q_τ is the quality of team τ and Q_{it} is the quality of team i in season t. Quality of team i in season t is defined by a third equation that is linear in a vector of the club's attributes (x) and violence (v).

$$Q_{it} = 1 + ax_{it} + av_{it} \tag{3}$$

Violence shifts demand for team i directly (the "blood lust" effect) in (1) and indirectly through (2) and (3) (the effect on team quality). After some substitutions and solving the club owner's revenue-maximizing problem, a system of four linear equations is derived that determines the club's revenue-maximizing winning percentage, ticket price, attendance, and violence. These equations were then estimated using data from the 1981–1982 and 1982–1983 NHL seasons for a total of 63 pooled observations. This equation system is specified in more detail in a later section of this paper. The system was estimated simultaneously using a full information maximum likelihood search algorithm with instrumental variables for the endogenous variables. Violence was measured by the total number of penalties, including misconduct penalties, over the season for home games only. The coefficient estimates suggest that violence does shift ticket demand significantly due to the "blood lust" effect in (1) by only a small amount (attendance elasticity = 0.075), but that the negative effect of violence on winning percentage outweighs the "blood lust" effect so that the overall effect of violence on attendance is slightly negative.

Subsequent papers to Stewart et al. (1992) do not use the same detailed structural model, which is unfortunate. Instead they specify a two-equation regression model best represented by Jones et al. (1993). Jones et al. (1993) also tests for any difference in fan preferences toward violence between Canadian and American clubs with the argument being that American clubs that operate in weaker markets might promote violence to a greater extent as a way to maintain revenues. The authors specify a price equation and an attendance equation with violence appearing in the latter. Winning percentage is not modeled as a function of violence, hence only the "blood-lust" effect is estimated. The innovation in the paper is the use of game-by-game attendance instead of total season attendance. Violence is measured as the average number of penalty minutes prior to the game in question, although the majority of these penalty minutes probably do not punish violent behavior. To address this issue, the authors also break penalty minutes down into major and minor penalties in separate regressions. The equations were estimated using the seemingly unrelated regression technique with data from the 1983–1984 NHL season. When violence is measured as major penalty minutes and misconduct penalties, American fans responded positively to violence (about 1,500 more fans per misconduct penalty) but Canadian fans responded negatively (about 680 fewer fans per misconduct penalty). These results ignore the negative effect of violence on team quality (winning percentage) found in Stewart et al. (1992) and are most likely overestimates. Jones et al. (1996) repeated the estimation using a single attendance equation and data from the 1989–1990 NHL season and found qualitatively identical results: American fans prefer violence and Canadian fans do not.

Isolating very violent behavior is difficult when penalty minutes are used as the measure of violence. Most penalties are not violent, but segmenting penalty minutes into major and minor penalties is not sufficient since fighting is only one type of major penalty. Without being a behavioral expert, I would guess that fighting is the form of violence that best represents the type of "blood-lust" that fans desire, but major penalties include other rule violations besides fighting. Fortunately, historical data on the number of fights has recently become available, so penalty minutes can be dispensed with as the violence proxy.[4] Paul (2003) replicated the method of Jones et al. (1996) using the number of fights per game, instead of major and minor penalty minutes, for each club from the 1999–2000 NHL season, . The study found that both American and Canadian fans preferred fighting, with American fans somewhat more responsive (about 4,700 more fans per game compared to 3,100 fans per game for Canadian fans). Again the nagging issue of how fighting affects a clubs winning percentage, and hence attendance, is not a feature of the model.

A different approach to determining if violence affects ticket demand for NHL clubs is to consider how violent behavior affects the salaries of particularly violent players. This approach borrows from human capital theory in which a higher demand for violence by fans will increase the marginal revenue product (MRP) for violent players. If club owners are not monopsonists, salaries for players should reflect their relative MRPs. Higher salaries for violent behavior can then be a reflection of higher ticket demand. Jones et al. (1997) tested this hypothesis using data for a sample of NHL players from the 1989–1990 season. Two categories of players were defined: "grunt" players who are more physical and less skilled, and non-grunt players who are everyone else. Differences in the salary structures of grunt and non-grunt players were estimated using a log-linear salary equation with the independent variables including player-specific and market-specific factors. Because a player cannot be observed to be a grunt or not, a switching regressions procedure utilizing a grid search method was used to estimate the grunt and non-grunt coefficients. Significant differences in salary structures were found between grunt and non-grunt players, suggesting that grunt players do serve a role in the NHL, but there was no statistically significant advantage to being a grunt player, ceteris paribus. This result seems to conflict with the findings of the previously mentioned studies that suggest that fans respond positively to violence in the NHL. The contradiction might be explained by two shortcomings of the paper. First, free agency was very restricted in the NHL up to the 2005 collective bargaining agreement, leaving much room for owners to capture monopsony rents from the players. Second, the salary = MRP rule applies for free-agent players only (Krautmann (1999)) because players under contracts cannot renegotiate their salaries every season. Jones et al. (1997) should have limited their sample to free-agent players only, of which there were very few in the 1989–1990 season.

The effect of violence on salaries was also estimated by Haisken-DeNew and Vorell (2008). Using data from the 1996–1997 to 2007–2008 NHL seasons, the authors found that violence (measured by the number of fights for each club) had a positive effect on team performance and player salaries (between $10,000 and $18,000 per fight won), suggesting a positive effect of fighting on attendance. Unfortunately this paper suffers the same shortcomings as those previously mentioned (using only free-agent data instead of all players, endogeneity issues, etc.).

THE EFFECTS OF GREATER
ENFORCEMENT ON VIOLENCE

A recent literature has used NHL games as a laboratory to test economic models of crime. The hypothesis is straightforward: greater enforcement should reduce the incidence and severity of violent offenses. The basic model of the individual's decision to commit an offense was developed by Becker (1968). Its first application to the NHL is Allen (2002). The model specifies the trade-off between the expected benefits and the expected costs of crime. Let t_L and t_G be the individual's time spent on legal (L) and illegal (G) activities respectively. Typically the total time spent on all activities is left unconstrained in these models, a potential shortcoming. The return to the time spent on legal activities is given by the function $L(t_L, \delta)$ where δ is a shift parameter, and the return to time spent on illegal activities is given by the function $G(t_G, \alpha)$ where α is a shift parameter.[5] If the illegal activity is detected, the offender will incur a penalty given by the function $C(t_G, \beta)$ where β is also a shift parameter. Let V represent accumulated wealth.

If the offense is not detected, the offender receives the income

$$I_u = V + L(t_L, \delta) + G(t_G, \alpha) \tag{4}$$

If the offense is detected, the offender receives the income

$$I_d = V + L(t_L, \delta) + G(t_G, \alpha) - C(t_G, \beta) \tag{5}$$

Let the function $p(N)$ be the probability of an offense being detected that is increasing in N, the number of enforcement officers (referees on the ice in hockey). It is quite likely that, in fact, $p = p(N, t_G)$ because greater time spent on illegal activities offers more opportunities for detection for a given N, but that is not a feature of the model in Allen (2002). The individual's maximization problem is then to maximize utility with respect to t_L and t_G.[6]

$$MAX \, E(U) = (1 - p(N))U(I_u) + p(N)U(I_d) \tag{6}$$

The solution to Eq. (6) reveals that an individual will equate the expected marginal utilities from not being detected and being detected when deciding on t_L and t_G. Allen (2002) derives several comparative static results: an increase in the return to legal activities (larger δ) reduces the incidence of illegal activities, but an increase in the return to illegal activities (larger β) may or may not increase the incidence of illegal activities, depending upon the magnitude of the increase in the penalty (C), if detected. An increase in the cost when detected (larger α) unambiguously reduces the incidence of illegal activities, as does an increase in the probability of detection by hiring more enforcement officers (larger N).

Allen (2002) tests these predictions using data from the 1998–1999 NHL season. Between October 15 and February 28 of this season, the NHL experimented with adding a second referee to the standard crew of one referee and two linesmen (the linesmen are not allowed to call penalties). The total sample size included all roster players in the 270 games played. The dependent variable was the number of penalties incurred by each player in a single game, which is a binomial random variable that is non-negative. This property necessitated the use of a negative binomial regression procedure that was estimated using maximum likelihood. The vector of independent variables included measures of legal and illegal gains in a contest (points scored, shots on goal, fights, and so on), the costs of illegal activity (penalty-killing percentage, opponent's power-play percentage and so on) and several control variables (player is a rookie, player is a defenseman, years of tenure and so on). Focusing on the incidence of violent penalties, the most significant explanatory variables were career penalty minutes per game, total number of fights in the contest, the player's average ice-time per game, and a dummy variable capturing the introduction of the two referees on the ice. The introduction of the extra referee was found to *increase* the number of major penalties. The results suggest that the introduction of additional enforcement (extra referee) did not reduce the incidence of violent behavior, but did increase its probability of detection.[7]

The two-referee experiment was repeated by the NHL in the 1999–2000 season. Heckleman and Yates (2003) found results consistent with Allen (2002), whereas Depken and Wilson (2004) found that the addition of the second referee increased scoring and reduced fighting but had no impact on attendace and competitive balance in the league, but television viewership increased slightly. Wilson (2005) used the same sample period and found that the incidence of major penalties was reduced by a relatively larger amount than the incidence of minor penalties. Major penalties are easier to detect (typically fighting) so the results are consistent with the economic model of crime.

Allen (2005) extended his earlier model of crime by adding a new variable c that is an index measuring the "culture of illegality" on a club. This can be interpreted as a measure of a coach's preference for disciplined play (few penalties) or aggressive play (more penalties). Players must adopt the coach's preference (c) and play more or less aggressively. Using the same notation as Allen (2002), $G = G(t_G, c, \alpha)$ and $C = C(t_G, c, \beta)$ where $\partial G/\partial c > 0$ and $\partial C/\partial c < 0$ (the social cost of offending is lower in a culture that is more accepting of offending [larger c]). Performing the same maximization problem as before[8] yields the same comparative static predictions as Allen (2002) with the addition of an additional prediction: an increase in c increases illegal activity $\partial t_G/\partial_c > 0$ if an increase in wealth does not diminish the marginal utility of illegal gains, but the result is not certain. This leaves the door open for empirical testing. Using the same sample period as Allen (2002), the author estimates the same regression model with the addition of a set of explanatory variables thought to capture situational culture toward offending (1) the change in the average number of team penalty minutes per game when a player moves from one club to another, and (2) the change in the average ice time per game when a player moves from one club to another. Large changes in these variables could reflect changes in cultural values on the club toward violence and offending. Unfortunately, the regression results do not support this hypothesis, perhaps because only a handful of players changed clubs over the sample period, although the author does not state the exact number.

Overall, this group of papers tends to agree that adding an additional referee did reduce the incidence of major penalties, providing some confirmation of the economic model of crime. Levitt (2002) is an exception. Using the same sample period as the other papers already cited, Levitt (2002) found that the additional referee had no effect on the incidence of violent offenses, arguing that the probability of detection was left unaffected. In the standard notation of the economic model of crime, $p \neq p(N)$, and, hence, there is no action in the model when N is increased.

AN EMPIRICAL TEST FOR THE EFFECT OF VIOLENCE ON DEMAND

The most elegant model, which estimates the effect of violence on the demand for NHL hockey, is the model of Stewart et al. (1992). It models the two effects of violence, the "blood-lust" effect and the effect on team performance, in a simultaneous equation framework. It also treats the ticket price, attendance, measure of violence, and winning percentage as endogenous variables. Finally, the assumption of using violence as an input to maximize club profit can be tested by testing the cross-equation restrictions this assumption imposes on the regression equations. We estimate this model over a more comprehensive sample period (1997–2008 NHL seasons, giving 330 observations for each variable) that reflects the recent rapid decrease in violence as measured by fighting. The Stewart et al. (1992) paper estimated the model using the 1981–1982, 1982–1983 NHL seasons when fighting was increasing rapidly. It could be that the decrease in fighting since the 1989–1990 NHL season (see Figure 9.1) was caused by a consumer preference for less fighting, rather than just NHL rule changes designed to reduce fighting. The model and the variable definitions are given below using the same notation as Stewart et al. (1992).

$$p_{it} = \frac{1}{2d}\left(\beta v_{it} + bw_{it} + cy_{it}\right) \tag{7}$$

$$A_{it} = \frac{1}{2}\left(\beta v_{it} + bw_{it} + cy_{it}\right) \tag{8}$$

$$v_{it} = -\frac{b}{\beta}\left(1 - w_{it}\right)w_{it} - \frac{1}{\alpha}ax_{it} \tag{9}$$

$$w_{it} - \frac{1}{2} = \frac{1}{2}\left(ax_{it} + av_{it}\right) \tag{10}$$

where

P_{it} = Average ticket price in US dollars

A_{it} = Annual home attendance for regular season games

v_{it} = Total number of fights, or Total number of hits given

w_{it} = Total points divided by maximum number of possible points (164) in the regular season

y_{it} = Total metropolitan area population (c_1), Total income in metropolitan area in U.S. dollars (c_2), a dummy variable set equal to one for a Canadian home city (c_3), arena capacity (c_4)

x_{it} = Power play percentage (a_1), Penalty kill percentage (a_2), Total goals allowed (a_3), Number of all-star players (a_4)

A list of sources for the variables is given in the appendix. Descriptive statistics for each of the variables appear in Table 9.1.

The coefficients of particular interest are α and β, which give the indirect (effect on winning percentage) and direct ("blood-lust") effects of violence on demand, respectively. Given the number of instruments in the x and y vectors, each equation is just identified or overidentified so that full information maximum likelihood could be used using the E-Views econometrics program. The first estimation used the total number of fights for each club as the measure of violence. The results appear in Table 9.2.

The dummy variable for a Canadian home city and the arena capacity variable both possess statistically significant coefficients that are the anticipated positive sign; however, the metropolitan-area-population variable and the metropolitan-area-income variable coefficients are not statistically significant. This can be explained by the high correlation coefficient between the population and income variables (0.8677) that resulted in multicollinearity and a lack of efficiency. Nevertheless, the coefficient on population is the wrong sign. It could also be that these coefficient estimates are heavily influenced by a few of the cities in the sample. Los Angeles and New York are the largest metropolitan areas in the sample by a wide margin, yet their NHL clubs (Islanders, Ducks, and Kings in particular) typically do not perform well and suffer at the gate.

All the coefficients that explain winning percentage are statistically significant (a_1 to a_4) and each carries the correct sign. The price coefficient d has a positive sign because it entered the demand equation with a negative sign. The price elasticity of demand, evaluated at the point of the mean ticket price ($45.22) and the mean attendance (16,713), is computed to be –1.009. Revenue maximizing firms that face primarily fixed costs will set output to where demand is unit elastic. The fact that the model confirms this behavior suggests that the model is correctly structured (Stewart et al. (1992) estimated a price elasticity of –0.99). An increase in winning percentage affects demand positively ($b > 0$) and significantly, resulting in an increase in ticket revenue.

Violence affects demand in two offsetting ways. The negative and statistically significant coefficient for α suggests that fighting reduces a club's winning percentage, resulting in a drop in ticket demand. It would appear that there is no apparent

Table 9.1 Descriptive Statistics for System Variables

Variable	Mean	Standard Deviation	Minimum	Maximum
Average ticket price	45.22	9.68	21.90	88.32
Annual attendance	16,713	2,234.86	8,188	22,247
Total number of fights per season	45.47	16.98	6.0	117.0
Total number of hits per season	822.90	294.87	133.0	1,734.0
Total points per season	87.40	15.69	39.0	124.0
Total metropolitan area population	6,539,717	6,939,650	721,528	23,102,699
Total metropolitan area income	1.92E+08	2.21E+08	14,506,560	1.00E+09
Arena capacity	18,343	1,238.6	14,703	21,273
Power play percentage	16.76	2.86	9.30	25.50
Penalty kill percentage	82.80	5.87	74.90	89.20
Goals against per season	2.74	0.37	2.00	3.82
Number of all-star players	1.41	0.96	0.0	6.0

Table 9.2 Full Information Maximum Likelihood Estimates of Equations 7–10 (Total Number of Fights Used as Violence)

	Coefficient	Std. Error	z-Statistic	Prob.
β	41.1215	6.988167	5.88444	0
d	372.8297	5.527089	67.44499	0
b	13226.23	2141.550	6.176008	0
$c(1)$	5.70E−07	2.03E−06	0.281031	0.7787
$c(2)$	−1.36E−05	6.76E−05	−0.20122	0.8405
$c(3)$	1.324869	0.077965	16.99308	0
$c(4)$	1998.579	603.4892	3.311706	0.0009
α	−0.004221	0.000522	8.089062	0
$a(1)$	0.004648	0.000667	6.968627	0
$a(2)$	0.000870	0.000175	−4.96535	0
$a(3)$	−0.05647	0.006862	−8.23004	0
$a(4)$	0.011788	0.002169	5.433312	0

intimidation effect of fighting on opponent clubs that might increase winning percentage. The winning elasticity with respect to fighting, evaluated at the mean level of fights (45.47) and winning percentage (0.5), is computed to be −0.384. Stewart et al. (1992) found the same result but with a much higher elasticity (−2.88). This difference could be due to the significantly lower number of fights per season in the sample period used here. The direct "blood-lust" effect of violence is measured by the coefficient β that is positive and statistically significant. The attendance elasticity of violence evaluated at the mean levels of fights per game and attendance

is computed to be 0.112, which is slightly larger than Stewart et al.'s (1992) estimate of 0.075. Although fighting declined in frequency over the sample period,
fans were still attracted by fighting for its blood-lust effect. Overall however, the
blood-lust effect and the effect on winning percentage work against each other, so
the overall effect of fighting on attendance must be calculated using the following
elasticity formula:

$$\frac{dA}{dv}\frac{\overline{v}}{\overline{A}} = \frac{1}{2}\left(\beta + \frac{b\alpha}{2}\right)\frac{\overline{v}}{\overline{A}} = \frac{1}{2}\left(41.1215 + \frac{13226.23(-0.00422)}{2}\right)\frac{45.47}{16713} = 0.0179$$

Doubling the number of fights per season increases attendance by just under two
percent, so fans are not particularly responsive to fighting. Whether NHL clubs
actually use fighting as a method to increase attendance relies on the validity of the
profit-maximizing behavior assumed in the model. The cross-equation non-linear
restrictions derived from the model of a profit-maximizing club owner are rejected
with a p-value of 0.000. Stewart et al. (1992) attribute this rejection to a sensitivity
of the Wald test to small sample sizes; however, the sample size used here is much
larger, so this argument is not relevant.

The equation system was re-estimated using the total number of hits given by
each club for each season in place of the total number of fights.[9] The results appear
in Table 9.3. Generally, the results using hits are inferior to the results using fights
as the measure of violence. The price elasticity of demand evaluated at the mean is
computed to be −1.007, a consistent result, but after that the results are not good.
Five of the system coefficients are not statistically significant, compared to only
two when fights were used as the measure of violence. The winning elasticity with

Table 9.3 Full Information Maximum Likelihood Estimates of Equations 7–10
(Total Number of Hits Used as Violence)

	Coefficient	Std. Error	z-Statistic	Prob.
β	1.475675	0.693065	2.129201	0.0332
d	372.4784	5.498428	67.74270	0
b	341.4866	185.8499	1.837432	0.0661
$c(1)$	−2.90E−07	2.15E−06	−0.13519	0.8925
$c(2)$	2.39E−05	7.28E−05	0.328108	0.7428
$c(3)$	1.725546	0.035128	49.12117	0
$c(4)$	1818.736	638.3774	2.848998	0.0044
α	3.86E−05	6.77E−06	5.690859	0
$a(1)$	2.41E−05	2.16E−05	−1.11599	0.2644
$a(2)$	3.00E−06	7.79E−06	0.384621	0.7005
$a(3)$	−0.00017	0.000163	−1.05188	0.2929
$a(4)$	0.000147	6.13E−05	2.396203	0.0166

respect to hits, evaluated at the mean level of hits (822.9), is computed to be 0.0872. More aggressive play, as measured by hits inflicted, improves winning percentage, but only marginally. The elasticity of attendance with respect to hits, evaluated at the mean, is computed to be 0.081. This is very close to the attendance elasticity using fights as the measure of violence. The blood-lust effect of hits on attendance demand is very close to the effect using fights, so fans might view these different types of violence as being close substitutes. However, hitting improves winning percentage, whereas fighting reduces winning percentage, so there is no trade-off in attendance by encouraging more hitting as a profit-maximizing strategy.

CONCLUDING REMARKS

Violence has always had an accepted place in NHL hockey at levels that go beyond its acceptability in other professional sports. This could be due to the speed of the game, the close physical contact of the players, and hockey's long reputation as a sport that demands toughness from its players. The economic literature on violence in hockey has taken two different directions: (1) determining whether violence in hockey is the result of profit-maximizing club owners who respond to the public's demand for it, and (2) testing whether rule changes and increases in refereeing have reduced the incidence of violent behavior according to economic models of crime. Each literature has its shortcomings, but the overall results suggest that hockey fans respond mildly positively to greater violence (in the form of fighting) and that efforts made by the NHL to reduce the frequency and severity of violent behavior have met with modest success. The new empirical in this paper suggests that violence measured by hitting, but not by fighting, has a greater effect on fan attendance than fighting. This makes sense because there are many alternative forms of violence that are available for the blood-lust fan to pay to watch. Since the early 1990s, professional wrestling experienced a tremendous increase in popularity, as did NASCAR racing with its crashes and spills. More recently, mixed martial arts fighting pits two opponents in a caged ring with little in the way of rules. Hockey fights might seem tame in comparison to these sorts of violent entertainment.

The next direction that this literature could take is to consider the broader business strategy of the NHL with regards to violence and the availability of entertainment substitutes for NHL violent behavior. This could take the form of including ticket prices, attendance, television viewership, and measures of violence from these other forms of entertainment in the demand functions for NHL attendance to determine if they are substitute goods in the eyes of consumers who like to watch violence. Past empirical studies have treated the NHL as a closed league that does not compete with any other leagues or other forms of entertainment.

The average attendance-capacity ratio was 91.1 percent over the 1997–2008 sample period, with little variation during the sample period (excluding the 2004–2005 strike season). There would not appear to be a lot of room for the NHL to somehow use violence as a means to increase attendance, however, the average attendance-capacity ratio hides some disturbing attendance figures in a few cities, particularly in the southern United States (Atlanta, Phoenix, and Tampa Bay in particular). Profit-maximizing club owners in these cities could develop some sort of strategy to take advantage of the mildly positive effect of fighting and the strong effect of hitting on attendance, but the NHL cannot adopt a leaguewide strategy that addresses only the local concerns of these clubs. A leaguewide strategy could be developed that increases attendance for low-attendance cities while raising ticket prices for clubs that operate at full capacity. The existing literature and the new evidence presented here suggest that encouraging violence in the form of hitting would be an effective strategy, but this should be evaluated relative to the other forms of violent entertainment that exist in the market. The NHL has a solid core of devoted fans, particularly in Canada, but to attract new fans away from other forms of violent entertainment, the NHL may have its work cut out for it.

Notes

1 The fall of the Berlin wall and the collapse of the Soviet Union in 1990 allowed for a significant increase in the number of skilled players imported to the NHL from behind the iron curtain.

2 There is a great debate among economists whether revenue sharing promotes competitive balance or not. No clear winner has emerged since the answer depends on the form of revenue function that is assumed. A good reference to this literature is Kesenne (2005).

3 Ticket price data is available from http://www.teammarketing.com/

4 Fight data can be obtained from http://www.hockeyfights.com/ going back to the 1984–1985 season. Data for previous seasons can be obtained from http://www.dropyourgloves.com/

5 Assume that $\partial^2 L/\partial t_L \partial \delta > 0$ and $\partial^2 G/\partial t_G \partial \alpha > 0$.

6 Note that if total time available is constrained to a fixed amount, the maximization problem reduces to maximizing with respect to t_L or t_G.

7 In the notation of the model, players responded to a higher p by increasing t_G to maintain utility.

8 Allen (2005) imposes a constraint on t_L and t_G that Allen (2002) does not.

9 Fights often result in offsetting five-minute penalties leaving each club with the normal five skaters. Excessive hits often result in a two-minute penalty for one of the clubs, leaving its opponent with one more skater and a definite advantage. The number of power plays and penalty kills are then endogenous with the number of hits, although we use power play percentage and penalty kill percentage rather than the number of power plays and penalty kills.

REFERENCES

Allen, W. D. 2002. Crime, punishment and recidivism: Lessons from the National Hockey League. *Journal of Sports Economics*, 3: 39–60.

Allen, W. D. 2005. Cultures of illegality in the National Hockey League. *Southern Economic Journal*, 71(3): 494–513.

Becker, G. S. 1968. Crime and Punishment: An Economic Approach. *Journal of Political Economy*, 76 (March/April): 169–217.

Bernstein, R. 2006. The Code: The unwritten rules of fighting and retaliation in the NHL. Chicago, IL: Triumph Books.

Depken II, C., and D. Wilson. 2003. Wherein lies the benefit of the second referee in the NHL? *Review of Industrial Organization*, 24(1): 51–71.

Haisken-DeNew, J., and M. Vorell. 2008. Blood money: Incentives for violence in NHL hockey. *Ruhr Economics Papers 47*, RWI Essen.

Heckelman, J., and A. Yates. 2003. And a hockey game broke out: Crime and punishment in the NHL. *Economic Inquiry*, 41(4): 705–712.

Jones, J.C.H. 1984. Winners, losers and hosers: Demand and survival in the National Hockey League. *Atlantic Economic Journal*, 12(3): 54–63.

Jones, J.C.H., D. Ferguson, and K. Stewart. 1993. Blood sports and cherry pie: Some economics of violence in the National Hockey League. *American Journal of Economics and Sociology*, 52(1): 63–78.

Jones, J.C.H., K. Steward, and R. Sunderman. 1996. From the arena into the streets: Hockey violence, economic incentives and public policy. *American Journal of Economics and Sociology*, 55(2): 231–243.

Jones, J.C.H., S. Nadeau, and W. Walsh. 1997. The Wages of sin: Employment and salary effects of violence in the National Hockey League. *Atlantic Economic Journal*, 25(2): 191–206.

Kesenne, S. 2005. Revenue sharing and competitive balance: Does the invariance proposition hold? *Journal of Sports Economics*, 6(1): 98–106.

Krautmann, T. (1999). What is wrong with Scully-estimates of a player's marginal revenue product? *Economic Inquiry*, 37: 369–381.

Levitt, S. D. 2002. Testing the economic model of crime: The National Hockey League's two-referee experiment. *Contributions to Economic Analysis and Policy*, 1(1): Article 2.

Paul, R. J. 2003. Variations in NHL attendance: The impact of violence, scoring and regional rivalries. *American Journal of Economics and Sociology*, 62(2): 345–364.

Stewart, K., D. Ferguson, and J.C.H. Jones. 1992. On violence in professional team sport as the endogenous result of profit maximization. *Atlantic Economic Journal*, 20(4): 55–64.

Wilson, D. P. 2005. Additional law enforcement as a deterrent to criminal behavior: Empirical evidence from the National Hockey League. *Journal of Socio-Economics*, 34(2): 319–330.

APPENDIX
DATA SOURCES

P_{it} = Average ticket price in U.S. dollars: http://www.rodneyfort.com and http://www.teammarketing.com

A_{it} = Annual home attendance for regular-season games: http://www.andrewsstarspage.com/index.php/site/comments/nhl_average_attendance_since_1989_90/118-2008-09

v_{it} = Total number of fights, or Total number of hits given: http://www.dropyourgloves.com and http://www.nhl.com

w_{it} = Total points divided by maximum number of possible points (160) in the regular season: http://www.nhl.com

y_{it} = Total metropolitan area population (c_1): http://www.bea.gov/regional/ Total income in metropolitan area in U.S. dollars (c_2): http://www.bea.gov/regional/a dummy variable set equal to one for a Canadian home city (c_3), arena capacity (c_4): http://www.statshockey.net/nhlarenas.html

x_{it} = Power play percentage (a_1), Penalty kill percentage (a_2), Total goals allowed (a_3), Number of all-star players (a_4): all taken from http://www.nhl.com

CHAPTER 10

HOCKEY

GAME DESIGN AND OVERTIME

JASON ABREVAYA

1. INTRODUCTION

ECONOMISTS have long recognized the value of field data coming from the world of sports. With clearly defined rules and perfectly observed outcomes, sports offer a unique opportunity to examine the effects of incentives upon effort and performance. In certain cases, sports leagues implement rule changes that affect the incentive structures faced by competitors.[1] These rule changes often have predictable effects, which can be empirically tested using data from periods before and after the rule change in question.

This chapter focuses specifically upon rule changes that have been implemented by the National Hockey League (NHL) to change how points are awarded in overtime games.[2] The NHL is the major professional hockey league in North America and currently consists of 30 teams (24 in the United States, 6 in Canada). In a regular-season NHL game, there are 60 minutes of regulation play, divided into three 20-minute periods. Since the number of goals scored in an NHL game is relatively low (an average of about 6 goals per game), the frequency of tied games has been quite high—about one of every five NHL games is tied after regulation time.

Although the NHL has the most severe problem with tied games among North American sports leagues (compared to football, basketball, and baseball), this problem is similar to that faced by soccer leagues worldwide. The NHL introduced its first overtime rule in the 1983–1984 season in an effort to lower the number of tied outcomes. This overtime rule (which we refer to as the "old overtime rule") specified a five-minute overtime period to be played if the score was tied after the end of regulation time. If either team scored during this overtime period, the game ended ("sudden-death overtime") and the scoring team received a win; if no goal was scored during this overtime period, the game ended in a tie.

The basic structure of the overtime period (five-minute, sudden-death format) has remained unchanged since it was originally introduced. The NHL has, however, introduced two important changes to the overtime system, both with the intention of further reducing the number of tied outcomes and increasing excitement for fans. Under the old overtime rules (which lasted through the 1998–1999 season), a team received two points in the league standings for a win (whether in regulation or overtime), zero points for a loss (whether in regulation or overtime), and one point for a tie. The total number of points accumulated by a team during the season determines whether or not the team makes the playoffs and, if the team reaches the playoffs, its playoff seeding. Under the point scheme of the old overtime rule, teams were often willing to "settle" for a tie by playing conservatively in overtime (guaranteeing themselves one point) rather than playing aggressively and risking a (zero-point) loss. Between the 1991–1992 and 1998–1999 seasons, nearly 70 percent of overtime games remained tied after the 5-minute overtime period.

1999–2000 Overtime Rule Changes

To deal with the huge percentage of overtime games that ended in ties, the NHL introduced two rule changes beginning with the 1999–2000 season.[3] The first change was to guarantee both teams one point for games that went into overtime, thereby eliminating the "risk" of receiving zero points for an overtime loss.[4] This change had the strange implication that overtime games could be worth a total of three points (if a goal is scored in overtime) whereas non-overtime games would be worth a total of two points. The second change was to reduce the number of skaters on the ice (from five to four, plus a goalkeeper), thereby creating more space on the ice for increased scoring opportunities. While these two rule changes were implemented simultaneously in the NHL, the same two rule changes were implemented sequentially in the American Hockey League (AHL) (a professional North American minor league). The AHL started guaranteeing one point for overtime losses in 1995 and then reduced the number of skaters (from five to four) in 1999. Table 10.1 summarizes the effects seen in the AHL from these two rule changes, with the one-point guarantee leading to a 9 percentage-point increase in non-tied overtime games and the skater reduction leading to an additional

Table 10.1 American Hockey League Overtime Rules and Results

Time Period	Overtime Rules	Percentage of Games Going into OT	Percentage of OT Games Ended by a Goal
1991–1994	5-on-5 play, 0-point loss	18.5%	31.8%
1995–1997	5-on-5 play, 1-point loss	20.4%	40.8%
1999–2001	4-on-4 play, 1-point loss	20.4%	45.0%

Source: Abrevaya (2004, *Journal of Sports Economics*).

4.2 percentage-point increase in non-tied overtime games. These numbers suggest that both rules introduced by the NHL would have the intended consequence. Table 10.1 also indicates that the one-point guarantee implemented by the AHL led to a slight increase in the overall percentage of overtime games, an effect that we will examine for the NHL in this chapter.

2005–2006 Overtime Rule Change

To put an end to tied games altogether, the NHL introduced a shootout beginning with the 2005–2006 season. If no goals are scored during the 5-minute overtime period, a shootout is used to decide the game's winner. The NHL official rules provide details on how the shootout proceeds:

> The home team shall have the choice of shooting first or second. The teams shall alternate shots. Three players from each team shall participate in the shootout and they shall proceed in such order as the Coach selects. . . . Each team will be given three shots, unless the outcome is determined earlier in the shootout. After each team has taken three shots, if the score remains tied, the shootout will proceed to a "sudden death" format. No player may shoot twice until everyone who is eligible has shot." (currently Rule 84.4, NHL Official Rules)

The loser of the shootout is still guaranteed one point, continuing the point scheme introduced in 1999–2000. The main difference from the 1999–2000 rule is that *all* overtime games under the shootout rule are worth three points (two for winner, one for loser) as opposed to just those overtime games in which an overtime goal is scored.

Table 10.2 provides a summary of the point-reward schemes under the three different NHL overtime rules (old overtime rule, new overtime rule without shootout, and new overtime rule with shootout). As discussed above, the main differences concern the treatment of overtime losses (zero points under the old overtime rule) and the guarantee of a winner under the new overtime rule with shootout. It is important to note that the rule changes implemented in 1999–2000 and 2005–2006 applied only to regular-season games. Since the introduction of

Table 10.2 Point Schemes for Different NHL Overtime Rule Regimes

	Old overtime rule (through 1998–1999)	New overtime rule (1999–2000 to 2004–2005)	New shootout rule (since 2005–2006)
Points awarded for			
Win	2	2	2
Loss (in regulation)	0	0	0
Loss (in overtime)	0	1	n/a
Loss (in shootout)	n/a	n/a	1
Tie (no overtime goal)	1	1	n/a

regular-season overtime, the playoff overtime format has remained the same—20-minute sudden-death overtime periods until a winner is determined. As such, the sample of playoff games provides a good "control" sample since we would not expect to see the same incentive effects (due to rule changes) as the regular-season sample.

The outline of this chapter is as follows. Section 2 reviews the existing literature on overtime incentives within hockey and introduces a simple theoretical framework for analyzing the different overtime regimes in the NHL. While the previous literature has considered the 1999 rule change, this chapter provides the first analysis of the shootout rule introduced in 2005. Section 3 provides empirical analysis for a comprehensive sample of NHL games played between the 1991–1992 and 2008–2009 seasons. Trends in tied-regulation outcomes and goal-in-overtime outcomes are examined, and regression analysis is used to estimate the effects of the new overtime rules on game outcomes. Section 4 concludes.

2. A SIMPLE FRAMEWORK AND A LITERATURE REVIEW

In this section, we provide a very simple (and intentionally informal) framework for analyzing end-of-regulation and overtime-play incentives. This basic framework yields some basic predictions about the likelihoods of end-of-regulation ties and overtime goals. The previous literature has included studies that provide more formal treatments of this problem and allow for more nuanced analysis (e.g., allowing for comparative advantage in aggressive or defensive play, considering the effects of in-conference versus out-of-conference play, etc.). Therefore, after introducing our basic theoretical framework, we review the existing literature on NHL overtime rules and summarize their main theoretical and empirical findings.

2.1 A Simple Framework

For the framework, several simplifying assumptions are made. (Extensions to more realistic assumptions have been considered elsewhere in the literature and are described more fully in Section 2.2.) First, we assume that teams are completely homogenous and symmetric. That is, opponents are of equal quality and have the same probability of winning (or losing) conditional on game situation. Second, we assume that each team is risk-neutral and, therefore, is interested in maximizing the expected number of points in a given game.

Some notation is introduced. The following point-award parameters are exogenous variables given by the particular scoring rule in place:

X_W^R (X_L^R) = points for a win (loss) in regulation

X_W^O (X_L^O) = points for a win (loss) in overtime or shootout

X_T = points for a tie.

As previously summarized in Table 10.1, the three NHL regimes mostly have the same point-award parameters ($X_W^R = X_W^O = 2$, $X_L^R = 0$, $X_T = 1$). The exception is that the old overtime system (prior to the 1999–2000 season) had $X_L^O = 0$, whereas the new overtime rules had $X_L^O = 1$.

The following probability parameters describe the likelihood of a win/loss/tie for games that are tied either late in regulation time or in overtime:

p^R = probability of a win (or loss) in regulation, conditional on being tied late in regulation (thus, the probability of a tie after regulation is $1-2p^R$)

p^O = probability of a win (or loss) in overtime, conditional on reaching overtime (thus, the probability of a tie after overtime, conditional on reaching overtime, is $1-2p^O$)

p^S = probability of a win (or loss) in shootout, conditional on reaching a shootout (under symmetry, we have $p^S = \frac{1}{2}$).

Note that the assumption of symmetry simplifies matters here, since the probability of a win is the same as the probability of a loss. Since we are interested in examining the incentives of different point-scoring rules on play toward the end of games, the first probability parameter (p^R) should be thought of as the probability of winning a game in regulation conditional on a tie score with, say, 5 or 10 minutes left to play.

The win-probability parameters p^R and p^O are endogenous since they will depend upon how aggressively (or defensively) the teams play. (Under symmetry, we restrict team behavior to be the same; again, this symmetry has been relaxed by previous studies with similar conclusions.) Aggressive play at the end of regulation time leads to a higher probability of winning (higher p^R value) but also to a higher probability of losing (since the losing probability is also p^R). Such aggressive play therefore leads to fewer tied games that remain tied at the end of regulation. Similarly, aggressive play during overtime leads to a higher probability of winning (higher p^O value), a higher probability of losing, and a lower probability of a tie at the end of overtime.

For analyzing the incentives for aggressive versus defensive play, we analyze the expected-point expressions for teams under the different NHL scoring regimes. We start from the latest point in the game and move backward: shootout (when relevant), overtime, and late in regulation.

Shootout

We assume that shootouts are essentially coin flips ($p^S = \frac{1}{2}$), so that the expected points, conditional on reaching a shootout, are given by:[5]

$$E(X|\text{shootout}) = \frac{1}{2}\left(X_W^O + X_L^O\right) \tag{1}$$

This expression is equal to 3/2 under the NHL shootout rule adopted in 2005–2006.

Overtime

For the overtime period, there are two different expressions for the expected points conditional on reaching overtime. The first expression is for a regime with no shootout rule, where the game ends in a tie after overtime if no goal is scored:

$$E(X|\text{overtime, no shootout rule}) = p^O X_W^O + p^O X_L^O + \left(1 - 2p^O\right)X_T \tag{2}$$

Note that the expected overtime points increased when the NHL adopted the one-point-for-loss guarantee in 1999–2000. Specifically, the expected points conditional on reaching overtime before and after this change are:

Old overtime rule (prior to 1999–2000): $E(X|\text{overtime, no shootout rule}) = 1$

New overtime rule (1999–2000 to 2004–2005):
$E(X|\text{overtime, no shootout rule}) = 1 + p^O$

The second expression is for a regime with a shootout rule, where the game goes to a shootout after overtime if no goal is scored:

$$E(X|\text{overtime, shootout rule}) = p^O X_W^O + p^O X_L^O + \left(1 - 2p^O\right)E(X|\text{shootout})$$

$$= p^O X_W^O + p^O X_L^O + \left(1 - 2p^O\right)\left(\tfrac{1}{2}\left(X_W^O + X_L^O\right)\right) \tag{3}$$

Plugging in the relevant point values under the NHL's shootout rule yields:

New overtime rule with shootout: $E(X|\text{overtime, shootout rule}) = \dfrac{3}{2}$

Under symmetry, note that the NHL shootout rule implies that the win probability (p^C) does not enter into the expected-points expression; once overtime is reached, the outcome is a coin flip with outcome of 1 or 2. In comparing the expected-point expressions across the three regimes, we see that the NHL rules have successively increased the expected points conditional on reaching overtime (regardless of p^O), going from 1 (old rule) to $1 + p^O$ (new rule, no shootout) to 3/2 (new rule, shootout). Moreover, the overtime-win probability p^O only affects the expected points under the new overtime rule without a shootout; under this point system, there is an incentive for teams to increase p^O (play more aggressively) during overtime (to have a chance at two points), whereas there is no such incentive present under either the old overtime rule or the new shootout rule. The basic prediction, then, is the following:

> Prediction for overtime play: The greatest incentive for aggressive play in overtime should be in the system with the one-point guarantee and no shootout (regime from 1999–2000 to 2004–2005), which should lead to more overtime games ending with goals during this regime.

Regulation play (tied late)

Finally, we consider the expected points for a team conditional on being tied late in regulation time. The general expression is given by:

$$E(X) = p^R X_W^R + p^R X_L^R + (1 - 2p^R)\,E(X|\text{overtime}) \qquad (4)$$

For each of the three NHL rule regimes, we can plug in the appropriate $E(X|\text{overtime})$ expression (as given above) into equation (4) to yield the following expected point values:

> Old overtime rule (prior to 1999–2000): $E(X) = 1$
>
> New overtime rule (1999–2000 to 2004–2005): $E(X) = 1 + p^O - 2p^O p^R$
>
> New overtime rule with shootout: $E(X) = \dfrac{3}{2} - p^R$

Again, these expected values have increased with the successive rule changes. How about the incentives for aggressive play? Note that the partial derivatives of the three formulas with respect to p^R are 0, $-2p^O$, and -1, respectively, for the old overtime rule, new overtime rule without shootout, and new overtime rule with shootout.[6] Thus, there is an incentive for more defensive play (lower p^R) under the new overtime rules, both with and without shootout, with a bigger incentive for more defensive play under the shootout rules. The intuition for the latter result is that more points, in expectation, are guaranteed for overtime games under the shootout rule. The basic prediction, then, is the following:

> Prediction for regulation play: The incentives for preserving a tie in regulation are strongest in the shootout regime (starting in 2005–2006), next strongest under the new overtime rule without shootout (from 1999–2000 to 2004–2005),

and weakest under the old overtime rule. Therefore, we should see more games go into overtime under the new overtime rules (and even more so with a shootout) than under the old overtime rules.

2.2 Literature Review

Several previous studies have examined, both empirically and theoretically, the incentive effects of the 1999–2000 rule change adopted by the NHL. The empirical study by Abrevaya (2004) confirmed two of the predictions of the simple framework above: (1) more games went into overtime after the 1999–2000 rule change, and (2) more overtime games ended with a goal after the 1999–2000 rule change. In addition, using individual game data (with shots-on-goal and time-of-goal information), Abrevaya (2004) found that games were more likely to remain tied in regulation after the rule change and also that play was less aggressive in tied games (on average, about 0.5 fewer shots in the third period) after the rule change.

Several papers have offered more formal treatments of the incentive structure and team-strategy choice than that offered in Section 2.1. Easton and Rockerbie (2005) provide a two-period model in which the incentive effects depend on (1) the relative quality of contestants and (2) whether they compete in the same conference. Banerjee, Swinnen, and Weesink (2007) offer a dynamic game-theoretic model teams in which teams can have comparative advantage in playing aggressively or defensively. Longley and Sankaran (2007) also make the point that the choice of aggressive versus defensive strategy can depend on relative quality of the opposing teams.

The simple framework of the previous subsection ignores any concerns about eventual playoff standings, which depend upon not only the team's point totals but also the team's standing relative to other teams in its division or conference. The model of Easton and Rockerbie (2005) predicts higher expected points per game when playing non-conference opponents. Although it would not be captured by the risk-neutral framework of Section 2.1, intuition suggests that a risk-averse team ahead of its opponent in the standings would play conservatively in order to avoid a loss (a net loss of 2 points relative to its opponent). This idea has been supported by empirical evidence. Shmanske and Lowenthal (2007), using data on 628 overtime games from the 2002–2003 and 2003–2004 seasons, found that home teams are seven percentage points less likely to get the extra point in overtime when playing an opponent from the same conference. Abrevaya (2004) finds that it is significantly more likely for divisional contests (24.7%) to go to overtime under the new rules than non-divisional contests (21.4%).

Another possible scoring scheme that has been discussed in the literature is the awarding of three points (rather than two points) for a win during regulation time. The model of Banerjee, Swinnen, and Weersink (2007) predicts that such an increase in rewards for a regulation win would prevent teams from playing defensively during regular time.[7] Note that a similar prediction can be derived from the framework in Section 2.1.[8] Although this rule has not been adopted by the NHL, Franck and Theiler (2009) offer empirical evidence from a Swiss hockey league (which adopted the three-point rule in 2006) that the rule is effective in reducing the incentive to tie in regulation time.

Finally, we briefly mention some studies that touch upon other aspects of the overtime system. Brocas and Carrillo (2004) consider the incentives of sudden-death (versus non-sudden-death) play in soccer overtime. Carrillo (2007), also within the context of soccer, recommends a shootout *prior* to overtime with the shootout outcome binding only if the overtime ends without a goal; this rule change would cause the shootout loser (winner) to become more aggressive (defensive) in overtime. Brimberg and Hurley (2008) fit a statistical model to NHL overtime results (and goal timing in overtime) and predict that over 70 percent of overtime games would end with a goal if overtime were extended to 10 minutes (as compared to the roughly 45 percent that currently end with a goal under the five-minute overtime format).

3. Data and Empirical Analysis

The data for this chapter were compiled from game-by-game NHL season logs starting with the 1991–1992 season and ending with the 2008–2009 season.[9] The NHL regular season begins in October and ends the following April. Two work stoppages affected games during the period of analysis. The first work stoppage shortened the 1994–1995 season to just 48 regular-season games (as opposed to the usual 80-plus regular-season games), with play commencing in January rather than October. The second work stoppage was more serious, resulting in cancellation of the entire 2004–2005 season (including the Stanley Cup Playoffs that season). The complete sample consists of 18,897 regular-season games between the 1991–1992 and 2008–2009 seasons. A sample of 1,451 playoff games during this time period was also compiled.

Table 10.3 provides descriptive statistics on the percentage of overtime games under the three NHL overtime rules, with the top panel summarizing the regular-season games and the bottom panel summarizing the playoff games. For regular-season games, the percentage of overtime games ended by a goal is also reported for the three overtime rules. The effects of the 1999–2000 overtime rule are as predicted in the previous section. The percentage of overtime games increased from 19.0 percent under the old overtime rule (between 1991–1992 and 1998–1999) to 23.6 percent under the new overtime rule (1999–2000 to 2004–2005), an increase of about a quarter. For regular-season overtime games, the percentage ended by a

Table 10.3 Descriptive Statistics for Different NHL Overtime Rule Regimes

	Old overtime rule (1991–1992 to 1998–1999)	New overtime rule (1999–2000 to 2004–2005)	New shootout rule (2005–2006 to 2008–2009)
Regular season games			
Percentage of games that go into overtime (s.e. in parentheses)	19.02% (0.44%)	23.60% (0.55%)	22.68% (0.60%)
Percentage of overtime games ended by a goal (s.e. in parentheses)	30.85% (1.19%)	45.95% (1.32%)	44.09% (1.49%)
number of games	7,909	6,068	4,920
number of overtime games	1,504	1,432	1,116
number of shootout games	n/a	n/a	624
Playoff games			
Percentage of games that go into overtime (s.e. in parentheses)	22.42% (1.60%)	21.51% (1.97%)	20.54% (2.21%)
number of playoff games	678	437	336

goal increased by about a half, from 30.9 percent under the old overtime rule to 46.0 percent under the new overtime rule. Both of these percentages remained approximately the same (decreasing 1–2 percentage points) when the overtime rule was changed to include a shootout (2005–2006 to 2008–2009). At first glance, then, there do not seem to be additional effects on these quantities from the addition of the shootout rule. The overtime percentages for playoff games are reasonably similar across the three different rule regimes, which is expected since the rule changes affected only regular-season games; these percentages indicate that the pattern in regular-season percentages is attributable to the rule changes rather than some other time trend in overtime-game prevalence (e.g., caused by a change in league parity).

Figures 10.1 and 10.2 provide additional detail on the likelihood of overtime games and the likelihood of overtime games being ended by a goal, respectively. These figures plot the respective season-by-season percentages (excluding the cancelled 2004–2005 season). A vertical line is drawn at 1999–2000 to indicate the first rule change (guarantee of one point in overtime), and another is drawn at 2005–2006 to indicate the second rule change (introduction of a shootout). In both plots, the difference prior to and after the 1999–2000 seasons is evident; each percentage from 1999–2000 and beyond is larger than all of the percentages prior to the 1999–2000 season. Again, however, there seems to be little evidence of a change in either the overtime percentage or the overtime-ending-in-goal percentage after the introduction of the shootout rule in 2005–2006.

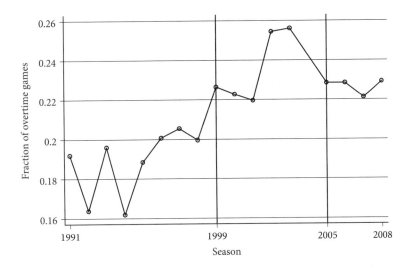

Figure 10.1 Likelihood of an overtime game in the NHL,
1991–1992 to 2008–2009.
(*Notes*: Season labels correspond to the beginning year (e.g., 1991 refers
to the 1991–1992 season). The vertical line at 1999 indicates the first
season of the new overtime rule. The vertical line at 2005 indicates
the first season of the shootout rule).

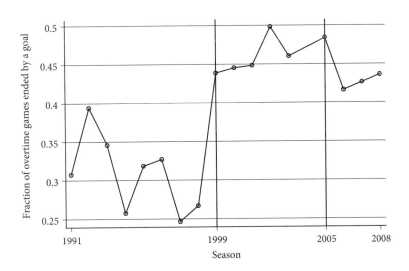

Figure 10.2 Likelihood of a goal an overtime game in
the NHL, 1991–1992 to 2008–2009.
(*Notes*: Season labels correspond to the beginning year (e.g., 1991
refers to the 1991–1992 season). The vertical line at 1999 indicates
the first season of the new overtime rule. The vertical line
at 2005 indicates the first season of the shootout rule).

Table 10.4 Regression Results, Full Sample

	Dependent variable (with relevant sample in parentheses)			
	Overtime (all games)	Goal in Overtime (overtime games)	Home Win in Overtime Game (non-tied overtime games)	Home Win in Shootout Game (shootout games)
New overtime rule (1999–2000 and after)	0.0462** (0.0070)	0.1507** (0.0178)	0.0836** (0.0298)	
New shootout rule (2005–2006 and after)	−0.0118 (0.0081)	−0.0206 (0.0199)	−0.0334 (0.0296)	
Absolute value of difference in team winning percentage	−0.1673** (0.0281)	0.0171 (0.0803)		
Home-team winning percentage			0.4496** (0.1029)	0.0073 (0.1880)
Visiting-team winning percentage			−0.4419** (0.1075)	−0.0636 (0.1912)
Days into season	0.000070 (0.000058)	0.000360** (0.000149)	0.000009 (0.000241)	0.000045 (0.000394)
number of observations	18,897	4,052	1,614	624

Notes: Each column represents a separate regression. Each dependent variable is binary, and the reported coefficient estimates are from linear regression models (linear probability models). Robust standard errors are reported. Asterisks indicate statistical significance based upon a two-sided test (**: p-value < 0.05, *: p-value < 0.10).

To assess the statistical significance and magnitude of the changes caused by the overtime rule changes, Table 10.4 reports regression results for the complete sample of regular-season games. Four different binary outcomes are considered: (1) overtime (i.e., a tie at the end of regulation); (2) goal in overtime (conditional on being in overtime); (3) home win in overtime (conditional on a goal being scored in overtime); and (4) home win in a shootout (conditional on being in a shootout). For ease of interpretation, linear probability models (estimated by linear regression) were used for each of the four outcomes.[10] Indicators for the two new overtime rules were included for the first three regressions; the shootout-outcome regression includes only games from the latest rule regime. The estimates on the "new shootout rule" variable should be interpreted as incremental effects above and beyond the post-1999 "new overtime rule" variable. Team winning percentages are included as control variables, with the absolute difference in winning percentage used for the overtime and goal-in-overtime regressions and the home-team and visiting-team winning percentages separately included for the overtime-home-win and shootout-home-win regressions.[11] Finally, the date of the game (as measured by the number of days since the beginning of the season) is included as a control variable, to allow for the possibility that the incentive effects may differ later in the season.

The overtime rule introduced in 1999–2000 increased the probability of overtime games by 4.62 percentage points (s.e. 0.70), which is in line with the prediction above. The addition of the shootout format in 2005–2006 had an insignificant (and negative) effect on the probability of an overtime game, which does not support the prediction that the shootout format would lead to a greater incentive for reaching overtime. A possible explanation is that the incremental incentive was not that large (going from an additional 0.20–0.25 points in expectation to an additional 0.50 points in expectation),[12] and the number of seasons under the shootout format (four in the sample) is not large enough to estimate the effect precisely enough. For the other control variables, the absolute difference in team quality has a significant negative effect on the likelihood of overtime but the days-into-season variable is statistically insignificant.

The goal-in-overtime regression results are somewhat similar to the overtime regression results, with a significant positive effect found after the 1999–2000 rule change (15.07 percentage point (s.e. 1.78) increase in overtime-goal likelihood) and no significant effect for the introduction of the shootout rule. The negative estimate on the shootout-rule coefficient is in line with the prediction that fewer overtime goals would be scored under the shootout regime, but this estimate is statistically insignificant (z-statistic slightly over one). The absolute difference in team quality has a positive, but insignificant, effect. Unlike the overtime regression, the days-into-season variable has a significantly positive effect. For example, a game that occurs three months later (90 days) has a goal probability that is 3.24 percentage points higher.

Among games that have goals scored in overtime, the estimates indicate that the home team was more likely to win (8.36 percentage points (s.e. 2.98)) after the new overtime rule was enacted in 1999–2000. Although the previous section does not offer predictions about the home-team win probability in overtime (due to assumptions about symmetry), it is possible that the reduction in skaters is more advantageous for the team with crowd support. Again, there is no additional significant effect found for the introduction of the shootout. Not surprisingly, the home-win probability is also significantly positively (negatively) related to the winning percentage of the home (visiting) team.

For shootout games (a sample of 624 games between the 2005–2006 and 2008–2009 seasons), the probability of a home win in the shootout does not depend upon the team winning percentages. Both the home-team winning percentage and visiting-team winning percentage are statistically insignificant (very low z-statistics), supporting our basic assumption that the shootout is essentially a coin flip. Of course, it is possible that more subtle factors (goalie save percentage, quality of top offensive players, etc.) affect the shootout-win probability, but such a consideration is a topic for future research.

To determine whether the effects of the control variables vary over the three overtime rule regimes, Table 10.5 reports regression results when the sample is split on the basis of the overtime rule regime. The same dependent variables from Table 10.4, except for the shootout win, are considered. Some interesting

Table 10.5 Regression Results, by Overtime Rule Regime

	Dependent variable (with relevant sample in parentheses)		
	Overtime (all games)	Goal in Overtime (overtime games)	Home Win in Overtime Game (non-tied overtime games)
Old overtime rule (1991–1992 to 1998–1999)			
Absolute value of difference in team winning percentage	−0.1770** (0.0389)	0.2345* (0.1248)	
Home-team winning percentage			0.5979** (0.1803)
Visiting-team winning percentage			−0.4207** (0.1903)
Days into season	−0.000001 (0.000083)	0.000232 (0.000230)	−0.000233 (0.000455)
number of observations	7,909	1,504	464
New overtime rule, no shootout (1999–2000 to 2004–2005)			
Absolute value of difference in team winning percentage	−0.1581** (0.0532)	−0.1162 (0.1356)	
Home-team winning percentage			0.5359** (0.1566)
Visiting-team winning percentage			−0.4997** (0.1651)
Days into season	−0.000062 (0.000108)	0.000692** (0.000259)	−0.000357 (0.000385)
number of observations	6,068	1,432	658
New overtime rule, shootout (2005–2006 to 2008–2009)			
Absolute value of difference in team winning percentage	−0.1592** (0.0607)	−0.1273 (0.1620)	
Home-team winning percentage			0.1357 (0.2061)
Visiting-team winning percentage			−0.3208 (0.2153)
Days into season	0.000347** (0.000117)	0.000112 (0.000289)	0.000692 (0.000427)
number of observations	4,920	1,116	492

Notes: Each column contains three separate regressions, one for each overtime regime (old overtime rule, new overtime rule without shootout, and new overtime rule with shootout). Each dependent variable is binary, and the reported coefficient estimates are from linear regression models (linear probability models). Robust standard errors are reported. Asterisks indicate statistical significance based upon a two-sided test (**: p-value < 0.05, *: p-value < 0.10).

differences and similarities emerge in the results. For overtime probabilities, the effect of relative team quality is quite similar across the three rule regimes, but the effect of the days-into-season variable is significantly positive only for the shootout regime. For the goal-in-overtime probability, the difference in team winning percentage has a positive and significant effect only under the old overtime rule (prior to 1999–2000). Recall that teams were playing more conservatively (and also with five skaters) under the old rules, in which case we would expect team quality to have more of an impact. Finally, for the home-win probability in overtime games, the effects of team winning percentage are statistically significant and quite similar in magnitude for the first two rule regimes, but the effects of team winning percentage are insignificant under the shootout regime.

4. CONCLUSION

This chapter has considered the effects of different overtime rule schemes within the National Hockey League. Section 2 introduced a simple framework for analyzing the two important changes that affected how points were awarded for NHL games, the first guaranteeing a point for overtime losses starting in 1999–2000 and the second introducing a shootout format in 2005–2006. Section 2 reviewed the literature that has looked at the incentive effects of the 1999–2000 rule change. Since no previous work has considered the effect of the shootout rule, we compiled a large sample of NHL games over a period (1991–1992 through 2008–2009) that included both rule changes. Section 3 provided an empirical analysis of this dataset. The basic results were in line with the predictions (and previous work) regarding the 1999–2000 rule change: both overtime games and overtime goals became significantly more likely under the new rule. Interestingly, despite the framework's prediction that the shootout rule would intensify these incentive effects, the empirical analysis did not uncover any additional significant effects from the introduction of the shootout format in 2005–2006.

The empirical analysis undertaken here is admittedly a first step, and further research is warranted. A more detailed look at the shootout incentives, both theoretically (in models allowing for team heterogeneity) and empirically (using additional control variables and, in the future, more seasons of data), would be interesting. In addition, aside from using naïve controls for how late in the season a game occurs, no previous research has taken a serious look at how the overtime incentives dynamically change over the course of the season for individual teams. While the examination of conference versus non-conference (or division versus non-division) contests is a step in this direction, it would be interesting to actually track exactly how many points behind (or ahead) teams are at different times in the season to get a better measure of how teams should be affected by the incentives. Such a study would be similar, say, to the work on professional golf done by Ehrenberg and Bognanno (1990).

NOTES

1 Alternatively, variation in compensation schemes can cause incentives to differ depending upon a competitor's relative standing in comparison to other competitors. For example, Ehrenberg and Bognanno (1990) study nonlinear incentive effects associated with tournament payouts in professional golf, and Taylor and Trogdon (2002) study the (perverse) incentive effects caused by the National Basketball Association's draft lottery system.

2 While the NHL has implemented many other rule changes over the last two decades, this chapter focuses only on those changes that directly affected the way points are awarded to teams.

3 The exact wording of the new rules: "During regular-season games, if at the end of the three regular 20-minute periods, the score shall be tied, each team shall be awarded one point in the League standings. The teams will then play an additional overtime period of not more than five minutes with the team scoring first declared the winner and being awarded an additional point. The overtime period shall be played with each team at a numerical strength of four skaters and one goalkeeper" (currently part of Rule 84 in the NHL Official Rules).

4 There is one exception to the one-point guarantee. If a team pulls its goalie to have an extra skater on the ice during overtime, that team will not receive the one point if they allow a goal. A team might pursue such a strategy near the end of the season when it needs two points for playoff-seeding (or playoff-making) reasons. Examples of this rule exception occurred on April 7, 2000 (Vancouver Canucks losing their point versus the Edmonton Oilers), and March 25, 2003 (Los Angeles Kings losing their point versus the Columbus Blue Jackets).

5 This assumption is a good first-order approximation. As shown in Section 3, there is no significant relationship between shootout-win probability and team quality (as measured by winning percentage).

6 It makes sense to treat p^O as fixed here. The style of play for overtime would not be "chosen" by the team until overtime play begins. At this stage, however, the team can fully anticipate what value of p^O it will subsequently choose.

7 Brocas and Carrillo (2004) offer the same theoretical prediction for the three-point rule in soccer.

8 If $X_W^R = 3$ (instead of $X_W^R = 2$), expected points for tied games in regulation are given by $1 + p^R$, $1 + p^O + (1 - 2p^O)p^R$, and $\frac{3}{2}$, respectively, for the old rule, new rule without shootout, and new rule with shootout. The partial derivative of the first two expressions w.r.t. p^R is positive, indicating an incentive to pursue more aggressive play. Note, however, that the extra points available due to a shootout exactly counterbalance this effect so that there is no incentive for either aggressive or defensive play under the new rule with shootout.

9 The sample was compiled from http://www.hockey-reference.com.

10 Probit regressions qualitatively yielded very similar results.

11 To be comparable across the three different rule regimes, winning percentage was defined as the percentage of *non-overtime* games that a team won in that season.

12 Looking at Figure 10.2, the likelihood of a goal in overtime is between 0.40 and 0.50 between 1999–2000 and 2004–2005, meaning that the expected incremental points (under symmetry) is between (0.5)(0.40) and (0.5)(0.50).

References

Abrevaya, Jason. (2004). Fit to be tied: The incentive effects of overtime rules in professional hockey. *Journal of Sports Economics* 5: 292–306.

Banerjee, Anurag N., Johan F. M. Swinnen, and Alfons Weersink. (2007). Skating on thin ice: Rule changes and team strategies in the NHL. *Canadian Journal of Economics* 40: 493–514.

Brimberg, Jack, and W. J. Hurley (2008). Is the overtime period in an NHL game long enough? An example for teaching estimation and hypothesis testing in the presence of censored data. *The American Statistician* 62: 151–154.

Brocas, Isabelle, and Juan D. Carrillo. (2004). Do the "three-point victory" and "golden goal" rules make soccer more exciting? *Journal of Sports Economics* 5: 169–185.

Carrillo, Juan D. (2007). Penalty shoot-outs: Before or after extra time? *Journal of Sports Economics* 8: 505–518.

Dilger, Alexander, and Hannah Geyer. (2009). Are three points for a win really better than two? A comparison of German soccer league and cup games. *Journal of Sports Economics* 10: 305–318.

Easton, Stephen T., and Duane W. Rockerbie. (2005). Overtime! Rules and incentives in the National Hockey League. *Journal of Sports Economics* 6: 178–202.

Ehrenberg, Ronald G., and Michael L. Bognanno. (1990). Do tournaments have incentive effects? *Journal of Political Economy* 98: 1307–1342.

Franch, Egon, and Philipp Theiler. (2009). One for sure or three maybe: Empirical evidence for overtime play from Swiss ice hockey. Institute for Strategy and Business Economics (University of Zurich) Working Paper Series, Working Paper No. 93.

Longley, Neil, and Swaminathan Sankaran. (2007). The incentive effects of overtime rules in professional hockey: A comment and extension. *Journal of Sports Economics* 8: 546–554.

Shmanske, Stephen, and Franklin Lowenthal. (2007). Overtime incentives in the National Hockey League (NHL): More evidence. *Journal of Sports Economics* 8: 435–442.

Taylor, Beck A., and Justin G. Trogdon. (2002). Losing to win: Tournament incentives in the National Basketball Association. *Journal of Labor Economics* 20: 23–41.

SECTION 4

FOOTBALL

CHAPTER 11

FIELD POSITION AND STRATEGY IN AMERICAN FOOTBALL

KEVIN G. QUINN

1. INTRODUCTION

SPORTING contests feature a unique combination of a relatively pure utility func-tion, a clear set of rules, and well-understood institutions. The choices that on-field managers make are quite public, and highly detailed records of these choices and their pay-offs are a fundamental part of modern sport spectatorship. The result is a hybrid of real and laboratory behavior that lends itself well to analysis of in-game strategic decision-making using the optimization and rationality assumptions that underpin classical economic thinking—and that have been challenged by the bur-geoning field of behavioral economics.

Game strategy as analytical fodder for academic inquiry is not a new concept. Modern probability theory traces its beginning to an exchange of letters between Blaise Pascal and Pierre Fermat in 1654 concerning the equitable division of the stakes in prematurely stopped games of chance. Jakob Bernoulli's thirty-five page "Letter to a Friend on Sets in Court Tennis," published posthumously in 1713 as part of *Ars Conjectandi* (The Art of Conjecturing), was another early landmark in the field (Hald, 2005). Interest in analyzing games with *a priori* unknown out-comes provided inspiration for the first probability theory textbook five years later (de Moivre, 1718). More recently, Zermelo's Theorem (1913), widely recognized as game theory's first formal theorem, resulted from ruminations about the mathe-matics of chess outcomes (Schwalbe and Walker, 2001).

The application of probability and game theory to questions of strategy in athletic contests remains a particular area of interest to probability theorists, sports economists, behavioral economists, and sports team decision-makers. Among the major North American sports, baseball enjoys the deepest tradition of using statistical information to steer on-field strategy. Henry Chadwick, a journalist best known for his nineteenth-century evangelism of the game, also advocated assiduous analysis of statistical data to assign appropriate credit for teams' competitive outcomes (Schiff, 2008). His philosophy and approach to questions of management and productivity are remarkably similar to those found in *The Principles of Scientific Management* (Taylor, 1911), but Chadwick's work predates Taylorism by nearly half a century.

While the recording and calculation of various and sundry statistics continued to be regarded as an integral element of baseball throughout the first half of the twentieth century, rigorous analyses of common "by-the-book" strategies were virtually nonexistent until the publication of *Percentage Baseball*, an ambitious but flawed 400-page volume (Cook, 1964). The modern manifestation of such analysis, sabermetrics, is now widely, but not universally, used in the daily strategy choices made by field managers and general managers. Basketball strategy in recent years has been the focus of similar analyses (e.g., Oliver, 2003, and Berri, Schmidt, and Brook, 2006). By comparison, rigorous and sophisticated statistical treatments of the game of football have been relatively uncommon in the academic literature, and the state of the art yet lags both baseball and basketball (Schatz, 2005).

The discussion that follows will assume that readers have a functional knowledge of the game of American football, as well as the relatively small differences between the two major forms of the game in the United States: as played by National Football League (NFL) teams, and as played by college teams under the auspices of the National Collegiate Athletic Association (NCAA).[1,2]

2. THE QUANTITATIVE ANALYSIS OF FOOTBALL: THEORETICAL CONSIDERATIONS

Background

Interest in the "science" of American football was part of the sport's earliest days in the last half of the nineteenth century (Oriard, 1991), with large amounts of data available for individual NFL games becoming available as early as the

1930s (Stern, 1997).[3] In the 1940s, legendary coach Paul Brown began to apply statistical analysis to opponent play-calling tendencies, as well to player physical and mental evaluations. Twenty years later, Dallas Cowboys general manager Tex Schramm pioneered the use of computers in the collection and analysis of entering player talent (Lahman, 2008). These efforts, and likely many others, remained proprietary, and academic econometricians and statisticians today would regard this work as relatively unsophisticated. More recently, a few publicly available web sites have investigated the creation and analysis of new statistics for use in ranking the competitive quality of National Football League teams. Generally meant as an aid for wagering on the sport, either via legal and illegal gambling markets, or through the proxy of fantasy games, these analyses have not typically been subjected to the usual scholarly peer-review process.[4,5] Consequently, much of this work has not gained universal acceptance by academic sports economists.

While these new quantitative machinations are beginning to have an impact on the way that football teams make on- and off-field decisions, they seem far less influential than is sabermetrics on baseball. Perhaps the most notable user of sophisticated statistical analysis in the NFL is Bill Belichick, head coach of the New England Patriots since 2000. Between the 2000 and 2008 seasons, the Patriots posted a 102–42 regular season record (.708), and have had four Super Bowl appearances (three wins, one loss). The tradition of the team's reliance on advanced statistical analysis may predate Belichick, however. From 1973 through 2005, the team employed statistician Pete Palmer, co-author of decidedly sabermetric-like compendia such as *The Football Abstract* and *The Hidden Game of Football*. It may well be that several other teams have been more favorably disposed to such analysis than has been generally recognized, but there is no reliable evidence of this readily available.

In any event, it is obvious that most football coaches rely more on heuristic traditions than on sophisticated data-driven statistical analysis. This is well-illustrated by the following comments by a former head coach of the NFL's Pittsburgh Steelers:

> "It's easy to sit there and apply a formula," said Bill Cowher, "but it's not the easiest thing to do on Sunday. There's so much more involved with the game than just sitting there, looking at the numbers and saying, 'Okay, these are my percentages, then I'm going to do it this way,' because that one time it doesn't work could cost your team a football game, and that's the thing a head coach has to live with, not the professor." To which he added: "If we all listened to the professor, we may be all looking for professor jobs." (Lewis, 2006)

Cowher's remarks are notable given his on-field success during his 1992–2006 Steelers coaching tenure: a 240–149 (.623) regular season record, and a 12–9 postseason record, including two Super Bowl appearances (1–1). Rules-of-thumb clearly dominate decision-making processes for at least some of football's most successful decision-makers.

Dynamic Programming Modeling

Perhaps the lesser degree of acceptance of sophisticated statistical analysis among football coaches than among baseball managers is due to an inherently greater analytical complexity in football than in baseball, at least insofar as on-field strategy typically has been modeled by academics. Game-theoretic concepts of in-contest decisions treat them as nodes in a sequential games under imperfect information, that is, as dynamic programming problems in which strategy choices are control variables in Bellman equations.[6] Sporting contests, of course, are necessarily zero-sum games in which the rationality assumption implies that win probability be maximized over the available control variables. However, in-contest strategy models in the literature often have used offensive production as the maximand. In either case, the relevant Bellman equation is solved via backward induction, a technique first used theoretically by von Neumann and Morgenstern (1944; Schwalbe and Walker, 2001).

In the analysis of actual sporting contest problems, backward induction can become computationally intensive. Bellman's (1977) own analysis of baseball strategy considered a total of 2,593 possible states in each inning, a large number, but hardly challenging for the computer capability available even at that time. Indeed, the tractability of dynamic programming models for baseball is evidenced by the set of similar academic papers published in the decades preceding and following Bellman's. These studies examined several common strategy choices that managers make, including batting order decisions, whether or not to attempt a stolen base or a sacrifice bunt, whether to issue an opposing player an intentional walk.[7]

In general, the Achilles heel of the dynamic programming analysis of in-contest decision-making is the volume of data necessary to estimate the relevant nodal probabilities. However, the nature of the Major League Baseball (MLB) season provides a large number of trials over which probabilities can be calculated; given the range of baseball problems' state space, one or a few seasons of information generally is sufficient to obtain reasonably precise estimates of the probabilities needed to solve many interesting strategy problems.[8] Unfortunately, the same cannot be said for football—the state space is not only much larger in models designed to address the most interesting football strategy problems, but data issues render considerably less certain the probability estimates required by those models.

The fundamental unit of football strategy analysis typically is the individual play. The game conditions during which any given play occurs include down, field position (any one of 99 different yard lines), quarter, time left in the quarter, differential game score, field conditions, and so on. Play strategy choices include all manner of runs and passes involving individual players of widely varying skills across a large number of dimensions. Play outcomes are: advancing the ball from −98 to +98 yards, scoring a touchdown (+7 points), kicking a field goal (+3 points), giving up a safety (−2 points), or a turnover of possession via a punt, downs, fumble, or interception (each with its own range of individual outcomes).[9] The Bellman equations that result from realistic models of in-contest football strategy choices become quite large compared to those for baseball. One "simple" student project analysis found approximately 500,000 possible states could exist for each first-half play in a game (Johnston et al., 2004). This number represents perhaps as much as an order of magnitude (or more) greater than even the more complex models considered for the analysis of interesting in-contest baseball strategy problems.

These bulky state spaces imply that football's dynamic programming problems require very large data sets to estimate the relevant decision node probabilities with any precision and confidence, considerably larger than for a typical dynamic programming model of a baseball contest. Worse, the number of relevant events in any given football season (from which these data must be drawn) is considerably smaller than those available during one baseball season. In the NFL, there are only a total of 512 regular season contests annually (16 games per season for 32 team-seasons). In college football, the data situation is a little better—NCAA Division I FBS (the top tier of the sport) features a total of about three times as many games per season as the NFL (approximately 12 or 13 games per team-season for approximately 120 teams). (Interestingly, despite its popularity, in-contest strategy analysis of the college game has enjoyed very little rigorous quantitative attention in peer-reviewed academic journals.)[10] The 1,171 offensive possessions (that average 5.54 plays each) that occurred during the 2007 NFL season represent only about 0.6 percent of the plate appearances in a typical MLB season. More finely, the just-under 6,000 individual plays in an NFL season number correspond to less than 1 percent of the number of pitches every year in MLB (Quinn and von Allmen, 2008; Kovash and Levitt, 2009).

Furthermore, the specific data necessary to estimate the relevant nodal outcomes in dynamic programming models of interest are typically far more readily and economically available for MLB baseball than for either NFL or NCAA football, although this is beginning to change. For example, STATS, Inc., offers a product that provides real-time textual descriptions of more than 200 potential play-by-play events during an NFL game (STATS, 2009). Even so, the football statistics that have traditionally been collected and recorded bear significantly less relationship to those necessary for the estimation of relevant nodal probabilities for dynamic programming models than is the case for baseball.

Football's inherent complexity combined with insufficient data availability have meant that dynamic programming analyses of the game in the academic literature typically have been limited to small set of dichotomous strategy decisions—whether to punt, try a field goal or go for a first down on fourth down (e.g., Carter and Machol, 1971 and 1978; Romer, 2006), whether to attempt an on-side kick (e.g., Sackrowitz, 2004), or whether to try for a one- or a two-point-after-touchdown conversion (e.g., Sackrowitz, 2000). Interestingly, these analyses often conclude that real-world decision-making in these relatively tractable problems is convincingly suboptimal.

Production Function Analysis

The estimation of production functions in sport begins with Scully's (1974) marginal revenue product investigation into the degree to which MLB's reserve system resulted in the economic exploitation of players. This paper used team data to estimate a production function that suggested the marginal contribution of individual statistics to winning. A large literature patterning itself after Scully has since emerged. However, there has been relatively little application of production function theory to the matter of point-scoring during a game, particularly to sports other than baseball.

Production function analysis of in-contest strategy requires far less data than necessary in the use of dynamic programming to investigate the same questions. The application of these models to basketball and football typically involve estimation using regression analysis of offensive possession outcomes over a relatively small number of explanatory variables using data sets from one or a few seasons. The degrees of freedom in such estimates allows for fairly sharp t-scores and F-statistics, and therefore a good degree of precision in the interpretation of those analyses. This is a significant advantage over dynamic programming studies. On the other hand, these production function models have an important disadvantage in the study of in-contest strategy: they necessarily aggregate all similar decision-making opportunities in the data set. Model coefficients therefore only represent averages across those situations considered, not true marginal contributions, significantly blurring insight into whether and how decision-making is suboptimal. Given that this is precisely the question of interest in strategy, this is a considerable compromise indeed. Furthermore, there are myriad complementarities, particularly in football, that simple production function models often do not capture very well.

Examples of early work in production function analysis of in-contest strategy estimate the marginal contributions of various actions in basketball; e.g., rebounds, three-point vs. two-point shooting, turnovers (e.g., Zak, et al., 1979; Berri, 1999; and Berri et al., 2006). Berri et al. (2006), in particular, find some interesting results that suggest suboptimality in the NBA's version of the sport, at least in the market for players with certain skills. Production function estimation also was used in Carmichael et al. (2000) to evaluate strategies in English Premier League Football. Discussion of similar other work can be found in Hadley et al. (2000) and Borland (2006).

Stochastic Analysis of Managerial Efficiency

Porter and Scully (1982) pose the sport team manager's problem as a Darwinian game of transforming inputs into outputs, allowing for "considerable dispersion" in the efficiency with which managers employ their talent endowments in the pursuit of wins. They also note that the data that are available in sports do not exist for other kinds of managers, so that estimates in this dispersion among sports managers may provide insight into similar dispersions in other industries. They employed the frontier production function method as developed by Timmer (1971), Forsund and Hjalmarsson (1974), and Schmidt and Lovell (1979) in their analysis. Scully (1994) further applied stochastic production function models to relate manager survival in his job to his managerial efficiency in baseball, basketball, and football. He found that while baseball and basketball coaches saw a similar relationship between efficiency and tenure, a football coach's tenure appeared to be considerably less dependent on his efficiency in using the factor endowments (player inputs) available to him.

Stochastic frontier production functions and data envelope analysis have become oft-used tools in the pursuit of questions of managerial efficiency in sports (e.g., Einolf, 2004).[11] While much of what is captured by these models does not involve the direct assessment of in-contest strategy allocation of salary dollars across different player characteristics (training routines, etc.), and the quality of in-contest strategy choices clearly has an impact on their findings.

There is evidence that differences in managerial efficiency among NFL teams are significant. Hadley et al. (2000) use a Poisson regression model to evaluate NFL head coaching efficiency over the 1969–1992 seasons. They consider efficiency to be teams' ability to convert a number of team-season offensive and defensive statistics (e.g., yards per rush, turnovers, number of first downs, pass completion percentage, etc.) into team wins for that season. They find that the difference between the average and the most efficient head coaches during that period is the equivalent of about 3.5 games per season—approximately one standard deviation of the distribution of NFL team wins per year.[12] However, due to their choice of inputs analyzed, the extent to which differences in in-contest decision-making are specifically responsible for differences in wins is cannot be determined.

3. SURVEY OF FINDINGS IN THE ACADEMIC LITERATURE

In general, the search for competitive advantage provides strong incentive for coaches and teams to keep their strategy research secret. This renders impossible any systematic review of the analyses that might have been undertaken by football practitioners throughout the history of the sport, or how reliable or theoretically rigorous any such analyses might have been, or how well diffused their conclusions might have been among other teams and coaches.

Major academic journals remained silent on matters regarding football field position and strategy until a research note by Mottley (1954). The article suggests that operations research techniques in use at the time to evaluate decision making in military and industrial settings might also be applied to questions of strategy in sports. By way of example, the note includes a discussion of a high school foot-ball team's cumulative distribution of yards gained on running plays, comparing results for plays "up the middle" versus those "around the end." Other than pro-viding a relatively simple figure of one team's data during a season, however, no detailed analysis is offered. No further mention is made of football strategy analy-sis in any of the major journals in statistics, mathematics, or economics for another seventeen years. Perhaps sports strategy problems were regarded as trifling uses of scarce, limited, and expensive electronic computing capabilities. Certainly, the data necessary to address interesting questions in football via quantitative analysis were difficult, if not impossible, to obtain until fairly recently.

Whatever the reasons for the paucity of published research on football issues, only the simplest of questions were addressable until the last decade or so. More advanced work necessary to put the analysis of football contests on a footing with that of baseball is only beginning to occur. Consequently, surveys of the academic economics and statistical literature on in-contest decision-making strategy in the sport mostly fall into just a few categories: the value of field position, fourth down strategy, and very elementary work on the run/pass play calling mix.[13]

Quinn and von Allmen (2008) compiled data on NFL team offensive drive statistics—average data for the 2003 through 2007 seasons, and detailed individual drive data for the 2007 season. Descriptive statistics for these data are shown in Table 11.1, Table 11.2, and Figure 11.1.[14]

The Value of Field Position

The first substantially sophisticated analysis of football field position was pro-vided by Carter and Machol (1971). Virgil Carter, then a quarterback for the NFL's Cincinnati Bengals, had met Robert Machol, a professor of systems analysis, while earning his MBA degree at Northwestern during his career with the Chicago Bears. After leaving Chicago for Cincinnati following the 1969 season, Carter taught math and statistics part-time at Xavier University. He also lent both his name and exper-tise on the use of statistical analysis to dinner sales seminars hosted by software vendor A. O. Smith (Levin, 2003).

The analysis in Carter and Machol (1971) made use of A. O. Smith's computing resources to analyze play-by-play data for the first half of the 1969 NFL season (56 games, 8,373 individual plays, 53 separate variables per play). An expected value of points scored was associated with first down field position; that is, for each yard line of starting field position, X, an expected value, E(X), of points scored from that yard line. The same analysis was performed on a subset of this data, 1,258 first down plays following a change of possession (i.e., first plays of offensive drives), with similar results. These analyses created a system of 99 equations in 99 unknowns, the solution to which was beyond the capability of the data set gathered, so indi-vidual field position observations were grouped into ten yard intervals. Figure 11.2

Table 11.1 2003–2007, Team-Season Drive Averages

	Mean	Std Dev	Max	Min
Beginning field position of drive (own goal = 100)	70.9	1.77	86.3	76.3
Average points scored per offensive drive	1.72	0.430	3.37	0.78
Average yards gained per offensive pass attempt	6.39	0.805	8.77	4.52
Average yards gained per offensive rushing attempt	4.08	0.449	5.50	3.144

Notes: N = 160.
Source: Quinn and von Allmen (2008).

Table 11.2 Descriptive Statistics for Individual Drives during the 2007 NFL Season

	Mean	Std Dev	Max	Min
Beginning offensive field position of drive (own goal = 100)	68.1	18.6	100	1
Net yards on drive	27.4	27.3	99	−33
Number of plays on drive	5.54	3.32	24	0
Time of possession on drive (seconds)	155.5	111.1	900	0
Drive ends with TD	0.189	0.391	1	0
Drive ends with FG	0.134	0.341	1	0
Drive ends with turnover	0.143	0.352	1	0
Points resulting from drive	1.72	2.74	8	−2
Drive begins in final two minutes of half or game	0.155	–	1	0

Notes: N = 5,968. 53.4% of drives end with a punt or turned-over-on-downs.
Source: Quinn and von Allmen (2008).

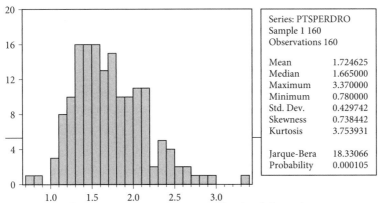

Figure 11.1 Drive outcomes: points per offensive drive using 2003–2007 team-season averages.
(*Source*: Quinn and von Allmen, 2008).

depicts the expected values derived—on the order of about 0.08 additional points in expected scoring for every additional yard of beginning field position.[15]

Quinn and von Allmen (2008) used modern statistical software to similarly analyze the relationship between starting field position for a drive and the average number of points scored on that drive for the 5,962 possessions during the 2007 NFL season. These data suggest that the marginal contribution of field position during the 2007 season was less than half (0.03 points per additional yard) of what Carter and Machol (1971) found for the 1969 season.[16]

Kovash and Levitt (2009) construct a measure of the value of field position in the NFL that measures the expected points scored before and after running a play via use of a regression model:

Y = f(down, yards to first down, distance to goal)

where Y is the change in the game score between the current time and the end of the half. They estimate their model over 127,885 first, second, and third down plays during the 2001–2005 seasons. They find that an offensive team gaining twenty yards on first down from their own twenty yard line has increased their expected

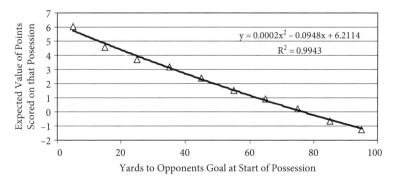

Figure 11.2 Carter and Machol (1971) Field Position Expected Values.

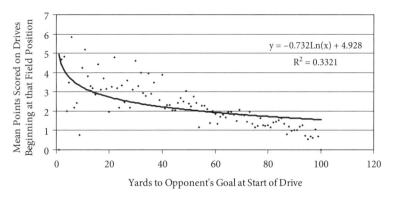

Figure 11.3 Mean Points Scored on Drive versus Starting Field Position.
(*Notes*: Average points scored by starting field position
calculated from 5,968 drives).
(*Source*: Quinn and von Allmen, 2008).

scoring in the half by approximately 0.9 points. This corresponds to an a marginal value of 0.45 points per yard of field position—a value closer to that suggested by Quinn and von Allmen (2007) than to Carter and Machol (1971).[17]

The differences in these estimates have two sources. First, the Carter and Machol (1971) and the Kovash and Levitt (2009) estimates take into account the effect on opponents' scoring associated with field position, while the Quinn and von Allmen (2008) only consider the scoring implications for the current offensive drive. Second, there have been substantial changes in the NFL game in the forty years since the 1969 season. In addition to the natural evolution of the sport during this time (better training techniques, innovations in both offensive and defensive strategy, equipment changes, etc.), a variety of important NFL rules changes affecting the balance between offensive and defensive play at different points on the field have occurred (see Table 11.3). Interestingly, these rules changes did not result in statistically significant changes in overall offensive production during this period. NFL team scoring did increase by about 4 percent between 1969 and 2007 (20.9 and 21.7 points per team per game, respectively; Pro-FootballReference.com, 2009b and 2009c), but an equality of means test does not find that this difference to be significant at even the 20 percent level. Perhaps the rules changes were designed and implemented so as to preserve the offensive-defensive balance but had as their consequence a mitigation of the importance of field position on scoring outcomes.

Figure 11.3 suggests why turnovers are of such consequence. For example, the expected scoring value to Team A of beginning a drive on their own forty yard line (sixty yards away from the goal line) is on the order of 2.0 points. On the other hand, the expected value to their opponent, Team B, of starting their drive at that field position (forty yards away from their objective) is about 2.5 points. That is about 0.8 points better than Team B's expected points associated with beginning a drive on their own thirty yard line (1.7 points), which is approximately the average starting offensive field position for teams during a season. Therefore, the difference to Team A between having the ball on their own forty, and turning the ball over at that spot is −3.3 points (−2.5−0.8). Since the average margin of victory in NFL games is approximately 3.0 points (Gray and Gray, 1997), this effect is not trivial.

The Value of a Yard Gained Running or Passing

Dynamic programming analysis of individual play situations requires considerably more data to estimate probabilities than has been readily available to researchers, and therefore does not have much of a presence in the published academic literature. Exceptions include Sahi and Shubik (1988), Boronico and Newbert (1999 and 2001), and Jordan et al. (2009). Not surprisingly, these efforts have yet to yield much in the way of comprehensive results, so production function approaches, with their lower data requirements, have become attractive to sports economists investigating the issue. A summary of the relatively small literature using production function

Table 11.3 Selected Significant NFL Rules Changes, 1969–2007

Year	Selected Significant NFL Rules Change
1969	NFL-AFL merger
1972	Hashmarks moved nearer to the center of the field
1974	Sudden-death overtime implemented; kickoffs moved from the 40- to the 35-yard line; opponent's possession following a missed field goal from beyond the 20-yard line begins at the former line of scrimmage; restrictions placed on punting team coverage to make returns easier; downfield contact with pass receivers restricted; penalties for offensive holding reduced to 10 yards; goal posts moved from the goal line to the end line
1977	Season increased from 14 to 16 games; pass defenders further restricted from contact with receivers
1978	Pass defenders even further restricted from contact with receivers; offensive pass blocking rules liberalized
1979	Blocking below the waist prohibited on punt and kickoff returns; plays now whistled dead when the quarterback ruled "in the grasp" of a tackler
1980	List of personal fouls expanded
1988	Change in the play clock timing rules to speed up the game
1994	Two-point conversion option added; kickoffs moved from the 35- to the 30-yard line; max height of kickoff tees reduced; opponent's possession following a missed field goal from beyond the 20-yard line begins at the spot of the kick (or at the 20-yard line if the kick was from inside the 20-yard line)
1995	Receivers knocked out of bounds by a defender can return to the field to make a play; quarterbacks can receive helmet radio transmissions from the bench
1996	Helmet-to-helmet hits by defenders banned
1998	Defensive players can no longer flinch to draw offensive players into an illegal procedure penalty
2001	Tighter enforcement of passer protection rules
2002	Game clock no longer stopped when quarterback is sacked
2005	"Horse collar" tackling banned; minor play clock rules change to speed up play; punt and kickoff penalty rules changed to speed up play
2006	Passers cannot be hit below the knees by tacklers; horse collar tackling further restricted

Source: The Sports Attic (2009).

estimation in football is presented in Quinn and von Allmen (2008). Such work, limited to the NFL, includes Berri (2007) and Simmons and Berri (2007). These find that find that average starting position, rushing and receiving yards, opponents' penalty yards, and number of plays run each have a statistically significant impact on the points scored by a team during a season. Berri et al. (2006) and Berri (2007) use season-long NFL team data to estimate linear regression models of net points scored for and against teams based on factors associated with ball possession acquisition, moving the ball down the field, avoiding turnovers, and conversion of scoring opportunities into points. These analyses find that an increase in the average yards per pass attempt has the same average net contribution to season points scored as an increase in average yards per rush attempt.

The sense of this finding—that a yard gained rushing is equivalent to a yard gained passing—is mirrored in Quinn and von Allmen (2008), which uses individual offensive drive data during the 2007 NFL season to estimate a left-censored (at zero) TOBIT production function model of points scored on each drive (see Table 11.4).[18] This analysis only considers offensive production and field position, but aggregates other variables by incorporating offensive and defensive team fixed effects. The TOBIT coefficient values for the average contribution to scoring on a given of one additional yard rushing on that drive (0.198) is quite similar to that of one additional yard passing (0.194), but each is a bit higher than the TOBIT coefficient value of an additional yard of starting field position (0.170).

These results should not be terribly surprising. Points scored on an individual drive (productive output) is the result of advancing the ball down the field (productive input). The marginal product of an additional yard gained is indifferent to the specific raw input (passing yards or rushing yards) used to supply that additional yard.

The "Passing Premium Puzzle"

Perhaps the most basic strategy decision facing an offensive football team is the choice on any given play between a run and pass. While a yard gained via passing might be identically as productive as a yard gained via running, it is not necessarily the case that the expected number of yards gained will be identical for each option in each instance. In a risk-neutral environment, assuming declining marginal returns to each strategy, efficiency suggests that the return to each strategy be equalized at the margin.[19] The equalization of expected outcomes of running and passing choices does not necessarily solely depend on neoclassical diminishing marginal returns, however. Von Neumann's minimax theory for two-person zero sum games—an apt description of the offense/defense strategy decision situation—also requires that the expected pay-offs across all options must be equalized (Kovash and Levitt, 2009). Furthermore, the minimax theorem also requires that the strategies chosen by offensive coaches be random; that is, that there should be no serial correlation, in run/pass play selection. Rational, efficient offensive play callers would not only mix runs and passes so as to have identical expected values for yards gained, but would choose them without any detectable patterns that might be exploited by defenses.

There is substantial evidence that the simultaneous criteria of expected value equalization and no serial correlation are not met in the NFL. Instead, there is a higher yards return to passing plays than to running plays that has remained

Table 11.4 TOBIT Regression for Individual Drives during the 2007 NFL Season

Variable	Coefficient	z	Variable	Coefficient	Z
C	4.217***	8.404			
FP	-0.170***	-42.100			
YDS_PASS	0.194***	53.937			
YDS_RUSH	0.198***	42.069			
DEFTEAM=ATL	-0.778	-1.696	DRIVINGTEAM=ATL	-0.528	-1.087
DEFTEAM=BAL	0.198	0.431	DRIVINGTEAM=BAL	-0.391	-0.806
DEFTEAM=BUF	-0.911	-1.889	DRIVINGTEAM=BUF	-0.824	-1.616
DEFTEAM=CAR	-1.042**	-2.236	DRIVINGTEAM=CAR	-0.275	-0.563
DEFTEAM=CHI	-1.215**	-2.561	DRIVINGTEAM=CHI	-0.213	-0.443
DEFTEAM=CIN	-0.403	-0.860	DRIVINGTEAM=CIN	-0.207	-0.447
DEFTEAM=CLE	-0.437	-0.945	DRIVINGTEAM=CLE	-0.218	-0.474
DEFTEAM=DAL	-0.410	-0.831	DRIVINGTEAM=DAL	0.828	1.793
DEFTEAM=DEN	-0.841	-1.712	DRIVINGTEAM=DEN	0.454	0.904
DEFTEAM=DET	-1.083**	-2.289	DRIVINGTEAM=DET	0.596	1.232
DEFTEAM=GB	-1.578***	-3.266	DRIVINGTEAM=GB	0.716	1.553
DEFTEAM=HOU	-0.699	-1.484	DRIVINGTEAM=HOU	0.486	1.008
DEFTEAM=IND	-1.298	-2.531	DRIVINGTEAM=IND	0.814	1.732
DEFTEAM=JAC	-1.577***	-3.192	DRIVINGTEAM=JAC	0.340	0.713
DEFTEAM=KC	-1.090**	-2.239	DRIVINGTEAM=KC	0.284	0.550
DEFTEAM=MIA	-0.197	-0.422	DRIVINGTEAM=MIA	-0.229	-0.450

DEFTEAM=MIN	−1.242**	−2.548	DRIVINGTEAM=MIN	0.665	1.363
DEFTEAM=NE	−1.247**	−2.474	DRIVINGTEAM=NE	0.233	0.514
DEFTEAM=NO	−0.293	−0.637	DRIVINGTEAM=NO	0.470	0.999
DEFTEAM=NYG	−0.310	−0.639	DRIVINGTEAM=NYG	0.456	0.968
DEFTEAM=NYJ	−0.476	−1.061	DRIVINGTEAM=NYJ	−2.439***	−5.301
DEFTEAM=OAK	−1.249**	−2.209	DRIVINGTEAM=OAK	0.931	1.655
DEFTEAM=PHI	−1.369***	−2.813	DRIVINGTEAM=PHI	−0.104	−0.219
DEFTEAM=PIT	−0.063	−0.126	DRIVINGTEAM=PIT	−0.081	−0.173
DEFTEAM=SD	−3.462***	−6.872	DRIVINGTEAM=SD	0.130	0.273
DEFTEAM=SEA	−0.654	−1.382	DRIVINGTEAM=SEA	0.140	0.310
DEFTEAM=SF	−0.414	−0.901	DRIVINGTEAM=SF	−0.461	−0.926
DEFTEAM=STL	−0.711	−1.583	DRIVINGTEAM=STL	−2.151***	−4.506
DEFTEAM=TB	−0.887	−1.747	DRIVINGTEAM=TB	−0.112	−0.241
DEFTEAM=TEN	−1.146**	−2.306	DRIVINGTEAM=TEN	0.524	1.098
DEFTEAM=WAS	−0.753	−1.545	DRIVINGTEAM=WAS	−0.019	−0.039
R^2	0.579		Prob(F)	0.000	

Notes: N = 5032. Dependent variable = Points Scored on Drive. Left-Censored at 0. FP = Beginning field position of drive (own goal =100); Yds_Pass and Yds_Rush = yards gained on drive via passing and via rushing, respectively; ARI dummies dropped. *** = significant at 1% level; ** = significant at 5% level.
Source: Quinn and von Allmen (2008).

stubbornly robust. In fact, Alamar (2006) finds that the return to passing in the NFL has been increasing, but that there has been no commensurate increase in the use of that strategy.

Between 1960 and 2006, NFL completion rates have steadily increased from just under 50 percent to about 60 percent, while interception rates have steadily fallen from above 6 percent to about 3 percent. Meanwhile, average yards gained per pass attempt have also increased. During the 1960s and 1970s, average yards per pass attempt ranged between 4.5 and 5.0, with a sharp increase between 1978 and 1985 to about 5.7, and since have again become relatively constant. On the other hand, average yards gained per rushing attempt have barely deviated from about 4.0 since 1960.

These changes seem to be fairly disconnected from how coaches have opted to mix passing and running. From 1960 through about 1970, passing annually accounted for approximately 52 percent of called plays. It fell to 42 percent by the mid-1970s, returning to 1960s levels by the early 1980s. Since then, passing has accounted for a very slowly increasing percentage of offensive plays, climbing to 54 percent by the mid-2000s. Alamar terms this curious set of phenomena the "passing premium puzzle."

Quinn and von Allmen (2008) consider a three-factor Cobb-Douglas model of offensive production on a data set of teams' average season drive statistics for the 2003–2007 seasons (160 team-season observations). The three factors were average starting field position for drives during each team-season, average yards gained per rush attempt for each team-season, and average yards gained for each team-

Table 11.5 Cobb-Douglas Production Function Model of Average Team Points Scored per Offensive Drive

Variable	Coefficient	T
C	−5.132***	−6.226
ln (offensive team's average drive starting field position during season)	0.656***	2.911
ln (offensive team's average passing yards gained per pass attempt during season)	1.295***	12.681
ln (offensive team's average rushing yards gained per rushing attempt during season)	0.720***	6.019
R^2	0.565590	
Adjusted R^2	0.557236	
F	67.70***	
Prob(F)	0.000	
N	160	

Notes: Dependent Variable = ln (team average points scored per drive during season). N = 160. Data = 2003–2007 team-seasons. *** = significant at 1% level; ** = significant at 5 percent level.
Source: Quinn and von Allmen (2008).

season. The explained variable was average points scored per drive during each team-season. This estimation is shown in Table 11.5; the coefficients are interpreted as the elasticity of points scored per drive with respect to each of the three factors.

The model estimation suggests that the elasticity of points per drive vis-à-vis field position and rushing efficiency (as measured by yards per rushing attempt) have roughly similar values (i.e., .66 and .72, respectively). On the other hand, the elasticity of points per drive vis-à-vis passing efficiency (as measured by yards per pass attempt) is considerably higher (i.e., 1.30), suggesting a higher return to gains in the quality of a team's passing game than to gains in rushing or field position. This finding, like Alamar's, seems inconsistent with efficient play calling.

Rockerbie (2008) addresses the passing premium puzzle by applying portfolio theory to the run/pass decision. Coaches are assumed to know the mean yards gained by each strategy, as well as the variance of possible outcomes, in each play-calling situation. They are also assumed to have differing levels of risk aversion. This model is tested empirically using 2006 NFL data, and leads to the conclusion that teams are not passing enough.

Kovash and Levitt (2009) also find systematically higher returns to passing over running, but add another dimension to the puzzle by noting that there is serial correlation in teams' NFL run/pass strategy mixes. They estimate that the average NFL team costs itself one point per game because of these deviations from efficiency, which leads to forgoing one half a win per season—and that these mistakes translate into an opportunity cost of $5 million annually (presumably for a team that were to eliminate this inefficiency while other teams did not).

There may be some explanations for why the passing premium endures in some optimal fashion. Perhaps teams run more than they "should" because certain game situations call more for running down the clock to winning the game than for maximizing yards per play or even points. Alamar (2006) mentions possible values associated with "establishing the run" that may pay off elsewhere. However, the magnitude of the premium seems to strongly suggest that non-optimality is in the mix.

Decision Making on Fourth Down

Carter and Machol (1971) use their field position value calculations to evaluate fourth down strategy, and conclude that coaches should be considerably more willing to try for a first down than kick (either punt or try a field goal) than they do. A later paper, Carter and Machol (1978), investigates this question in greater detail. They determine the probability of success on fourth down with between one yard and five yards to go for a first down (or touchdown), then determine the probability of success for field goal attempts from various points on the field. These results are used to calculate which fourth down option (kicking or trying for a first down or touchdown) is optimal, depending on which has the highest expected points scored. They again find that coaches opt for field goal attempts on fourth down far more frequently than is optimal.

This result has survived subsequent analyses, most notably by Carroll et al. (1988), Stern (1997), and Romer (2006). Romer (2006) states that teams are "dramatically more conservative than the choices recommended by the dynamic programming analysis." The paper analyzed a total of 2,672 fourth down situations over 732 games during the 1998–2000 seasons. In 1,604 of those cases, kicking was found to be the optimal strategy, while "going for it" was found optimal in 1,068 cases. Teams rarely chose to go for it when kicking was best (only 9 times), but kicked when going for it was optimal on all but 109 occasions. All told, teams made the wrong fourth down choice a striking 36 percent of the time.[20] The pay-off of optimal fourth down strategy choices over the observed actual choices corresponds to an increase in the probability of winning each game of about 2.1 percentage points, or about one additional win every three seasons.

While Adams (2006) has disputed Romer's main result, another dynamic programming analysis by Johnston et al. (2004) supports more aggressive fourth down strategy than is currently practiced. They find that implementation of optimal policies in fourth down situations would improve NFL teams' probability of winning any given game by as much as an average of 6.5 percent.

4. BEHAVIORAL ECONOMICS CONSIDERATIONS

The fourth down findings of suboptimal policy detailed above and the passing premium puzzle are problematic for the strong form win maximization assumption commonly adopted by sports economists. The object of a contest indeed would seem to be winning, and at the highest level of sport, researchers seemed justified in assuming that this objective is relatively unadulterated by other social considerations (at least compared to many other business decision-making situations).

Perhaps football coaches have much to learn about strategy, even at the highest levels of the game. Hadley et al. (2000) find that coaches with more experience are more efficient managers and provide evidence that this is not simply a survivor effect. This suggests that coaches learn through experience. While some of this learning may have to do with matters other than in-game strategy (e.g., personnel management), it is likely that learning is occurring on this front as well. Indeed, the most experienced and successful coaches do seem to be those who are most likely to make better kick-or-try decisions on fourth down (Berri, 2006).[21] This learning hypothesis of fourth down suboptimality seems wanting, however, given the particularly long-standing findings in the literature. For example, Carter and Machol (1971) confessed to being puzzled by why these strategy errors endure, and mention "non-quantitative" factors such as "personalities."

Both Romer (2006) and Lewis (2006) both dismiss analytic errors, offering a variety of explanations for the fourth down problem. Romer (2006) also dismisses rational risk aversion. One possibility is that the complexity of football not only stymies computational analysis of game strategy, but also creates a bounded rationality situation in human decision makers. Heuristic rules evolve to deal with common problems, but that evolution continues. Baseball coaches, for example, once believed that weight training would harm batters' ability to quickly swing a bat; this fallacy did not lose widespread appeal until well into the 1970s or perhaps even later. Even so, forty years of academic findings ought to have some effect on faulty fourth down strategy if slow technology diffusion were the only reason for it.

A more plausible explanation for cognitive bias may be found in behavioral economics. For example, it may well be that coaches are not trying to win so much as they are trying to keep their very high-paying jobs. While winning clearly contributes to that goal, perhaps "playing by the book" is more important. Fired head coaches who "are good football people" have a good probability of being rehired elsewhere, but that probability may be negatively impacted by a reputation as an unconventional decision maker.[22] Bandwagon effects, herding behavior, or other social consensus pressures could cause deviations from win maximizing behavior. Furthermore, confirmation biases may offer resistance to the Darwinian forces toward adoption of better strategy.

Fourth down strategy decisions are perceived as both very public and very consequential. This suggests that endowment effects, anchoring effects, and even denomination effects could cause cognitive biases in decision making. Coaches could erroneously undervalue the expected value of points via a possible but somewhat uncertain touchdown compared to the more certain points from a field goal—especially if going for it means the perceived risk of giving up an opponent's field goal or touchdown.

5. SUMMARY OF DISCUSSION

The analysis of game strategy has a long academic record, and has been the inspiration for a number of important advances in mathematics and statistics. The subject of this essay, the analysis of American football field position value and in-contest strategy, has not enjoyed the depth of attention afforded to baseball strategy found in the peer reviewed literature. The primary reason for this oversight is the level of complexity involved in football strategy decisions of interest, compared to that required for the analysis of many important baseball decisions.

Dynamic programming is the most comprehensive theoretical approach to modeling in-contest strategy in many sports. However, the models of football strategy imply very large game state spaces. Sufficient real world data required to estimate all the relevant nodal probabilities used by such models have not until recently been available for football, and even now are often not recorded in an amenable manner. Consequently, estimates of these probabilities for such models can be inadequately precise to address interesting strategy questions. Production function models for strategy analysis in football require smaller data sets, but compromise the fine analytical detail possible with dynamic programming. A number of other approaches to the analysis of managerial decision-making efficiency in football have been borrowed from other management research, but they too offer duller insights into specific game situational strategy analysis than can dynamic programming.

The majority of academic inquiry into football strategy can be put into one of three categories: the value of field position, the passing premium puzzle, and fourth down strategy. The main finding is that field position matters, and its marginal contribution is on the order of the marginal value of an additional offensive yard gained either by passing or rushing. There is evidence, however, that the marginal value of field position has declined, at least in the NFL, over the last several decades, perhaps because of changes to the game's rules and how the game is played.

More intriguingly, there is a growing body of research on the NFL indicating that some strategies chosen by offensive coaches are suboptimal. In particular, the passing premium puzzle suggests that teams opt for runs over passes significantly more than they should, and that such inefficiencies are costly. As data sets become more readily available, particularly in college football, these phenomena will be further investigated, but coaches might be overly risk averse. Fourth down strategy analysis, which has been more deeply studied in the academic literature, finds nearly universal agreement among researchers that suboptimal decision making endures—coaches seem far too conservative compared to what win maximization implies.

These suboptimality findings challenge the pure win maximization models that are favored in most of the North American sports economics literature. Rather, they might best be explained in terms of behavioral economics, but considerably more research into this matter is required.

NOTES

1 For a basic outline of NFL football, see http://www.nfl.com/rulebook/ beginnersguidetofootball.

2 For a basic outline of the differences between NFL and NCAA football rules, see: Wesley, Tad (no date).

3 Walter Camp, the medical doctor and Yale graduate who is generally credited as the "Father of American Football," embraced the application of scientific thinking to decision making in his sport. He published a number of articles in *Harper's Weekly* and other periodicals that emphasized the intellectual elements of the game. Similarly, in 1894, famed University of Chicago coach, who was a contemporary of Camp, published the book *Scientific and Practical Treatise on American Football*, which also sought to position the sport as a thinking man's endeavor.

4 For two examples of such web sites, see Football Outsiders (www.footballoutsiders. com) and Two Minute Warning (www.twominutewarning.com).

5 A notable exception is the work published in the relatively new *Journal of Quantitative Analysis of Sports*.

6 Norman (1995) and Haigh (2009) contain discussions of the use of dynamic programming in a number of sports applications.

7 Dynamic programming models of baseball strategy in the peer-reviewed literature typically consider each batter's plate appearance as a contest's event quantum. Any given plate appearance has only a few different outcomes (i.e., the player reaches base via a walk, single, double, etc., or the player is out), each with relatively well-established real-world frequencies (i.e., on-base-percentages of batters are well-known and derived from relatively large sample sizes). Furthermore, plate appearances take place across a fairly small number of game situation dimensions (home-visitor differential score, inning, number of outs, and number of players on each base). Plate appearance outcomes can be modeled in finer detail than simply as getting on base or making an out. For example, balls hit into play can be considered to be any one of several types (e.g., ground ball, line drive, fly ball) to any one of a dozens or even hundreds of zones on the field (e.g., left of the third baseman, deep right-center field, etc.) (Lewis, 2003). In addition the game's quantum can be treated as an individual pitch rather than an entire plate appearance. Here, the analysis must consider ten possible batting counts with pitches of a few types (fastball, changeup, slider, curve, etc), each intended to arrive in any of nine "zones" (e.g., up and inside, belt-high and inside, down and inside, up over the middle, middle-middle, low over the middle, etc.) as they cross the plate.

8 Each MLB season features about 185,000 individual plate appearances: 38.2 plate appearances per team per game for 30 MLB teams over 162 games per team per season. (Author calculation based on 2000–2006 MLB team-season data). Furthermore, increasingly detailed pitch-by-pitch and balls-hit-into-play data for the approximately 700,000 individual pitches in an MLB season about 3.8 pitches per plate appearance (Baxamusa, 2007) have become commercially available.

9 Note that touchdowns are six points, with a choice of either a one- or a two-point-after-touchdown conversion attempt. According to Sackrowitz (2000), teams converted 98% of their one-point attempts, and 39% of their two point attempts in 1998. In 2008, NFL teams scored a total of 1,246 touchdowns, kicked 1,170 successful one-point conversions, and made 28 two-point conversion tries, so the true average number of points scored per touchdown in the NFL is 6.984 (Pro-Football Reference.com, 2009a).

10 A notable exception is Porter (1967).

11 Data envelopment analysis is a technique that seeks to estimate peak organizational efficiency within a group of like organizations via linear programming analysis of the relationships between organizational inputs and output (Charnes, Cooper, and Rhodes, 1978).

12 Author calculation based on data from Fort (2009).

13 A few exceptions include consideration of one- versus two-point-after-touchdown conversion attempts (e.g., Porter, 1968), overtime strategy choices (e.g., Rosen and Wilson, 2007), and how to position players on the field (Brimberg et al., 1999).

14 Amy Seeger and Kristopher Foulk are to be credited for their dedicated research assistance in the assembly of the 2007 individual drive data.

15 Stern (1997) notes that Carroll et al. (1988) redid this analysis with a richer data set than was used for Carter and Marchol (1971) and obtained similar results.

16 Quinn and von Allmen (2008) gathered a data set of average drive-starting field position by team-season for the 2003–2007 seasons. An analysis done for the present article finds a similar marginal contribution of an improvement in average field position; i.e., 0.03 pts per yard.

17 Also note that Kovash and Levitt attempt to estimate the effect of changes in field position on scoring during the remainder of the current half, while Quinn and von Allmen only consider scoring on the current drive.

18 The left-censored (at zero) model estimated in Quinn and von Allmen (2008) over the 2007 season data is: $Pts_i = \beta_0 + \beta_1(FP)_i + \beta_2(PassYds)_i + \beta_3(RunYds)_i + \beta_4(OffTeam)_i + \beta_5(DefTeam)_i + e_i$; where Pts_i = points scored on drive i, FP_i = beginning field position of drive i, $PassYds_i$ = the yards gained via passing on drive i, $RunYds_i$ = the yards gained via rushing on drive i, $OffTeam_i$ and $DefTeam_i$ are vectors of dummies for the offensive and defensive teams on drive i (respectively), and the e_i are the stochastic noise terms.

19 A declining marginal return to both passing and running is reasonable given how defenses would adjust to doing "too much" of one strategy over the other. For example, offenses that run more can expect defenses to stack "eight in the box" (forgoing one of the four defensive backs in order to add another lineman or linebacker), while offenses that pass more likely will be met with a "nickel package" (five defensive backs), a "dime package" (six defensive backs), or a "prevent" defense (seven or even eight defensive backs).

20 Adams (2006) questions Romer's results based on a Heckman selection bias model of the data. The paper also evaluates various fourth down situations via Monte Carlo simulation using the Madden NFL 07 video game.

21 Berri, David J. (2006) Rational irrationality in pro football, *The Sports Economist* (18 December). Accessed August 30, 2009 from http://thesportseconomist.com/2006/12/rational-irrationality-in-professional.htm.

22 For example, consider the decision made by Detroit Lions head coach Marty Mornhinweg going into the sudden death overtime period in a game with the Chicago Bears on November 24, 2002. There was a substantial wind, and upon winning the toss, the Lions opted to kickoff to the Bears and take the wind. One analysis suggests that a "ten yard wind" (i.e., a headwind sufficient to make the success probability of a field goal attempt from x yards away into that wind equal to the probability of an attempt x +10 yards away with no wind) is enough to have made Mornhinweg's decision the proper one (Krasker, 2004). However, the Bears ended up scoring on the resulting drive; the Lions offense never took possession. This decision was frequently cited among the reasons why Mornhinweg was fired following his one and only season as head coach (although the 3–13 record clearly was a factor).

References

Adams, Christopher (2006). Estimating the value of 'going for it' (when no one does). SSRN Working Paper Series (12 December). Available at http://ssrn.com/abstract=950987.

Alamar, Benjamin C. (2006). The passing premium puzzle. *Journal of Quantitative Analysis in Sports* 2(4), Article 5.

Baxamusa, Sal (2007). The long and short of plate appearances. *The Hardball Times.* Accessed August 25, 2009 From http://www.hardballtimes.com/main/article/the-long-and-the-short-ofplate-appearances.

Berri, David J. (1999). Who is most valuable? measuring the player's production of wins in the National Basketball Association. *Managerial and Decision Economics* 20(8): 411–427.

Berri, David J. (2006) Rational irrationality in pro football. *The Sports Economist* (18 December). Accessed August 30, 2009, from http://thesportseconomist. com/2006/12/rational-irrationality-in-professional.htm.

Berri, David J. (2007). Back to back evaluations on the gridiron. In Jim Albert and Ruud. H. Konig (eds.) *Statistical Thinking in Sports.* Ann Arbor: CRC Press, 235–256.

Berri, David J., Martin Schmidt, and Stacy Brook (2006). *The wages of wins: Taking measure of the many myths of modern sport.* Palo Alto, CA: Stanford.

Borland, Jeffrey (2006). Production functions for sporting teams. In Wladimir Andreff and Stefan Szymanski (eds.) *Handbook on the economics of sport*, 610–615. Cheltenham, UK: Elgar.

Boronico, Jess S., and Scott L. Newbert, S. (1999). play calling strategy in American football: A game-theoretic stochastic programming approach. *Journal of Sports Management* 13:103–113.

Boronico, Jess S. and Scott L. Newbert (2001). An Empirically Driven Mathematical Modelling Analysis for Play-Calling Strategy in American football. *European Sport Management Quarterly* 1(1): 21–38.

Brimberg, Jack, W. J. Hurley, and R. E. Johnson (1999). A punt-returning location program. *Operations Research*, 47(3): 482–487.

Carmichael, Fiona, Dennis Thomas, and Robert Ward (2000). Team performance: The case of English premiership football. *Managerial and Decision Economics* 21(1): 31–45.

Carroll, Bob, Pete Palmer, and John Thorn (1988). *The hidden game of football.* New York: Warner Books.

Carroll, Bob, Pete Palmer, John Thorn, and David Pietrusza (1998). *The hidden game of football: The next edition.* Kingston, NY: Total Sports.

Carter, Virgil, and Robert E. Machol (1971). Operations research on football. *Operations Research* 19(2): 541–544.

Carter, Virgil, and Robert E. Machol (1978). Optimal strategies on fourth down. *Management Science* 24(16): 1758–1762.

Charnes, A., W. Cooper, and R. Rhodes (1978). Measuring the efficiency of decision making units. *European Journal of Operational Research* 2(6): 429–444.

Cook, Earnshaw (1964). *Percentage baseball.* Baltimore: Waverly Press.

de Moivre, Abraham (2000). *The Doctrine of Chances: A Method of Calculating the Probabilities of Events in Play (Third Edition).* New York: Chelsea.

Einolf, Karl W. (2004). Is winning everything?: A data envelopment analysis of Major League Baseball and the National Football League. *Journal of Sports Economics* 5(2): 127–151.

Forsund, F., and Hjalmarsson, L. (1974). On the measurement of productive efficiency. *Swedish Journal of Economics* 76: 131–153.

Fort, Rodney (2009). Sports business data page. Accessed August 30, 2009, from http://rodneyfort.com/SportsData/BizFrame.htm.

Gray, Philip, and Stephen F. Gray (1997). Evidence from the nfl sports betting market. *Journal of Finance* 52(4): 1725–1737.

Hadley, Lawrence, Marc Poitras, John Ruggiero, and Scott Knowles (2000). Performance evaluation of National Football League teams, *Managerial and Decision Economics* 21(2): 63–70.

Haigh, John (2009). Uses and limitations of mathematics in sport. *IMA Journal of Management Mathematics* 20(2): 97–108.

Hald, Anders (2005). *A history of probability and statistics and their applications before 1750*. Hoboken, NJ: Wiley.

Johnston, Rick, Brad Null, and Mark Peters (2004). Optimal decision making in football: MS&E Project. Stanford University. Accessed August 27, 2009, from http://www.google.com/url?sa=t&source=web&ct=res&cd=1&url=http%3A%2F%2Fwww.stanford.edu%2F~null%2FFootball%2520Presentation.ppt&ei=7BKUSqzJKMiolAeIhv2bDA&usg=AFQjCNE5yvQdCAd4Mopn8gvme15DPKy3xQ.

Jordan, Jeremy D., Melouk, Sharif H., and Perry, Marcus B. (2009) Optimizing football game play calling, *Journal of Quantitative Analysis in Sport* 5(2), Article 2.

Kahneman, Daniel, Paul Slovic, and Amos Tversky (1982). Judgment under uncertainty: Heuristics and biases. Cambridge: Cambridge University Press.

Krasker, William S. (2004). Overtime and the wind. Football Commentary. Accessed August 30, 2009, from http://www.footballcommentary.com/wind.htm.

Kovash, Kenneth, and Steven D. Levitt (2009). Professionals do not play minimax: Evidence from Major League Baseball and the National Football League. National Bureau of Economic Research Working Paper 15347 (Cambridge, MA: NBER). Accessed October 25, 2009, from http://www.nber.org/papers/w15347.

Lahman, Sean (2008). *The Pro football historical abstract: A hardcore fan's guide to all-time player rankings*. Guilford, CT: Globe Pequot.

Lavin, James (2005). *Management secrets of the New England Patriots:* Volume 2. St. Petersburg, FL: Pointer Press.

Levin, Josh (2003). Number crunching: Why doesn't football have a Bill James? Slate (19 December). Accessed August 20, 2009, from http://slate.msn.com/id/2092863/.

Lewis, Michael (2003). *Moneyball: The art of winning an unfair game*. New York: Norton.

Lewis, Michael (2006). If I only had the nerve. *ESPN the Magazine*. Accessed August 27, 2009, from http://sports.espn.go.com/espnmag/story?id=3641375.

Mottley, Charles M. (1954). The Application of operations-research methods to athletic games. *Journal of the Operations Research Society of America* 2(3): 335–338.

NFL (no date). Beginner's guide to football. Accessed August 25, 2009, from http://www.nfl.com/rulebook/beginnersguidetofootball.

NFLdata.com (2009). NFL play-by-play database (2006–2008). Accessed August 29, 2009, from http://www.nfldata.com/playbyplay/.

Norman, J. M. (1995) Dynamic programming in sport: A survey of applications. *IMA Journal of Mathematics Applied in Business and Industry* 6(2): 171–176.

Oliver, Dean (2003). *Basketball on paper: Rules and tools for performance analysis*. Dulles, VA: Potomac Books.

Oriard, Michael (1991). *Sporting with the gods: A rhetoric of play and game in American culture*. Cambridge: Cambridge University Press.

Palmer, Pete (1989). *The football abstract*. New York: Warner Books.

Porter, Philip, K. and Gerald W. Scully (1982). Measuring managerial efficiency: the case of baseball. *Southern Economic Journal* 48(3): 642–650.

Porter, Richard C. (1967). Extra point strategy in football. *The American Statistician*, 21(5): 14–15.

Pro-Football-Reference.com (2009a). 2007 NFL standings, team & offensive statistics. Accessed August 30, 2009, from http://www.pro-football-reference.com/years/2007/.

Pro-Football-Reference.com (2009b). 1969 NFL standings, team & offensive statistics. Accessed August 30, 2009, from http://www.pro-football-reference.com/years/1969/.

Pro-Football Reference.com (2009c). 2008 NFL standings, team & offensive statistics. Accessed August 29, 2009, from http://www.pro-football-reference.com/years/2008/.

Quinn, Kevin G., and Peter von Allmen (2008). Using drive level data to estimate a production function for National Football League offenses. Paper presented to North American Association of Sports Economists at the 83rd Annual Conference of the Western Economic Association International.

Rockerbie, Duane W. (2008). The passing premium puzzle revisited. *Journal of Quantitative Analysis in Sports* 4(2), Article 9.

Romer, David (2002). It's fourth down and what does the bellman equation say? A dynamic programming analysis to football strategy. National Bureau of Economic Research paper no. 9024 (June).

Romer, David (2006). Do firms maximize? Evidence from professional football. *Journal of Political Economy* 114(2): 340–365.

Rosen, Peter A., and Wilson, Rick L. (2007). An analysis of the defense first strategy in college football overtime games. *Journal of Quantitative Analysis in Sports* 3(2), Article 1.

Sackrowitz, Harold B. (2000). Refining the point(s) after touchdown decision. *Chance* 13: 29–34. Available at http://www.stat.duke.edu/~dalene/chance/chanceweb/133.sackrowitz.pdf.

Sackrowitz, Harold B. (2004). Dynamic programming and time related strategies in sports. In Sergiy Butenko, Jaime Gil-Lafuente, and Panos M. Pardalos (eds.) *Economics, management and optimization in sports*. New York: Springer.

Sahi, S., and M. Shubik (1988). A model of a sudden-death field-goal football game as a sequential duel. *Mathematical Social Sciences* 15(3): 201–215.

Schatz, Aaron (2005). Football's Hilbert problems. *Journal of Quantitative Analysis in Sports* 1(1), Article 2.

Schiff, Andrew J. (2008). *The father of baseball: A biography of Henry Chadwick*. Jefferson, NC: McFarland.

Schmidt, P., and Lovell, C. A. K. (1979. Estimating technical and allocative inefficiency relative to stochastic production and cost frontiers. *Journal of Econometrics* 9(3): 343–366.

Schwalbe, Ulrich, and Paul Walker (2001). Zermelo and the early history of game theory. *Games and Economic Behavior* 34(1): 123–137.

Scully, Gerald W. (1974). Pay and performance in Major League Baseball. *The American Economic Review* 64(6): 915–930.

Scully, Gerald W. (1994). Managerial efficiency and survivability in professional team sports. *Managerial and Decision Economics* 15(5): 403–411.

Simmons, Rob, and David J. Berri (2007). Does it pay to specialize? The story from the gridiron. Working Paper. The Department of Economics, Lancaster University. Accessed August 29, 2009, from http://eprints.lancs.ac.uk/6924/1/005290.pdf.

Stagg, Amos A., and Henry L. Williams (1983). *Scientific and practical treatise on American football*. New York: D. Appleton & Company. Available at http://books.google.com/books?id=5FcVAAAAYAAJ&oe=UTF-8.

STATS, Inc. (2009). NFLOffering.pdf. Accessed August 29, 2009, from http://www.stats.com/images/PDFS/NFLOffering.pdf.

Stern, Hal S. (1997). American football. Iowa State University Department of Statistics. Accessed August 27, 2009, from http://homepages.cae.wisc.edu/~dwilson/rsfc/rate/papers/footstatchap.pdf.

The Sports Attic (2009). History of NFL rules. Accessed October 28, 2009, from http://www.sportsattic.com/araig/NflRulesHistory.htm.

Timmer, C. (1971). Using a probabalistic frontier production function to measure technical efficiency. *Journal of Political Economy* 79: 776–794.

Taylor, Frederick W. (1911). *The principles of scientific management*. New York: Harper Bros.

von Neumann, John, and Oskar Morgenstern (1944). *Theory of games and economic behavior*. Princeton, NJ: Princeton University Press.

Wesley, Tad. (no date). *Helium*. Accessed August 25, 2009, from http://www.helium.com/items/304857-how-college-football-rules-are-different-from-nfl-rules.

Zak, T. A, Huang, C. J., and Siegfried, J. J. (1979). Production efficiency: The case of professional basketball. *Journal of Business* 52: 379–392.

Zermelo, Ernst (1913). Uber eine Anwendung der Mengenlehre auf die Theorie des Schachspiels, *Proceedings of the Fifth Congress of Mathematicians*, 501–504. Cambridge: Cambridge University Press.

CHAPTER 12

NETWORK TELEVISION REVENUE SHARING AND COMPETITIVE BALANCE IN THE NFL

IRA HOROWITZ AND G. E. WHITTENBURG

INTRODUCTION

THE All-American Football Conference ended its four-year existence in December 1949. Three of its teams, the Cleveland Browns, the Baltimore Colts, and the San Francisco 49ers, joined the ten-team National Football League (NFL). A fourth team, the Brooklyn-New York Yankees, were morphed with the NFL's New York Bulldogs, neé Boston Yanks, into the New York Yanks. Thirteen teams then celebrated the league's thirtieth anniversary and began a new era in professional football. The Colts, however, folded after one year, and the Yanks mutated into the Dallas Texans and then into the Baltimore Colts in 1953 when the NFL stabilized into a twelve-team league.

In 1948, some 172,000 nine- to twelve-inch black-and-white television sets made programs accessible to a select few urban areas, including most prominently New York and Chicago, and a year later NFL television rights totaled $75,000 (MacCambridge, 2005, pp. 104–106). Some teams, such as the Chicago Bears, actually *paid* stations to televise their games (Powers, 1964, p. 79) reflecting the fact that pro football played a poor-third sports fiddle to baseball and the college game and sought public exposure. By 1955, however, in excess of 25 million sets sat in two out of every three households, and five years later only about one in ten *lacked* a set.

In 1956, a two-year-old national magazine, *Sports Illustrated*, "began publishing weekly reports on pro football" (Maraniss, 1999, p. 170) lending further credibility to the sport. And when the Colts defeated the New York Giants 23–17 in sudden-death overtime on December 28, 1958, in a historic nationally televised championship game, the rights to which the National Broadcasting Company (NBC) had acquired for $100,000, pro football gained a genuine foothold on the public's attention. It took another thirty years, however, before the sport was to equal and subsequently surpass baseball in popularity among sports fans, with twice as many respondents preferring pro football to baseball in the latest Harris Interactive poll (2008), and two-and-a-half times as many preferring it to the college game.

Bert Bell, who served as commissioner of the NFL from 1946 until his death in October 1959, was attuned to the growth in the new medium and recognized its potential as an additional, if addictive, source of team and league revenue that wouldn't require the teams to do anything beyond what they were going to be doing anyway: notably, playing football on twelve Sundays from mid-September through early December. In the course of doing so, and particularly doing it through a network package of the entire schedule, Bell, however, hoped to achieve a complementary objective of competitive balance. It was his belief that "pro football is like a chain (that is) no stronger than its weakest link ..." (MacCambridge, 2005, p. 43). That belief initially manifested itself in his 1935 proposal that introduced the reverse-order-of-finish collegiate draft (MacCambridge, 2005, p. 44), and was later reinforced when, as commissioner, he set the annual schedule in accordance with the philosophy that "weak teams should play other weak teams while strong teams are playing other strong teams early in the year (as) the only way to keep more teams in contention longer into the season" (MacCambridge, 2005, p. 40).

The initial network television package with the Columbia Broadcasting System (CBS) in 1956 was actually a patchwork of twelve individually negotiated packages. Each package was subject to Bell's approval and his adamancy "that no signal could be broadcast from a transmitter within seventy-five miles of a game site" and that they be "transmitted back to the network of the visiting team" (Mickelson, 1998, p. 178). The so-called blackout rule was designed to protect local gate receipts and catered to Bell's belief that it was dishonest to sell "a person a ticket and then, after you've taken his dollars, decide to put the game on television, where he could've seen it for nothing" (MacCambridge, 2005, p. 106). Bell further stated "No Green Bay, no deal," in response to the network's reluctance to televise Packer games. The result was that CBS paid the Packers a $50,000 fee (Mickelson, 1998, p, 179).

Bell's vision was finally realized under his successor Pete Rozelle's watch. In 1962, each of the now fourteen NFL teams received about $320,000 for its broadcast rights. Previously, the sale of local rights ranged from $105,000 for the Packers to $340,000 for the Giants. Currently, and through 2011, the broadcast and cable networks will pay each of the 32 teams an annual $95 million to televise their games, with 99 percent of all households having at least one television set and 75 percent wired for cable. These equal shares dwarf in size, perhaps by as much as a factor of 20, the revenues the teams obtain through the sale of pre-season television and local/regional radio rights. The blackout restriction also remains, but since 1973 it has been limited to games that fail to sell out 72 hours before the kickoff, although in most cases local businesses, including TV stations, assure that the blackout will be lifted by purchasing any unsold tickets and the accompanying goodwill.

The twofold purpose of this chapter is to set out the role of television in the post-1949 history of the NFL, with specific respect to the network contracts and more recent media trends, and to explore the extent to which the revenue-sharing codicil, which commissioner Bell saw as helping the weak, has contributed to achieving competitive balance. It will be seen that the teams' shared rights have grown at an annual rate of 14.5 percent, even as the league was expanding from fourteen to thirty-two teams, and the number of telecasts were expanding from a single Sunday game and, starting in 1956, a Detroit Lions Thanksgiving Day game, to four-game Sundays, the occasional Monday night double header, and Thursday night and Saturday games. It will also be seen that whether competitive balance is measured in terms of competitive division/conference races, competitive games, or the distribution of championships, it has not been enhanced, and may have been reduced, by the revenue-sharing policy. Inasmuch as network revenues now exceed the salary cap, one might infer that a principal impact of that policy has been to relax any short-term minimum-profit constraint that may have deterred some owners from increasing payroll in an effort to improve team performance and gate receipts, while allowing others to field an inferior product to the dismay of their paying customers.

HISTORICAL DEVELOPMENTS

In The Beginning

The 1951 championship game between the Los Angeles Rams and the Browns was the first national broadcast of an NFL game. Two years later, the broadcaster, the Dumont Television network, "experimented with the first regular national broadcast of NFL games" through a *Saturday Night Game of the Week* (Maraniss, 1999, p. 170). Local broadcasts and regional networks, however, were springing up, subject to the league's territorial-blackout policy, and in 1953 TV income made the difference between profit and loss for two of the nine profitable teams (Heldenfels, 1994, p. 167).

The blackout policy provoked a federal lawsuit, *United States v. National Football League et al.* (116 F.Supp. 319 (1953)), alleging a violation of the Sherman Anti-Trust Act, §1. District Court Judge Alan K. Grim gave the plaintiff partial satisfaction.

Judge Grim upheld a team's right to enforce a gate-protecting blackout of any radio or television broadcast of another game into its territory when it is playing at home. But he also ruled that when the team is telecasting an away game into its home territory, barring another team from offering a competitive telecast constituted an unreasonable restraint of trade. Implicit in the decision is the notion that an attempt to extend a playing-field monopoly to a territorial broadcast market would violate Sherman §2. Jacobson (2007, pp. 302–304) discusses the principle.

In a courtroom reprise eight years later, Judge Grim similarly held in violation of §1 Commissioner Pete Rozelle's first NFL-CBS two-year contract that gave the network the sole right, with certain exceptions, to choose which games to televise and where to televise them. Judge Grim, confining his decision to the NFL, found that "by agreement, the member clubs of the League have eliminated competition among themselves in the sale of television rights to their games" (196 F.Supp. 445, 447 (1961)).

In a related development, the rival eight-team American Football League, kicked off in 1960 with a five-year $11 million contract with the American Broadcasting Company (ABC), which assured each team $185,000 annually. As AFL commissioner Joe Foss remarked: "Pro football survived without television, but the sport's period of expansion, solvency, and growth is directly equated to its entrance into the field of television" (*Broadcasting*, July 24, 1961, p. 61). Pro football and television were wed, and Congress reacted to the marital partners' petition to pool rights with hearings that resulted in Public Law 87–331 (75 Stat. 732), approved September 30, 1961. Specifically as it pertained to pro football, the law permitted the pooling of rights, provided that the resulting telecasts did not compete with college games and that any blackouts were restricted to a team's home territory. The *raison d'être* was fan interest in preserving the league, which was in danger of failure should only a few teams be able to avail themselves of the then limited access to television coverage and its income-generating potential, absent a television package (Anderson, 1995). The rest, as they say, is history.

The Growth in Network Revenues

The second column of Table 12.1 ("TV") gives revenue, per team, from the first 1960–1961 contract with NBC to broadcast the championship game between the Philadelphia Eagles and the Packers, which in 1960 brought each of the thirteen teams about $23,000, through the current complex of contracts worth about $117 million to each of the thirty-two teams. In this complex, CBS, NBC, and the Fox Broadcasting Company (FOX) are the over-the-air "free" providers; ESPN, originally the Entertainment and Sports Programming Network, is the cable-television

Table 12.1 Shared Revenues and Competitive Balance

Year	Network Revenues Per Team TV	($000's) Competitive Balance Measures SD	RE
1950	0	10.16	0.9518
1951	0	8.44	0.9577
1952	0	8.42	0.9666
1953	0	10.09	0.9426
1954	0	10.03	0.9644
1955	0	4.88	0.9773
1956	0	5.58	0.9793
1957	0	4.79	0.9779
1958	0	7.99	0.9543
1959	0	6.90	0.9619
1960	23.08	7.88	0.9578
1961	21.43	7.42	0.9662
1962	336.71	7.74	0.9534
1963	415.43	8.47	0.9554
1964	1157.14	6.79	0.9752
1965	1196.43	5.77	0.9739
1966	1456.67	8.89	0.9782
1967	1606.25	7.93	0.9688
1968	1575.00	9.46	0.9568
1969	1606.25	7.45	0.9517
1970	1807.69	7.02	0.9734
1971	1807.69	6.93	0.9772
1972	1807.69	8.36	0.9668
1973	1810.00	8.82	0.9656
1974	2100.00	6.15	0.9749
1975	2100.00	8.70	0.9609
1976	2022.22	9.06	0.9569
1977	1932.14	6.06	0.9715
1978	5775.00	4.74	0.9816
1979	5775.00	4.72	0.9798
1980	5775.00	6.01	0.9771
1981	5775.00	5.85	0.9804
1982	7142.86	5.98	0.9702
1983	10714.29	5.44	0.9803
1984	14821.43	7.26	0.9730
1985	16071.43	6.50	0.9759
1986	17678.57	6.00	0.9732

(Continued)

Table 12.1 (*Continued*)

	Network Revenues Per Team	($000's) Competitive Balance Measures	
Year	TV	SD	RE
1987	17000.00	5.56	0.9819
1988	17321.43	4.84	0.9825
1989	18964.29	6.05	0.9784
1990	32160.71	6.41	0.9742
1991	32160.71	6.81	0.9687
1992	32160.71	6.23	0.9730
1993	32160.71	5.54	0.9842
1994	39178.57	5.22	0.9801
1995	36566.67	5.21	0.9860
1996	36566.67	5.80	0.9779
1997	36566.67	5.44	0.9806
1998	73333.33	6.84	0.9733
1999	70967.74	6.58	0.9793
2000	70967.74	7.18	0.9750
2001	70967.74	6.03	0.9740
2002	68750.00	5.46	0.9830
2003	68750.00	6.34	0.9793
2004	68750.00	5.62	0.9790
2005	68750.00	6.51	0.9732
2006	116718.80	5.67	0.9806
2007	116718.80	7.15	0.9741
2008	116718.80	6.60	0.9696

Note: The network revenues are from www.rodneyfort.com/SportsData/BizFrame.htm, amended by data from Broadcasting (August 4, 1986, and August 3, 1987). The per-team computation assumes that expansion franchises immediately participate in the revenue-sharing process. The competitive-balance measures are the authors' computations.

provider; and the league's own NFL Network package is brought to subscribers through a direct satellite service, DirecTV. ESPN partnered with ABC in 1984 and the full-integration process began after ABC was acquired in 1996 by the Walt Disney Company. ESPN, which is now the sole cable provider, the Turner Broadcasting System (TBS) having dropped out a decade ago, has also assumed ABC's role and accounts for about a third of the rights.

To put those rights in perspective, in 1960 $23,000 would have paid the average salary of about 1.5 players on an active NFL roster of some forty players. In 2008, teams were allowed fifty-three players on their rosters and eight on their practice squads. The average salary, including bonuses, was $1.95 million. Television rights alone now cover player salaries. Indeed, in 2008 the rights marginally exceeded the $116 million salary cap.

Under the anti-trust cover of PL 87–331, CBS and the NFL negotiated successive two-year contracts (1961–1962 and 1963–1964), followed by a four-year contract (1965–1969). In the first three of those contract years, NBC retained control of the championship game.

On June 8, 1966, following secret negotiations, the two leagues committed to a merger that received congressional antitrust dispensation in October. Pete Rozelle would be commissioner of the new National Football League. The league was to be divided into two separate but equal thirteen-team conferences, the National Football Conference (NFC) and the American Football Conference (AFC), but would only start playing what was initially a partially integrated schedule in 1970. The twenty-six teams shared equally in the revenues from three new network contracts to the tune of about $1.8 million each. Specifically, CBS and the NFC continued their previous arrangement with the expanded NFL; NBC and the AFC continued an arrangement with the AFL, begun in 1965, when its contract with ABC expired; and the expanded NFL began a new and legendary relationship with ABC for a program to be known as *Monday Night Football* (*MNF*), which is now broadcast on ESPN. NBC and CBS would alternate in televising the NFC-AFC championship Super Bowl and Pro Bowl All-Star game. The average player's salary was about $40,000 and approximately forty-five players were on the active rosters. Network television rights were now and henceforth capable of footing the bill for player salaries, and while gate receipts, concessions, merchandise, and local broadcast revenues may not have been all gravy, television eased direct fan pressure on management to field a quality product.

A complex of rules surrounded the telecasts, with the most salient being that the visiting team's "network" was responsible for inter-conference telecasts and the game would have to be shown in that team's home territory. Starting in 1965, CBS began televising doubleheaders, which potentially meant three telecasts on most Sundays. Currently, the networks coordinate activities and, subject to local blackout restrictions, three games are telecast every Sunday during the regular season, along with Thanksgiving games and Saturday games that do not violate PL 87–331, and NBC televises a Sunday-evening game. First-game telecasts start at 1:00 pm and the second starts at 4:15 pm. The doubleheader game alternates between broadcasters, though not on an every-other-week basis. Aside from local and regional considerations in determining which game is telecast where, the networks might have a national telecast of a game that projects as being of widespread interest. Indeed, "once a broadcast contract is signed a partnership is formed with the objective of creating a television programming schedule that attracts the most viewers for NFL games ... (that) ... includes the strategic placement of games and the selection of teams playing in those games" (Fortunato, 2008, p. 27).

The initial arrangement continued through the next two four-year contracts and the five-year contracts for the 1982–1986 telecasts. But problems were starting to occur.

The Rest of the Story

In the early 1950s CBS was plagued by low ratings, and its affiliates were reluctant to carry its Sunday-afternoon programs. Football telecasts offered a positive solution to the problem, and CBS was anxious to partner with the NFL (Cressman and Swensen, 2007, pp. 483–490). Given its first opportunity to participate, ABC saw similar benefits from its AFL partnership. And especially with late-game telecasts, pro football provided an excellent lead-in, along with promotional opportunities, for the networks' Sunday-evening programs, which for CBS, starting in 1968, included in particular the now long-running and still highly rated *60 Minutes*. Moreover, even if the two networks ended up providing competing pro-football telecasts, and even if the other drew the monopoly straw for a particular Sunday-afternoon time slot on a doubleheader Sunday, each could take some satisfaction from the fact that NBC and especially independent broadcasters and cable networks were being frozen out and denied the ancillary benefits accruing to them on Sunday evening, particularly if the second-game telecast ran long.

In addition to what turned out to be unfounded fears that *MNF* would cost ABC female viewers, the Monday-evening telecasts and the doubleheaders led to equally unfounded speculation about the negative saturation effects of too much televised football, in too short a time frame (Broadcasting, July 19, 1971, p. 35). In 1964, for example, numbered among the most prominent sponsors of pro football on CBS were Ford Motor and Philip Morris, which for almost seven more years was permitted to promote its Marlboro brand and four years later would acquire Miller Brewing. The network charged them $60,000 per minute. Ten years later, in 1974, the rate had risen modestly to $37,600 for a 30-second slot, and by leaps and bounds, to $159,000 for 30 seconds on a 1984 telecast. In 1984, however, the Supreme Court ruled against ABC and the NCAA (*National Collegiate Athletic Association v. Board of Regents of the University of Oklahoma*, 468 U.S. 85 (1984)) and the Saturday afternoon program *NCAA Football* was joined by an initial trickle that eventually became a flood of Saturday day and evening college-football telecasts. Further, from 1983 to 1985, football fans could satisfy some of their cravings for the sport via spring and summer telecasts of the United States Football League (USFL). As an inferred result of all this televised football, 1984 was "one of the worst ratings years in network NFL history" (*Broadcasting*, August 4, 1986, p. 53), suffering about a 20 percent decline from 1981, before rebounding in 1985, although still down in 1986 by about 15 percent from the 1981 peak. By 1989, however, *Broadcasting* was talking about a "brand new ball game" (*Broadcasting*, August 15, 1989, pp. 44–45) as cable television—TBS and especially ESPN—entered front and center into the pro-football picture. Steady ratings for both NFC and AFC telecasts over the preceding three years didn't hurt, and network rights surged in the 1990–1993 contracts, raising each team's revenues by some 70 percent to approximately $32 million. The average player's salary during this period was in the neighborhood of $0.5 million.

The networks, however, started to make noises about the fact that they were not going to be making money from the existing contracts and sought a $200 million rebate for the *quid pro quo* of a two-year rights extension, an offer that the owners narrowly rejected (*Broadcasting*, August 10, 1992, p. 44). They subsequently developed a strategy to keep rights within 10 percent of current levels, while alleging that they would need decreases of at least 25 percent just to break even. They claimed to have lost about $250 million on their $900 million investment (*Broadcasting*, August 16, 1993, p. 24).

Meanwhile, FOX, which had begun operations in October 1986, found itself in a position akin to that of CBS some thirty years earlier: notably, it sought a means of making a big splash and developing a lead-in to its Sunday-evening lineup. Its response was to step in and, in an astounding move, outbid CBS for the rights to the NFC. The result was that despite two new teams, the Carolina Panthers and Jacksonville Jaguars, starting play in 1995, each of the now thirty NFL teams got a 10 percent boost in rights payments in a new four-year set of deals. In 2005, when the next complex of eight-year contracts concluded, with the Houston Texans and the latest incarnation of the Browns joining the league, each team received $68.75 million in network revenues, while the average player's salary, including bonuses, now reached $1.3 million. This increase in rights was in the face of a steady decline in ratings for ABC, NBC, and FOX telecasts from 1994 through 1998, because "the NFL is still TV sport's biggest advertising draw" (*Broadcasting & Cable*, July 12, 1999, p. 29). The recent institution of late-season flexible scheduling as to which teams play at which times and on which days has been held to account for a surge in overall viewership in the early years of the new contracts (Fortunato, 2008, pp. 36–44).

The least-squares estimate of the annual growth rate in network revenues per team from 1960 through 2008 is 14.5 percent, which is almost 2.5 times the annual growth rate in (nominal) per capita gross domestic product. Moreover, this growth was accomplished while the number of participating teams more than doubled from thirteen to thirty-two. Concurrently, average annual attendance per team increased by 1.5 percent per year to about 540,000 for what is currently an eight-game home season, up from six games in 1960. With an average weighted ticket price of $72, this implies gate revenues of about $39 million, or 57 percent of network rights that comprise 53 percent of total revenues. Although not exactly chump change, it is apparent which tail is wagging the dog—something to remember when suffering through the next momentum-breaking TV time out, following the next critical fourth quarter turnover. By contrast, in Major League Baseball, where highly variable local rights outweigh network rights, the latter now comprise approximately 10 percent of total revenues, and in the National Basketball Association and National Hockey League network revenues are about 20 percent and 5 percent, respectively, of the totals.

COMPETITIVE BALANCE AND NETWORK BROADCAST REVENUE SHARING

Theoretical Considerations

Quirk and El Hodiri (1974) provided the theoretical structure to formally demonstrate Rottenberg's (1956) invariance principle and to show that with a set of profit-maximizing owners "the rules structure of professional sports is relatively ineffective in balancing playing strengths, and that imbalance is due to the differences in the drawing potentials of franchises" (1974, p. 58). That rules structure includes the sharing of network broadcast revenues. They freely acknowledge, however, that "when the assumption of profit maximization is abandoned, almost any conclusion may be rationalized by imputing sufficient strength to nonprofit motivating factors" (1974, p. 76). This is especially the case in the NFL, which prohibits ownership by publicly traded corporations (Ross, 2003, p. 325), although the Packers are community-owned by over 110,000 shareholders on a not-for-profit basis. Profit, assuredly, was not a concern of George Allen when, while having organizational control of the Washington Redskins in the 1970s, in an oft-quoted remark he was said by owner Edward Bennett Williams to have been "given an unlimited budget and he exceeded it." And when Denver Broncos' owner Pat Bowlen fired his long-time friend and fourteen-year head coach and general manager Mike Shanahan at the end of the Broncos' 2008 also-ran season, he did so reluctantly, but he had only "so many years left in this chair. The way that I will be judged after I'm gone is how many Super Bowls did I win. To my mind, that's tantamount to everything else" (Mike Kiis, *Denver Post*, December 30, 2008, p. C1). Nonprofit motivating factors are indeed alive and well in the NFL.

More pointedly and recently, Fort and Quirk (1995, pp. 1291–1292) argue that under the NFL structure the strong-drawing teams are subsidizing the weak-drawing teams, and that while "revenue sharing per se should have no effect on competitive balance because payments to teams are independent of each team's win-percent," the league itself has a television-revenue profit incentive to adopt policies that favor those stronger-drawing teams. That incentive, they suggest, along with the growing importance of those revenues, should prompt policies that lessen competitive balance. Building on that analysis, Noll (2007, p. 418) argues that the principal effect of the revenue-sharing policy is to reduce player salaries, enhance the financial viability of the weaker teams, and make the league more profitable by reducing costs, while not affecting player allocation (and, by implication, competitive balance).

Cave and Crandall (2001, p. F14) confine to a footnote the observation that "pooling of broadcast revenues does not eliminate the advantages of large-market teams at securing talent, and therefore it does not necessarily contribute to competitive balance." Atkinson et al. (1988), however, show that revenue sharing encourages an optimal distribution of playing talent, which in this context further implies a movement towards parity—or increasing competitive balance, a movement that is mitigated when owners maximize utility that depends on winning. Vrooman (1995) provides a theory that leads to the inference that the NFL, where at the time of his writing the shared and winning-inelastic broadcast revenues accounted for two-thirds of total revenue, would increase competitive balance "to virtual parity" and result in "self-imposed mediocrity." Palomino and Sákovics (2004) similarly conclude that in a league such as the NFL *full* revenue sharing leading to full competitive balance is optimal, and Késenne (2000) shows that when the impact on revenues of the *absolute* quality of the members is taken into account, regardless of whether ownership is profit *or* utility oriented, revenue-sharing improves balance. By contrast, Szymanksi and Késenne (2004) show that "under reasonable assumptions" the revenue-sharing process reduces the league's investment in talent and reduces competitive balance. And in apposition, Grossman et al. (2008) conclude that with a constant-elasticity-of-marginal-cost class of convex cost functions, increased revenue sharing reduces balance. Késenne (2005) subsequently concludes that the impact of revenue sharing on competitive balance depends upon one's assumptions!

In sum, then, and contrary to Bert Bell, Pete Rozelle, and instinctively popular belief in general, "the effect of revenue sharing on competitive balance, although likely modest, could go in either direction" (Sanderson and Siegfried, 2003, p. 269).

Franchise Decision Factors, Owner Motivations, and Tax Implications

These views of ownership, however, fail to explicitly consider the full complexity of the motivations behind an investment in a sports franchise, which comprise both short-term and long-term factors.

Personal gratification is a short-term factor. A sports franchise is a "cool toy" to own, and owners who are ego-involved with the ownership role may be satisfied with a break-even return on their investment on an *annual* basis. An owner is a member of a very exclusive club; there are 100 United States Senators, but only 31 NFL principal owners/partners who enjoy locker-room access. Lucrative network contracts take some of the short-term risk out of team ownership because of the annual guaranteed cash flow.

There are, however, also long-term factors in the decision to invest in a sports franchise. Indeed, the potential long-term appreciation of its value can make annual returns a secondary factor in owning a franchise, with or without positive cash flows, in part thanks to those who specifically desire a sports franchise and thereby tend to "bid up" its value for non-economic reasons. The sports news is replete with stories of owners who purchased teams, held them for, say, ten to twenty years, and then sold them for a large gain. The Miami Dolphins and Wayne Huizenga are a recent case in point.

Huizenga paid $168 million to become the majority owner of the Dolphins and assumed a $100 million debt on their Joe Robbie Stadium. Subsequent upgrades to the stadium brought his total investment to approximately $580 million. The latter was amply covered by the $1.1 billion that Stephen M. Ross paid for the team and its properties fifteen years later. The Dolphins are also estimated to have booked an annual profit of upward of $10 million during the Huizenga years. In all, Huizenga is estimated to have earned some $730 million on his initial investment (Dave Hyde, *South Florida Sun-Sentinel*, January 27, 2009, p. C1), while enjoying the perks and prestige that go along with owning a sports franchise, albeit not a single appearance in an AFC Championship Game.

An indirect reason to invest in a franchise is to enhance associated investments. An owner may have real-estate holdings in the immediate area and a team can have a positive impact on those holdings. Hotels, condominiums, and office developments adjacent to a team locale may get a strong boost in value. This seems to be a trend when structuring a deal for a franchise and/or stadium in a new or redevelopment location.

Tax considerations may also affect the investment potential of a franchise. Team owners have one thing in common: a lot of wealth and alternative sources of income. Thus, any *losses* arising from the team ownership can reduce the income for tax purposes from other investments. Put otherwise, the tax law helps subsidize any short-term team-ownership losses. In the long-term future, when the team is sold for a large gain, the gain may be taxed at the preferential long-term capital-gains rate, which is currently 15 percent. In many respects, team ownership is similar to a classic tax shelter. Competent accounting and legal advice could often turn team ownership into a tax-advantaged investment.

There are, however, several tax-law provisions that can have a negative impact on those tax advantages. As an exemplar, under Section 183 (Hobby Losses) of the Internal Revenue (IRS) Code, if a taxpayer enters into an activity without a profit motive, the law limits the available tax deductions. Under the hobby-loss provisions, one cannot net against other income a loss from an activity that is not engaged in for profit. An economist, say, might breed racehorses on the weekend. The IRS might contend that the activity was for personal enjoyment and disallow any loss for tax purposes. Despite the limitation on losses, any profits from hobbies must be included in taxable income.

Individual taxpayers or S corporations can avoid the hobby-loss rules by showing that the activity was conducted with the *intent* to earn a profit. To resolve the issue, the IRS may look at some or all of the following factors:

1. Whether the activity is conducted like a business;
2. The expertise of the taxpayer,
3. The time and effort expended;
4. Previous success of the taxpayer in similar activities;

5. Income-and-loss history from the activity;
6. Relationship of income to losses in the activity;
7. Financial status of the taxpayer; and
8. Elements of personal recreation in the activity.

As regards an NFL ownership, there is a rebuttable presumption that if an activity shows a profit for three of the five previous years, the activity is engaged in for profit and presumed to be a trade or business. It is then up to the IRS to establish that it is a hobby.

If a business activity is not a hobby, the allocable expense that may be claimed as deductions against its income is unlimited. But for an activity determined to be a hobby and subject to the hobby-loss rules, expenses are allowed as deductions only to the extent of the income they generate. Consider the NFL owner who sells a business and has an investment portfolio worth about $2 billion that produces an annual income of $100 million, and whose team loses $25 million a year. If the activity is deemed a hobby, the $25 million loss cannot be deducted from the $100 million income for tax purposes. Good and well-taken accounting and legal advice followed carefully can normally prevent hobby losses and other undesired tax consequence from being a tax problem.

Measuring Competitive Balance

Competitive balance within a league relates to the teams' relative playing strengths, which manifest themselves in three different ways: the competitiveness of the individual games, the league standings, and the distribution of championships and/or the carryover effects of championships from one season to the next (Neale, 1964, p. 4). Our interest in determining whether and how the NFL's revenue-sharing policy has affected competitive balance over time leads us to focus primarily on the first two approaches to the issue, but we shall also take a briefly deferred look at the third approach

In order to objectively measure how competitive games were during a particular season, one might proceed by taking the weighted average of the average margins by which a team won the games that it won and by which it lost the games that it lost. Doing this for every team over the 59-year period from 1950 through 2008 requires a daunting data-gathering task. We thus chose a more feasible, if modestly flawed, compromise.

For each season and team, we first divide the difference between total points scored and allowed by the number of games the team played and measure that year's competitiveness of play by the standard deviation of the average differences. In a league of N equally matched teams where each finished at 0.500 and allowed as many points as it scored, the standard deviation would be zero. Assuredly, there are highly competitive games that end with one team winning by a final score of, say, 31–14, which might hint at a minor rout, as well as seemingly nail-biting 24–22 games that "weren't as close as the final score indicates." And while the average difference of –15.6 points for the winless Lions in 2008 would seem to accurately reflect the excitement that their games generated, the average difference of +2.44 for the Packers, who compiled a 6–10 win-loss record, would not. Those cherry-picked examples notwithstanding, we believe that the measure generally paints a reasonable picture of game competition in each season. The annual figures for the measure appear in the third column of Table 12.1 ("SD"). Thus, in 1950 about two-thirds of the teams might be expected to have had average differentials between points scored and allowed of plus or minus ten points (one standard deviation), whereas in 2008 the range would have been about two-thirds as large, suggesting that games tended to be more competitive in the latter year than in the former year.

Our metric to assess competition in the league standings is based on Shannon's (1948) classical entropy measure of information or equivalently uncertainty, which in this context reflects the degree of uncertainty as to which team will have won a game chosen at random from all the games played that season, or intra-league competition. Theil (1967, pp. 290–291), among others, proposed entropy as an inverse measure of industrial concentration that proxies the degree of market competition.

Let W_{it} denote the number of wins for team i in year t, and let W_t denote the total number of wins that season. Then, $w_{it} = W_{it}/W_t$ is the proportion of league wins attributable to team i and entropy in year t is defined as $H_t = -\Sigma_i w_{it} \text{Log}_2(w_{it})$. The measure, which is highly dependent upon the number of teams in the league N_t, is maximized at $\text{Log}_2(N_t)$ when each teams finishes at 0.500 and the league has seemingly achieved perfect competitive balance. To account for differences in the number of teams, we employ as our metric relative entropy $RE_t = H_t/\text{Log}_2(N_t)$, which reflects how close the league comes to the maximum-entropy condition of perfect balance (Horowitz, 1997).

For example, in the current $N_t = 32$-team league with a 16-game schedule, $W_t = 16^2 = 256$. If each team wins eight games: $w_{it} \equiv 8/256 = 1/32$ and H_t is maximized at:

$$H_{tmax} = -32(1/32)\text{Log}_2(1/32) = \text{Log}_2(32) = 5;$$

$RE_{tmax} = 1$. Suppose, however, that the league is perfectly imbalanced in the sense that one team in each conference goes undefeated, one wins 15 games, etc., with no 0.500 teams and a winless team bringing up the rear. H_t attains its minimum value at:

$$H_{tmin} = -2(16/256)\text{Log}_2(16/256) - 2(15/256)\text{Log}_2(15/256) \cdots -0 = 4.48363.$$

The antilogarithm, 22.4, is the numbers-equivalent (Adelman, 1969) of 0.500 teams in a perfectly balanced league that yields the same degree of competition, or uncertainty of outcome, as in the imbalanced league where relative entropy is $RE_{tmin} = 4.48363/5 = 0.89$.

The fourth column of Table 12.1 ("RE") gives the annual relative-entropy figures, which as implied in the previous paragraph necessarily fall within a very narrow range. That range notwithstanding, the low-end figure of 0.9426 implies that the 1953 season was the least competitive in the 59-year sample period when the one-loss Browns were the class of the league, losing only their final game to the Eagles, although closely trailed by the two-loss and eventual-champion Lions. The Chicago Cardinals, who won only one of their 12 games, edged the Packers for the cellar by virtue of one less win and one more loss. At the high end of 0.9860, the 1995 season was the most competitive: the Kansas City Chiefs, with 13 wins in 16 games, were only three games better than three teams that tied for sixth place, and even the last-place New York Jets won three games.

We now consider whether fluctuations in these measures and the implied changes in competitive balance can be "explained" by changes in network broadcast revenues.

Empirical Results

We suspect that fan interest in competitive contests is largely a myth—at least as regards rabid fans of the participants, virtually all of whom in our experience would rather see their team win a one-sided contest than to lose (or even to win) a nail-biter, particularly against a traditional and hated rival. The same, however, is not necessarily true of the (relatively) neutral observer who tunes into NFL football games for love of the sport, interest in the race to the Super Bowl, and in the hope of seeing an exciting contest whose outcome will not be decided until the very end of a seemingly interminable final two minutes of football-clock time. On the one hand, then, each NFL team has a stake in putting the best possible team on the field in order to draw fans to the stadium and assure as many season-ticket sales as possible. On the other hand, the league and the networks have an interest in equalizing playing strengths to achieve the promise of competitive games that will retain viewer interest, and the close and compelling conference standings that provoke fan interest in the outcomes of games that might otherwise be ignored. That is, the NFL and the networks have a joint interest in at a minimum "foster[ing] the perception of inter-club competitiveness" (Mason, 1999, p. 404). Networks and sponsors want to encourage the *ex ante* expectation of a competitive game that will draw viewer interest, and the follow-up *ex post* realization of a game that will retain the viewers' interest and capture their attention—even and especially through the commercials.

The response of the league, which holds mutual-interest sway in these matters, has been to adopt a series of policies that the commissioners and managements believe, aptly or otherwise, will contribute positively toward improving competitive balance, with the reverse-order draft and broadcast revenue sharing being prime cases in point. The salary cap and floor, introduced in 1994 and periodically modi-fied, would seem to act in favor of competitive balance, while having the further vir-tue to the league and individual owners of simultaneously restricting player salaries and holding down costs. The NFL scheduling process, which as temporized from previous years currently has each team playing one game against each of the other two teams in its conference that finished in the same position in the previous season, is another attempt to assure competitive games and tight races. The impact of free agency, which initially came to the NFL in 1989 and was later modified in 1993, on competitive balance is subject to the muting argument of the invariance principle.

Insofar as the assorted rules-and-policy changes since 1950 have been under-taken with the television audience in mind, which we would argue was at worst a tertiary consideration, we hypothesize that they have tended to contribute toward competitive balance. The success of *Sports Illustrated* and especially that of ESPN might also be expected to have contributed toward competitive balance by assur-ing that all managements, both on the field and off, have access to full informa-tion as to every other team and both current and upcoming players. Managerial deficiencies are now more readily exposed and correctable than ever before, which means greater balance beyond the rosters of eligible players. Thus, we hypothe-size a long-run trend toward heightened competitive balance. We are, however, less inclined to speculate on the resolution of the debate on the impact of shared television revenues on balance.

To test the hypothesis and resolve the debate, we posit a two-equation linear model that uses the following notation:

t = current year—1950;

RE_t is the league's relative entropy at time t; SD_t is the standard deviation of the average scoring differential at time t; and TV_t is the shared revenue that each team received at time t.

The first equation models relative entropy as a linear function of network rev-enue and time:

$$RE_t = \alpha_0 + \alpha_1 TV_t + \alpha_2 t + \varepsilon_{1t}. \tag{1}$$

The α_j are regression parameters whose estimates are denoted a_j; ε_{1t} is a random-error term with the usual normality properties. Our trend hypothesis translates into $\alpha_2 > 0$, while the sign of α_1 will resolve the debate with respect to competition in the standings.

Implicit in the second equation is the notion that the degree of competition in the individual games is in the main dependent upon the overall level of competi-tion within the league. That is, a set of equally strong teams will produce a set of highly competitive games, rather than the reverse. To the extent that the shared revenues contribute to producing highly competitive games—or otherwise—we hypothesize that this would be accomplished by the impact that the revenues have on the degree of competition among the teams. The second equation therefore models the standard deviation in the averages as a liner function of relative entropy and time:

$$SD_t = \beta_0 + \beta_1 RE_t + \beta_2 t + \varepsilon_{2t}. \tag{2}$$

As in Equation (1), the β_j are regression parameters whose estimates are denoted b_j, and ε_{2t} is the random-error term. Our trend hypothesis translates into $\beta_2 < 0$. Our shared-revenue-impact hypothesis translates into $\beta_1 < 0$, since this implies that increased competitive balance within the league results in narrower victory margins and consequently smaller spreads in the average differentials between points scored and allowed, while lesser balance results in larger spreads. If, therefore, the shared-revenue policy has a positive (negative) impact on competitive balance in the standings, it will also have a positive (negative) impact on competitive balance in individual games.

The ADF tests strongly reject ($p \leq 0.001$) the unit-root hypothesis for both RE_t and SD_t, or both time series are presumptively stationary. Equations (1) and (2) are therefore estimated by two-stage least squares. Letting e_{kt} denote the residual for Equation ($k = 1$ or 2), the following are the least-squares estimates of the model:

$$RE_t = 0.9589 - 0.000000124 TV_t + 0.000534 t + e_{1t}; \tag{1e}$$
$$(<0.0001) \quad\quad (0.0374) \quad\quad\quad (<0.0001)$$

$$SD_t = 163.8040 - 161.974 RE_t + 0.012502 t + e_{2t}. \tag{2e}$$
$$(0.0036) \quad (0.0054) \quad\quad (0.5375)$$

The figures in parentheses are p values.

The first estimated equation (Adj $R^2 = 0.42$) supports the hypothesis of a statistically significant positive trend in competitive balance in the standings, as $a_2 = 0.000534 > 0$. Popular belief notwithstanding, $a_1 = -0.000000124 < 0$ implies that the revenue-sharing process has lessened balance and that higher absolute shared revenues led to less competition in the standings. The argument, however, is not immune to the conjecture that absent revenue sharing the large-market teams in particular would have dominated the television screens and broadcast rights, although at much lower than current levels due to seller competition. If the argument were valid, that domination would extend to the standings. The argument might be tempered or reversed if shared revenues were replaced as the independent variable by shared revenues as a percent of total revenues. Unfortunately, the data that would permit us to do so are not available.

The second estimated equation (Adj $R^2 = 0.37$) supports the hypothesis that greater competitive balance in the standings results in more competitive games, with a statistically significant $b_1 = -161.974 < 0$. Contrary to our hypothesis, $b_2 = 0.012502 > 0$ implies a positive if statistically insignificant trend toward less-competitive games. Qualitatively equivalent results are obtained when TV_t is introduced into Equation (2), with or without a trend. In effect, competitive games result solely from competitive teams. Thus, with constant network revenues, the trend toward increased competition among the teams would result in increased competition in the games. Any such trend, however, is offset and perhaps reversed when the revenues are increasing, because that will tend to reduce competitive balance among the rivals.

The Distribution of Championships

Since 1950, only one of the thirty-two teams, the Pittsburgh Steelers, has won as many as six NFL championships, and while five have won five championships, fourteen others have never won. Indeed, six have never even made it to the championship game and seven have only qualified once. Two teams earned eleven appearances, another has participated once, and no others have made more than seven appearances. There would seem to be a distinct lack of competitive balance in the distribution of championships.

The lack of balance, however, is not unusual in the "pursuit of excellence" (Murray, 2003). Murray documents this to be the case whether he is discussing significant figures in astronomy, Indian literature, or golf, where, for example, of the 361 players who made the cut to the final two rounds of the men's PGA Championship at least once from 1970 to 1989 and completed their careers by the end of 2001, only four had more than 30 PGA Tour victories, with Jack Nicklaus (71) and Arnold Palmer (61) leading the way (Murray, 2003, pp. 98–100), and Tiger Woods already having injected himself into the out-of-sample and theory-supportive mix.

Table 12.2 The Pursuit of Championships

Number of Events n	Percent of Successful Pursuers	Championship Game Championship
0	18.75	43.75
1	21.88	9.38
2	3.13	12.50
3	3.13	9.38
4	12.50	6.25
5	9.38	15.62
6	15.62	3.13
7	6.25	0
8	0	0
9	3.13	0
10	0	0
11	6.25	0

Note: The data are the authors' computations.

Murray quantifies the phenomenon via a Lotka curve, $y = cd^n$, a hyperbolic function where in this context y is the percentage of eligible teams and n is the number of championships or playoff appearances. His explanation for the phenomenon is that while "anybody" can accomplish an "easy" task, only the truly excellent can accomplish a really difficult task (Murray, 2003, pp. 102–103), such as getting to the championship game. In a minor modification of Murray's approach, we specify all teams to be eligible. Nevertheless, there are still too few data points to permit a meaningful estimate of the curve, and so we provide the raw data in Table 12.2. There would seem to be somewhat greater balance in those given the opportunity to play for the championship than there is with respect to the actual winners, but in neither regard is there anything approaching competitive balance in the sense of a flat or rectangular distribution of winners.

Moreover, if the revenue-sharing policy had any impact on that distribution, it is not readily apparent from a more detailed inspection of the data. In each of the six decades of our sample period, one or at most three teams stand out as dominant. In the 1950s, the Browns, Lions, and Colts won eight of the ten championships, and in the 1960s the Packers won half of the championships and no other team won more than once. The Steelers won four championships in the 1970s, as did the 49ers in the 1980s, and both the Dallas Cowboys and the New England Patriots won three in the 1990s and the first nine seasons of the current decade, respectively. Quarterbacks Otto Graham (Browns), Bart Starr (Packers), Terry Bradshaw (Steelers), Joe Montana (49ers), Troy Aikman (Cowboys), and Tom Brady (Patriots), and their respective coaches Paul Brown, Vince Lombardi, Chuck Noll, Bill Walsh, Jimmy Johnson, and Bill Belichick would seem to have had a greater impact on the championship aspect of competitive balance than did the league's television policy and the steady growth in broadcast rights.

Conclusions

Almost sixty years ago, the NFL embraced, adopted to, and exploited the post–World War II television era with five primary objectives in mind: (1) promote the product; (2) preserve territorial monopolies and if at all possible extend them to local broadcast markets; (3) protect gate receipts from the competition of either a same-game telecast or that of an out-of-territory game; (4) shore up the financial status of small-market teams that might need it; and (5) maximize the league's network broadcast revenues in conjunction with an equal-revenue-sharing policy that would help maintain competitive balance. It has succeeded admirably in *almost* all regards.

(1) Professional football has gone from being a pre-war afterthought to becoming the most popular team sport in the United States. The NFL has grown from a 13-team league in 1950 to a 32-team league in 2009. It has accomplished this partially from absorbing franchises through merger with the AFL, and principally through relocating and/or establishing franchises in the untapped television markets of Seattle, Minneapolis/St. Paul, Atlanta, New Orleans, Phoenix, Charlotte, Nashville, and a Florida triad comprising Jacksonville, Miami, and Tampa Bay.

(2) The league's premier status and its franchises have survived challenges from the AFL and the USFL, despite the failed attempt to extend the territorial monopolies (or duopolies in the cases of New York and the Bay area) to include the television market.

(3) Thanks to an act of Congress, the NFL has been able to maintain its local-television blackout policy and prevent the telecasting of a competing game when such might have the effect of hurting the local gate. In 2008 more than two-thirds of the teams recorded attendance in excess of 95 percent of stadium seating capacity, with only four teams charging an average of less than $60 for a ticket and twelve charging in excess of $75.

(4) All franchises are thriving. The Cowboys, with a new stadium having opened in 2009, have a Forbes-estimated franchise value of $1.6 billion, closely trailed by the Redskins at $1.5 billion, with the Oakland Raiders ($861 million) and Minnesota Vikings ($839 million) bringing up a highly valued rear. As for the Packers, they stand smack in the middle of the pack at $1 billion. The Packers are profiting at the gate and through their share of network revenues, but ironically—and future Hall of Famer Brett Favre notwithstanding—until the 2010 season they had not won a championship since Bart Starr and Vince Lombardi retired and since the NFL started sharing broadcast revenues in an effort to help them and other small-market teams compete financially and thus on the gridiron.

(5) Even with two-and-a-half times as many teams participating, the network revenue per team has grown by some 14.5 percent annually and shows no sign of abating. Indeed, the NFL is moving with the times as it extends its involvement with cable television, satellite television, films, videos, and most recently the Internet through revenue-generating options offered by nfl.com. As the NFL Network "suggests a very real possibility of further siphoning of games and programming [from over-the-air television] at the expense of the consumer," it could, however, attract Congressional attention and raise Sherman antitrust concerns (Paolino, 2009, p. 43).

Each team now earns broadcast revenues that exceed the salary cap. In 2008, however, 18 of the 32 teams had player payrolls that fell short of the cap, and some substantially so. Also-rans such as the 2–14 Chiefs, the 0–16 Lions, the 6–10 Packers, and the 8–8 Broncos, along with the highly-competitive 11–5 Patriots, did not come within $19 million of the cap; but neither did the playoff-bound 12–4 Colts, 11–5 Baltimore Ravens, or the 11–5 Atlanta Falcons. Thanks to paying signing bonuses that allow a team to pay salaries in excess of the cap, the Super Bowl opponents, the 9–7 Arizona Cardinals and the 12–4 Steelers, both exceeded the cap—as did the salary-pacing but otherwise struggling 5–11 Raiders, who exceeded it by some $36 million. The television-rights annuity, which relaxes any short-term minimum-profit constraint that might otherwise have kept some owners and managements from pursuing a win-at-all costs expected-utility-maximizing policy, also allows others the luxury of focusing solely on the overall profitability of the enterprise and future resale value of the franchise. This implies that the rights-revenue-sharing scheme ought to perhaps be accompanied by one that rewards investment in pay-roll and provides an additional incentive for small-market teams to compete with their large-market rivals (Lewis, 2008, p. 547).

The sharing of television revenues has not, however, contributed to maintaining competitive balance. In fact, just the opposite has been the case. Competition in the standings has declined in concert with the steady increases in the shared revenues, and games have tended to become somewhat less competitive. Nor has the policy succeeded in spreading the wealth, insofar as the latter is measured in terms of either championships or the opportunity to play in a championship game. Organizational excellence appears to be a fleeting thing, although persistent incompetence, at least in the NFL with wealthy owners and substantial shared television revenues, is more readily attained. Bert Bell might have been somewhat dismayed to learn of this, but we suspect that after having studied bottom lines, franchise values, and the overall health of the industry, he would have been a very happy man, indeed.

ACKNOWLEDGMENTS

Except when we felt a citation was absolutely necessary, we have included data without attribution. Those data come primarily from Rodney Fort's web site www.rodneyfort.com/SportsData/BizFrame.htm. Additional data are from Horowitz (1974), Quirk and Fort (1992), Staudohar (1996), the annual football issue of *Broadcasting*, which appeared in late July or early August, from 1960 through 1994, and subsequent *ad hoc* articles in both *Broadcasting* and its successor, *Broadcasting & Cable*, and various issues of the *Statistical Abstract of the United States*. The blame-free comments of Mr. Philip R. Hochberg are gratefully acknowledged.

REFERENCES

Adelman, M. A. (1969). Comment on the "H" concentration measure as a numbers-equivalent. *The Review of Economics and Statistics* 51: 99–101.

Anderson, David L. (1995). The Sports Broadcasting Act: Calling it what it is—Special interest legislation. *Hastings Law Journal* 17: 945–959.

Atkinson, Scott E., Stanley, Linda R., and Tschirhart (1988). Revenue sharing as an incentive in an agency problem: An example from the National Football League. *RAND Journal of Economics* 19: 27–43.

244   ECONOMICS OF MAJOR LEAGUE SPORTS

Cave, Martin, and Crandall, Robert W. (2001). Sports rights and the broadcast
industry. *The Economic Journal* 111: F4–F26.

Cressman, Dale L., and Swenson, Lisa (2007). The pigskin and the picture tube: The
National Football League's first full season on the CBS television network. *Journal
of Broadcasting and Electronic Media* 51: 479–497.

Fort, Rodney, and Quirk, James (1995). Cross-subsidization, incentives, and outcomes
in professional team sports leagues. *Journal of Economic Literature* 33: 1265–1299.

Fortunato, John A. (2008). NFL agenda-setting. *Journal of Sports Media* 3: 27–49.

Grossman, Martin, Dietl, Helmut A., and Trinkner, Urs (2008). The effect of
marginal cost elasticity on competitive balance. *Journal of Sports Economics* 9:
339–350.

Heldenfels, Rich D. (1994). *Television's greatest year.* New York: Continuum.

Horowitz, Ira (1974). Sports broadcasting. In Roger G. Noll (ed.), *Government and the
sports business.* Washington, DC: Brookings Institution.

Horowitz, Ira (1997). The increasing competitive balance in Major League Baseball.
Review of Industrial Organization 12: 373–387.

Jacobson, Jonathan M. (2007). *Antitrust law developments,* 6th ed. Chicago: American
Bar Association.

Késenne, Stefan (2005). Revenue sharing and competitive balance. *Journal of Sports
Economics* 6: 98–106.

Késenne, Stefan (2000). Revenue sharing and competitive balance in professional
team sports. *Journal of Sports Economics* 1: 56–65.

Lewis, Michael (2008). Individual team incentives and managing competitive
balance in sports leagues: An empirical analysis of Major League Baseball. *Journal
of Marketing Research* 45: 535–549.

MacCambridge, Michael (2005). *America's game.* New York: Knopf.

Maraniss, David (1994). *When pride still mattered.* New York: Simon & Schuster.

Mason, Daniel S. (1999). What is the sports product and who buys it? The marketing
of professional sports leagues. *European Journal of Marketing* 33: 402–418.

Mickelson, Sig (1998). *The decade that shaped television news.* Westport, CT: Praeger.

Murrary, Charles (2003). *Human accomplishment.* New York: HarperCollins.

Neale, Walter C. (1964). The peculiar economics of professional sports. *Quarterly
Journal of Economics* 78: 1–14.

Noll, Roger G. (2007). Broadcasting and team sports. *Scottish Journal of Political
Economy* 54: 400–421.

Palomino, Frédéric, and Sákovics, József (2004). Inter-league competition for talent
vs. competitive balance. *International Journal of Industrial Organization* 22:
783–797.

Paolino, Ross C. (2009). Upon further review: How NFL network is violating the
Sherman Act. *Sports Lawyers Journal* 16: 1–46.

Powers, Ron (1984). *Supertube: The rise of television sports.* New York: Coward-
McCann.

Quirk, James, and El Hodiri, Mohammed (1974). The economic theory of a sports
league. In Roger G. Noll (ed.), *Government and the sports business.* Washington,
DC: Brookings Institution.

Quirk, James, and Fort, Rodney D. (1992). *Pay dirt.* Princeton: Princeton University
Press.

Ross, Stephen F. (2003). Antitrust, professional sports, and the public interest.
Journal of Sports Economics 4: 318–331.

Rottenberg, Simon (1956). The baseball players' market. *Journal of Political Economy* 64: 242–258.21.

Sanderson, Allen R., and Siegfried, John J. (2003). Thinking about competitive balance. *Journal of Sports Economics* 4: 255–279.

Shannon, Claude E. (1948). A mathematical theory of communication. *The Bell System Technical Journal* 27: 379–423, 623–656.

Staudohar, Paul. D. (1996). *Playing for dollars.* Ithaca, NY: ILR Press.

Szymanski, Stefan, and Késenne, Stefan (2004). Competitive balance and gate revenue sharing in team sports. *Journal of Industrial Economics* LII: 165–177.

Theil, Henri (1967). *Economics and information theory.* Amsterdam: North-Holland Publishing.

Vrooman, John (1995). A general theory of professional sports leagues. *Southern Economic Journal* 61: 971–990.

....

CHAPTER 13

COMPETING LEAGUES, MERGERS, AND EXPANSIONS

AJU J. FENN

THE purpose of this chapter is to review the existing literature pertaining to the origins of American football leagues and their subsequent evolution in the United States. The chapter will also review the economic literature on themes pertaining to contemporary issues in American Football. The material in this chapter is linked to the themes expressed in Part I of this volume on league design and competitive balance. This chapter will consist of three sections. Section 1 will summarize and review the relevant economic literature pertaining to the birth and evolution of football as a sport in the United States. This section will track the game from its birth until the formation of the National Football League (NFL). The subsequent section will briefly touch on some of the themes regarding football that have been explored in the rest of the literature. The chapter will conclude with theoretical insights into the main economic issues pertaining to the NFL.

THE BIRTH AND EVOLUTION OF AMERICAN FOOTBALL

....

The Early Days

American football as we know it today has its origins in association football (soccer) and rugby, (Carrol et al., 1999). As both of these sports came to the United States, they grew in popularity and gave birth to American football.[1] The first college football game was played on November 6, 1869, between Princeton and Rutgers. As college football evolved with uniform rules and increased violence, the professional version of the game took root through athletic clubs on the East Coast of the United States. These clubs allowed men to participate in and bet on outcomes of sporting events. Athletic clubs were seen as stepping-stones for their members to gain access to exclusive metropolitan men's clubs. In order to survive financially, these clubs needed to win games in order to give their members access to the men's clubs. Athletic clubs sought to attract good athletes, who often hailed from a lower social class, by offering them partial memberships. In exchange for playing for the club they received use of the club's facilities and payment of their dues. The semi-professional football player was born.

Athletic clubs soon began paying their players. The first professional football player was William (Pudge) Hefflinger in 1892. Controversy over paying players erupted and the Allegheny Athletic Association (AAA) was banned from playing in the Amateur Athletic Union (AAU). The AAA responded by hiring the best players and coaches and played two games against other athletic clubs before folding. Thus the first completely professional football team was formed.

Birth of the NFL

In 1902 John Rogers, Ben Shibe, and Dave Berry put together three teams that competed against each other and united to form the first professional football league in U.S. history: the National Football League. Canton and Massilon fielded teams that competed with each other. This rivalry ended up with teams paying players and resulted in the birth of the Ohio League. In 1905 President Theodore Roosevelt, who was troubled by the number of deaths and injuries in the sport, demanded a safer game. The Intercollegiate Athletic Association of the United States, a pre-cursor to today's National Collegiate Athletic Association (NCAA), was formed. Several rule changes (such as the legalization of the forward pass) followed, which made the game safer and more popular. Since professional football followed collegiate rules, these changes had an immediate impact on the professional game as well. Players began to drive up salaries by switching teams. The Ohio League owners responded by contacting all professional teams in the country, forming the American Professional Football Association (APFA). George Halas organized this league with 14 teams. It was founded to raise the standard of the game and to eliminate bidding for players. Joe Carr succeeded Jim Thorpe as the president of APFA. He was able to enforce the league rules that prevented teams from approaching players that were under contract with another team. He also passed a rule that prohibited teams from signing college athletes whose class had not yet graduated. The APFA was renamed the NFL after 1921.

Birth of the First AFL

When C. C. (cash and carry) Pyle, an agent for the Bears running back Red Grange, demanded a five figure salary and part ownership of the Bears from owner George Halas he was rebuffed. This led Pyle to form a nine-team rival league called the American Football League (AFL) in 1926. The team from New York was called the New York Yankees. The AFL started competing with the NFL for talent. The struggle continued until Tim Mara, the owner of the New York Giants (an NFL team), and C. C. Pyle reached an uneasy truce in 1927 with the Yankees joining the NFL.

Teams came and went as their economic fortunes dictated. The next significant event was the institution of the reverse order college draft. In 1936 Bert Bell—one of the co-owners of the Pittsburg football franchise, the Pirates—convinced fellow owners that a draft was good idea for the league. Prior to the draft the Bears, Giants, Packers, and Redskins dominated the league.

The Birth of the All America Football Conference

Arch Ward, a sports editor for the *Chicago Tribune,* had the idea that, like baseball, football would benefit from a two-league structure. In 1944 several owners who had been shut out of the NFL jumped at the chance to form a rival league, and the advent of air travel made cross-country games feasible.[2] The All America Football Conference (AAFC) was born; it existed from 1946–1949 (Quirk and Fort, 1997). This rival league had teams in New York City, Brooklyn, Los Angeles, San Francisco, Chicago, Cleveland, Miami, and Buffalo. The league did not institute a college draft. Over time the Cleveland franchise became dominant and the AAFC competed successfully with the NFL for attendance. After some of the AAFC franchises in Chicago and Los Angeles ran into financial trouble, the two leagues agreed to merge.

The AFL

As average game attendance rose by about 60 percent during 1950–1960, some NFL owners favored expansion (Quirk and Fort, 1997). George Halas and Art Rooney were in favor of expansion but George Marshall and the Wolfners used their veto power under NFL bylaws at the time to thwart expansion. In 1957 Lamar Hunt applied for an expansion NFL franchise in Dallas. He was turned down by the NFL. In 1958 the Houston Sports Association tried to get an NFL franchise for Houston with similar results. In Minneapolis, Max Winter, H. P. Skoglund, and Bill Boyer tried to get an NFL franchise for the Twin Cities. Their bid was also rejected by the NFL. In 1958, after Lamar Hunt tried unsuccessfully to buy the Chicago Cardinals and move them to Dallas, he decided to form his own football league. He was joined by a group of entrepreneurs, including Bud Adams from Houston, Bob Howsam from Denver, Barry Hilton, Harry Wismer, Max Winter, and Bill Boyer. They founded teams in New York, Boston, Buffalo, Houston, Dallas, Denver, Los Angeles, and Minneapolis. The only team to defect to the NFL was the Minnesota Vikings. The AFL began operations in 1960 and also filed an antitrust lawsuit against the NFL. The AFL contended that the NFL sought to destroy competition by expanding into new cities with specific intent to destroy the AFL. The verdict was in favor of the NFL. Several NFL players who did not make it in the NFL got a second chance in the AFL and became stars. The AFL was originally designed to enter smaller markets like the Twin Cities. Once their franchises were rejected by the NFL they had to compete in larger markets as well. The AFL placed teams in New York and Los Angeles (Quirk and Fort, 1997). The AFL did not pose a severe threat to the NFL in terms of attendance, even though it drew healthy numbers. Initially the AFL did not compete with the NFL for players. Like many rival leagues before it, the AFL chose to sign NFL cast-offs or collegiate players. The difference between the AFL and its predecessors was that it had a national television contract to compensate for lower attendance figures (Quirk and Fort, 1997).

Carrol et al. cite several important reasons for the survival of the AFL and its eventual viability. In 1963, Lamar Hunt moved his team from Dallas to Kansas City, where they became a viable franchise (Carrol et al., 1999). Oakland hired Al Davis as a coach and general manager, and he stabilized the team and made it successful. The New York Titans went bankrupt and were sold to a syndicate led by Werblin. They were renamed the Jets and moved into a new stadium built for the World's Fair in 1964. The AFL signed a five-year $36 million contract with NBC, which bolstered their hopes for survival. Al Davis was named AFL commissioner and he aggressively pursued NFL stars. The AFL began to sign NFL players. In 1966 the AFL signed Mike Ditka of the Bears to a contract for the Houston Oilers for the 1967 season. There were also preliminary plans for an AFL expansion franchise in Chicago (Quirk and Fort, 1997). These events paved the way for a merger between the two leagues.

The hostilities ended by the start of the 1966 season. This move eventually led to the NFL and AFL champions playing each other in the Superbowl. Peace broke out and the two leagues merged in 1970 after their respective national television contracts expired. The NFL as we know it today was born.

Other Leagues after the Birth of the 1970 AFL-NFL merger

The 12-team World Football League (WFL) started in 1974 and played a 20 game per team season. It was founded by Gary Davidson, who had also started the American Basketball Association and the World Hockey Association. It was disbanded midway through the 1975 season because of economic problems stemming from a cancellation of its television contract (Quirk and Fort, 1997). The next rival league was the USFL, which played its game in the spring and was operational from 1983 to 1985. The expansion by five teams in the second year proved detrimental to the health of the league. Teams were relocated and sold several times. The USFL television revenue and attendance figures paled in comparison to the NFL. Several franchises lost money, and eventually the league went under in 1985 (Quirk and Saposnik, 1992). On the other hand, the Arena Football League ran from 1987–2008. This league focused on an indoor version of the game that put an emphasis on scoring. Economic debts caused the league to suspend its activities after the 2008 season. Furthermore, the NFL founded a developmental league, the World League of American Football (WLAF) that had teams based in the United States, Canada, and Europe. It ran from 1991 and 1992 and it reemerged as NFL Europe from 1995–2007. At that point the NFL shut it down, choosing to focus its international marketing efforts by having regular NFL teams play a regular season game in a foreign country. The XFL was formed via collaboration between the World Wrestling Federation and NBC and they began playing games in 2001. Jesse Ventura, the governor of Minnesota at the time, served as a color commentator for select games. It dissolved after one season due to a lack of fan interest. The United Football League (UFL) began playing games in 2007 and is still in existence. They located teams in cities such as Orlando, Las Vegas, Hartford, and Sacramento where the NFL has no presence. Another proposed league is the All American Football League, which is supposed to start its season in the spring of 2011. The Canadian Football League (CFL) began operations in 1956 and is in existence today with nine teams. The CFL expanded briefly into the United States from 1993 to 1995. In 1996 the league returned to a Canadian venture. As time passes, one will no doubt see the birth of various football leagues in uncontested markets. If NFL television contracts become too expensive, one might even see a rival league backed by television corporations make an appearance. The NFL already has its own cable/satellite network. The next phase in the evolution of American football may well be a battle between NFL-owned networks and other television networks each putting their own teams on the air. Another opportunity for a rival league may present itself if there is a work stoppage in the NFL. If owners and players cannot settle their contract negotiations, the demand for football may present an opportunity for a rival league.

THE ECONOMIC LITERATURE ON AMERICAN FOOTBALL

There is a substantial literature on American football. Vrooman presents an extensive analysis of league expansion and franchise relocation in the post AFL-NFL merger era (Vrooman, 1997). His paper discusses franchise relocations in the wake of league expansion for both Major League Baseball (MLB) and the NFL. He contends that the early NFL was forced to expand, as that was the only viable option to contend with rival leagues in larger cities. Expansion in the post-1970 merger was done to maximize national television contracts, so franchises were located in Tampa Bay and Seattle. The NFL selected five finalist cities for these expansion franchises in an effort to maximize the concessions obtained from these cities. Even cities that did not get teams proved useful for teams that wished to relocate. The NFL always pitted multiple cities against each other, either for franchise expansion or relocation purposes. This tactic proved useful, as cities understood the credibility of the threat of losing their existing or expansion franchise. This maximized the concessions from host cities, whether it came to building new stadiums for existing teams or giving teams favorable stadium rental terms. Vrooman contends that the NFL is capable of constraining franchise relocation without being granted an antitrust exemption similar to that of MLB. When the NFL voted to block the Raiders from relocating from Los Angeles to Anaheim in 1978, the Raiders sued the league for a violation of the Sherman Act and prevailed. The court ruled that individual teams conspired to keep the Raiders from relocating and that constituted a violation of the Sherman Act. Vrooman argues that since the institution of revenue sharing and a salary cap, the league is now effectively a single firm, and as such its members can no longer conspire to violate the Sherman Act. Its members are now part of a single firm. The NFL, however, only restricts franchise movement when it is in the best interest of the league. The issue of the NFL being a single identity is now under review by the U.S. Supreme Court. The case of *American Needle vs. NFL* is one that the court is considering. If the Supreme Court sides with the Seventh Circuit Court that the NFL is indeed a single entity, the decision will exempt the NFL from the Sherman Act, as its corporate members (the teams) will not be deemed as conspiring against teams that seek to relocate (McCann, 2010).

Some of the best sources for the birth and evolution of American football are the ones that have been summarized above. Carroll at al. provides excellent details about the birth of American football and its early history (Carroll et al., 1999). Quirk and Fort provide more detailed insights into the birth of rival leagues and the resulting mergers and competition between these leagues after the formation of the NFL in 1922 (Quirk and Fort, 1997). The reader who is interested in even greater detail regarding the football wars is referred to Quirk and Saposnik (1992). Readers who are interested in mergers, expansions and team relocations of any major American sport between 1876 and 1950 are referred to Jozsa (2006). He has an excellent account of these issues during this historical time period in American sports.

There is an extensive literature on the formation and evolution of sports leagues in general. Noll examines the incentive structure and efficiency of different forms of league organization (2003). His work concludes that European league promotion-relegation structures are superior to their closed league North American counterparts. El Hodiri and Quirk examine the structure of professional sports to determine the extent to which current operating rules justify an exemption from antitrust law (2001). Vrooman constructs a general theory of professional sporting leagues based on evidence from the NFL, the National

Basketball Association (NBA), and Major League Baseball (MLB). His conclusions regarding the NFL are as follows: "The extensive sharing of winning-inelastic revenue in the NFL increases competitive balance ... whereas the extensive sharing of winning-elastic revenue leads to the depression of player salaries. Thus, the NFL is predictably the most competitively balanced, but also the most exploitive of the leagues" (2001).

The rest of the literature on the NFL can be classified according to the following major themes: the creation of NFL institutions that have lead to increased competitive balance; the impact of race on players' and coaches' success in the NFL; betting on NFL games; issues of market power and profitability; and finally, the cost-benefit analysis of hosting an NFL team. There are also some papers that may be put in the miscellaneous category.

Larsen et al. demonstrate that the institution of free agency and a salary cap led to an increase in competitive balance in the league (Larsen et al., 2006). Teams that tend to pay their players more equally tend to do better than teams that have a few superstars that are paid much more than the rest of the team (Borghesi, 2008). The determinants of winning are important in professional sports, and there are studies that have looked at this question from different angles. Off the field arrests do not have a significant impact on team wins (Stair et al., 2008). Quinn (2003) finds that getting a new stadium does not significantly impact the winning percentage of an NFL team. Terry (2007) examines the impact of team averages for speed, strength, and intelligence on winning while controlling for the career win percentages of the head coach, strength of schedule, team payroll, and average player tenure. He finds that the only significant variable is average team speed.

The issue of race has been investigated extensively in sports economics. The NFL is no exception. Malone et al. (2008) find that black coaches are held to higher standards than their white counterparts. Simmons and Berri (2009) find that black and white quarterbacks play the game differently. Black quarterbacks are more likely to run with the ball but are not compensated for this skill. Conlin and Emerson (2006) find that nonwhite players face hiring discrimination in the NFL but are treated more equitably in retention and promotion decisions.

There is a decent literature on efficient markets and wagering in the NFL. Boulier et al. (2006) find that the NFL betting market was efficient from 1994–2000. There are other studies that look at factors that impact the efficiency of betting markets from weather to late-season home underdogs. This strand of the literature is more about using NFL data to test hypotheses about efficient markets and betting than it is about shedding light on the NFL.

We turn next to issues of market power and profitability. Brook and Fenn (2008) find that the NFL does possess market power based on the data used from 1995–1999. Brunkhorst and Fenn (2010) find that NFL teams do maximize profits. They find that about 80 percent of NFL teams set ticket prices in a manner consistent with gate receipt maximization.

Most academic studies done on the economic value of professional sports teams to their communities conclude that the benefits generated by the team fall short of the costs of a new stadium. Fenn and Crooker (2009) find that in the face of a credible threat of relocation, the welfare estimates of a team to a community are higher than previously thought. They find that the range of welfare contribution by the Vikings to households in Minnesota is $445.3 million to $1,571.3 million. The literature on the NFL is small compared to the amount of academic studies done on MLB, but it is a growing field.

PAST AND FUTURE ECONOMIC ISSUES PERTAINING TO THE NFL

The NFL started as the response of a league to rising player salaries, and the league expanded in order to prevent rival leagues from becoming viable threats. Football teams were originally the tenants of MLB teams. As the game grew in popularity and the average capacity of stadiums increased, so did the revenue streams from concessions, parking, and the use of stadiums on non-game days. Some football teams were the sole tenants of their facilities. Other NFL teams that were joint tenants wanted their own stadiums, with an increased number of luxury suites and club seating levels. NFL teams share gate revenues, with 60 percent going to the home team and 40 percent going to the away team. The revenue from luxury suites and from club seats is a windfall for the home team because they keep all revenues over and above the average ticket price for general admission. The average ticket price for a club seat or a seat in a luxury suite is much higher. It is this fact that prompted several NFL teams to move or to threaten relocation if they did not get new stadiums that were largely funded by taxpayer dollars. Being a sole tenant of a stadium also gives the team exclusive control over the use of the stadium on days that the team is not playing in the stadium. Teams regularly rent out their stadiums for events such as rock concerts and monster truck rallies. They also rent out parts of the stadium, such as larger end zone luxury suites, for corporate team building events, weddings, and trade shows. Some of the teams to get new stadiums in the last two decades or so have been the Denver Broncos, the Detroit Lions, the Seattle Seahawks, the Houston Texans, and the New England Patriots. The most recent recipients of new stadiums have been the Dallas Cowboys and the New York Jets. Details about costs and the taxpayer burden may be found in Komisarchik and Fenn (2010).

While stadiums are often the subject of discussion, the NFL has also made progress in the broadcasting arena. The NFL owns its own cable/satellite channel, the NFL network, which carries football content all the time. During the season the focus is often on match-ups before games and post-game analysis after games have been played. The NFL also selectively televises live games during the regular season exclusively on the NFL network. During the off-season the NFL network carries classic games and coverage of the owners meetings, the NFL free agency period, and the NFL combine, as well as the draft. The network is a way for fans to stay connected to their teams during the off-season.

The NFL has also partnered with DirecTV to tap into another revenue source. Fans who leave their hometown and still wish to follow their home teams on Sunday can do so if they purchase the NFL Sunday Ticket. This is an exclusive service provided by DirecTV and retails for about $315 per household. In addition, this service caters to those who are pressed for time by presenting entire games in 30 minutes or less without commercials by Sunday night. NFL Sunday Ticket subscribers can also have games streamed to their laptops or cell phones. DirecTV renewed its deal to serve as the NFL's exclusive satellite carrier through the 2014 season. Fox and CBS have broadcasting rights deals with the NFL, worth more than $712 million a year (Fox) and $622 million a year (CBS); the NFL gets about $1 billion annually from this deal. The NFL has a four-year $720 million agreement with Verizon to become the league's exclusive wireless partner.[3] All of these broadcasting innovations have helped the NFL to increase the size of the revenue pie.

On the cost side, players do not have guaranteed contracts but do get large signing bonuses. The amount of NFL revenue that is spent on players is about 60 percent, according to the last collective bargaining agreement (CBA), supervised by former NFL commissioner Paul Tagliabue. The buzz among NFL insiders is that owners did not wish to give up such a large piece of the revenue pie to players and are looking for more favorable terms in the next CBA. The NFL now has a new commissioner, Roger Goodell, and the players union has a new executive director, DeMaurice Smith. Both sides will be eager to impress their constituencies with favorable terms of the new CBA. If the NFL and NFLPA do not reach a new CBA by March 5, 2011, there will be a work stoppage during the ensuing fall season. The NFL has enjoyed relative labor peace with few work stoppages. The last two stoppages were in 1982 for 57 days and in 1987 for a month.

The economic model on the negotiations between a single buyer and a single seller (of labor) is called a bilateral monopoly. The majority of the pie being negotiated over usually goes to the party with the more favorable bargaining position and ability. While the NFL owners are the only employer of elite professional football players, the NFL players are not the only source of players. The NFL may choose to go with college recruits and replacement players from other football leagues such as the CFL and the USFL. Contract negotiations are going to dominate the NFL economic landscape in the days and months ahead.

Another issue that has far-reaching implications for the NFL will be the ruling of the U.S. Supreme Court in *American Needle vs. NFL*. If the Court deems the NFL to be a single firm, it becomes virtually immune to anti-trust action based on the charge stemming from conspiracy among NFL teams to prevent team relocation. Another court case that is pending may also have a bearing on the pending negotiations. Last year the NFL suspended Pat and Kevin Williams of the Minnesota Vikings for testing positive for a steroid masking agent. The players sued the NFL and the case is still in progress. If the judge ultimately rules that the NFL and not the Vikings employed Pat and Kevin Williams, then the Minnesota workplace drug testing laws will keep the league from carrying out its suspension. Substance abuse and NFL player health are issues that will remain constant as long as the game is played.

Conclusion

This chapter has reviewed the history of the early football leagues in America and the birth and evolution of the National Football League. Rival leagues were either absorbed into the NFL or they went out of business. The chapter also discussed the main economic themes pertaining to the NFL. The institution of free agency, combined with a salary cap and revenue sharing, has done much to promote the success of the league. The United Football League has quietly entered markets where the NFL does not have a presence, such as Orlando, Omaha, Hartford, Las Vegas, and Sacramento. It started play in 2007 and may gain market share if the NFL locks its players out for the 2011–2012 season. It appears as if the NFL is headed for a work stoppage that will be the next milestone in the storied history of this great American pastime. Given the deep devotion of its fans, a short work stoppage will probably not have much of an effect on the long-term popularity of the sport.

Notes

1 A detailed history of the game can be found in (Carrol et al., 1999). This section draws heavily upon their work.
2 Prior to the formation of the AAFC there were two other rival leagues that should be noted briefly. (Quirk and Fort, 1997) report the formation of two other rival leagues: AFL 2 from 1936–1937 and AFL 3 from 1940–1941. They state that both leagues failed and that neither was a credible threat to the NFL. AFL 2 failed due to the dominance by the Los Angeles Bulldogs and AFL 3 was seen as a minor league masquerading as a major league.
3 The broadcast deal values are reported on the NFLPA web site at http://www.nflplayers. com/Articles/CBA-News/Lockout-Steps

References

Berri, David J., and Simmons, Rob. (2009). Race and the Evaluation of Signal Callers in the National Football League *Journal of Sports Economics* 10(1): 23–43.
Borghesi, R. (2008). Allocation of scarce resources: Insight from the NFL salary cap. *Journal of Economics and Business* 60(6): 536–550.

Boulier, B., Stekler, H., and Amundson, S. (2006). Testing the efficiency of the National Football League betting market. *Applied Economics* 38(3): 279–284.

Brook, S., and Fenn, A. (2008). Market power in the National Football League. *International Journal of Sport Finance* 3(4): 239–244.

Brunkhorst, John P., and Fenn, Aju J. (2010). Profit maximization in the National Football League. *Journal of Applied Business Research* 26 (1): 45–58

Carrol, Bob, Gershman, Michael, Neft, David, and Thorn, John (1999). *Total football II: The official encyclopedia of the National Football League.* New York: Harper Collins Publishers.

Conlin, M., and Emerson, P. (2006). Discrimination in hiring versus retention and promotion: An empirical analysis of within-firm treatment of players in the NFL. *Journal of Law, Economics, and Organization* 22(1): 115–136.

El-Hodiri, Mohamed, and James Quirk. (2001). An economic model of a professional sports league. *The economics of sport* 1: 80–97. Elgar Reference Collection. International Library of Critical Writings in Economics, vol. 135. Northampton, MA

Fenn, Aju J., and Crooker, John R. (2007). Estimating local welfare generated by an NFL team under credible threat of relocation. *Southern Economic Journal* 76 (1): 198–223

Jozsa, Frank P. (2006). *Big sports big business: A century of league expansions, mergers, and reorganizations.* Westport, CT: Praeger.

Komisarchik, Mayya M., and Fenn, Aju J. (2010). Trends in stadium and arena construction, 1995–2015. Colorado College Working Paper Series.

Larsen, A., Fenn, A., and Spenner, E. (2006). The impact of free agency and the salary cap on competitive balance in the National Football League. *Journal of Sports Economics* 7(4): 374–390.

Malone, K., Couch, J., and Barrett, J. (2008). Differences in the success of NFL coaches by race: A different perspective. *Journal of Sports Economics* 9(6): 663–670.

McCann, M. (2010). American Needle v. NFL: An opportunity to reshape sports law. *Yale Law Journal* 119(4): 726–781.

Noll, Roger G. (2003). The organization of sports leagues. *Oxford Review of Economic Policy* 19(4): 530–551

Quinn, K. (2003). Do new digs mean more wins? The relationship between a new venue and a professional sports team's competitive success. *Journal of Sports Economics* 4(3): 167–182.

Quirk, James, and Fort, Rodney D. (1997). *Paydirt: The business of professional team sports.* Princeton, NJ: Princeton University Press.

Quirk, James, and Saposnik, Rubin. (1992). The great football wars. In *Advances in the economics of sports,* ed. Gerald Scully. New York: JAI Press.

Stair, A., Day, A., Mizak, D., and Neral, J. (2008). The factors affecting team performance in the NFL: Does off-field conduct matter? *Economics Bulletin* 26(2): 1–9.

Terry, N. (2007). Investing in NFL prospects: Factors influencing team winning percentage. *International Advances in Economic Research* 13(1): 117.

Vrooman, J. (1997). Franchise free agency in professional sports leagues. *Southern Economic Journal* 64(1): 191–219.

Vrooman, John. (2001). A general theory of professional sports leagues. *The economics of sport.* 1: 152–171. Elgar Reference Collection. International Library of Critical Writings in Economics, vol. 135. Northhampton, MA

SECTION 5

SOCCER

CHAPTER 14

....

THE BOSMAN RULING
AND LABOR MOBILITY
IN FOOTBALL
(SOCCER)

....

JOHN GODDARD,
PETER J. SLOANE, AND
JOHN O. S. WILSON

1. INTRODUCTION

....

IN this chapter, we trace the historical development of free agency in professional football using the English leagues as representative of what has happened in Europe. We then summarize work that has been undertaken to unravel the effects of the Bosman ruling. We conclude by presenting some data on changes in the patterns of employment of professional footballers in the English leagues since the mid-1980s, which enable several effects of the Bosman ruling to be identified.

2. THE HISTORICAL DEVELOPMENT OF FREE AGENCY IN FOOTBALL (SOCCER)

There are a number of special features of sporting labor markets that distinguish them from other labor markets. First, teams can only field a set number of players, so that additional signings are substitutes for existing players, though a larger squad may enable players to be rested more frequently. Second, team work is crucial, and players may be complements or substitutes. Third, players are not homogeneous:— star players can turn games. Fourth, given all the previously mentioned distinctions, the supply of labor must be measured in quality units, which are defined as enough additional talent to win one more game per season, given that the talent of the other teams in the league is constant. Fifth, contract length is of crucial importance. Given that no team can produce on its own, and clubs must not be too unequal, the allocation of players among clubs becomes paramount.

League organizers and club owners seem to have been aware of these special features from the start.

> At its formulation in 1888 the Football League's expressly set out the twin aims of imposing a maximum wage and preventing the movement of a player from one club to another without the permission of the former (Szymanski and Kuypers, 1999, p. 99).

A maximum wage was eventually introduced in 1905 at £4 per week, with sanctions for infringement. As outlined by Sloane (1969) and Thomas (2006), players had to be registered both with the Football League and the Football Association, and mobility of labor between clubs required the consent of both clubs, with a transfer fee often required. Until 1963 a player who wished to move to another club would request to be placed on the club's transfer list. If, however, the club refused to do this, the player had to continue to play for that club if he wished to remain as a professional footballer. At the end of the playing season, a club was free to place a player either on the transfer list or the retained list on whatever terms it wished, provided only that they were no lower than the minimum agreed wages and conditions.

After World War II these arrangements were frequently challenged by the Professional Footballers' Association (PFA). The basis of the Football Leagues' defense, when challenged, was the principle of equality among clubs. The maximum wage clause, it was claimed, gave clubs more equal chances of obtaining the services of the best players, and this maintained competition to the long-run benefit of both players and the public. The League believed in the principle of mutuality as typified by the division of receipts in the FA Cup competition in which a third of gate receipts from the third round onward was shared equally among all the competing clubs, regardless of size. When the Minister of Labor set up a Committee of Investigation (under John Forster) in 1952 the League claimed that the removal of either the maximum wage or the retain-and-transfer system would lead to the disintegration of the competition. Broadly speaking, the Forster committee accepted the weight of these arguments.

In 1959, the PFA again reopened talks with the Football League and managed to negotiate the abolition of the maximum wage in January 1961. Within the next few years, a wage spiral ensued with salaries more than doubling and, between 1960–61 and 1966–67, the number of professionals employed by the ninety-two Football League clubs fell by 20 percent. In 1963 the PFA was again successful in supporting George Eastham who had been refused a transfer by Newcastle United. The High Court judge held that the existing rules were an unreasonable restraint of trade. This decision led to revised rules being introduced, which specified an initial period (usually of two-years duration) and an option period (which was required to be the same as the initial period). If a club failed to exercise this option, which must offer renewal on terms no less favorable than the initial terms, the player was free to sign for another club, with no transfer fee required. If, however, the club wished to retain the player but there was no agreement between player and club, either party could appeal to the Management Committee of the Football League to adjudicate. If there was still no agreement, further appeal could be made to an independent tribunal, whose decision was binding on both parties.

In other European countries and elsewhere, similar though not identical arrangements applied. Thus, under UEFA rules a board of experts could make a binding judgement in the case of a disputed transfer fee, but differences remained across countries. Thus, within France, a transfer fee was payable only in the case of a player's first change of club, and within Spain, players aged twenty-five or more could move freely between clubs without a fee being required.

These arrangements turned out, however, not to be stable in the long run, as became evident in a landmark decision before the European Court of Justice in December, 1995. This case concerned a Belgian player Jean Marc Bosman who played for RC Liege on a contract consisting of a basic salary of 75,000 Belgian francs a month, plus bonuses amounting to 45,000 francs. In April 1990, his club offered him a new contract at the minimum basic wage allowed by the Belgian FA (contractual arrangements in Belgium being somewhat different than elsewhere in Europe). When Bosman refused this offer, he was placed on the transfer list at a fee just under 12 million Belgian francs. Because no offer was forthcoming from other clubs, Bosman went on loan to a French second division club, Dunkirque, at a salary of 90,000 Belgian francs per month, with an agreement that Dunkirque would purchase his services for a sum of 1.2 million Belgian francs on receipt of a clearance certificate. However, when doubts arose about Dunkique's ability to pay, the deal lapsed. When Liege suspended Bosman's contract he took legal action demanding payment of 100,000 Belgian francs per month. The Belgian court ordered a payment of 30,000 Belgian francs to be made and referred the case to the European Court of Justice (ECJ).

In reaching his decision, the Advocate General, Heinz Otto Lenz considered both rules on foreign players and transfer rules. In the former case, many national associations had, from the 1960s onward, introduced rules restricting the employment of players of foreign nationality. Following a 1976 ECJ case (*Dona v. Mantero*), UEFA agreed with the European Commission in 1978 that it would relax restrictions on the number of foreign players from the European Community that a club could have under contract. Further, it would fix at two the number of such players who could take part in a match with players resident in the country concerned for five years exempted from this provision. After further discussions with the Commission, the so-called 3+2 rule was imposed in 1991, under which the number of foreign players to be included on the team sheet could be restricted to not less than three per team, plus two players resident for five years. This rule was to be extended to all professional leagues by the 1996–97 season. It was, however, open to national associations to impose no limit, if they so wished, and this was the case, for example, in Scotland. Lenz noted that there were three arguments under which the rule could be defended, namely, that spectators identified themselves with players of their own nationality; that there was a need to protect the development of young players; and that there was a need to preserve a balance between clubs. However, he observed that the vast majority of clubs had non-local or foreign players, that the presence of the latter could improve the development of young players, and that the influx of foreign players was in itself insufficient to cause any major problem. He concluded that these rules amounted to discrimination because of nationality and were, therefore, in breach of Article 48 of the Treaty of Rome.

In relation to the transfer issue, Lenz found that such rules could only be lawful if they were justified by "imperative reasons in the general interest" and did not go beyond what is necessary for attaining these objectives. He did regard the maintenance of financial and sporting equilibrium as the most significant argument in favor of such institutions as articulated in the following quote:

> I share the opinion that a professional league can only flourish if there is not a glaring imbalance between the clubs taking part. If the league is clearly dominated by one team, the necessary tension is absent, and the interest of spectators will thus probably lapse within a foreseeable period.

However, he concluded that it was doubtful whether transfer rules were capable of achieving that objective, given that transfers tended to be from smaller to larger clubs and there were alternative means of attaining the objective, which did not reduce freedom of movement. Such alternatives included a collective wage agreement specifying limits to the salaries paid to the players by the clubs and more equal income sharing of gate receipts from home games and from television. Transfer fees might be lawful in some cases, however, where they were linked to the costs of training, provided that the size of the fees was limited to the amount spent on training by the previous club and was also limited to the first change of club. Because this was not presently the case, they found that the current arrangements were unlawful. He recognized that his recommendation would lead to an increase in player wages and that the payment of transfer fees to non-EU clubs may well create some difficulties. Further, there would be some appropriation from those clubs that had recently invested in players, but it was their own responsibility to sign players on long-term contracts.[1]

Following the ECJ judgement there were protracted discussions on what should replace the existing system. In March, 2001 the EU, UEFA, and FIFA finally agreed on a new system. This involved compensation to clubs for the training and development of young players moving before the age of twenty-four; the creation of one transfer period per season, and a further limited mid-season window, with players allowed to move just once a season; a minimum contract duration of one year and a maximum of five years; contracts are to be protected for a period of three years up to the age of twenty-eight and for two years after that age; when a player breaks a contract within these periods, he will be banned from playing for his new club for four months; financial compensation can be paid if a contract is breached, whether by the player or the club. These arrangements went into effect in 2003. The new system still allows transfer fees to be negotiated for in-contract players, but if a player is unhappy about the size of fee demanded, he can appeal to an arbitration body made up of an equal number of members representing players and clubs.

3. Assessing the Impact of the Bosman Ruling

Testing of the effect of the Bosman case is rendered difficult because of the lack of detailed data on individual player contracts and also because of the contemporaneous substantial increase in gate, TV broadcasting, and other revenues that would have caused salaries to increase sharply even in the absence of freedom of contract. Further, studies differ with respect to the assumptions made about individual club behavior and on whether the labor market should be viewed as competitive or not. In part, this can explain why some authors regard the impact of Bosman as being major, whereas others regard the impact as limited.

If one assumes that clubs are profit maximizers and the invariance principle holds, then restrictions on employment mobility should not alter the distribution of playing talent. If a player is worth more to a large club than to a small club, it will still be possible for the two clubs to come to an agreement. However, if the potential value of a player is greater in a small club, it is not inevitable that a player will end up there, because the small club may not be able to pay a sufficiently high fee to encourage the large club to part with a player or a large enough salary to attract the player.[2] If clubs are win maximizers, the distribution of playing talent should change in a manner that reduces competitive inequality with the abolition of the transfer system; although Kesenne (2006) argues that this effect may not be very significant.

Several potential direct effects of the Bosman ruling on the market for playing talent were identified by Simmons (1997), as follows:

1. The collapse of transfer markets
2. The loss of transfer income to smaller clubs
3. Increased and more unequal player salaries
4. A reduction in transfer fees
5. Longer-term contracts

We consider these in turn. Simmons believed the collapse of transfer markets was unlikely, because an important role of the transfer market is efficient matching of players, managers, and clubs. A player's contribution to team performance can vary considerably across clubs. Antonioni and Cubbin (2000) believed that most transfers would be relatively unaffected by Bosman. The majority of transfers have always involved players who are within contract. In the year preceding Bosman, Antonioni and Cubbin claim that 90 percent of transfers involving top-flight players in the UK had involved in-contract players. It should be relatively straightforward, therefore, for clubs to adapt their behavior to the changed circumstances by placing their most valuable players on long-term contracts.

On the question of the potential loss of income to smaller clubs, Simmons notes that many smaller clubs generated transfer surpluses that offset operating losses, but suggests that the transfer market was not an effective mechanism for redistributing income through the divisions of the league. Ericson (2000) argues that free agency might reduce the quality of play because the marginal cost of talent increases for small market clubs, which no longer receive adequate compensation for producing talent, because the large-market clubs free ride on the talent developed by the small market clubs. Such a free-rider effect could be mitigated by allowing transfer fees for non-contracted players.[3] In contrast, Fees and Muehlheusser (2003a, 2003b) distinguish between pre-Bosman, Bosman, and post-Bosman contracts, and find that each type leads to the same levels of player effort, investment incentive, and payoffs, provided the desired payoffs to players can be achieved by varying the contract length. If this is not possible, there are ambiguous results with respect to social welfare.[4]

On the question of increased and more unequal player salaries, Simmons suggests that transfer fees will be converted into higher player salaries and sign-on fees, whereas players in the lower leagues may face lower salaries. Tervio (2006) suggests that restricting the length of *enforceable* contracts to three years (or less for older players) will increase salaries for all types of player by more than their corresponding transfer-fee cost under the previously unregulated system, with the salaries of the highest star talent increasing the most.

The expected reduction in the size of transfer fees is linked to the question of contract duration, discussed later. What may be more apparent is a reduction in the proportion of players for whom no fee is demanded. Frick (2007) reports that, in Germany, the percentage of player moves involving the payment of a transfer fee declined from over 95 percent in the 1980s and early-1990s to below 40 percent more recently. Frick attributes this change to the effects of Bosman. Fees, Frick and Muehlheusser (2004) find evidence to support their hypothesis that the higher the remaining length of a player's contract, the higher the transfer fee that will ensue if the player is sold, and the lower the player's salary at his new club. They could, however, find no evidence that these effects were higher at the margins in the post-Bosman period than the pre-Bosman period.

There is general agreement that contract length should tend to be longer following Bosman, especially for the most talented players, though contracts are now constrained to be no longer than five years.[5] There is, however, a moral hazard problem if longer contracts increase the tendency for contracted players to shirk.[6] Fees, Frick, and Muehlheusser (2007) report that, in Germany, average contract length increased by about six months (or 20 percent) after the Bosman ruling, from around two-and-a half years to three years. Longer contracts, however, are not necessarily honored for the entire duration, and there are clear incentives for both clubs and players to either renegotiate or transfer before present contracts expire. Post-Bosman, football clubs are still able to realize a transfer fee by selling an in-contract player to another club. Accordingly, the incentive for the club to negotiate a transfer before the contract expires and the player becomes a free agent is strong. A player who allows his present contract to expire runs the risk that injury or loss of form could prevent him from either negotiating a new contract with his present club or transferring elsewhere.

Evidence of racial discrimination in English football is investigated by Goddard and Wilson (2009), using data for the period 1986–2001. Over this period, there was an increase of over 60 percent in the number of players employed in English football, reflecting rapid increases in revenues as a result of rising gate, commercial, and TV income. The proportion of black players also increased, and the rate of increase became faster in the post-Bosman period. Pre-Bosman, black players tended to gravitate toward teams with higher divisional status, suggesting that they were more talented than average football players employed with any Premier League or Football League club. Goddard and Wilson interpret this pattern as symptomatic of an element of hiring discrimination affecting opportunities for black players to become established as professionals. Although the most talented players were able to overcome whatever barriers existed, less talented black football players found it harder to do so than their (equally averagely talented) white counterparts. Post-Bosman, however, increased competition between clubs in the market for playing talent may have helped reduce the extent of racial discrimination.

Broader concerns over the impact of the Bosman ruling and the subsequent relaxation of restrictions on the employment of both non-British EU nationals and non-EU nationals in English football have centered on the following issues:

1. An increase in competitive inequality resulting from a tendency for the most talented players to gravitate more easily in a flexible market for playing talent to the richest and highest-paying clubs

2. Damage to the solvency of smaller football clubs that were previously reliant on "windfall" transfer-fee income resulting from the sale of talented discoveries to leading clubs

3. An erosion of professional career opportunities for locally born players, due to two factors: a lack of incentives for domestic clubs to invest in the development and training of new playing talent, and a displacement effect arising from an influx of foreign-born talent.

The received wisdom with respect to point 1 is that competitive inequality in English football has increased significantly during the first fifteen years post-Bosman; for empirical evidence, see Dobson and Goddard (2004). The extent to which the rising trend in competitive inequality is attributable to Bosman, however, is difficult to determine. It is clear that the financial windfalls experienced by the leading English clubs from increased TV and commercial revenues, following the formation of the English Premier League in 1992, and (for the very top clubs) from the revenues generated by the expansion of the pan-European Champions League have pushed similarly in the direction of increased competitive inequality.

Regarding point 2, the turnover of clubs in and out of the English Football League has risen during the 2000s, partly by design through an increase in the number of clubs automatically promoted and relegated between the Football League and the highest non-league division, from one to two per season from the 2002–03 season onward. Several clubs that have lost Football League status have done so against a background of severe financial duress. However, the sale of talented young players was always a highly volatile and unpredictable source of income for the smaller clubs, and it is not clear that dependence on such income ever formed a basis for a truly viable business model, even during the pre-Bosman period. Finally with respect to point 3, the influx of foreign players is one of the most visible and, in view of its effect on playing standards, surely welcome developments of the post-Bosman period. The verdict remains open, however, on the impact of this influx on employment opportunities for locally born players. This is one of the issues we investigate in the next section of this chapter.

4. Trends in Employment Patterns of Professional Footballers in England and Wales, 1986–2009

The principal data source for the empirical analysis reported in this section is the Premier League (PL) and Football League (FL) retained list, published annually in *Sky Sports Football Yearbook* (known as *Rothmans Football Yearbook* prior to 2003). This source provides an annual snapshot of the employment history and current status of all players employed with the ninety-two English league member clubs at an end-of-season (May) census point, enabling career progression to be tracked at the micro (individual player) level. In addition, we used the comprehensive post-war listing of players' career records compiled by Hugman (1998) to cross-check the data for the earlier years, and to complete some of the early-career details for players whose records would otherwise have been left-censored. As an employment sector, professional team sports are possibly unique in having available in the public domain regular and comprehensive data on the employment status of a principal category of employee.

At the time of writing in 2009, the top twenty clubs in England and Wales compete in the PL, and the next seventy-two clubs compete in 3 twenty-four-club divisions of the FL (currently known as the Championship, League One and League Two). The PL was formed at the start of the 1992–93 season. Previously, the top ninety-two clubs were all members of the FL, which was organized into four divisions numbered 1 to 4. Over the period under review, there have been occasional and relatively minor changes to the numbers of clubs per division, and there have been several changes to the names of the four divisions. For simplicity and consistency, throughout this section we refer to the current PL and three divisions of the FL, and the four pre-1992 divisions of the FL, as "tiers" T1, T2, T3, and T4.

Table 14.1 reports the number of players recorded at each end-of-season census point from 1986 to 2009, in total and disaggregated between the four tiers (divisions). During this period as a whole, there has been significant growth in the numbers of players employed by PL and FL clubs in all four tiers. Overall, the total number of professional football players was 46.0 percent higher in 2009 than it was in 1986. The rate of growth was somewhat faster in T1 and T2 (55.2 percent and 55.4 percent, respectively), and somewhat slower in T3 and T4 (38.5 percent and 31.9 percent, respectively). Employment growth appears to have been concentrated mainly in T2, T3, and T4 in the late-1980s, with most of the growth in T1 having occurred a few years later, during the 1990s. Employment in T2, T3, and T4 continued to grow throughout the 1990s, but at a slower rate than in T1. The peak numbers of professional football players were recorded between 1999 and 2002. Between 2002 and 2009, total employment dropped by around 10 percent. A reduction in employment in T2, T3, and T4 accounts for most of this decline.

Table 14.1 also reports the mean and standard deviation of the average age (last birthday) of all players recorded in each end-of-season census. Table 14.2 reports a more detailed analysis of changes in the age distribution of professional footballers, based on comparisons drawn at five-year intervals using the 1989, 1994, 1999, 2004, and 2009 end-of-season censuses. Although there was little change in the average age of professional footballers between 1986 and 2009, during the 1990s there was a pronounced increase in the standard deviation of players' ages. This increase appears to have been driven by improvements in training regimes and in the treatment of injuries, which enabled more players to prolong their playing careers into their mid- or late-thirties. Between 1989 and 1999 the proportion of professional footballers aged thirty-three or more increased from 5.4 percent to 8.3 percent. During the 2000s, however, there are signs of a reversal of this trend toward career

Table 14.1 Employment Totals for Professional Football Players in the PL and FL by Tier (Division), 1986–2009

	T1	T2	T3	T4	Total	Mean age	S.D. Age
1986	623	509	501	476	2109	24.0	4.7
1987	649	522	546	536	2253	23.9	4.7
1988	613	574	579	585	2351	24.1	4.8
1989	610	655	600	595	2460	24.1	4.8
1990	627	717	630	616	2590	24.1	4.8
1991	679	721	634	626	2660	24.2	4.8
1992	749	718	670	581	2718	24.3	4.9
1993	779	727	617	546	2669	24.3	4.9
1994	779	792	634	622	2828	24.5	5.0
1995	846	753	654	596	2849	24.5	5.1
1996	830	820	675	686	3011	24.4	5.2
1997	825	812	688	691	3016	24.4	5.2
1998	859	884	732	704	3179	24.3	5.3
1999	980	848	767	728	3323	24.2	5.3
2000	937	910	804	741	3392	24.2	5.4
2001	944	946	785	733	3408	24.3	5.3
2002	952	924	776	772	3424	24.3	5.3
2003	958	848	728	687	3221	24.4	5.3
2004	881	776	676	680	3013	24.4	5.2
2005	803	785	726	714	3028	24.6	5.3
2006	815	771	715	686	2987	24.4	5.3
2007	834	765	659	645	2903	24.5	5.2
2008	939	797	700	651	3087	24.2	5.1
2009	967	791	694	628	3080	24.2	5.0
Percent growth, 1986–2009	+55.2	+55.4	+38.5	+31.9	+46.0		

prolongation. By 2009 the proportion of footballers aged thirty-three or more had fallen back to 6.6 percent, and there was a downward drift in the standard deviation of football players' ages.

At the other end of the age distribution, Table 14.2 suggests that over the period there has been a shift in the burden of responsibility for the development of new playing talent away from clubs in T3 and T4, and toward clubs in T1 and T2. During the mid- to late-1990s following the formation of the PL in 1992 and the Bosman ruling in 1995, much of the growth in employment in T1 was concentrated among footballers in the younger age groups, as newly cash-rich clubs cast the net more widely in their efforts to unearth new playing talent. During the 2000s, however,

Table 14.2 Percentage Distribution of Professional Football Players in the PL and FL by Age Band and Tier (Division), Selected Years

	T1	T2	T3	T4	All
1989					
under 21	35.9	28.7	30.0	29.2	30.9
21–24	24.3	28.1	26.0	27.7	26.5
25–28	23.9	23.2	22.0	23.0	23.0
29–32	12.8	15.0	15.2	13.4	14.1
over 32	3.1	5.0	6.8	6.6	5.4
	100.0	100.0	100.0	100.0	100.0
1994					
under 21	32.0	30.2	25.6	24.6	28.4
21–24	24.3	24.7	24.9	32.3	26.3
25–28	20.3	22.6	24.8	20.3	21.9
29–32	17.2	16.5	15.8	14.0	16.0
over 32	6.3	5.9	9.0	8.8	7.4
	100.0	100.0	100.0	100.0	100.0
1999					
under 21	45.3	33.7	29.3	27.9	34.8
21–24	16.7	21.5	20.6	25.4	20.7
25–28	18.2	21.1	22.4	22.0	20.7
29–32	14.0	16.3	17.7	13.7	15.4
over 32	5.8	7.4	9.9	11.0	8.3
	100.0	100.0	100.0	100.0	100.0
2004					
under 21	36.4	29.1	26.6	20.7	28.8
21–24	20.7	26.0	31.1	35.4	27.7
25–28	18.5	17.3	20.4	21.3	19.2
29–32	17.4	18.7	13.0	13.2	15.8
over 32	7.0	8.9	8.9	9.3	8.4
	100.0	100.0	100.0	100.0	100.0
2009					
under 21	40.7	28.7	27.4	22.5	30.9
21–24	20.1	25.0	27.5	30.3	25.1
25–28	20.6	24.0	23.6	24.7	23.0
29–32	13.9	15.9	14.7	12.9	14.4
over 32	4.8	6.3	6.8	9.7	6.6
	100.0	100.0	100.0	100.0	100.0

the employment share of the under-twenty-one age group in T1 appears to have stabilized (but there is significant year-on-year variation). Over the period 1986–2009
as a whole, the employment share of the under-twenty-one age group in T3 and T4
clubs fell by 2.6 percent and 6.7 percent, respectively. As suggested in section 3, this
reduction may be related to the introduction of free agency through the Bosman

Table 14.3 Employment Totals for Professional Football Players in the PL And FL
by Birthplace (Country), 1986–2009

	England and Wales	Scotland	Northern Ireland	Republic of Ireland	Rest of the world	All
1986	1820	157	39	33	60	2109
1987	1949	160	41	41	62	2253
1988	2038	160	40	48	65	2351
1989	2126	169	44	50	71	2460
1990	2218	174	49	54	95	2590
1991	2288	167	40	62	103	2660
1992	2328	153	40	69	128	2718
1993	2277	144	46	61	141	2669
1994	2408	156	48	60	156	2828
1995	2415	140	48	64	182	2849
1996	2514	134	51	76	236	3011
1997	2443	140	61	79	293	3016
1998	2486	144	67	98	384	3179
1999	2517	153	69	105	479	3323
2000	2521	152	69	133	517	3392
2001	2427	153	71	155	602	3408
2002	2407	147	81	165	624	3424
2003	2268	133	72	153	595	3221
2004	2129	126	67	135	556	3013
2005	2098	121	65	124	620	3028
2006	2084	103	68	122	610	2987
2007	1993	98	53	124	635	2903
2008	2086	102	58	122	719	3087
2009	2057	104	48	127	744	3080
Percent growth, 1986–2009	+13.0	-33.8	+23.1	+284.8	+1140.0	+46.0

ruling which, despite safeguards in the form of financial compensation when players below the age of twenty-four change clubs as free agents, have made it more difficult for lower-division clubs to realize large windfall financial gains through the sale of their most talented young players to top clubs. Accordingly the incentive to invest in the training and development of young footballers is reduced.

Table 14.3 reports the number of players recorded at each end-of-season census point from 1986 to 2009, disaggregated by country of birth. The categories are England and Wales, Scotland, Northern Ireland, Republic of Ireland, and the rest of the world. Although sustained growth in the employment of footballers from outside the British Isles (the rest of the world category) had been underway for a number of years prior to the Bosman ruling, the rate of growth was markedly faster throughout the second half of the 1990s. After a short pause between 2001 and 2004, when the employment of players from outside the British Isles went into decline, the upward trend has resumed subsequently, with a record total of 744 (24.2 percent of total employment) recorded in 2009.

Among the other categories reported in Table 14.3, the number of players born in England and Wales who were employed in 2009 was only 13 percent higher than the corresponding figure in 1986. The period 1986–2000 witnessed a significant increase in employment opportunities for locally-born players, but most of this gain was reversed subsequently during the 2000s. The number of Scottish-born players playing in the PL and FL has declined, gradually during the 1990s and more sharply during the 2000s. For players born in Northern Ireland, there was employment growth over the period 1986–2002, followed by decline during 2002–2009. For players born in the Republic of Ireland the pattern is similar, but with markedly faster growth recorded for 1986–2002, and a slower rate of decline for 2002–2009.

Table 14.4 reports a more detailed analysis of changes in the distribution of players by country of birth and by tier (division), based on comparisons drawn at five-year intervals using the 1989, 1994, 1999, 2004, and 2009 end-of-season censuses. The relationship between divisional status and the employment of players from outside the British Isles is monotonic at each of these observation points. Accordingly, most of the employment growth in this category is concentrated on T1, followed by T2, T3, and T4, respectively. For the rest of the world category, three factors are likely to have contributed toward this skewed distribution of employment by divisional status. First, the top English clubs have the financial resources to be able to search for playing talent internationally, but the lower-division clubs may not be able to do so. Second, the financial rewards in T1 and (to a lesser extent) T2 are sufficient to induce the most talented players to relocate to England, but the financial rewards in T3 and T4 may be insufficient. Third, the rules governing the issue of visas and work permits for the employment of non-EU nationals are more favorable to the most talented sports professionals, but less favorable to journeyman non-EU professionals, in order to protect the employment of locally born players.

Table 14.4 Total Numbers of Professional Football Players in the PL and FL by Birthplace (Country) and Tier (Division), Selected Years

	T1	T2	T3	T4	All
1989					
E+W	484	546	557	539	2126
Scotland	47	64	20	38	169
NI	18	12	8	6	44
Ireland	28	8	7	7	50
RoW	33	25	8	5	71
	610	655	600	595	2460
1994					
E+W	606	665	569	568	2408
Scotland	56	51	22	26	156
NI	21	14	10	3	48
Ireland	24	19	8	9	60
RoW	72	43	25	16	156
	779	792	634	622	2828
1999					
E+W	617	646	607	647	2517
Scotland	49	36	41	27	153
NI	22	22	21	4	69
Ireland	61	21	14	9	105
RoW	231	123	84	41	479
	980	848	767	728	3323
2004					
E+W	448	543	547	591	2129
Scotland	53	27	30	16	126
NI	17	23	13	14	67
Ireland	54	43	19	19	135
RoW	309	140	67	40	556
	881	776	676	680	3013
2009					
E+W	451	505	553	548	2057
Scotland	18	47	23	16	104
NI	22	12	6	8	48
Ireland	33	48	31	15	127
RoW	443	179	81	41	744
	967	791	694	628	3080

It is likely that the first two of these three factors are also partly responsible for the skewed distribution by tier (division) of employment of players born in Scotland, Northern Ireland and the Republic of Ireland. The skewness was more pronounced in the earlier years than it has been in the later ones, with T2 having overtaken T1 with respect to the employment of both Scottish- and Irish-born players by 2009. In 1989, Scotland was the principal source of non-indigenous playing talent for T1 clubs in England and Wales. By 2009, however, the T1 clubs were casting their nets further afield in their quest to unearth new playing talent. The contribution of the Scottish contingent at the top level in English football, in both relative and absolute terms, was considerably diminished.

The data reported in Tables 14.3 and 14.4 suggest that there have been significant changes in employment opportunities in the PL and FL for players born in England and Wales. Employment prospects of may have benefited to some extent from the increase in total employment over the period 1986–2009, but prospects have also been damaged by the sharp influx of players born outside the British Isles. Table 14.5 presents an analysis of the distribution of the employment of players at the level of standard English regions (for those born in England) or by country (using the same categories as Tables 14.3 and 14.4 for players born outside England).

Table 14.5 indicates some sharp regional disparities in changes in the employment prospects for English-born players. The numbers of professional footballers born in the East, London, North West, and South East regions increased, by 38.2 percent, 24.0 percent, 17.9 percent, and 16.2 percent, respectively, between 1989 and

Table 14.5 Total Numbers of Professional Football Players in the PL and FL by Birthplace (Country and English region), Selected Years

	1989	1994	1999	2004	2009	% growth, 1989–2009
London	337	392	392	369	418	+24.0
South East	162	191	205	180	191	+17.9
South West	114	132	142	117	112	−1.8
East	110	157	173	155	152	+38.2
East Midlands	154	181	186	169	125	−18.8
West Midlands	220	252	241	191	196	−10.9
Yorks and Humber	316	329	329	256	221	−30.1
North West	389	440	479	411	452	+16.2
North East	214	222	217	178	119	−44.4
Wales	110	112	153	103	71	−35.5
Scotland	169	156	153	126	104	−38.5
Northern Ireland	44	48	69	67	48	+9.1
Rep. Ireland	50	60	105	135	127	+154.0
Rest of the world	71	156	479	556	744	+947.9
Total	2460	2828	3323	3013	3080	+25.2

2009, but the numbers born in the South West, West Midlands, East Midlands, Yorks and Humber, Wales, and North East regions decreased by 1.8 percent, 10.9 percent, 18.8 percent, 30.1 percent, 35.5 percent, and 44.4 percent, respectively. Some of these shifts might be explained by shifts in the fortunes of the PL and FL clubs from each region. For example, the number of North West clubs in T1 increased from three in 1989 to seven in 2009. London and the adjacent South East region have also remained strongly represented at the highest level throughout the period. In contrast, the sharp reduction in the employment of players born in the North East is especially noteworthy, in view of this region's renowned historical tradition as a producer of high-quality playing talent. Clearly there are some affinities between the experiences of the North East and Scotland in this respect.

Table 14.6 reports several indicators of the trend toward rising turnover in player employment in the PL and FL at five-year intervals between 1989 and 2009: the average number of career appearances in PL and FL matches made by players recorded in the end-of year censuses, the average number of appearances for the player's current club, the average number of end-of season censuses in which each employed player had appeared, and the average number of seasons in which the player was employed by his current club. These data are reported for all players, and for players that had made at least one PL or FL appearance by the time of the relevant census (to avoid possible distortions caused by variations in the numbers of youth- or reserve-team players employed). All of the data reported in Table 14.6 point in the direction of an increase in the turnover of employment.

Tables 14.1 to 14.6 provide snapshots of the characteristics of the population of football players employed by PL and FL clubs at various points in time. The data set, however, also permits us to track the career progression of individual players over time. Table 14.7 reports empirical transition probabilities based on

Table 14.6 Indicators of Employment Turnover for Football Players in the PL and FL, Selected Years

	1989	1994	1999	2004	2009
All football Players					
Average number of PL/FL appearances	138.3	133.8	117.2	118.0	112.1
Average number of appearances for current club	51.9	52.1	42.6	47.8	40.7
Average number of seasons employed	6.05	6.14	5.75	5.89	5.48
Average number of seasons with current club	2.53	2.74	2.49	2.70	2.36
Footballers who have appeared in the PL or FL					
Average number of PL/FL appearances	156.3	157.5	147.8	138.5	133.5
Average number of appearances for current club	58.7	61.3	53.7	56.1	48.5
Average number of seasons employed	6.66	6.94	6.82	6.58	6.22
Average number of seasons with current club	2.69	2.96	2.73	2.84	2.51

comparisons between the divisional status (T1, T2, T3, or T4) of players employed at each of two start-years of 1989 and 1994, and the status of the same players five years later in 1994 and 1999, respectively. Table 14.8 reports the equivalent analysis for start-years 1999 and 2004 and end-years 2004 and 2009, respectively. Transition probabilities are reported for all players in the top panels of Tables 14.7 and 14.8, and for players in the under- twenty-one, twenty-one to twenty-four, twenty-five to twenty-eight, twenty-nine to thirty-two, and over-thirty-two age bands in the remaining panels. Using the first row of Table 14.8 as an example, 21.7 percent of players who were employed by a T1 club in 1999 were also employed by a T1 club in 2004, 12.0 percent of those employed in T1 in 1999 were employed in T2 in 2004, 7.8 percent and 5.8 percent of those employed in T1 in 1999 were employed in T3 and T4 in 2004, respectively, and 56.3 percent were not employed by any PL or FL club in 2004. Similarly, the percentages of T1 players in 2004 employed in T1, T2, T3, and T4 and not employed in 2009 were 19.6 percent, 14.4 percent, 5.9 percent, 3.7 percent, and 56.3 percent, respectively.

The probability of not being employed at the end of each five-year period is directly related to the divisional status of the player's employer at the start of the period: T1 players are the most likely and T4 players are the least likely to be employed five years later. These data indicate that employment growth has been accompanied by a rise in employment turnover. Between 1989 and 2004 total employment increased by 22.5 percent from 2,460 to 3,013. However, a comparison between the numbers of players who were employed in both 1989 and 1994, and the numbers who were employed in both 2004 and 2009, shows a decline of 21.7 percent from 1,683 to 1,317. This increase in turnover is only partially attributable to the influx of players born outside the British Isles, who are more likely than their British or Irish counterparts to exit from employment in the PL or FL in order to join an overseas club, and who, therefore, tend to exhibit a faster rate of turnover. Excluding the rest of the world category, between 1989 and 2004 total employment increased by 2.8 percent, whereas the comparison between the numbers employed in both 1989 and 1994 and the numbers employed in both 2004 and 2009 shows a decline of 20.2 percent.

The tabulation of five-year transition probabilities by age group indicates that the transition probabilities are highly non-linear in age. By age band, the five-year transition probabilities out of employment between 1989 and 1994 were 0.402 (under twenty-one), 0.189 (twenty-one to twenty-four), 0.226 (twenty-five to twenty-eight), 0.397 (twenty-nine to thirty-two) and 0.684 (over thirty-two). The corresponding probabilities between 2004 and 2009 were 0.583, 0.390, 0.491, 0.686, and 0.855. The under-twenty-one age band includes a high proportion of youngsters who subsequently fail to make the grade as professionals, whereas the over-thirty-two age band naturally includes older professionals who are approaching retirement. Among those players who remain in employment, there is a consistent tendency for divisional status to decline as a player's career progresses. In other words, players who eventually become unemployable at the highest level are able to prolong their

Table 14.7 Five-Year Employment Transition Probabilities by Tier (Division), 1989–1994 and 1994–1999

	Start = 1989, End = 1994 End Status					Start = 1994, End = 1999 End Status				
	T1	T2	T3	T4	Not emp.	T1	T2	T3	T4	Not emp.
all ages										
start: T1	.316	.193	.105	.069	.316	.240	.167	.127	.091	.375
T2	.153	.206	.136	.110	.395	.100	.160	.140	.119	.481
T3	.060	.092	.153	.138	.557	.024	.080	.150	.148	.598
T4	.020	.106	.104	.109	.661	.016	.064	.103	.116	.701
All	.139	.151	.125	.107	.479	.103	.123	.130	.117	.526
under 21										
start: T1	.187	.160	.151	.100	.402	.169	.116	.129	.116	.470
T2	.154	.229	.096	.133	.388	.079	.151	.113	.105	.552
T3	.083	.072	.122	.144	.578	.043	.086	.117	.130	.623
T4	.034	.161	.098	.098	.609	.033	.078	.111	.092	.686
All	.120	.156	.118	.118	.488	.091	.113	.118	.111	.567
21–24										
start: T1	.480	.223	.054	.054	.189	.333	.233	.127	.069	.238
T2	.223	.277	.141	.092	.266	.179	.194	.179	.143	.306
T3	.096	.160	.244	.141	.359	.032	.108	.209	.203	.449
T4	.024	.139	.176	.164	.497	.020	.109	.129	.149	.592
All	.201	.202	.155	.113	.329	.144	.162	.158	.140	.396
25–28										
start: T1	.411	.233	.075	.055	.226	.335	.228	.127	.095	.215
T2	.112	.224	.204	.105	.355	.117	.218	.179	.128	.358
T3	.045	.106	.174	.159	.515	.019	.108	.197	.185	.490
T4	.015	.080	.088	.131	.686	.008	.040	.135	.143	.675
All	.150	.164	.136	.111	.439	.126	.156	.161	.137	.419
29–32										
start: T1	.256	.192	.115	.038	.397	.187	.134	.149	.082	.448
T2	.102	.071	.133	.133	.561	.031	.107	.099	.122	.641
T3	.000	.033	.099	.121	.747	.000	.020	.110	.080	.790
T4	.000	.013	.050	.025	.913	.000	.011	.046	.103	.839
All	.086	.075	.101	.084	.654	.064	.077	.106	.097	.655
over 32										
start: T1	.053	.053	.158	.053	.684	.082	.061	.061	.061	.735
T2	.091	.000	.030	.030	.848	.000	.000	.085	.043	.872
T3	.000	.000	.000	.073	.927	.000	.018	.018	.070	.895
T4	.000	.000	.000	.026	.974	.000	.000	.000	.018	.982
All	.030	.008	.030	.045	.886	.019	.019	.038	.048	.875

Table 14.8 Five-Year Employment Transition Probabilities by Tier (Division), 1999–2004 and 2004–2009

| | Start = 1999, End = 2004 End status | | | | | Start = 2004, End = 2009 End status | | | | |
	T1	T2	T3	T4	Not emp.	T1	T2	T3	T4	Not emp.
all ages										
start: T1	.217	.120	.078	.058	.527	.196	.144	.059	.037	.563
T2	.067	.143	.114	.104	.572	.079	.151	.115	.093	.563
T3	.035	.100	.123	.107	.635	.016	.078	.130	.133	.642
T4	.005	.040	.065	.122	.768	.015	.056	.103	.103	.724
All	.091	.104	.094	.095	.616	.085	.111	.099	.088	.617
under 21										
start: T1	.155	.099	.113	.090	.543	.128	.156	.072	.062	.583
T2	.063	.108	.087	.098	.643	.080	.119	.106	.080	.615
T3	.053	.076	.107	.080	.684	.028	.072	.133	.128	.639
T4	.010	.054	.039	.118	.778	.021	.050	.135	.064	.730
All	.087	.089	.092	.095	.636	.077	.112	.104	.081	.627
21–24										
start: T1	.335	.128	.079	.061	.396	.341	.165	.066	.038	.390
T2	.104	.231	.187	.115	.363	.144	.223	.168	.119	.347
T3	.051	.152	.152	.203	.443	.024	.124	.138	.171	.543
T4	.005	.054	.135	.184	.622	.021	.100	.124	.116	.639
All	.120	.141	.139	.141	.459	.121	.150	.126	.114	.490
25–28										
start: T1	.309	.197	0.039	.028	.427	.282	.178	.043	.006	.491
T2	.078	.196	0.140	.106	.480	.067	.261	.127	.075	.470
T3	.041	.163	0.157	.110	.529	.007	.087	.181	.181	.543
T4	.006	.044	0.063	.150	.738	.014	.048	.117	.159	.662
All	.112	.152	0.100	.097	.538	.100	.143	.114	.102	.541
29–32										
start: T1	.219	.109	.044	.007	.620	.124	.105	.052	.033	.686
T2	.036	.072	.087	.123	.681	.028	.069	.097	.117	.690
T3	.000	.051	.118	.081	.750	.000	.023	.091	.068	.818
T4	.000	.010	.030	.060	.900	.000	.000	.033	.100	.867
All	.068	.065	.072	.068	.726	.048	.059	.069	.078	.746
over 32										
start: T1	.070	.053	.000	.018	.860	.081	.032	.032	.000	.855
T2	.016	.048	.016	.048	.873	.014	.000	.000	.043	.942
T3	.000	.013	.039	.026	.921	.000	.000	.033	.000	.967
T4	.000	.000	.013	.013	.975	.000	.000	.016	.016	.968
All	.018	.025	.018	.025	.913	.024	.008	.020	.016	.933

playing careers by a few years by accepting a transfer that entails a move to a lower tier (division). Consistently across Tables 14.7 and 14.8, the probabilities of playing in a lower tier after five years (above the main diagonal) exceed the probabilities of playing in a higher tier (below the main diagonal). For all except the youngest age group, the probabilities of moving to a higher tier tend to decrease monotonically with age, and the probabilities of moving to a lower tier tend to increase monotonically.

5. Conclusion

In this chapter, we have traced the historical development of free agency in professional football. The European Court of Justice's landmark 1995 ruling in the case of Jean-Marc Bosman versus his employer, the Belgian football club RFC Liege, established the principle of complete freedom of movement across national borders within the EU for out-of-contract professional football players over the age of twenty-four who seek renewed employment with another football club. The European football industry quickly adapted to this imposed change in the legal environment by introducing similar provisions for freedom of movement between clubs within national borders, and by reducing, but not completely eliminating, restrictions on the employment by EU football clubs of non-EU nationals.

With more than fifteen years having elapsed since the Bosman ruling, it is possible to make an evidence-based assessment of the impact of Bosman. In this chapter, we have presented data on changes in the patterns of employment of professional footballers in the English Premier League and Football League since the mid-1980s, using a data set that straddles both the pre- and post-Bosman periods. The influx of foreign players is one of the most visible post-Bosman developments. Its effects on the employment prospects of locally born players, however, are more difficult to disentangle, because the latter are also influenced by fluctuations in the financial fortunes of football clubs attributable to other factors. Although the employment of players born in the British Isles increased during the 1990s, it has fallen back again during the 2000s, whereas the size of the international contingent has continued to increase relentlessly.

Although there is evidence that Bosman increased the average duration of players' employment contracts, employment turnover has also risen, in part because there are incentives for both clubs and players to either renegotiate their contracts or transfer before contracts reach expiry. There appears to have been a shift in the overall burden of responsibility for the development of young players away from the smaller English clubs toward their larger counterparts, perhaps because the financial incentive for small clubs to invest in player development is reduced if they are unable to realize windfall financial gains by selling their talented discoveries to larger clubs. This shift has been accompanied by sharp regional disparities in the effect on the prospects for locally born youngsters to become professional footballers. Employment prospects have improved for youngsters born in regions with a preponderance of top-level professional clubs, such as London and the North West; but prospects have diminished, in several cases substantially, for youngsters born elsewhere. The decline is especially noticeable in certain regions, such as the North West and Scotland, with a strong history of producing high-quality football talent.

NOTES

1 For a more detailed discussion of the judgement see Campbell and Sloane (1997).
2 As Bourgheas and Downward (2003) note, the invariance principle may not hold in an incomplete contracting environment, so that there may be negative effects on competitive balance even in a profit maximizing framework.
3 But see Dilger (2002).
4 For a discussion of the effect in particular on small clubs see Szymanski (1999).
5 However, five years is long in relation to a player's expected length of career. Frick (2007) reports that the average duration of career for current players in the Bundesliga is four years and less than ten per cent of careers extend beyond nine years.
6 As Fees and Muehlheusser (2003) put it, "the shorter the initial contract the higher the player's stake in the renegotiation game, because he benefits from being out of contract. This induces him to exert greater effort. Shorter contracts also benefit a purchasing club since it is less costly to buy an out of contract player."

REFERENCES

Antonioni, P., and J. Cubbin, 2000. The Bosman ruling and the emergence of a single market in soccer talent. *European Journal of Law and Economics* 9(2): 157–173.

Bourgheas, S., and P. Downward, 2003. The economics of professional sports leagues: Some insights on the reform of transfer markets. *Journal of Sports Economics* 4(2): 87–107.

Campbell A.I.L., and P.J. Sloane. 1997. The implications of the Bosman case for professional football. *Scottish Law and Practice Quarterly* 2(3): 230–248.

Dilger, A. 2001. The Ericsson case. *Journal of Sports Economics* 2(2): 194–198.

Dobson, S., and J. Goddard, 2004. Revenue divergence and competitive balance in a divisional sports league. *Scottish Journal of Political Economy* 51(3): 359–376.

Ericson, T. 2000. The Bosman case: Effects of the abolition of the transfer fee. *Journal of Sports Economics* 1(3): 203–218.

Fees, E., and G. Muehlheusser. 2003. Transfer fee regulations in European football. *European Economic Review* 47: 645–668.

Fees, E., and G. Muehlheusser. 2003. The impact of transfer fees on professional sports: An analysis of the new transfer system for European football. *Scandinavian Journal of Economics* 105(1): 139–154.

Fees, E., B. Frick, and G. Muehlheusser. 2004. Legal restrictions on buyout fees: Theory and evidence from German soccer. IZA Discussion Paper No. 1180, Bonn.

Frick, B., 2007. The football players' labour market: Empirical evidence from the major European leagues. *Scottish Journal of Political Economy* 54(3): 422–446.

Goddard, J., and J.O.S. Wilson. 2009. Racial discrimination in English professional football: Evidence from an empirical analysis of players' career profession. *Cambridge Journal of Economics* 3392: 295–316.

Hugman, B. 1998. *The PFA Premier and Football League players' records*, 1946–1998. Harpenden: Queen Anne Press.

Kesenne, S. 2006. The Bosman case and European football. In *Handbook on the Economics of Sport,* eds. W. Andreff and S. Szymanski, 636–642. Edward Elgar.

Simmons, R. 1997. Implications of the Bosman ruling for football transfer markets. *Economic Affairs* 17(3): 13–18.

Sloane, P.J. 1969. The labour market in professional football. *British Journal of Industrial Relations.* 181–199.

Szymanski, S. 1999. The market for soccer players in England after Bosman: Winners and losers. In *Competition Policy in Professional Sports: Europe after the Bosman Case,* eds. C. Jeanrenaud and S. Kesenne, 133–160. University of Neuchatel, Switzerland: CEIS.

Szymanski, S., and T. Kuypers. 1999. *Winners and losers: The business strategy off Football.* London: Viking.

Tervio, M. 2006. Transfer fee regulations and player development. *Journal of the European Economic Association* 4(5): 957–987.

Thomas, D. 2006. The retain and transfer system. In *Handbook on the Economics of Sports,* eds. W. Andreff and S. Szymanski, 630–635. Edward Elgar.

CHAPTER 15

LABOR SUPPLY AND HUMAN CAPITAL FORMATION IN PROFESSIONAL TEAM SPORTS

EVIDENCE FROM THE FA PREMIER LEAGUE

BILL GERRARD

INTRODUCTION

COMMON sense tells us that the more successful sports teams tend to have better quality players. It is this expected positive association between player quality and team success that underpins much of the economic analysis of professional team sports, which is pervaded by a belief in financial determinism—"wallets will win." Financial determinism is the proposition that larger-market teams can use their superiority in economic and financial resources to acquire the best playing talent and increase their probability of sporting success. It is the belief in financial determinism combined with the belief that uncertainty of outcome is an essential source of utility for sports fans that together provide the rationale for league interventionist strategies to maintain an adequate degree of competitive balance between teams with varying degrees of economic potential. Professional sports leagues have sought to close the economic gap between large- and small-market teams by both product market and labor market regulations (Fort and Quirk, 1995). Product market regulations have usually taken the form of cross-subsidization through revenue-sharing arrangements such as sharing gate receipts between home and away teams, and collective selling by the league of media and other image rights. Labor market regulations have involved limiting how much teams can spend on player salaries through salary caps as well as limiting the scope for competitive auctions between teams for playing talent by, for example, player reservation systems and centralized drafting arrangements for rookie players.

But, as always, reality tends to be much more complex. The link from individual talent to team performance is complex. The main proposition of this chapter is that although team performance is crucially dependent on the team's stock of human capital, there is a need to develop a multidimensional human capital model of team performance to more fully understand the complex causal nexus. The chapter is structured as follows. Following this introduction, the next section provides a short review of the relevant literatures on coaching efficiency and the resource-based view of the firm and develops a multidimensional human capital model of team performance. The following section provides an initial empirical application of the multidimensional human capital model by examining labor supply and human capital formation in the FA Premier League in England, the leading domestic soccer league globally in financial terms. The chapter concludes with a summary of the principal theoretical and empirical findings, some discussion of the limitations of the proposed model, and suggestions for future research.

A MULTIDIMENSIONAL HUMAN CAPITAL MODEL OF TEAM PERFORMANCE

There are two starting points in the existing literatures for the multidimensional human capital model of team performance: the coaching efficiency literature in sports economics, and the resource-based view of the firm in strategic management. Research on coaching efficiency has sought to quantify how much of team performance can be attributed to the coaching staff. This research involves specifying a sporting production function to capture the link between inputs and outputs within a professional sports team. Clearly, in order to quantify the effectiveness of the input of the coaching staff (usually identified by the head coach), it is crucial to control for the other principal input, namely, the quantity and quality of playing talent available to the team. At least four different approaches have been used by different studies to control for playing talent: (1) the financial approach; (2) the player characteristics approach; (3) the player rating approach; and (4) the on-the-field player performance approach. The financial approach involves using the financial expenditure by teams on playing talent as a measure of the team's playing resources. The team's expenditure on player wages is the most obvious financial proxy of playing resources, although this may need to be adjusted to include capital expenditures if teams are required to pay a transfer fee to other teams to acquire a player's playing services as in soccer. The financial approach has been adopted quite widely in research on coaching efficiency in soccer (see, for example, Szymanski and Smith, 1997; Szymanski and Kuypers, 1999; Haas, 2003) although the lack of public availability of reliable individual player salary data in European soccer has required the use of accounting data on total salary expenditure by teams that includes the salaries of coaches and managerial and administrative staff.

The player characteristics approach to measuring team quality is to use team averages for certain key characteristics of individual players such as age, career experience, and career achievements such as international or all-stars selections. Rather than using team averages of player characteristics, an alternative approach is to use either published player ratings or to construct a player quality index using player characteristics data combined with an appropriate weighting system. One early example of using a player ratings system to control for team quality was by Fizel and D'itri (1996) who employed the *Hoop Scoop* talent index in their study of coaching efficiency in NCAA Division 1 basketball. Gerrard (2001) proposed a player quality index for soccer players using current and career data on age, experience, and achievements. Gerrard used a hedonic-pricing analysis of soccer transfer fees to identify both the relevant player characteristics and the appropriate weightings. This approach was used by Gerrard (2005) in a study of sporting and financial performance in the FA Premier League. Dawson et al. (2000a, b) used all three of these approaches in their study of coaching efficiency in English professional soccer.

The final approach to controlling for playing resources is on-the-field performance data. The use of player performance data in sports economics can be traced back to Scully (1974), who estimated the marginal productivity of Major League Baseball players using hitting and pitching data. The availability of equivalent data for more complex and continuous invasion team sports such as soccer is a more recent phenomenon, reliant on video and tracking systems. Carmichael et al. (2000) was one of the first studies in soccer to use player performance data to identify efficiency differences. More recently, Gerrard (2007) used player performance data within a hierarchical structural model of soccer to compare the coaching efficiency of two leading English soccer teams over a four-year period. Of course, these types of study take a much more limited view of coaching efficiency, since player on-the-field performance could be considered as an intermediary output, with the coaching input encompassing both the training and motivational function to enable players to produce their best individual performances given their *ex ante* playing potential as well as the more tactical/strategic function of combining individual player performances to produce the optimal team performance. The training and motivational function is not captured by those coaching efficiency studies that use player performance as the measure of playing resource.

Studies of coaching efficiency have used a variety of statistical methods: regression analysis, data envelopment analysis, and stochastic frontier analysis. As Dawson et al. (2000) show, the estimates of coaching efficiency can be very sensitive to both the measures of playing resources and the statistical methods employed. Some studies have gone beyond simply attributing the unexplained residual variation in team performance (i.e., after controlling for player quality) to coaching efficiency and have attempted to tunnel down to investigate the possible effects of coaching characteristics such as career playing and coaching experience and achievements on coaching efficiency. The first study of this type was the analysis on coaching efficiency in Major League Baseball by Porter and Scully (1982).

An important consideration for understanding the link between player quality and team performance that emerges from the coaching efficiency literature is the game structure of the team sport being analyzed. In simple atomistic striking-and-fielding sports such as baseball, there is little interdependency between the performances of individual players within a team with the consequence that the tactical/strategic coaching function is limited. Smart et al. (2008), for example, find that field managers in baseball have "very limited influence" on team performance and highlight "the independence of the players during the game" (p. 318). Clearly, any analysis of more complex invasion team sports such as soccer, other codes of football, hockey, and basketball needs to allow for the interdependency effects.

It is the importance of interdependency effects in invasion team sports that has been a focus of the other literature on which this chapter draws. The resource-based view of the firm in strategic management emerged in the late 1980s and early 1990s as an alternative to market structure explanations of the sources of competitive advantage, such as Porter's five-forces model (1980). The resource-based view focuses more on the firm's own internal attributes rather than external market condition, with sustainable competitive advantage being seen as ultimately dependent on the firm possessing strategic resources that are unique to the firm and difficult to imitate by competitors (Wernerfelt, 1984; Barney, 1991). One particular type of strategic resource identified in this literature as an important source of sustainable competitive advantage is the tacit knowledge that employees accumulate through on-the-job training and experience in the firm. Tacit knowledge by its very nature is not easily transferable between firms, since it is not codified and relates to the specific ways of doing things in a particular firm. For example, players acquire experience of playing with teammates within the specific tactical system determined by the team's head coach. Although some of the tactics may be codified in the team's playbook, much of the players' team-specific knowledge will be acquired on the practice field through a trial-and-error learning process. And little of this knowledge will be transferable if the player moves to another team with different teammates and a different tactical system.

The notion of tacit knowledge as a source of sustainable competitive advantage has been developed and empirically tested in the sporting context by Berman et al. (2002). Using data from the National Basketball Association, Berman et al. argued that tacit knowledge could be conceptualized empirically as shared team experience (i.e., the weighted average of each player's total number of appearances for the team in previous seasons weighted by the player's time on court in the current season). Berman et al. found shared team experience to be a highly significant determinant of team performance.

Gerrard and Lockett (2007) have criticized Berman et al. on both theoretical and empirical grounds. They refute the theoretical argument that shared team experience is a good proxy of tacit knowledge since shared team experience will reflect the accumulation of both codified and tacit knowledge. For example, team tactics are often codified in a team playbook, and it could be expected that the longer that players spend training and playing with a team, the better their knowledge of the team's codified plays. Gerrard and Lockett are also critical of the empirical specification of the sporting production function estimated by Berman et al. Specifically, the failure to allow for the dynamics of team performance is likely to imply that the shared team experience variable is capturing in part the momentum effects of past performance. There is also clearly the likelihood of two-way causation. Successful teams will tend to stay together and therefore exhibit increasing shared team experience, whereas losing teams will be broken up, with current players replaced by new acquisitions and consequently decreasing shared team experience. Berman et al. find evidence of residual autocorrelation but interpret this as an error specification problem requiring a change in estimation method (i.e., GLS instead of OLS regression) rather than a dynamic misspecification problem requiring re-specification of the deterministic component of the sporting production function.

Gerrard and Lockett argue that it is more appropriate to view the relationship between shared team experience and team performance using the human capital lens. Rather than focusing the distinction between tacit and codified knowledge, Gerrard and Lockett adopt Becker's distinction between general and specific human capital (Becker, 1975, 1993) but applied at the level of teams/workgroups rather than firm level. They argue that shared team experience is better viewed as a measure of team-specific human capital comprising both tacit and codified knowledge acquired through formal and informal training and experience. Gerrard and Lockett propose a dynamic human capital model that also allows for the momentum effects of past performance on current performance. Testing the model empirically on data for ten seasons of the FA Premier League, the top-tier division in professional soccer in England, they find that the impact of team-specific human capital of team performance is highly dependent on the mediating effects of past team performance. Increased shared team experience has a positive effect on team performance only in teams that were successful in the previous season. One interpretation is that, unlike Berman et al. whose findings are consistent with "practice makes perfect," Gerrard and Lockett's findings fit more with "practice makes permanent." Increased shared team experience in losing teams tends to perpetuate the losing streak. The context or *quality* of the shared team experience is as important as the *quantity* of shared team experience. Gerrard and Lockett suggest that one possible interpretation of their findings is as evidence of self-efficacy effects at the team level (Bandura, 1997).

Gerrard and Lockett's dynamic human capital model is suggestive of a more general model of team performance. The human capital approach highlights the importance of the stock of skills in determining the individual player produc-tivity and team performance. Four dimensions of the skills and experience that constitute the stock of human capital can be distinguished: transferability, mode of acquisition, individuality, and management style. The first skill dimension is that of transferability, highlighted by Becker (1975, 1993) in the distinction drawn between general and firm-specific skills, and subsequently adopted by Gerrard and Lockett (2007) and applied at the level of teams/workgroups. General skills are easily transferable between individuals, team/workgroups, and organizations. As a con-sequence, general skills cannot be a source of sustainable competitive advantage. In contrast, specific skills are not easily transferable between team/workgroups and organizations. Hence specific skills are a potential source of sustainable com-petitive advantage. Specific skills create a mutual dependency between the indi-vidual and the team/workgroup/organization with both individual and collective productivity higher if the employment relationship is maintained.

The second skill dimension focuses on the mode of skill acquisition. Skills may be developed internally within the team or organization, or externally by other teams and organizations, including educational and training institutions such as schools, colleges, and universities. The mode of acquisition relates closely to the general-specific dichotomy. Specific skills are developed internally through train-ing programs and on-the-job experience. Firms are the sole providers of specific skill training, but as the sole beneficiary of these skills they are able to extract a return on their investment, since the value of specific skills is low or zero to other teams/organizations. The value of an individual's stock of specific skills is maxi-mized by remaining with the current team/organization. General skills are more amenable to provision by the state education system since teams/organizations may find it more difficult to extract the return on their investment given that individu-als with general skills are highly mobile. In the context of professional team sports, there is a clear difference between leading sports in Europe and North America in the mode of skill acquisition for young players. Whereas the North American major leagues source their young players from the educational system with the youth development function effectively outsourced to high schools, colleges, and universities, in Europe (particularly in soccer) the teams themselves undertake youth development from a very young age through the academy system.

The third skill dimension relates to the scope for a particular skill to be devel-oped and practiced by an individual in his or her own unique way. Some skills are very mechanistic with little or no scope for individual choice and creativity. Other skills can offer much more scope for the individual to develop a unique style.

Also the skill acquisition process can be affected by social and cultural factors. For example, general skills acquired in one country might differ in quite subtle ways from the same skills acquired in another country. In the case of European soccer, which has operated with an open international players' labor market since the mid-1990s, there has been an increasing trend in the top leagues and top teams to highly diverse team squads in terms of the nationality of players. This raises obvious issues over the impact of diversity on team performance and the potential trade-off between the benefits of diversity on creative problem-solving but the possible difficulties for resolving conflicts and achieving effective cooperation.

The final skill dimension relates to management style. Makadok (2001) differentiates between the resource-picking and capability-building functions of management. Resource-picking management concerns the identification and recruitment of skilled individuals. Resource-picking management involves correctly assessing and valuing the expected future productivity of an individual's stock of human capital. One aspect of resource-picking management is identifying individuals whose expected future productivity has been undervalued by the market and exploiting this market inefficiency to maximize the quantity of human capital obtained per dollar spent. Capability-building management refers to those functions of management concerned with achieving the maximum performance from current members of the organization. Capability-building management involves the development and enhancement of the existing skills of the individuals within the team or organization as well as the integration of individuals to optimize collective productivity. The distinction between the resource-building and capability-building functions of management relates to the other dimensions of the human capital model. Resource-picking management is associated primarily with general skills that can be acquired externally, although a crucial element may be the evaluation of an individual's ability to acquire specific skills and fit in effectively with the team or organization. Capability-building management is more closely associated with specific skills developed internally within the team or organization as well as the ability of the manager to integrate a diverse set of individuals into an effective unit. Gerrard (2007) has applied Makadok's distinction to soccer, arguing that general skills can be measured by player actions. These team totals of player actions are highly correlated with team wage costs. Teams that achieve a level of sporting performance consistent with their wage costs can be considered as efficient resource-pickers. Teams that achieve performance levels significantly higher than predicted by their wage costs and team totals of player actions may be efficient capability-builders. Gerrard provides empirical evidence for English Premiership soccer over the period 1998/1999–2001/2002. He found Manchester United to be an efficient resource-picking team, whereas the closest rivals, Arsenal, spent significantly less but closed the resource gap by not only efficient resource-picking but also efficient capability-building.

In summary, in order to better understand the intricacies and interdependencies of labor supply and human capital formation in affecting team performance in professional sports, it is suggested that the most useful framework is provided by a multidimensional human capital model of team performance that recognizes the complex nature of skills in terms of transferability, mode of acquisition, individuality, and management style. Furthermore, this model must be dynamic to allow for the important feedback processes between labor supply, human capital formation, and team performance. The multidimensional human capital model is illustrated in the next section by examining labor supply and human capital formation in the FA Premier League in England, the world's leading domestic soccer league in financial terms.

EMPIRICAL APPLICATION: LABOR SUPPLY AND HUMAN CAPITAL FORMATION IN THE FA PREMIER LEAGUE

Professional soccer in England is organized as a merit hierarchy known as the FA pyramid with a system of promotion and relegation between the different tiers. The top tier consists of the FA Premier League, formed in 1992 but dating back to 1888 when the Football League was formed with a single division of 12 teams. The Football League gradually expanded into a four-divisional structure with 92 teams. From 1921 to 1958 the Football League operated a three-tier system with the third tier organized as two divisions on a regional basis, Division 3 North and Division 3. The Football League moved to a four-tier structure in 1958, with Division 3 and Division 4 replacing the two regional divisions. The FA Premier League was formed as a separate entity from the Football League when the top tier teams broke away and formed their own self-managed league in 1992 but remained within the FA pyramid with promotion and relegation between the FA Premier League and the top tier of the Football League (now known as the Football League Championship). The Football League now consists of three divisions with 72 teams. Below the Football League the semi-professional teams are organized into a series of tiers on a national (tier 5 currently known as the Blue Square Premier) and regional basis (tier 6 and below). The number of tiers in the FA pyramid in any particular locality depends on the number of teams in the area. For example, the University of Leeds soccer team, the Leeds Gryphons, entered the FA pyramid in August 2009 in the West Yorkshire League Division 2, which is tier 13, with nine promotions required to reach the Football League. The FA pyramid embodies "the Dream" that if a team is good enough in sporting terms, no matter what its size it can progress up through the leagues and eventually compete with the bigger, more established teams. The only criterion for advancement is sporting success, although higher tier leagues do make promotion conditional on adequate facilities.

The FA Premier League currently has 20 teams who play each other home and away in a pure round-robin tournament between August and May. Each team, therefore, has a 38-game schedule. Three points are awarded for a win, one point for a tied match, and no points for a loss. There are no tie-breaker procedures for games that are tied at the end of the scheduled playing time. The team finishing with most points are the Premiership champions and, along with the second-, third-, and fourth-placed teams, qualify for the UEFA Champions League the following season, a midweek tournament involving the top teams from all 52 national soccer associations in Europe. The next placed teams qualify for the Europa League in the following season, again a Europe-wide tournament organized by the UEFA, the regional governing body for soccer in Europe. Teams qualifying for these UEFA tournaments continue to play in their domestic soccer leagues as well. The bottom three teams in the FA Premier League are relegated to the Football League Championship and replaced by three promoted teams comprising the first- and second-placed teams in the Championship, plus the winners of the Championship promotion playoffs involving the third- to sixth-placed teams in the Championship.

The FA Premier League has been a massive commercial success since its formation in 1992. In season 2007/2008 the 20 Premiership teams had combined revenues of €2.4bn, the largest of any domestic soccer league in the world and well ahead of the other Big Five European top-tier soccer leagues (i.e., France, Germany, England, Italy and Spain). As Table 15.1 shows, the FA Premier League has maintained its first-mover advantage as the first major soccer league to break away from the existing domestic league structure, using this autonomy to fully exploit the commercial opportunities in the sale of the league's media and sponsorship rights. By 1997/1998 and the internationalization of the soccer players' labor market (see below), the English Premiership teams generated total revenues that were 37.7 percent higher than their counterparts in the Italian Serie A, the next largest soccer

Table 15.1 Revenue Growth in the Big Five Leagues, 1997–2008

	League Revenues 1997/1998 €millions	League Revenues 2007/2008 €millions	Average Annual Revenue Growth Rate, 1997–2008
England	895	2,441	10.55%
France	323	989	11.84%
Germany	569	1,438	9.71%
Italy	650	1,421	8.14%
Spain	513	1,438	10.86%
All	2,950	7,727	10.11%

Note: Local currencies converted into Euros using closing exchange rate on June 30 of the relevant years.

Source: Deloitte Annual Review of Football Finance 2009; own calculations.

league in financial terms. Over the following decade, revenues across the Big Five have grown on average at 10.1 percent annually. In season 2007/2008, the Spanish Primera Liga and German Bundesliga had both matched the Italian Serie A in revenues, but the gap between these three leagues and the English Premiership had widened significantly to 69.7 percent. The French Ligue 1, despite experiencing faster revenue growth than any of the other Big Five over the last ten years, remains the smallest of the Big Five leagues with total revenues in 2007/2008 that were only 40.5 percent of those in the FA Premier League.

Until the mid-1990s, the players' labor market in European soccer was largely balkanized into small domestic markets with significant cross-border flows typically only in bordering countries with close ties, such as the four home nations in the United Kingdom and the Republic of Ireland. In the first weekend of games in the FA Premier League in August 1992, the 22 Premiership teams fielded only 11 foreign players in their starting line-ups (i.e., 4.5 percent). There were several reasons for the balkanization of the soccer players' labor market, including cultural and institutional factors. The player transfer system in soccer may have inhibited the international mobility of players since it acted as a reservation system akin to the reserve clause in Major League Baseball. Teams retained property rights over their players' playing services, even after contract expiry, such that if an out-of-contract player moved to a new team a transfer fee by way of compensation had to be paid to the player's former team. Players in England had achieved "freedom of contract" in the late 1970s, which allowed players the right to move to new teams at the end of their contract but subject to the payment of a transfer fee either agreed between the teams or through an arbitration process. Another barrier to international player mobility was UEFA's requirement for its tournaments that teams could not field more than three foreign players at any time in the game.

Both these institutional barriers to international player mobility were abolished by the Bosman ruling in the European Court of Justice in 1995. The Bosman ruling established the principle that the concept of a single market, as embodied in the Treaty of Rome, applied to players' labor markets in professional team sports. The Court did not recognize any exemption on the grounds of the specificity of sport. The Court ruled that both UEFA's restrictions on foreign players from other EU member states and the payment for transfer fees for out-of-contracts players moving between EU member states were in contravention to the Treaty of Rome. The immediate effect of the Bosman ruling was the introduction of international free agency in European soccer for out-of-contract players moving to a new team in another EU member state. Transfer fees remained payable in many European leagues for out-of-contract players moving to a new team within a domestic league, but this dual transfer system gradually disappeared as free agency was extended to all out-of-contract players, irrespective of whether or not the transfer was domestic or cross-border.

The internationalization of the Big Five leagues is shown in Table 15.2. In the three seasons between 2005 and 2008, around 40 percent of the players appearing

Table 15.2 Percentage of Foreign Players in the Big Five Leagues, 2005–2008

	2005/2006	2006/2007	2007/2008
England	55.25%	55.38%	59.52%
France	34.57%	32.06%	33.42%
Germany	40.85%	44.63%	46.45%
Italy	30.51%	28.94%	36.46%
Spain	31.64%	34.25%	36.81%
All	**38.38%**	**38.80%**	**42.36%**

Source: www.eurofootplayers.org.

in the Big Five were foreign nationals. The highest penetration rate was in the English Premiership with just under 60 percent of the players appearing in season 2007/2008 from outside the British Isles. The FA Premier League was the only one of the Big Five leagues in which the majority of players were foreign nationals. The league with the lowest penetration rate by foreign players was the French Ligue 1. Only one in three of the players playing in the top division in France come from outside the country. These differential penetration rates broadly reflect the relative financial power of the Big Five leagues and the ability of teams to offer high salaries. Given the revenue generation capabilities of English Premiership teams, it is no surprise that they have been able to attract the top soccer players from around the world. Players acting as rational economic agents will move to those leagues in which they can maximize their marginal revenue product, provided that the incremental salary gains from moving to another country outweigh the net non-financial costs of doing so.

Although teams in the Big Five operate in a global players' labor market, scouting around the world for the best talent, they have also invested heavily in developing home-grown talent. Youth development in European soccer is mainly the responsibility of the teams themselves through the academy system. In England, for example, professional teams scout players as young as five or six years old and provide coaching to the best prospects. Professional teams are able to register players from eight years old upward. Registration confers exclusivity over the player to the registering team so that at this point the best talent drop out from playing in local youth leagues (and often also stop playing for their school teams as well) and train and play exclusively with the professional academy teams. Players still attend school but will train several times a week with their team's academy in the evenings and weekends as well as during school holidays. These players are continuously assessed, with the best prospects being offered a two- or three-year full-time training contract when they reach school-leaving age (i.e., 16 years old). It is a highly competitive process with very high drop-out rates. There are no reliable statistics on the number of players of school age training with professional teams, but it is estimated that in excess of 10,000 children may be attached to the 92 Premiership and Football League teams. These teams recruit between 600 and 700 full-time trainees annually. An internal survey by the Professional Footballers Association, the players union in England, found that only around 15 percent of full-time trainees entering the academy system at age 16 are still under contract with one of the 92 professional teams by age 21.

An illustration of the drop-out rate in the soccer academy system is provided in Table 15.3, which charts the career survival rates of full-time trainees at Manchester United over the period 1990–2007. Manchester United has been the most successful team in the English Premiership and has a reputation for developing its own talent. It could be expected that Manchester United would be able to attract the best trainees and that these young players would have the best prospects

Table 15.3 Career Survival Rates, Manchester United, All Trainees, 1990–2007

Age	Entry	Exit	Truncated	Survival Rate
16/17	222	41	16	80.10%
18	165	9	9	74.62%
19	147	32	6	57.07%
20	109	19	8	44.81%
21	82	7	4	39.66%
22	71	3	4	36.57%
23	64	7	8	29.34%
24	49	4	3	25.61%
25	42	3	4	21.88%
26	35	2	3	19.11%
27	30	5	3	14.29%
28	22	2	3	11.26%
29	17	2	3	8.11%
30	12	1	0	7.43%
31	11	0	7	2.84%
32	4	0	2	1.44%
33	2	0	0	1.44%
34	2	0	2	

Explanatory Note:

Entry = the number of trainees/player still under contract with Manchester United or another professional soccer team at the specified age.

Exit = the number of trainees/players that exit from full-time professional soccer at the specified age.

Truncated = the number of trainees/players of the specified age at May 2007, the end-point of the data.

Survival rate = Entry, Next Year Group/(Entry, Current Year Group—Truncated, Current Year Group).

Example: Survival rate, 16/17 age group = 165/(222−16) = 80.10%.

Source: Rothmans/Sky Sports Football Yearbook (various editions); own calculations.

for a professional career. As Table 15.3 shows that this is indeed the case, but even Manchester United trainees face a high drop-out rate. Of those who were offered and accepted a full-time training contract with Manchester United at age 16 or 17, by age 21 only 39.7 percent can expect to still be professional soccer players. By age 24 only 25.6 percent of Manchester United trainees are still under contract with Manchester United or another professional soccer team. As expected, the survival rate of Manchester United trainees at age 21 is well above the average of 15 percent across all English professional soccer teams but shows that even full-time trainees recruited by Manchester United have a less than one-in-two chance of a professional career stretching into their twenties. And even of those who remain in the professional game, most will play outside the Premiership.

The benefits of academy system can be interpreted as an extension of the research of Berman et al. (2002) and Gerrard and Lockett (2007) that show the positive effects of shared team experience on team performance. Supporting evidence for this argument is provided in Table 15.4, which tracks the impact on youth development of the introduction of Bosman free agency and the globalization of the players' labor market in the mid-1990s. Table 15.4 considers the success rate of the academies of 12 leading English Premiership teams. Success is defined as the percentage of starting league appearances during the season provided by home-grown players (i.e., players who joined the team as full-time trainees in the academy). The data covers 11 seasons and is split into a pre-Bosman period, 1992/1993–1996/1997, and a post-Bosman period, 1997/1998–2002/2003. What is remarkable about this data is the stability across all years, both before and after the Bosman ruling, of around 22 percent of starting league appearances being provided by home-grown players. On average these Premiership teams started every game with two or three players who had come through the team's own academy system. There is a high degree of variability across teams, and even year-to-year with individual teams. For example, Manchester United averages around five home-grown players in their starting line-up for league games over the six seasons, 1997/1998–2002/2003. These were the years of the so-called "Golden Generation" of Beckham, Butt, Giggs, Gary and Phil Neville, and Scholes, the exceptional group of players who all came though the Manchester United academy in the early 1990s and who all went on to become top Premiership players and full internationals. Yet in season 1993/1994, Manchester United averaged less than one home-grown player in their starting line-up. The stability in the percentage of starting league appearances accounted for by home-grown players, even after the Bosman ruling and the influx of foreign players, suggests that teams continued to value the benefits of the academy system in human capital formation. Foreign players did not supplant home-grown talent to any significant extent, implying that it was domestic players acquired from other English teams particularly from the lower divisions (i.e., Football League teams) who were squeezed out of the Premiership labor market.

Despite having the highest penetration rate by foreign players, the English Premiership is not out of line with the other Big Five leagues (except France) in the

Table 15.4 Home-Grown Starting League Appearances, Leading English
Premiership Teams, 1992–2003

(i) Seasons 1992/1993–1996/1997

Club	1992/1993	1993/1994	1994/1995	1995/1996	1996/1997	1992–1997
Arsenal	40.91%	37.45%	27.71%	24.40%	22.49%	30.59%
Aston Villa	17.53%	12.99%	12.34%	9.57%	10.05%	12.50%
Chelsea	39.18%	28.14%	21.86%	29.90%	24.64%	28.74%
Everton	11.26%	12.12%	15.37%	16.27%	16.99%	14.40%
Leeds United	16.67%	19.70%	22.51%	26.56%	19.14%	20.92%
Liverpool	14.50%	19.48%	18.18%	18.90%	22.25%	18.66%
Manchester United	14.50%	8.23%	17.53%	37.80%	35.41%	22.69%
Newcastle United	26.88%	24.46%	16.23%	16.75%	18.90%	20.64%
Southampton	38.96%	38.74%	40.91%	36.84%	24.88%	36.07%
Tottenham Hotspur	22.94%	31.82%	31.82%	28.23%	34.45%	29.85%
West Ham United	24.70%	12.55%	18.40%	17.46%	10.53%	16.73%
Average	24.37%	22.33%	22.08%	23.88%	21.79%	22.89%

(ii) Seasons 1997/1998–2002/2003

Club	1997/ 1998	1998/ 1999	1999/ 2000	2000/ 2001	2001/ 2002	2002/ 2003	1997– 2003
Arsenal	16.51%	15.55%	12.92%	16.51%	17.46%	12.44%	15.23%
Aston Villa	12.92%	19.62%	13.40%	14.83%	21.05%	31.82%	18.94%
Chelsea	23.21%	8.13%	8.13%	9.09%	8.61%	8.85%	11.00%
Everton	12.68%	20.81%	14.83%	11.96%	3.83%	8.85%	12.16%
Leeds United	19.38%	30.62%	42.58%	29.67%	26.08%	42.34%	31.78%
Liverpool	31.34%	32.54%	33.49%	22.49%	24.40%	23.44%	27.95%
Manchester United	44.74%	39.23%	37.80%	47.85%	40.43%	45.45%	42.58%
Newcastle United	10.05%	10.77%	11.96%	13.16%	9.81%	14.11%	11.64%
Southampton	33.25%	27.51%	25.12%	25.12%	21.53%	18.66%	25.20%
Tottenham Hotspur	30.86%	29.19%	31.34%	30.62%	8.61%	13.16%	23.96%
West Ham United	18.42%	19.62%	24.88%	23.92%	17.94%	25.60%	21.73%
Average	23.03%	23.05%	23.31%	22.29%	18.16%	22.25%	22.02%

Source: Rothmans/Sky Sports Football Yearbook (various editions); own calculations.

percentage of home-grown players appearing in the league. As Table 15.5 shows,
in season 2007/2008, the English Premiership was on a par with the German
Bundesliga and Spanish Primera Liga with around 20 percent of the players being
home-grown talent coming through team's own training systems. Only top-
division French teams have averaged well above this with 30–40 percent home-
grown players, but in part this is due to the French academy system being much

Table 15.5 Percentage of Home-Grown Players in the Big Five Leagues, 2005–2008

	2005/2006	2006/2007	2007/2008
England	24.32%	21.82%	19.13%
France	40.06%	33.30%	35.34%
Germany	22.87%	24.11%	22.94%
Italy	14.73%	14.65%	11.67%
Spain	31.65%	28.08%	22.94%
All	26.91%	24.33%	22.05%

Source: www.eurofootplayers.org.

Table 15.6 Home-Grown Players and League Performance, FA Premier League, 1998–2003

Correlation between Home-Grown Starting Appearances and League Points	All Home-Grown Players	"Senior" Home-Grown Players*
1998/1999	0.093	0.038
1999/2000	0.239	0.291
2000/2001	0.567	0.568
2001/2002	0.513	0.545
2002/2003	0.207	0.238
1998–2003	0.308	0.323

*Senior home-grown player defined as player over 21 years old at start of season (i.e., July 31) recruited from team's own youth development program.

Source: Rothmans/Sky Sports Football Yearbook (various editions); own calculations.

more long-standing and dating back in some teams to the late 1960s, compared to, for example, the early 1990s in many English Premiership teams.

More direct evidence of the benefits of the academy system and team per-formance is provided in Table 15.6, which reports the simple correlation between home-grown starting league appearances and league performance in the English Premiership over five seasons, 1998/1999–2002/2003. Although the correlation var-ies from season-to-season, it is statistically significant in four out of five individ-ual seasons (the exception is season 1998/1999), as well as across the whole sample period. The relationship tends to be slightly stronger if only "senior" (i.e., aged 21 or more) home-grown players are included. Focusing on only senior home-grown players excludes young players who may be tried out in end-of-season games in which there is nothing at stake. Of course it also excludes the young prodigies who become established players at an exceptionally young age, but overall the data sug-gests the try-out effect outweighs the prodigy effect.

Summary and Conclusions

This chapter has considered aspects of labor supply and human capital formation in professional team sports. A multidimensional human capital model of team performance has been proposed that considers four inter-related dimensions of skills: transferability, mode of acquisition, individuality, and management style. The model has been outlined more as a framework than a formalized predictive tool. The theoretical development of the model is the obvious next stage, particularly the formalization of the complex causal nexus between the different skill dimensions and team performance.

As an illustration of its potential, this multidimensional human capital model has been applied to investigating labor supply and human capital formation in the FA Premier League in England, the leading domestic soccer league in the world. Regarding labor supply, it has been shown that the English Premiership has the highest penetration rate by foreign players among the top European soccer leagues, as would be expected given the league's financial advantage.

An important focus of the chapter has been the role of the academy system in human capital formation in European soccer, with professional teams recruiting and training players from the age of five and six years old. This institutional structure stands in total contrast to the North American major leagues, where youth development is largely outsourced to high schools, universities, and colleges. The academy system is highly competitive, with only an estimated 15 percent of full-time trainees at age 16 remaining under contract by age 21. Even at a top academy such as Manchester United, as shown by the evidence reported here, the "failure" rate is around 60 percent between ages 16 and 21.

One possible explanation of the academy system in the European soccer is the perception that team-specific human capital is a key source of sustainable competitive advantage. Berman et al. (2002) and Gerrard and Lockett (2007) have both provided evidence of a significant link between shared team experience and team performance. The academy system can be seen as an attempt to develop team-specific human capital from a very young age and not just when the player joins the first-team squad. Preliminary evidence has been presented here to show that there is some evidence of a positive relationship between home-grown talent and team performance in the FA Premier League. Furthermore, it has been shown that, despite the internationalization of the soccer players' labor market in the mid-1990s after the Bosman ruling, there was no discernible impact in the English Premiership on the number of starting league appearances by home-grown players, despite the huge influx of foreign players. This suggests that European soccer coaches continue to place value on home-grown talent, even when able to search the global players' labor market for new acquisitions. The issue remains to what extent the perceived benefits of the academy system are real benefits. This is an obvious line for future research. One possible starting point would be to include starting home-grown appearances in a fully specified multivariate model of team performance. Such a model could also be used to test the impact of skill diversity. Gerrard and Lockett (2007), for example, include several team heterogeneity measures in their model of team performance in the English Premiership. Heterogeneity is measured as the standard deviation across players of selected human capital variables. Interestingly, most of these team heterogeneity measures were found to have a negative effect on team performance, with the exception of age heterogeneity, which was found to have a positive but insignificant effect on team performance. In other words, teams with greater dispersion in their player ages tended to be more successful, *ceteris paribus*. The possible trade-off between conflict and creativity in teams with greater diversity in their stock of human capital is another area for future research.

REFERENCES

Bandura, A. (1997). *Self-efficacy: The exercise of control.* New York: Freeman.

Barney, J. B. (1991). Firm resources and sustained competitive advantage. *Journal of Management* 17: 99–120.

Becker, G. S. (1975). *Human capital.* New York: National Bureau of Economic Research.

Becker, G. S. (1993). Nobel lecture: The economic way of looking at behaviour. *Journal of Political Economy* 101: 385–409.

Berman, S. L., Down, J., and Hill, C. W. (2002). Tacit knowledge as a source of competitive advantage in the National Basketball Association. *Academy of Management Journal* 45: 13–31.

Carmichael, F., Thomas, D., and Ward, R. (2000). Team performance: The case of English Premiership football. *Managerial and Decision Economics* 21: 31–45.

Dawson, P. M., Dobson, S. M., and Gerrard, B. (2000a). Estimating coaching efficiency in professional team sports: Evidence from English association football. *Scottish Journal of Political Economy* 47: 399–421.

Dawson, P. M., Dobson, S. M., and Gerrard, B. (2000b). Stochastic frontiers and the temporal structure of managerial efficiency in English soccer. *Journal of Sports Economics* 1: 341–362.

Fizel, J. L., and D'itri, M. (1996). Estimating managerial efficiency: The case of college basketball coaches. *Journal of Sport Management* 10: 435–445.

Fort, R. M., and Quirk, J. (1995). Cross-subsidisation, incentives, and outcomes in professional team sports leagues. *Journal of Economic Literature* 33: 1265–1299.

Gerrard, B. (2001). A new approach to measuring player and team quality in professional team sports. *European Sport Management Quarterly* 1: 219–234.

Gerrard, B. (2005). A resource-utilisation model of organisational efficiency in professional team sports. *Journal of Sport Management* 19: 143–169.

Gerrard, B. (2007). Is the Moneyball approach transferable to complex invasion team sports? *International Journal of Sport Finance* 2: 214–230.

Gerrard, B., and Lockett, A. (2007). Team-specific human capital, team momentum and team performance. Unpublished mimeo.

Haas, D. J. (2003). Technical efficiency in the Major League Soccer. *Journal of Sports Economics* 4: 203–215.

Makadok, R. (2001). Toward a synthesis of the resource-based and dynamic-capability views of rent creation. *Strategic Management Journal* 22: 387–401.

Porter, M. (1980). *Competitive strategy: Techniques for analyzing industries and competitors.* New York: Free Press.

Porter, P. K., and Scully, G. W. (1982). Measuring managerial efficiency: The case of baseball. *Southern Economic Journal* 48: 642–650.

Scully, G. W. (1974). Pay and performance in Major League Baseball. *American Economic Review* 64: 915–930.

Smart, D., Winfree, J., and Wolfe, R. (2008). Major League Baseball managers: Do they matter? *Journal of Sport Management* 22: 303–321.

Szymanski, S., and Kuypers, T. (1999). *Winners and losers: The business strategy of football.* London: Viking.

Szymanski, S., and Smith, R. (1997). The English football industry: Profit, performance and industrial structure. *International Journal of Applied Economics* 11(1): 135–153.

Wernerfelt, B. (1984). A resource-based view of the firm. *Strategic Management Journal* 5: 171–180.

PART III

ECONOMICS OF OTHER SPORTS

CHAPTER 16

REMEMBERING THREE ECONOMIC STUDIES ON PROFESSIONAL GOLF

MATTHEW HOOD

AN economics education nearly forces some academics to apply economic theories everywhere, even to their favorite pastimes. Waiting for the foursome ahead of them to finish putting prompts them to envision scheduling tee times as a queuing problem. They turn naturally to a production function when they hear "drive for show, putt for dough" (Sommers, 1994). They wonder if the disparity between the earnings on the men's tour and the ladies' tour is evidence of discrimination (Shmanske, 2000). Searching for a lost ball causes them to consider their play to have a positive externality on a future duffer (Barro, 2000). When announcers extol the virtues of consistency, they speculate heroics might be better (Shmanske, 2007, and Hood, 2008).

One of the most published avenues in the application of economics to golf has been on the participation decision of professional golfers. One of the ways golf is unique among professional sports is that the individual chooses when and where to play. As such, it provides a fertile source of data to apply the theories of labor economics. This article remembers three papers on the participation of professional golfers and supports their work by finding their results hold for a decade of professional golf (1999–2008) and further, that natural extensions of their conclusions also appear valid.

One of the most cited papers in sports economics was written by Ehrenberg and Bognanno (1990a). They use data from the PGA TOUR in 1984 to determine that richer tournaments entice stronger fields and that the more money is at stake, the better the play. In a subsequent paper they use data from the European Tour in 1987 (Ehrenberg & Bognanno, 1990b). Orszag (1994) agrees with their assessment that richer tournaments entice stronger fields using data from the PGA TOUR in 1992.

These findings go back to the beginning of economics: supply and demand. They determine that the labor supply curve for professional golf is upward sloping, but not vertical. If it were vertical, the size of the purse would make no difference, and if it were downward sloping, richer tournaments would entice weaker fields.

This article seeks to substantiate their findings about the labor supply curve with ten years of data for European Tour events. A natural extension of their work is that celebrated opportunities outside of Europe will cause the elite players to skip regular European Tour events. The shape of the labor supply curve is dependent upon opportunity costs. This article considers the possibility of special events outside of the tour as viable alternatives for players ranked in the top fifty in the world. If elite players on the European Tour skip regular tour events to play in them, this further supports the findings of Ehrenberg and Bognanno. Therefore the first research question is:

QUESTION 1:   *Is the field for richer purses stronger and do elite players skip regular European Tour events when there is a strong viable alternative?*

Hood (2006) researched factors besides the size of the purse to explain participation rates. Using data from 1997 to 2003 for the PGA TOUR he finds that players were more likely to play an event if they played there the previous year and much more likely if they had played well. Golfers go with what they know.

Golfers are not alone in staying with the familiar. Investors favor stocks from their own country, Americans prefer to own stock in their local utility company rather than one from another region, and Grinblatt and Keloharju (2001) find that Finnish investors particularly favor stocks of firms that are headquartered nearer to their house.

This article seeks to substantiate his findings about golfers' preference for the familiar with ten years of data from European Tour events. A natural extension of his work is that golfers will also prefer to play in tournaments in their home countries. Therefore, the second research question is:

QUESTION 2:   *Do European golfers favor events they played last year and do they favor events in their home country?*

The advantages of full membership in the PGA TOUR are great but tenuous. By winning a major championship event, a player gets an exemption for the next five years. If he struggles to perform at a high level one year, he can still keep his membership and try again the next year. A golfer who does not finish in the top 125 on the money list does not automatically keep his tour card. In 2007 Ben Curtis finished 126th with $772,321, and in 2008 Shane Bertsch finished 126th with $841,248. Ben Curtis did not lose his tour card because his victory in the British Open four years earlier gave him an exempting through 2008. Ben Curtis rebounded in 2008 to win $2,615,798. Shane Bertsch had no exemption for 2009 and did not play any events that year.

A key factor in the work of Lazear and Rosen (1981) and Rosen (1986) on the incentives of elimination tournaments is that a highly skewed prize structure makes performance in an early round important, not because of the slight change in the guaranteed prize for winning that round, but because it allows the competitor to continue on to later rounds with much larger prizes. Rhoades (2007) studies the impact of exemptions using a sample of non-elite PGA TOUR players from 1995 to 2002. Players who were already exempt through the next year played 0.7 fewer events. When individuals face elimination in a lucrative and continuing game, they respond with more effort.

This article seeks to substantiate Rhoades' findings about golfers with tenuous exemption status with ten years of data from European Tour events. Therefore, the third research question is:

QUESTION 3:   *Do European golfers with fewer years of exemptions remaining play fewer events?*

These three questions will be answered empirically, but first it would be helpful to understand the nature of professional golf and the data.

PROFESSIONAL GOLF

Professional golf tours began before World War I as organizers of events in a region began coordinating their events. In 1916 the PGA of America was founded to help golf professionals, mostly club professionals laboring for their local golf and country clubs. By the 1930s the PGA of America sanctioned tournaments for professionals who made a living on tour. The PGA TOUR split from the PGA of America in 1968 because the smaller, more famous, group of tournament professionals had different needs than the club professionals. The PGA TOUR established a tour for players over fifty (now known as the Champions Tour) and a development tour (now known as the Nationwide Tour) in the 1980s, but the Ladies Tour (LPGA) is organized separately and was actually founded in 1950. Although there are tours specifically for older players and for women, the PGA TOUR is open to any golfer regardless of age or gender (Wikipedia, PGA Tour).

The European Tour was established in 1972 and has been fully independent since 1984. Besides creating its own senior and development tours, it has increased its geographic scope dramatically. Its American counterparts now have events in Canada, Mexico, and Puerto Rico, but the European Tour now has events in Africa, the Middle East, the Orient, and Australia. One way the European Tour has done this is by expanding directly into the Middle East, which is now an important part of their tour. Another way is by co-sanctioning events with weaker tours: the Asian Tour, Australasian Tour, and Sunshine Tour (Southern Africa). Instead of diluting their own tour, it has acted as a draw to bring the best players from these tours into the fold and added exposure for new global sponsors. The European Tour is clearly the second strongest tour in the world, in terms of prize money and prestige (Wikipedia, European Tour).

Golf has four major events, the Masters, the U.S. Open, the British Open, and the PGA Championship; all predate the PGA TOUR and European Tour. Although the tours do not organize any of the majors, they do recognize them and qualifying tour members love to play them.

One of the first published papers using economics to study golf was by Cottle (1981). He describes a professional tour as a cartel. The tours have the explicit goal of financially aiding their members and collectively they accomplish much more than they could individually. Like all cartels, a professional golf tour must govern and police itself. This requires that the same people that receive the benefits and face the punishments are the ones that establish the structure and its rules. Borrowing from Abraham Lincoln's Gettysburg Address, a professional golf tour is of the members, by the members, and for the members. A common theme in economics is the principal-agent problem in which an individual, the principal, establishes a structure of prizes and penalties so as to encourage another, the agent, to do what is in the principal's best interest. A cartel or professional golf tour, is better described as an agents-agent problem (Carmichael, 1983). The individuals setting the rules must live by the rules.

Economists believe cartels to be a natural development when a small group of individuals each have limited market power. However natural, they have also been found to be unstable and difficult to maintain because they face governments intervention, changes in demand, outsiders working to push their way in, and internal conflict—such as subsets of the group with their own agenda or desire to form a smaller and more exclusive cartel, and the prisoners' dilemma problem. The professional tours have succeeded for more than thirty years without harassment from government, who rarely intercede in sporting matters, and by careful collaboration, expansion, and management of prospective members. Some examples of their efforts to combat the conflicts from inside the tour and outside the tour are the World Golf Championship events, the FedEx Cup, and the current system of exemptions to decide membership.

Tour members are not homogeneous; there are a few players that command great attention because of their reputation and skill. These players are overwhelmed in numbers by the rank-and-file members of the tour. Cottle (1981) writes that a similar cause drove the touring professionals out of the PGA of

America to form the PGA TOUR in 1968. It has been surmised that a world tour of superstars will emerge when the current tours do not meet their needs. These superstars do not need a season full of mediocre tournaments. Instead, they want more exclusive and famous events to build their reputation and endorsement potential.

In an effort to satisfy these members, the PGA TOUR and European Tour worked together to create the International Federation of PGA Tours in 1996. They brought in three much weaker tours: the Japan Golf Tour, the PGA Tour of Australasia, and the Sunshine Tour (Southern Africa), and later allowed three even weaker tours: the Asian PGA, the Canadian Professional Golf Tour, and the Tour de las Americas (Latin America) to join in order to establish it as a truly international federation. This body began organizing three elite and rich tournaments known as the World Golf Championships in 1999. These events are successful because they are popular with player, fans, and sponsors (Wikipedia, World Golf Championships).

The World Golf Championships events give a mini-tour to the best players, reducing their incentive to form a super-exclusive tour apart from the PGA TOUR and European Tour. These players rarely want to play much more than twenty events, and with the four majors, the three World Golf Championships, plus the most prestigious tournaments on their own tour there is little need to start their own tour. They would have a great deal of difficulty establishing three events of more world-renown than the World Golf Championships. The European Tour receives the added benefit of providing the Europeans a way to play for large purses without leaving for the PGA TOUR.

The PGA TOUR added the FedEx Cup and Fall Series in 2007. The FedEx Cup was added to build more excitement heading into the season-ending TOUR Championship and the Fall Series was added to provide players another opportunity to keep their tour membership. With the FedEx Cup the regular season now culminates with a series of four tournaments that decide $35 million in bonus money (Wikipedia, FedEx Cup). The FedEx Cup adds luster and value to these four tournaments, so it attracts excellent fields and aids the top players on the PGA TOUR in their need for prestigious tournaments. This works to further diminish their incentive to create a new tour, just like the World Golf Championships. After the season-ending TOUR Championship, the last event in the FedEx Cup, there are about five tournaments that are scheduled to help golfers struggling in their quest to keep their tour card. These tournaments are for the players who do not qualify for THE TOUR Championship, which is limited to the top thirty in the FedEx Cup points (Wikipedia, Fall Series).

The World Golf Championship events, FedEx Cup, and Fall Series stratify the tour. The standard deviation of the strength of the field is increasing; there are more tournaments with strong fields, more with weak fields, and fewer tournaments with moderate fields. A stratified tour is able to satisfy more members, heterogeneous tour members benefit from heterogeneous events.

The members in a cartel do not want others usurping their position, yet all golfers recognize the benefits of new, young professionals that can improve the status of the tour. Where would the PGA TOUR be if its members had kept Tiger Woods out? To satisfy their members and allow for new talent, a complex series of exemption rules have evolved for the tours.

Professional golf tours have developed a unique set of rules to govern who may enter their open tournaments to help their current members retain their tour privileges, give extra benefits to the most powerful members on the tour, and allow for enough new golfers to compete and build their reputations. It is comprised mostly of a series of exemptions based upon winning tournaments and year-end finishes. The priorities established by the exemption categories are long and detailed (both the PGA TOUR and European Tour list more than thirty categories) to handle most contingencies. A very basic summary, as of 2009, for the two tours follows (PGA TOUR and European Tour, 2009).

To be exempt beyond the current year typically requires winning an event. Winning the Masters Tournament, U.S. Open, British Open, or PGA Championship is worth a five-year exemption on the PGA TOUR and a ten-year exemption on the European Tour. Winning a World Golf Championship event is worth a three-year exemption on both tours. The winner of THE PLAYERS Championship is exempt on the PGA TOUR for five years and the winner of THE TOUR Championship is exempt on the PGA TOUR for three years. The winner of the Dubai World Championship will be exempt on the European Tour for five years and the winners of the European Open, Open de France ALSTOM, and the Barclays Scottish Open will be exempt on the European Tour for three years. The winner of the FedEx Cup and the leader on the PGA TOUR's official earnings will gain a five-year exemption for the PGA TOUR and the winner of The Race to Dubai will gain a ten-year exemption for the European Tour.

Winning any other PGA TOUR approved event yields a two-year exemption, with additional wins adding additional years—up to five years—for the PGA TOUR. Winning a Race to Dubai tournament with at least €1.5 million in total prize funds is worth a two-year exemption on the European Tour and winning one with a less than €1.5 million in total prize funds is worth a one-year exemption. Lastly, members of the European side of the Ryder Cup are exempt the following year on the European Tour.

All these players have a high priority for entering regular tour events. Below them in priority is the largest group with a tour card: those that finish in the top 125 on the PGA TOUR or top 118 on the European Tour. Beyond these groups are the ways for newcomers to join the tour. The top performers from their development tour, the Nationwide Tour for the PGA TOUR and the Challenge Tour for the European Tour, receive a tour card. Also, both tours have a multistage qualifying tournament, known as Q-school, to permit more newcomers and allow those who failed to keep their card with good play during the year to compete for a tour card.

Cottle (1981) recognizes the dynamic conflict between the individual and the collective interests of professional golfers. Although the issues and responses have changed since 1981, conflicts remain. The economic behavior of cartels aids in understanding the creation of the World Golf Championship events, FedEx Cup, and Fall Series and the evolution of the tours' exemption rules. All are essential pieces of modern professional golf.

DATA

This article remembers three studies on the participation decision of professional golfers and tests their conclusions, and two natural extensions, concentrating on the European tournaments of the European Tour. The European Tour is much less lucrative than the PGA TOUR and has much more variety. In addition to events throughout Europe, between 2000 and 2008 the tour sanctioned or co-sanctioned: two events in Morocco; four in Argentina and Brazil; twenty in Australia and New Zealand; twenty-two in South Africa; twenty-one in Qatar and the United Arab Emirates; twenty-six in China and Hong Kong; and twenty-six in India, Indonesia, Malaysia, Singapore, South Korea, Taiwan, and Thailand. However, the heart of the tour is in Europe. The tournaments in the British Isles and on the European continent are the oldest and among the richest. They still have a great deal of variety in the prize money, prestige, and player experiences but with much less variability in travel and appearance bonuses. To answer the three questions about the attitudes of professional golfers, the events outside Europe are eliminated from the sample because they differ in more aspects than can be controlled. Despite the advantages of the variety on the European Tour, most golf work is focused on the more lucrative and famous American PGA TOUR, perhaps evidence that the superstar effect (Rosen, 1981) carries over into golf research as well.

Three other events are also eliminated from the sample for their differences from regular tour events: the British Open, known as the Open Championship to golfers outside the United States; the World Match Play, sponsored by Cisco and HSBC during this time and not to be confused with the World Golf Championship event, which is also a match play format event; and the season-ending championship tournament, the Volvo Masters. As one of golf's major events, the British Open brings in talent from around the world, it is too different from the other tournaments to lump it in with them in a statistical study. The World Match Play is contested by only sixteen top players from around the world with the largest first-place prize in golf—£1 million—so it is also not a satisfactory fit for a statistical study. The exclusion of the season-ending tournament for the European Tour is more difficult but necessary because of the questions posed. The decision to play

Table 16.1 Mean and Standard Deviations for the Total Purse and Percentage of
European Tour Members for All Events in Sample, Broken Down According
to Year and Division of Members into the Elite and Regular Members.*

		Purse		Elite			Regular		
Year	Events	Mean	St Dev	Players	Mean	St Dev	Players	Mean	St Dev
2000	25	€ 1,420,631	€ 627,308	11	37%	26%	89	61%	22%
2001	26	€ 1,840,740	€ 1,114,220	15	38%	31%	85	65%	22%
2002	25	€ 1,913,776	€ 1,019,536	15	39%	31%	85	69%	23%
2003	26	€ 1,874,227	€ 986,467	17	31%	28%	83	64%	27%
2004	25	€ 1,955,221	€ 1,033,317	16	28%	25%	84	66%	25%
2005	24	€ 2,051,799	€ 1,149,489	20	21%	22%	82	67%	26%
2006	23	€ 2,135,456	€ 1,121,779	18	27%	23%	82	67%	26%
2007	26	€ 2,219,857	€ 1,106,420	25	24%	21%	75	67%	25%
2008	25	€ 2,102,794	€ 1,013,990	21	27%	22%	79	65%	25%

*To be included in the list, one must have finished in the top one hundred on last year's European Tour
Order of Merit. To be distinguished as an elite member the player must also have finished in the top fifty
on last year's Official World Golf Ratings. The sample only includes European Tour events in Europe but
does not include the British Open, World Match Play, and Volvo Masters.

this tournament has less to do with the three questions posed in this article (issues
relating to the purse familiarity, and exemptions) and more to do with whether the
golfer earned his spot into the field that year.

This leaves the sample with 225 events taking place in Europe between 2000
and 2008 (Table 16.1). For each of these events in the sample the European Tour
members who finished in the top one hundred on the previous year's Order of
Merit are studied. These golfers are split into two groups: those who also finished
last year in the top fifty in the Official World Golf Rankings, "elite" in this chapter,
and those who did not, "regular" in this chapter. The data for each golfer in each
group for each year are assembled and modified to answer the questions and provide adequate control variables for a logit regression. The dependent variable is the
individual's decision to play or not, represented by a binary choice variable, *Play*.

Question 1 seeks to understand the impact of the size of purse and those of
simultaneous events on the strength of the field. The necessary explanatory variables to answer this question are: *Purse*, *Special*, and *USA*. *Purse* is a modification of
the total purse of the tournament. The total purse of the tournament is divided by
the average purse for the events in Europe that year so that the prize money in the
nine years can be used together in the same sample. *Special* is a binary variable that
indicates if a prestigious special event is played on the same weekend. These special
events are: the Masters, the U.S. Open, the PGA Championship, the Ryder Cup, the
Presidents Cup, the three annual World Golf Championship events, and the World
Match Play. *USA* is a modification of the total purse of the PGA TOUR's coincidental tournament. The total purse of the PGA TOUR's tournament is converted

into Euros using the tournament dates' exchange rate and then divided by the total purse of the European Tour's event so that the PGA TOUR event is relative to the European Tour event.

Question 2 recognizes that familiar settings impact the individual players' decisions to enter a tournament. If golfers played the event the preceding year, particularly if they played it well, they are familiar with the tournament. Also, if the tournament is in their own country, they are familiar with the tournament. This question requires three more explanatory variables: *Home*, *Played Before*, and *Prize Before*. *Home* is a binary indicator variable taking the value of 1 if the event is in the player's home country. Players and events in the British Isles are separated into their five nationalities. Therefore, Colin Montgomerie is not treated as playing a home event for the BMW PGA Championship because it takes place in England and he is from Scotland. *Played Before* is also a binary indicator variable for the player's participation last year. (In a tournament's debut season, all the golfers will have a 0 value.) *Prize Before* is a continuous variable ranging from 0 if the player skipped or missed the cut up to 16.67 percent for a victory.

Question 3 considers how the exemption status affects the entry decision of professional golfers. The only extra variable necessary to answer Question 3 is *Exemptions*. *Exemptions* is a count variable that indicates the years of exemption the player currently possesses. At a minimum, all the players in the sample are exempt through the current season because of their finish in the top one hundred on the previous year's Order of Merit. All the exemption categories listed earlier are considered. However, because of data concerns, some other exemption status rules are not considered, including lifetime exemptions and possible reinstatements due to injury.

From previous works on golf, several control variables are necessary. *Before British* and *After British* are binary variables indicating if the tournament is one week before or after the British Open or a Ryder Cup or World Golf Championship event taking place in Europe. *Before Major* and *After Major* are binary variables indicating whether the tournament is one week before or after a major, Ryder Cup, Presidents Cup, or World Golf Championship event taking place in America. It is expected that the overseas travel for a tournament of this stature will draw elite players away from tournaments in Europe the week before or after. If these variables are significant it gives further weight to the argument that the opportunity costs of affects their entry decision. *Events Before* is a count variable for the number of official European Tour events the golfer played the previous year. This is an important variable for the amount the players play on the tour without having dummy variables for each player, which causes a large multi-collinearity problem. *Age* is the player's age at the time of the tournament. Lastly, *Week*, is the number of weeks from the British Open, a negative number represents a tournament before the British Open.

The data necessary for this undertaking is large and varied. The date, total purse, and location for each tournament sanctioned by the PGA TOUR or European Tour (official and unofficial) from 1999 to 2008 are gathered from the PGA TOUR's web site, www.pgatour.com, and the European Tour's web site, www.europeantour.

com, and need to be complemented with Yahoo! Sport's web site on golf, sports. yahoo.com/golf. The top fifty golfers with their ranking and rating in the Official World Golf Ratings for the end of every calendar year and the top 100 golfers with their official earnings from the European Tour Order of Merit for 1999 to 2007 are found at the Official World Golf Ranking's web site, www.officalworldgolfrank-ing.com and the European Tour's web site. For every golfer on the list, their birth date, nationality, tournaments entered, tournament finishes, and tournament prize money is found from the European Tour Official Guide 09 (2009), the European Tour's web site, the PGA TOUR's web site, Yahoo! Sport's golf web site, and their individual pages from Wikipedia's web site: www.wikipedia.org. The prize money for the tournaments comes in dollars, pounds, and euro from these web sites and is converted to a common currency, as needed, by using the historical exchange rates for the final day of play found at Oanda's FX record, www.oanda.com, and Yahoo! Finance's exchange rates, finance.yahoo.com. Exemptions are determined by combing through the history of each exemption category and matching them to the players. Careful attention and double-checking information led to the discov-ery of errors and omissions in the data; hopefully few and inconsequential errors remain in the sample.

Figure 16.1 shows the average purse for tournaments on both the American PGA TOUR and the European Tour; the European Tour events are split into those in Europe and those taking place elsewhere. The two tours' purses are compared to golf's four majors and the three World Golf Championships. It is clear from this picture that the PGA TOUR is far more lucrative than the European Tour.

Separate logit regressions are run for both groups of European Tour mem-bers, those in the top fifty in the world (elite) and those that are not (regular). The logit regressions are run in GAUSS, borrowing from the codes of Fernando Rizzo (www1.american.edu/academic.depts/cas/econ/gaussres/qcuice/rizzo.src). The two groups are very different. Those high in the world rankings played 29.4 percent of the events in the sample whereas those not high in the rankings played 65.1 percent of the events.

RESULTS

QUESTION 1: *Is the field for richer purses stronger and do elite players skip regular European Tour events when there is a strong viable alternative?*

For both the elite and non-elite groups the *Purse* coefficient is positive and sig-nificant (Table 16.2). This is the expected result, playing for more money should encourage greater participation for both groups. The coefficient for *Special* is also negative and significant for both groups. This is the expected result for the elite sample because these tournaments provide unique opportunities for prestige. The

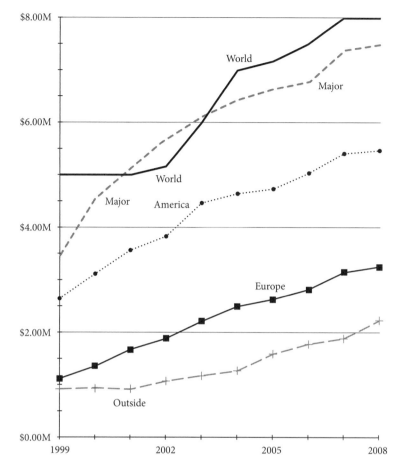

Figure 16.1 The mean purse from 1999–2008 by type and location.
The three annual World Golf Championship events, the four majors
of golf, the official tournaments organized by the American PGA
TOUR, and the official tournaments organized or co-organized by
the European Tour in Europe and Outside Europe.

reaction is so strong for elite players that travel considerations cause them to be less likely to play the week before or after a special event in America; the coefficients for *Before Major* and *After Major* are negative and significant beyond 0.1 percent.

The coefficient for *USA* is significant in both cases, negative for the elite, and positive for the regular members. The result for the elite is as expected because they have opportunities to play in America and it is sensible that they would go to America when the disparity in the purses is the greatest. Regular European Tour members do not have the opportunity to play in America and would not be expected to change their behavior. That it is positive and significant is of little concern unless the response is also strong.

The responses are determined by using the estimated coefficients at their median levels to reflect a typical situation. These responses are important because it is not only necessary to understand the statistical significance but the economic meaningfulness of the results. (A very strong statistical significance in data may still not be noticeable or important.) A 20 percent change in the purse changes the participation of the elite players by about 4.5 percent and regular players by nearly 5 percent (Table 16.3, Panel A). From another perspective, a tournament with a 20 percent greater purse than the median will have 83 percent more of the elite Tour members than a tournament with a 20 percent smaller purse than the median. And 57 percent more of the regular tour members skip tournaments with a purse that is 20 percent smaller than the median than tournaments with a purse that is 20 percent larger than the median. A difference in the purse of this size is large, but not extreme for the European Tour (Table 16.1). Only eleven of the twenty-five tournaments in the sample for 2008 were within 20 percent of the median of €1,984,350, the smallest purse was €604,470 and the largest was €4,500,000. European Tour members react strongly to the purse.

Elite tour members are usually invited to special events, and so they are expected to skip their own tour events for the prestige of the alternative. They decrease their likelihood of participating in a European Tour event from 15.3 percent to 6.8 percent when a special event is held simultaneously. Regular tour members are not invited to special events. However, they, too, are also less likely to play their own tour event that weekend, because their probability of playing drops from 78.2 percent to 64.5 percent.

The relative prize money of tournaments in America has little effect on the European Tour members. A 20 percent increase in the purse causes elite players to only decrease their likelihood of playing the European event by 0.8 percent. The tournaments on the PGA TOUR are not a strong substitute for events on their own tour. Regular members of the European Tour respond to increases in American purse by actually playing their own tour more by 0.5 percent. It cannot be explained by their desire to play tournaments without the elite members of their tour because they both seek richer tournaments and avoid playing European Tour events when a special event, such as a major, is scheduled for that same weekend. In addition to replicating the Ehrenberg and Bognanno (1990a) finding that the prize money matters in a player's decision to enter, this article also finds that opportunity costs matter. This provides a more complete picture for the theory that players respond to prize money incentives.

QUESTION 2: *Do European golfers favor events they played last year and do they favor events in their home country?*

Golfers are expected to play events in their home country more frequently and to return to events they played the previous year, particularly if they played well. The probability values for all three variables, *Home, Played Before*, and *Prize Before*, are all positive and significant beyond 0.1 percent (Table 16.2) for both the elite and regular member samples. Players want to play in their home country and like to return to the same events they played last year, particularly if they played well.

The economic significance of these variables is determined by examining the effect of reasonable changes on the margin by using the estimated coefficients from the logit regressions, and the effects are dramatic. Elite members only play 15.3 percent of the European events in foreign countries that they skipped the previous year (Table 16.3, Panel B). These players play 40.3 percent of events in foreign countries that they played the previous year and missed the cut and 45.0 percent of the events in foreign countries that they played well (winning 2 percent of the purse is equivalent to a tenth-place finish). Regular tour members play more events in general, playing 56.8 percent of the events in foreign countries that they skipped the previous year. If they played it but missed the cut, their likelihood of playing is 78.2 percent, and if they won 2 percent of the purse, their likelihood is 80.5 percent. The probability of playing an event at home is much larger. Even if they skipped the event last year, elite members play 50.6 percent and regular members play 77.0 percent of home events. If they played it the previous year and played well (represented with winning 2 percent of the purse), the elite members play 82.3 percent and regular members play 91.3 percent of home events. Some of the most important factors in a player's decision to play or skip are the tournament's location and their experiences at that tournament. In addition to replicating the Hood (2006) finding that previous experiences with the tournament are important factors in a player's decision to play or skip, this article also finds that the tournament's location affects this decision. This provides a more complete picture for the theory that players prefer the familiar.

QUESTION 3: *Do European golfers with fewer years of exemptions remaining play fewer events?*

A player with *Exempt* equal to 1 has already guaranteed their playing privileges for the next year. Keeping your tour card is very valuable, as shown earlier with Ben Curtis and Shane Bertsch. The coefficient for the *Exempt* variable is significant for both samples (Table 16.2); however, it is positive for the elite players on the European PGA. The elite players with more years of future exemptions play more than those with fewer years of future exemptions. The sign is negative, as expected by theory, for the regular tour members. This is the group for which the response is expected to be the strongest because these players do not have the option of the PGA TOUR and are the most vulnerable to losing their playing privileges (the median for *Exempt* is 2 for elite players and 0 for regular players).

The estimations from the logit regressions are performed using the medians of the two samples with the *Exempt* variable to determine the economic meaningfulness of the estimations (Table 16.3, Panel C). The median years of automatic exemption for regular players is 0; if this is increased to 2, their participation rate for a tournament falls from 78.2 percent to 70.4 percent. Just during the season when the European Tour is in Europe this would be about two fewer tournaments, which is a sizable impact. The median years of automatic exemptions for elite players is 2; if this is reduced to 0, their participation rate for a tournament at the median falls from 15.3 percent to 14.0 percent—a difference of just 0.3 tournaments over the

Table 16.2 The Logit Regression Results for the Two Groups of Golfers on the European Tour, Those Who Began the Year in the Top Fifty in the Official World Golf Rankings (Elite) and Those Who Did Not (Regular).*

	Elite						Regular				
Observations	3,951					Observations	18,549				
	Median	Estimate	St. Err.	P–Value	Margin		Median	Estimate	St. Err.	P–Value	Margin
Constant	1	−5.553	0.431	0.0%	−0.72	Constant	1	−3.543	0.190	0.0%	−0.60
Purse	0.92	1.388	0.137	0.0%	0.18	Purse	0.92	1.631	0.064	0.0%	0.28
Special	0%	−0.908	0.222	0.0%	−0.12	Special	0%	−0.681	0.065	0.0%	−0.12
USA	2.47	−0.127	0.041	0.2%	−0.02	USA	2.34	0.065	0.011	0.0%	0.01
Home	0	1.736	0.201	0.0%	0.22	Home	0	0.932	0.092	0.0%	0.16
Played Before	0	1.317	0.108	0.0%	0.17	Played Before	1	1.004	0.042	0.0%	0.17
Prize Before	0.0%	9.747	1.709	0.0%	1.26	Prize Before	0.0%	7.009	1.359	0.0%	1.19
Before British	0	0.184	0.190	33.3%	0.02	Before British	0	0.149	0.105	15.5%	0.03
After British	0	−0.311	0.190	10.1%	−0.04	After British	0	−0.346	0.086	0.0%	−0.06
Before Major	0	−0.930	0.149	0.0%	−0.12	Before Major	0	−0.307	0.049	0.0%	−0.05
After Major	0	−0.578	0.134	0.0%	−0.07	After Major	0	0.029	0.051	57.5%	0.00
Exemptions	2.0	0.052	0.015	0.1%	0.01	Exemptions	0.0	−0.207	0.016	0.0%	−0.04
Events Before	20.0	0.088	0.010	0.0%	0.01	Events Before	26.0	0.085	0.004	0.0%	0.01
Age	34.1	0.032	0.009	0.0%	0.00	Age	32.6	0.000	0.003	98.0%	0.00
Week	−2.0	0.031	0.006	0.0%	0.00	Week	−2.0	0.013	0.002	0.0%	0.00

*Both groups consist solely of members who finished in the top one hundred on the previous year's Order of Merit. The sample is events sanctioned by the European Tour that took place in Europe between 2000 and 2008, not including the British Open (Open Championship), World Match Play, and Volvo Masters.

Table 16.3 The Probability of Participating, Using the Logit Model Regressions Shown in Table 16.2, at the Median Value for the Explanatory Variables Except for Those Being Studied. Entries in Bold Are the Standard Case When All Values Are at Their Median

Panel A: Changes in the prize money and simultaneous events

	Elite	Regular
Standard case, all values at the median	**15.3%**	**78.2%**
20% increase in the purse (*Purse*)	19.8%	83.1%
20% decrease in the purse (*Purse*)	10.8%	73.4%
20% increase in the PGA TOUR purse (*USA*)	14.5%	78.7%
20% decrease in the PGA TOUR purse (*USA*)	16.1%	77.7%
Simultaneous to a special event (*Special* = 1)	6.8%	64.5%

Panel B: Changes in the location of the event and the player's participation and finish from last year

	Elite	Regular
Not home and didn't play (*Home* = 0, *Last Played* = 0, *Last Prize* = 0	**15.3%**	56.8%
Not home and missed cut (*Home* = 0, *Last Played* = 1, *Last Prize* = 0	40.3%	**78.2%**
Not home and tenth place finish (*Home* = 0, *Last Played* = 1, *Last Prize* = 2%	45.0%	80.5%
Home and didn't play (*Home* = 1, *Last Played* = 0, *Last Prize* = 0)	50.6%	77.0%
Home and missed cut (*Home* = 1, *Last Played* = 1, *Last Prize* = 0)	79.3%	90.1%
Home and tenth place finish (*Home* = 1, *Last Played* = 1, *Last Prize* = 2%)	82.3%	91.3%

Panel C: Changes in the player's exemption status

	Elite	Regular
Not exempt for next year (*Exempt* = 0)	14.0%	**78.2%**
Exempt for next year (*Exempt* = 1)	14.6%	74.5%
Exempt for next two years (*Exempt* = 2)	**15.3%**	70.4%

course of the season. The sign is as expected for the regular tour members, and the effect is larger for this group than for the elite tour members. This result substantiates Rhoades (2007) finding with a different tour and different set of seasons.

Regular tour members appear to enter fewer tournaments if they have longer exemptions, but elite players enter slightly more tournaments when they have longer exemptions. The other question with this type of response is with the impact of an increase in the purse of a PGA TOUR tournament. In both cases the group that is most affected react as expected and in a meaningful way, but the other group reacts weakly but in the opposite direction.

Conclusions

The understanding of professional golf is aided by economic theory and econometric techniques. This article approaches three questions from economic studies of golf, traces their roots to economic theory, and answers them again with a new data set. The results are statistically significant and economically meaningful.

Ehrenberg and Bognanno (1990a) show that golfers respond to financial incentives. The logic of using incentives to influence participation and performance is at the heart of economics. This paper confirms that European Tour members are more likely to play richer tournaments and that the elite members of the tour, defined as those who were in the top fifty in the Official World Golf Rankings at the beginning of the year, are less likely to play when there is a strong alternative event that is run simultaneously by a different organization, including the PGA TOUR. Professional golfers respond to incentives.

Hood (2006) reveals that professional golfers are more likely to play the events they played the previous year, particularly if they played well. Behavioral finance establishes that investors are more likely to trade in local stocks. Individuals prefer the familiar. This article verifies that European Tour members strongly prefer events in their own country and that they are much more likely to play the same events they played the previous year—particularly those they played well. Professional golfers prefer the familiar.

Rhoads (2007) establishes that non-elite players recognize the value of their tour card by playing in more events when their playing privileges for the next year are at stake. Future earnings are an important reason to play today. Economics teaches that rational individuals contemplate the expected value of their decisions, which includes side effects and future opportunities. This article corroborates this finding. Professional golfers who are in danger of losing their playing privileges enter more tournaments. Professional golfers consider the future consequences when making their participation decision.

References

Barro, R. 2000. Economics of golf balls. *Journal of Sports Economics,* 1(1): 86–89.

Carmichael, H. L. 1983. The agent-agents problem: Payment by relative output. *Journal of Labor Economics,* 1(1): 50–65.

Cottle, R. 1981. Economics of the Professional Golfers' Association Tour. *Social Science Quarterly,* 62(4): 711–734.

Ehrenberg, R., and M. Bognanno. 1990. Do tournaments have incentive effects? *Journal of Political Economy,* 98(6): 1307–1324.

Ehrenberg, R., and M. Bognanno. 1990. The incentive effects of tournaments revisited: Evidence from the European PGA Tour. *Industrial and Labor Relations Review,* 43(3): 74S–88S.

European Tour. 2009. *European Tour Official Guide 09.* 38 ed.

Grinblatt, M., and M. Keloharju. 2001. How distance, language, and culture influence stockholdings and trades. *The Journal of Finance,* 56(3): 1053–1073.

Hood, M. 2008. Consistency on the PGA Tour. *Journal of Sports Economics,* 9(5): 504–519.

Hood, M. 2006. The purse is not enough: Modeling professional golfers entry decision. *Journal of Sports Economics,* 7(3): 289–308.

Lazear, E., and S. Rosen. 1981. Rank-order tournaments as optimum labor contracts. *The Journal of Political Economy,* 89(5): 841–864.

Orszag, J. 1994. A new look at incentive effects and golf tournaments. *Economic Letters,* 46(1), 77–88.

PGA TOUR. (n.d.). *PGA TOUR—2009 Exemptions.* Retrieved 2009, from PGA TOUR. http://www.pgatour.com/players/pgatour-exempt/2009/

Rhoads, T. 2007. Labor supply on the PGA TOUR: The effect of higher expected earnings and stricter exemption status on annual entry decisions. *Journal of Sports Economics,* 8(1): 83–98.

Rosen, S. 1986. Prizes and incentives in elimination tournaments. *American Economic Review,* 76(4): 701–715.

Rosen, S. 1981. The economics of superstars. *American Economic Review* 75(5): 845–858.

Shmanske, S. 2007. Consistency or heroics: Skewness, performance, and arnings on the PGA TOUR. *Atlantic Economic Journal,* 35: 463–471.

Shmanske, S. 2000. Gender, skill, and earnings in professional golf. *Journal of Sports Economics,* 1(4): 385–400.

Sommers, P. 1994. A bread-and-putter model. *Atlantic Economic Journal,* 22(4): 77.

CHAPTER 17

....

THE ECONOMICS
OF NASCAR

....

ANDREW ABERE,

PETER BRONSTEEN, AND

KENNETH G. ELZINGA

INTRODUCTION

....

In the scholarly literature on sports economics, most of the research has focused on team sports, in which a league sanctions the sporting activity among discrete teams, amateur or professional, most of which are located in different cities. For example, in classic articles, Simon Rottenberg examined problems concerning the labor market for baseball players, Walter Neale studied industrial organization and labor-related phenomena within professional sports leagues, and Roger Noll analyzed the organization of sports leagues.[1]

A sport that is not often analyzed in the sports economics literature is stock car racing. This is peculiar in part because, in its NASCAR form, stock car racing is one of the largest spectator sports in the United States.[2] NASCAR holds seventeen of the top twenty highest-attended sporting events in the United States and is rated second among all regular season sports on television.[3] One reason for the inattention may be because NASCAR, although a sanctioning body, does not follow the economic model of most professional sports. In NASCAR events, it is as though all the "teams" compete simultaneously and not two at a time; the "teams" are not identified with particular cities or individual schools; indeed most fans root for a particular driver (e.g., Dale Earnhart, Jr. versus Jimmie Johnson); some fans have a favorite brand of automobile (e.g., Ford versus Chevrolet); and some fans (the minority) have a favorite team (e.g., Hendrick versus Roush).

Several books have attempted to describe the culture of NASCAR,[4] but there has been little systematic attempt to place NASCAR under the lens of economic analysis.[5] This chapter endeavors to develop an economic understanding of this popular and (from an economic standpoint) idiosyncratic sport.

This chapter stands on three legs. The first is a description and brief history of NASCAR, placing it in the context of other auto sports, which it has, so to speak, outraced. The second explains the economic logic of the NASCAR business model. The third offers a partial explanation, based on outcome uncertainty, about the popularity of NASCAR and why it has outpaced other professional sports competitors.

1. NASCAR AND THE MOTORSPORTS INDUSTRY

There is an old saying, usually attributed to the iconic NASCAR driver Richard Petty, that the first automobile race occurred right after the second car was built. In reality, the first formal automobile race in the United States involved six cars, and took place on November 28, 1895. It covered 54 miles from Chicago to Evanston, Illinois, and back. The winner was J. Frank Duryea, who averaged 7.3 miles per hour and won $2,000.[6]

Today, auto racing is among the most popular spectator sports in the world. There are numerous races involving different types of cars and different types of courses. The largest auto racing category in the United States, in terms of attendance, media exposure, and sponsorships, is stock car racing. Stock car racing evolved from equipment once derived from standard passenger automobiles, and races are typically staged on oval courses. Professional stock car racing developed in the southeastern United States in the 1930s.

The most prominent sanctioning body in stock car racing today is NASCAR, which was founded in 1948 and has been influential in the growth and development of motorsports. NASCAR's success in competing for consumer patronage against other sports and other forms of auto racing has made stock car racing the largest auto racing category in the United States, and NASCAR has become the most prominent organizing body in stock car racing.

NASCAR racing began in 1949 with its Strictly Stock series of eight races generally run on short (e.g., half-mile) dirt tracks in the southeastern portion of the United States. In the following years, NASCAR expanded the number of races in its Grand National series (the successor to the Strictly Stock series and a predecessor to the current Cup series). In 1950, there were nineteen races, and the number of races in the series reached a maximum of 62 in 1964.[7] NASCAR also began to have more races hosted on longer paved tracks (speedways) rather than dirt tracks, which allowed for higher speeds and more exciting racing for fans. In 1957, William H.G. France, the founder of NASCAR, established what is now International Speedway Corporation (ISC) in order to build a state-of-the art speedway as a showplace for NASCAR. In 1959, ISC opened the Daytona International Speedway, which, at 2.5 miles in length was more than twice as long as most other speedways at the time.[8]

With such a large number of races in the Grand National series, not all drivers competed in all races in the series. In 1971, the last year of this series, the number of cars in the forty-eight races ranged from a low of fourteen (at Houston) to a high of fifty-one (at Ontario). In 1972, R.J. Reynolds became the sponsor of NASCAR's top series, which was renamed the Winston Cup series.[9] At the sponsor's request, NASCAR reduced the number of races that season to thirty-one. Less was believed to be more. R. J. Reynolds predicted that a shorter season profiling bigger events would generate more exposure for its brand and would be a more cost-efficient use of sponsorship dollars.[10] A shorter season also allowed the better drivers to compete in a higher percentage of the races in the series. This increased the quality of racing for fans. By 2006, there were forty-three cars in each of the Cup races, and the top drivers participated in each race.[11]

NASCAR sanctions most of its Cup races on oval tracks, which are closed circuits often banked at varying angles. NASCAR sanctions some of its races on road courses which are built solely for auto racing and are designed with left and right turns, straight-aways, and elevation changes to simulate driving on a road. Some venues contain both oval tracks and road courses (e.g., the road course is inside the oval).

NASCAR sanctions a number of local, regional, and national racing series. The top three are the NASCAR Sprint Cup series, the NASCAR Nationwide series,[12] and the NASCAR Craftsman Truck series. The most popular stock car race in the United States today is the Daytona 500, traditionally the first race of the NASCAR Cup series. This race has been held at Daytona International Speedway since 1959. During 2006, there were thirty-six races that counted toward determining the annual Cup champion, NASCAR's equivalent of the World Series or the Super Bowl champion (except that it is an individual driver who is named champion, not the team that sponsors the driver or the car driven by the Cup winner).

Rival Motorsports Sanctioning Bodies

NASCAR is not the only auto-sport sanctioning body. Stock car races also are sanctioned by the Automobile Racing Club of America (ARCA), founded in 1953. ARCA's top series is the ARCA RE/MAX series, which consisted of twenty-three races in 2006, many on tracks that also hosted one or more races in NASCAR's top three series.[13]

Internationally, the most recognized form of auto racing is open-wheel racing. These races are held on oval tracks and road courses (including some of the same venues that host NASCAR stock car races), as well as on temporary street courses. The latter typically are built on closed-off city streets, but can also be built on airport runways or similar facilities that have a primary purpose other than as a racing venue.

The most prominent open-wheel sanctioning bodies in the United States are Champ Car and the Indy Racing League (IRL), which have recently agreed to merge.[14] The most famous open-wheel race in this country is the Indianapolis 500, sanctioned by IRL and held annually at the Indianapolis Motor Speedway. The IRL was formed in 1996 by the owner of the Indianapolis Motor Speedway who broke away from the predecessor of Champ Car (the predecessor was Championship Auto Racing Teams, or CART) taking many of the predecessor's participating teams and drivers. In 2006, IRL put on fourteen races (including one race overseas). During the same year, there were fourteen Champ Car World Series races with six of them in foreign countries. Champ Car tends to run its races on road and street courses whereas IRL tends to favor oval courses. The split between IRL and Champ Car was generally viewed as detrimental to open-wheel racing but beneficial to NASCAR.[15]

Relative to open-wheel racing, winning NASCAR Cup races may not be as easy as some might think. Although a half-dozen or so top drivers from the leading open-wheel circuits have migrated to NASCAR, only Tony Stewart has had substantial success as a NASCAR driver. Stewart, who was the IRL Rookie of the Year in 1996 and won the IRL championship in 1997, came to the Cup series in 1999, has raced to average finishing positions ranging from 9.9 to 14.6, and won two NASCAR Cup championships in 2002 and 2005. The other open-wheel transplants, although newer to NASCAR, have not fared as well. Juan Pablo Montoya, who finished sixth or better in each of his five full seasons with Formula 1, finished 34th in his only Cup race in 2006. Thereafter, his average finishing positions were 22.7 in 2007 and 18.8 for the first eleven races in 2008. Sam Hornish, Jr., who is the only three-time IRL champion in the history of that series, has an average finishing position in two partial seasons with NASCAR of 23.9. Patrick Carpentier, who has raced in the IRL, Champ Car, and CART open-wheel series, has an average finishing position in two partial seasons with NASCAR of 26.4. Finally, Dario Franchitti, who was the 2007 IRL champion, raced to an average finishing position in seven NASCAR races in 2008 of 31.6. The critics of stock car racing who contend that the only skills required are to go fast and turn left do not understand the motor skills (no pun intended) and endurance required to succeed in this sport.

Other open-wheel sanctioning bodies include the Federation Internationale de L'Automobile (FIA), and the United States Automobile Club (USAC). The FIA's top series, Formula 1 (F1), is held primarily outside the United States and is considered the most prestigious open-wheel series in the world. In 2006, there was only one F1 event held in the United States (the Grand Prix of the United States held at Indianapolis Motor Speedway). USAC, formed in 1956, was a prominent open-wheel sanctioning body in the United States but was largely

displaced in 1979, when CART was formed, retaining the Indianapolis 500 as
its only major event until IRL sanctioned that event in 1997. USAC's top series
today is the Silver Crown series. In 2006, there were fourteen Silver Crown races
held in the United States.[16]

Sports car races are held on road courses and temporary street courses
throughout the United States. These races are sanctioned by organizations such as
International Motor Sports Association (IMSA), the Grand-American Road Racing
Association (Grand-Am), and Sports Car Club of America (SCCA). The IMSA was
founded in 1969, and its top series is the American Le Mans Series, which was
started in 1999. In 2006, there were nine American Le Mans races in the United
States. The Grand-Am, established in 1999, is located in Daytona Beach, on the
same corporate campus that is home to NASCAR and ISC. The Grand-Am's top
series is the Rolex Sports Car Series. In 2006, there were fourteen Rolex Sports Car
races in the United States. The Sports Car Club of America (SCCA) was founded in
1944. Its leading series is the SCCA World Challenge, which promoted ten races in
2006, including one race in Canada.

Drag racing is another automotive speed contest. In this racing format, drivers and their vehicles compete in short races (usually a quarter mile) on a straight-
line strip. Some venues contain both oval tracks and drag strips. The National
Hot Rod Association (NHRA), founded in 1951, is the most prominent sanctioning body in drag racing in the United States. The NHRA's premier series is the
POWERade series. In 2006, there were twenty-three POWERade events in the
United States.

NASCAR's Growth and the Cup Series

Unlike most sanctioning bodes in professional sports in which the fundamental relationship is between the league and its team owners, NASCAR contracts
with racetracks to host its events. In 2006, NASCAR's Cup series was run at
twenty-two different tracks in the United States, with several hosting two races
in the series. Many of these tracks are owned and operated by public corporations, such as ISC with twelve tracks;[17] SMI with six tracks; and Dover with
four tracks (one track hosts two Cup events and the three other tracks host
Nationwide series races). Other tracks, often referred to as independents, are
not affiliated with public corporations and are often privately owned by family groups, such as the Indianapolis Motor Speedway (owned by the Hulman-
George family), Pocono Raceway (owned by the Mattioli family), and New
Hampshire International Speedway.[18]

In 1994, NASCAR embarked on a strategy to expand from its traditional base
in the southeastern United States. In that year, NASCAR added a Cup race at the
Indianapolis Motor Speedway, which, until then, had only hosted the Indianapolis
500, the most famous open-wheel race in the United States.[19] Following the success

Table 17.1 NASCAR Cup Series Races: New Race Awards and Relocations*

Year	New Race Location	Former Race Location
1997	California Speedway	**
	Texas Motor Speedway	North Wilkesboro Speedway, NC
	New Hampshire Int'l Speedway	North Wilkesboro Speedway, NC
1998	Las Vegas Motor Speedway	**
1999	Homestead-Miami Speedway	**
2001	Chicagoland Speedway	**
	Kansas Speedway	**
2004	California Speedway	North Carolina Speedway, NC
2005	Phoenix Int'l Raceway	Darlington Raceway, SC
	Texas Motor Speedway	North Carolina Speedway, NC

*The NASCAR Cup series was called the Winston Cup series from 1972 through 2003 and was called the Nextel Cup series from 2004 through 2007. Since 2008, it has been renamed the Sprint Cup series.

**New race award.

Sources: www.racing-reference.info; www.na-motorsports.com; Penske 10-K405 for the fiscal year ended 12/31/1996; ISC 10-K for fiscal year ended 11/30/2004; Robert G. Hagstrom, *The NASCAR Way: The Business That Drives the Sport* (New York: Wiley, 1998: pp. 109–10); SMI 10-K for the fiscal year ended 12/31/2004.

of the inaugural stock car race at Indianapolis, NASCAR began to add more races to the series and did so at tracks outside the southeastern United States. NASCAR added Cup races at tracks in southern California (1997), Las Vegas (1998), Miami (1999), Kansas City (2001), and Chicago (2001),[20] each a relatively new facility that had been open for four seasons or less. NASCAR moved races from older, smaller tracks such as Darlington, North Wilkesboro, and Rockingham, all located in the Carolinas, to tracks serving larger markets outside the Southeast.[21]

NASCAR also redesigned the manner in which stock car racing would be viewed by the television audience.[22] In the late 1990s, each track owner sold the television rights for its Cup race(s). Although all the races in the series were televised, they were broadcast on a hodgepodge of different channels, three of which were only available on cable television (ESPN, TBS, and TNN), which required a monthly subscription. In 1999, NASCAR began to sell the rights for all Cup races for the 2001 to 2006 period. Although this resulted in the races being broadcast on fewer channels, it led to a greater number of races appearing on network television, making the sport accessible to more viewers.[23] Viewers responded, as the average number of households watching Cup races increased from 3.5 million in 2000 to more than 5 million thereafter.[24]

Similarly, ISC contributed to the growth of NASCAR Cup racing. To compete against other sports and entertainment options, ISC expanded output to make stock car racing accessible to more track customers and increased the quality of races and venues where they are hosted. ISC has grown from owning just one track in Daytona in 1959 to owning or operating a dozen tracks today from coast to coast.

Table 17.2 Growth of NASCAR Cup Series: 1998–2006*

Statistics**	1998	1999	2000	2001	2002	2003	2004	2005	2006
Number of Races	33	34	34	36	36	36	36	36	36
Number of States Hosting Races	17	17	17	19	19	19	19	19	19
US Population Within 200 Miles of Races (millions)	675	683	683	714	714	714	722	711	711
Total Seating Capacity (millions)***	3.4	3.6	3.8	4.0	4.0	4.0	4.1	4.2	4.3
Average TV Viewing Households (millions)	3.3	3.7	3.5	4.9	5.0	5.2	5.4	5.8	5.4

*The NASCAR Cup series was called the Winston Cup series from 1972 through 2003 and was called the Nextel Cup series from 2004 through 2007. Since 2008, it has been renamed the Sprint Cup series.
**Excludes non-points races.
***2001 seating capacity used for Pocono Raceway for 1998, 1999 and 2000 because data for these years are not available.
Sources: www.racing-reference.info; Dover 10-Ks; ISC 10-Ks; SMI 10-Ks; www.covers.com; Census 2000 (Landview 6); Robert G. Hagstrom, *The NASCAR Way: The Business That Drives the Sport* (New York: Wiley, 1998: pp. 109–10); data provided by NASCAR.

2. THE ECONOMICS OF NASCAR AND HOST TRACKS

Beginning with the 2001 season, NASCAR's consolidated television contract dramatically increased the media revenues flowing into the sport.[25] From an economic perspective, the consolidation was a watershed event in the history of NASCAR and its host tracks. Much of these revenues flowed to host tracks instead of to NASCAR, the negotiator of the contracts and the sanctioning body of the sport. From the perspective of NASCAR's business model, this (at first glance) seemed myopic. However, when one considers the economics of operating a racetrack and NASCAR's dependence on tracks, the allocation makes sense.

Tracks typically have excess capacity. Speedways hosting NASCAR's Cup Series, NASCAR's Nationwide Series, and/or NASCAR's Craftsman Truck Series races usually run only about five to eight races per year.[26] As a result, the opportunity cost of a given race is low. In other words, hosting one race probably does not mean not hosting another. Consequently, tracks have an economic incentive to host any event that covers the track's incremental costs of offering the event.

Prior to NASCAR's 2001 consolidated television agreement, tracks obviously were willing to host Cup races under the terms and conditions offered by NASCAR. There do not appear to be any instances in which a track turned down the chance to host a Cup race in those days. The new broadcast contract produced a substantial increase in the money flowing into the sport. Indeed, television revenue became far more important as a source of revenue than ever before.

Table 17.3 Average Televison Revenue and Net Sanction Revenue Per Race Received by NASCAR Cup Tracks: 2000–2006* (Index Values: Base Value of 100; Base Year 2000)

Statistics**	2000	2001	2002	2003	2004	2005	2006
Television Revenue***	100	193	223	258	313	369	427
Net Sanction Revenue[†]	100	976	1,191	1,455	1,947	2,452	2,981

*The NASCAR Cup series was called the Winston Cup series from 1972 through 2003 and was called the Nextel Cup series from 2004 through 2007. Since 2008, it has been renamed the Sprint Cup series.

**Excludes non-points races.

***Defined as the share (65%) of live television revenue paid to the track.

[†]Defined as the live television revenue allocated to the event minus all expenses specified in the sanction agreement, which include the sanction fee, awards and purse money, the share of television revenue paid to NASCAR and the teams and drivers, and other costs. Net sanction revenue does not include the additional receipts the track takes in from the sale of tickets, concessions, and sponsorships for hosting a race.

Sources: NASCAR sanction agreement summary tables (NAS 216932-6, NAS 216939-43, NAS 216946-50, NAS 216953-7, NAS 216960-4, NAS 216967-71, and NAS 216974-8); www.racing-reference.info; Robert G. Hagstrom, The NASCAR Way: The Business That Drives the Sport (New York: Wiley, 1998: pp. 109–10).

Under these conditions, NASCAR might have been able to capture all this incremental money for itself, but, instead, NASCAR continued to split broadcast revenue as it had in the past: 65 percent going to the tracks, 25 percent going to the teams and drivers, and 10 percent going to NASCAR. This proved to be a substantial benefit for the host tracks.

Table 17.3 shows the dramatic increase in television revenue and net sanction revenue received by tracks hosting Cup races as a result of the consolidated television contract. Using 2000 as the base year, which was the year before the consolidated contract went into effect, the base index value representing average annual television revenue received by Cup tracks has been set to 100. In 2001, under the consolidated contract, that index value rose to 193 and reached 427 in 2006. Similarly, in 2000, the base index value for average annual net sanction revenue received by Cup tracks has been set to 100.[27] With the consolidated contract, that index value rose almost tenfold to 976 in 2001 and then to 2,981 in 2006.

Track Income and NASCAR Cup Events

On top of the income flowing from the sanction agreement between NASCAR and the host tracks (which averaged $6.5 million in 2006), tracks earn additional revenue on their sale of tickets, sponsorships, concessions, and merchandise.[28] One consulting firm estimated that in 1997, a Cup race generated total revenues of over $10 million and profits of over $6 million.[29] Given the rise in television income since that time, the figure could now be close to double the estimate for 1997.

The Dover Motorsports SEC filings indicate the importance of the Cup races to the financial health of the company. Its 2004 Annual Report states, "Our two

Dover NASCAR weekends once again produced record revenues and profits."[30] Speedway Motorsports, which operated six tracks at the time, states, in its 2005 Annual Report, "We produce minimal operating income during our third quarter when we host only one major NASCAR race weekend."[31] The *Wall Street Journal* reports that Infineon Raceway, an SMI track in Sonoma, California, will have about 330 revenue producing days in a year, but the NASCAR weekend accounts for about two-thirds of the track's total revenue.[32]

Hosting Cup Events and Economic Value

Cup events typically are more profitable than any other events conducted by host tracks. The profits generated by hosting Cup events are reflected in the market values of tracks hosting these events. For example, in 1998, SMI purchased Las Vegas Motor Speedway, which hosted one Cup race, for $150 million (after deducting additional payments for other assets); in 1999, ISC purchased Richmond International Raceway, which hosted two Cup races, for approximately $215.6 million.[33]

Why NASCAR Shares Revenues with Host Tracks

We believe there are two reasons why NASCAR shares its revenues with host tracks. The first requires a discussion of the cost structure of these tracks.

Operating a racetrack capable of hosting a Cup event entails relatively high fixed and relatively low variable costs.[34] When fixed costs are high relative to variable costs, a firm (in this case a track) runs the risk of failing to earn at least a normal return on its *total* costs, that is, fixed *and* variable, if it does not host a substantial number of events. As a result, if NASCAR charged high prices in the form of sanction fees—that is, high enough to extract all revenues in excess of the track's variable costs—tracks would not be sufficiently profitable to cover all their costs and maintain their fixed assets. Tracks might deteriorate and eventually shut down. Because NASCAR is interested in preserving a healthy group of tracks to host its races, it is economically prudent for NASCAR to subsidize the tracks to help them cover their fixed costs.[35]

The second reason for NASCAR's revenue sharing is that these funds align the incentives of the track with those of NASCAR. Incentive compatibility helps ensure that the track will host a successful event and that the value of NASCAR's brand name, which is affected by the performance of the track, will be protected and enhanced. Here's how this works.

If NASCAR sets its prices to extract the entire value of its Cup events, tracks would earn, at best, a normal return on their invested capital (assuming as discussed earlier that the track is compensated for its cost of capital), with all the additional profits flowing to NASCAR. NASCAR then would earn substantially more per event than the track would. At the margin, this would affect the incentive of the track to ensure that the event was conducted properly, safely, and in the best interests of NASCAR. If there were a problem at a Cup event, perhaps due to lax security, inadequate medical care, poor preparation of the racing surface, or insufficient parking space, NASCAR would have more to lose than the track. In the event of a problem, NASCAR might pull the event from the track, but the track would lose relatively little because the event covered little more than the track's incremental costs. However, NASCAR would have a lot to lose, because problems at one event would adversely affect attendance at any future event. NASCAR's brand name would suffer the consequences, not just at one track but potentially at other tracks where Cup events are held. This would impose a substantial cost on NASCAR, with little or no consequences to the track.

As the promoter of one track put it:

> NASCAR wants things that are going to look good because the track represents NASCAR. We pay a sanction fee to be a part of NASCAR, which averages anywhere from a thousand to a couple thousand dollars a night. NASCAR will not sanction facilities that are potential problems for its reputation. Over the years a lot of strange things have occurred. Promoters did not have a good name because it was perceived that they would screw the drivers over at any opportunity. That was not necessarily the case, but all it took was a couple occurrences and the image was created. When I went out to Altamont our main problem getting started was that previous fly-by-night promoters had ripped off so many sponsors. Those are the kind of things NASCAR does not want. A lot of it comes down to tracks that are versatile. We run an all pro race, a NASCAR truck race, and a Goody's dash race. That is why we are a NASCAR track.[36]

One way to overcome this problem—that is, one way to efficiently align incentives between NASCAR and its host tracks—is for NASCAR to share the profits from the event with the track. NASCAR accomplishes this by keeping its sanction fee low and the share of broadcast revenues to tracks high. When NASCAR shares its profits with the track, the track has a strong interest, as does NASCAR, in a successful event. If the event does not go well, the track will lose its Cup races and the substantial profits that flow from these events. In short, the seemingly excess payments to the tracks are a means of ensuring incentive compatibility between NASCAR and the track.

These practices are familiar to economists as a means of overcoming a principal-agent problem, a form of market failure in which the promoter, who otherwise would have little riding on the success of the event, would not be incentivized to act in NASCAR's best interests. One implication of this insight is that that NASCAR would not want, even if it could, to charge monopoly prices. Charging higher fees would eliminate the incentive structure that NASCAR has adopted that ultimately expands the demand for Cup races and benefits consumers.

Vertical Integration between NASCAR and ISC

Economic theory teaches that a non-integrated or stand-alone NASCAR will expand its annual Cup schedule until the incremental revenue to NASCAR from additional races is offset by the incremental costs that NASCAR would incur from organizing additional races. As discussed earlier, NASCAR pays a premium to tracks hosting Cup races. Tracks receiving this payment would gladly host additional races above and beyond the number NASCAR has an economic interest in organizing. The premium is comparable to a tax on NASCAR that is collected by the tracks. The tax discourages output expansion by NASCAR, but leaves tracks with excess or unmet demand for additional races.

When NASCAR vertically integrates (at least partially through ownership or influence of NASCAR upon ISC), it becomes profitable for NASCAR to expand the number of races held at integrated tracks (i.e., those owned by ISC).[37] In deciding on the optimum number of races to organize, an integrated NASCAR will consider, not only its incremental revenues and costs, but also those of its integrated tracks. The excess demand by integrated tracks becomes relevant to NASCAR, which will find it profitable to expand the number of contests by adding races at these locations. Comparing the premium payment to a tax, integration eliminates the output-restraining impact of the tax because the payment made by the sanctioning body now simply represents a transfer to its integrated tracks. As a consequence, integration benefits consumers because the total number of Cup races expands as NASCAR places additional races at the integrated tracks.[38]

The second economic characteristic of vertical integration is that integration stimulates investment in tracks that host Cup races. This happens because some of the risk associated with owning and operating a race track goes away when the track is owned (at least partially) by NASCAR. To the extent that the financial performance of a track depends on having one or more Cup races, one would not expect non-integrated entities to invest as much to build and maintain a premium facility.[39] It is riskier to invest the requisite $100 to $150 million dollars when the return hinges on decisions made by others. For this reason, one would expect vertical integration to take place in this industry because vertical integration reduces the risk associated with such investments. Risk reduction through vertical integration benefits consumers who can attend races in newer and more accommodating facilities.[40] Even after a track has been built, acquisition by NASCAR/ISC likely will reduce the risk the facility faces by encouraging investments in maintaining and upgrading the facility. It is likely to be more risky for an independent track to fund these investments than it would be for ISC.

3. NASCAR Success and Outcome Uncertainty

Many factors contribute to NASCAR's growth in competing for consumer patronage against other sports and other forms of auto racing. Several factors include NASCAR's efforts to balance competition across large and small teams, incentives

NASCAR provides for marquee drivers to participate in all races, and the points system and the Chase for the Cup that heighten spectator interest. One element we observed in our research is how races organized by NASCAR are structured so that the outcome remains largely uncertain right up until the very end of the contest. Indeed the results of NASCAR's races are significantly more uncertain during the course of the contest than in other major sports leagues.[41] NASCAR organizes contests in which the outcome may be in doubt right through the last turn on the last lap.[42]

In this part of our paper, Cup races are compared with competition in five sports: Major League Baseball (MLB), the National Basketball Association (NBA), the National Football League (NFL), the National Hockey League (NHL), and the Professional Golfers' Association (PGA). For NASCAR, each of the thirty-six-point races from the 2006 Cup series was studied. The MLB data consisted of all Saturday games during the 2006 regular season. The NBA and NHL data consisted of the 2006–2007 regular season Saturday games, through January 6, 2007; the NFL data consisted of all Sunday games during the 2006–2007 regular season; and the PGA data consisted of the 2006 United States PGA Tour events.[43] The focus of the investigation was on Saturday and Sunday games in the MLB, NBA, NFL, and NHL to make the comparisons with the weekend events of NASCAR (and the PGA) more analogous. This also made the number of individual contests considered in each of those sports a manageable number.

To measure the uncertainty of a contest's outcome, for each of the sports leagues the percentage of the contests when the leader at the halfway point of the contest went on to win the event was calculated.[44] The halfway point would be the end of the second quarter in basketball and football, the end of the second round in golf, and the completion of half the laps in NASCAR races. For baseball and hockey, in which the contests are not readily divisible into halves but are divisible into thirds, the first third of the contest was used. This would be the third inning in baseball and the end of the first period in hockey.[45]

The eventual winner was determined by taking into account the outcome of any overtime (including shootouts and extra innings) or playoff (as in the case of golf). For example, if a baseball game was decided in the thirteenth inning, the analysis compares the leader at the end of the third inning to the winner of the game (after all thirteen innings). In the event of a tie at the halfway point, neither team (or player or driver) is considered to be the leader.

Our research shows that, in NASCAR events, the leader at the halfway mark is much less likely to win the contest than in any of these other professional sports. For NASCAR, the early leader wins only 22 percent of the races. In golf, the early leader wins 27 percent of the contests. In hockey and baseball, the early leader wins roughly 50 percent to 60 percent of the time. In basketball and football, the early leader wins about 70 percent of the time. Table 17.4 summarizes the results of this study.[46]

Having compared early leaders and eventual winners, we sought a second measure to better understand what happens with lead changes. This entailed

Table 17.4 Percentage of Contests in which the Halfway Leader is the Final
Winner: Selected Sports

Organization	Sport	Percentage
NASCAR*	Auto Racing	22.2%
PGA*	Golf	2%
NHL**	Hockey	53.4%
MLB**	Baseball	57.3%
NBA*	Basketball	70.1%
NFL*	Football	70.9%

*Halfway is 1/2 point of contest.

**Halfway is 1/3 point of contest.

Note: MLB data from 2006 regular season Saturday games; NASCAR data from 2006 Nextel Cup Series
points races; NBA and NHL data from 2006–2007 regular season Saturday games, current as of 1/6/07;
NFL data from 2006–2007 regular season Sunday games; and PGA data from 2006 United States PGA
Tour (excluding Bob Hope Chrysler Classic (five rounds) and four special rules tournaments: WGC-
Accenture Match Play Championship, The International, Ryder Cup, and WGC-World Cup).

Sources: www.espn.com, www.mlb.com, www.nba.com, www.nfl.com, www.nhl.com, www.pga.com,
and data provided by NASCAR.

calculating the percentage of events when the leader at the halfway point was not
the leader at the start of the final period and the leader at the start of the final
period was not the eventual winner. In an event with two teams, this statistic shows
the percentage of times the leader at halftime was trailing at the end of the third
quarter, but then came back to win the contest. With more than two participants,
the statistic shows the percentage of times the leader at halftime is not the leader
at the end of the three-quarters mark, and the leader at the end of three-quarters
is not the eventual winner. The results reveal the percentage of contests in which
there are at least two lead changes after the first half (or, in the case of baseball and
hockey, after the first third). Higher percentages reflect more uncertainty—that is,
lead changes are more common late in the contest.[47]

In NASCAR Cup races, nearly half the time the leader at the midpoint of the
race is not the leader at the three-quarters point, and that leader does not win the
race. In golf, this happens nearly 44 percent of time. In all other sports, there are
similar lead changes only about 7 percent to 18 percent of the time.[48] Table 17.5 summarizes the results of this analysis.

Because there are forty-three drivers in NASCAR races, but only two teams in
NFL, MLB, NBA, and NHL games, one might expect to observe that lead changes
and uncertain outcomes are more likely to occur in NASCAR than in these
other sports.[49] However, that only underscores the point we are making: the way
NASCAR has structured its races (and the rules the driving teams operate under)
allows the outcome of the contest to remain uncertain right up until the checkered
flag, which keeps spectators engaged throughout the entire length of the race.

Table 17.5 Percentage of Contests with at least Two Lead Changes after the Halfway Point: Selected Sports

Organization	Sport	Percentage
NASCAR*	Auto Racing	47.2%
PGA*	Golf	44.4%
NHL**	Hockey	18.4%
MLB**	Baseball	11.6%
NFL*	Football	8.4%
NBA*	Basketball	

*Halfway is 1/2 point of contest. Lead changes after the halfway point are measured at the 3/4 point and the end of the contest.

**Halfway is 1/3 point of contest. Lead changes after the halfway point are measured at the 2/3 point and the end of the contest.

Note: MLB data from 2006 regular season Saturday games; NASCAR data from 2006 Nextel Cup Series points races; NBA and NHL data from 2006–2007 regular season Saturday games, current as of 1/6/07; NFL data from 2006–2007 regular season Sunday games; and PGA data from 2006 United States PGA Tour (excluding Bob Hope Chrysler Classic (five rounds) and four special rules tournaments: WGC-Accenture Match Play Championship, The International, Ryder Cup, and WGC-World Cup).

Sources: www.espn.com, www.mlb.com, www.nba.com, www.nfl.com, www.nhl.com, www.pga.com, and data provided by NASCAR.

4. CONCLUSION

This article discusses the economic structure and development of NASCAR stock car racing, a sport that has grown dramatically in the past decade or so. Our analysis indicates that NASCAR keeps its fees to host tracks low and the share of broadcast revenue to these tracks high in order to provide a strong incentive for tracks to act in the best interests of NASCAR by ensuring successful and well-run events. This fee structure makes track ownership particularly attractive to NASCAR, which has come, through its common ownership of NASCAR and ISC, to own a share of the tracks that host NASCAR's Cup events. This integration has stimulated output expansion as NASCAR has placed new and additional races at tracks owned by ISC. Many analysts have contemplated why demand for NASCAR events has grown so dramatically over time. Our analysis suggests one additional factor: races are structured so that the outcome is more uncertain than in most other sports right up until the very end of the event.

Andrew Abere is Senior Economist with the Princeton Economics Group, Inc.; Peter Bronsteen is President of the Princeton Economics Group, Inc. Kenneth G. Elzinga is Robert C. Taylor Professor of Economics at the University of Virginia. All three authors served as consultants to NASCAR and ISC on an antitrust matter. The views expressed in this article are their own. The authors wish to thank Craig Depken II, Leo Kahane, Jeremy Schwartz, Robert Tollison, Peter von Allmen, and William Wood for helpful comments and suggestions and Wyatt Allen, Michelle Cleary, Daniel Savas, Chia Shen, and Tripti Thapa for research assistance.

NOTES

1 See Rottenberg (1956); Neale (1964); Noll (2003).

2 NASCAR stands for the National Association for Stock Car Auto Racing. NASCAR is privately owned and controlled by members of the France Family Group. International Speedway Corporation (ISC) was originally founded as Bill France Racing, Inc. by William H.G. France, who was also the founder of NASCAR. ISC is now a publicly traded corporation.

3 NASCAR, "About NASCAR," http://www.nascar.com/guides/about/nascar/ (accessed May 8, 2008).

4 See Hembree (2000); MacGregor (2005); Menzer (2001); Garner (2006).

5 But see O'Roark and Wood (2004); von Allmen (2001); Depken and Wilson (2004); Schwartz, Isaacs, and Carilli (2007).

6 About.com: Inventors, "The Duryea Brothers," inventors.about.com/library/inventors/blDuryea.htm (accessed on May 21, 2008).

7 www.racing-reference.info (accessed May 22, 2007).

8 France, though, had visions of an even bigger and faster speedway for NASCAR. In 1969, ISC opened Talladega Superspeedway, which is 2.66 miles in length. www.iscmotorsports.com (accessed May 22, 2007).

9 In 2004, the Winston Cup series was renamed the Nextel Cup series. In 2008, the Nextel Cup series was renamed the Sprint Cup series. Hereafter, we refer simply to the NASCAR Cup races.

10 See Hagstrom (1998).

11 www.racing-reference.info (accessed May 22, 2007).

12 The Nationwide series was formerly known as the Busch series from 1982 through 2007.

13 A comprehensive listing of active U.S. race tracks may be found in: Brown (2006).

14 As of February 2008, these two sanctioning bodies have signed an official agreement to merge together. The Champ Car World Series has promised to cease operations and cede control to the IRL. "IRL, Champ Car Agree to Unify Open-Wheel Series," *The Washington Post*, February 23, 2008, http://www.washingtonpost.com/wp-dyn/content/article/2008/02/22/AR2008022202652_pf.html (accessed May 9, 2008). Associated Press, "After 12 Years of Conflict, IRL and Champ Car Merge," *ESPN.com*, February 22, 2008, http://sports.espn.go.com/rpm/news/story?id=3259364 (accessed May 5, 2008).

15 Ryan McGee, "Did 12-Year Split Between Champ Car, IRL Cause Irreparable Damage?" *ESPN.com*, http://sports.espn.go.com/rpm/columns/story?seriesId=1&columnist=mcgee_ryan&id=3257069 (accessed on May 9, 2008).

16 NASCAR, "Tony Stewart," http://www.nascar.com/news/headlines/cup/stewart.bio (accessed May 16, 2008). NASCAR, "Juan Montoya," http://www.nascar.com/news/headlines/cup/montoya.bio (accessed May 16, 2008). NASCAR, "Sam Hornish Jr.," http://www.nascar.com/news/headlines/cup/hornishjr (accessed May 16, 2008). NASCAR, "Patrick Carpentier," http://www.nascar.com/news/headlines/cup/carpentier.patrick.bio (accessed on May 16, 2008). NASCAR, "Dario Franchitti," http://www.nascar.com/news/headlines/cup/franchitti.bio (accessed on May 16, 2008).

17 This includes Chicagoland Speedway, an acquisition ISC completed in early 2007.

18 New Hampshire International Speedway was a privately owned track under Bob and Gary Bahre. However, SMI agreed to purchase the speedway from Bob and Gary Bahre in the fourth quarter of 2007. "Speedway Motorsports

Purchases New Hampshire International Speedway," *Speedway Motorsports, Inc.*, November 2, 2007, http://phx.corporate-ir.net/phoenix.zhtml?c=99758&p=irol-newsArticle&t=Regular&id=1071914& (accessed May 9, 2008).

19 www.indianapolismotorspeedway.com (accessed May 22, 2007).

20 See Hurt (2005).

21 See Table 17.1, which lists race awards and relocations.

22 We do not discuss here the innovations in televising NASCAR sporting events as a factor in growing demand for the sport. However, the use of multiple camera angles, from above (blimp), from trackside, to below ("Digger" the in-ground camera locations), to in-car cameras have been important innovations in visual perspectives for fans not at the tracks.

23 See John Mansell et al., *U.S. TV Sports Databook 2003* (Carmel, CA: Kagan World Media, May 2003), 134.

24 See Table 17.2, which lists the growth of output statistics for the Cup series.

25 NASCAR negotiated the consolidated television contract for the 2001 through 2006 racing seasons and allocated the proceeds to tracks, teams/drivers, and NASCAR. Prior to the 2001 season, NASCAR permitted host tracks to negotiate their own broadcast contracts for Cup races.

26 Other than hosting automobile races, some tracks generate income from renting the facility for racing schools, automobile testing, and non-motorsports events (such as concerts and other special events).

27 The net sanction revenue represents the excess of the track's share of broadcast revenue minus the costs of obtaining the Cup event, which include the sanction fee paid to NASCAR, the purse and award money paid to the teams and drivers, and other costs specified in the sanction agreements.

28 For example, ISC reported total revenues of $740 million for the fiscal year ended Nov. 30, 2005. Of that amount, 32 percent ($235 million) was generated by admissions and 12 percent ($87 million) was generated by food, beverage, and merchandise sales. International Speedway Corporation, Annual Report (2005): 29 and 34.

29 Dennis B. McAlpine, "The Motorsports Industry," *Josephthal & Co., Inc. Institutional Research* (Dec. 1, 1997): 5.

30 Dover Motorsports, Inc. Annual Report 2004, "Shareholders' Letter."

31 Speedway Motorsports, Inc. Annual Report 2005, 40.

32 Mark Yost, "At Speedways, Nonracing Events Accelerate," *Wall Street Journal* (June 20, 2006): D8.

33 Speedway Motorsports, Inc., Form 8-K for the period of December 1, 1998, Exhibit 99.5. International Speedway Corp., Form 10-K405 for the period January 30, 2001, 5.

34 Examples of fixed costs incurred by track operators would be the upfront cost of building the track facility and paving the surface, taxes on the land and property where the track resides, and interest payments on debt. Examples of variable costs incurred by track operators would be the cost of labor to host an event, the cost of concessions sold at an event, the cost of promotional material for each event, and the cost of cleaning up after each event. We use the terms *incremental* and *variable* interchangeably.

35 This explains why NASCAR would encourage other forms of racing. As tracks handle more races, these other events share a portion of the tracks' fixed costs, and a smaller burden falls on NASCAR.

36 P. Scott Douglas, "P. Scott Douglas: Promoter/Director of Media, Louisville Motor Speedway," in *Profiles of Sport Industry Professionals: The People Who Make the*

Games Happen, Matthew J. Robinson et al. (Gaithersburg, Maryland: Aspen Publishers, 2001), 215–216.

37 James C. France, Chairman of the Board and Chief Executive Officer of ISC, and Lesa France Kennedy, President of ISC and one of ISC's directors, are both members of the France Family Group, which controls NASCAR. Additionally, they both hold positions with NASCAR. France Family Group members, together, beneficially own approximately 35.0 percent of ISC's capital stock and over 65.0 percent of the combined voting power of both classes of ISC's common stock. International Speedway Corporation, Form 10-K for the fiscal year period ended Nov. 30, 2007: 3 and 8.

38 NASCAR has done just this by issuing new race dates to tracks that, at the times of the date awards, were at least partially owned by ISC in Miami, Kansas City, and Chicago, and NASCAR is interested in expanding the schedule once more by placing a new race in New York.

39 Public filings made by SMI and Dover indicate that their profitability could be adversely impacted by a deterioration in their relationship with NASCAR or NASCAR's decision not to renew events now hosted by these companies. See, for example, Speedway Motorsports, Inc., Form 10-K for the fiscal year ended Dec. 31, 2005:15, and Dover Motorsports, Inc., Form 10-K for the fiscal year ended Dec. 31, 2005: 16.

40 That vertical integration leads to greater investment is not unique to NASCAR and tracks. For an analysis of vertical integration between physicians and hospitals, see Ciliberto (2006).

41 The literature on sports economics identifies uncertainty of outcome as one of the key drivers of demand or fan interest. See, for example, Borland and MacDonald (2003).

42 See also Hagstrom (1998), p. 35, where the author notes that: "Five decades of experience have taught NASCAR that lopsided races lead to fan apathy and a drop in gate receipts. The reason 100,000 fans and millions more watching television stay glued to their seat for the entire race is that, until the checkered flag drops, it is still almost anyone's race to win. It is not unusual for a race to end with fifteen cars on the lead lap, separated by less than two or three seconds."

43 We excluded the Chrysler Classic, which has five rounds, and four other tournaments with different rules or scoring systems (e.g., match play, etc.). The four excluded tournaments are: WGC-Accenture Match Play Championship, The International, Ryder Cup, and WGC-World Cup.

44 This approach has been utilized in other studies of the outcomes of sports contests. Magnus and Klaassen, for example, found in their analysis of a sample of singles tennis matches at Wimbledon, that the player who had won the next-to-last set also won the final set about 50 percent of the time (1999, pp. 461–468).

45 A baseball game consists of nine innings and a hockey game consists of three periods.

46 We also performed this analysis using the three-quarters mark instead of the halfway point. This involved looking at the end of the third period in football and basketball; the end of the third round in golf; and the end of three-quarters of the laps in NASCAR. Again, for baseball and hockey, which are not divisible into quarters, this meant looking at the end of the two-thirds point, which is the end of the sixth inning in baseball and the end of the second period in hockey.

   The resulting pattern is very similar to that shown in Table 17.4, except all the percentages are higher. The leader in NASCAR races at the three-quarters mark wins the event only about 40 percent of the time. The leader after three rounds in golf wins about 50 percent of the time. The leaders in the remaining sports win the contests about 70 percent to 80 percent of the time.

47 To perform these calculations, the halfway and three-quarters points for football, basketball, golf, and NASCAR were used. The end of the third and sixth innings for baseball, and the end of the first and second periods for hockey, were used.

48 A mirror image of this analysis examines the proportion of contests in which the leader at the midpoint also leads at the start of the final period and ultimately wins the contest. For NASCAR, the eventual winner led at the halfway point and before the start of the final quarter less than 15 percent of the time. For all other sports, the eventual winner leads at halftime and at the start of the fourth quarter in about 25 percent to nearly 67 percent of the contests.

49 Like NASCAR, golf tournaments have multiple participants.

REFERENCES

Borland, Jeffery, and Robert MacDonald. 2006. Demand for sport. *Oxford Review of Economic Policy* 19: 478–502.

Brown, Allan E., and Nancy L. Brown. 2006. *2006 National speedway directory.* Comstock Park, MI: Allan E. Brown and Nancy L. Brown.

Ciliberto, Federico. 2006. Does organizational form affect investment decisions? *Journal of Industrial Economics* LIV: 63–93.

Depken II, C. A., and D. P. Wilson. 2004. The efficiency of the NASCAR reward system: Initial empirical evidence. *Journal of Sports Economics* 5: 371–86.

Garner, Joe. 2006. *Speed, guts, & glory: 100 unforgettable moments in NASCAR history.* New York: Warner Books.

Hagstrom, Robert G. 1998. *The NASCAR Way: The business that drives the sport.* New York: Wiley.

Hembree, Mike. 2000. *NASCAR: The definitive history of America's sport.* New York: HarperCollins Publishers.

Hurt, Douglas A. 2005. Dialed in? Geographic expansion and regional identity in NASCAR's Nextel Cup Series. *Southeastern Geographer* 45: 125.

MacGregor, Jeff. 2005. *Sunday money.* New York: HarperCollins Publishers.

Magnus, Jan R., and Franc J.G.M. Klaassen. 1999. The final set in a tennis match: Four years at Wimbledon. *Journal of Applied Statistics* 26: 461–468.

Menzer, Joe. 2001. *The wildest ride: The history of NASCAR.* New York: Simon & Schuster.

Neale, Walter C. 1964. The peculiar economics of professional sports: A contribution to the theory of the firm in sporting competition and in market competition. *Quarterly Journal of Economics* 78: 1–14.

Noll, Roger G. 2003. The organisation of sports leagues. *Oxford Review of Economic Policy* 19: 530–551.

O'Roark, J. Brian, and William C. Wood. 2004. Safety at the racetrack: Results of restrictor plates in superspeedway competition. *Southern Economic Journal* 71: 118–29.

Rottenberg, Simon. 1956. The baseball players' labor market. *Journal of Political Economy* 64: 242–258.

Schwartz, Jeremy T., Justin P. Isaacs, and Anthony M. Carilli. 2007. To race or to place? An empirical investigation of the efficiency of the NASCAR points competition. *Journal of Sports Economics* 8: 633–641.

von Allmen, Peter. 2001. Is the reward system in NASCAR efficient? *Journal of Sports Economics* 2: 62–79.

PART IV

ECONOMICS OF COLLEGE SPORTS

CHAPTER 18

TO BE OR NOT TO BE

THE NCAA AS A CARTEL

ROBERT D. TOLLISON

1. INTRODUCTION

THE National Collegiate Athletic Association (NCAA) is commonly seen as a benign administrator of the rules of college athletics and as an organization that promotes the ideals of amateurism. In a word, the NCAA serves the public interest. Economists, on the other hand, tend to view the NCAA as a cartel (Alchian and Allen 1972, Becker 1985, 1987). Barro, for example, called the NCAA, the "best monopoly in America" (Barro 2002, p. 22).

Economists hold this view because the NCAA has historically devised rules to restrict output (the number of games played and televised) and to restrict competition for key inputs (student-athletes). Economists have focused primarily on the latter restrictions, or the input or monopsonistic aspects of NCAA behavior. NCAA rules concerning recruiting and financial aid are seen as transferring rewards from players to schools and coaches so that the rules are seen as an expression of an agreement among buyers to restrict competition for inputs.

The purpose of this paper is to explain the various aspects of the analysis of the NCAA as a cartel. Kahn (2007) performs a similar analysis in a comparison of cartel theory with competing explanations of NCAA behavior. In effect, this paper uses the economic theory of cartels to analyze the institutional practices of the NCAA with respect to its regulation of student-athletes. The paper is, therefore, an exercise in the "economics of sports" rather than "economics in sports."

2. An Economic Approach to the NCAA

In spite of the unique features of college sports, approaching the NCAA and its members as economic entities is warranted. In most cases the peculiar aspects of college athletics change only the relevant variables to consider and not the appropriate analytical framework. For instance, professional sports are for-profit ventures. The typical assumption of profit maximization is normally appropriate in this case. Can the same be said of college athletics? Yes, because revenue is still an important objective to collegiate decision makers. The difference with professional sports in this regard lies mainly in the form that net revenues assume on the balance sheet. Instead of being clearly listed as dividends to stockholders or retained earnings, NCAA member surpluses end up in expense items such as salaries, equipment, buildings, or even transfers to the general fund. Similarly, college athletes do not receive an explicit wage or salary. Instead, they receive in-kind payments from schools. Additionally, they provide implicit revenues to schools even if these values get allocated to other budgetary units. The NCAA's unique qualities do not require a different kind of economic analysis, only careful application of the appropriate and existing analysis.

3. The NCAA Is Transparent

The NCAA provides a useful setting for applications and tests of cartel theory. The NCAA operates largely, though not entirely, without antitrust constraints so that it has a long and, to a large extent, public history. In the *National Collegiate Athletic Association v. Board of Regents of the University of Oklahoma et al.* (1984), the Association ran afoul of U.S. antitrust laws (more on this case later). In spite of the ruling, the NCAA continues to restrict output (other than through television rights) and to regulate competition for inputs. The NCAA does not have a legislative exemption from antitrust laws; still, it has two factors that have worked in its favor with respect to its legal status and its ability to continue to behave as a cartel. First, sports in the United States have historically been given a great deal of leeway in terms of their treatment under the antitrust laws. Federal courts largely ignored or sidestepped antitrust issues in sports until the 1970s and the onset of unionization by professional athletes. Second, the NCAA is strongly linked to higher education and traditions of amateurism. Member schools have successfully hidden cartel behavior behind the rhetoric of support for academic achievement and the nonproprietary setting of universities, as well as the fanciful idea that intercollegiate sports competition actually takes place between amateurs.

4. THE CARTEL VERSUS COMPETING EXPLANATIONS OF THE NCAA

The question of whether an association of rival producers implies cartel-like behavior is debatable. Some industrial cooperation may function to establish standard weights, measures, or the like, which provide benefits to producers and consumers. Even among economists, the cartel interpretation of the NCAA has met some strenuous objection. McKenzie and Sullivan (1985) suggest that the Association is a necessary vehicle for scheduling, rules standardization, and provision of amateur standards. In this view, although a few star players may have value to their schools in excess of their in-kind compensation, the same condition does not hold for the average college player. What can be said about this argument?

First, a convincing *prima facie* case that the NCAA is a cartel can be derived from the explicit behavior of the NCAA. The open collusion among schools extends far beyond rules standardization, scheduling, and the like. For example, the football contract with a single television network, until voided by the Supreme Court, was not necessary for rules standardization. It restricted competition among members and increased NCAA revenues.

Second, although revenues to schools, coaches' salaries, and expenditures on athletic programs have exploded over the years since 1950 (the time that the present version of NCAA enforcement emerged), allowable compensation to athletes has remained essentially the same: a full grant-in-aid equal to tuition and fees, room and board, and books. Any athlete receiving more than a full grant-in-aid is automatically ineligible for NCAA participation. This differential growth in allowable compensation is easy to explain with cartel theory. Schools have successfully colluded to restrict growth in student-athlete compensation to levels below the value of these athletes to the schools. A non-cartel explanation of such developments is not so obvious. Such a framework must explain the huge increases in the compensation of two inputs (schools and coaches), whereas players' compensation has remained almost constant (in real terms) over the same period of time. In a rent-redistribution framework of cartel theory, this seeming paradox vanishes.

Third, the exclusion of school brand-name and other capital assets from NCAA regulation also suggests a cartel scheme. Proponents of the NCAA restrictions have pointed to educational requirements, standardized rules, and maintenance of amateurism as rationales for such things as the television plan and eligibility rules. Yet the NCAA policy is not consistent across all types of inputs, automatically according certain advantages to some schools in recruiting and performance. Specifically, one can point to stadiums, training facilities, food, living accommodations, and the like as examples of unregulated physical capital across schools. If a quest for education, amateurism, and standardized rules were truly at the heart of NCAA behavior, these inputs would be regulated along with labor inputs. Indeed, if such purposes were goals of the NCAA, some schools would not be allowed to offer recruits a more attractive package of complements than other schools, and student-athletes would not be allowed to choose schools freely. Indeed, athletes might be subject to a draft system, as are most professional athletes.

Fourth, the value of many athletes to schools, or what economists call their marginal-revenue products (MRPs), are large in relation to the market value of the educational product that they are given, at least in football and basketball. College athletes possess skills that are relatively rare in the population as a whole and that are in demand by a large segment of sports fans. Conservative estimates of the career MRPs of certain college athletes, such as Patrick Ewing, Doug Flutie, or Bo Jackson, are in the millions of dollars and over $10 million in some cases. Certainly, the MRP of the average starter in college football or basketball is less than this; yet average salaries in the same professional sports, which run into hundreds of thousands and millions of dollars per year, provide a rough shadow price for at least the largest revenue producers in college sports. Even if the average college player's MRP is one-quarter that of the average professional player, the in-kind educational compensation of college players falls several times short of this level.

Fifth, the very existence of illicit payments to student athletes and their families indicates the presence of rents attempting to find their way to the relevant input. Producers and loyal patrons of Burger King do not offer large cash and in-kind enticements to lure skillful workers away from McDonald's. If college athletics are in financial deficit, as is often claimed, such illicit enticements to athletes would not make any sense.

The available evidence of price fixing, output controls, compensation of athletes below their MRPs, the absence of regulation of brand-name and capital assets, and so on, taken together, indicate cartel behavior. If these behavioral aspects do not suggest a cartel, one could fairly ask, what would? In this case it seems that there is no evidence short of tape recordings of the NCAA Council reviewing graphs of cartel theory that would refute the no-cartel proposition.

5. The NCAA's Monopoly Power

In spite of the evidence that the NCAA behaves as a cartel, some questions linger about the source of the NCAA's cartel power. Clearly, athletes are not forced to accept scholarship offers nor are schools forced to join the NCAA. One key factor contributing to the NCAA's monopoly power is U.S. antitrust policy. As noted earlier, the sports industry in the United States has historically enjoyed lenient antitrust treatment. This is especially so with respect to college sports. The impact of antitrust enforcement on NCAA collusive power is clearly seen in the decision on the NCAA television plan (*National Collegiate Athletic Association v. Board of*

Regents of the University of Oklahoma et al., 1984). Before the Supreme Court decision, with relative immunity from the antitrust laws, the NCAA enforced a television plan that severely limited the total number of games that could be broadcast per season, limited the number of appearances per school, and increased NCAA revenues from television rights. In the wake of the Court's decision, the output of college football in terms of the number of games televised per weekend increased dramatically, as did the quality of the matchups presented. Before the decision, a fan might have been able to see two or sometimes three games per weekend. Since the decision, Saturdays have provided morning-to-night college football coverage. Of course, this is exactly what economic theory predicts when a market shifts from monopoly to competition. Quantity (number of televised games) increases and price (payment by the networks per game) falls. It is not a great leap to suggest that the lenient posture of antitrust policy toward the NCAA input restrictions on compensation for student-athletes serves a similar function in maintaining the NCAA's monopsony or buyer power.

Lenient antitrust policy provides a necessary condition for successful collusion; yet, given that the NCAA is a voluntary association, its antitrust status alone is not a sufficient condition for long-lasting monopoly or monopsony power. Two other factors provide this condition. One factor is the discontinuous, or "lumpy," entry conditions in college athletics. One or even a few schools cannot produce a viable ten- or eleven-game football season or a thirty-game basketball season. Coordination among several schools would be necessary for a successful breakaway from the NCAA and establishment of a competitive league or association. In other words, there is a first-mover problem. Although this does not render disassociation from the NCAA and new competitive entry impossible, it does increase the costs and decrease the likelihood of such behavior.

A second factor plays a major role in keeping schools in the NCAA. This is the threat of sanctions against a school's *academic* programs. Obviously, the NCAA does not directly control the academic accreditation process; however, NCAA sanctions and pressure have influenced this process. For instance, in the early 1950s, Oklahoma A&M (now Oklahoma State) came under NCAA scrutiny because of its athletic scholarships. Because of these scholarships, the North Central College and Secondary Schools Association compiled a report on the school and considered repealing its accreditation. Alchian and Allen (1972, p. 444) mention a similar episode. A school placed on probation will be less likely to exit the cartel if, by exiting, they draw upon themselves the threat of academic sanctions. Moreover, many conferences are not just simply athletic affiliations; they are also academic associations operated directly by university presidents. Organizationally, the NCAA does not separate athletics and academics. The NCAA Council and Infractions Committee are not staffed simply by coaches and athletic directors. Faculty, deans, and college executives fill these positions. Thus, the NCAA can threaten the brand-name capital of academic institutions in such a fundamental way as to make exit from the Association very costly. Loss of accreditation would seriously harm many schools in the market for students, endowments, and grants. The linkage between academics and athletics is probably the real source of the NCAA's cartel power.

6. A Short Digression on the Formation of the NCAA

College athletics producers faced an organizational problem in the late 1800s and early 1900s. Violence during college football contests had reached alarming proportions (a number of players were killed) due largely to the absence of effective punishment of such behavior. No one school had an incentive to reduce such tactics because other teams would continue to use them and win. In addition to violent play, football was still in a formative period as far as its basic playing rules were concerned. The roots of rugby lingered in some rules recognized by some teams.

The initial reason for cooperation among producers often centers on solving a common externality problem, such as violence in college football. The resulting association may provide such public goods as measurements, standards, and the like, but over time, an association can evolve into an organization with a different purpose. The primary purpose may remain constant, that is, the management of potential externalities; yet the organizational format can turn from reducing externalities to increasing joint profits. The scenario has been referred to as the by-product theory of interest-group organization.

The initial or startup costs of an organization are often high. These fixed and quasi-fixed costs hinder the effective solution of externality problems. As stressed in the case of the NCAA, the extent of the initial cost is evidenced by the degrees to which violent play and other problems were allowed to grow before they were addressed. In spite of these large start-up costs, once an association is organized and such origination costs have been incurred, the continuing costs of association may be quite low. In other words, variable and marginal costs are low with respect to the fixed costs, and the association enjoys economies of scale. In addition, the costs of expanding the scope of the association to include additional areas may be quite low; the association may enjoy economies of scope. The factor behind such economies is that the association already has a management and decision-making apparatus in place. Once an association is organized, given that the initial organizational costs are borne, the marginal costs of agreeing to extend the scale and scope of the association are low.

The areas into which the association extends its reach can vary. The firms and organizations may agree on additional rules and institutions to reduce other externalities. However, producers may also use the cooperative apparatus to behave like a cartel. Such behavior includes making price-fixing agreements, placing restrictions and quotas on the quantity of the product sold, colluding on the purchase of inputs, and so on. To paraphrase Adam Smith, producers seldom get together without the discussion turning to plots against consumers and input suppliers.

The NCAA is no exception to this general maxim. The colleges and universities did not originally cooperate for cartel purposes. Instead, the association that became the NCAA bore the initial costs of organization in order to provide public goods. Very shortly thereafter, the discussion turned from the reduction of violence and on-the-field rule standardization to price and output restrictions and restrictions on the recruiting of student-athletes. For the most part, the evolution of the NCAA as a cartel took place over the first half of the 1900s. By 1950, these restrictions on college athletic product and resource markets had become the primary preoccupation of the NCAA.

7. Cartel Enforcement

Now that some of the basic economic principles concerning cartel behavior and the NCAA have been addressed, the problem of cartel enforcement can be discussed. This topic has been saved for last because some of the foregoing analysis is important in understanding the nature of the enforcement process. This is especially true in the specific application to the NCAA.

A necessary condition for successful cartel operation is a viable enforcement and punishment process. Yet the mechanism must be cost-efficient. It is on this point that a cartel faces a dilemma. Widespread cheating on the cartel agreement signals the end of the cartel, and such behavior must be controlled. However, if members of the cartel are spatially dispersed when selling their products and purchasing inputs, enforcement may be expensive.

In general, the cartel has two ways to determine if firms are violating a collusive agreement. First, it can monitor each member directly, that is, engage in constant surveillance of each firm's practices. Second, it can use probabilistic evidence to infer when producer's behavior diverges from agreed-upon principles. Unless cartel members sell and purchase in centrally located and well-organized markets, direct surveillance is prohibitively costly. With dispersed firms, the cartel enforcement agency is not able to monitor all members directly.

Without direct monitoring, the enforcement agency must monitor imperfectly. A relatively inexpensive way to infer cheating is by using a probabilistic model. If data are available on firm performance (profits, revenues, costs), probabilistic inferences can be drawn about behavior. The enforcement process, at least in a stylized way, is not difficult to imagine. Suppose the enforcement agency uses an end-of-year performance statistic as its guide. It knows past historical performance, and from this data can compute the probability of various levels of firm performance relative to the cartel as a whole for the present year. Using some decision rule, the enforcement agency infers that a violation has occurred if firm-level performance exceeds its average performance relative to the cartel by a large amount; that is, the probability of such an outcome occurring by random chance is small. One would expect to see enforcement and punishment actions brought against members performing extraordinarily well, given their historical performance.

Application of this analysis to NCAA enforcement is direct. Consider the rules regarding compensation to athletes. Given the number and location of schools and the diversity of places visited by schools in recruiting, direct surveillance is not possible. This is especially true in view of the limited enforcement staff of the NCAA, but would still hold for an even larger NCAA staff. The number of possible contacts between schools, athletes, coaches, and alumni is far too large for a cost-efficient system of direct surveillance monitoring. As a result, the NCAA uses probabilistic evidence to infer violations (at least at the initial stages of an investigation). The most obvious statistic from which to draw inferences is on-the-field performance. If a school's winning percentage increases dramatically relative to its historical average, illegal activity may be occurring. (Fleisher, Goff, and Tollison 1992, 1998).

Enforcement has interesting implications for the allocation of rents within the NCAA. If the enforcement process is relatively successful at keeping compensation to athletes close to its agreed-upon value, secret cash and in-kind payments will have little impact on the distribution of rents (or who wins) in the cartel. Instead, the allocation of rents to a particular school will depend primarily upon that school's ability to compete in non-regulated areas of competition. As we have seen already, these areas are largely physical and brand-name capital expenditures. Generally, traditional winners with a large stock of brand-name capital and schools with the financial resources to build up their physical capital will gain from the enforcement process. These programs have a built-in group of fans, large stadiums, and plush facilities, and are, therefore, in a natural economic position to benefit from good teams, high rankings, conference championships, and bowl games.

NCAA enforcement based on probabilistic evidence also affects performance on the playing field. A simple and testable theory follows. First, the traditional football powers in the NCAA capture the organization and its various committees from its modern inception in 1950 and maintain this power over time. Schools are judged by their win-loss records. Teams that win all the time (the traditional powers) and teams that lose all the time are not placed on probation. However, when teams that usually lose start to improve and win more games, they are put on probation by the NCAA. The penalties, such as lost scholarships, promptly return the offending school to its losing ways. In this way, traditional football and basketball schools are able to protect their rents (television, bowls, and so on) from the interloping or "improving" programs. The testable implication of this theory is that variability in the win-loss records of teams should be a positive predictor of enforcement actions.

Fleisher, Goff, and Tollison (1992) offer an empirical test of this hypothesis. Using data on NCAA enforcement actions against college football programs for the 1953–1983 time period, they estimate a LOGIT model of whether a school was placed on probation during this period as a function of the coefficient of variation of the school's win-loss record in football and several control variables, such as the size of the stadium and the age of the school. The sign on the variable of interest is positive and significant. More variability in a school's win-loss record is a good predictor of enforcement actions. The placeholder variables are significant and carry the expected signs. Stadium size, for example, is positive and significant. Overall, the model is significant and explains about 33 percent of the variation in NCAA enforcement actions.

So enforcement can lead to different outcomes. If it is effective, schools will compete through facilities and reputation. If not, student-athletes will be compensated beyond the NCAA levels, and some schools will be penalized for such behavior, others not. It is a good guess that enforcement is effective because the episodic evidence with respect to payments to players is wide spread and because such practices would be hard to cover up.

Lastly, what keeps the cartel together? This goes back to the earlier discussion of the extent of monopoly power held by the NCAA. Surely, a school cannot opt out by itself (who would it play?) or without the strong prospect that its academic accreditation may be at stake as well.

So we have a trifecta. The NCAA was formed for a good economic reason, but its organizational capital was later used to cartelize output and input markets. The enforcement process is predictably carried out to benefit traditional winners in college football, and there is no easy way to break down the cartel. If it walks like a duck and talks like a duck, it is a duck.

8. Conclusion

This chapter is a positive economic analysis of the NCAA. The normative issue would be whether players *should* be paid. This issue is beyond the scope of this paper, but it is an interesting question with interesting implications. For example, what if payments to players led to a migration of college sports to off-campus venues such as for-profit minor leagues and conferences? As a fan, I have a simple reaction: YIKES!

REFERENCES

Alchian, Armen A., and William R. Allen. 1972. *University Economics*. Belmont, CA: Wadsworth Publishing.

Barro, Robert J. 2002. The best little monopoly in America. *Business Week*, December 9: 22.

Becker, Gary. 1983. College athletes should get paid what they are worth. *Business Week*, September 30: 18.

Becker, Gary. 1987. The NCAA: A cartel in sheepskin clothing. *Business Week*, September 17: 24

Fleisher, A. A., B. C. Goff, and R. D. Tollison. 1988. Crime or punishment?: Enforcement of the NCAA football cartel. *Journal of Economic Behavior and Organization*, 10: 433–51.

Fleisher, A. A., B. C. Goff, and R. D. Tollison. 1992. *The National Collegiate Athletic Association: A study in cartel behavior*. Chicago: University of Chicago Press.

Kahn, L. 2007. Cartel behavior and amateurism in college sports. *Journal of Economic Perspectives*, 21: 7–23.

McKenzie, R. B., and E. T. Sullivan. 1985. Does the NCAA exploit college athletes? An economics and legal interpretation. *Antitrust Bulletin*, 32: 373–399.

CHAPTER 19

WHAT DOES INTERCOLLEGIATE ATHLETICS DO TO OR FOR COLLEGES AND UNIVERSITIES?

MALCOLM GETZ AND JOHN SIEGFRIED

FIELDING high quality athletic teams that generate substantial revenues for colleges and universities by competing against rival universities is a peculiarly American phenomenon. Unlike many American innovations, virtually no other country in the world has copied it. Such uniqueness ought to provoke reflection about the role of big-time sports in the American academy (Clotfelter, Chapter 1, 2011).

One explanation for this sports–scholarship partnership is that inputs used in higher education complement those used in athletics. The primary input for both production processes is young adults. In the presence of diminishing marginal returns both to academic study and physical exercise, engaging in sports and study over a similar period might increase productivity. Why, then, would many universities partner with quasi-professional sporting teams, but not with, say, landscape architects, construction firms, or, as former University of Chicago President Robert Hutchins once asked, racing stables? University students could plant shrubs, carry bricks, or ride horses just as easily as they can participate in commercialized athletic competitions against other universities, and all of these activities require intense physical exertion.

Roger Noll (1999) argues that universities field athletic teams to attract students who want to participate in organized sports. Many prospective students have played on organized youth teams, and have represented their high school on athletic teams. They enjoy uniforms, teammates, and trophies. This preference for participation can explain the prevalence of a wide array of athletic programs from the Ivy League, whose members field as many sports teams as any university in the United States, to elite liberal arts colleges that play in the National Collegiate Athletic Association's Division 3 without athletic scholarships (although its members do give admissions preferences to some athletes). Of course, collegiate athletics were important in America when kids played sports on an empty lot with whoever showed up, wearing T-shirts and jeans. So, there must be more to the demand for college athletic competitions than just uniforms and trophies. Although the desire to be part of a team can rationalize student demand for sporting opportunities in the form of intramurals and club sports, it does not explain the high level of spending on coaches, recruiting, travel, and facilities, particularly for the large commercialized operations of Division 1 football, or men and women's intercollegiate basketball. The discussion that follows reviews available evidence on the returns to universities from supporting big-time televised college sports, including effects on government support, philanthropy, admissions, and on students themselves.

Direct Effects on Institutional Revenue

In light of the substantial ticket prices charged for big-time college sporting events such as football at the University of Michigan, men's basketball at Duke, or women's basketball at the University of Tennessee, a tempting explanation for the peculiar partnership is that universities sell sports entertainment services to the public to raise revenue that they then can reallocate to the (academic) mission of their institutions. Indeed, a 2006 survey found that 78 percent of Americans believe college athletics programs are profitable (Knight Commission on Intercollegiate Athletics, 2006). But reports by university administrators (Duderstadt, 2000), economists (Zimbalist, 1999), and even the NCAA itself (Osborne, 2004; NCAA, 2009), raise considerable doubt that revenues garnered by university athletic departments contribute much to supporting the academic enterprise financially.

In the first place, there seem to be relatively few Division 1 universities that actually earn net positive revenues from their football and basketball programs (Duderstadt, 2000). In 2007–2008, for example, only 25 of the 119 Football Bowl Subdivision universities in the NCAA ran an athletic department surplus.

Individually, a majority of football programs failed to cover their operating costs from 2004 to 2006 (Fulks, 2008). If capital costs and an allocation for general university overhead (e.g., administrative time, security costs, etc.) were included, the financial results would look even worse. This is partly the result of a zero-sum game that encompasses universities fielding Division 1 sports (Frank, 2004). It is also a function of the large variation in revenues earned by Division 1 athletic departments. The reliably more successful teams earn greater revenues, which can (but often do not) leave them with a net surplus. Athletic success is largely positional—that is, what is valuable is winning the game, the league championship, or the national championship. Unfortunately, for every winner, there is a loser; for every league champion, there is a doormat; and for every national champion, there are many more "also-rans." If the teams that do not achieve positional success fail to garner anticipated revenues, they may be tempted to invest in improving their circumstances so that they can be more successful in the future. They may boost the salaries of coaches so as to attract what appear to be more successful team leaders, they may remodel or replace expensive physical facilities so that better players will be interested in playing for their university, and they may expand their game schedules geographically in order to appeal to recruits who have never ventured far beyond their own neighborhood. Such efforts cost money, which could and would generate success except that rival institutions are doing the same thing, and in the end, there can be only one winner of each game, only one league champion, and only one national champion.

Although colleges and universities have a built-in demand for athletic services from their alumni that helps them attract paying fans and television contracts, collegiate teams lack the controls imposed by professional leagues to avoid competitively spending themselves into poverty. This puts them in an incessant quest for athletic superiority that is collectively doomed to mediocrity and inevitably leads to the dissipation of revenues through aggressive rent-seeking behavior (Frank, 2004). Indeed, the athletics arms race may be escalating, with large television revenues bringing ever greater focus on just a few premier teams. Coaches and athletic administrators earn salaries substantially above their best alternative pay, and stadium architects and construction firms gain business they would otherwise not receive. Even though the student stars that fill the enormous stadiums are not paid, there is usually little left from athletics profits to subsidize the academic missions of the colleges and universities the teams represent. Indeed, the flow of funds seems to move in the opposite direction. A 2010 report concluded that "more than $800 million in student fees and university subsidies are propping up athletics programs at the nation's top sports colleges, including hundreds of millions in the richest conferences" (Gillium, Upton and Berkowitz, 2010). Indeed, the concentration of television revenues on post-season play and national champions may be molding a winner-take-all market with outsized rewards for the teams at the pinnacle, and losses for all the rest. In spring 2010, the NCAA expanded its men's basketball tournament to sixty-eight teams as it signed a fourteen-year contract for television broadcast rights for $10.8 billion. Rampant press speculation in 2010 suggested that there might be fewer, larger major-college-football conferences in the years ahead, perhaps only four superconferences, that will increase television revenues from conference football championships (Thamel, 2010). With a larger reward at the pinnacle, the climb to the top will get steeper, yet more enticing. Nevertheless, if history is informative, the competition will be no more profitable for the colleges.

The lack of reported financial surpluses from commercial college and university athletics is partly a function of academe's unusual accounting practices. If a university is not at its maximum enrollment, the incremental cost of adding scholarship athletes is likely to be significantly less than the full-tuition scholarship that is reflected on the university's books as an accounting cost, because the athletes will fit into existing classes, without hiring additional instructional staff, and will live in housing that may otherwise have stood vacant. Even if a recruited athlete did displace another student, the net average cost of losing that other student may be less than the cost of the athlete. Many students in the general student body receive scholarships and/or subsidized loans, whereas athletic departments typically provide extensive and expensive tutoring and other academic support to athletes, which are not furnished to other students. Because an ordinary student who might replace a student-athlete may not pay the full tuition sticker price and likely consumes fewer academic support services, he or she would cost less than a scholarship athlete.

On the other hand, conventional university-fund accounting does not charge to athletics (or any other operating unit) the full depreciation cost of facilities, and some institutions do not charge any of the costs of scholarships for student athletes to the athletic department. The true net effect of these various accounting quirks is unknown. Borland, Goff, and Pulsinelli's (1992) study of Western Kentucky University suggests that athletic-department losses may be overstated by exaggerated costs, but, of course, their conclusion is based on the experience of only one university. On the revenue side, big-time athletics generates ticket sales, royalties on logos, and television contracts, usually shared among conference members. Yet, expenditures continuously expand to consume even more than the available revenue.

INDIRECT EFFECTS

If big-time collegiate athletics is not a direct financial bonanza to colleges and universities, why then, does the vast majority of America's leading universities spend large sums of money on coaches, facilities, and scholarships to field competitive teams in football, men's and women's basketball, and often intercollegiate ice hockey (in the north) or baseball (in the south)? The conventional answer to this question is indirect benefits. For example, as a form of advertising, public relations, and consumption (entertainment), intercollegiate athletics may increase financial donations to a university from former athletes, from sports fans who are not alumni, from alumni who are not necessarily sports fans, or from people who are not directly connected to the institution. Athletic success may attract more students with academic talent, enhancing a university's academic prestige. Success in athletics may be interpreted (correctly or not) as a signal of excellence in all pursuits, including academic, and thus attract the attention of those who fancy themselves as people associated with success. This view is summed up succinctly by David Schmidly, president of the University of New Mexico, who said: "One of the most effective ways to market your university nationally is to have a really quality athletic program. It helps recruit faculty, students, and donors. It helps with the image of the whole university" (Zengerle, 2010).

INDIRECT EFFECTS ON GOVERNMENT SUPPORT

At public institutions, athletic success might attract larger university appropriations from state legislators concerned more with the perception of the university by the majority of voters among their constituents who do not hold a college degree than by the minority in their districts who have earned a baccalaureate degree. Allen (1999), for example, reports that the University of Connecticut managed to secure an additional billion dollars from its state legislature by capitalizing on the success of its men's and women's basketball teams in 1999, when the men won the national championship. More systematic evidence supports Allen's anecdote. Using data on 570 public universities, Humphreys found that those fielding Division 1 football teams receive about 8 percent more from their state legislature than otherwise comparable universities that do not participate in Division 1 football. Participation seems to be what matters. Success is less important. State subsidies appear to be no greater for universities with top-twenty or bowl-participating football teams.

Government may also be interested in increases in sales tax revenue emanating from taxable sales of tickets to large-scale college events. Local officials may expect that increased ticket sales to the large crowds add more to their revenues than local government lays out for the extra police and ambulance services required by the crowds. State officials might value the visitors attracted to the state by popular sporting events. Coates and Depken (2008) use daily sales tax receipts for cities in Texas to investigate whether sales tax revenues rise or fall on game days. They find that for a typical highly attended game, local sales tax revenues fall, suggesting the local residents and visitors spend less on the congested game days than crowded-out locals would spend on a non-game day. However, in-conference games with in-state rivals seem to generate sufficiently more sales than the average game day to about offset the usual dampening effect of game day congestion on local sales. Rees and Schnepel (2009) report evidence that crime is higher on game days. We know of no direct measure of the inconvenience to locals of the extra traffic and noise created by popular college sporting events. Public officials' enthusiasm for college sports appears to be motivated by something other than fiscal effects.

INDIRECT EFFECTS ON DONATIONS

There are over a dozen empirical studies of the effects of participation and success in intercollegiate athletics on private donations to colleges and universities. They vary substantially in quality. Early ones failed to employ adequate controls and used small and sometimes inappropriate samples or suspect statistical techniques (e.g., step-wise regression), but the pioneers deserve recognition for directing attention to this question.

The studies differ in important ways and draw divergent conclusions that do not yield simple, general findings. Some examine Division 1 universities with expensive sports programs, while others investigate Division 3 (mostly liberal arts) colleges with no athletic scholarships. Some look only at donations made by former athletes, some examine donations by all alumni, and some investigate donations made by people with no obvious association with the university. Some studies focus on donations restricted to use for athletics, some look at donations that can be used for anything except athletics, and some consider unrestricted donations. Some compare contributions to a single university as its athletic fortunes wax and wane. Others are cross-sectional, comparing donations to different institutions at a point in time, while trying to hold constant other differences among them. More recent work has employed panel data to exploit variation in sports participation and success across both institutions and over time. Finally, some studies focus on how intercollegiate sports affects the fraction of potential givers (usually alumni) who donate, whereas others correlate sports participation and success with the dollar value of the donations received.

Among American colleges and universities, 124, about 13 percent, changed the level of their intercollegiate athletics participation between 1991 and 1999 (Sandy and Sloan, 2004). Of those, 109 went up and 15 went down in classification. Harrison, Mitchell, and Peterson (1995) explore the effect of an institution's participation in Division 1 intercollegiate sports *per se* on alumni donations. Comparing eighteen heterogeneous colleges and universities, ranging from Berea and Baylor Medical College to the Universities of Chicago and Georgia, they observed no correlation between Division 1 sports status and alumni donations. This may be the most important empirical result we review, because choice of level of play is not a zero-sum game. Teams at each level win about 50 percent of their contests. On average, moving to a higher level of play adds costs without changing the average winning percentage.

At the level of individual donors, Clotfelter (2003), Monks (2003), and Wunnava and Lauze (2001) all find that alumni who participated in intercollegiate athletics when they were students donate more than alumni who never saw the inside of a locker room. More recently, Holmes, Meditz, and Sommers (2008), studying 22,000 Middlebury College alumni, found that former athletes are 22 percent more likely to donate than non-athletes, and, on average, former athletes donate about 20 percent more than non-athletes. Meer and Rosen (2008) find that at one university, alumni male athletes who had played on national championship teams as undergraduates contributed about 7 percent more per year (with the exception of football and basketball players); there was no similar effect for women. Only Shulman and Bowen (2001) found contrary evidence, reporting systematically lower unrestricted donations by former athletes than non-athletes. Because Shulman and Bowen analyze data on 111,000 individual graduates of 30 colleges and universities over 40 years, however, their evidence is important (Siegfried and Getz, 2002). Consequently, it seems premature to draw a conclusion about whether athletic participation by individuals alters the level of future donations a university might expect to receive from them.

Although the first published study of the effect of athletic success on donations (Sigelman and Carter, 1979) reported no relation between total alumni giving (to both the athletic department and to other parts of their alma mater), three other early cross-section studies [Brooker and Klastorin (1981), Sigelman and Bookheimer (1983), and Coughlin and Erekson (1984)], did observe higher contributions associated with athletic success. These early studies used limited data sets and did not adequately control for other important determinants of alumni contributions.

Donation studies in the 1990s employed better data and statistical techniques. McCormick and Tinsley (1990) and Grimes and Chressanthis (1994) switched the focus from cross-section to time-series analysis, studying donations to Clemson and Mississippi State Universities, respectively, as the success of their intercollegiate football teams waxed and waned. Both found a positive correlation between athletic success and general giving. McCormick and Tinsley found that the success of the Clemson football team initially increased athletic contributions. They also observed that, over time, Clemson's general endowment increased when athletic contributions rose. Later, Goff (2000) looked at the effect of football success on fund raising at Georgia Tech, which shared the national football title in 1990, and Northwestern, after its 1995 Rose Bowl appearance, a relatively infrequent event for the Wildcats. He found no evidence that Georgia Tech's football success improved general fund raising at the university, but did observe a significant increase in Northwestern's endowment immediately after its unprecedented football achievements. The President of Northwestern, however, indicated that a simultaneous financial reorganization probably created the appearance of financial returns to the football success.

Baade and Sundberg (1996) were first to use panel data with many observations, a giant leap forward in estimation procedures. They correlated general giving information collected from the Council for Aid to Education with athletic success for 142 universities and 167 liberal arts colleges from 1973 to 1990, capitalizing on both cross-section and time-series variation, while controlling for differences in other characteristics of the institutions and their students. They considered two dimensions of athletic success: the football and men's basketball teams' regular-season winning percentages, and postseason bowl or tournament participation by each team. Regular-season winning percentage was unrelated to donations for both private and public universities, but for private universities, a football bowl appearance was associated with an increase in general alumni contributions, boosting the average contribution by about 50 percent. It is possible, however, that the expansion of bowl games in the decades since Baade and Sundberg completed their study might have diminished the donations effect of bowl appearances. Basketball tournament participation did not affect donations. For state universities, whose external fund raising is generally less than that of privates, playing in a postseason football bowl game or the men's basketball tournament were both associated with a statistically significant increase in contributions of about 40 percent. For liberal arts colleges, which do not go to bowl games or the NCAA Division 1 basketball tournament, the average football regular-season winning percentage was statistically significantly related to greater contributions, but the size of the effect was trivial. Basketball success does not seem to matter for donations to liberal arts colleges either.

Following Baade and Sundberg, Rhoads and Gerking (2000) analyzed panel data on donations collected by the Council for Aid to Education for 87 Division 1 universities for the decade starting in 1986–1987. They used a fixed effects model that relies primarily on changes over time for individual institutions. Although they examined only the effects of success in postseason bowl games and basketball tournament appearances, they did consider contributions made by alumni separately from contributions made by others. They found that winning a football bowl game stimulates contributions by alumni, but is unrelated to contributions from others. Basketball tournament victories do not seem to affect donations of either group. A football bowl victory is associated with a 7 percent increase in alumni donations.

The largest sample of individuals in which a correlation between generosity and athletic success has been explored is the Andrew W. Mellon Foundation's College and Beyond database containing about 75 percent of all graduates from the entering classes of 1951, 1976, and 1989 at thirty selective colleges and universities, including eight that play football in Division 1-A, the Football Bowl Subdivision (Shulman and Bowen, 2001). Those data reveal no evidence that winning in high-profile sports promotes alumni giving. There is no connection between football winning percentages and the level of general contributions from donors who did not personally participate in intercollegiate athletics. Contribution rates from former athletes do seem to rise with subsequent athletic fortunes of their schools, but since the 1970s former athletes have been *less generous* alumni than non-athletes, and they constitute a small proportion of total alumni at most universities, although they are a larger fraction of selective liberal arts college graduates. Survey responses indicated that graduates who made the largest contributions favor a de-emphasis of sports at their alma maters.

In a more focused panel analysis of giving by 15,351 alumni of fifteen private institutions from the College and Beyond data for the decade starting in 1989, Turner, Meserve, and Bowen (2001), found no effect of football winning on the proportion of alumni who contributed to either a university's general fund or to the athletics department for the eight Division 1 universities in the sample mentioned. The value of contributions actually declined when the football team was more successful.

Litan, Orszag, and Orszag (2003) studied the effects of football success for the NCAA. They had access to confidential data that are not available to other scholars. Using a fixed effects model, they found no statistically significant relationships between football winning percentages and either total alumni contributions or donations restricted to football programs. Tucker (2004) related the percentage of undergraduate alumni who gave money to their school during the 1999–2000 and 2000–2001 academic years to average winning percentages, post-season bowl and tournament appearances, and final Associated Press (AP) rankings for both football and men's basketball at seventy-eight Division 1 universities. He found no association between basketball success and the fraction of alumni donating, but did observe significant positive correlations for football achievements. A 10 percent increase in football winning percentage (about one win per year) was predicted to increase the proportion of alumni who make contributions by about 1 percentage point. One additional bowl appearance or appearance in the top-twenty final AP football poll over a six-year period also was predicted to increase the giving rate by about 1 percentage point.

Humphreys and Mondello (2007) used a comprehensive panel data set for 320 colleges and universities drawn from the Integrated Postsecondary Education Data System for the period 1976–1996, a previously untapped source for donation studies. Their data include giving by alumni, foundations, corporations, and others. They studied both restricted and unrestricted donations, although the restricted donations were not necessarily restricted to athletics. They found no increase in unrestricted donations as a result of any measure of success of either the football or men's basketball teams. Restricted giving appeared to rise at both public and private universities in response to success of the basketball team, and at public universities when the football team is invited to a bowl game.

In sum, the more recent studies (by Baade and Sundberg; Shulman and Bowen; Turner, Meserve, and Bowen; Litan, Orszag, and Orszag; Tucker; and Humphreys and Mondello) use a variety of data sources, consider different donors, separate gifts into those restricted to athletics and those donated for general purposes, and rely primarily on the variation in giving over time for individual institutions in samples of more than one university. These studies do an adequate job of controlling for other influences on contributions. Some find no effect of athletic success, whereas others find a modest effect, usually on restricted giving. Participation in post-season play by the football team seems most likely to function like advertising for the institutions, increasing awareness of the university, and perhaps allowing the university to capture a larger share of the donations market. This evidence, however, is not sufficient to show that the financial subsidies most universities provide to their athletics programs reap rewards sufficient to improve the institutions' overall financial conditions, because, for every winner, there is a loser. The average gain is nil, but the subsidies spent in pursuit of the gain are incurred by all teams.

The analysis of giving patterns using regression analysis tends to focus on the number of givers and average level of donations. In dollar terms, however, the behavior of a few of the largest donors may dominate the averages. T. Boone Pickens' gift of $160 million to Oklahoma State's athletic program in 2006 topped Ralph Engelstadt's $100 million gift to North Dakota's ice hockey program in 1998 as the largest on record (Associated Press, 2006). A university may sensibly focus on total dollars. A statistical analysis that accounts for only occasionally observed large gifts requires use of different methods and larger data sets than have been available so far.

The analysis of benefits should be balanced against an assessment of costs. If athletic success increases donations, a next step in the analysis might be to estimate the cost of increasing athletic success. How much more spending is associated with increased winning and how is more spending most effectively deployed? Of course, if all of the competitors increase spending in proportion, the likely effect on winning will be nil. The analysis might then ask how often institutions in a given competitive group increase spending that is not matched immediately by their rivals? Showing that winning stimulates more giving isn't sufficient to conclude that devoting more resources to athletics will pay. The literature on college sports offers little guidance on how to produce winners.

THE OPPORTUNITY COST OF
INCREASED DONATIONS

What, then, should we conclude from these results? Although the evidence is scant, suppose contributions to colleges and universities do increase when the institutions enjoy intercollegiate athletics success. Is this a good thing?

Evidence correlating university donations to athletic success reveals only half the effects of a resource reallocation. *What is the opportunity cost of additional*

donations received by an institution that wins a bowl game or the national champi-
onship in football or basketball? Would the funds otherwise have been donated to
another college or university? If so, by how much does the reallocation of donations
among academic institutions on the basis of their athletic success increase welfare?
Or is it possible that the donations could have alternatively constituted more valuable incremental contributions to other charitable organizations, for example, the
Red Cross, American Cancer Society, or a local repertory theater group?

In whose view might the donations' next-best use have been more valuable?
Presumably, donors value their contributions be directed as they prefer more than
their next-best alternative. But are the donors fully informed, or is there a "winner's myopia?" If donors knew that winning is partly random, would they still
value gifts to winners? If winning is mostly random but donors attribute wins to
deeper forces, would the pattern of giving have as much social value as gifts made
on other grounds? Is society better off if donations go to the athletic department
of a university with winning intercollegiate athletic teams, boosting salaries of the
coaching staff or building plush skyboxes, with no clear effect on either winning
or on improved academic performance of the institution? Or would society be better off with the donations directed to the use they would find if intercollegiate
athletics did not exist, or was not hyped to the degree it is? At the very least, the
opportunity cost of the donations is surely not zero; thus, the net social value of
donations stimulated by athletic success is undoubtedly less than their gross value
to the university that receives them.

Alternatively, the donated funds might have been spent on the donors' consumption or they could have been added to savings. Is a diversion of consumption
or savings to collegiate donations stimulated by high-profile athletic participation
or success desirable? These important questions are never asked when the fund-
raising prowess of successful athletic teams is proudly reported. It seems to us
impossible to intelligently judge the desirability of additional contributions that
may be stimulated by athletic success without knowing the source and opportunity
cost of the money.

INDIRECT EFFECTS ON APPLICATIONS
AND ENROLLMENT

As a form of advertising and public relations or as the consumption of entertainment services, intercollegiate athletics may attract students, thereby substituting
for alternative recruitment expenditures. Simply having Division 1 sports teams
seems to matter more than success of the teams. Describing a fifteen-year, $3 billion
agreement with ESPN to televise Southeastern Conference intercollegiate athletics,

Wolverton (2009) reported that the universities "hope the exposure will help them attract students who would otherwise not have considered their universities."

There is systematic empirical evidence bearing on the question. Sandy and Sloane (2004) found that institutions with Division 1 sports programs attract more applications and enroll students with higher average SAT scores than similar institutions that do not participate in Division 1 sports. McCormick and Tinsley (1987) discovered the same thing when they distinguished those sixty-three universities in one of the six big-time athletic conferences (and a few independents) from other colleges and universities. Osborne (2004) found that students actually are willing to pay for big-time athletic programs, and, indeed, do so, because those universities with big-time athletic programs charge higher tuition and fees, *ceteris paribus*. However, there is important contradictory evidence about the attractiveness of big-time sports to students, at least for more academically oriented colleges and universities. Looking at the huge College-and-Beyond sample of alumni from thirty selective colleges and universities, Shulman and Bowen (2001) found compelling evidence that average graduates of universities with Division 1 sports claim to prefer less emphasis on intercollegiate athletics.

The choice of level of competition (Division 1, 2, or 3) and perhaps the decision of which conference to join is less susceptible to the zero-sum game problem than the decision about whether to accelerate expenditures in an effort to be more competitive at whatever level of play has been selected. Although Division 1 is much more costly than Division 2, which, in turn, is more expensive than Division 3, the decision to move up in level does not mean that another institution necessarily moves down, and revenues as well as costs rise as one moves to a more competitive level of play.

Nevertheless, winning also may attract the attention of prospective students. It has been reported (*USA Today*, April 3, 1985) that North Carolina State enjoyed a 40 percent rise in applications after winning the NCAA men's basketball championship in 1983 with charismatic coach Jim Valvano, and that Boston College received close to 4,000 more applications in 1985 than in 1984, after its highly publicized football season, during which Doug Flutie beat favored University of Miami with a long last-play pass, and won the Heisman Trophy.

Systematic evidence concerning the effect of success at Division 1 sports in attracting the interest of prospective students is ambiguous, but the better studies suggest that winning or participating in post-season competition does not generate much additional student interest. Two types of outcomes have been examined: the size of the applicant pool, and the academic credentials of the enrolled class. Although the academic credentials of enrolled students would seem to be the objective, a larger applicant pool could permit an institution to enroll fewer students requiring financial assistance or to choose a more diversified student body, and thus be a goal in and of itself. A larger applicant pool reduces the admission rate and boosts national rankings even when there is no change in the students who enroll because the ratio of enrolled students to applicants is an element of many college-ranking systems.

Applying a fixed-effects model to panel data on universities in the six big-time football leagues, Murphy and Trandel (1994) found that football-conference-winning percentage is correlated with the number of undergraduate applications received the following year. Although statistically significant, the size of the effect is modest. If a school increases its winning percentage from half to three-quarters of its games, for example, the application pool is predicted to increase by only 1.3 percent.

Toma and Cross (1998) looked explicitly at the effect of winning a national football championship or men's basketball championship during the period 1979 through 1992 on applications received the year after the championship. They contrasted changes in applications experienced by championship universities to contemporaneous changes at five other colleges and universities that each champion identified as its competitors for students. For football, ten of the sixteen champions in the sample enjoyed a subsequent boost in applications of at least a few percentage points more than the average of their peer institutions. In basketball there was only one anomalous spike in admissions applications following a championship season, after Michigan won the 1989 men's championship. Applications appeared to grow primarily at more academically selective institutions that enjoyed athletic success.

McEvoy (2005) also found that increased winning in football boosted undergraduate applications, but showed no effect for men's or women's basketball. Schools whose football in-conference winning record increased by at least three wins per year realized a subsequent average gain of 6.1 percent in undergraduate applicants. Schools with no change in their in-conference football-winning record experienced virtually no change in their application pool. Zimbalist (1999) also found a tendency for intercollegiate athletic success to boost applications.

Asking whether the increased applicant pool made any difference for the college, McCormick and Tinsley (1987) were among the first to relate intercollegiate athletics success to freshmen academic credentials. They found that universities with a winning trend in football from 1971 through 1984 enjoyed higher average freshmen SAT scores from 1981 to 1984. Tucker and Amato (1993) observed a greater increase in the average freshmen SAT score at universities with a higher average final top-twenty football AP rating during the 1980s. An increase of three places in the AP ranks over the decade was predicted to raise SAT scores by 3 percent. Again, success in basketball did not appear to matter. Bremmer and Kesselring (1993) related changes in SAT scores for the freshmen class to appearances in football bowl games and the NCAA basketball tournament over a nine-year period, finding no evidence that athletic success improves the academic credentials of the freshman class. Zimbalist (1999) also found no correlation between athletic success and SAT scores.

Using an unusually comprehensive data set, including proprietary NCAA data, Litan, Orszag, and Orszag (2003) reported no effect of football winning percentages on average freshmen SAT score. Mixon, Trevino, and Minto (2004) found that institutions with better big-time football winning percentages during the 1990s landed a 2001 freshman class with higher SAT scores, *ceteris paribus*. Again, however, the effect was small. Improving from a 3–9 record to 9–3, a dramatic change, was predicted to increase the average freshmen SAT score by only 4 percent. Goff (2000) found that postseason achievements attract more applications, but only at academically select institutions.

Tucker (2005) looked at the period after the Bowl Championship Series began to generate more hype for post-season football. He first set a baseline for comparison. Like Bremmer and Kesserling, he found no measures of football success related to freshmen SAT scores before 1996. When he repeated the analysis for 1996 to 2002, however, he found that football winning percentage, AP rank, and bowl appearances were associated with higher SAT scores. A 50-percentage-point increase in winning (e.g., from a 3–9 record to 9–3) was associated with a 6 percent increase in SAT scores. One extra bowl appearance over six years was related to a 1 percent increase in SAT scores. Examining the effect of men's basketball on a school's academic credentials, Smith (2008) found that, neither membership in a power basketball conference, nor success in basketball (winning percentage, appearing in the NCAA basketball tournament, or making the Final Four of the tournament) were associated with stronger student academic credentials. If there is an advertising effect of intercollegiate sports, it apparently does not operate through basketball.

The most comprehensive and careful study of the advertising effects of intercollegiate sports is by Pope and Pope (2009), using data from 1983 through 2000 for all 330 NCAA Division 1 universities with football or basketball programs. To isolate the influence of athletic success in attracting students, they controlled for unobserved effects due to each school, trends in each school's admissions, effects on admissions that apply similarly to all schools in a given year, and for other attributes of the institutions that might influence admissions, including the cost of attendance and real income in the state. Basketball success was measured by participation in the NCAA tournament, the Sweet 16, the Final Four, and winning the National Championship. Football success was based on the final AP ranking, and National Champion. They employed zero-, one-, and two-year lags.

In contrast to most other studies, Pope and Pope report significant effects for basketball that persist over two years, particularly for private universities. Appearing in the NCAA tournament boosts applications by 1 percent, making the Sweet 16 bumps the gain to 3 percent, with a 4–5 percent gain for the Final Four, and 7–8 percent for the Champion. The biggest effect is in the following year, with little effect remaining after three years. For football, a top-20 finish adds 2.5 percent to applications and a Championship adds 7–8 percent, with a big effect in the immediate year and little effect after one year. Private institutions gain more than public universities from success in basketball, with less difference for football.

Pope and Pope also estimate whether universities expand their enrollments following athletic success. Success in football is associated with increased enrollment at public universities, but success in basketball shows no enrollment effect. In contrast to Osborne (2004), Pope and Pope find little evidence that athletic success allows universities to raise tuition.

To consider the effect of athletic success on academic credentials, Pope and Pope estimated how athletic success affects the number of students sending SAT scores to various universities. Although students with lower SAT scores appear to be more sensitive to athletic success, students with all levels of SAT scores send more scores to universities that have enjoyed recent athletic success. The influence of winning on applications, enrollment, and SAT scores, however, is not sufficient to show that universities with big-time athletics programs come out ahead for their effort. For every winner that gains a positive effect, there is an offsetting effect for a loser. The winning and losing effects average to zero, but the costs are incurred by all.

Athletics also plays a role in admissions, but the effect is little studied. Anecdotal evidence suggests that fielding intercollegiate sports teams can draw more students from under-represented groups. For example, Shenandoah University revived its football program in 2000 to attract more males to its then-female-dominated student body (Pennington, 2006). In contrast, Stevens Institute of Technology introduced women's athletics to attract more females. In 2004, 43 percent of Stevens' athletes were women whereas the student body was only 24 percent female (Wolverton, 2006). Sports opportunities may draw students from different demographic groups that enrich college life for all students.

Even the best studies of enrollment effects are limited to documenting how relatively small changes in athletic performance effect applications and enrollment. They provide little guidance about the consequences of substantial change. Suppose what is now college football and basketball were no longer supported by institutions of higher education, but instead shifted to professional player development systems operated by the premier leagues. What would happen to enrollment in higher education? Would it decline? Would the few dozen universities with teams now featured regularly on television experience declining enrollment? Would the enrollment level and possible shifts among colleges and universities lower the general welfare of the population? Without the responsibility of intercollegiate athletics competition, Division 1 universities could redirect funds currently used to subsidize athletics to other uses, such as recruiting students directly or enhancing their academic programs in ways that might yield better outcomes for the institutions and the students who attend them. Existing studies do not address such larger possibilities.

THE OPPORTUNITY COST OF INDIRECT EFFECTS ON APPLICATIONS AND ENROLLMENT

Evidence seems to support the notion that Division 1 intercollegiate athletics provides consumption benefits for students, thereby attracting applications. There may, however, be an opportunity cost of this consumption if students spend relatively more time enjoying the success of their team than studying. So far, however, there seems to be no reason to worry about this, as Rishe (2003) found that average institutional graduation rates are unrelated to football success. This is no surprise, as there are undoubtedly many important determinants of institutional graduation rates other than distractions from study caused by enthusiastic student supporters of athletic teams.

There is some evidence that the presence and success of intercollegiate athletics at colleges and universities may increase the applicant pool, and possibly may improve the academic credentials of the student body of institutions that win national championships. However, for every institution that wins a national championship, there are hundreds that do not. Although no one has devised a way to test the hypothesis that the presence of intercollegiate athletics increases the overall proportion of high school graduates who attend college, there is no evidence to suggest that this might even be possible beyond the important but small effect of increasing the prospects of the athletes themselves attending college.

National intercollegiate athletics championships may alter the mix of institutions to which college prospects apply, and may affect the yield (the fraction of admitted students who enroll) on admitted applicants experienced by various institutions. In other words, sports success may *rearrange* students among colleges and universities. But, is this a good thing? Is learning improved if prospective students decide which universities should receive their applications and which university they should attend from among those that admit them based on the knowledge of different institutions they gain by watching the hype surrounding successful intercollegiate athletic teams on television? Are the student-university matches better or worse if sports success reshuffles students?

If, ultimately, the athletic success of football and basketball teams is decided in recruiting battles to sign high school athletes, as many successful coaches claim, are we comfortable with decisions about which college or university some non-athlete students will attend being influenced by which institution can hire a coach who can best persuade a seventeen-year-old star high school athlete that he or she will be best served playing for that coach? It seems a peculiar way to choose a college. For more conventional criteria for college choice, see Getz (2007).

One might challenge the argument that college athletics is a zero sum game by noting that colleges engage in arms races in many areas, including academic disciplines. Colleges compete to build more highly ranked programs like physics, English, and economics. These competitions bid up the salaries of visible faculty stars, diminish the amount of contact research-active faculty must endure with undergraduates, and redirect financial aid to merit scholarships for academically superior affluent students. Positional competition causes a misallocation of resources. Athletics differs, however, in that the athletic arms race draws resources away from the academic missions of universities, while academic arms races likely promote at least some dimensions of academic achievement that were contemplated when the institutions' charters were written. The arms race in athletics is most evident in the bowl-active football and leading basketball programs in which the resource commitments are substantial and the relationship to academic goals is minimal.

EFFECTS ON STUDENTS

The preceding evidence suggests that college sport is a zero-sum game among universities. However, from other points of view, the competition could spawn positive or negative sums. One case for a negative involves NCAA rules against paying players. Payments-in-kind of tuition plus room and board, offered as athletic scholarships, may be less valuable than the cash equivalent that at least some college athletes might receive if professional-training-level athletic competition were organized by competitive entities with free entry or by the corresponding professional leagues themselves, in the style of minor league baseball (Zimbalist, 1999). Moreover, press accounts of college athletes who have lived in enclaves isolated from the rest of the student body, who could not read, and who took courses only open to athletes, suggest that some colleges do not even deliver on the promise of a college education (Rather, 1985). Recent changes in NCAA policies now require that student-athletes be able to read before they enroll in college, that coaches be rewarded in part for the academic as well as athletic performance of their charges, and that athletes at least attend class (Brand, 2009). The worst abuses may be over. Although the NCAA imposes sanctions on universities that violate its rules, such scandals may also have adverse effects on donations, applications, and enrollments. Grimes and Chressanthis (1994), for example, show a decline in alumni giving after the NCAA imposed penalties on the football program at Mississippi State University. Goff (2000) finds a $31 million annual decline in donations and a 7 percent decline in the three-year average number of applications received after the NCAA closed Southern Methodist University's football program (the so-called death penalty) in 1987 and 1988 after repeated rules violations. Zimbalist (1999), however, argues that the NCAA's enforcement process is largely a paper tiger.

On the other hand, because athletics heighten human performance, collegiate competition could be a positive-sum game. Plato saw athletic training as a complement to intellectual development. Modern psychology shows that gains in the vascular system from exercise stimulate neural activity at all ages (Reynolds, 2009). As a consequence, athletic participation correlates with other kinds of success. Long and Caudill (1991) estimate that athletes earn about 4 percent more than non-athletes approximately ten years after graduation, controlling for other personal characteristics. Using the College-and-Beyond data, Shulman and Bowen (2001, p. 95) similarly find that athletes enjoy higher lifetime incomes compared with non-athletes, *ceteris paribus*. The premium earned by athletes, however, is apparent only among those who pursue careers in financial services, a sector differentially favored by former athletes. Moreover, there is evidence that questions whether sports actually teach skills that improve earnings, namely, the fact that earnings are not related to the number of years former athletes played (Shulman and Bowen, 2001). The evidence contradicts the popular hypothesis that sports helps to develop leaders. There is no greater proportion of future CEOs from among former athletes than from among non-athletes in the College-and-Beyond sample (Bowen and Shulman). The connection between sport and lifetime performance is complicated.

One link is from fitness to level of play. Students can pursue fitness without participating in intercollegiate competition. Many who participate in competition do so at the intramural and club level. The level of play that involves paid coaches typically requires a higher degree of effort and physical performance. Those collegiate sports that offer paths to professional athletic careers are likely to stimulate the highest levels of physical, mental, and emotional performance. We don't know what dimensions of athletic participation contribute to lifetime performance. Moreover, intense athletic competition generates injuries that are particularly severe in football. The effect of big-time college revenue sports on lifetime fitness could conceivably be negative.

The link from athletics to academic performance is complex. The direct evidence from Shulman and Bowen (2001, p. 67) is that athletes earn lower grades than their non-athlete colleagues, even after controlling for their lower average high school grades and standard test scores. This finding is consistent with anecdotal evidence that many athletes are less serious students or make time commitments to athletics that undermine academic performance. In a study of grades at Penn State, Fizel and Smaby (2004) find that the lower grades earned by athletes are limited to a few sports like football, men's fencing, and women's field hockey, whereas grades of athletes in some other sports (e.g., women's swimming) are above average.

A different perspective is offered by the concept of stereotype threat. Dee (2009) compares the performance of athletes to non-athletes on an academic test at Swarthmore College. Before taking the test, half of the subjects got a verbal cue that evokes an image of athletics, the other half got a non-athletic cue. The athletes who got the non-athletic cue performed the same as non-athletes who got either cue. However, athletes who were reminded of athletics by the cue performed below both the other athletes and non-athletes. Apparently, participation in athletics builds a psychological frame that reduces measured academic performance. It would be interesting to learn whether the stereotype threat differs by gender, by sport, by type of college, and by level of competition. Fizel and Smaby's (2004) results suggest the possibility of differences by sport.

Another view of the link from athletics to academic performance considers graduation rates. Long and Caudill (1991) found a 4 percent higher rate of graduation for athletes, *ceteris paribus*. Amato et al. (1996) correlated graduation rates for football players with attributes of their college. They found post-season appearances by Division 1 universities were associated with lower graduation rates, suggesting lower academic emphasis at the highest levels of play. In a follow-up study, Amato et al. (2001) found that evolving NCAA rules apparently have eliminated the negative effect of post-season play on graduation rates. Importantly, they find much higher graduation rates for football players on campuses where graduation rates are higher for all students. Shulman and Bowen (2001, p. 61) also observed higher graduation rates for athletes (particularly for participants in low-profile sports) but with non-athletes closing the gap more recently. Shulman and Bowen have the advantage of using information about individual students (rather than college averages) in estimating relationships. In the time since these studies were conducted, the NCAA has adopted rules that reward athletic programs that achieve higher levels of academic performance by athletes. As a consequence, graduation rates by athletes are likely to continue to increase. In addition, the higher level of financial aid received by scholarship athletes is likely to increase graduation rates by reducing attrition caused by financial problems.

Because students affect the performance of their peers, athletes may affect the learning of other students. Sacerdote (2001), Zimmerman (2003), and others took advantage of colleges that randomly assign students to dormitory rooms to demonstrate that residential peers influence academic performance. The evidence on athletic stereotype threats suggests hypotheses about the influence of athletes on the academic and social behaviors of roommates and other students. Shulman and Bowen (2001, p. 41) make clear that athletes have a significant advantage in admission, even at academically selective colleges. On average, they have much lower standardized test scores than their peers, a gap that has grown over time and is largest in revenue sports. Consequently, athletes may be less attractive as academic peers both because of their weaker academic backgrounds and because they earn even lower grades than predicted on the basis of those weaker admissions credentials.

Swarthmore chose to eliminate football, along with two other sports in 2001, primarily to limit the number of admission slots with an athletic nod to 10 to 15 percent of the class (Suggs, 2000). With an enrollment of only 1,400, including about 700 men, Swarthmore found that about 10 percent of entering males would need to be recruited as football players to field a successful team. They seem to have decided that the football culture, the lower academic performance of recruited players, and the likely peer effects made the cost too high.

Another link is from athletics to personal satisfaction. It seems likely that athletes have goals in addition to income. Performing before a crowd of thousands of enthusiasts may offer its own satisfactions. Many athletes value the camaraderie that comes from being part of a team. The higher level of giving by athletes than non-athletes at Middlebury College (Holmes, et al., 2008) may reflect the sense of identity athletes achieve from participation, but the effect may be idiosyncratic to particular sports at some colleges.

Athletic performance may be an end in itself. Running faster, leaping higher, and lifting more may lead to satisfaction not measured by income. Winning times for track and swimming events and winning distances for field events have steadily improved over a long time. The trend is apparent for both men and women. Similar trends appear in winning Olympic performances. Performance may improve for many reasons, among them higher levels of spending on college athletics. Advances may result from better techniques, coaching, and selectivity, as more children explore athletics, or they may result from better facilities, year-round training, and higher rewards from national and international competition. Long-term trends in performance in team sports are more difficult to document, but in many sports, the level of athleticism and skill seems to increase over time.

The social value of sustained improvement in athletic performance by the most successful is difficult to determine. Surprisingly, the dramatic increase in childhood and adult obesity has occurred simultaneously with continued improvement in the performance of athletic elites. The biggest rewards and primary emphasis may arise because of spectator values in revenue sports rather than the direct value of participation.

Athletics builds a sense of community that transcends the participants. The trustees of many universities seem to value intercollegiate athletic competition as an end in itself (Clotfelter, 2011). Perhaps the big-time sports enterprise reflects the personal utility these individuals enjoy. The experience of spectators may create bonds that extend to a substantial number of students, staff, faculty, alumni, and fans from the local area. A college that seeks to be more than the sum of its parts may promote its mascot, its colors, and its athletic rituals as a way of drawing its many constituencies together. In this way, intercollegiate athletics enhances the value of a university's brand, and consequently the value of sweatshirts, license plates, and coffee cups that promote the brand. In 2009, Georgia State University, for example, decided to add a $170 per year charge to its students to finance a new Division 2 football program to create a collective identity for the ninety-seven-year-old school (Tierney, 2009). In an era when female enrollments are well over half of many student bodies, the male-dominated sport may have extra appeal.

Conclusion

A lot of anecdotes and marketing hype are devoted to the prospect that winning university sports teams stimulate private donations to the successful schools. Systematic empirical evidence generally supports the anecdotes, although the effects appear to be small, and result primarily from the appearance of football teams in post-season bowl games. There are similar stories of individual universities attracting more applications following athletic achievements, although, in this case, the empirical evidence is equivocal, and there appears to be little effect on the academic credentials of classes enrolled subsequent to the athletic achievements. Although there has been much less attention focused on the effects of intercollegiate sports on the athletes themselves and other students, there appear to be a number of conflicting implications for the intellectual atmosphere and achievements of university students from adopting a big-time sports program and its attendant culture.

What has received virtually no attention is the opportunity cost accompanying any of these possible changes. If athletic success does boost donations and attract more and better credentialed applicants to the successful institutions, from where do the donations and students come, and is the reallocation of these resources efficient and equitable? It is impossible to decide if the indirect effects of college athletics are desirable or undesirable by looking at just one side of a reallocation of resources. If a university wants to attract more or different students or to increase donations that support general academic purposes, might the funds currently spent subsidizing intercollegiate athletics be more productive in addressing these goals directly by bolstering the budgets of university development and admissions offices? Up to this point, the net social welfare and equity implications of any indirect effects of college sports on the institutions that host big-time intercollegiate teams really remain unknown. It is possible that these effects could be sufficiently large and undesirable to outweigh the consumers surplus created by the direct entertainment value of intercollegiate athletic competition.

The authors thank Charles Clotfelter, Brad Humphreys, Leo Kahane, Kevin Quinn, Stephen Shmanske, Peter Sloane, and Andrew Zimbalist for helpful comments on an earlier draft.

References

Allen, M. 1999. UConn finds rich off-court gains in basketball power. *The New York Times on the Web*, March 31, 1999, 1–4.

Amato, Louis, John M. Gandar, Irvine B. Tucker III, and Richard A. Zuber. 1996. Bowls versus playoffs: The impact of football player graduation rates in the National Collegiate Athletic Association. *Economics of Education Review*, 15(2): 187–195.

Amato, Louis, John M. Gandar, and Richard A. Zuber. 2001. The impact of Proposition 48 on the relationship between football success and football player graduation rates. *Journal of Sports Economics*, 2(2): 101–112.

Associated Press. 2006. Pickens sets record with $165M Oklahoma State gift. January 10, http://sports.espn.go.com/ncaa/news/story?id=2286820

Baade, Robert A., and Jeffrey O. Sundberg. 1996. Fourth down and gold to go? Assessing the link between athletics and alumni giving. *Social Science Quarterly*, 77(4): 789–803.

Borland, Melvin V., Brian L. Goff, and Robert W. Pulsinelli. 1992. College athletics: Financial burden or boon? *Advances in the Economics of Sport*, 1: 215–35.

Brand, Myles. 2009. APR: Mission accomplished. *NCAA Champion Magazine*, Summer: 5.

Bremmer, D. S., and R. G. Kesselring. 1993. The advertising effect of university athletic success: A reappraisal of the evidence. *Quarterly Review of Economics and Finance*, 33(4): 409–421.

Brooker, George, and T. D. Klastorin. 1981. To the victors belong the spoils? College athletics and alumni giving. *Social Science Quarterly*, 62(4): 744–50.

Clotfelter, Charles. 2003. Alumni giving to elite private colleges and universities. *Economics of Education Review,* 22: 109–120.

Clotfelter, Charles. 2011. *Big-time sports in American universities.* New York: Cambridge University Press.

Coates, Dennis, and Craig O. Depken II. 2008. Do college football games pay for themselves? The impact of college football games on local sales tax revenue. SSRN Working Paper, http://ssrn.com/abstract=1140271.

Coughlin, Cletus, and Homer Erekson. 1984. An examination of contributions to support intercollegiate athletics. *Southern Economic Journal,* 51(1): 180–195.

Dee, Thomas S. 2009. Stereotype threat and the student athlete. NBER Working Papers 14705, February.

Duderstadt, James. 2000. *Intercollegiate athletics and the American university.* Ann Arbor: University of Michigan Press.

Fizel, John L., and Timothy Smaby. 2004. Participation in college athletics and academic performance. In *Economics of College Sports,* eds. J. L. Fizel and R. Fort, 163–173. Westport CT: Praeger.

Frank, Robert H. 2004. Challenging the myth: A review of the links among college athletic success, student quality, and donations. Essay prepared for the Knight Commission on Intercollegiate Athletics, May.

Fulks, D. L. 2008. *2004–06 NCAA revenue and expenses of division 1 intercollegiate athletic programs report.* Indianapolis, IN: NCAA.

Getz, Malcolm. 2007. *Investing in college: A guide for the perplexed.* Cambridge, MA: Harvard University Press.

Gillium, Jack, Jodi Upton, and Steve Berkowitz. 2010. Amid funding crisis, college athletics soak up subsidies, fees. *USA Today,* January 13.

Goff, Brian. 2000. Effects of university athletics on the university: A review and extension of empirical assessment. *Journal of Sport Management,* 14(2).

Grimes, Paul W., and George A. Chressanthis. 1994. Alumni contributions to academics: The role of intercollegiate sports and NCAA sanctions. *American Journal of Economics and Sociology,* 53(1): 27–40.

Harrison, William B., Shannon K. Mitchell, and Steven P. Peterson. 1995. Alumni donations and colleges' development expenditures: Does spending matter? *Journal of Economics and Sociology,* 54(4): 397–412.

Holmes, Jessica A., James A. Meditz, and Paul A. Sommers. 2008. Athletics and alumni giving. *Journal of Sports Economics,* 9(5): 538–52.

Humphreys, Brad R. 2006. The relationship between big-time college football and state appropriations for higher education. *International Journal of Sport Finance,* 1: 119–128.

Humphreys, Brad R., and Michael Mondello. 2009. Intercollegiate athletic success and donations at NCAA division 1 institutions. *Journal of Sports Management.*

Knight Commission on Intercollegiate Athletics. 2006. *Public Opinion Poll.*

Litan, Robert E., Jonathan M. Orszag, and Peter R. Orszag. 2003. The empirical effects of collegiate athletics: An interim report. National Collegiate Athletic Association.

Long, James E., and Steven B. Caudill. 1991. The impact of participation in intercollegiate athletics on income and graduation. *Review of Economics and Statistics,* 73(3): 525–31.

McCormick, Robert E., and Maurice Tinsley. 1987. Athletics versus academics? Evidence from SAT scores. *Journal of Political Economy,* 95(5): 1103–1116.

McCormick, Robert E., and Maurice Tinsley. 1990. Athletics and academics: A model of university contributions. In *Sportometrics*, eds. B. Goff and R. D. Tollison, 193–204. College Station, TX: A&M University Press.

McEvoy, Chad. 2005. The relationship between dramatic changes in team performance and undergraduate admissions applications. *The Smart Journal*, 2(1): 17–24.

Mixon, Franklin G. Jr., L. J. Trevino, and T. C. Minto. 2004. Touchdowns and test scores: Exploring the relationship between athletics and academics. *Applied Economic Letters*, 11(7): 421–424.

Monks, James. 2003. Patterns of giving to one's alma mater among young graduates from selective institutions. *Economics of Education Review*, 22(2): 121–130.

Murphy, Robert G., and Gregory A. Trandell. 1994. The relation between a university's football record and the size of its applicant pool. *Economics of Education Review*, 13(3): 265–270.

National Collegiate Athletic Association. 2009. *2004–2008 NCAA revenues and expenses of division 1 intercollegiate athletics programs report*. Indianapolis, IN: August.

Noll, Roger G. 1999. The business of college sports and the high cost of winning. *Milliken Institute Review*, Third Quarter: 24–37.

Osborne, Evan. 2004. Motivating college athletes. In *Economics of College Sports*, eds. J. L. Fizel and R. Fort, 51–62. Westport, CT: Praeger.

Pennington, Bill. 2006. Small colleges, short of men, embrace football. *The New York Times*, July 10.

Pope, Devin G., and Jaren C. Pope. 2009. The impact of college sports success on the quantity and quality of student applications. *Southern Economic Journal*, 75(3): 750–780.

Grube, G.M.A., trans. 1992. *The Republic* of Plato Part III. Indianapolis: Hackett Publishing

Rather, Dan. 1985. When the Cheering Stops. *CBS Evening News*, October 7.

Rees, Daniel, and Kevin T. Schnepel. 2009. College football games and crime. *Journal of Sports Economics*, 10(1): 68–87.

Reynolds, Gretchen. 2009. What sort of exercise can make you smarter. *New York Times Magazine*, September 20: 24.

Rhoads, Thomas A., and Shelby Gerking. 2000. Educational contributions, academic quality, and athletic success. *Contemporary Economic Policy*, 18(2): 248–58.

Rishe, Patrick James. 2003. A reexamination of how athletic success impacts graduation rates. *American Journal of Economics and Sociology*, 62(2): 407–27.

Sacerdote, Bruce. 2001. Peer effects with random assignment: Results for Dartmouth roommates. *Quarterly Journal of Economics*, 116(2): 681–704

Sandy, Robert, and Peter Sloane. 2004. Why do U.S. colleges have sports programs? In *Economics of College Sports*, eds. J. L. Fizel and R. Fort, 87–109. Westport CT: Praeger.

Shulman, James, and William G. Bowen. 2001. *The game of life: College sports and educational values*. Princeton: Princeton University Press.

Siegfried, John J., and Malcolm Getz. 2002. Economic issues in intercollegiate athletics: A book review essay. *Southern Economic Journal*, 68(4): 972–978.

Sigelman, Lee, and Robert Carter. 1979. Win one for the giver? Alumni giving and big-time college sports. *Social Science Quarterly*, 60(2): 284–294.

Sigelman, Lee, and Samuel Bookheimer. 1983. Is it whether you win or lose? Monetary contributions to big-time college athletic programs. *Social Science Quarterly,* 64(2): 347–359.

Sigelman, Lee, and Paul J. Wahlenbeck. 1999. Gender proportionality in intercollegiate athletics: The mathematics of Title Ix compliance. *Social Science Quarterly,* 80(3): 518–538.

Smith, D. Randall. 2008. Big-time college basketball and the advertising effect, does success really matter? *Journal of Sports Economics,* 9(4): 387–406.

Suggs, Welch. 2000. Swarthmore kicks football out of the college. *Chronicle of Higher Education,* December 15.

Thamel, Pete. 2010. College conferences ponder expansion, and their extinction. *New York Times,* April 19.

Tierney, Michael. 2009. Georgia State hoping football builds community in a football town. *New York Times,* April 19.

Toma, J. Douglas, and Michael E. Cross. 1998. Intercollegiate athletics and student college choice: Exploring the impact of championship seasons on undergraduate applications. *Research in Higher Education,* 39(6): 633–661.

Toma, J. Douglas, and Michael E. Cross. 2004. A reexamination of the effect of big-time football and basketball success on graduation rates and alumni giving rates. *Economics of Education Review,* 23(3): 656–661.

Tucker, Irvine B. 2005. Big-time pigskin success: Is there an advertising effect? *Journal of Sports Economics,* 6(2).

Tucker, Irvine B., III, and Louis Amato. 1993. Does big-time success in football or basketball affect Sat scores? *Economics of Education Review,* 12(2): 177–181.

Turner, Sarah E., Lauren A. Meserve, and William G. Bowen. 2001. Winning and giving: Football results and alumni giving at selective private colleges and universities. *Social Science Quarterly,* 82(4): 812–826.

Wolverton, Brad. 2007. Growth in sports gifts may mean fewer academic donations. *Chronicle of Higher Education,* October 5.

Wolverton, Brad. 2009. A powerful league piles up its advantages. *Chronicle of Higher Education,* September 4: A-1, A-26, A-27, A-28.

Wunnava, Phanindra V., and Michael A. Lauze. 2001. Alumni giving at a small liberal arts college: Evidence from consistent and occasional donors. *Economics of Education Review,* 20(6): 533–543.

Zengerle, Jason. 2010. Special report: Compensation. *Business Week,* April 5: 58–62.

Zimbalist, Andrew. 1999. *Unpaid professionals: Commercialism and conflict in big-time college sports.* Princeton: Princeton University Press.

Zimmerman, David J. 2003. Peer effects in academic outcomes: Evidence from a natural experiment. *Review of Economics and Statistics,* 85(1): 9–23.

CHAPTER 20

IS MARCH MADNESS CONTAGIOUS?

POST-SEASON PLAY AND ATTENDANCE IN NCAA DIVISION I BASKETBALL

CRAIG A. DEPKEN, II

1. INTRODUCTION

In April 1939, eight basketball teams participated in the first NCAA Championship Tournament. The Western regional, held in San Francisco, involved Oregon, Texas, Oklahoma, and Utah State. The Eastern Regional, held in Philadelphia, involved Villanova, Brown, Wake Forest and Ohio State. The national championship game, played in central Evanston, Illinois, pitted Ohio State against Oregon; the latter winning 46 to 33. The total attendance to the first NCAA tournament was 15,025 with 5,500 watching the final game (NCAA, 2009). Seventy years later, the 2009 NCAA tournament, often called "March Madness," involved sixty-five teams playing in seventeen different cities, with total attendance of 826,989 and with 72,922 watching the final game (NCAA, 2009).

The inaugural National Invitational Tournament (NIT), held in March 1938 in New York's Madison Square Garden, involved six teams: Bradley, Colorado, Long Island, New York University, Oklahoma A&M (later Oklahoma State), and Temple. The championship game set Temple against Colorado, with the former winning by a score of 60 to 36. The total attendance to the first NIT was 40,326 with 14,497 watching the final game (Daley, 1938, multiple).[1]

In the early years of both tournaments, the NIT was generally perceived to be of higher quality. However, by the end of the 1970s this perception changed as the NCAA tournament expanded to include more teams, offered automatic bids to conference-tournament winners and the majority of regular-season conference champions, and the long-running dominance of UCLA came to an end.[2] As the media focus and revenue potential of the NCAA tournament continued to grow, the NCAA tournament eventually came to be the superior tournament, relegating the NIT to secondary status.

In 2009, only 97 of 347 Division I basketball programs participated in post-season play (65 in the NCAA tournament and 32 in the NIT). As such, post-season play not only provides an experience enjoyed by just a minority of Division I basketball players but selection into the NCAA tournament especially is regularly used as a barometer for overall program quality. On the other hand, participation in the NIT can be accepted as a signal of improving quality for an up-and-coming program but also as a signal of marginal or declining quality for more established programs. If these perceptions reflect reality, different benefits may be associated with playing in either tournament.

"Selection Sunday," during which the at-large bids and the seeding of each team in the NCAA tournament are revealed, is a media event watched by thousands. This focus points to the perceived and actual importance that being invited to participate in the tournament provides. Indeed, each year there is considerable debate in the popular press and the general population concerning which schools are "on the bubble" and which are not invited to the NCAA tournament. Some might dismiss this as simply reflecting short-run fan frustration, yet there are considerable financial benefits associated with being invited to the NCAA tournament. Primarily, the NCAA distributes to the various conferences revenues generated from the NCAA tournament. The allocation formula is based on the total number of tournament games in which a conference's members have played over the past six years (less championship games). In the 2008–2009 school year the amount distributed per unit, or game played, was $206,200.

Table 20.1 recreates the distribution report of the NCAA for the 2008–2009 school year (NCAA, 2010). As can be seen, the traditional basketball powerhouse conferences such as the Big Ten, the Big East, and the Atlantic Coast, have considerably more units in a given year than smaller conferences such as the America East or the Southwestern Athletic Conference. The majority of the conferences with a single unit in a given year are smaller conferences in which the conference post-season tournament winner receives an automatic bid to the NCAA tournament. Lower quality conferences often receive only one bid to the NCAA tournament, which is often given a lower seed (higher in number). In the first round of the NCAA tournament, the number one (highest) seed plays the number sixteen (lowest) seed, the number two seed plays the number fifteen seed, and so forth. Thus, many lower seeded teams and the conferences of which they are members face substantial challenges to participating in more than one game in a given tournament.[3]

The data reported in Table 20.1 also reveal a potential source of antagonism within the ranks of the NCAA Division I membership. Many claim that the at-large selection process is biased against members of small and mid-major conferences in favor of teams in the bigger conferences. This bias, if it exists, harms smaller

Table 20.1 Distributions from NCAA Basketball Fund 2008–2009

Conference	2003	2004	2005	2006	2007	2008	Total Units	Projected Distribution
America East Conference	1	1	2	1	1	1	7	$1,442,140
Atlantic 10 Conference	4	10	1	3	3	6	27	$5,562,539
Atlantic Coast Conference	9	19	15	10	14	10	77	$15,863,538
Atlantic Sun	1	1	1	1	1	1	6	$1,236,120
Big 12 Conference	19	14	12	8	10	16	79	$16,275,578
Big East Conference	14	16	13	19	13	19	94	$19,365,877
Big Sky Conference	1	1	1	2	1	1	7	$1,442,140
Big South Conference	1	1	1	1	2	1	7	$1,442,140
Big Ten Conference	13	6	16	9	14	9	67	$13,803,338
Big West Conference	1	2	3	1	1	1	9	$1,854,180
Colonial Athletic Association	1	1	1	6	3	1	13	$2,678,260
Conference USA	9	11	10	5	4	5	44	$9,064,879
Horizon League	4	1	3	2	4	2	16	$3,296,320
Ivy Group	1	1	1	1	1	1	6	$1,236,120
Metro Atlantic Athletic Conf.	1	2	1	1	1	2	8	$1,648,160
Mid-American Conference	2	1	1	1	1	1	7	$1,442,140
Mid-Eastern Athletic	1	1	1	1	1	1	6	$1,236,120
Missouri Valley Conference	2	2	4	8	4	1	21	$4,326,419
Mountain West	4	3	4	2	4	3	20	$4,120,399
Northeast Conference	1	1	1	1	1	2	7	$1,442,140
Ohio Valley Conference	1	1	1	1	1	1	6	$1,236,120
Pacific-10 Conference	11	4	9	11	16	14	65	$13,391,298
Patriot League	1	1	2	2	1	1	8	$1,648,160
Southeastern Conference	12	13	10	17	14	10	76	$15,657,518
Southern Conference	1	1	1	1	1	4	9	$1,854,180

(Continued)

Table 20.1 (*Continued*)

Conference	2003	2004	2005	2006	2007	2008	Total Units	Projected Distribution
Southland Conference	1	1	1	2	1	1	7	$1,442,140
Southwestern Athletic Conf.	1	1	1	1	1	1	6	$1,236,120
Summit League*	1	1	1	1	1	1	6	$1,236,120
Sun Belt Conference	1	1	1	1	1	4	9	$1,854,180
West Coast Conference	3	2	3	3	1	4	16	$3,296,320
Western Athletic Conference	2	4	3	2	3	1	15	$3,090,300
GRAND TOTALS:	125	125	125	125	125	126	751	$154,721,003
						Amount per unit:		$206,020

Notes: *Formerly Mid-Continent Conference. Obtained from *www.ncaa.org*, last accessed January 2010. The NCAA defines a unit as a game, other than the championship game, in which a conference member participated.

conferences because they do not earn as many units, thereby creating an ever widening gulf between the bigger, richer conferences and the smaller, poorer conferences. However, these claims ignore an endogeneity problem: the value of each unit might be the result of a biased selection process, that is, a biased selection process might increase or maintain a high interest in the NCAA tournament, which increases the value of the tournament's media contract, which, in turn, translates into a higher unit value. Thus, including more small and mid-major conference teams in the tournament could reduce the unit value sufficient to offset the benefits of having more teams in the tournament.

Nevertheless, Table 20.1 shows that the selection process for the NCAA tournament, regardless of bias, provides both internal and external benefits in the form of revenue distributions to other conference members, including those that do not participate in the NCAA tournament. However, distributions from the NCAA basketball fund are not the only benefits that programs and institutions might enjoy from post-season play. For instance, some benefit of post-season play redounds on the coaching staff inasmuch as success in the NCAA tournament (and to a lesser degree the NIT) provides an exogenous signal of coaching staff quality. Additional non-monetary benefits are reaped by players in terms of experience and exposure and by other stakeholders in the basketball program, such as cheerleaders, band members, and fans, who receive benefits from their team playing in the tournament. Finally, monetary and non-monetary benefits might accrue to the institution itself as participation in post-season play provides an advertising effect, often referred to as the Flutie Effect.[4]

The central hypothesis of this paper is to test whether there are internal and external benefits associated with post-season play in the form of additional future attendance. To the extent that teams earn revenue in the form of ticket sales, concession sales, and perhaps increased value in media contracts and sponsorships, any increases in attendance associated with a program's participation in post-season play would represent internal benefits associated with the selection process not accounted for in the existing literature. Yet, the impacts of tournament participation need not be zero-sum or mutually exclusive. Indeed, more conference members participating in post-season play can provide a signal of the quality about the entire conference, thereby increasing interest in the home games of all conference members in the future, especially for intra-conference games. This suggests the potential for external benefits from post-season play that have also not been considered in the literature.

2. LITERATURE REVIEW

In the current context, the existing literature focusing on the impacts of March Madness, and college basketball in general, can be divided into three parts. The first focuses exclusively on internal benefits of basketball success to parent institutions. Several papers investigate the impact of basketball program quality, usually measured by team winning percentage and/or participation in post-season play, on the number of applications, the quality of the incoming class, the graduation rate of current students, and the level and rate of contributions to the athletic and general endowment.

The empirical evidence provided in these papers is rather mixed, primarily because of different samples of schools, different time periods, and different control variables. These mixed results suggest that the internal benefits of basketball success for these aspects of parent institutions are difficult to isolate and causally link to basketball success. For example, basketball success might provide an advertising effect that increases interest in the school on the part of potential students. Toma and Cross (1988) show that winning the NCAA tournament increased applications for as many as three years. Pope and Pope (2009) reinforce this finding by showing a positive relationship between the quantity of applications and basketball success, as measured by reaching the Sweet Sixteen of the NCAA basketball tournament.[5]

An increase in the number of applications might allow institutions to become more selective and increase the quality of the incoming students. Although there seems to be some relationship between football success and the quality of incoming students (for example, Murphy and Trandel, 1994), Mixon (1995) finds only slight evidence that playing in more NCAA tournament games corresponds with higher SAT scores for incoming students, as does Pope and Pope (2009). In contrast,

Amato and Tucker (1993) find no evidence that basketball success, as measured by top-twenty end-of-season rankings, is related to incoming SAT scores.

Basketball success might distract students from their academic pursuits, thereby reducing retention and graduation rates. On the other hand, basketball success might increase the desire to be an alumnus of the school, thereby increasing graduation rates. Tucker (1992 and 2004) and Rishe (2003) find no evidence that basketball success is related to overall graduation rates.

Basketball success might encourage alumni to increase donations to either the athletic foundation or the general endowment of the institution. Sigelman and Carter (1979) find no evidence that basketball winning percentage influenced alumni giving rates. In contrast, Baade and Sundberg (1996) find that NCAA tournament appearances (rather than winning percentage) are statistically related to alumni donations. However, Rhoads and Gerking (2000) find that the relationship between basketball success and alumni giving is no longer statistically meaningful when controlling for unobserved institution heterogeneity.

A second portion of the literature focuses on whether the selection process of the NCAA tournament is biased against smaller conferences.[6] The most popular approach is to test whether the initial seeding of the teams, which reflects the NCAA selection committee's estimation of relative team strengths, is accurate on average. Bryan, et al. (2006) show that from 1985–2005 first-round upsets in the NCAA tournament were predictable, suggesting bias in the original seeding. Schwertman, et al. (1991), Smith and Schwertman (1999), and Caudill (2002) all show that the original seeding is not as good a predictor of whether a team will win a particular game as exogenously available information such as third-party ratings. West (2006, 2008) shows that third-party rating systems predict margin of victory better than seeding. Zimmer and Keuthe (2008) show that teams from bigger conferences win NCAA tournament games by less than predicted by their regular season winning percentages. These empirical papers seem to present overwhelming evidence that the selection process is biased against smaller conference teams.

Indeed, in 2009 the Big-Six conferences contained 73 of the 347 Division I basketball schools but had earned 102 of 116 Final Four tournament spots between 1981 and 2009.[7] Despite this dominance, Sanders (2007) argues that the selection committee uses third-party rankings, such as the Ratings Percentage Index (RPI), that favor programs that dominate their conferences. Given that intra-conference dominance is rare in the Big-Six conferences and more common in the smaller and mid-major conferences, the selection process might actually be biased toward the small conferences. Boulier and Stekler (1999) argue that the original seeding is a good predictor of which team wins, all else equal. Shapiro, et al. (2009) argue that the selection committee is not biased, citing evidence from logistic models explaining which teams receive at-large bids to the NCAA tournament.

A third portion of the literature, and that which seems the least developed, focuses on the analysis of basketball attendance. Pan, et al. (1997) investigate the characteristics of individuals who purchase season tickets to college basketball and find that the winning percentage of the program is but a minor factor to the

purchase decision. Schurr, et al. (1988) investigate the attendance of college sopho-
mores to two basketball games for a single program in sequential seasons and find
that race, gender, and living on campus all contributed positively to the odds of
attending a basketball game; this study did not control for team quality at the time
of the game. Drea (1995) investigates attendance to a single Division II basketball
program over the course of four seasons and finds that team quality, as measured by
average win/loss margin, is positively related to attendance. In a similar approach,
Walls and Bass (2004) investigate the influences of attendance to basketball games
at a single Division I basketball program over four seasons and find that the quality
of the home team and visiting team, measured as being ranked in the *USA Today/
ESPN* Top 25 at the time of the game, are both positively related to attendance.
Fanney (2009) investigates the relationship between so-called one-and-done players, who play only one year in college before moving to the National Basketball
Association (NBA), and finds that, although these players seem to increase NCAA
tournament victories, they do not correspond with increases in winning percentage, attendance, roster turnover, or merchandise sales.

3. The Impact of Post-season Basketball Tournaments on Basketball Attendance

Hypothesis Development

As described in the previous section, there is mixed evidence in the existing literature of bias in the NCAA tournament selection process. Although this paper
does not address the existence of bias, if the bias exists, what are the immediate
implications? Those conferences consistently seeded high play weaker opponents
earlier in the tournament (when higher-seeded teams exclusively play lower-seeded
teams) and, all else equal, stand to win, therefore, in more games. Playing in more
games provides internal benefits to the team by an increased advertising effect and
generates external benefits in the form of increased revenue distributions from the
NCAA basketball fund.

These external benefits might be implicitly recognized by basketball coaches
and players, and, by extension, the institutions. Balsdon, Fong, and Thayer (2007)
provide empirical evidence of teams that win a regular season conference championship and are seemingly assured an at-large bid to the NCAA tournament
might tank the conference post-season tournament to (1) rest their players for the
upcoming NCAA tournament, and (2) allow another conference member to win
the conference tournament to maximize the conference's returns from the NCAA
basketball revenue pool.

The question asked here is whether participation in the NCAA tournament and the NIT generate internal and external benefits to teams in the dimension of basketball attendance. Internal benefits of post-season play would be reflected in current and lagged NCAA tournament and the NIT participation being related to per-game attendance. External benefits would be reflected in current and lagged success of the team's fellow conference members in the NCAA tournament and the NIT being related to per-game attendance. External benefits might arise if post-season success by more teams in the conference provides an advertising effect that is partly a public good, much like generic advertising in product markets (see, for example, Depken, Kamerschen and Snow, 2000). A test for this is to estimate the impact of a conference's total post-season participation and success, differentiated by each post-season tournament, on individual team attendance. To the extent that participation in either tournament provides the public good impact, we expect to see inter-season impacts on attendance.

Another potentiality is that the internal and external benefits of post-season participation and play differ across conferences. Big-Six conference teams might find it harder to internalize the benefits of playing in the NCAA because these programs already enjoy relatively large levels of attendance and television exposure. Smaller conference teams, on the other hand, generally play to smaller crowds and have more locally based fans who might respond more, on the margin, to post-season appearances. Similarly, more participation of Big-Six conference teams might generate smaller external benefits compared to smaller conferences because the bigger conferences are already viewed as being comprised of the best basketball programs, already play to large audiences, and generally play against more prestigious opponents.

4. EMPIRICAL STRATEGY AND DATA

The previous section provided the intuition for how external benefits might arise from having more teams in a conference participating in either the NCAA or the NIT tournament. To formalize, the null hypotheses tested are as follows:

H1: Current and previous winning percentages have no impact on per-game attendance.

H2: Current and previous probationary status has no impact on per-game attendance.

H3 and H4: Current and previous participation in the NCAA tournament (H3) and in the NIT (H4) has no impact on per-game attendance.

H5 and H6: Current and previous participation in the NCAA tournament (H5) and in the NIT (H6) by other conference members has no impact on per-game attendance.

H7 and H8: The impact of current and previous participation in the NCAA tournament (H7) or the NIT (H8) on per-game attendance in the Big Six conferences is not systematically different than in the smaller and mid-major conferences.

H9 and H10: The impact of current and previous participation in the NCAA tournament (H9) or the NIT (H10) by other conference members on per-game attendance in the Big Six conferences is not systematically different than in the smaller and mid-major conferences.

To test each hypothesis, per-game attendance to Division I men's basketball programs from the 1990–1991 through the 2008–2009 seasons is related to variables that describe the school, the program's current and recent success, the program's current and recent probationary status, the program's current and recent participation in the NCAA tournament and the NIT, the participation in both tournaments of the other members of the team's conference, and interaction terms to test for differences between the Big-Six conferences and the other conferences.[8]

The regression model estimated is of the form:

$$ATTEND_{i,t} = f(X_{i,t}, POSTSEASON_{i,t}, CONFPOST_{i,t}, BIG6POST,$$
$$BIG6CONFPOST; \beta) + \varepsilon_{i,t},$$

where $ATTEND_{i,t}$ is the per-game attendance for team i in year t, $f()$ is a linear transformation function, the β's are parameters to be estimated, and ε is a zero-mean composite error term comprised of stochastic white noise and a team-specific effect.

The regressors included in the vector X are the current and previous six years of the team's winning percentage (*WINPCT*), the current and previous six years of whether the program was on probation by the NCAA (*PROB*), whether the school is private (*PRIVATE*), whether the school is a member of a Big-Six conference (*BIG6*), and whether the school moved from one conference to another in the previous year (*NEWCONFERENCE*).

It is anticipated that current and lagged winning percentage is positively related to per-game attendance with a declining impact into the past. A formal test for this direct quality impact is a test of joint significance of the current and lagged values of winning percentage (H1). NCAA probations are intended to punish programs for violations of the NCAA membership agreement, ostensibly through lost reputation and scholarships, which reduce the ability to recruit. A test for any additional reduction in attendance caused by probations is a test of joint significance of the current and lagged values of probation (H2).

It is anticipated that private schools enjoy lower attendance, primarily because they generally have fewer students and smaller alumni bases. It is anticipated that teams in the Big-Six conferences enjoy greater attendance for the opposite reason: the majority of the Big-Six schools have relatively more students and larger alumni bases. Schools that move from one conference to another might enjoy an increase in attendance if the realignment is to a more compelling basketball conference but might see a reduction in attendance if the realignment reduces interest in the program.

The vector *POST* is comprised of the current-year and six lagged values of two variables: the number of NCAA and NIT units for team i in year t (*NCAAUNITS, NITUNITS*).[9] Here, a unit is defined as a game played in the NCAA tournament or the NIT tournament.[10] The current-year NCAA and NIT units are included as a proxy for team quality that might draw people to the team's games beyond the team's win-loss record. The lagged values indicate whether there are intertemporal impacts on attendance after participating in the NCAA tournament or the NIT. Given the greater popularity and selectivity of the NCAA tournament, it is anticipated that the impacts of NCAA participation are greater than for NIT participation. A formal test of H3 (H4) is to test the joint significance of the current and six lags of *NCAAUNITS* (*NITUNITS*); rejection of either H3 or H4 would indicate internal benefits from participating in the NCAA tournament or the NIT.

For each team and year the total number of NCAA units and NIT units associated with the *other* conference members are aggregated (*CONFNCAAUNITS, CONFNITUNITS*). The vector *CONFPOST* includes the current-year and six lagged values of these two variables that indicate whether there are external benefits to post-season play. A formal test of H5 (H6) is a joint test of statistical significance of the current-year and six lagged values of *CONFNCAAUNITS* (*CONFNITUNITS*); rejection of either H5 or H6 would indicate external benefits from participating in the NCAA tournament or the NIT.[11]

To test for any difference in internal benefits between the Big-Six conferences and the smaller and mid-major conferences, the vector *POST* is interacted with the BIG6 indicator variable to yield two sets of variables *BIG6NCAAUNITS* and *BIG6NITUNITS*. The current-year and six lagged values of these two variables are included to test for differences in internal benefits across the two tournaments and the two types of conferences. A formal test of H7 (H8) is a joint test of statistical significance of the current-year and six lagged values of *BIG6NCAAUNITS* (*BIG6NITUNITS*); rejection of either H7 or H8 would indicate that the Big-Six conferences enjoy different internal benefits from participating in the NCAA tournament or the NIT.

To test for any difference in external benefits between the Big-Six conferences and the smaller and mid-major conferences, the vector *CONFPOST* is interacted with the BIG6 indicator variable to yield two sets of variables *BIG6CONFNCAAUNITS* and *BIG6CONFNITUNITS*. The current-year and six lagged values of these two variables are included to test for differences in external benefits across the two tournaments and the two types of conferences. A formal test of H9 (H10) is a joint test of statistical significance of the current-year and six lagged values of *BIG6CONFNCAAUNITS* (*BIG6CONFNITUNITS*); rejection of either H9 or H10 would indicate that the Big-Six conferences enjoy different external benefits from participating in the NCAA tournament or the NIT.

Data

The data employed to test these hypotheses constitute an unbalanced panel of 323 Division I men's basketball programs from the 1990–1991 through the 2008–2009 seasons.[12] For each team, per-game home attendance is calculated as the ratio of total attendance as reported by the NCAA to the number of regular-season home games. For each team the regular-season winning percentage is used, including both conference and non-conference games. For each conference, the total number of teams participating in the NIT and NCAA tournaments and the total number of wins in each tournament were tallied. Data on basketball probations were gathered from the NCAA major infractions database, whether the school was private was obtained from the Integrated Post-Education Database System of the Department of Education, and whether a school changed from one conference to another was determined by comparing each team's men's basketball conference from one year to the next. The upper panel of Table 20.2 reports the descriptive statistics for the entire sample of schools and the lower panel reports the descriptive statistics for the subsample of schools that play in the Big-Six conferences.

From the upper panel of Table 20.2, the average attendance to Division I men's basketball games was approximately 4,900 with a minimum of 253 per game

Table 20.2 Descriptive Statistics of the Data (Sample Period: 1990–1991 through 2008–2009)

All Division 1 Conferences (N = 3965)

Variable	Mean	Std. Dev.	Min	Max
AVEATTEND	4920.22	4372.60	253.00	23946.00
WINPCT	0.51	0.17	0.03	0.95
NCAAUNITS	0.41	1.00	0.00	6.00
NITUNITS	0.22	0.73	0.00	5.00
CONFNITUNITS	2.28	3.04	0.00	16.00
CONFNCAAUNITS	4.19	4.94	0.00	24.00
BIG6	0.23	0.42	0.00	1.00
PROBATION	0.03	0.18	0.00	1.00
PRIVATE	0.33	0.47	0.00	1.00
NEWCONF	0.03	0.16	0.00	1.00
BIG6NCAAUNITS	0.26	0.89	0.00	6.00
BIG6NITUNITS	0.11	0.58	0.00	5.00
BIG6CONFNCAAUNITS	2.72	5.37	0.00	24.00
BIG6CONFNITUNITS	1.19	2.79	0.00	16.00

(Continued)

Table 20.2 (*Continued*)

Big Six Conferences (*N* = 900)

Variable	Mean	Std. Dev.	Min	Max
AVEATTEND	10284.04	4304.76	2257.00	23946.00
WINPCT	0.59	0.16	0.17	0.95
NCAAUNITS	1.14	1.57	0.00	6.00
NITUNITS	0.49	1.14	0.00	5.00
CONFNITUNITS	5.24	3.62	0.00	16.00
CONFNCAAUNITS	11.98	4.03	1.00	24.00
BIG6	1.00	0.00	1.00	1.00
PROBATION	0.05	0.21	0.00	1.00
PRIVATE	0.23	0.42	0.00	1.00
NEWCONF	0.01	0.10	0.00	1.00
BIG6CAAUNITS	1.14	1.57	0.00	6.00
BIG6NITUNITS	0.49	1.14	0.00	5.00
BIG6CONFNCAA UNITS	11.98	4.03	1.00	24.00
BIG6CONFNITUNITS	5.24	3.62	0.00	16.00

(Chicago State in 1997) and a maximum of 23,946 (Kentucky in 1997). Average winning percentage was .512, which is greater than five hundred because some games are against non-Division I opponents. The average NCAA units in a given year were 0.41 and the average number of NIT units was 0.22. The average conference NCAA units were 4.19, and the average conference NIT units were 2.28. Approximately three percent of Division I basketball programs were on probation in a given year, approximately 33 percent of all Division I schools in the sample are private, approximately 22 percent of Division I schools play in one of the Big-Six conferences, and approximately 2.7 percent of the teams in the sample changed conferences from one year to the next.

From the bottom panel of Table 20.2, schools in the Big Six conferences enjoy considerably more attendance (on average, 10,284), have a higher winning percentage at 0.593, and average more NCAA units and NIT units (1.13 and 0.49, respectively). The average number of conference NCAA units and conference NIT units are also considerably higher than non-Big-Six conference schools, being 11.93 and 5.23 units, respectively. Approximately 5 percent of Big-Six basketball programs are on probation in a given year, approximately 22 percent of Big-Six conference members are private, and 1 percent of Big-Six conference schools joined a different conference from one year to the next during the sample period.[13]

Table 20.3 lists the frequency distribution of *NCAAUNITS* and *NITUNITS* and for *CONFNCAAUNITS* and *CONFNITUNITS*. As can be seen, the vast majority of schools have no *NCAAUNITS* or *NITUNITS* in a given year, primarily because only ninety-six Division I teams participate in any given post-season.[14] On the other hand the vast majority of Division I teams have at least one conference NCAA unit, those that do not are independents or come from a conference without an automatic bid to the tournament.[15]

Table 20.3 Frequency Distribution of Individual and Conference NCAA and NIT Units

Units	NCAA Units		Conference NCAA Units		NIT Units		Conference NIT Units	
	Freq	Pct	Freq	Pct	Freq	Pct	Freq	Pct
0	3135	79.07	269	6.78	3514	88.63	1544	38.94
1	410	10.34	1739	43.86	228	5.75	783	19.78
2	212	5.35	386	9.74	107	2.70	360	9.08
3	104	2.62	225	5.67	60	1.51	308	7.77
4	52	1.31	186	4.69	30	0.76	222	5.60
5	26	0.66	97	2.45	26	0.66	187	4.72
6	26	0.66	114	2.88			114	2.88
7			41	1.03			100	2.52
8			93	2.35			105	2.65
9			140	3.53			74	1.87
10			111	2.8			78	1.97
11			84	2.12			27	0.68
12			85	2.14			17	0.43
13			87	2.19			28	0.71
14			67	1.69			8	0.20
15			71	1.79			2	0.05
16			48	1.21			8	0.20
17			47	1.19				
18			16	0.4				
19			36	0.91				
20			11	0.28				

(Continued)

Table 20.3 (*Continued*)

Units	NCAA Units		Conference NCAA Units		NIT Units		Conference NIT Units	
	Freq	Pct	Freq	Pct	Freq	Pct	Freq	Pct
21			1	0.03				
22			1	0.03				
23			1	0.03				
24			9	0.23				

5. EMPIRICAL RESULTS AND DISCUSSION

The full random effects estimation results, with robust standard errors, are reported in Appendix A.[16] The first column presents the estimates from estimating the full specification as described in the preceding section. The specification reported in the second column removes insignificant variables from the initial specification. The majority of the parameters take the expected sign and significance. Rather than discuss all the parameters individually, Table 20.4 reports joint significance tests associated with the hypotheses developed in the previous section.

From Table 20.4 it can be seen that there is a direct quality effect ($\chi^2 = 414.99$, $p = 0.000$); teams with higher winning percentages enjoy greater attendance with the impact of winning decreasing over time (see results in column 1 of Appendix A). Interestingly, there is no statistically significant evidence of an additional impact of probation beyond probation's impact on winning percentage ($\chi^2 = 11.12$, $p = 0.13$). This suggests that fans do not punish the team for violating the NCAA arrangement in addition to whatever impact the probation has on team winning percentage and tournament appearances.

As can be seen in Table 20.4 there are internal benefits to participating in the NCAA tournament ($\chi^2 = 175.65$, $p = 0.00$). From the results in Appendix A, it appears that the impact of NCAA success fades over time. There are also significant effects of NIT participation ($\chi^2 = 21.09$, $p = 0.00$), but from Appendix A it seems that the impact of NIT participation fades rather quickly. As shown in Table 20.4, one is not able to reject the secondary test that the fourth, fifth, and sixth lagged values of *NITUNITS* are jointly insignificant ($\chi^2 = 3.43$, p = 0.33). This suggests that the impacts of the NIT on average attendance are less and not as long lived as the impact of NCAA tournament, that is, the internal benefits of the NCAA tournament are greater, on average, than the internal benefits of the NIT.

The internal benefits that arise from NCAA tournament and NIT participation are not surprising. However, the results in Table 20.4 suggest that there are also external benefits to NCAA participation. ($\chi^2 = 45.62$, $p = 0.00$). This suggests

Table 20.4 Tests for Internal and External Benefits of NCAA and NIT
Appearances

Hypothesis	Variable Group	Lags Included	Hypothesized impact on per-game attendance (Sign: Description)	Chi-square Statistic
H1	Winning percentage	0–6	Positive: Direct quality	414.99***
H2	Probation	0–6	Negative: Indirect penalty/ Reputation	11.12
H3	NCAA units	0–6	Positive: Internal benefits of NCAA Appearances	175.65***
H4	NIT units	0–6	Positive: Internal benefits of NIT appearances	21.09***
H4	NIT units (secondary test)	4–6	Positive: Internal benefits of NIT appearances	3.43
H5	Conference NCAA units	0–6	Positive: External benefits of NCAA appearances	45.62***
H6	Conference NIT units	0–6	Positive: External benefits of NIT appearances	7.80
H7	Big-six x NCAA units	0–6	Positive: Different internal benefits of NCAA appearances for major conferences	12.37*
H8	Big-six x NIT units	0–6	Positive: Different internal benefits of NIT appearances for major conferences	2.72
H9	Big-six x Conference NCAA units	0–6	Negative: Different external benefits of NCAA appearances for major conferences	24.66***
H9	Big-six x Conference NCAA units (secondary test)	1–6	Negative: Different external benefits of NCAA appearances for major conferences	5.99
H10	Big-six x Conference NIT units	0–6	Negative: Different external benefits of NIT appearances for major conferences	18.13**
H10	Big-six x Conference NIT units (secondary test)	0,1,3,5,6	Negative: Different external benefits of NIT appearances for major conferences	4.66

Notes: * significant at 10%; ** significant at 5%; *** significant at 1%.

that, when more conference members play in the NCAA tournament, there are positive spillovers to attendance for other teams in the conference. This external benefit is in *addition* to the conference-level dollar distributions from the NCAA basketball fund, which are also based upon the number of conference units over the past six years.

Unlike the case of the NCAA tournament, there is no evidence of external benefits associated with having more conference members participating in the NIT ($\chi^2 = 7.80$, $p = 0.35$). However, from the results in Appendix A it appears that the current-year conference NIT units might have a slight positive impact on the attendance of other conference members. This is supported by the fact that we can (weakly) reject the null that the parameter on the contemporaneous value of *CONFNITUNITS* is equal to zero ($\chi^2 = 3.01$, $p = 0.08$) but cannot reject the null that the parameters on the first through sixth lagged values are jointly equal to zero ($\chi^2 = 3.31$, $p = 0.77$).

The remaining tests listed in Table 20.4 investigate whether there are differences in the internal and external benefits of the NCAA tournament and the NIT across the Big Six and non-Big Six conferences. There is evidence of slightly different (and smaller) impacts of NCAA units in the Big Six conferences ($\chi^2 = 12.37$, $p = 0.08$). However, it seems that the impacts are on the fifth and sixth lags. A joint test that the parameters on the current-year and first four lagged values of *BIG6NCAAUNITS* are jointly equal to zero cannot be rejected ($\chi^2 = 3.36$, $p = 0.64$) and the joint test that the fifth and sixth lags are jointly equal to zero is rejected ($\chi^2 = 9.47$, $p = 0.01$). This suggests that a biased NCAA selection process would harm programs in smaller conferences as they do not enjoy an increase in attendance associated with participating in the NCAA tournament.[17]

However, from Table 20.4, there seem to be no differences in the internal benefits of participating in the NIT between the Big-Six and non-Big-Six conferences ($\chi^2 = 2.72$, $p = 0.90$). This is perhaps not surprising if the majority of the teams invited to play in the NIT are not as good as those that play in the NCAA tournament, although there might be some NIT teams of higher quality than some automatic bids for the NCAA tournament. If relatively lower quality teams in the Big-Six conferences and relatively higher quality teams in the smaller conferences are the teams invited to the NIT, then the lack of significant differences in the internal benefits of the NIT might not be surprising.

The next hypothesis tests for differences in external benefits between the Big-Six conferences and the non-Big-Six conferences. There appear to be differences ($\chi^2 = 24.66$, $p = 0.00$) and that, from the results in Appendix A, the impact of *CONFNCAAUNITS* is smaller for the Big-Six conferences. However, it seems that the only differences are with the current-year conference NCAA units, which is supported by the fact that the hypothesis that the parameters on the first through sixth lagged values of *BIG6CONFNCAAUNITS* are jointly equal to zero cannot be rejected ($\chi^2 = 5.99$, $p = 0.42$).

Finally, there seem to be differences in the external benefits from conference participation in the NIT tournament between the Big-Six and non-Big-Six conferences ($\chi^2 = 18.13$, $p = 0.01$). These differences seem isolated to the second and fourth lagged values of *BIGS6CONFNIT*. The null hypothesis that the parameters on the current-year, first, third, fifth, and sixth lagged values of *BIG6CONFNIT* are jointly equal to zero cannot be rejected ($\chi^2 = 4.66$, $p = 0.45$), whereas the null that the parameters on the second and fourth lagged values are jointly equal to zero can be rejected ($\chi^2 = 10.02$, $p = 0.01$).

Thus, if the NCAA selection process is biased against smaller and mid-major conferences, the selection process reduces future attendance to smaller conference teams through two avenues. First, small-conference teams not included in the tournament miss out on the internal benefits, which are statistically the same as for the Big-Six conference teams for up to four years into the past and then perhaps greater for the smaller conferences five and six years in the past. However, the smaller-conference teams also miss out on the external benefits that accompany more conference participation in the tournament, which are generally greater than they are for big-conference teams. This suggests that if the NCAA were solely concerned about how the selection process influences home-game attendance of the teams selected, the organization would include more teams from smaller and mid-major conferences.

6. CONCLUSIONS

This chapter undertakes an analysis of how current and recent-past participation in post-season play in Division I men's college basketball influences current and future attendance. Similar to studies of other sports, team quality, measured by winning percentage, has a positive impact on current and future attendance levels. However, being on NCAA probation does not reduce attendance beyond the impact of probation on team quality. Private colleges and universities enjoy lower attendance levels, on average, and universities in the Big-Six conferences enjoy higher attendance levels on average. Schools that switch conferences do not suffer reductions in attendance in the subsequent year.

Of primary focus here is the impact of recent NCAA tournament and NIT participation on current and future attendance levels. It is shown that participating in more NCAA tournament games increases attendance up to six years into the future. The intuition for this is that NCAA tournament success provides an additional signal of quality for fans and can also engender greater fan loyalty to the program, which translates into greater attendance levels. On the other hand, participation and success in the NIT has only a short-run impact on attendance, consistent with the common wisdom that participation in the NIT is not as coveted as in the NCAA tournament.

Overall, there seem to be additional internal benefits from participating in the NCAA tournament and the NIT as reflected in additional attendance in the future. These benefits are internal to the extent that the individual team benefits from their participation. However, there appear to be external benefits to participating in the NCAA tournament; the more other conference members participate in the NCAA tournament, the greater is attendance to a particular team. This might arise through an increased reputation effect that encourages individuals to attend games in part for the teams that visit as much as for the home team. However, there do not seem to be long-lived external benefits to conference participation in the NIT.

There are also differences between the internal and external benefits of participating in the NCAA tournament and the NIT between the Big-Six conferences and the smaller and mid-major conferences. This suggests that, if the NCAA selection process is biased against smaller and mid-major conferences, then it introduces a negative-sum outcome, at least in terms of average attendance. Teams in a Big-Six conference do not enjoy as much an increase in attendance as their small-conference counterparts from participation in the NCAA tournament. These impacts are in addition to the reduced revenue distributed to the smaller conference because it will have fewer NCAA units with which to claim shares of the NCAA basketball fund. It is also demonstrated that the external benefits of the NCAA Tournament and the NIT differ across the Big-Six and smaller conferences.

If critics of the NCAA selection process are correct that it is biased against teams in smaller conferences, then it seems that the lack of inclusion of otherwise qualified teams hit the pocketbook of these teams in at least two ways. The more obvious impact is the reduced distribution from the NCAA basketball fund to the team's conference that arises because the team's conference has fewer units over time. This paper documents a less obvious impact: attendance to teams that participate in the NCAA tournament, and to a lesser degree, the NIT is greater, all else equal. Thus, if smaller conferences suffer a bias in the selection process, their attendance is lower than it otherwise would be, and this would have a negative impact on the team's revenue, thereby introducing an additional cost not heretofore considered.

Notes

1 Annual attendance to the National Invitational Tournament is not as readily available as for the NCAA Tournament. Contemporaneous newspaper accounts of the first National Invitational Tournament in 1938 report aggregate attendance for each of the tournament's three nights; each night had two games played. Therefore, attendance to the final game might be somewhat misleading, depending on exactly when the attendance count was taken during the course of the evening.
2 Between 1964 and 1975 UCLA won the NCAA Tournament ten times, which included an unmatched streak of seven championships between 1967 and 1973.
3 In the history of the modern NCAA tournament, no sixteen-seed (lowest seeded) team has beaten a number one seed (highest seeded) team.

4 The Flutie Effect is used to describe the documented short-term impact of sports success on applications to an institution as was documented after Doug Flutie led Boston College to a dramatic, last-second football victory against Miami (FL) in 1984. McCormick and Tinsley (1987) indicate that North Carolina State University received 40 percent more applications the year its basketball program won the national championship in 1983, and that Boston College received 3,700 (29.6 percent) more applications after Flutie won the Heisman Trophy in 1984. Similar experiences were documented at Miami (FL) in 1987 and Georgia Tech in 1990 after those schools enjoyed dramatic and unexpected football success (Toma and Cross, 1998). Recently, success in the NCAA tournament has provided advertising effects for George Mason University in 2006 and Davidson College in 2008.

5 The "Sweet Sixteen" is the term applied to the last sixteen teams playing in the tournament. These teams have each won two games (maximum three games if one of the teams participated in the play-in game) to reach this stage of the tournament.

6 These papers do not consider whether the NIT selection process is biased.

7 This was first mentioned by Sanders (2007), and the tally has been updated through the 2009 tournament. This was done by using the current Big-Six conferences, the Atlantic Coast Conference, the Big East, the Big Twelve, the Big Ten, the Southeastern, and the Pacific Ten, and the teams that played in the Southwest and Big Eight Conferences which merged in 1996 to create the Big Twelve.

8 Appendix B reports the schools included in the sample.

9 The NCAA includes the last six years of participation data in determining the revenue distributions and, therefore, six lags of NCAA and NIT units are used here. Thus, the first year in the sample is the 1996–1997 school year.

10 The NCAA defines a unit as a game played in the NCAA tournament that is not the final game. This avoids double counting as the two teams in the final game receive a separate payout from the tournament revenue. Here, the most NCAA units (NIT units) a given team can have in a given year is six (five).

11 For example, assume six Atlantic Coast Conference schools participated in the NCAA tournament, and these six teams won a combined twelve games. If Duke participated in the tournament and won three games, then for Duke *NCAAUNITS* would be coded as a three and *CONFNCAAUNITS* would be coded as nine. If Florida State did not participate in the NCAA tournament that year, then for Florida State *NCAAUNITS* would be coded as a zero and *CONFNCAAUNITS* would be coded as a twelve. For those teams that participated in the NCAA tournament, *NITUNITS* is necessarily coded as zero, although *CONFNITUNITS* is coded as the number of total NIT games in which conference members participated; a similar coding is done for those teams that participate in the NIT.

12 The sample of 3,965 observations is unbalanced because some schools were promoted to Division I status in the middle of the sample. Still other schools dropped out of Division I status for one or more years of the sample.

13 These teams include, in alphabetical order, Boston College (2005), Cincinnati (2005), DePaul (2005), Louisville (2005), Marquette (2005), Miami-Florida (2004), South Florida (2005), and Virginia Tech (2004). These movements coincide with realignment in the Atlantic Coast Conference in 2004 and 2005 and the Big East conference in 2005.

14 Except for 2002, 2003, 2004, 2005, and 2006, during which the NIT expanded to include forty teams.

15 When conferences are promoted to Division I status, they are generally held on
    "probation" for a number of years before they are granted an automatic bid. For
    instance, the recently created Great West conference will not receive an automatic bid
    to the NCAA tournament until 2020.

16 The random effects estimator was employed for three reasons. First, the fixed effects
    model would remove the ability to estimate parameters on time invariant variables
    such as *PRIVATE*. Second, there is more variation in attendance between college
    basketball programs than within college basketball programs. Thus, the fixed effects
    model sacrifices a considerable amount of information and degrees of freedom. Finally,
    the fixed effects model assumes the unobserved heterogeneity of each college basketball
    program is time-invariant; likely a strong assumption in the current context. Over
    the nineteen years of the sample period, there are any number of coaching changes,
    dynamics in player retention, changes in facilities, and other aspects of the program
    that suggest the random effects model is perhaps conceptually superior. Nevertheless,
    the Hausman test rejects the random-effects model ($c^2 = 217.63$, $p = 0.00$). Fixed effects
    estimates, which are not quantitatively but are somewhat qualitatively different from
    the random effects estimates, are available from the author upon request.

17 It should be stressed that these effects are in the context of a 64- (and 65-) team
    tournament. In early 2010, there were discussions about expanding the NCAA
    tournament to ninety-six teams, essentially folding the NIT into the NCAA
    tournament. The results presented here do not necessarily suggest that such a move
    would be good or bad because the attendance and tournament participation figures
    are not based on a ninety-six-team field.

References

Baade, Robert, and J. S. Sundberg. 1996. Fourth down and gold to go? Assessing
    the link between athletics and alumni giving. *Social Science Quarterly*, 77(4):
    789–803.

Balsdon, Ed, Lesley Fong, and Mark A. Thayer. 2007. Corruption in college
    basketball? Evidence of tanking in postseason conference tournaments. *Journal of
    Sports Economics*, 8(1): 19–38.

Boulier, Bryan, and H. O. Stekler. 1999. Are sports seeds good predictors? An
    evaluation. *Journal of Forecasting*, 15(1): 83–91.

Bryan, Kevin, Michael Steinke, and Nick Wilkins. 2006. Upset special: Are March
    Madness upsets predictable? available at ssrn.com/abstract=899702, last accessed
    January 2010.

Carlin, Bryan P. 1996. Improved NCAA Basketball Tournament modeling via point
    spread and team strength information. *The American Statistician*, 50(1): 39–43.

Caudill, Steven B., and Norman H. Godwin. 2002. Heterogeneous skewness in
    binary choice models: Predicting outcomes in the men's NCAA Basketball
    Tournament. *Journal of Applied Statistics*, 29(7): 991–1001.

Daley, Arthur J. 1938. 13,829 in Garden See N.Y.U. and Temple fives triumph in
    national tourney. New York Times, March 10.

Daley, Arthur J. 1938. "Colorado Five Thrills 12,000 in Garden with Last-Minute
    Victory over N.Y.U.," *New York Times*, March 15.

Daley, Arthur J. 1938. Temple crushes Colorado, 60–35. *New York Times*, March 17.

Depken, Craig A., David R. Kamerschen, and Arthur Snow. 2000. Generic advertising of intermediate goods: Theory and evidence on free riding. *The Review of Industrial Organization,* 20(3): 205–220.

Drea, John. 1995. The effects of winning, weather, scheduling, and promotion on attendance at NCAA Division II men's college basketball games. In *Proceedings of the Southern Marketing Association,* available at www.sbaer.uca.edu/Research/sma/1995/pdf/62.pdf, accessed January 2010.

Fanney, S. Brandon. 2009. The effect of one-and-done players on Division I men's college basketball programs. The University of North Carolina at Chapel Hill, Publication Number 1463777.

McCormick, Robert E., and Maurice Tinsley. 1987. Athletics versus academics? Evidence from SAT scores. *Journal of Political Economy,* 95(5): 1103–1116.

Mixon, Franklin. 1995. Athletics versus academics? Rejoining the evidence from SAT scores. *Education Economics,* 3(3): 277–283.

NCAA. 2009. Division I championship statistics. Available at www.ncaa.org, accessed January, 2010.

NCAA. 2010. Current division I total revenue distribution information. Available at www.ncaa.org, accessed January 2010.

Murphy, Roger G., and Gregory A. Trandel. 1994. The relation between a university's football record and the size of its applicant pool. *Economics of Education Review,* 13(3): 265–270.

Pan, David W., Trent E. Gabert, Eric C. Mcgaugh, and Scott. E. Branvold. 1997. Factors and differential demographic effects on purchases of season tickets for intercollegiate basketball games. *Journal of Sport Behavior,* 20(4): 124–142.

Pope, Devin G., and Jaren C. Pope. 2009. The impact of college sports success on the quantity and quality of student applications. *Southern Economic Journal,* 75(3): 750–780.

Rhoads, Thomas, and Shelby Gerking. 2000. Educational contributions, academic quality, and athletic success. *Economic Inquiry,* 18(2): 248–258.

Rishe, Patrick. 2003. A reexamination of how athletic success impacts graduation rates: Comparing student-athletes to all other undergraduates. *American Journal of Economics and Sociology* 62(2): 407–421.

Sanders, Shane. 2007. A cheap ticket to the dance: Systematic bias in college basketball's ratings percentage index. *Economics Bulletin,* 4(34): 1–7.

Schurr, K. Terry, Arno Wittig, Virgil Ruble, and Arthur Ellen. 1987. Demographic and personality characteristics associated with persistent, occasional, and nonattendance of university male basketball games by college students. *Journal of Sport Behavior,* 11(1): 3–17.

Schwertman, Neil C., Thomas McCready, and Lesley Howard. 1991. Probability models for the NCAA Regional Basketball Tournament. *The American Statistician,* 45(1): 35–38.

Shapiro, Stephen, Joris Drayer, Brendan Dwyer, and Alan Morse. 2009. Punching a ticket to the big dance: A critical analysis of at-large selection into the NCAA Division I Men's Basketball Tournament. *Journal of Issues in Intercollegiate Athletics,* 2: 46–63.

Sigelman, Lee, and Robert Carter. 1979. Win one for the giver? Alumni giving and big-time college sports. *Social Science Quarterly,* 60(2): 284–294.

Smith, Tyler, and Neil C. Schwertman. 1999. Can the NCAA Tournament seeding be used to predict margin of victory. *The American Statistician,* 53(2): 94–98.

Toma, J. Douglas, and Michael Cross. 1998. Intercollegiate athletics and student college choice: Understanding the impact of championship seasons on the quantity and quality of undergraduate applicants. *Research in Higher Education,* 39(6): 633–661.

Tucker, Irvin. 1992. The impact of big-time athletics on graduation rates. *Atlantic Economic Journal,* 20(4): 65–72.

Tucker, Irvin. 2004. A reexamination of the effect of big-time football and basketball success on graduation rates and alumni giving rates. *Economics of Education Review,* 23(6): 655–661.

Tucker, Irvin, and Louis Amato. 1993. Does big-time success in football or basketball affect SAT scores. *Economics of Education Review,* 12(2): 177–181.

Walls, Thomas L., and Ellen Bass. 2004. A regression-based predictive model of student attendance at UVA men's basketball games. In *Proceedings of the 2004 Systems and Information Engineering Design Symposium,* eds. Matthew H. Jones, Stephen D. Patek, and Barbara E. Tawney. Available at ieeexplore.ieee.org, accessed January 2010.

West, Brady T. 2006. A simple and flexible rating method for predicting success in the NCAA Basketball Tournament. *Journal of Quantitative Analysis in Sports,* 2(3): Article 3.

West, Brady T. 2008. A simple and flexible rating method for predicting success in the NCAA Basketball Tournament: Updated results from 2007. *Journal of Quantitative Analysis in Sports,* 4(2): Article 8.

Zimmer, Timothy, and Todd Kuethe. 2008. Major conference bias and the NCAA Men's Basketball Tournament. *Economics Bulletin,* 12(17): 1–6.

APPENDIX A
RANDOM EFFECTS REGRESSION RESULTS

	(1)	(2)
	Per-Game Attendance	Per-Game Attendance
WINPCT	2,028.937***	2,071.036***
	(121.441)	(118.638)
WINPCT (first lag)	758.478***	753.252***
	(120.877)	(117.940)
WINPCT (second lag)	195.811*	199.358*
	(116.728)	(113.105)
WINPCT (third lag)	128.805	158.015
	(114.243)	(112.841)
WINPCT (fourth lag)	144.035	214.976*
	(117.156)	(112.707)

	(1) Per-Game Attendance	(2) Per-Game Attendance
WINPCT (fifth lag)	400.084***	437.917***
	(117.781)	(113.048)
WINPCT (sixth lag)	190.842	269.921**
	(118.636)	(115.274)
PROBATION	86.085	
	(124.399)	
PROBATION (first lag)	145.287	
	(133.871)	
PROBATION (second lag)	64.380	
	(145.550)	
PROBATION (third lag)	116.649	
	(141.126)	
PROBATION (fourth lag)	177.040	
	(145.180)	
PROBATION (fifth lag)	39.268	
	(138.433)	
PROBATION (sixth lag)	−151.982	
	(135.422)	
PRIVATE	−891.969***	−892.894***
	(212.194)	(218.623)
BIG6	2,567.936***	2,185.910***
	(422.909)	(363.894)
NEWCONF	−100.177	−96.978
	(65.213)	(66.199)
NCAAUNITS	281.483***	239.103***
	(46.850)	(28.984)
NCAAUNITS (first lag)	263.152***	288.221***
	(41.614)	(28.708)
NCAAUNITS (second lag)	228.450***	215.344***
	(39.736)	(29.427)

(Continued)

	(1)	(2)
	Per-Game Attendance	Per-Game Attendance
NCAAUNITS (third lag)	198.866***	156.262***
	(42.903)	(29.877)
NCAAUNITS (fourth lag)	117.029**	98.093***
	(47.230)	(29.119)
NCAAUNITS (fifth lag)	109.748**	105.942**
	(44.806)	(41.507)
NCAAUNITS (sixth lag)	183.986***	150.640***
	(46.775)	(44.656)
NITUNITS	154.271***	101.262***
	(52.048)	(31.182)
NITUNITS (first lag)	133.791***	143.665***
	(47.316)	(28.708)
NITUNITS (second lag)	93.830**	31.911***
	(43.468)	(29.427)
NITUNITS (third lag)	66.132	39.132
	(45.332)	(31.830)
NITUNITS (fourth lag)	40.661	
	(38.989)	
NITUNITS (fifth lag)	11.306	
	(40.684)	
NITUNITS (sixth lag)	62.273	
	(41.096)	
CONFNCAAUNITS	68.730***	74.607***
	(16.593)	(15.366)
CONFNCAAUNITS (first lag)	15.730	11.598
	(16.257)	(9.941)
CONFNCAAUNITS (second lag)	40.034**	31.910***
	(16.506)	(9.742)
CONFNCAAUNITS (third lag)	33.683**	20.816**
	(16.719)	(9.477)

(Continued)

	(1)	(2)
	Per-Game Attendance	Per-Game Attendance
CONFNCAAUNITS (fourth lag)	−8.910	17.116*
	(15.549)	(9.648)
CONFNCAAUNITS (fifth lag)	31.419*	20.482**
	(16.036)	(10.338)
CONFNCAAUNITS (sixth lag)	55.073***	35.327***
	(17.723)	(9.122)
CONFNITUNITS	21.406*	15.869*
	(11.957)	(9.033)
CONFNITUNITS (first lag)	11.179	
	(11.513)	
CONFNITUNITS (second lag)	−1.461	
	(11.679)	
CONFNITUNITS (third lag)	−1.206	
	(11.332)	
CONFNITUNITS (fourth lag)	−19.461	
	(13.569)	
CONFNITUNITS (fifth lag)	−4.178	
	(14.750)	
CONFNITUNITS (sixth lag)	8.276	
	(13.902)	
BIG6NCAAUNITS	−71.492	
	(56.004)	
BIG6NCAAUNITS (first lag)	43.557	
	(53.714)	
BIG6NCAAUNITS (second lag)	−26.462	
	(54.375)	
BIG6NCAAUNITS (third lag)	−63.094	
	(55.859)	
BIG6NCAAUNITS (fourth lag)	−15.048	
	(57.970)	

(Continued)

	(1)	(2)
	Per-Game Attendance	Per-Game Attendance
BIG6NCAAUNITS (fifth lag)	−96.799*	−97.876**
	(55.122)	(50.820)
BIG6NCAAUNITS (sixth lag)	−129.553**	−118.425***
	(57.598)	(55.494)
BIG6NITUNITS	−70.092	
	(65.703)	
BIG6NITUNITS (first lag)	41.724	
	(62.913)	
BIG6NITUNITS (second lag)	25.054	
	(61.410)	
BIG6NITUNITS (third lag)	−23.829	
	(64.725)	
BIG6NITUNITS (fourth lag)	22.625	
	(58.820)	
BIG6NITUNITS (fifth lag)	33.843	
	(59.772)	
BIG6NITUNITS (sixth lag)	23.453	
	(58.957)	
BIG6CONFNCAAUNITS	−87.985***	−77.409***
	(20.984)	(19.129)
BIG6CONFNCAAUNITS (first lag)	−7.839	
	(20.341)	
BIG6CONFNCAAUNITS (second lag)	−18.709	
	(20.316)	
BIG6CONFNCAAUNITS (third lag)	−22.351	
	(19.691)	
BIG6CONFNCAAUNITS (fourth lag)	25.081	
	(19.912)	
BIG6CONFNCAAUNITS (fifth lag)	−23.307	
	(19.988)	

(Continued)

	(1) Per-Game Attendance	(2) Per-Game Attendance
BIG6CONFNCAAUNITS (sixth lag)	−23.452 (20.859)	
BIG6CONFNITUNITS	−13.202 (18.757)	
BIG6CONFNITUNITS (first lag)	1.718 (17.671)	
BIG6CONFNITUNITS (second lag)	25.857 (18.230)	
BIG6CONFNITUNITS (third lag)	18.725 (17.979)	
BIG6CONFNITUNITS (fourth lag)	60.599*** (20.589)	29.469** (14.658)
BIG6CONFNITUNITS (fifth lag)	16.676 (20.538)	
BIG6CONFNITUNITS (sixth lag)	31.140 (20.173)	
Constant	1,259.727*** (181.018)	1,288.037*** (177.146)
Observations	3965	3965
Number of teams	323	323

Robust standard errors in parentheses. * significant at 10%; ** significant at 5%; *** significant at 1%.

APPENDIX B
TEAMS INCLUDED IN THE SAMPLE

Air Force	Brigham Young	College of Charleston
Akron	Brown	Colorado
Alabama	Bucknell	Colorado State
Alabama A&M	Buffalo	Columbia
Alabama State	Butler	Connecticut
Alabama-Birmingham	Cal Poly	Coppin State
Albany	Cal State-Fullerton	Cornell
Alcorn State	Cal State-Northridge	Creighton
American	Cal State-Sacramento	Dartmouth
Appalachian State	California	Davidson
Arizona	California-Irvine	Dayton
Arizona State	California-Riverside	Delaware
Arkansas	California-Santa Barbara	Delaware State
Arkansas State	Campbell	Denver
Arkansas-Little Rock	Canisius	DePaul
Arkansas-Pine Bluff	Centenary	Detroit
Army	Cent. Connecticut State	Drake
Auburn	Central Florida	Drexel
Austin Peay	Central Michigan	Duke
Ball State	Charleston Southern	Duquesne
Baylor	Charlotte	East Carolina
Belmont	Chattanooga	East Tennessee State
Bethune-Cookman	Chicago State	Eastern Illinois
Binghamton	Cincinnati	Eastern Kentucky
Boise State	Citadel	Eastern Michigan
Boston College	Clemson	Eastern Washington
Boston University	Cleveland State	Elon
Bowling Green	Coastal Carolina	Evansville
Bradley	Colgate	Fairfield

Fairleigh Dickinson	Iona	MD-Baltimore County
Florida	Iowa	MD-Eastern Shore
Florida A&M	Iowa State	Massachusetts
Florida Atlantic	IUPUI	McNeese State
Florida International	Jackson State	Memphis
Florida State	Jacksonville	Mercer
Fordham	Jacksonville State	Miami-Florida
Fresno State	James Madison	Miami-Ohio
Furman	Kansas	Michigan
Gardner Webb	Kansas State	Michigan State
George Mason	Kent	Middle Tennessee State
George Washington	Kentucky	Minnesota
Georgetown	Lafayette	Mississippi
Georgia	Lamar	Mississippi State
Georgia Southern	LaSalle	Mississippi Valley State
Georgia State	Lehigh	Missouri
Georgia Tech	Liberty	Missouri State
Gonzaga	Lipscomb	Missouri-Kansas City
Grambling	Long Beach State	Monmouth
Hampton	Long Island	Montana
Hartford	Louisiana State	Montana State
Harvard	Louisiana Tech	Morehead State
Hawaii	Louisiana-Lafayette	Morgan State
High Point	Louisiana-Monroe	Mount St. Mary's
Hofstra	Louisville	Murray State
Holy Cross	Loyola-Chicago	Navy
Houston	Loyola-Maryland	Nebraska
Howard	Loyola-Marymount	Nevada
Idaho	Maine	Nevada-Las Vegas
Idaho State	Manhattan	New Hampshire
Illinois State	Marist	New Mexico
Illinois-Chicago	Marquette	New Mexico State
Indiana	Marshall	New Orleans
Indiana State	Maryland	Niagara

Nicholls State	Princeton	Southern Utah
Norfolk State	Providence	St. Bonaventure
North Carolina	Purdue	St. Francis-NY
North Carolina A&T	Quinnipiac	St. Francis-PA
North Carolina State	Radford	St. John's
NC Asheville	Rhode Island	St. Joseph's
NC Greensboro	Rice	St. Peter's
NC Wilmington	Richmond	Stanford
North Texas	Rider	Stephen F. Austin
Northeastern	Robert Morris	Stetson
Northeastern Illinois	Rutgers	Stony Brook
Northern Arizona	Sacred Heart	Syracuse
Northern Illinois	Saint Louis	Temple
Northern Iowa	Saint Mary's	Tennessee
Northwestern	Sam Houston State	Tennessee State
Northwestern State	Samford	Tennessee Tech
Notre Dame	San Diego	Tennessee-Martin
Oakland	San Diego State	Texas
Ohio	San Francisco	Texas A&M
Ohio State	San Jose State	Texas Christian
Oklahoma	Santa Clara	Texas Southern
Oklahoma State	Seton Hall	Texas State
Old Dominion	Siena	Texas Tech
Oral Roberts	South Alabama	Texas-Arlington
Oregon	South Carolina	Texas-El Paso
Oregon State	South Carolina State	Texas-Pan American
Pacific	South Florida	Texas-San Antonio
Penn State	Southeast Missouri State	Toledo
Pennsylvania	Southeastern Louisiana	Towson
Pepperdine	Southern	Troy State
Pittsburgh	Southern California	Tulane
Portland	Southern Illinois	Tulsa
Portland State	Southern Methodist	UCLA
Prairie View	Southern Mississippi	Utah

Utah State

Valparaiso

Vanderbilt

Vermont

Villanova

Virginia

Virginia Commonwealth

VMI

Virginia Tech

Wagner

Wake Forest

Washington

Washington State

Weber State

West Virginia

Western Carolina

Western Illinois

Western Kentucky

Western Michigan

Wichita State

William & Mary

Winthrop

Wisconsin

Wisconsin-Green Bay

Wisconsin-Milwaukee

Wofford

Wright State

Wyoming

Xavier

Yale

Youngstown State

CHAPTER 21

GENDER EQUITY IN INTERCOLLEGIATE ATHLETICS

ECONOMIC CONSIDERATIONS AND POSSIBLE FIXES

ANDREW ZIMBALIST

INTRODUCTION

THIS chapter will first briefly review the history of Title IX. I will then consider ways that women's sports can continue to be promoted without reducing men's sports and without increasing athletics' budgets. I will propose that Congress grant the NCAA a limited antitrust exemption, so that universities can cap coaches' compensation levels. Finally, as part of the argument for capping coaches' salaries, I will present econometric evidence that suggests coaches' salaries do not bear a significant relationship to team performance.

Title IX is about gender equity. It is a law that was passed in June 1972 as part of the educational amendments to the Civil Rights laws of the 1960s. The law simply states: "No person in the United States shall, on the basis of sex, be excluded from participation in, be denied the benefits of, or be subjected to discrimination under any education program or activity receiving federal financial assistance." As such, it applies broadly to all educational programs and activities, not just athletics. Athletics stands out for a number of reasons, one of which is that almost all sports have gender-segregated teams.

Title IX encompasses a wide range of issues, including: equity in facilities, equity in marketing and promotional resources, pay equity for coaches, equity in financial aid, retaliation against employees or students who speak out against discrimination, sexual harassment of female students and employees, equity in travel and accommodations, among many others. Nonetheless, most of the public discussion around Title IX concentrates on the opportunities for athletic participation by female students. Simply put, without female participation in sports, most other forms of unequal treatment cannot occur.

One fact that stands out about Title IX is its enormous success.

Let us take a step back and consider the history of Title IX.

Table 21.1 Female Participation Numbers

	1971	2007	Increase
High School Sports	294,015	3.06 million	10.4X
College Sports	31,852	166,800	5.2X

Source: Nancy Hogshead-Makar and Andrew Zimbalist, *Equal Play: Title IX and Social Change*. Philadelphia: Temple University Press, 2007, p. 2.

EARLY YEARS

Prior to the emergence of the women's movement in the 1960s, female participation in organized sports was minimal. The prevailing ideology asserted that playing competitive sports was incompatible with women's reproductive role and that women who played competitive sports risked being masculinized; frequently it was claimed that these masculinized athletes must be homosexuals. Indeed, many leagues and organizations, including the AAU (Amateur Athletic Union), the All-American Girls Baseball League, and the women's golf tour, found it necessary to promote the high percentage of its players who were married or looking for husbands as a way to combat this prejudice.

Attitudes began to change with the resurgent women's movement, catalyzed by the 1963 publication of Betty Friedan's *The Feminine Mystique*. In 1967, the Commission on Intercollegiate Athletics for Women (CIAW) was formed "to give college women more opportunities for high level competition in athletics." The CIAW evolved into a permanent organization in 1972, the Association for

Intercollegiate Athletics for Women (AIAW). At the time, the NCAA's policy still banned women from its championships. Throughout the 1970s the AIAW effectively promoted and organized women's college sports under its own philosophy, which was based on the social and psychological value of athletics participation to women. This philosophy was encapsulated in the first clause of the AIAW policy statement which stipulates: "The enrichment of the life of the participant is the focus and reason for the existence of any athletic program. All decisions should be made with this fact in mind." Insistent on keeping women's athletics as an amateur activity, subordinate to academics, the AIAW adopted many policies, such as one that prohibited coaches from recruiting off campus. Student athletes would try out for a team on campus, just as student thespians tried out for school plays and student musicians tried out for the orchestra.

Meanwhile, as women began to participate increasingly in sports, the emotional, social, and physiological benefits therein became more and more apparent. Research has shown, *inter alia*:

- High school girls who play sports are less likely to be involved in an unwanted pregnancy; less likely to watch television; less likely to be overweight; more likely to have a positive body image; more likely to get better grades in school, and more likely to graduate than girls who do not play sports.
- Girls involved in organized sports are less likely to smoke cigarettes or marijuana or to use recreational drugs; and the more teams they play on, the less likely they are to indulge in these habits.
- As little as four hours of exercise a week may reduce a teenage girl's risk of breast cancer by up to 60 percent; breast cancer is a disease that afflicts one out of every eight American women.
- 40 percent of women over the age of fifty suffer from osteoporosis (brittle bones). Proper physical exercise is believed to lower the incidence.
- Girls and women who play sports have higher levels of confidence and self esteem.
- Sport teaches teamwork, discipline, goal-setting, the pursuit of excellence in performance and other achievement-oriented behaviors—critical skills necessary for success in the workplace. In an economic environment in which the quality of our children's lives will be dependent on two-income families, our daughters cannot be less prepared for the highly competitive workplace than our sons. It is no accident that 80 percent of the female executives at Fortune 500 companies identified themselves as former "tomboys"—having played sports.[1]

The NCAA did not know what to make of the surge in women's athletics. Initially, as a men's organization, they saw it as a threat to their domain. The NCAA spent most of the 1970s first lobbying in Congress and then fighting in the courts to clip the wings of women's college sports. The NCAA's first plan was to lobby Congress to remove the entire realm of intercollegiate athletics from coverage by Title IX.

That having failed, they then supported Senator Towers' amendment to exempt the "revenue-producing" sports from Title IX. When that effort foundered, the NCAA in 1976 sued the HEW[2] over its regulations to implement Title IX. Among other things, the NCAA here claimed that athletic departments that did not directly receive federal subsidies should not be covered, even if the university did. Having also lost in the courts, and given the rapid growth in women's sports and in their popularity during the 1970s, the NCAA decided its next best option was to use its financial muscle to take over the administration of women's sports from the AIAW, which it did.

In 1979, the Office of Civil Rights (OCR) of the HEW issued what were to become the most controversial regulations regarding the implementation of Title IX. These regulations related to how to identify whether women were being discriminated against with regard to the level of women's sports participation relative to men's. The goal of Title IX and these regulations is to promote equal opportunity for women, not necessarily equal outcome. These regulations included the infamous three-prong test. This test stipulated that to be in compliance, one of the following three criteria (or prongs) must be met:

- Opportunities for males and females must be substantially proportionate to their respective enrollments.
- When one sex has been underrepresented, the program must show a history and continuing practice of program expansion responsive to the developing interests and abilities of that sex.
- When one sex is underrepresented and the school cannot show a continuing practice of program expansion, it must be demonstrated that the interests and abilities of that sex have been fully and effectively accommodated by the existing program.

This three-pronged test has been litigated heavily, but its legality has been upheld by every one of the eight federal appeals courts that has considered it.[3]

The early success during the 1970s of Title IX led to a backlash. In 1981, the incoming Reagan administration cut funding for the Department of Education and took the position that Title IX should only apply to those departments within a university that received direct federal funding. This position was tested in the courts and upheld in the 1984 Supreme Court decision in the Grove City College case. Four years later Congress overturned it with the Civil Rights Restoration Act. The administration of George Herbert Walker Bush showed little interest, however, in supporting Title IX implementation and, by 1992, the share of women in all intercollegiate athletes leveled off at 32 percent, just 2 percentage points higher than a decade earlier.

Gains resumed under the Clinton administration, with women's share among intercollegiate athletes rising a full 10 percentage points, to 42.3 percent. Title IX's detractors, however, regrouped and made hay during the two administrations of George W. Bush. The last available figures show the proportion of women in all NCAA athletes had risen by only a half a point to 42.8 percent. Indeed, the October

Table 21.2 Share of Women in Intercollegiate Athletics

1971–1972	15%
1981–1982	30%
1991–1992	32%
2001–2002	42.3%
2005–2006	42.8%

Source: Nancy Hogshead-Makar and Andrew Zimbalist, *Equal Play: Title IX and Social Change*. Philadelphia: Temple University Press, 2007 pp. 3, 302–303.

2008 Gender Equity Report of the NCAA finds that there has even been backsliding in many areas during the Bush administration. For instance, in Division 1, the share of all athletic spending going to women fell from 37 percent in 2003–2004 to 34 percent in 2005–2006.[4]

Bush's Secretary of Education, Rodney Paige, established a Commission on Opportunities in Athletics with the purported role of making a balanced assessment of Title IX. However, the Commission's composition and the selection of preponderantly anti-Title IX witnesses laid bare the intention of weakening the law. After a year and a half of investigating, the Commission came out with a series of recommendations, many of which would have set back gender equity in athletics (e.g., excluding walk-on athletes in the proportionality count, or allowing relative interests to be determined solely by a survey of prospective or current students). After the Commission's recommendations were made public, there was a strong and persistent critical reaction, leading Secretary Paige to assert that only recommendations that were supported unanimously by the Commission's members would be adopted. Secretary Paige's pledge notwithstanding, following Bush's reelection in November 2004, in March 2005 the OCR issued a new clarification, which stated that, henceforth, it would be acceptable for a school to do an e-mail survey of its current student body as the only evidence to ascertain whether the school was meeting prong three by fully and effectively accommodating the interests and abilities of the underrepresented sex. This stood in direct contradiction to the OCR's 1996 clarification which stipulated that several tests, such as high school participation in the sport, the existence of club sports, the petition of students to add a sport, among others, should be used. Now an e-mail survey could stand as the sole determinant of students' interests. Ironically, the OCR itself was about to release a study that showed that between 2002 and 2006 student response rates to these surveys varied between 1 and 78 percent, and in more than two-thirds of the surveys the response rate was below 40 percent. Further, the March 2005 clarification indicates that non-responses can be counted as no interest. The clarification says not a word about the OCR or any other body providing oversight to ensure that the surveys are properly designed and carried out. Both the NCAA and the U.S. Congress subsequently rejected the use of e-mail surveys as the sole determinant of relative athletic interests.

In this context, it should be underscored that, in 2007, the number of women participating in intercollegiate sports was 160,800, whereas the number of girls participating in high school sports was 3.06 million. Thus, today, for every 100 girls playing high school sports, there are only 5.5 playing in college. This is *prima facie* evidence that the interest and ability level is there to support continued growth in intercollegiate athletic opportunities for women.[5]

Despite tremendous outcry from Title IX detractors about OCR activism, there were just 44 Title IX participation cases before the OCR during the eight-year time frame 1992–2000. Further, no college has ever lost any funds for a violation of Title IX standards, despite OCR being responsible for overseeing the athletics programs at more than 1,200 colleges and universities. Notably, between 2002 and 2006, out of the 416 complaints filed regarding Title IX's implementation, only 1 of these was initiated by the OCR.

The Bush administration also encouraged a suit brought by the National Wrestling Coaches Association. One of their main claims was that Title IX had promoted the growth of women's participation at the expense of cutting men's teams. The evidence suggests otherwise. The greatest drop in the number of men's wrestling teams occurred between 1982 and 1992. The number fell from 363 to 275. These were years, as we saw earlier, when Title IX was virtually unenforced. Title IX cannot fairly be blamed for this drop. Also, during this time period, the number of men's gymnastics teams decreased from 79 to 40; men lost 39 gymnastics teams, women lost 83 gymnastics teams. Again, Title IX is not responsible. What, then, explains the drops in these sports? Men's allegiances have been shifting to football and soccer; and with both gymnastics and wrestling, there have been growing college concerns about serious injury and liability.

More generally, Title IX's critics have argued that women's participation gains have come at the expense of men. But a 2007 U.S. government report finds that the number of male participants in intercollegiate athletics grew by 21 percent between 1991–1992 and 2004–2005.[6]

The critics have pointed out that the reported growth in the absolute number of male student-athletes can be misleading. This is because the NCAA has experienced rapid growth in its membership, because schools have moved from the NAIA to the NCAA. The number of four-year colleges in the NCAA grew from 847 colleges in 1991–1992 to 1,045 in 2004–2005.

To adjust for this factor, the General Accounting Office (GAO) considered a group of 750 colleges that were consistently members of the NCAA throughout the 1991–2005 period. Even in this fixed group, however, the report finds that the number of male athletes grew by almost 14,000, or 9 percent during the fourteen-year period.

Thus, although it is true that the number of male wrestling teams has diminished, the overall level of male athletic participation continues to rise. Title IX cannot properly be blamed for reducing the number of male athletes, because, simply put, there has been no reduction.[7]

THE ROAD AHEAD

Nonetheless, there are no free goods, and devoting resources to women's sports means that fewer resources are available elsewhere. If gender equity in intercollegiate athletics is to continue to advance, it is desirable to find the new resources for women's sports without cutting men's sports and without straining university budgets. The most obvious source for such resources is the elimination of extravagant and superfluous expenditure. The reality that college athletics departments do not have shareholders who are residual claimants means that they do not face the typical pressure of private sector firms to economize on resources and generate profit. This feature, along with some others, engenders endemic waste.

One example of extravagance is the size of Division 1A (FBS) football teams. FBS football does not need eighty-five scholarships. Sixty would do fine. NFL teams have a maximum active roster of forty-five, plus a maximum inactive roster of eight additional players.[8] The average FBS team has thirty-two walk-ons plus eighty-five scholarship players.[9] If football scholarships were cut to sixty, the average college would save approximately $750,000 annually, enough to finance more than two wrestling teams (whose average cost is $330,000 per team).

Other examples of waste abound, but perhaps the most egregious is the salaries paid to head football and men's basketball coaches, which often exceed the salaries of the university's president by a factor of five to ten. Today, there are over 100 college football coaches with compensation packages exceeding $1 million, and there are more than a dozen exceeding $3 million. Men's basketball coaches are not far behind: in 2005–2006, the coaches of the sixty-five Division 1 teams in the NCAA tournament had an average maximum compensation of $959,486, with the top-paid coach earning a guaranteed salary of $2.1 million and a maximum salary of $3.4 million.[10] These figures exclude extensive perquisites, including free use of cars, housing subsidies, country-club memberships, private jet service, exceptionally generous severance packages, and more.

Back in 1924, Centenary College in Shreveport, Louisiana, the nation's first liberal arts college west of the Mississippi, was denied accreditation by the Southern Association of Colleges and Schools because the school placed an "undue emphasis on athletics." The primary evidence of Centenary's misplaced priorities by the Southern Association was that the college paid its football coach more than it paid its college president. The next year the football coach was gone and the college gained accreditation.[11]

More recently, the legendary head football coach at the University of Alabama (1958–1982), Bear Bryant, adhered to a firm policy of always keeping his salary $1 below that of the school president. Bryant believed that it was symbolically important for the university president to be paid more than the head football coach.[12]

Defenders of the multimillion-dollar head coaches' salaries are wont to repeat the mantra: "Coaches' compensation packages are driven by market forces." Fair enough, but what drives the market forces? It is clear that the market for coaches is sustained by artificial factors: (1) there is no compensation paid to the athletes; (2) intercollegiate sports benefit from substantial tax privileges; (3) there are no shareholders demanding dividend distributions or higher profits to bolster stock prices; (4) athletic departments are nourished by university and state-wide subsidies; and, (5) coaches' salaries are negotiated by athletic directors whose own worth rises with the salaries of their employees.

In a normal competitive market, college football coaches would not be getting compensated almost at the same level as NFL coaches. The top thirty-two college football programs generate average revenues in the $40–$50 million range; the average NFL team generates around $230 million.

The real point is that, if the NCAA placed, say, a $500,000 limit on coaches' compensation packages, it would not affect the quality of coaching or the level of intercollegiate competition one iota. This is because the next best alternative for top college coaches (the reservation wage) is likely to be well below this level. Anything above the reservation wage, then, is what economists call economic rent.

It is clear that coaches are being paid in part for the value produced by the athletes they recruit, who do not get paid. That is, the marginal revenue product of the star players accrues largely to the head coach, rather than to the players. This is reason enough to cap coaches' salaries. It is more reason because much of the work of recruiting is done by assistant coaches and much of the attraction a school has to a player has to do with the school's reputation and facilities, both factors independent of the head coach.

RESULTS

I have collected data on compensation levels of head coaches in Division 1 men's basketball and Division 1A football and compared these levels to different measurements of team performance. I run multiple regressions and panel regressions to explore the extent of correlation between coaches' salaries and team performance. Because of data limitations, the regressions do not represent formal models to predict either compensation levels or team performance; rather, they are simple efforts to observe whether teams with more highly compensated coaches

Table 21.3 Dependent Variable: BKGuarComp Adj $R^2 = .44$, $n = 75$

Independent Variable	Coefficient	t-statistic	p-value
Constant	−749,021	−2.37	0.02
BCSConf	+390,184	4.33	0.00
WinPct	+266,357	0.63	0.53
Rec10Yr	+1,700,468	3.73	0.00
ConfChamp	−34,872	−0.29	0.77
MarchMad	+80,481	0.75	0.46
Sweet 16	+169,322	1.31	0.19
Finals	+369,300	1.30	0.20

are also teams with more competitive success. The regression results do not suggest that the more highly paid coaches are associated with more successful teams in current years; rather, they suggest that higher salaries are positively correlated with a school's historical success. That is, team success appears to be correlated with longstanding institutional factors rather than the performance of the current coach.

I employed three distinct data sets.[13] One for head Division 1 men's basketball coaches in 2005–2006 ($n = 75$), another for head Division 1A football coaches in 2006–2007 ($n = 109$) and another for both basketball and football coaches from 2000–2001 to 2006–2007 ($n = 241, 274$, respectively).

Men's Basketball Head Coaches

Consider first the regression analysis for men's basketball coaches in 2005–2006. The results of the most robust linear model were the following:

Where BKGuarComp denotes a coach's guaranteed compensation for teams in the March Madness tournament in 2005–2006,[14] BCSConf is a dummy variable equaling 1 if the school plays in one of the six BCS conferences,[15] WinPct is the team's win percentage in 2005–2006, Rec10Yr is the team's win percentage over the last ten years, ConfChamp is a dummy variable equaling 1 if the team came in first in its conference in 2005–2006, MarchMad is a dummy variable equaling 1 if the team was among the sixty-five schools participating in the year-end tournament, Sweet 16 is a dummy variable equaling 1 if the team made it to the final sixteen teams in this tournament, and Finals is a dummy variable equaling 1 if the team made it to the finals in this tournament. Only BCSConf and Rec10Yr are statistically significant at the 10 percent level. Each of these variables represents characteristics of the school's historical standing, rather than its current performance.

The various measurements of the team's current performance, more directly connected to the coach's efforts than the school's conference or its ten-year record, do not come close to significance at the 10 percent level.

In fifty-four of the seventy-five schools, I was able to confirm the starting date and length of the coach's contract, and, hence, was able to consider the coach's performance over the span of his contract, rather than just the current year. When this variable was included (and the sample size reduced to fifty-four), it was not significant at the 10 percent level.[16]

The regression was modified to include dummies for each of the rounds of the March Madness tournament as well as other performance measures, but none of the added variables were significant or added to the explained variance. It was also modified to take natural logs of the independent and (non-binary) dependent variables and the explained variance and significant variables remained the same. Finally, the regressions were run again using BKMaxComp as the dependent variable.[17] BKMaxComp represents BKGuarComp plus all the yearly bonuses in the coach's contract and the amortized value of any one-time longevity bonuses. The pattern of significant variables remained the same, though the explained variance (adjusted R^2) dropped four points.

Table 21.4 Dependent Variable: FTEstComp Adj R^2 = .59, $n = 1$

Independent Variable	Coefficient	t-statistic	p-value
Constant	−282,137	−1.42	0.16
WinPct	−24,235	−0.07	0.94
Rec10Yr	2,517,515	3.98	0.00
ConfChamp	193,056	0.98	0.33
BCSBowl	312,562	1.30	0.20
BCSConf	943,644	8.13	0.00
TRec3YrBCC	−897,627	−2.05	0.04

Descriptive Statistics for Cross Section Analysis

Variable	Obs	Mean	St. Dev.	Min. Value	Max. Value
BK GuarComp	75	$731,758	$472,336	$99,000	$2,073,307
FT GuarComp	109	$1,060,880	$792,645	$144,225	$4,048,571
FT EstComp	109	$1,142,196	$838,466	$171,042	$4,272,071
FT ConfChamp	109	119	326	0	1
FT BCSBowl	109	.073	.262	0	1
TRec3YrBCC	106	.457	.180	.119	.863

It is important to recall that these tests are based on the sixty-five schools in the March tournament, augmented by an additional fifteen schools for which I was able to procure data about coaches' compensation.[18] As such, my sample is skewed toward the more successful programs and, hence, probably reduces the correlation between a team's performance and its coach's compensation. Nonetheless, the historical variables remain significant determinants of a coach's salary. In contrast, the data set for football coaches includes over 90 percent of all FBS programs, so it does not suffer from this possible bias.

Football Head Coaches

Consider next the result for football head coaches during the academic year 2006–2007 in Division 1A.

Where FTEstComp is the coach's estimated compensation during 2006–2007,[19] WinPct is the team's win percentage in that year, Rec10Yr is the team's average win percentage over the last ten years, ConfChamp is a dummy variable equal to one if the team came in first place in its conference in 2006–2007, BCSBowl is a dummy variable equal to one if the team played in a BCS bowl game in 2006–2007, BCSConf is a dummy variable equal to one if the team was in one of the six BCS conferences and TRec3YrBCC is the team's average win percentage during its three years immediately before the current coach was hired. The results echo those for basketball coaches' salaries. The variables representing the team's current performance (WinPct, ConfChamp, BCSBowl) do not come close to statistical significance. In contrast, the variable representing the team's history (Rec10Yr, BCSConf) are both highly statistically significant (at the .01 level), with the expected sign. Lastly, the TRec3YrBCC variable is significant at the .05 level with a negative sign, indicating that teams that were performing more poorly were more anxious to hire a top coach to reverse the team's fortunes, and, hence, other things equal, paid more for the coach. Again, as in basketball, paying more for a coach is not correlated with better current year performance.

It is also interesting to note that despite the fact that football revenues in DIA average approximate 3.2 times higher than basketball revenues, for the teams in my samples football coaches' average guaranteed compensation ($1.06 million in 2006–2007) was only 44.8 percent above that of basketball coaches' average guaranteed compensation ($731,758 in 2005–2006).[20] In this regard as well, it appears that a coach's compensation does not reflect his revenue contribution to the team.

When the foregoing model is run using FTGuarComp as the dependent variable, rather than FTEstComp, the results are almost identical. The adjusted R^2 falls by less than one point and the same variables remain significant.

Further, the inference that it is the historical characteristics of the institution rather than a coach's performance that drives salary level is reinforced when the model is expanded to include the coach's record in the prior year (regardless of whether it was with current team) and the coach's record during his entire contract.[21] Because data for these variables was not available for all teams, the number of observations drops to eighty. Neither of these new variables comes close to statistical significance, and the same pattern of significance remains for the original variables.

Panel Data, 2001–2007

Finally, I assembled a longitudinal data set for the fiscal years 2001 through 2007 for both basketball and football coaches from schools in the six Bowl Championship Series (BCS) conferences. This data set has the advantage of covering multiple years (and, hence, contains more total observations, $n = 241$ for basketball and $n = 274$ for football), but, due to data limitations, the number of observations in each year is reduced. I ran fixed effects models that control for the institution (university). The basic model for

Table 21.5 Descriptive Statistics for Panel Data

Variable	Obs	Mean	Std Dev	Min. Value	Max. Value
BKCOMP	241	$896,875	$534,511	$26,550	$3,089,017
BK Revenues	299	$7,229,919	$3,913,627	$551	$23,320,000
BK Expenses	299	$2,924,524	$1,804,218	−$502,010	$22,900,000
FTCOMP	274	$1,315,281	$812,285	$115,000	$4,440,000
FT Revenues	299	$22,000,000	$13,000,000	0	$66,300,000
FT Expenses	299	$9,739,449	$4,094,532	$587,038	$30,200,000

Note: BK and FT Expenses deduct the head coach's compensation from the EADA reported figures for total expenditures for the sport.

Table 21.6 Fixed Effects: Men's Basketball, 2001–2007

Dependent Variable: BKCOMP

R^2: within = 0.27	No. of observations = 201
between = 0.25	No. of schools = 50
overall = 0.19	Robust standard errors

Independent Variable	Coefficient	*t*-statistic	*p*-value
Constant	199,557	1.08	0.28
TIME	68,727	2.52	0.15
BK Revenues	.011	0.43	0.67
BK Win Pct	186,744	1.18	0.25
BK Lagged Win Pct	370,530	3.16	0.00
New Coach	−46,387	−0.45	0.65

Table 21.7 Fixed Effects: Men's Basketball, 2001–2007

Dependent Variable: WinPct (basketball)

R^2: within = 0.08	No. of observations = 201		
between = 0.38	No. of schools = 50		
overall = 0.24	Robust Standard Errors		

Independent Variable	Coefficient	t-statistic	p-value
Constant	.448	5.55	0.00
BK Revenues	1.14e−08	1.29	0.21
WinPctLagged	.034	0.40	0.69
BKCOMP	2.20e−08	0.50	0.62
New Coach	.062	1.25	0.22
BK Expenses	1.12e−10	0.01	0.99

each sport ran the highest reported coach's salary or COMP (from coaches' contracts and 990 filings)[22] on TIME (2001 = 1, 2002 = 2, etc.), sport revenue (EADA reports[23]), current sport win percentage, lagged sport win percentage, and "New Coach," a variable equaling 0 when there is no change of head coach in the given year,[24] 1 when the school changes the head coach of the team in question and equaling 2 when the school makes such a change a second time in the seven-year period.

When controlling for the school, current year win percentage is not significantly correlated with a coach's compensation, but the previous year's win percentage is. Assuming a roughly thirty-two-game schedule, the coefficient on lagged win percentage indicates that winning all thirty-two games the year before would raise this year's compensation by $370,530 for the fifty institutions included in my sample. Alternatively, for each additional game won by the team the previous year, the coach's compensation would increase by $11,579. Thus, while this variable is statistically significant at the .01 level, the magnitude of its effect is rather small given that the average value of BKCOMP was $896,875 during 2001–2007 for the schools in my sample. It implies that, on average, each additional win increases a coach's compensation the next year by 1.29 percent, or an increase of 10 games in the number of wins, increases a coach's next year salary by only 12.9 percent.

An alternative perspective on this relationship might consider a team's win percentage as the dependent variable and, controlling for other relevant factors, whether it is positively correlated with a coach's compensation.

BK Expenses is the total expenditure (minus the compensation paid to the head coach) on the basketball program in each year, as reported by the schools in their EADA report. None of the independent variables is a statistically significant correlate of a team's win percentage. Higher coach compensation is not associated with a higher win percentage, nor is higher basketball expenses or higher revenues.

Table 21.8 Fixed Effects: Football, 2001–2007

Dependent Variable: FTCOMP

R^2: within = 0.44	No. of observations = 226		
between = 0.24	No. of schools = 58		
overall = 0.26	Robust Standard Errors		

Independent Variable	Coefficient	t-statistic	p-value
Constant	493,632	1.93	0.06
TIME	102,327	4.08	0.00
FT Revenues	.024	2.26	0.03
WinPct	−404,329	−2.13	0.04
WinPctLagged	58,329	0.45	0.66
New Coach	2,632	0.03	0.98

Interestingly, the team's previous year's win percentage is not significantly correlated with the current year's with these control variables.[25] Because of the possibility that collinearity among some independent variables is yielding insignificant coefficients, I tested this model several times, dropping first BK Revenues, then WinPctLagged, then BK Expenses, and in each model the BKCOMP coefficient remained insignificant at the .01, .05 and .10 levels.

The results for football suggest in stronger terms that higher coaches' salaries are not associated with higher win percentages, other things equal. Indeed, the coefficient on WinPct is significant and negative, indicating an inverse relationship between performance and pay, whereas the coefficient on WinPctLagged

Table 21.9 Fixed Effects: Football, 2001–2007

Dependent Variable: WinPct (football)

R^2: within = 0.10	No. of observations = 226		
between = 0.02	No. of schools = 58		
overall = 0.04	Robust Standard Errors		

Independent Variable	Coefficient	t-statistic	p-value
Constant	.512	6.19	0.00
FT Revenues	3.13e-09	1.21	0.23
FT Expenses	1.04e-08	2.19	0.03
WinPctLagged	.077	1.04	0.30
FTCOMP	−1.05e-08	−2.79	0.01
New Coach	−.036	−0.83	0.41

is not significant. The negative coefficient on WinPct in theory could reflect a strong positive correlation FT Revenues and WinPct, but the correlation coefficient between the two variables is only 0.45. In the case of football, a new coach is not associated with a higher compensation level.

These results largely mirror those in Table 21.6, with the addendum that higher football expenditures are associated with a higher win percentage in the current year at the .05 level of statistical significance. (As with BK Expenses, the compensation of the head coach has been deducted.) When FT Expenses and FT Revenues are dropped as independent variables, the coefficient on FTCOMP remains negative but its p-value falls to 0.136.[26]

CONCLUSION

In this chapter I have reviewed the history of Title IX. Although Title IX has helped to promote enormous gains for women in intercollegiate athletics, there is still a strong and well-organized opposition to its advance. Given the demonstrated physical, emotional, academic and career benefits associated with women participating in school sports, it is important to continue to push gender equal opportunity in this area. In 2007, women constituted 56 percent of undergraduate students, but less than 43 percent of intercollegiate athletes.

The question thus emerges: If gender equity is to move forward, from where will the resources come? I have argued that it is possible to obtain large resources from reducing the waste and inefficiency in men's programs. One area of extravagant and unnecessary expenditures is in the compensation packages of head coaches in men's basketball and football. Not only do such astronomical remuneration levels engender an ethical issue, they are also superfluous to the efficient allocation of resources. I have conducted a variety of statistical tests which all lend support to the claim that higher coaches' salaries are not associated with higher levels of team success. Beyond that, it is clear that the lion's share of head coach compensation constitutes economic rent.

If the Bear Bryant rule were followed—not paying head coaches more than the university president, universities could save millions of dollars in their athletic budgets.[27] A typical Division 1, non-revenue intercollegiate sports team costs a couple of hundred thousand dollars to support. Several such teams could be added and there still would be savings leftover to reduce the university subsidy to athletics.

The obvious hurdle to such a policy is the inevitable confrontation with the nation's antitrust laws. The NCAA already saw its limitation on payment to the fourth basketball coach rejected by the courts in *Law v. NCAA*. Although the NCAA may be able to defend a restriction on head coaches' salaries on the grounds that it is necessary to preserve the amateur branding and financial viability of intercollegiate sports (rule of reason), the more prudent course would be for the association to go to Congress to ask for an antitrust exemption. There would be no good reason for Congress to reject such an appeal.

The problem is motivating the NCAA, which essentially functions as a trade association for coaches, athletic directors, and conference commissioners, to make this appeal. They would be legislating lower salaries for themselves.

The good news is that there are many sources of waste in intercollegiate athletic departments and, hence, various opportunities to free up resources. In the end, Title IX needs to advance. As with all social progress, however, it will take the political will and organization to achieve the goal of equal athletic opportunity for men and women.

NOTES

The author wishes to thank Leigha Miyata for superb research assistance.

1 A study published by the Women's Sports Foundation ("Her Life Depends On It," May 2004) elaborates on some of the benefits from sports participation.

- Breast Cancer Risk: One to three hours of exercise a week over a woman's reproductive lifetime (the teens to about age 40) may bring a 20–30 percent reduction in the risk of breast cancer, and four or more hours of exercise a week can reduce the risk almost 60 percent. L. Bernstein, B. Henderson, R. Hanisch, J. Sullivan-Halley, and R. Ross, "Physical Exercise and Reduced Risk of Breast Cancer in Young Women," *Journal of the National Cancer Institute* 86 (1994): 1403–1408.
- Smoking: Female athletes on one or two school or community sports teams were significantly less likely to smoke regularly than female nonathletes. Girls on three or more teams were even less likely to smoke regularly. M.J. Melnick, K.E. Miller, D. Sabo, M.P. Farrell, and G.M. Barnes, "Tobacco Use Among High School Athletes and Nonathletes: Results of the 1997 Youth Risk Behavior Survey," *Adolescence* 36 (2001): 727–747.
- Illicit Drug Use: Two nationwide studies found that female school or community athletes were significantly less likely to use marijuana, cocaine or most other illicit drugs, although they were no less likely to use crack or inhalants. This protective effect of sports was especially true for white girls. K. E. Miller, D. Sabo, J. J. Melnick, M. P. Farrell, and G. M. Barnes, *Health Risks and the Teen Athlete*. The Women's Sports Foundation Report (East Meadow, NY, 2000).
- Sexual Risk: Female athletes are less likely to be sexually active, in part because they tend to be more concerned about getting pregnant than female non-athletes. T. Dodge, and J. Jaccard, "Participation in Athletics and Female Sexual Risk Behavior: The Evaluation of Four Causal Structures," *Journal of Adolescent Research* 17 (2002): 42–67.
- Depression: Women and girls who participate in regular exercise suffer lower rates of depression. G. Nicoloff, and T. S. Schwenk, "Using Exercise to Ward Off Depression," *Physician Sports Medicine* 23 (1995): 44–58. R. M. Page and

L.A. Tucker, "Psychosocial Discomfort and Exercise Frequency: An Epidemiological Study of Adolescents," *Adolescence* 29(1994):183–191.

- Suicide: Female high school athletes, especially those participating on three or more teams, have lower odds of considering or planning a suicide attempt. D. Sabo, K. E. Miller, M. J. Melnick, M. P. Farrell, and G. M. Barnes, "High School Athletic Participation and Adolescent Suicide: A Nationwide Study," *International Review for the Sociology of Sport* (2004).
- Educational Gains: The positive educational impacts of school sports were just as strong for girls as for boys including self-concept, educational aspirations in the senior year, school attendance, math and science enrollment, time spent on homework, and taking honors courses. H. W. Marsh, "The Effects of Participation in Sport During the Last Two Years of High School," *Sociology of Sport Journal* 10 (1993): 18–43.
- A 2008 survey by Harris Interactive of over 2,000 3rd through 12th graders also finds significant psychological and social benefits from participation in organized sports. *Go Out and Play: Youth Sports in America.* Women's Sports Foundation, October 2008.

2 HEW was the Department of Health, Education and Welfare, which, in 1980, was divided into two cabinet level departments, the Department of Health and Human Services and the Department of Education.

3 Clearly, a precise determination of whether or not the underrepresented gender is being provided equal opportunity will be elusive. The three-pronged test, where only one prong must be met for their to be a subjective determination that equal opportunity is being provided, was subject to an extensive period of public comment before it was promulgated. Since its promulgation, it has been extensively tested (and upheld) in the courts.

4 NCAA, *Gender Equity Report, 2005–06.* October 2008, pp. 5, 10, 22.

5 In 2007, there were 4.32 million boys participating in high school athletics (www.nfhs. org/custom/participation_figures/default.aspx, accessed January 1, 2009); thus, girls constituted 41.1 percent of all high school athletes—a slightly lower proportion than at the college level. The conversion of high school athletes into college athletes, then, was slightly more efficient for females than males. One possible inference here is that the provision of equal opportunity for female athletes in high school was more deficient at the secondary school, than the university, level.

6 General Accounting Office (GAO). *Intercollegiate Athletics: Recent Trends in Teams and Participants in NCAA Sports.* Retrieved February 22, 2008, from www.gao.gov/new.items/d07535.pdf.

7 To be sure, there are some methodological issues that render the number of male and female participants less than perfectly precise. The GAO corrects for some of these issues. Other issues, such as, when the schools count the number of athletes in each sport (e.g., when the team is first selected at the beginning of the season, at midseason or at season's end), remain because schools follow different practices. But there is no evidence that suggests such irregularities bias the reported statistics in favor of one gender or the other.

8 Teams are also allowed to carry up to eight additional players on their practice squad.

9 NCAA, *Gender Equity Report, 2005–06.* (October 2008): 27.

10 The sources for these figures are discussed in the statistical section that follows.

11 James Johnson, "The Suicide Season," *The Shreveport Times*, September 4, 2008.

12 Allen Barra, *The Last Coach: A Life of Paul "Bear" Bryant.* (New York: W. W. Norton, 2005).

13 The data for basketball coaches' salaries comes from a variety of sources. *USA Today* published an extensive survey of the head coaches of the 65 teams that participated in the March tournament in 2006. It included access to the actual contracts, at http://www.usatoday.com/sports/college/mensbasketball/2007–03–08-coaches-salarycover_N.htm. These data were supplemented by making freedom of information act requests to the other Division 1A schools and, in a few cases, with data from the 990 tax forms filed by nonprofits, which are available at www.guidestar.org. (Only in the roughly ten cases in which the athletic department is run by a separate foundation do the 990 forms contain coach compensation information. Even in these instances, the data is often partial. Typically, because coaches receive the bulk of their pay from third parties, they do not figure among the top-five salaried employees paid by the university. All told, we assembled men's basketball coach compensation data for 75 schools. The data for football coaches' salaries in 2006–2007 comes from http://www.usatoday.com/sports/college/football/2007–12–04-coaches-pay_N.htm, which also provided access to actual contracts. These data were supplemented in the same manner as were the basketball coaches' contracts and together include data for 109 Division 1A head coaches. Further, by obtaining earlier contracts, we were able to assemble an annual data set for football and basketball coaches going back to 2000–2001. This panel data set encompasses a more restricted set of schools, including 274 observations for football coaches and 241 for basketball coaches over seven years.

14 Includes base salary, annualized deferred payments, annuities, and contractual expense accounts.

15 These conferences, whose champions are guaranteed an appearance in one of the five annual BCS bowl games are: ACC, Big East, Big Ten, Big 12, Pac10, and SEC. Together these Division 1A conferences include 73 universities.

16 Because of possible collinearity between the coach's record over the life of his current contract and the team's ten-year record, I ran this regression with and without the team's ten-year record and the coach's record during his contract was not statistically significant in either case.

17 For the seventy-five schools in my sample, the mean value of BKMaxComp was $937,834, with a minimum value of $104,300 and a maximum value of $3.37 million.

18 Five of the sixty-five schools did not provide coach's contracts or compensation data to *USA Today,* to me, or on their Form 990s.

19 Estimated compensation is the guaranteed compensation plus 30 percent of potential bonuses.

20 To be sure, in a more limited sample of forty-five schools, the average compensation of basketball coaches increased 24.5 percent between 2005–2006 and 2006–2007. On this basis, football coaches' average compensation was only 16.4 percent higher than men's basketball coaches in 2006–2007.

21 Again, these variables were added together and separately to adjust for the possibility of collinearity producing imprecision in the standard errors.

22 I took the highest reported because some reports only listed the coach's base salary or that part of his compensation that was paid directly by the university, as opposed to being paid by third parties (such as marketing agencies or sneaker companies). For this variable, I also assumed that all bonuses were earned. Again, these contracts were procured either from FOIA requests or from the *USA Today* data bank. The

compensation variable in the longitudinal set is slightly different than that used in the cross-sectional tests because not all the data was available for all the years.

23 EADA stands for Equity in Athletics Disclosure Act. Universities to the Department of Education have filed these reports annually since the mid-1990s, pursuant to the monitoring of Title IX's progress.

24 Where there is a change in head coach during a season, this variable is also given a value of 0.

25 The simple correlation coefficient between WinPct and WinPctLagged in basketball is 0.51.

26 My results here are consistent with those found in a study performed for the NCAA by Robert Litan, Jonathan Orszag, and Peter Orszag, "The Empirical Effects of Collegiate Athletics: An Interim Report," August 2003 (http://ncaa.org/databases/ baselinestudy/baseline.pdf), section 4 and appendix I. The authors use fixed effects models for Division 1A football and find: no association between team spending and net revenue; no statistically significant relationship between spending and winning; no statistically significant relationship between winning and revenue; and, a low correlation of a team's win percentage from one year to the next.

27 It is, of course, possible that if coaches' compensation was capped, the athletic departments would simply use the savings to seek other ways to attract the best athletes to the school (e.g., hiring more coaches, providing yet fancier facilities and travel amenities, etc.) Although some such squandering of resources may occur, it is also likely that universities would be better able to control these forms of expenditure than they are coaches' salaries.

PART V

ECONOMICS OF MEGA EVENTS

CHAPTER 22

ECONOMICS OF THE OLYMPICS

PETER DAWSON

> Holding an Olympic Games means evoking history.
> —Pierre de Coubertin

The Olympic Games are truly a global event and are considered the most prestigious multi-sport event in the world. The Games of the XXIX Olympiad, held in Beijing, attracted competitors from over 200 nations who competed in over 300 events, ranging from archery to Greco-Roman wrestling.[1] It was the most watched sports event in history, enabling viewers to watch events on a variety of media platforms (TV, via video content on the Internet and on mobile phones). The American network NBC Universal provided a total of 3,600 hours of coverage across TV and the Internet and in the UK it had been reported that 41.1 million (approximately 67 percent of the population) had watched at least fifteen minutes of the BBC's Olympic broadcast. By way of contrast, the 1948 London Olympics were watched by an estimated 500,000 viewers, mostly residing within a fifty-mile radius of London.

Given the plethora of coverage associated with the Olympics, it comes with very little surprise that corporations are willing to pay vast sums of money to sponsor the Games (Preuss, 2004). The Olympic Partner Programme (TOP), introduced by the International Olympic Committee (IOC) in 1985, is the most lucrative, and currently includes multinational companies such as the fast-food chain McDonalds, the Coca-Cola Company and Visa International. TOP companies are granted exclusive worldwide marketing rights to both Winter and Summer Games and provide the third largest source of revenue to the IOC (see Table 22.1).

Table 22.1 Total Revenue Generated by the Olympics 1993–2004

Revenue Source	1993–1996	1997–2000	2001–2004
Broadcast	1,251,000,000	1,845,000,000	2,232,000,000
TOP Programme	279,000,000	579,000,000	663,000,000
Domestic Sponsorship	534,000,000	655,000,000	796,000,000
Ticketing	451,000,000	625,000,000	411,000,000
Licensing	115,000,000	66,000,000	87,000,000
Total	2,630,000,000	3,770,000,000	4,189,000,000

Source: Olympic Marketing Factfile (2008 edition). Figures quoted in U.S. dollars (rounded up).

Table 22.1 also highlights that broadcasting provides the single largest source of revenue to the Games and has largely been responsible for the commercialization of the Olympics in much the same way as it has in other major professional sports over the last twenty-five years. The value of TV rights has increased exponentially. The amount paid by American broadcaster NBC to secure the rights for the Beijing Olympics was $893 million, and represented a threefold increase on the amount paid by ABC for the 1984 Los Angeles Olympics. Over the same period, the European Broadcasting Union (EBU) experienced a twentyfold increase in the value of the rights fee.

The 1984 Summer Olympics held in Los Angeles is often highlighted as a watershed in the development of the Games. Previously the common perception was that hosting the Olympics would leave the host region servicing a significant amount of debt and, following the colossal debts associated with the 1976 Montreal Olympics, only two cities—Los Angeles and New York City—expressed an interest in hosting the 1984 Games.[2] Los Angeles was chosen, and by using existing arenas to minimize the need for new stadiums managed to generate a profit of more than $200 million.

Nowadays, competition to host the Olympics is fierce. The competition to host the 2012 Summer Olympics involved nine candidate cities officially recognized by the International Olympic Committee (IOC) and a further twenty-six cities who had reportedly expressed a desire to host the Games. On July 6, 2005 the International Olympic Committee (IOC), having by this stage reduced the number of candidate cities from nine to five, chose London as the host for the XXX Olympiad, to be held in 2012.

The focus of this chapter is on the impact of Olympics. First, an overview of the literature on the impact of the Olympics is presented. Essentially two strands to the literature are identified: one based on the economic impact associated with tangible effects, such as employment, consumption, and GDP. This area is well developed and a substantial body of literature exists. The second strand is based on discussions and measurement of intangible effects. In this area the literature remains relatively sparse.

The second part of the chapter presents empirical findings relating to the announcement effect associated with the Olympics, using London 2012 as a case study. Original research based on the impact of the 2012 announcement on participation rates in sport and physical activity in the UK is included.

Background

Together with the soccer World Cup (see Simmons and Deutscher, chapter 23 of this volume) the Olympic Games are considered to be highly prized assets with host countries spending vast sums of money in developing infrastructure and stadiums. In the case of London, initial estimates placed the total cost of hosting the event at £2.4 billion. By March 2007, it was reported that the total cost had quadrupled to around £9.3 billion ($15.4 billion). Such dramatic increases, however, are not unusual: the cost of both the Sydney and Athens Olympics were double the initial projections whereas the cost of the Barcelona Olympics increased fivefold over an eight-year period. Precise estimates of the 2008 Beijing Olympics are difficult to obtain. Official sources claim the total cost is comparable to the Athens Olympics; other sources suggest the true cost is closer to $40 billion (Leeds et al., 2009). In contrast, the 1984 Los Angeles Olympics cost just $546 million.

Is the quest for major sporting events such as the Olympics the "holy grail" people perceive them to be? Urban planners and policy makers typically view the Olympic Games as the catalyst for urban and, increasingly, environmental improvement and argue that, despite the costs, significant economic benefits will accrue. In their Bid Books for 2012, London and Paris identified significant economic impact. In the case of London, it was said that:

> Every sector of the economy will benefit from the staging of the Olympic Games. The recently approved planning application for the Olympic Park predicted the need for 7,000 full-time equivalent jobs in the construction industry alone and assumed that around 12,000 jobs could be created as a result of the legacy development of the Olympic Park area. While many of the economic benefits will accrue to the Lea Valley, the whole of the UK will gain from the prosperity generated by the Olympic Games.

Similarly the Paris document claimed:

- The impact of the Games will be significant:
- from 2005 to 2012 there will be a USD 7.2 billion (EUR 6 billion) direct economic impact, with immediate effects on tourism, the sport-related economy, entertainment and construction industries. Additionally the equivalent of 60,000 jobs per year will be created;
- from 2012 to 2019, there will be a USD 42 billion (EUR 35 billion) additional economic impact, resulting from an additional 7 million tourists annually 4 million new people playing sport on a regular basis, and the creation of 42,000 permanent jobs.

The academic literature has generally been sceptical over claims such as these and in the legitimacy of using public subsidies to contribute toward costs (Baade, 2007). Focusing on the 1984 Los Angeles and 1996 Atlanta Summer Olympics, Baade and Matheson (2002) found the (ex-post) impact on unemployment in both regions were entirely transitory and concluded that long-run changes in steady-state equilibrium were only possible when new infrastructure and facilities were appropriate for the present and future economy. These results contrast to the work of Economics Research Associates (1984) and Humphreys and Plummer (1995) who had predicted positive results on an ex-ante basis for Los Angeles and Atlanta, respectively. Studies by Madden (2006) and Giesecke and Madden (2007) conclude that initial ex-ante assessments of the impact of the 2000 Sydney Olympics overestimated the financial gain because the assumptions relating to induced tourism and the responsiveness of the labor market were overly optimistic.

The main approach to assessing the economic impact of major sporting events, such as the Olympics, involves the measurement of multiplier effects. The multiplier works on the principle that initial (direct) spending in the local economy leads to further (indirect and induced) spending. Typically, the multiplier is calculated using macroeconomic models, of which input-output (I-O) and computable general equilibrium (CGE) are the most common.[3] The basic principle of these models is to trace the flows of expenditure between the various sectors of the economy and provide estimates of the effect on income, output, and jobs. In the absence of detailed disaggregated data, a third approach, the development of small macroeconometric models, has been recently added to the literature (see, for example, Kasimati and Dawson, 2009).

Typical values for the multiplier tend to lie within the 1.5–3 range, although relatively small changes can lead to substantial differences in the impact on output and employment. The misapplication of the multiplier has been seen by many commentators (Crompton, 1995; Matheson, 2006) as the main reason for the exaggerated benefits often associated with studies carried out on behalf of organizing committees or local chambers of commerce.

An alternative approach to impact assessment is to use retrospective (ex-post) econometric analysis. This involves the construction of regression equations in which employment or GDP figures are used as the dependent variable.[4] A number of explanatory variables are included to explain the variation in the dependent variable. These include population size, per capita income, and wage rates, and the impact of the Olympics is captured through the inclusion of a dummy dichotomous variable. Baade and Matheson (2002) applied this methodology to assess employment changes from the Los Angeles (1984) and Atalanta (1996) Olympics.[5] A European perspective is provided by Jasmand and Maennig (2008), based on the 1972 Munich Olympics.

Academic interest has also been directed toward the impact of the announcement of the Olympics on the stock market. Event analysis studies have been carried out on Sydney (Berman et al. 2000), Athens (Veraros et al. 2004), and Beijing (Leeds et al. 2009).[6] Veraros et al. and Leeds et al. find an immediate positive (but ultimately short-lived) impact for the overall market index. Neither study finds a statistically negative effect on the stock market on the main rival competing for the prize. Leeds et al. suggest the modest, short-term impact is reminiscent of the winner's curse: The "successful" recipient of the Games is often the one with the most optimistic expectations, and it is possible that the market quickly realized that the bid was more about winning the prize than any tangible gains associated with employment and tourism.

Another approach has been offered by Rose and Spiegel (2011) who look at the impact of the Olympics on export trade patterns. Using a cross-country cross-event (i.e., Summer and Winter Olympics) comparison for the period 1950–2006, a positive effect is found for both host and candidate countries, and the effect is robust across a variety of specifications that account for both endogeneity and sample selection effects. The comparability of magnitudes implies there is no obvious gain in trade for the host over other countries bidding to stage the event. This, they argue, implies that the bidding process essentially acts as a signaling device toward trade liberalization.

The focal point of all of these studies is on measurable (or tangible) outcomes. Claims that major sporting events such as the Olympics can provide important intangible benefits, such as civic pride and community spirit, generating psychic income to residents within the host region have come to prominence in the last 10 years or so and have featured frequently in policy documentation. A typology of intangible benefits and costs is provided in Table 22.2. The consideration of intangible effects provide an additional set of factors which policy-makers can, and have, used to justify the hosting of major sporting events. The potential importance of intangible effects has been acknowledged in the academic literature but remain difficult to quantify.

Table 22.2 Typology of Intangible Benefits and Subjective Costs

Intangible Benefits

Uniting people / Feel good factor / National pride	Anticipation of event (excitement of event, boosting nation's morale and image), excitement during the event (flags displayed, people watching and talking about events together, increased medal success for national athletes, national heroes), shared memories after the event
Motivating / Inspiring children	Inspiring children to play sports, sports champions as role models
Legacy of sports facilities	Local facilities for children, new stadiums and sports venues continuing to be used after the event
Environmental improvements	Speeding up planned environmental regeneration, creation of new green spaces and recreational areas.
Promoting healthy living	Promoting healthy diet and nutrition, benefits of sports and outdoor activities
Cultural and social events	Other (non-sport) cultural and social activities accompanying the event

(Continued)

Table 22.2 (*Continued*)

Intangible Costs	
Crowding	In streets, transport, public spaces, restaurants, and pubs during the event
Crime	Increased risk of petty crime
Safety and security	Risks associated with potential terrorist activities
Local disruption during construction phase	Congestion, pollution around construction sites
Transport delays	
Excessive (or negative) media coverage	Saturated coverage and / or presence of scandals

Source: Adapted from Atkinson et al. (2008). We could describe equally some or all of these intangible benefits (costs) as subjective measures or measures that are difficult to quantify.

One attempt to generate monetary estimates of intangible effects that has recently been applied to major sporting events such as the Olympics is the contingent valuation method (CVM).[7] Atkinson et al. (2008) sampled households in London, Manchester and Glasgow whilst Walton et al. (2008) surveyed individuals in the city of Bath. Despite differences in survey mode, method of elicitation and statistical methods, both estimate the total value of intangibles to be in the region of £2 billion.

But what can be said of the importance attached to specific intangible effects? Some ranking analysis based on the subjective judgements of respondents is provided in Atkinson et al. (2008) and reproduced in Table 22.3.

The benefit associated with uniting people/feel-good factor/national pride generated high scores in all three regions, although, in the case of London, the mean score for motivating/inspiring children was higher. There was also importance attached to the legacy of sports facilities. On the cost side, transport delays and increased safety and security risks appeared to be the main concerns.

Empirical analysis associated with specific intangible effects have recently appeared in the literature. In the first example of its kind, Kavetsos and Szymanski (2010) focus on the link between happiness and major sporting events. Using happiness data from the Eurobarometer Surveys for twelve countries over the period 1974–2004, two hypotheses are tested: (1) better than expected national athletic performance increases happiness; (2) hosting major sporting events increases happiness. The dataset is applied to both soccer tournaments (World Cups and European Championships) and the Olympics. The results provide some qualified support that hosting major soccer tournaments increases happiness, but the effect appears to be transitory. No significant effect is associated with better-than-expected performance in the Olympics whereas no definitive conclusions can be made on the impact of hosting the Olympics because only one observation (Barcelona, 1992) is included.

Table 22.3 Importance of Intangible Effects Associated with Hosting
the 2012 Olympics

Category of Intangible Impact	London	Manchester	Glasgow
Benefits			
Motivating / Inspiring children	18.85	16.54	18.68
Uniting people / Feel good factor / National pride	16.87	18.01	17.59
Legacy of sports facilities	16.07	16.62	16.52
Environmental improvements	13.94	14.69	10.55
Improving awareness of disability	13.77	14.68	13.97
Promoting healthy living	11.94	11.87	13.57
Cultural and social events	8.39	7.57	9.47
Costs			
Transport delays	20.24	18.69	15.57
Increased safety and security risks	18.88	18.20	23.18
crowding	17.64	17.74	17.65
Local disruption During construction	17.17	18.80	15.09
Increased risk of petty theft	16.25	16.47	17.45
Excessive media coverage	8.75	8.84	10.41

Source: Adapted from Atkinson et al. (2008). Respondents were asked to assign each benefit (cost) a score out of 100. Cell entries represent mean scores.

There is also a limited amount of literature relating participation in sport and physical activity with major sporting events. As part of an investigation into sources of data on leisure and leisure trends over time, Veal (2003) estimates the impact of the Sydney Olympics on Australian sporting participation. The findings suggest that seven Olympic sports experienced a small increase in participation (running, soccer, and basketball) but there was a noticeable decline in nine other sports (including cycling, swimming, and tennis). Veal argues that the extent to which these changes are attributable to the Olympics is difficult because of methodological changes to the survey before and after the Games. Murphy and Bauman (2007) cite work by the Australian Bureau of Statistics and Australian Sports Commission, who also analyzed trends in physical activity before and after the Sydney Olympics, and they conclude there was no significant change in levels of physical activity.

In the following section, after a brief discussion of existing literature relating to the impact of the 2012 announcement, new findings are presented that attempt to assess the impact of the 2012 announcement on sporting participation in the UK.

The Impact of the 2012 Announcement: Existing Literature

As previously detailed, the announcement that London was to be awarded the 2012 Summer Olympics was made on July 6, 2005. This section reviews two studies that have analyzed the impact of the announcement.

The Impact on the London and Paris Stock Exchanges

In the immediate aftermath of the announcement, there were notable gains on the London Stock Exchange experienced by companies in the construction sector and the leisure and hospitality sectors. In contrast, French stocks in a number of construction and hotel groups fell. Unfortunately, an event analysis of the impact on the stock market is complicated because of the terrorist attacks on London, which were carried out on the morning of July 7, 2005, the day after the announcement.

In order to distinguish the impact associated with terrorist attacks from the impact associated with the announcement, Kavestos and Szymanski (2008) include decaying specifications for both the announcement and terrorist effects. The estimation of Auto-Regressive Conditional Heteroskedasticity (ARCH) and Generalized-ARCH models indicate a positive effect associated with the announcement and negative effect associated with the terrorist attacks on the British Indices. A negative effect relating to the terrorist attacks is also observed on a number of French markets. The positive effect associated with the Olympic announcement on many of the French markets appears surprising, but as Kavetsos and Szymanski (2008) argue, it can be explained by the correlated nature of international markets. However, the specifications are sensitive to the index chosen, and the magnitudes, in general, appear to be very small.

Impact on London House Prices

In a similar manner, Kavetsos (forthcoming) also considers the impact of the Olympic Games announcement on residential property prices in London. The approach was to establish the contribution of intangible effects associated with peoples' demand to live in areas close to the site of the Olympic stadium. Previous studies on franchise (Carlino and Carlson, 2004; Tu, 2005) and venue location (Dehring et al. 2007) in American sports suggest positive externalities exist, particularly for properties located closer to the stadium. The extent to which these increases are attributable to notions of civic pride and such represents a further way of estimating intangible effects associated with sporting events.

Controlling for dwelling and neighborhood characteristics, Kavetsos finds that there was indeed a positive, and statistically significant, reaction on residential property prices in the area immediate surrounding the proposed area for the Olympic stadium. Moreover, the investigation also constructs radius rings in order to establish whether the effect on house prices diminishes the further away they are from the epicenter. The results of difference-in-difference hedonic price equations suggest a premium of 3.3 percent is paid on properties in the host boroughs relative to other (non-host) boroughs. Based on the total housing stock and the average property price, the total monetary contribution is estimated to be around £1.4 billion or 15 percent of the current cost.

The Impact of the 2012 Announcement on Leisure Participation in the UK

This section considers the impact of the Olympic announcement on participation in sport and physical activities in the UK and represents, to the best of the author's knowledge, a first attempt to link participation with the Olympic announcement using econometric methods.

Data

In estimating the empirical relationship between participation in sport and physical activity and the 2012 Olympic announcement, longitudinal data from the British Household Panel Survey (BHPS) is used. The BHPS is an annual household survey that commenced in 1991.[8] For the purpose of this study, the sample period 1996–2006 is used. Unlike other surveys, which carry questions on sport and leisure participation (such as the General Household Survey), the BHPS has the advantage of allowing one to track the same individuals enabling the analyst to control for unobserved individual heterogeneity.

The BHPS since Wave 6 (1996) has included questions relating to sport and leisure participation. Questions on leisure participation are part of the set of rotating core questions and are included in the questionnaire every other year. Respondents are asked the following:

> We are interested in the things people do in their leisure time, I'm going to read out a list of some leisure activities. Please look at the card and tell me how frequently you do each one.

Several activities are listed, including frequency of visits to the cinema, theatre, meals out, and voluntary work. The interest here is the response to the question relating to how often the individual plays sports or goes walking or swimming. The outcome variable has the following categories: At least once a week /at least once a month/several times a year/once a year or less/never, almost never.

Figure 22.1 displays trends in frequency of participation in playing sport or going walking or swimming for the period 1996–2006.[9] The results reveal an

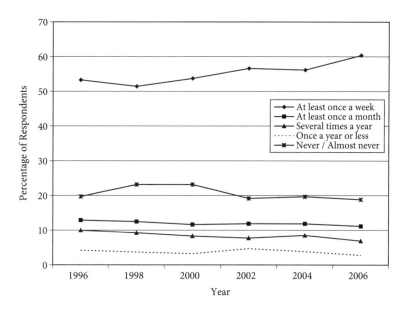

Figure 22.1 Frequency of Participation in Sport and Physical Activities in the UK, 1996–2006.

Table 22.4 Leisure Participation: Transition Probabilities

t *t*-1	At least once a week	At least once a month	Several times a year	Once a year or less	Never/ almost never	Total
At least once a week	78.70	8.80	3.93	1.37	7.20	100
At least once a month	48.92	25.18	12.92	2.69	10.30	100
Several times a year	35.48	18.47	21.60	7.35	17.10	100
Once a year or less	29.84	12.76	12.35	9.47	35.60	100
Never/almost never	25.14	5.60	4.99	3.65	60.62	100
Total	59.40	11.10	7.01	2.78	19.72	100

Note: cell entries represent row percentages.

increase in those respondents whose participation is within the at-least-once-a-week category between 2000 and 2002 and a further increase between 2004 and 2006, and a corresponding decline in the never/almost never category over the same period.

To better exploit the panel nature of the dataset, Table 22.4 presents transition probabilities. A high level of persistence is evident: Over three-quarters of respondents who participate in sports and physical activity at least once a week in one period continue to do so in the following period. Likewise, just over 60 percent of respondents remain in the never/almost-never category across the two periods. There is, however, some movement across categories as revealed by the entries in the off-diagonal cells. In general, around 20 percent of respondents increased their level of participation.

Methodology

To what extent are these increases a consequence of the Olympic announcement effect? In order to test this hypothesis, the following econometric model is estimated:

$$p_{it}^* = x_{it}'\beta + v_{it} \qquad i = 1, 2, \ldots, n \text{ and } t = 1, 2 \ldots, T \qquad (1)$$

$$v_{it} = \alpha_i + u_{it} \qquad (2)$$

The observed dependent variable, p_{it}, is constructed in binary form with:

$$p_{it} = \begin{cases} 1 \text{ if } p_{it}^* > 0 \\ 0 \text{ otherwise} \end{cases}$$

where $p_{it} = 1$ if the respondent participates in sport, goes walking or swimming at least once a week.[10] In equation (1), x_{it} represents exogenous socioeconomic and demographic characteristics affecting participation and v_{it} is an independently and identically distributed error term. In equation (2), α_i denotes the individual-specific but time-invariant unobserved heterogeneity, and u_{it} is a random error term that varies among individuals and across time. Assuming $\alpha_i \sim IIN(0, \sigma_\alpha^2)$ and is independent of both x_{it} and u_{it} leads to a random probit model.

As noted in the previous paragraph, we control for socioeconomic and demographic characteristics of respondents based on previous cross-sectional studies that have analyzed the determinants of participation (Inter alia: Downward and Riordan, 2007; Humphreys and Ruseski, 2007; Farrell and Shields, 2002). Table 22.5 provides a list of the socioeconomic and demographic characteristics included in the model together with their (pooled) sample mean and standard deviation.

The next step is to capture the announcement effect. The simple approach taken here is to augment equation (1) as follows:

$$p_{it}^* = x_{it}'\beta + \lambda z_t + v_{it} \qquad (3)$$

where z_t represents a vector of major-sporting-event dummies. During the sample period, the UK, and England in particular, took part in a number of major

Table 22.5 Variable Labels, Definitions and Summary Statistics (Pooled Adult Data)

Variable Label	Definition	Mean	Standard Deviation
Dependent Variable			
PARTFREQ	1 if does sport, goes walking or swimming at least once a week, 0 otherwise	.556	.497
Explanatory Variables			
AGE1619	1 if the aged between 16 and 19, 0 otherwise	.066	.249
AGE2024	1 if the aged between 20 and 24, 0 otherwise	.081	.273
AGE2529	1 if the aged between 25 and 29, 0 otherwise	.084	.277
AGE3034	1 if the aged between 30 and 34, 0 otherwise	.093	.290
AGE3539	1 if the aged between 35 and 39, 0 otherwise	.101	.301
AGE4044	1 if the aged between 40 and 44, 0 otherwise	.093	.290
AGE4549	1 if the aged between 45 and 49, 0 otherwise	.083	.277
AGE5054	1 if the aged between 50 and 54, 0 otherwise	.080	.271
AGE5559	1 if the aged between 55 and 59, 0 otherwise	.073	.260
AGE6064	1 if the aged between 60 and 64, 0 otherwise	.060	.238
AGE6569	1 if the aged between 65 and 69, 0 otherwise	.052	.223
AGE7074	1 if the aged between 70 and 74, 0 otherwise	.049	.217
MALE	1 if respondent is male	.458	.498
MARRIED	1 if respondent is married, 0 otherwise	.532	.499
SINGLE	1 if respondent has never been married, 0 otherwise	.288	.453
HHSIZE	Number of people in household	2.863	1.394
NCHILD	Number of children in household	.514	.934
DEGREE	1 if respondent has a first or higher degree, 0 otherwise	.124	.330
INCOME	Annual income	12976.7	13260.2
HRSWRK	Number of hours normally worked per week	17.854	18.825
SELFEMPLOY	1 if self-employed, 0 otherwise	.069	.253
EMPLOYED	1 if employee, 0 otherwise	.505	.500
UNEMPLOYED	1 if unemployed, 0 otherwise	.034	.182
RETIRED	1 if retired, 0 otherwise	.205	.403
STUDENT	1 if student, 0 otherwise	.059	.236
CIGS	Usual number of cigarettes smoked per day	3.966	7.930

(Continued)

Table 22.5 (*Continued*)

Variable Label	Definition	Mean	Standard Deviation
GOODHEALTH	1 if respondent's self-reported health status over the last 12 months was good or excellent	.691	.462
VSATISFIED	1 if respondent's overall satisfaction with life is recorded as completely or close to completely satisfied, 0 otherwise	.470	.499
WATCHFREQ	1 if respondent goes to watch live sport at least once a week, 0 otherwise	.061	.240
WATCHNEVER	1 if respondent never or almost never goes to watch live sport, 0 otherwise	.615	.487
LONDON	1 if respondent lives in inner or outer London	.060	.238
SOUTH EAST	1 if respondent lives elsewhere in South East	.130	.336
SOUTH WEST	1 if respondent lives in South West	.064	.244
EAST ANGLIA	1 if respondent lives in East Anglia	.030	.171
EASTMIDS	1 if respondent lives in East Midlands	.059	.236
GREATERMAN	1 if respondent lives in Greater Manchester	.027	.161
MERSEYSIDE	1 if respondent lives in Merseyside	.015	.121
NORTHWEST	1 if respondent lives elsewhere in North West	.032	.176
SYORKSHIRE	1 if respondent lives in South Yorkshire	.018	.133
WYORKSHIRE	1 if respondent lives in West Yorkshire	.023	.150
YORKHUM	1 if respondent lives elsewhere in Yorkshire or Humberside	.023	.151
TYNEWEAR	1 if respondent lives in Tyneside or Wearside	.015	.123
NORTH	1 if respondent lives elsewhere in the North	.027	.162
WALES	1 if respondent lives in Wales	.148	.355
SCOTLAND	1 if respondent lives in Scotland	.165	.371
NIRE	1 if respondent lives in Northern Ireland	.103	.303

sporting events. Specifically and of most significance, England hosted two major international spectator events: the soccer European Championships in 1996 and the Commonwealth Games, which took place in Manchester in 2002. England also competed at the soccer World Cups held in France (1998), in South Korea and Japan (2002), and in Germany (2006). In terms of success in major tournaments, as well as notable achievements in a number of sports (e.g., rowing, sailing, and cycling) during the Summer Olympics held in 2000 (Sydney) and 2004 (Athens),[11] two other successes are identified. The first was England winning the 2003 Rugby World Cup. The second was England's victory over Australia in the 2005 (summer) Ashes series. Arguably the most notable event, however, took place on July 6, 2005 when the announcement was made that London was to host the 2012 Summer Olympics.

Because of the presence of several events taking place in any one year, it is perhaps difficult to disentangle event-specific impacts. A similar difficulty can also arise when distinguishing between hosting and success because the two tend to be correlated (Bernard and Busse, 2004). However, success in soccer has historically led to increases in passive participation (spectator demand) rather than active participation, and the successes associated with the minority sports of rugby and cricket have tended to be short lived.[12] As such, attention here is restricted to the inclusion of three dummy dichotomous variables: two representing the effect on hosting associated with the European Championships in 1996 in (EURO96) and the Commonwealth Games in 2002 (COMM02), and a third representing the impact of the Olympic announcement (OLYMPIC). Note that, in the case of the latter, the dummy relates to 2006 (the year after the announcement), which is a characteristic of the sample (i.e., participation questions were not asked in 2005), but it is convenient because it reduces the possibility of spurious effects that might have occurred in the immediate aftermath of the announcement.

Results

Table 22.6 presents the results using a random-effects probit specification, and the estimation routines were undertaken using STATA version 10. The default method of 12-point Gauss-Hermite quadrature was used to solve the likelihood function. A comparison using a different number of quadrature points suggests the method is appropriate.

The importance of individual heterogeneity is confirmed by the estimate of rho, which is relatively important, attaining a value of just over 0.5 in each of the four models estimated. The likelihood ratio test for rho indicates that a panel approach generates more information than a standard (pooled) probit.

Individual and household characteristics are in line with existing literature. The calculation of marginal effects in a random-effects probit model is problematic because the value depends on the unknown individual-specific effect. However, the relative size of coefficients can be assessed. For example, the relative difference between ages 16–19 and ages 70–74 implies that individuals in the former group are three times more likely to regularly participate in sports and physical activity.

As well as the decline with age, the results also reveal that men participate more frequently than females, as do respondents who have never married.

Table 22.6 Random Effects Probit Results

Variable	(1)	(2)	(3)	(4)
AGE1619	1.264 (0.065)***	1.266 (0.065)***	1.273 (0.065)***	1.266 (0.065)***
AGE2024	1.170 (0.059)***	1.170 (0.059)***	1.181 (0.059)***	1.173 (0.059)***
AGE2529	1.213 (0.055)***	1.210 (0.055)***	1.223 (0.055)***	1.216 (0.055)***
AGE3034	1.132 (0.054)***	1.131 (0.054)***	1.141 (0.054)***	1.135 (0.054)***
AGE3539	1.128 (0.054)***	1.130 (0.054)***	1.136 (0.054)***	1.131 (0.054)***
AGE4044	1.030 (0.053)***	1.032 (0.053)***	1.038 (0.053)***	1.032 (0.053)***
AGE4549	1.021 (0.052)***	1.028 (0.052)***	1.029 (0.052)***	1.024 (0.052)***
AGE5054	1.023 (0.051)***	1.027 (0.051)***	1.030 (0.051)***	1.025 (0.051)***
AGE5559	0.947 (0.049)***	0.949 (0.049)***	0.953 (0.049)***	0.949 (0.049)***
AGE6064	0.860 (0.045)***	0.864 (0.045)***	0.865 (0.045)***	0.861 (0.045)***
AGE6569	0.733 (0.042)***	0.734 (0.042)***	0.736 (0.042)***	0.734 (0.042)***
AGE7074	0.429 (0.039)***	0.432 (0.039)***	0.431 (0.039)***	0.429 (0.039)***
MALE	0.168 (0.020)***	0.166 (0.020)***	0.169 (0.020)***	0.169 (0.020)***
MARRIED	0.003 (0.024)	0.004 (0.024)	0.002 (0.024)	0.003 (0.024)
SINGLE	0.085 (0.032)***	0.086 (0.032)***	0.084 (0.032)***	0.085 (0.032)***
HHSIZE	−0.035 (0.008)***	−0.036 (0.008)***	−0.035 (0.008)***	−0.035 (0.008)***
NCHILD	−0.026 (0.012)**	−0.024 (0.0124)*	−0.027 (0.012)**	−0.027 (0.012)**
DEGREE	0.210 (0.029)***	0.211 (0.029)***	0.211 (0.029)***	0.210 (0.029)***
INCOME	3.85×10^{-7} (6.63×10^{-7})	4.03×10^{-7} (6.63×10^{-7})	3.92×10^{-7} (6.63×10^{-7})	3.92×10^{-7} (6.63×10^{-7})
HRSWRK	−0.007 (0.0008)***	−0.007 (0.0008)***	−0.007 (0.0008)***	−0.007 (0.0008)***
SELFEMPLOY	−0.246 (0.037)***	−0.243 (0.037)***	−0.244 (0.037)***	−0.246 (0.037)***
EMPLOYED	0.023 (0.032)	0.025 (0.032)	0.024 (0.032)	0.024 (0.032)
UNEMPLOYED	0.072 (0.041)*	0.076 (0.041)*	0.073 (0.041)*	0.072 (0.041)*
RETIRED	0.319 (0.037)***	0.323 (0.037)***	0.320 (0.037)***	0.319 (0.037)***
STUDENT	0.212 (0.043)***	0.214 (0.043)***	0.215 (0.043)***	0.213 (0.043)***
CIGS	−0.024 (0.001)***	−0.024 (0.001)***	−0.024 (0.001)***	−0.024 (0.001)***
GOODHEALTH	0.338 (0.016)***	0.340 (0.016)***	0.338 (0.016)***	0.338 (0.016)***
VSATISFIED	0.166 (0.014)***	0.165 (0.014)***	0.166 (0.014)***	0.166 (0.014)***
WATCHFREQ	0.392 (0.032)***	0.393 (0.032)***	0.391 (0.032)***	0.392 (0.032)***

(Continued)

Table 22.6 (*Continued*)

Variable	(1)	(2)	(3)	(4)
WATCHNEVER	−0.259 (0.016)***	−0.258 (0.016)***	−0.258 (0.016)***	−0.258 (0.016)***
LONDON	−0.002 (0.052)		−0.003 (0.052)	−0.002 (0.052)
SOUTH EAST	0.127 (0.045)***		0.126 (0.045)***	0.127 (0.045)***
SOUTH WEST	0.120 (0.052)**		0.120 (0.052)**	0.120 (0.052)**
EAST ANGLIA	0.166 (0.065)**		0.164 (0.065)**	0.165 (0.065)**
EASTMIDS	−0.042 (0.053)		−0.042 (0.053)	−0.041 (0.053)
GREATERMAN	−0.214 (0.067)***		−0.218 (0.067)***	−0.216 (0.067)***
MERSEYSIDE	−0.097 (0.084)		−0.103 (0.084)	−0.101 (0.084)
NORTHWEST	−0.004 (0.064)		−0.007 (0.064)	−0.006 (0.064)
SYORKSHIRE	−0.219 (0.080)***		−0.216 (0.080)***	−0.218 (0.080)***
WYORKSHIRE	0.003 (0.070)		0.003 (0.070)	0.003 (0.070)
YORKHUM	0.105 (0.070)		0.104 (0.070)	0.104 (0.070)
TYNEWEAR	−0.118 (0.082)		−0.115 (0.082)	−0.119 (0.082)
NORTH	0.0002 (0.068)		−0.003 (0.068)	−0.002 (0.068)
WALES	0.058 (0.044)		0.065 (0.044)	0.054 (0.044)
SCOTLAND	0.305 (0.044)***		0.313 (0.044)***	0.300 (0.044)***
NIRE	0.155 (0.046)***		0.169 (0.047)***	0.156 (0.046)***
EURO96	**−0.009 (0.019)**		**−0.009 (0.019)**	**−0.022 (0.020)**
COMM02	**0.058 (0.015)***		**0.060 (0.015)***	**0.051 (0.016)***
OLYMPIC	**0.182 (0.016)***		**0.176 (0.016)***	**0.182 (0.016)***
TEMPERATURE			0.005 (0.002)**	
RAINFALL				−0.0003 (0.00015)**
LONDON* EURO96		−0.083 (0.056)		
LONDON* COMM02		−0.004 (0.062)		
LONDON* OLYMPIC		0.132 (0.071)*		
SOUTH EAST* EURO96		0.039 (0.040)		
SOUTH EAST* COM02		0.119 (0.042)		
SOUTH EAST* OLYMPIC		0.284 (0.044)***		

Table 22.6 (*Continued*)

Variable	(1)	(2)	(3)	(4)
SOUTH WEST* EURO96		0.051 (0.059)		
SOUTH WEST* COMM02		0.006 (0.061)		
SOUTH WEST* OLYMPIC		0.234 (0.062)***		
EAST ANGLIA* EURO96		0.011 (0.086)		
EAST ANGLIA* COMM02		0.119 (0.088)		
EAST ANGLIA* OLYMPIC		0.123 (0.086)		
EASTMIDS* EURO96		−0.031 (0.061)		
EASTMIDS* COMM02		−0.113 (0.063)		
EASTMIDS* OLYMPIC		0.122 (0.064)*		
GREATERMAN* EURO96		−0.120 (0.090)		
GREATERMAN* COMM02		−0.156 (0.095)		
GREATERMAN* OLYMPIC		0.037 (0.097)		
MERSEYSIDE* EURO96		−0.221 (0.117)		
MERSEYSIDE* COMM02		0.040 (0.116)		
MERSEYSIDE* OLYMPIC		0.008 (0.125)		
NORTHWEST* EURO96		−0.111 (0.083)		
NORTHWEST* COMM02		−0.015 (0.085)		
NORTHWEST* OLYMPIC		0.151 (0.090)*		
SYORKSHIRE* EURO96		−0.088 (0.109)		

(*Continued*)

Table 22.6 (*Continued*)

Variable	(1)	(2)	(3)	(4)
SYORKSHIRE* COMM02		0.023 (0.113)		
SYORKSHIRE* OLYMPIC		−0.112 (0.115)		
WYORKSHIRE* EURO96		0.011 (0.097)		
WYORKSHIRE* COMM02		−0.007 (0.102)		
WYORKSHIRE* OLYMPIC		0.067 (0.105)		
YORKHUM* EURO96		−0.070 (0.095)		
YORKHUM* COMM02		0.266 (0.101)***		
YORKHUM* OLYMPIC		0.118 (0.102)		
TYNEWEAR* EURO96		−0.045 (0.112)		
TYNEWEAR* COMM02		0.009 (0.126)		
TYNEWEAR* OLYMPIC		0.189 (0.132)		
NORTH*EURO96		−0.074 (0.090)		
NORTH*COMM02		−0.047 (0.092)		
NORTH*OLYMPIC		0.193 (0.094)**		
WALES*EURO96		−0.106 (0.078)		
WALES*COMM02		−0.001 (0.034)		
WALES*OLYMPIC		0.175 (0.037)***		
SCOTLAND* EURO96		0.034 (0.060)		
SCOTLAND* COMM02		0.243 (0.034)***		
SCOTLAND* OLYMPIC		0.346 (0.037)***		
NIRE*COMM02		0.010 (0.002)***		
NIRE*OLYMPIC		0.008 (0.046)		
CONSTANT	−0.919 (0.064)***	−0.831 (0.053)***	−0.980 (0.069)***	

Table 22.6 (*Continued*)

Variable	(1)	(2)	(3)	(4)
n	23,267	23,267	23,267	23,267
n × T	74,594	74,594	74,594	74,594
Log likelihood	−43515.98	−43559.44	−43513.24	−43513.89
σ_α	1.030	1.034	1.031	1.030
ρ	0.515	0.516	0.515	0.515
Likelihood-ratio test of $\rho = 0$	8732.50	8788.09	8737.65	8732.70

Notes: Standard errors in parentheses. *** significant at the 1% level; ** significant at the 5% level; * significant at the 10% level. $\rho = \sigma_\alpha^2 / (\sigma_\alpha^2 + \sigma_u^2)$. In Model 2, NIRE*EURO96 is excluded because of collinearity.

Household dynamics are also important with larger households, and the presence of children reduces the probability of regular participation.[13] A negative effect is also associated with the number of hours worked. Respondents who have acquired a first or higher degree are significantly more likely to participate regularly relative to those who hold other or, indeed, no qualifications. Smokers, particularly heavy smokers, are less likely to regularly participate, whereas the probability of regular participation is higher for those respondents who report that they are in good or excellent health. A similar finding is also observed with respect to self-reported life satisfaction. The results also reveal a complementary effect between regular participation and the frequency of spectating at live sporting events.[14]

The findings reveal that region is important. Relative to the West Midlands (the reference category) regular participation is particularly prominent in the South East, South West, and East Anglia. Negative and statistically significant effects are observed in Greater Manchester and South Yorkshire. There is no statistically significant effect for residents in London. Finally the dummy variables associated with the Commonwealth Games and the Olympic announcement are significant at better than the 1 percent level, whereas the coefficient associated with the European Championship is negative but statistically insignificant. These findings confirm the probability of regular participation increasing following the announcement of the decision to award London the 2012 Olympics. The potential importance of the Olympic Games announcement is also reflected in the size of the coefficient, which is three times the size of the Commonwealth Games coefficient.

To explore the impact of wave/event-specific effects in more detail, Model 2 replaces event and region dummies with their interacted equivalents. The rationale is to determine whether changes in participation following these events are region specific. The results confirm the existence of regional differences. Relative to the other events, the Olympic Games announcement is particularly prominent in the South East and South West. The case of London is also interesting as the results suggest a positive effect on participation following the announcement (despite being significant at no better than the 10 percent level). Although the relative sizes of the coefficients indicate that there is some evidence of a distance-decay effect, neighboring countries (Wales and Scotland) also appear to benefit from the announcement.

Can we be sure that the estimated impact is due to the Olympics? To what extent is the announcement effect confounded with other factors? One potentially important factor is the influence of climate.[15] Because many sporting and leisure activities are undertaken outdoors, temperature and rainfall are likely to be important determinants. Of significance for the present sample is the observation that the UK experienced higher-than-average temperatures in July 2006 (17.8 degrees Celsius compared to an average of 15.2 for the month of July for the entire sample period 1996–2006). Levels of rainfall were also lower (41.8mm compared to 55.8mm).

To explore the possibility that participation is influenced by climate, Model 3 includes temperature and Model 4 includes rainfall. Both temperature and rainfall are significant, at the 5 percent level but, more importantly, have little effect on the relative size (and significance levels) of the event dummies.[16] It would appear, therefore, that the event dummies are not simply acting as proxies for differences in weather patterns.

Overall the evidence reported here suggests a positive and statistically significant effect on the Olympic announcement on participation in sport and leisure activity. Although the results of the BHPS are limited to an assessment of general patterns of sport and physical activity,[17] evidence from other surveys such as the Active People Survey highlights significant increases in athletics and cycling participation over the period 2005/06 to 2007/08.[18] However, over the same period, significant reductions in participation were found in other sports, including swimming. Therefore, there appears to be evidence to suggest that people are participating more in some, but not all, Olympic-related events.

What is the transmission mechanism that links the hosting of major sporting events with participation rates? This is not an easy question to answer. Whether competitive excellence is the optimal approach to promoting mass participation is debatable. Currently only 21 percent of the adult UK population participate in moderate intensity sport and physical activity for at least thirty minutes for three days per week and less than 10 percent do so via competitive sport. It is also questionable whether success in the Olympics can offer sufficient inspiration to change the behaviour of those currently undertaking little or no physical activity.[19] Nonetheless, the results provide some cautious optimism that *hosting* the Olympics can help toward the promotion of more healthy lifestyles. Only time will tell whether participation will continue to increase in the immediate lead-up to the Olympics and, more importantly, in the post-event period.

Conclusion

This chapter has provided a review of the economic impact of the Olympics and presented new findings relating to the impact of the 2012 announcement on participation levels in sport and physical activity in the UK. Although there appears to be a consensus that the tangible economic benefits associated with the major sporting events are, at best, transitory, there is much less literature that has considered evaluating intangible effects.

The findings presented in this chapter suggest there are potential intangible benefits associated with hosting the Olympics, but more work is required to unpick the mechanism that links the Olympics to participation in sport and to establish whether the legacy effects are permanent.

Notes

1 In a similar manner, the first Winter Olympics, held in Chamonix, France, involved sixteen nations competing in sixteen events, whereas the most recent (2006, in Turin, Italy) saw competitors from eighty nations compete in eighty-four events.

2 However, as pointed out by Preuss (2004), when long-term investment items are excluded the deficit is transformed into a surplus.

3 For further details on economic multipliers, see von Allmen, this handbook, volume 2.

4 Often in first difference form due to the non-stationary nature of the data.

5 See also Hotchkiss et al., (2003).

6 For a general discussion on the use of event analysis as applied to sport see Leeds, this handbook, volume 2.

7 More details on CVM are provided in Whitehead, this handbook, volume 2.

8 For details see, for example, http://www.iser.essex.ac.uk/survey/bhps/about-bhps/the-sample.

9 Each Wave is associated with interviews that are carried out over nine months, which transcend two years. For example, interviews for Wave 16 started in September 2006 and were completed in April 2007. The majority of respondents however were interviewed in September and October. Similar patterns emerge for other Waves.

10 More complicated structures, based on ordered probit specifications are also possible. In the interest of space they are not included here but the results are comparable.

11 Apart from success in curling and bobsleigh, the UK's achievements in the Winter Olympics have been rare.

12 Evidence from other surveys also suggests participation rates in these sports are historically low.

13 The data is not sufficiently detailed to distinguish between infants and older children.

14 The relationship between participation, spectator demand, and TV viewing habits is explored further in Dawson and Downward (2009).

15 A further limitation of the analysis offered here is the absence of the counterfactual: the level of participation that would have occurred had London not won the bid to host the 2012 Olympics.

16 Similar results are found when temperature and rainfall are included as additional factors in Model 3.

17 A new UK longitudinal study, Understanding Society, introduced in 2009, incorporates the BHPS. It includes more specific information on individuals involvement in sports and physical activity.

18 The Active People Survey first carried out in 2005–2006 is described as the largest ever survey on sport and leisure participation in the England. Sponsored by Sport England and administered by Ipsos Mori, the first wave generated a sample size of 363,724, covering all 354 local authorities in England. A fourth wave was released in December 2010.

19 According to the Department of Culture, Media, and Sport web site, it is claimed that the Olympics will provide the inspiration to increase sports participation at the grassroots level. However, it is the case that some of the costs associated with the Olympics will be paid for by funds that would have otherwise gone directly to grassroots sport.

References

Atkinson, G., S. Mourato, S. Szymanski, and E. Ozdemiroglu. 2008. Are we willing to pay enough to 'Back the Bid'?: Valuing the intangible impacts of London's bid to host the 2012 Summer Olympic Games. *Urban Studies,* 45: 419–444.

Baade, R. A. 2007. The economic impact of mega-sporting events. In *Handbook of the Economics of Sport,* eds. Andreff and Szymanski, 177–82. Cheltenham: Edward Elgar.

Baade, R. A., V. Matheson. 2002. Bidding for the Olympics: Fool's gold? In *Transatlantic Sport: the comparative economics of North America and European Sports,* eds. C. P. Barros, M. Ibrahimo, and S. Szymanski, 127–151. Cheltenham: Edward Elgar.

Berman, G., R. Brooks, and S. Davidson. 2000. The Sydney Olympic Games announcement and Australia stock market reaction. *Applied Economic Letters,* 7: 781–84.

Bernard, A., and M. Busse. 2004. Who wins the Olympic Games: Economic resources and medal totals. *Review of Economics and Statistics,* 86: 413–417

Carlino, G., and N. E. Coulson. 2004. Compensating differentials and the social benefits of the NFL. *Journal of Urban Economics,* 56: 25–50.

Crompton, J. 1995. Economic impact analysis of sports facilities and events: Eleven sources of misapplication. *Journal of Sport Management,* 9: 14–35.

Dawson, P., and P. M. Downward. 2009. Participation, spectatorship and media coverage in sport. Bath Economics Research Papers 24/09. Accessible from: http://www.bath.ac.uk/economics/research/working-papers/2409.pdf.

Dehring, C., C. Depken, and M. Ward. 2007. The impact of stadium announcements on residential property values: Evidence from a natural experiment in Dallas-Fort Worth. *Contemporary Economic Policy,* 25: 627–638.

Downward, P. M., and J. Riordan. 2007. Social interactions and the demand for sport: An economic analysis. *Contemporary Economic Policy,* 25: 518–537.

Economics Research Associates. 1984. Community economic impact of the 1984 Olympic Games in Los Angeles and Southern California. Los Angeles Olympic Organising Committee, Los Angeles.

Farrell, L., and M. A. Shields. 2002. Investigating the economic and demographic determinants of sporting participation in England. *Journal of the Royal Statistical Society Series A,* 165: 335–348.

Giesecke, J., and J. Madden. 2007. The Sydney Olympics, seven years on: An ex-post dynamic CGE assessment. Centre of Policy Studies Monash University Working Paper G-168.

Hotchkiss, J., R. Moore, and S. Zobay. 2003. Impact of the 1996 Summer Olympic Games on employment and wages in Georgia. *Southern Economic Journal,* 69: 691–704.

Humphreys, J. M., and M. K. Plummer. 1995. The economic impact on the state of Georgia of hosting the 1996 Olympic Games. Selig Center for Economic Growth, Georgia.

Humphreys, B., and J. Ruseski. 2007. Participation in physical activity and government spending on parks and recreation. *Contemporary Economic Policy,* 25: 538–552.

Jasmand, S., and W. Maennig. 2008. Regional income and employment effects of the 1972 Munich Olympic Summer Games. *Regional Studies,* 42: 991–1002.

Kasimati, E., and P. Dawson. 2009. Assessing the impact of the 2004 Olympic Games on the Greek economy: A small macroeconometric model. *Economic Modelling,* 26: 139–146.

Kavetsos, G. (Forthcoming). The impact of the London Olympics Announcement on Property Prices. *Urban Studies.*

Kavetsos, G., and S. Szymanski. 2010. National wellbeing and international sports events. *Journal of Economic Psychology,* 31: 158–71.

Kavetsos, G., and S. Szymanksi. 2008. Olympic Games, terrorism and their impact on the London and Paris stock exchanges. *Revue d'Economie Politique,* 118: 189–206.

Leeds, M. 2012. Event Studies. In *The Oxford Handbook of Sports Economics, Volume 2,* eds. L. Kahane and S. Shmanske. New York: Oxford University Press.

Leeds, M., J. Mirikitani, and D. Tang. 2009. Rational exuberance? An event analysis of the 2008 Olympics announcement. *International Journal of Sport Finance,* 4: 5–15.

Madden, J. 2006. Economic and fiscal impacts of mega sporting events: A general equilibrium assessment. *Public Finance and Management,* 6: 346–394.

Matheson, V. 2006. Mega-events: The effect of the world's biggest sporting events on local, regional and national economies. IASE Working Paper No. 06–22.

Murphy, N., and A. Bauman. 2007. Mass sporting and physical activity events: Are they "bread" and "circuses" or public health interventions to increase population levels of physical activity? *Journal of Physical Activity and Health,* 4: 193–202.

Preuss, H. 2004. *The economics of staging the Olympics: A comparison of the games 1972–2008.* Cheltenham: Edward Elgar.

Rose, A., and M. Spiegel. 2011. The Olympic Effect. *Economic Journal,* 121: 652–677.

Simmons, R., and C. Deutscher. 2012. Economics of the World Cup. In *The Oxford Handbook of Sports Economics, Volume 1,* eds. L. Kahane and S. Shmanske. New York: Oxford University Press.

Tu, C. 2005. How does a new sports stadium affect housing values? *Land Economics,* 81: 379–395.

Veal, A. J. 2003. Tracking change: Leisure participation and policy in Australia, 1985–2002. *Annals of Leisure Research,* 6: 245–277.

Veraros, N., E. Kasimati,and P. Dawson. 2004. The 2004 Olympic Games announcement and its effect on the Athens and Milan stock exchanges. *Applied Economics Letters,* 11: 749–753.

Von Allmen, P. 2012. The multiplier and local impact. In *The Oxford Handbook of Sports Economics Volume 2,* eds. L. Kahane and S. Shmanske, New York: Oxford University Press.

Walton, H., A. Longo, and P. Dawson. 2008. Contingent valuation of 2012 London Olympics: A regional perspective. *Journal of Sports Economics,* 9: 304–317.

Whitehead, J. C. 2012. Contingent valuation methods. In *The Oxford Handbook of Sports Economics, Volume 2,* eds. L. Kahane and S. Shmanske. New York: Oxford University Press.

....

CHAPTER 23

THE ECONOMICS OF THE WORLD CUP

....

ROB SIMMONS AND CHRISTIAN DEUTSCHER

INTRODUCTION

....

THE FIFA World Cup is an international soccer tournament played every four years in a different country to the previous location. FIFA stands for *Fédération Internationale de Football Association,* and is the governing body of world soccer. In addition to holding the rights to host the World Cup, and owning the World Cup brand, FIFA is responsible for the rules of soccer, as played at both professional and amateur levels worldwide. The World Cup is competed by teams representing countries, more specifically national soccer associations that are officially recognized by the organizers. The first World Cup was in 1930, and the tournament has been held every four years since, with breaks for wartime disruption in 1942 and 1946. Although the specific format of the finals has varied, the basic concept remains that a large number of national teams compete in a qualifying tournament organized around regional football associations for the right to participate in the World Cup finals. In 2010, thirty-two teams were awarded places in the finals, played in South Africa between June 11, 2010 and July 11, 2010. One place is traditionally reserved for the host nation (two places if there are co-hosts as in the case of Japan and South Korea in 2002). The 2010 finals comprised a round-robin league competition of eight divisions of four teams each, with places allocated by complex seeding principles; this was followed by a knock-out tournament involving single games, leading eventually to the final.

The World Cup final is the planet's most-viewed sports event. The 2006 final in Germany played between Italy and France, drew an estimated 75 million television viewers. FIFA estimated that an overall total of $3.4 billion would be generated from proceeds of the most recent World Cup finals (www.sportcal.com). This would represent an increase from $2.6 billion in the 2006 World Cup held in Germany (Maennig and du Plessis, 2007).

This chapter will present a general review of the economics of the FIFA World Cup. We shall proceed as follows. Section 1 explores the method by which host countries are selected by FIFA for the rights to organize the World Cup finals. Section 2 explores the benefits to host countries from organizing the World Cup finals. Because the literature consensus is that the direct benefits are at best modest, we move on to consider intangible benefits to host country residents from the World Cup finals. In Section 3 we consider the later benefits to soccer fans in a host country from new stadium infrastructure and other legacies of hosting the World Cup finals. Section 4 turns our attention to the players participating in the World Cup finals, examining their direct remuneration from participation plus later benefits in terms of career advantages. This section will present new evidence from the German Bundesliga of salary premiums to players associated with World Cup participation. In Section 5, we offer some views on attempts by some national soccer associations to restrict imports of foreign players, sometimes with the explicit goal of using import controls as a means of promoting national success in tournaments such as the World Cup.

1. SELECTION OF HOST COUNTRIES FOR THE WORLD CUP FINALS

FIFA is essentially an umbrella organization, comprising six confederations that, in turn, represent national associations. The six confederations are Africa (CAF), Asia (AFC), Europe (UEFA), North America, Central America and the Caribbean (CONCACAF), Oceania (OFC), and South America (CONMEBOL). Places for the World Cup finals are allocated by confederations so, for example, UEFA sent nine teams to the 2010 finals. On the executive committee, UEFA has the largest representation with nine seats out of twenty-four, followed by CONMEBOL, AFC, and CAF with four each.

The choice of host country for the World Cup finals is made by the FIFA Executive Committee from a set of national association bids. In several respects, the choice mechanism has some similarities with that of host city for the Olympic Games, also held every four years, but not in the same year as the World Cup finals. Hosting the World Cup finals is a right that the local soccer federation buys from FIFA. Similar to the Olympic Games, FIFA sets up an auction for the rights to hold the World Cup finals every four years. Also similar to the Olympic Games, FIFA extracts economic rent due to its position as monopoly provider of the tournament. FIFA does not take a fee from the successful bidder but instead insists on a number of favorable contract provisions that can be judged to be components of economic rent. For example, Maennig and du Plessis (2007) report that FIFA insisted that, for the 2010 finals in South Africa, advertising billboards within 1 kilometer of stadiums where Finals games were played, and along access roads to such stadiums, should be restricted to FIFA-endorsed enterprises. Profits from such advertising went to FIFA. A similar rule applied to the 2006 finals in Germany.

From 1958 to 2006, FIFA followed a rotation policy, although this was only ever explicit from 2000. Under this policy, the finals would be held every eight years in Europe, alternating with a venue from another continent (see Table 23.1). Ostensibly, this policy was designed to promote soccer in continents and countries where soccer leagues and soccer participation were less well established. The choice of South Korea and Japan as co-hosts in 2002 could be rationalized in this way.

A counter-argument to the rotation policy is that FIFA has taken the World Cup finals to countries where soccer is always likely to be a minority sport (USA) or where a club league is always going to be small in size and audience interest (South

Table 23.1 Hosts and Winners of the World Cup Finals since Origin

Year	Host	Winner
1930	Uruguay	Uruguay
1934	Italy	Italy
1938	France	Italy
1950	Brazil	Uruguay
1954	Switzerland	West Germany
1958	Sweden	Brazil
1962	Chile	Brazil
1966	England	England
1970	Mexico	Brazil
1974	West Germany	West Germany
1978	Argentina	Argentina
1982	Spain	Italy
1986	Mexico	Argentina
1990	Italy	Germany
1994	USA	Brazil
1998	France	France
2002	South Korea/Japan	Brazil
2006	Germany	Italy
2010	South Africa	Spain
2014	Brazil	
2018	Russia	
2022	Qatar	

Africa). Conversely, the continent on which soccer is most intensely followed as the dominant team sport is, of course, Europe. So why does FIFA not locate the World Cup finals in Europe at every opportunity so as to maximize attendances, broadcast audiences, and possibly revenues? One answer to this objection is that the stadium audience is much smaller than the global television audience, now enhanced by other media, such as cellphones and the Internet. With a huge global broadcast audience available, it may not matter where the games are actually played. It is notable that part of the revenue from sales of the 2010 finals broadcast rights came from the United States. FIFA negotiated a deal with the English-language networks, ABC, and ESPN for a total of $100 million for the two tournaments in 2010 (South Africa) and 2014 (Brazil). This sum was exceeded, however, by the amount of $325 million paid by the Spanish-language network, Univisión, over the same period. The reason for this large fee is the sizable and growing Hispanic/Latino minority group in the United States, and its passionate interest in soccer.

There may be a deeper reason for FIFA's rotation policy than an ambassadorial function for the finals. The Union of European Football Associations (UEFA), itself one of the FIFA confederations, hosts two tournaments: the prestigious club-level UEFA Champions' League contested by the most successful teams across national leagues within Europe, and the European Championship, a national team tournament contested by European national sides every four years and two years apart from the World Cup finals. Locating the World Cup finals on every occasion in Europe, would dilute the FIFA brand and would present UEFA with enhanced negotiating power within FIFA. Understandably, therefore, FIFA avoids the option of locating the Finals in Europe on every occasion.

After the 2018 finals, FIFA will operate a new system for allocation of host nation(s). Rotation will be formally abandoned in favor of a new rule whereby the confederations whose associations have hosted the two preceding World Cups are not eligible to bid, however. All the associations from Asia, North and Central America and the Caribbean, Oceania, and Europe could bid for the 2018 FIFA World Cup. The reason for this change in policy came about because Brazil emerged as sole (and successful) bidder for the rights to host the 2014 finals. As shown in the case of the Olympic Games, rights holders gain more rents from a larger number of bids.

Competition between bidders drives up the sums of money committed to stadium and other infrastructure, and these sums are an important part of any successful bid. For the 2006 finals in Germany, many club stadiums needed renovation and redevelopment rather than being built as new. The German Organizing Committee spent $1.9 billion over twelve locations with over 60 percent of this figure coming from clubs and private investors, meaning that the share of public spending on stadiums-development programs was relatively low. In contrast, Maennig and du Plessis (2007) estimated the spending on stadiums in South Africa at $1.4 billion over 10 venues, with five new and five renovated stadiums. The key difference from the German case was that, in South Africa, the government made virtually all the financial commitment. Another difference is that South Africa does not have a well-developed and vibrant team-level soccer league, which Germany clearly has.

In addition to stadiums and related infrastructure, such as roads and public transport networks, host associations must commit to various other expenses that include security, advertising, and cultural programs. Maennig and du Plessis (2007) estimate the profit for the German organizing committee in 2006 to be $206 million, aided by near capacity sales of match tickets. This surplus was distributed among the German Soccer Association (DFB), the German Premier League (DFL), and the German Olympic Federation. In contrast, the estimated profit to FIFA from the 2006 finals was $1.9 billion, although part of this was redistributed to FIFA development programs worldwide.

Despite the substantial costs involved, which extend to nontrivial costs of the bidding process itself, the likelihood of cost overruns and projections of fairly modest net profits to the host organizing committee, there has been no shortage of bids to host the 2018 and 2022 World Cup finals. FIFA decided to allocate both sets of finals simultaneously and, by the deadline of March 2009, had received seven bids for 2018 or 2022, featuring Australia, Belgium, and Netherlands as co-hosts, England, Japan, Russia, Spain, and Portugal as co-hosts, and the United States. A further four bids were received for 2022 only, including Indonesia, South Korea, and Qatar. As of November 2009, the betting odds offered by Sky Bet for host of the 2018 tournament were 11/8 for England, 3/1 for Spain and Portugal and 7/2 for Australia. However, the short odds on England may be driven by national sentiment, and odds do vary in response to news stories, such as internal arguments within the England bid team, which moved the odds from 11/10 to 11/8 in November 2009. In the end, Russia and Qatar were selected to host the 2018 and 2022 World Cups, respectively, both being heavy underdogs prior to the voting.

Given the high costs of stadium infrastructure, security, and advertising, and the ability of FIFA to extract economic rents as tournament rights holder, it is worth considering in more detail the likely pecuniary and non-pecuniary benefits from hosting the World Cup Finals. Benefits to host country populations are considered next.

2. Benefits to Local and National Economies from Hosting the World Cup Finals

The general consensus of the economic benefits from hosting large-scale sports events is that these are both exaggerated in ex ante studies and small ex post (Baade, 2003; Matheson, 2008). This consensus covers the Olympic Games (Baade and Matheson, 2002; Hotchkiss et al. 2003; Humphreys and Zimbalist, 2008) and the National Football League's Superbowl (Baade and Matheson, 2006). Ex ante estimates of expected economic benefits of large-scale sporting events tend to be optimistic, partly through booster studies undertaken by consultants who have an incentive to report large benefits. The events themselves are subject to a number of leakages and diversion effects. For example, hotel room rates rise around locations of large sporting events. Local residents may leave the area to avoid congestion and nuisance associated with the event. Projected employment gains may be misleading as the jobs involved may well be low skilled and temporary, and many services are actually performed by volunteer workers whose activity will not form any part of Gross Domestic Product.

In contrast, ex post studies of the economic benefits to local economies from hosting large-scale sports studies are more downbeat. There are two methods typically used to evaluate economic benefits ex post. The first is applied by Baade and Matheson (2004) to the World Cup finals hosted by the United States in 1994 and estimates a regression model of income growth with national GDP growth, demographic variables, and time trend as control variables. This study compared income growth in the seventy-five largest population centers (Metropolitan Standard Areas) before and after the World Cup, spanning a period of 1970 to 2000. The main finding was that actual growth in incomes was less than would have been expected prior to the World Cup event. Moreover, nine out of thirteen host cities suffered lower growth after the World Cup compared to before. Using a similar approach, Hagn and Maennig (2008) could not find any evidence of statistically significant positive benefits to German regions (in the old Federal Republic) from hosting the 1974 World Cup, whether assessed by GDP growth, income growth, or unemployment reductions.

The second approach involves use of local employment data and a difference-in-difference methodology in which employment levels in localities that hosted World Cup games are compared with those that did not host, using differences in employment as the dependent variable in a regression model. This method was applied by Hotchkiss et al. (2003) in a study of employment effects of the Atlanta Olympic Games on counties in the Atlanta area. Applying this method to German cities before and after the 2006 World Cup, Feddersen et al. (2009) find a lack of significant short-run or long-run employment or unemployment effects attributable to hosting the World Cup in Germany. The procedure was to consider twelve World Cup venues as a treatment group among the 118 largest population urban districts in Germany. Noting that construction projects on host city stadiums began several years before the World Cup actually took place, and using a time span of 1995 to 2005, the authors compare differences in outcome measured as per capita income, employment, and unemployment levels (separately) before and after the intervention, defined as the beginning of a large stadium construction project. The hypotheses of zero income and employment effects of the stadium construction projects in urban districts with completed work could not be rejected at the conventional five percent significance level.

At the microeconomic level, some particular industries may benefit from a country hosting the World Cup finals. For example, the German beer industry enjoyed high levels of sales during the 2006 World Cup finals. However, it is difficult to separate the effects of hot weather in the June and July period from the effects of the World Cup finals. Also, Hagn and Maennig (2009) report that hotel occupancy rates actually fell during the World Cup finals with substantial reductions in Berlin and Munich as host cities. Revenues held up as room rates rose. These results are very much in line with the skeptical analyses offered by Baade (2003) and Matheson (2008).

The absence of substantial direct economic benefits from hosting the World Cup has led several researchers to examine possible intangible or "feel-good" effects. Heyne, Maennig, and Sussmuth (2007) conducted a before-and-after contingent valuation study to extract willingness-to-pay values for 500 people, before and after the 2006 World Cup finals in Germany. The authors found that the average ex ante willingness-to-pay figure for respondents offering a positive value was $30.4. However, fewer than 20 percent of respondents had a positive willingness to pay, so the overall average was $5.66. After the event, 43 percent of respondents reported a positive willingness to pay, whereas over the whole sample before and after the event, willingness to pay had a mean of $13.4 per person. Many respondents switched from zero willingness to pay to positive willingness to pay, particularly respondents from the eastern Germany and also the less educated. The authors suggest that this is indicative of the World Cup as an experience good, and, also, that ex ante studies of willingness to pay might be biased downward.

As shown in the 2010 South Africa case, hosting the World Cup finals can entail considerable spending by the public sector on soccer stadiums and associated infrastructure. The case for such spending is stronger if it can be shown that the World Cup generates a net increase in social welfare. However, increased social welfare is not observed and is imperfectly correlated with objective measures, such as Gross Domestic Product. This problem has led to use of self-reported happiness indicators in questionnaire studies. The question typically put is, "Taking all things together, how would you say things are these days- would you say that you are happy, quite happy, or nor very happy." Responses are then coded on a Likert scale and applied ordinally in econometric analysis.

Kavetsos and Szymanski (2010) use happiness data taken from the Eurobarometer Survey covering 1,000 people per country over twelve countries for the period 1974–2004. In this case, there were four responses to the life satisfaction question: very, fairly, not very, and not at all satisfied. The authors propose two hypotheses (1) better than expected national athletic performance raises happiness and (2) hosting major sporting events increases happiness. These hypotheses are tested over the World Cup years 1978, 1982, 1986, 1990, and 1994. Thus, they included a dummy variable for the only host country in the data, Italy, 1990. By comparing national team ratings just before and just after the World Cup finals the authors tested the impact of team performance on happiness using an ordinal logit model. This model had a long list of control variables. Macroeconomic control variables comprised GDP per capita, unemployment rate, and inflation rate. Personal control variables included employment status, sex, age, age squared, marital status, household income quartiles, and educational level attained. The results showed that hosting the World Cup finals by Italy in 1990—which did not win the tournament—was positively and significantly correlated with reported happiness for the population as a whole and for a series of subgroups, with the notable exception of females. The authors also considered anticipation and legacy effects. A set of post-event dummies for two and four years after was jointly significant for all subgroups considered. Also, dummy variables for one year before and one year after gave positive effects on happiness, for the population as whole, for individuals under the age of 50, males, the unemployed and those who had not benefited from higher education.

3. BENEFITS OF HOSTING THE WORLD CUP FINALS TO SOCCER FANS

A criticism of public expenditure on purpose-built stadiums constructed for the World Cup finals is that they are underused after the event. In the case of the 2006 finals in Germany, all twelve stadiums used for the finals reverted to use by Bundesliga clubs after the event. This includes the venue for the final itself, the Olympiastadion in Berlin, currently occupied by Hertha Berlin. This club is a good example of how a team can successfully raise its attendance following a move into a new stadium. In the season directly after the World Cup finals, 2006–2007, Hertha Berlin's average league attendance was 25,000, but in 2008–2009, average attendance had grown to 52,300 including three sell-out games at a capacity limit of 74,000.

The German Bundesliga is notable for the enthusiasm of its fans, and it is no surprise that several teams that had renovated or new stadiums after hosting World Cup finals have experienced rising league attendances. As put in the baseball literature, the question is "If you build it, will they come?" A thorough empirical investigation of this question is offered, again for Germany, by Feddersen et al. (2006). Their analysis of 'novelty' effects of new or renovated stadiums follows the literature on baseball attendances (Coates and Humphreys, 2005) and distinguishes three effects:

1. Fans quickly get used to newly built or renovated stadiums. This is a short-term immediate novelty effect confined to the first season directly after opening, with a dummy variable set equal to one for this period only.

2. There may be a long-term novelty effect, as long as five years, but then ending abruptly. Hence, a dummy variable is set equal to one for time periods $t + 1$ to $t + 5$ after stadium opening.
3. The novelty effect begins on the date of stadium opening, has a maximum value after opening, but then decays over the following years; the dummy variable is then $D = aT$ where T is a five-year time trend and $a < 0$.

Looking first at the 1974 finals, Feddersen et al. find that there was an average increase in attendance for all clubs playing home games in new or renovated stadiums of 47 percent one season after the finals. This novelty effect shows some persistence: after five years, eight out of nine new or renovated stadiums had higher fan numbers than in the year prior to the completion of construction. For the 2006 Finals, new stadium projects began as early as 1998. For these stadiums, the authors find some evidence of novelty effects in the descriptive data.

The authors combine impacts of new and renovated stadiums for the 1974 and 2006 finals in an econometric analysis of Bundesliga 1 club attendances over 1963–2003, using club and season fixed effects and controls for regional income and team performance. In Germany, stadium capacity is rarely binding, so Tobit estimation is not required. Of the three novelty effects noted earlier, only the second is significant at the five percent level. This long-term novelty effect is estimated at 2,700 extra fans per game for five years, or 10.7 percent on a mean value of 25,000 fans. Higher novelty effects, estimated at an extra 10,300 fans per game, are found for two clubs, Hamburg and Schalke 04, who introduced the innovation (for Germany) of building new stadiums without the traditional running track to separate crowd from the pitch.

Feddersen et al. point out that a large part of the revenue gains from new or renovated stadiums comes from VIP and corporate seats, with around €8 millions accruing to Bundesliga clubs after the 2006 World Cup. It appears that extra revenue from new stadium developments comes from absorbing the purchasing power of a small group of affluent fans, a point that echoes the luxury box strategy of new stadium construction by Major League Baseball and National Football League franchises in North America. Since these affluent fans are willing to pay higher ticket prices then consumer surplus rises, but extra corporate boxes and seating may reduce the capacity available for less affluent fans, leading to "social exclusion" from games. Supporters' organizations often voice equity concerns as a result.

FIFA operates two key restrictions on stadium development for World Cup Finals. First, there must be a minimum capacity of 40,000. The capacity minimum is designed to ensure sufficient revenue from ticket sales but has the consequence that smaller teams using a World Cup stadium for regular League games may find they often have empty seats. This is a particular problem for countries such as South Korea and South Africa whose leagues are less mature than European leagues. In the case of South Africa, two new stadiums were built in Durban and Cape Town, holding 70,000 and 68,000 fans, respectively. The two stadiums in Johannesburg were renovated to reach capacities of 94,700 (Soccer City) and 65,000 (Ellis Park).

These are most unlikely to sell out, save for a few international rugby and possibly soccer matches and certainly not for club fixtures.

Second, FIFA prohibits the sponsorship of stadiums in the form of naming rights unless the stadium sponsors are also official sponsors. Thus, the AOL Arena in Hamburg became the FIFA Football World Cup Arena for the duration of the 2006 finals. A total of seven out of twelve German stadiums were affected in this way. This is another example of rent extraction by FIFA.

Regardless of newness of stadiums, hosting the World Cup finals may lead to a boost to soccer attendances at league level. In his analysis of English Football League, Bird (1982) used a World Cup dummy to capture the combined effects of England hosting and winning the tournament on annual league attendances after the 1966 finals. Controlling for admission prices, travel costs, and real incomes, Bird found that the World Cup contributed to a significant upward shift of 9.7 percent in the 1966–1967 season immediately following the finals. This was in the context of long-term decline in soccer attendances in England over the period 1946–1985. However, Bird could not differentiate between a World Cup effect and a possible uplift to attendances due to the extra publicity brought about by the introduction, for the first time, of a popular TV show *Match of the Day* featuring edited highlights of Saturday matches.

In 1998, France repeated England's achievement of hosting and winning the World Cup. Falter et al. (2008) argue that the period after France's success was one of "overwhelming joy," which led to a positive network externality on club attendances in the French league. In terms of raw data, average league attendances rose from 16,600 in the 1997–1998 season, just before the finals, to 19,800 in 1998–1999, just after, and rose again to 22,300 in 1999–2000. Falter et al. present an econometric demand model containing a host-city dummy, home and away standings, home-team payroll as a proxy for team quality, last score of the home team, transport costs, and dummies for seasons, matches involving local rivalry and sunshine, all as control variables alongside year dummies intended to capture World Cup effects. Unlike Bird's (1982) study, Falter et al. use match level data. Their World Cup dummy variables show statistically significant increases in club league attendances of 14 percent and 23 percent for the two years following France's World Cup success, ceteris paribus. There is also a positive and significant host city effect. That is, the World Cup effect on club attendances is stronger for cities that hosted tournament games. This is apparently a combination of new stadium (novelty) and advertising effects.

The authors make two robustness checks that do not affect their results. They deduct the more habitual season-ticket holds from their match attendance figures, and they also adopt tobit estimation to deal with sell-out fixtures. The authors also note that the rise in attendances in the French league was not matched by other leagues, such as England, Germany, Italy, and Netherlands. However, the rise in league attendances following a World Cup victory is also apparent in England (1966), Germany (1974, 1990), and Italy (1982). Hence, the authors conclude that average club league attendance tends to increase after a World Cup win, and, moreover, this effect persists for several years after the victory.

4. Benefits to Players from Participating in the World Cup Finals

Players who appear in national team squads in the World Cup finals, and in the earlier qualifying tournament, are selected by national associations, primarily by the national team head coach. These players will have employment contracts with clubs, with whom they play their regular soccer games in leagues, domestic Cup competitions, and in other competitions such as the UEFA Champions' League. However, national associations have the right to demand release of players from club duties for national selections. This right does not amount to conscription because players can "retire" from international soccer. Also, players may be injured with their club teams and hence be temporarily unavailable for selection for national teams. Clubs receive some compensation for release of players for national team games, but this is, nevertheless, a source of complaint, especially when players return from national games with injuries. Conversely, national associations complain that players withdraw from less important national team games, especially ad hoc friendly matches, with injuries that are not as serious as first appears. The international fixture calendar, including the World Cup qualifying competition, is carefully set so that club fixtures are removed from weekends or midweek periods when international games are played. Also, the finals themselves are always played in the close season for the vast majority of leagues.

In terms of career prestige, playing in, and better still, winning the World Cup finals offers a huge boost to player career incomes and also offers a high non-pecuniary reward. A player who appears in the winning team in the World Cup Finals can expect both national adulation for a long time to come and immense off-field-earnings prospects in the form of endorsements and lucrative after-dinner speaking engagements. Hence, players typically regard the possibility of playing in the World Cup finals as an important career goal.

The size of direct payments to players from participating in the World Cup finals has been assessed by Coupé (2007). He finds for the 2006 World Cup that most national associations had bonus schemes that rewarded performance but incentives did not rise monotonically as the tournament progressed. Table 23.2 shows the total and marginal (by tournament stage) team bonus in millions of euros paid to competitors in the 2006 finals. Prior to 2006, FIFA and the national associations had used a fixed bonus per match regardless of the stage of the tournament, presumably under the assumption that prestige effects dominated pecuniary considerations in terms of player effort and performance.

Across the competitors in the 2006 finals, Coupé finds that different bonus schemes were used. Croatia distributed a fixed percentage of FIFA prize money. Germany operated a fixed increase in prize for reaching the next stage together with a double bonus for winning the final. Spain applied a rising bonus level at each stage, and this was the method closest in spirit to the predictions of tournament theory. Generally, though, Coupé finds that bonuses did not have the convex

Table 23.2 Team Bonuses at the 2006 World Cup Finals

Round	Bonuses	Marginal Bonus
Elimination round	3.79	
Reach 8th finals	5.38	1.59
Reach quarter final	7.28	1.90
Semi final	13.61	6.33
Final	14.24	0.63
Winner	15.51	1.27

Source: Coupé (2007).

structure that tournament theory would predict. There was no discernable relationship between size or structure of bonuses and either match results or quality ratings of games played. Typically, all players in a finals squad (fixed at 22 by FIFA) got the same bonus regardless of playing time.

There are several episodes of disputes between players and national associations over the size of bonuses, for example, Germany in 2002 and Ghana in 2006. In Ghana's case, player pressure forced their national association to raise the level of bonuses. Bonuses can vary according to performance in previous World Cup finals. The bonus paid to the French national team squad was €244,000 in 1998 when they won, rose to €300,000 in 2002, as a reflection of player bargaining power, and fell back after a poor 2002 finals to €240,000 in 2006 (all values are nominal).

At the individual level, a number of studies have shown that soccer-player basic salary offered by clubs (before bonuses) can be successfully modeled as a Mincer-type earnings function, in which experience (or age) and its square and performance (assessed as goals scored and possibly assists to goals) are regressors that deliver statistically significant coefficients (Lucifora and Simmons, 2003; Frick, 2006). However, these models lack a full set of performance indicators for defenders and midfield players. Lucifora and Simmons (2003) had a sample of 533 players in the 1993–1994 season for Italy's series A and B with salary data gleaned from the players' association. Using dummy variables to denote players who had recently appeared for their national teams, they find that Italian international players received a 52 percent salary premium against non-internationals whereas other internationals obtained a higher premium of 75 percent. The study predates the Bosman ruling of 1995, which led to enhanced player mobility within the European Union. Using a suitable proxy measure of player salaries and with data spanning 1995 to 2005—therefore, after the Bosman ruling—Frick (2006) shows, again using a standard Mincer earnings function, that sizable nationality premiums for country of birth applied in the German Bundesliga over the period 1995–2003. On top of these ethnicity premiums are further salary returns for each career international appearance made. Frick enters the career international appearance variable in quadratic form and finds that salary is maximized at fifty appearances.

Both Lucifora and Simmons (2003) and Frick (2006) find large salary premiums accruing to players who represent their national teams. We suspect that much of these sizable premiums are a consequence of omitted variable bias because the only performance measure in Frick's study is goals scored, itself mostly a product of forwards, whereas Lucifora and Simmons consider goals and assists. Future data sets may well resolve this omitted variable problem as more detailed performance statistics become publicly available, including those for defenders. However, we do have detailed data on player performances in the Bundesliga top division for one season. These data include the number of tackles won or lost and both completed and incomplete passes made, plus several other performance measures. We find that the impact of these additional variables on player salary is statistically not significant, separately or jointly considered.

Neither Lucifora and Simmons or Frick attempt to separate international status or appearances into participation in World Cup finals and other World Cup games. Clearly, ad hoc "friendly" matches and World Cup finals are quite different in prestige and are likely to have different impacts on salary. At least, this is a proposition to be tested. Within the soccer industry, there has been much discussion of the World Cup finals as a "shop-window" effect for players, especially less well-known players from third-world countries. Rather than view misleading video clips or make expensive scouting trips to remote countries, clubs and their agents can view and assess players in the highest-level competition on a world stage.

At issue here is whether participation in the World Cup finals adds to a player's productivity at club level, that is, augments his human capital, or whether participation in the finals is simply a signal. In the labor- and education-economics literatures, there are longstanding debates about whether college education adds to human capital or is a signal to employers. In the sports-economics literature, we know of no attempt to distinguish signaling from human-capital explanations of player salary. In the major North American sports, appearances for a national team are rare. Playing for the United States national basketball team at the Olympic Games is a notable exception. Therefore, international soccer offers an excellent opportunity to discriminate empirically between human capital and signaling explanations of player salary. Arguments can be made for the conjecture that participation in World Cup finals augments a player's productivity at club level. At the finals, players must pit their wits against the best players from opposing national teams, and their experience of competition at this highest level could well spill over into more successful league performance. Learning effects may also result from playing with excellent peers in one's own national team. Moreover, the World Cup finals put great pressure on players because of the burden of expectations placed on national teams by citizens and media alike. The experience of playing under such intense pressure could also aid the mental development of a player.

On the other hand, the World Cup finals could be argued to be a unique exercise in competition among nations that is unlikely to be replicated at the league level, where teams play each other repeatedly, save for entry and exit occasioned by promotion and relegation. It is quite possible that participation in the World Cup finals adds little or nothing to a player's productivity at club level, yet it has the effect of raising a player's salary. This would be consistent with the signaling hypothesis. Indeed, Szymanski and Kuper (2009), in their entertaining account of world soccer, argue that clubs tend to overpay for players who have recently appeared in World Cup finals.

To properly discriminate between human capital and signaling explanations of soccer-player salary would require more detailed performance measures than current publicly available data sources permit. As an interim step, we can simply assess whether salary premiums for World Cup appearances are larger than for other appearances.

We have data on salaries for all players with positive appearances in the German Bundesliga top division from 1995–2006 to 2007–2008. The salary measure is a market value measure collected by *Kicker* magazine that is known to be a good proxy (in the sense of well correlated) with a subsample of actual salaries released by the German Football Association (Frick, 2006; Torgler and Schmidt, 2007). This sample comprises 1,993 players for a total number of 6,147 observations. We regress log salary against the following control variables: age and its square, number of appearances in the Bundesliga in the previous season, goals scored last season in the Bundesliga, career appearances in Bundesliga and its square, career goals scored in the Bundesliga and its square, and dummy variables for position played in the club team, seasons, and region of birth. Over and above these controls, we add our focus variables, which are number of World Cup finals games played in the previous season, number of non-World Cup finals games played in the previous season, career World Cup finals appearances up to the previous season, and career non-World Cup appearances up to the previous season. Non-World Cup games include World Cup qualifying matches, European Championship qualifying and finals games, and friendly matches. Table 23.3 shows ordinary least squares (OLS) and fixed effects (for players) results of our focus variables.

Table 23.3 OLS and Fixed Effects Results for German Bundesliga; Dependent Variable is Log Salary

Focus Variable	OLS Coefficient (*t* statistic)	Fixed effects coefficient (*t* statistic)
World Cup appearances	0.087 (6.16)	0.072 (5.58)
Other international appearances	0.033 (9.52)	0.015 (4.02)
Career World Cup appearances	0.029 (2.70)	0.004 (0.20)
Career other international appearances	0.007 (4.33)	−0.005 (1.32)
Career other international appearances squared	−0.0001 (4.02)	0.000 (1.05)

The results clearly show that one extra appearance in World Cup finals games delivers a greater salary benefit compared to one extra appearance in other international games. This result applies to both OLS and fixed effects estimates, although the latter may not be reliable because of the small of number of observations per player (three on average). Also, an extra career appearance in World Cup finals games up to the previous season delivers a greater salary increment than an extra game played in non-World Cup finals matches. Hence, we have support for a World Cup shop-window effect on player salaries.

The ordinary least squares results show impacts of international appearances at the means of variables. However, the salary distribution for soccer players is highly skewed, even more so than in standard occupations. Evaluating impacts at the mean may then be misleading, and it is useful to consider impacts over the whole salary distribution. Recently, a number of studies have looked at determinants of player salaries in various sports using quantile regression (for example, see Berri and Simmons, 2009 on NFL quarterbacks and Vincent and Eastman, 2009 on the NHL). This method allows us to estimate differing salary impacts of covariates through the salary distribution. Our own quantile regression results for soccer player in the Bundesliga are shown in Table 23.4.

The results of the quantile regression broadly support those of OLS. At the median salary, it is clear that salary returns to an extra World Cup finals match exceed returns to other international matches. However, above the median, the gap in returns is not significantly different at five percent level, despite the apparent gap in point estimates. The results point to diminishing returns of salary to recent World Cup finals appearances through the salary distribution. For career

Table 23.4 Quantile Regression Results for Log Salary

Focus Variable	0.1 Quantile	0.25 Quantile	0.5 Quantile	0.75 Quantile	0.9 Quantile
World Cup appearances	0.107***	0.102***	0.079***	0.069***	0.062**
Other international appearances	0.029***	0.022***	0.031***	0.037***	0.044***
Career World Cup appearances	0.029*	0.039**	0.030**	0.039**	0.035**
Career other international appearances	0.004+	0.005**	0.007***	0.008***	0.009***
Career other international appearances squared	0.000+	−0.0001**	−0.0001***	−0.0001***	−0.0001***

+ not significant; * $p < 0.10$; ** $p < 0.05$; *** $p < 0.01$.

appearances, the results are more clear-cut, with salary returns to career World Cup finals games always greater than returns to other international games, at all quantiles.

At club level, it is apparent that some national leagues are more prestigious and generate more revenues than others. Hence, one would expect the best players to gravitate towards those Leagues where these players' marginal revenue product would be at their highest. The Leagues where revenues and average player salaries are highest at present are the English Premier League and Spain's La Liga. UEFA gives each European team a score, based on standings in national Leagues and progress in European competitions, essentially the UEFA Champions' League and the European Cup (previously UEFA). The score variable ranges from one to thirty-one. We create a dummy variable, *mover*, for players who switch from lower ranked teams to higher ranked teams between seasons. We then estimate a probit regression for this variable using the same control variables as for the salary model earlier. This model is estimated for all players who switch teams, giving us 1,638 observations. Using our World Cup dummy variables already created, we can determine whether participation in World Cup games raises the probability of movement to a more highly ranked team. The estimated coefficients from our probit model are shown in Table 23.5.

It is clear that an extra recent appearance in a World Cup finals match raises the probability of a move to a more highly ranked team, conditional on moving at all. In contrast, an extra recent appearance in other internationals has no statistically significant effect on a move to a better team. Looking at the career variables, however, the results switch so that an extra career World Cup finals appearance has no effect on probability of a move to a more highly ranked team whereas an extra career appearance in other international matches does have a significant and positive effect on transition to a better team. Nevertheless, the marginal effect is smaller than for recent appearances in World Cup finals matches.

To summarize, recent appearances in World Cup finals matches do appear to have shop-window effects, both by raising player salaries paid by clubs and by helping players secure transitions to more highly ranked teams. This still leaves open the intriguing research question about whether participation in World Cup finals matches genuinely raises player productivity or whether it is just a signal that need not necessarily represent player ability.

Table 23.5 Probit Estimates of Movement to a More Highly Ranked Team

Focus Variable	Coefficient (*t* statistic)
World Cup appearances	0.335 (3.00)
Other international appearances	0.026 (1.57)
Career World Cup appearances	0.045 (0.81)
Career other international appearances	0.026 (2.92)
Career other international appearances squared	−0.0004 (3.38)

5. CLUB VERSUS COUNTRY?: THE DOMESTIC PLAYER QUOTA DEBATE

Up to the Bosman ruling of 1995, it was possible to restrict the number of foreign-born players in a national league by means of various rules. In the English Football League in the 1950s and 1960s, the word *foreigner* meant a player from Scotland or Wales and not someone from Africa or South America. Many European Leagues, such as England and Italy, operated with a rule that a club team could consist of a maximum of three foreign-born players plus two "assimilated" players who were foreign-born but had played at club level in their adopted country for at least two years.

After the Bosman ruling, such restrictions were deemed to be counter to principle of free movement of labor, at least as far as European Union countries were concerned. Restrictions remained in place for players attempting to move into European Union Leagues from outside the European Union. However, the increasing demands by clubs for quality players from outside the European Union grew, and restrictions became more relaxed over time. We now have a situation in which each major soccer League in Europe (England, France, Germany, Italy, and Spain) has a cosmopolitan mix of players from all continents. Indeed, it is quite possible for a team to field a starting eleven consisting entirely of non-domestic players, as practiced in recent years by Arsenal and Chelsea in the English Premier League.

Increased immigration of player talent has led to concerns that the displacement of domestic talent by foreign-born talent, a form of import substitution, might undermine the prospects for the national team. In England, these concerns were documented in a set of proceedings from the "feet drain" conference held at Birkbeck College, London in April 2008. These proceedings feature an address by Gordon Taylor, Chief Executive of the Professional Footballers' Association, which summarizes the arguments in favor of quotas of domestic nationals in team squads, using the term *meltdown* to describe the internationalization of playing talent in the English Premier League in particular (Taylor, 2009). Recently, UEFA has implemented a ruling whereby the squads of teams playing in its Champions' League football competition should comprise twenty-five players, eight of which should be "homegrown," meaning having trained for three seasons at a domestic club between the ages of fifteen and twenty-one, and, of these, at least half should have been trained at the club itself for the same period. Similar rules will be applied by the English Premier League from the 2010/11 season.

One of the arguments in favor of such quotas is that they encourage the development of promising young homegrown players who may eventually be selected for their national teams. Conversely, the present arrangements in several European Leagues, in which starting teams in England, in particular, feature relatively few English players, and youth academies also feature a high proportion of imported foreign players, are alleged to stifle the development of the national team. In

England, this translates into the notion of reduced prospects of winning the World Cup.

Looking at the general arguments surrounding fixed quotas for playing rosters at club level, we make several predictions drawing on simple economic theory:

- The supply curve for talent gets steeper as there is more competition for stars, giving richer clubs an advantage.
- There will be rising salaries for domestic stars.
- There will be less competition for foreign players which means that these get lower salaries and owners get more profits.
- Playing quality falls as some stars leave for Leagues that do not operate restrictions.
- Broadcasting deals become less attractive as the total pool of talent is less.
- Big clubs will be less able to win the UEFA Champions' League.
- Small countries will be less successful in national competitions such as the World Cup.

A number of papers have empirically modeled World Cup success using World Cup finals rankings or something similar as a dependent variable in a regression analysis. Monks and Husch (2009) present a panel data analysis of World Cup success, from 1982 to 2006, using tournament finals standings as their dependent variable. They find that playing on one's own continent and being seeded are each significant determinants of World Cup success. In purely practical terms, of course, the strong records of Brazil and Germany (previously West Germany) at the World Cup finals, as noted in Table 23.1, means that a national team aspiring to win the tournament has to be capable of beating one or both of these teams, or hope that some other team does so.

Leeds and Leeds (2009) adopt a cross-country (not panel) analysis with FIFA points assessed at 2006 as their dependent variable. They find a statistically significant positive effect of the international success of a country's *club* teams on *national* team success. A specific example supporting this result is France in 1998, who managed to win the World Cup with a majority of players in the national team being attached to clubs outside France, many of which had made successful progress in the Champions' League. As we showed earlier, in section 3 on impacts of World Cup finals on fans, Falter et al. (2008) report positive externalities from French national team success on club attendances and revenues. Szymanski and Kuper (2009) take the club versus country arguments a stage further by suggesting that England's prospects for World Cup success would be enhanced if more of the higher-quality English players actually played abroad, a suggestion that is directly counter to the arguments noted earlier in favor of domestic quotas. However, Szymanski and Kuper also suggest that the natural finals standing for an England team at the World Cup is the quarterfinals stage, and it is somewhat optimistic, based on historical data, to expect anything better.

Overall, the attempt to re-introduce domestic quotas in European League soccer appears to be a protectionist device with little merit. The case for such quotas to actually contribute to enhanced World Cup performance has yet to be made, and does not come with any supporting empirical observation. It is notable that the "internationalization" of teams in European soccer leagues has been accompanied by rising attendances in four out of five major European leagues since the mid-1990s (Italy being the exception, which can be explained by a host of specific circumstances relating to hooliganism and corruption scandals). Thus, fans, and also television viewers, appear to like the increasingly cosmopolitan makeup of their club sides.

6. Conclusions

The FIFA World Cup can make a legitimate claim to be the world's largest sporting tournament, even bigger than the Olympic Games in terms of broadcast audience and worldwide interest. The rights to hold this lucrative and prestigious tournament reside with FIFA, and it is no surprise to find that FIFA succeeds in rent extraction, even though FIFA does not take a direct payment from local organizing committees. FIFA does earn substantial revenues from sponsors and advertisers and employs restrictions to ensure that official FIFA partners receive favorable treatment on access to advertising space, for example, on billboards.

The consensus of the sports economics literature is that the World Cup, in common with other large-scale sports events, does not generate substantial benefits in terms of local real income and employment growth and unemployment reductions. In contrast, non-pecuniary benefits, in terms of enhanced satisfaction and happiness, have been identified by some recent research. Further research is needed to corroborate these findings. There is little doubt that hosting the World Cup Finals is costly in terms of stadium development, infrastructure, and security. Where public spending is involved in hosting the Finals, more cost-benefit studies on the net benefits to the host country would be welcome.

There are two impacts on soccer fans worth noting. First, there are novelty effects of new stadiums that persist for some time after new stadiums are constructed, at least as far as Germany 2006 was concerned. Second, hosting and winning the World Cup can lead to a boost to club attendances through a "warm-glow" effect.

Players who appear in the World Cup finals appear to benefit in terms of enhanced salary, although whether this is due to a signaling effect or to genuine improvement in productivity is a matter for future research to resolve. Finals participants also benefit from increased probability of a transfer to a better club, as measured by UEFA rankings for European clubs.

The FIFA World Cup finals are, no doubt, here to stay as a vital component of the sporting calendar. Avoiding excessive and wasteful expenditures is difficult to achieve, given the emotion and sentiment that surrounds the event. However, the World Cup does offer excellent opportunities for economists to make substantial contributions to the various public choice and policy issues surrounding the World Cup, including a more sober assessment of employment and income effects, than is present in consultancy and booster studies.

REFERENCES

Baade, R. 2003. Evaluating subsidies for professional sports in the United States and Europe: A public sector primer. *Oxford Review of Economic Policy* 19: 585–597.

Baade, R., and V. Matheson. 2002. Bidding for the Olympics: Fool's gold? In *Transatlantic Sport,* eds. C. Barros, M. Ibrahim, and S. Szymanski. Cheltenham: Edward Elgar.

Baade, R., and V. Matheson. 2004. The quest for the Cup: Assessing the economic impact of the World Cup. *Regional Studies,* 38: 341–352.

Baade, R., and V. Matheson. 2006. Padding required: Assessing the economic impact of the Super Bowl. *European Sport Management Quarterly,* 6: 353–374.

Berri, D., and R. Simmons. 2009. Race and the evaluation of signal callers in the National Football League. *Journal of Sports Economics,* 10: 23–43.

Bird, P. 1982. The demand for league football. *Applied Economics,* 14: 637–649.

Coates, D., and B. Humphreys. 2005. Novelty effects of new facilities on attendance at professional sporting events. *Contemporary Economic Policy,* 23: 436–455.

Coupé, T. 2007. Incentives and bonuses: The case of the 2006 World Cup. *Kyklos,* 60: 349–359.

Falter, J-M, C. Pérignon, and O. Vercruysse. 2008. Impact of overwhelming joy on consumer demand: The case of a soccer World Cup victory. *Journal of Sports Economics,* 9: 20–42.

Feddersen, A., W. Maennig, and M. Borcherding. 2006. The novelty effect of the new football stadiums: The case of Germany. *International Journal of Sport Finance,* 1: 174–188.

Feddersen, A., A. Grötzinger, and W. Maennig. 2009. Investment in stadiums and regional economic development: Evidence from FIFA World Cup 2006. *International Journal of Sport Finance,* 4: 221–239.

Frick, B. 2006. Salary determination and the pay-performance relationship in professional soccer: Evidence from Germany. In *Sports economics after fifty years: Essays in honour of simon rottenberg,* eds. P. Rodrígues, S. Késenne, and J. García, 125–146. Oviedo: Ediciones de la Universidad de Oviedo.

Hagn, F., and W. Maennig. 2008. Employment effects of the Football World Cup 1974 in Germany. *Labour Economics,* 15: 1062–1075.

Hagn, F., and W. Maennig. 2009. Large scale events and unemployment: The case of the 2006 soccer World Cup in Germany. *Applied Economics,* 41: 3295–3302.

Heyne, M., W. Maenning, and B. Süssmuth. 2007. Mega-sporting events as experience goods. *International Association of Sports Economists Working Paper* 0706.

Hotchkiss, J., R. Moore, and S. Zobay. 2003. Impact of the 1996 Summer Olympic Games on employment and wages in Georgia. *Southern Economic Journal,* 69: 691–704.

Humphreys, B., and A. Zimbalist. 2008. The financing and economic impact of the Olympic Games. In *The business of sports volume 1: Perspectives on the sports industry,* eds. B. Humphreys, and D. Howard, 101–124. Westport, CT: Praeger.

Kavetsos, G., and S. Szymanski. (2010). National well-being and international sports events. *Journal of Economic Psychology, 31: 158–171.*

Leeds, M., and E.M. Leeds. 2009. International soccer success and national institutions. *Journal of Sports Economics,* 10: 351–390.

Lucifora, C., and R. Simmons. 2003. Superstar effects in sport: Evidence from Italian soccer. *Journal of Sports Economics,* 4: 35–55.

Maennig, W., and S. du Plessis. 2007. World Cup 2010: Economic perspectives and policy challenges informed by the experience of Germany 2006. *Contemporary Economic Policy,* 25: 578–590.

Matheson, V. 2008. Mega-events: The effect of the world's biggest sporting events on local, regional and national economies. In *The business of sports volume 1: Perspectives on the sports industry,* eds. B. Humphreys, and D. Howard, 81–100. Westport CT: Praeger.

Monks, J., and J. Husch. 2009. The impact of seeding, home continent and hosting on FIFA World Cup results. *Journal of Sports Economics,* 10: 391–408.

Szymanski, S., and S. Kuper. 2009. Why England lose; and other curious phenonema explained. London: HarperCollins.

Taylor, G. 2009. Meltdown: The nationality of Premier League players and the future of English football. In *Labour market migration in European football: Key issues and challenges,* eds. G. Walters, and G. Rossi. *Birkbeck Sport Business Centre Research Paper Series.* Volume 2.

Torgler, B., and S. Schmidt. 2007. What shapes players' performance in soccer? Empirical findings from a panel analysis. *Applied Economics,* 39: 2355–2369.

Vincent, C., and B. Eastman. 2009. Determinants of pay in the NHL: A quantile regression approach. *Journal of Sports Economics,* 10: 256–277.

CHAPTER 24

ECONOMICS OF THE SUPER BOWL

VICTOR A. MATHESON

INTRODUCTION

THE Super Bowl, the season-ending championship game of the National Football League, is, by most measures, the most significant annual sporting event in the United States. The game routinely attracts a sellout audience willing to pay top dollar for seats. In 2008, the face value for a typical Super Bowl ticket averaged $700, and ticket scalpers could expect to receive many times that figure in the secondary market. Table 24.1 shows the average price for a Super Bowl ticket sold on StubHub, a large secondary market dealer, between 2003 and 2009.

The Super Bowl's television viewing numbers are even more astounding. The Super Bowl is far and away the most watched television program in the United

Table 24.1 Secondary Market Price for Super Bowl Tickets

Date	Teams	Average Price
2/1/09	Pittsburgh Steelers v. Arizona Cardinals	$2,790
2/3/08	New England Patriots v. New York Giants	$3,536
2/4/07	Indianapolis Colts v. Chicago Bears	$4,004
2/5/06	Pittsburgh Steelers v. Seattle Seahawks	$3,009
2/6/05	Philadelphia Eagles v. New England Patriots	$2,659
2/1/04	New England Patriots v. Carolina Panthers	$2,290
1/26/03	Oakland Raiders v. Tampa Bay Buccaneers	$2,767

Source: Darren Rovell, CNBC.com.

States every year. For example, nineteen of the forty most watched programs in U.S. television history are Super Bowls, and more recently, the last ten Super Bowls are the ten most watched programs of the past decade. Between 2000 and 2009, the average Super Bowl attracted just over 90 million viewers in the United States. By way of comparison, over the same period the National Basketball Association (NBA) finals drew 14.3 million per game, the World Series attracted an audience of just under 19 million per game, and the National Hockey League's (NHL) Stanley Cup drew a paltry 4.1 million viewers per game. The Super Bowl's television ratings also dwarf non-sports programming. The Academy Awards drew an average of 39.7 million viewers over the same time period, and even the top-rated non-football program of the entire decade, the series finale of *Friends,* attracted only 52.5 million fans, barely half that of the typical Super Bowl. See Table 24.2 for a comparison of television ratings for various sporting and non-sporting events.

Of course, sky-high television ratings also mean sky-high advertising revenues. A thirty-second television spot during the Super Bowl is the single most valuable piece of real estate in all of American broadcast television. In 2009, a thirty-second commercial during the Super Bowl sold for $3.0 million, an 11 percent increase over the previous year, despite the turmoil affecting the national economy. As shown in Table 24.3, advertising rates at the Super Bowl have experienced a rapid increase over the past two decades, far outpacing inflation as well as advertising rates for other major television events.

ECONOMIC IMPACT OF THE SUPER BOWL

Although the spectacle of the big game may be of the greatest interest to the media, marketing experts, and the general public, the economic impact of the Super Bowl on host cities has attracted the most interest from academic economists. Unlike

Table 24.2 Average Television audiences for Various Programming

Event	Years	Rating	Share	Households	Viewers
Super Bowl	2000–2009	41.7	62.6	45,115,000	90,421,000
World Series	2000–2009	12.1	20.3	13,161,000	19,053,000
NBA Finals	2000–2009	8.4	17	9,957,000	14,320,000
Stanley Cup	2000–2009	2.6	4.9	2,778,000	4,081,000
BCS Championship	2000–2009	16.4	26	17,385,000	26,448,000
Academy Awards	2000–2009	23.9	37.4	25,753,000	39,719,000
American Idol Finale	2002–2009	n.a.	n.a.	n.a.	30,938,000

Source: TVbythenumbers.com, 2009.

Table 24.3 Super Bowl 30-Second Advertising Spot Prices

Year	Super Bowl ad price	Real price	Percent change	Academy Awards ad price	Real price	Percent change
1990	$700,000	$1,164,882	n.a.	n.a.	n.a.	n.a.
1991	$800,000	$1,264,136	8.5 percent	n.a.	n.a.	n.a.
1992	$800,000	$1,229,478	–2.7 percent	n.a.	n.a.	n.a.
1993	$850,000	$1,265,241	2.9 percent	n.a.	n.a.	n.a.
1994	$900,000	$1,306,791	3.3 percent	n.a.	n.a.	n.a.
1995	$1,000,000	$1,411,577	8.0 percent	n.a.	n.a.	n.a.
1996	$1,100,000	$1,511,663	7.1 percent	n.a.	n.a.	n.a.
1997	$1,200,000	$1,600,554	5.9 percent	n.a.	n.a.	n.a.
1998	$1,300,000	$1,709,315	6.8 percent	n.a.	n.a.	n.a.
1999	$1,600,000	$2,069,285	21.1 percent	$1,000,000	$1,293,303	n.a.
2000	$2,100,000	$2,631,263	27.2 percent	$1,305,000	$1,635,142	26.4 percent
2001	$2,050,000	$2,481,047	–5.7 percent	$1,450,000	$1,754,887	7.3 percent
2002	$1,900,000	$2,273,670	–8.4 percent	$1,290,000	$1,543,702	–12.0 percent
2003	$2,100,000	$2,436,355	7.2 percent	$1,355,000	$1,572,029	1.8 percent
2004	$2,250,000	$2,567,037	5.4 percent	$1,503,000	$1,714,781	9.1 percent
2005	$2,400,000	$2,657,052	3.5 percent	$1,503,000	$1,663,979	–3.0 percent
2006	$2,500,000	$2,669,261	0.5 percent	$1,647,000	$1,758,509	5.7 percent
2007	$2,600,000	$2,710,053	1.5 percent	$1,666,000	$1,736,518	–1.3 percent
2008	$2,700,000	$2,701,865	–0.3 percent	$1,689,000	$1,690,166	–2.7 percent
2009	$3,000,000	$3,000,000	11.0 percent	$1,400,000	$1,400,000	–17.2 percent

Source: Advertising Age online, 2007 and TNS Media Intelligence, 2009.

championships in the NBA, NHL, and MLB, the Super Bowl takes place in a neutral site rather than being hosted by the participating teams. Furthermore, unlike the major bowl games played in college football, the location of the game changes from year to year. In this sense, the Super Bowl is most similar to major international competitions such as the Olympics or World Cup. The Union of European Football Association's (UEFA) annual Champions League final, arguably the biggest annual single day sporting event in Europe, also plays at rotating neutral sites in the same fashion.

The NFL and league boosters typically claim that the Super Bowl generates huge economic windfalls for the cities lucky enough to be selected as the host for the event. For example, a joint study conducted by the NFL and the W.P. Carey MBA Sports Business Program estimated an economic impact of $500.6 million from Super Bowl XLI on the greater Phoenix economy in 2008 (W.P. Carey Business School, 2008). As noted by Baade and Matheson (2006a), "If those (types of) numbers are accurate, 'Super' is an apt adjective for the event." Few other events aside from the Olympic Games or soccer's World Cup can generate such lofty claims of an economic windfall from such a short-term event.

The W.P. Carey MBA Sports Business Program is not alone in their heady claims. Consulting firms, local visitor and tourism bureaus, as well teams and the league annually publish eye-popping estimates of the economic impact of the big game. For example, an NFL-Sports Management Research Institute (SMRI) study attributed a $670 million ($863 million in 2009 dollars) increase in taxable sales in South Florida (Miami-Dade, Broward, and Palm Beach counties) and an increase in economic activity of $396 million ($510.1 in 2009 dollars) to the 1999 event (NFL, 1999). As with other economic impact reports, this NFL-commissioned study predicted that a horde of affluent tourists would descend on the three-county area. The NFL-SMRI team reported that the average income of Super Bowl attendees is more than twice that of the average visitor to South Florida during the peak tourist months of January and February ($144,500 compared to $40,000–$80,000), and they spend up to four times as much as the average visitor to South Florida ($400.33 per day compared to $99–$199 per day). As noted by Jim Steeg, the NFL's vice president for special events from 1977–2005,

> The Super Bowl is the most unique of all special events. Extensive studies by host cities, independent organizations and the NFL all try to predict the economic impact the big game will have on a community. They talk to tens of thousands of attendees, local businessmen, corporate planners, media and local fans—looking to see how they are affected.
>
> These studies have provided irrefutable evidence that a Super Bowl is the most dramatic event in the U.S. Super Bowl patrons are significantly more affluent, spend more and have more spent on them, and influence future business in the community more than attendees of any other event or convention held in the U.S. (Steeg, 1999).

Table 24.4 summarizes a variety of *ex ante* estimates of the impact of the Super Bowl on the host city's economy.

There are reasons to be skeptical of such claims, however, because the league has strong financial incentives to publicize studies that report a large financial windfall for host cities. The NFL explicitly uses the lure of the Super Bowl as a carrot to convince otherwise reluctant cities to provide public subsidies for the construction of new playing facilities. For example, just days before Arlington, Texas voters narrowly approved a $325 million tax increase to fund a new stadium for the Dallas Cowboys, NFL commissioner Paul Tagliabue visited the area and suggested that the construction of a new stadium would put the city in a prime position to host an upcoming Super Bowl. Indeed, the new $1.1 billion stadium hosted the 2011 Super Bowl. If the Super Bowl really provides a $400 or $500 million boost to a local economy, then, in effect, the benefits of the game could completely cover the public outlay. Of course, this logical reasoning only holds if the big game does, in fact, generate substantial economic benefits. Given the fact that over $5 billion in taxpayer money has been spent since 1995 on the construction or refurbishment of NFL stadiums, obtaining accurate measurements of the economic impact of NFL franchises and mega-events such as the Super Bowl is of significant public policy importance.

Table 24.4 Estimates of *Ex Ante* Economic Impact of Super Bowl

Year	Author	City	Estimate in millions of \$ and (millions of 2009 \$)
1994	Jeffrey Humphreys, Georgia State University	Atlanta	\$166 (\$240.7)
1995	NFL and Kathleen Davis, Sports Management Research Institute	Miami	\$365 (\$515.2)
1998	PriceWaterhouseCoopers	San Diego	\$295 (\$387.9)
1999	NFL and Kathleen Davis, Sports Management Research Institute	Miami	\$396 (\$510.1)
2000	Jason Ader, Bear Stearns	Atlanta	\$410 (\$513.7)
2000	Jeffrey Humphreys, Georgia State University	Atlanta	\$292 (\$365.9)
2003	Super Bowl Host Committee	San Diego	\$375 (\$435.1)
2006	David Allardice, Lawrence Technological University	Detroit	\$302 (\$322.4)
2007	PriceWaterhouseCoopers	Miami	\$390 (\$406.5)
2008	W.P. Carey MBA Sports Business Program	Phoenix	\$500.6 (\$500.9)
2009	PriceWaterhouseCoopers	Tampa	\$290 (\$290.0)

Source: Various news sources.

Table 24.5 shows the hosts of the Super Bowl from 1967 through 2013. It is interesting to note that during the early years of the game, it was common for the same city to host the game multiple times. Fourteen of the first fifteen games were held in either New Orleans, Miami, or the Los Angeles area. More recently, however, the clear tendency has been to spread out the game. Over the fifteen year period from 1999–2013, eleven different cities held games, and in at least six of these cases (Tampa, Dallas, Indianapolis, Glendale/Phoenix, Houston, and Detroit), the game was awarded immediately after the construction of a new publicly financed stadium. There can be little doubt that the NFL would not place its premier event in Detroit or Indianapolis except in exchange for a large public subsidy in the form of a new stadium for one of the league's franchises.

On the surface, measuring the economic impact of a large sporting event is a regularly straightforward task. One simply needs to add up the number of attendees at the game and estimate the average fan's expenditures in connection with the game. For example, in assessing the impact of Super Bowl XXVIII on the City of Atlanta and the State of Georgia, Jeffrey Humphreys (1994) estimated that the event generated 306,680 "visitor days" and that the average per diem expenditures per visitor was \$252 to arrive at a direct economic impact from the event of \$77 million. The indirect economic impact of an event is calculated by taking the direct impact and applying a multiplier to account for the initial round of

Table 24.5 Super Bowl Locations 1968–2013

City	Number	Years
Miami	10	1968, 1969, 1971, 1976, 1979, 1989, 1995, 1999, 2007, 2010
New Orleans	10	1970, 1972, 1975, 1978, 1981, 1986, 1990, 1997, 2002, 2013
Los Angeles/Pasadena	7	1967, 1973, 1977, 1980, 1983, 1987, 1993
Tampa	4	1984, 1991, 2001, 2009
San Diego	3	1988, 1998, 2003
Houston	2	1974, 2004
Detroit/Pontiac	2	1982, 2006
Atlanta	2	1994, 2000
Phoenix/Tempe/Glendale	2	1996, 2008
Palo Alto	1	1985
Minneapolis	1	1992
Jacksonville	1	2005
Dallas/Arlington	1	2011
Indianapolis	1	2012

expenditures recirculating in the economy. Although the magnitude of the multiplier can be affected by a large number of variables including the sectors in which the initial spending takes place and the size of the metropolitan area in which the event occurs, typically for major sporting events, the multiplier effect doubles the size of the initial round of spending. Humphreys estimated the indirect economic impact of the 1994 Super Bowl at $89 million for a total impact from the game of $166 million.

Although this type of *ex ante* prediction of the economic impact of the Super Bowl appears straightforward, in fact, there are numerous theoretical difficulties with this method of estimation. Three prominent problems frequently cited by economists are the substitution effect, the crowding out effect, and leakages.

The substitution effect occurs when consumers spend money on a sporting event that would normally have been spent elsewhere in the economy. For example, if a parent buys a child a Pittsburgh Steelers 2009 Super Bowl Champions sweatshirt for Christmas, it is unlikely that this sweatshirt represents an additional gift but instead will be given instead of another present. In this case, the Super Bowl has not increased total expenditures on gifts but instead has simply rearranged spending patterns toward sports paraphernalia and away from, say, ugly holiday sweaters. In a broader sense, spending on the Super Bowl by residents of the host city reduces the money available for these consumers to spend elsewhere in the economy. For this reason, most honest practitioners of economic impact analysis exclude spending by local residents from final economic impact numbers.

Of course, for mega-events like the Super Bowl, the substitution effect is likely to be much lower than for a regular season game because a much larger percentage of the attendees are from out of town. On average, the NFL distributes 75 percent of the available tickets to individual teams. Each participating team receives 17.5 percent of the tickets whereas non-participating teams get 1.2 percent of the tickets and the host team receives 5 percent of the tickets. The remaining quarter of the available tickets are retained by the NFL and distributed to sponsors, the broadcast networks, media, VIPs, and the host committee (Tampa Bay Super Bowl Host Committee, 2009). Because few of the attendees at the game are local residents, the substitution effect is likely to be low. On the other hand, the Super Bowl has become a weeklong event with numerous open events for fans that are more accessible to the local population. Spending at these events by local residents must be factored out of expenditure estimates in order to obtain an accurate assessment of the net economic impact.

Crowding out occurs when the crowds and congestion associated with a sporting event displaces regular economic activity. Although there is no doubt that the Super Bowl attracts large numbers of tourists, it is equally clear that others are dissuaded from visiting Super Bowl host cities during the time period around the game. Indeed, the situation is much like Yogi Berra's famous quote, "No one goes there anymore; it's too crowded." Traditionally, the Super Bowl has been held in warm-weather cities that are popular vacation destinations even when the Super Bowl is not in town. Therefore, even if a city's hotels during a Super Bowl are full to capacity with sports fans, if the hotels would have been 80 percent occupied anyway, the net effect of the Super Bowl is the incremental 20 percent of additional rooms that are sold, not the entire number of rooms sold to Super Bowl visitors.

A perfect example of this phenomenon occurred in January 2002 in the aftermath of the September 11 terrorist attacks. The attacks caused the NFL season to be pushed back by one week. Unfortunately, the host city that year, New Orleans, was initially unable to accommodate the Super Bowl on the succeeding weekend because of the presence of a large national auto dealers convention the next week. Only when the convention was moved was it possible to host the Super Bowl on the desired week. Although the Super Bowl filled every hotel room in the city, a large number of these hotel rooms would have been full of auto dealers even in the absence of the Super Bowl. Therefore, the economic impact of the Super Bowl should only include any hotel rooms sold to sports fans over and above the number of rooms that would have been sold anyway. Of course, the recent decisions to hold Super Bowls in cold weather locations such as Detroit and Indianapolis are likely to reduce any potential crowding out effects.

The third major consideration is the problem with leakages. Although a great deal of money may be spent within a city during a mega-event, much of the money may immediately leak out of the city and not end up in the pockets of local residents. In other words, the event may generate economic activity for the city but not generate income for its citizens. Of course, normal multiplier analysis as performed by software modeling packages such as the Bureau of Economic Analysis' Regional Input-Output Multiplier System (RIMS II) or IMPLAN (IMpact analysis for PLANing) does account for leakages in its modeling. However, the complex input-output matrices upon which these models rely are based on the normal inter-industry relationships that exist in local economies, and during a mega-event these relationships may be anything but.

For example, it is common practice for hotels to raise their rates to three or four times the normal level during the Super Bowl. Local hotel desk clerks and room cleaners, however, don't see a 300 percent or 400 percent increase in their wages. It is not the local workers but, instead, shareholders back at corporate head-quarters who benefit from the event. Because a smaller portion of visitor spending at hotels winds up in the hands of local residents during the Super Bowl, multi-pliers calculated using average spending patterns are likely to be biased upward (Matheson, 2009).

Capacity constraints in cities also lead to leakages. The Super Bowl is a large enough event that many services demanded by visitors, ranging from high-end catering to exotic dancing, cannot be fulfilled solely by local providers. Therefore, labor and capital must often be imported into the host city to meet the excess demand. Of course, payments to these imported factors of production do not rep-resent income for the city but instead increase incomes of the guest workers.

An obvious illustration of this situation occurred in Jacksonville in 2005. Jacksonville was a significantly smaller and less popular tourist destination than Super Bowl venues such as New Orleans or Miami, and the city, therefore, had significantly fewer hotel rooms available than most other host cities. To allevi-ate the shortage of hotel rooms, the Super Bowl host committee arranged for six large cruise ships to dock in the area, providing housing for up to 7,600 guests (Donovan, 2005).

Of course, after the big weekend, the ships pulled up anchor and sailed away, tak-ing any revenues they generated with them. In effect, all spending that occurred on these ships was subject to nearly 100 percent leakage from the Jacksonville economy.

Other issues that may affect the true net economic impact of an event include casual visitors and time switching. Casual visitors are tourists who attend a sport-ing event while traveling but whose primary purpose for traveling is not sports related. For example, a professor at a conference who attends a baseball game during his or her stay would get counted into a typical economic impact study. However, the sporting event had no influence on whether the individual visited the city, and the spending done at the ballpark simply substitutes away from spending that would have taken place elsewhere in the economy in the absence of the game. Of course, with a huge event like the Super Bowl, casual spending is unlikely to play a significant role because crowding will preclude large numbers of non-sports fans from being in the city during Super Bowl week anyway.

Time switching, however, may be an important factor when considering the economic impact of the Super Bowl. Time switching occurs when an individual is planning to visit a city but rearranges his or her schedule to coincide with a sport-ing event. The sporting event does not influence whether the person visits the city but instead only influences the timing. This factor can certainly be important for the Super Bowl. A person may have long desired to visit a tourist destination like

New Orleans, and the Super Bowl is what finally prompts the individual to take that trip. However, once the sports fan has seen the city, the tourist has crossed the city off of his or her future vacation destinations.

EMPIRICAL STUDIES OF THE SUPER BOWL

Given the theoretical shortcomings of traditional economic impact analysis as well as public-policy implications of publishing potentially inflated economic benefit numbers, numerous independent scholars not connected with the NFL or any Super Bowl host committees have examined the *ex post* impact of hosting the Super Bowl on a wide variety of economic variables including employment, personal income, per capita income, taxable sales, tax revenues, and visitor statistics. In general, these studies have all come to the same conclusion: the Super Bowl generates a fraction of the economic impact claimed by boosters.

Porter (1999) examines short-term data on sales receipts for several Super Bowls concluding,

> Investigator bias, data measurement error, changing production relationships, diminishing returns to both scale and variable inputs, and capacity constraints anywhere along the chain of sales relations lead to lower multipliers. Crowding out and price increases by input suppliers in response to higher levels of demand and the tendency of suppliers to lower prices to stimulate sales when demand is weak lead to overestimates of net new sales due to the event. These characteristics alone would suggest that the estimated impact of the mega-sporting event will be lower than the impact analysis predicts.

Baade and Matheson (2000) examine twenty-five Super Bowls from 1973 to 1997 and find that the game is associated with an increase in employment in the host metropolitan area of 537 jobs. Based on simple assumptions about the value of a job to a community, they estimate an average economic impact of roughly $30 million or approximately one-tenth the figures touted by the NFL.

Baade and Matheson (2006a) update their previous results by directly examining personal income in host cities. They find that for Super Bowls held between 1970 and 2001, the host city experienced an average increase in personal income of $91.9 million. Although this amount is not statistically significant at any generally accepted level, Baade and Matheson also calculate confidence intervals for their point estimate and conclude that there is less than a 5 percent probability that the true impact of the Super Bowl on personal incomes in host metropolitan statistical areas exceeds $300 million, and the chance that the true impact exceeds $400 million is less than 1 percent.

Coates and Humphreys (2002) look at all post-season play in American professional sports, not just the Super Bowl, and find that hosting the Super Bowl had no statistically significant effect on per capita income in the host city. Interestingly, however, they do find that the city of the winner of the Super Bowl experiences statistically significant increase of roughly $140 in per capita income. They attribute this finding to possible higher labor efficiency due to a "feel-good" effect although they concede that the most likely answer is simply spurious correlation. Matheson (2005), on the other hand, arrives at a figure of between a $50 and $60 increase in per capita income for winning cities, a figure that is not statistically significantly different from zero at the 5 percent significance level.

Davis and End (2009) extend the results of both of the previous papers. Although their paper focuses on the effects of team-winning percentage on city-wide wages and income per capita, they include variables for both hosting and winning the Super Bowl. Under various estimation methods the coefficient on winning the Super Bowl is nearly always positive and is statistically significant at the 5 percent level in roughly half the estimations. Interestingly, the coefficient on hosting the Super Bowl is nearly always negative and is again statistically significant at the 5 percent level in roughly half the regression models, suggesting that there is evidence that hosting the Super Bowl may actually have a significant negative impact on income per capita in host cities.

As noted previously, a major difficulty of measuring the economic impact of events like the Super Bowl is that even the effect of largest sporting events may be hard to isolate within the large, diverse metropolitan economies in which they take place. For example, even if the Super Bowl does result in a $500 million boost to the host city, this is less than 0.2 percent of the annual GDP of a large metropolitan area like Miami, the most frequent Super Bowl host. Any income gains as a result of the big game would likely be obscured by normal fluctuations in the region's economy. This problem is further compounded by the fact that the Super Bowl, even with its surrounding activities, lasts for only a few days. Even if the effects of the event are large in the time period immediately surrounding the Super Bowl, this impact is likely to be obscured in annual data. All the ex post studies described previously utilize annual data.

If a data source that covers a smaller geographical area or a shorter timeframe can be uncovered, however, any potential impact is more likely to be identified. For example, although the presence of the Super Bowl might have a large effect on neighborhood businesses, the overall effect on a state or country's economy will be minuscule and hard to identify. Furthermore, these same economic effects may be large for the time period immediately surrounding the event, but over the course of an entire year, the impact of a single weeklong period is not likely to show up as an important change.

For this reason, several researchers have turned to taxable sales, which are often available monthly and frequently cover areas as small as individual cities and counties instead of entire metropolitan areas. Furthermore, general sales tax collections or specific increases in the sales tax rate have been used to finance many publicly funded sports facilities making an examination of taxable sales especially relevant from a public policy standpoint. For example, of the twenty-three new stadiums constructed for NFL franchises between 1992 and 2009, seven were funded, at least in part, through increases in the local general sales tax rate, and another eight were funded through increased excise taxes, that is, sales taxes on specific goods and services such as rental cars or hotel rooms (Baade and Matheson 2006b). In addition, the single largest component of gross domestic product is consumer spending, much of which is captured by taxable sales, and, therefore, taxable sales are a good proxy for overall economic activity.

Baade, Baumann, and Matheson (2008) examine monthly taxable sales in Florida counties between 1980 and 2005. Three Florida cities (Miami, Tampa, and Jacksonville) hosted seven Super Bowls during this period. Six of the seven Super Bowls show no significant increase in taxable sales during the event, and the authors calculate that a typical game increased taxable sales by roughly $99 million.

Coates (2006) performs a similar analysis on monthly sales-tax collections for the city of Houston finding that the Super Bowl increases tax revenues by roughly $5 million. Given a tax rate of 5 percent, this approximates an increase in taxable sales of roughly $100 million, confirming the results of Baade, Baumann, and Matheson (2008). Coates and Depken (2006) extend this analysis to cover multiple cities in Texas, again finding a significant increase in taxable sales associated with hosting the Super Bowl although the estimated increase is only roughly half that estimated by Coates (2006).

Interestingly, the NFL itself has also examined the effect of the Super Bowl on taxable sales. In one of the few examples of a league-sponsored *ex post* study, the NFL reported that, "Thanks to Super Bowl XXXIII, there was a $670 million increase in taxable sales in South Florida compared to the equivalent January–February period in 1998" (NFL Report, 1999). Indeed, a cursory examination of the data shows that the three county region of Miami-Dade, Broward, and Palm Beach counties did experience an increase in taxable sales roughly the size of that claimed by the league. Unfortunately for the NFL, their study is woefully inept because the league neglected to account for factors besides the Super Bowl, such as inflation, population growth, and routine economic expansion, which could account for the rise in taxable sales. As noted as by Baade and Matheson (2000), over 90 percent of the increase can be accounted for by these variables.

Of further interest is the fact that if taxable sales are further broken down by county, both Broward and Palm Beach counties actually experienced lower-than-expected taxable sales in 1999 (by $14 and $16 million, respectively) despite the presence of the Super Bowl. Only Miami-Dade county (the actual location of the Super Bowl) experienced an increase in taxable sales (of $67 million) beyond expectations. This is further evidence that mega-events merely tend to shift resources from one area to another rather than generating new economic activity.

Finally, it is worth noting that taxable sales in the area during January–February 2000, the year after the game, were $1.26 billion higher than in the same months during the Super Bowl year. Strangely, the NFL never publicized a story announcing, "Thanks to the lack of a Super Bowl, there was a $1.26 billion increase in taxable sales in South Florida compared to the equivalent January–February period in 1999."

NON-MONETARY BENEFITS

If the monetary benefits of the Super Bowl generally fail to materialize at the level predicted by *ex ante* estimates, it is often claimed that the Super Bowl brings indirect or non-pecuniary benefits to host cities that add substantially to the direct monetary benefits. For example, in assessing the impact Super Bowl XLII in Glendale, Arizona, Michael Mokwa, chairman of the marketing department at the W.P. Carey School of Business stated, "'The money is just the tip of the iceberg. Thousands and thousands of people who came here for the Super Bowl, of whom many had never been to the Valley before, took away powerful memories and good feeling about Arizona.' This translates, he said, into coveted return visits, family and business relocations, and word-of-mouth marketing throughout the country. Priceless, as MasterCard is fond of saying." (W.P. Carey School of Business, 2008)

Alan Sanderson, a University of Chicago economist counters, however, that anyone who claims that the intangible benefits of an event like the Super Bowl are "priceless" or "immeasurable" either are "too lazy to go find the correct answer or are afraid of what the true answer might be."

Certainly the game brings potential intangible benefits to the host city. The game can serve to advertise the city to future conventions, businesses, and individual tourists. However, here, too, estimates of potential benefits can be inflated by the league. Overhead television shots broadcast during the game are often assigned a value at the same rate as commercial during the game. Thus, a 30-second shot of downtown Miami is valued at the same rate as a 30-second commercial spot, which sold for $3 million in 2009. Given the large number of times the stadium or the city is shown during the game, such advertising can easily add up to tens or hundreds of millions of dollars of imputed value. But such calculations must be flatly incorrect.

First, this technique implies that a simple thirty-second overhead shot has the same effect on the consumer as a targeted and professionally designed commercial. Such an implication is both unlikely and would invalidate the *raison d'être* of the entire advertising industry. Next, this technique assumes that advertising the city is not subject to diminishing marginal returns. Although the first shot of the city may have an advertising effect, it is almost certainly not the case that the thirtieth panoramic scene would have the same impact. Finally, when city tourism bureaus state that the Super Bowl provides more advertising for a city than the city would be able to purchase on its own, in fact revealed preference suggests that the game provides more advertising than the city would be willing to purchase on its own.

The very fact that cities rarely have tourism advertising budgets in the hundreds of millions of dollars suggests that cities typically don't value such advertising very highly.

There are several other considerations that should be mentioned. First, while the Super Bowl may generate some repeat visitors, if time switching is occurring, as discussed previously the Super Bowl may actually lead to less future tourism. Next, although it is frequently claimed that mega-events like the Super Bowl serve to "put a city on the map," most Super Bowl hosts are large, popular tourist destinations that are already homes to multiple Fortune 500 corporate headquarters and are frequent convention sites. By any definition, cities like Miami, New Orleans, and Los Angeles are already on everyone's map. Furthermore, not every host city comes away from the game with an enhanced reputation. Many visitors left Jacksonville, the host of Super Bowl XXXIX, with the impression that the city had little to offer in the way of excitement or cultural amenities. Finally, although it is possible that a company could decide to locate its corporate headquarters and production facilities to a new city based on the favorable impressions its CEO had while in town for the Super Bowl, there isn't even anecdotal evidence of any major corporate relocations associated with this or any other mega-sporting event. Although there is no denying that intangible benefits from the Super Bowl may exist, there does not appear to be much empirical evidence that they are very large.

Conclusion

There is little doubt that the Super Bowl is at the center of the American sports universe. It is the most watched sporting event, or any event for that matter, in the country every year. The game also has the highest priced tickets and the most expensive sponsorships among spectator sports. If one believes the *ex ante* estimates of economic impact provided by the NFL and civic boosters, the event also generates many hundreds of millions of dollars in benefits for the host city, and the league uses these promises of riches to convince cities that the construction of a new NFL stadium at significant public expense is a profitable investment, especially if it includes the promise of a future Super Bowl.

The lure of the Super Bowl is used to extract public financing from cities; this therefore creates ample reason to be skeptical of any claims made about the reported economic impact because the sponsors of the impact studies have a financial interest in results that show large economic benefits from the game. Aside from the inherent incentive problem associated with impact assessments, there are numerous theoretical reasons to be wary of economic impact statements. Such reports do a notoriously poor job of accounting for the substitution effect and the crowding out effect. In short, although *ex ante* economic impact studies often do a good job measuring activity that *does* occur because of an event, they do a poor job at measuring any economic activity that *does not* occur because of an event. In other words, economic impact studies typically measure gross economic activity when what is really desired is a measure of net economic activity. Furthermore, standard multiplier analysis may give misleading and inflated results when applied during mega-events.

Ex post economic analyses of the Super Bowl by scholars not financially connected with the game have typically found that the observed effects of the game on real economic variables such as employment, government revenues, taxable sales, GDP, and personal income, although generally positive, are a fraction of those claimed by the league and sports boosters. When considering optimal public policy with respect to sports infrastructure, it would be wise to take any claims of super benefits from the Super Bowl with a grain of salt. It appears that most economic impact reports are padded at least as well as the players on the field.

REFERENCES

Advertising Age. 2009. Super Bowl 2007—Advertising history: 40 years of prices and audience. http://adage.com/SuperBowlBuyers/superbowlhistory07.html; accessed November 15, 2009.

Baade, Robert, Robert Baumann, and Victor Matheson. 2008. Selling the game: Estimating the economic impact of professional sports through taxable sales. *Southern Economic Journal,* 74: 794–810.

Baade, Robert, and Victor Matheson. 2000. An assessment of the economic impact of the American Football Championship, the Super Bowl, on host communities. *Reflets et Perspectives,* 30: 35–46.

Baade, Robert, and Victor Matheson. 2006a. Padding required: Assessing the economic impact of the Super Bowl. *European Sports Management Quarterly,* 6: 353–374.

Baade, Robert, and Victor Matheson. 2006b. Have public finance principles been shut out in financing new stadiums for the NFL? *Public Finance and Management,* 6: 284–320.

Coates, Dennis. 2006. The tax benefits of hosting the Super Bowl and the MLB All-Star Game: the Houston experience. *International Journal of Sport Finance,* 1: 239–252.

Coates, Dennis, and Craig A. Depken II. 2006. Mega-events: Is the Texas-Baylor game to Waco what the Super Bowl is to Houston? *International Association of Sports Economists, Working Paper Series* 06–06.

Coates, Dennis, and Brad Humphreys. 2002. The economic impact of post-season play in professional sports. *Journal of Sports Economics,* 3: 291–299.

Davis, Michael C., and Christian M. End. 2009. A winning proposition: The economic impact of successful National Football League franchises. *Economic Inquiry,* in press.

Donovan, John. 2005. From downtown? Jax's urban sprawl makes for Super tough week. Sports Illustrated online. http://sportsillustrated.cnn.com/2005/writers/john_donovan/02/04/scene.jacksonville/; posted February 4, 2005; accessed November 15, 2009.

Humphreys, Jeffery. 1994. The economic impact of hosting Super Bowl XXVIII on Georgia. *Georgia Business and Economic Conditions,* May-June: 18–21.

Matheson, Victor. 2005. Contrary evidence on the economic effect of the Super Bowl on the victorious city. *Journal of Sports Economics,* 6: 420–428.

Matheson, Victor. 2009. Economic multipliers and mega-event analysis. *International Journal of Sport Finance,* 4: 63–70.

National Football League. 1999. Super Bowl XXXII generates $396 million for South Florida. NFL Report 58.

Porter, Philip. 1999. Mega-sports events as municipal investments: A critique of impact analysis. In *Sports Economics: Current Research,* eds. J. Fizel, E. Gustafson, and L. Hadley, 61–73. Westport, CT: Praeger Press.

Rovell, Darren. 2008. Super Bowl tickets: What they could cost this year. CNBC.com. http://www.cnbc.com/id/22647777; posted January 14, 2008; accessed November 15, 2009.

Steeg, Jim. 1999. Inquiring minds should know. *Fox Sports Biz online;* posted November 9, 1999.

Tampa Bay Super Bowl Host Committee. 2009. FAQs. http://tampabaysuperbowl.com/faqs.htm; accessed December 1, 2009.

TNS Media Intelligence. 2009. TNS media intelligence reports Academy Awards spending reached $691 million. TNS Media Intelligence online. http://www.tns-mi.com/news/02112009.htm; posted February 11, 2009; accessed November 30, 2009.

TVbythenumbers. 2009. Various pages, http://tvbythenumbers.zap2it.com/; accessed November 15, 2009.

W. P. Carey Business School. 2008. Economic impact study: Phoenix scores big with Super Bowl XLII. http://knowledge.wpcarey.asu.edu/article.cfm?articleid=1597; posted April 23, 2008; accessed November 30, 2009.

PART VI

ECONOMICS OF REFEREEING

....

CHAPTER 25

CAREER DURATION IN PROFESSIONAL FOOTBALL

THE CASE OF GERMAN SOCCER REFEREES

....

BERND FRICK

1. INTRODUCTION

....

IT is now commonplace belief, even among European economists, that professional team sports offer a unique opportunity for labor market research:

> There is no research setting other than sports where we know the name, face, and life history of every production worker and supervisor in the industry. Total compensation packages and performance statistics for each individual are widely available, and we have a complete data set of worker-employer matches over the career of each production worker and supervisor in the industry.... Moreover, professional sports leagues have experienced major changes in labor market rules and structure ... creating interesting natural experiments that offer opportunities for analysis. (Kahn 2000: 75; with similar arguments Rosen and Sanderson 2001)

Contrary to football players and head coaches, for whom salaries as well as information on contract length and career duration have been extensively analyzed in an already large (and still growing) number of publications,[1] referees have been almost completely neglected as far as remuneration and career duration is concerned. Apart from the literature that studies the behavior of and the decisions made by referees under particular circumstances (for an overview see Buraimo, Forrest and Simmons 2010), very little is known about the "last amateurs" in what has recently become a billion Euro industry.[2]

Thus, the following paper seeks to contribute to the discussion on labor markets in professional team sports by focusing on the careers of a particular group of actors, the referees. In the next section, I describe the institutional framework and the nomination procedure that is currently applied in the German "Bundesliga" (henceforth GBL). I then proceed in section 3 to present the data and some descriptive evidence on career length of soccer referees. Section 4 describes the estimation techniques used, and section 5 presents the empirical findings. Section 6 concludes with a plea for further research on the determinants of career length of referees from a comparative perspective (i.e. across leagues and across sports).

2. Institutional Framework and Nomination Procedure

In soccer, referees and their two assistants[3] are appointed to regulate matches under the rules set by the governing body of world soccer, Fédération Internationale de Football Association (FIFA).[4] In applying these laws, referees have sanctions in the form of cautions (yellow cards) and expulsions of players from the field (red cards). Although yellow cards are issued for less heinous offenses, such as dissent, deliberate handball, persistent fouling, obstruction, and shirt pulling, this sanction offers an important disincentive to persist in illegal behavior because a second caution to the same player is accompanied by dismissal (second yellow card). A red card results from serious misconduct such as hitting a player or a dangerous tackle or the so-called professional foul in which a player deliberately prevents a clear goal-scoring opportunity for an opponent by unfair means. Red cards are relatively infrequent. Contrary to the situation in most U.S. team sports, referees in soccer have to decide immediately, that is, they do not have the possibility to watch a foul, an offside, or a goal again in slow motion. Therefore, fans, players, and head coaches worldwide often complain about both inconsistent application of rules by referees and alleged bias against their team. Critical refereeing decisions can be pivotal for a team's prospects of winning championships, qualifying for lucrative European competition, or avoiding relegation. As revenue streams, especially sales of broadcast rights, have grown in European football, so criticism of referee behavior has intensified (Simmons 2009).

In an attempt to reduce the likelihood as well as the number of false decisions, the German Football Association (DFB) has implemented a specific tournament-style nomination procedure to select and motivate the best referees. At the beginning of each season, a pool of twenty-two referees[5] is created by identifying the previous season's top-performers who are still eligible (i.e., below a certain age threshold) plus a certain number of "junior" referees who demonstrated their talent and abilities in the previous season in the second division.[6] During each match that a referee is assigned to, he is monitored by a delegate of the GBL. Poorly performing referees are sanctioned immediately in the sense that they have to wait significantly longer until they are assigned to the next match. Because referees are remunerated on a match basis, longer waiting periods result in lower salaries.[7] Moreover, at the end of the season, poorly performing referees can be relegated to a lower division. Because referees have to retire at the age of forty-seven, each season two to four new referees enter into the pool, out of which nine persons are selected every weekend.[8]

In the early 1990s when the revenues of the league skyrocketed (see Frick and Prinz 2006) the DFB started to pay its referees more than just their travel costs plus a fixed daily allowance (until 1991–1992 that allowance amounted to approximately €100 per weekend). Starting in 1992–1993 referees received a match fee of €750, which was increased to €1,250 in 1995–1996 and to €2,000 in 1997–1998. Further increases occurred in 2000–2001 (to €3,068) and, finally, in 2005–2006 (to €3,600).[9] Match fees in the second division have always been set at 50 percent of what the referees were paid in the first division. Thus, there are pronounced financial incentives to maximize the number of appearances in the country's elite division.[10]

3. DATA AND DESCRIPTIVE EVIDENCE

The following empirical investigation is based on a data set including all referees who were assigned to at least one match in any of the forty-six GBL seasons 1963–1964 to 2008–2009. The data has been compiled from a compendium published by the GBL (Bender 2003) and various special issues of a highly respected soccer magazine (*Kicker*). During the period under investigation, 282 different referees appeared in the GBL, officiating between 1 and 338 matches. Of these 282 referees, 19 were still active at the start of the current season (2009–2010). Thus, the findings reported in Figure 25.1 are derived from analyses at the person level and not at the spell- or the person-year-level.[11]

Average career duration of referees is 6.3 years. Compared to players, for whom average career duration is four years and average spell length 3.4 years (see Frick, Pietzner, and Prinz 2007, 2009) and head coaches, for whom average

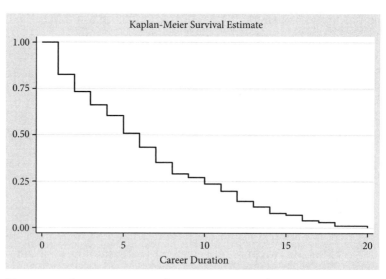

Figure 25.1 Career Duration of German Soccer Referees, 1963–2009.

career duration is 3.5 years and average spell length 2.1 years (Barros, Frick, and Passos 2009, Barros, Frick, and Prinz 2010), referees seem to survive much longer. However, as in the case of players and head coaches, this average hides a large variation: 18 percent of the match officials exit the labor market after just one season, another 17 percent after their second or third season. After five years, exactly half of the referees have been replaced, whereas the percentage of long-term survivors (more than twelve seasons) is less than 10 percent (see Figure 25.1).

A perhaps surprising finding is that the survivor curves are not significantly different from each other when distinguishing between the different decades or pay regimes.[12] This seems to suggest that (increasing) financial incentives do not motivate the referees to put forth higher levels of effort. However, there is yet another explanation—poorly performing match officials are replaced by better referees before the beginning of the new season—that will be tested later in section 5. Although the annual number of substitutions is quite low, ranging from zero to a maximum of three since the early 1990s, the league has implemented a powerful promotion-relegation system to select and motivate its referees, which does, indeed, induce match officials to put forth high amounts of effort in order to avoid relegation to the lower levels of the league hierarchy, where far less money can be earned. This, of course, does not necessarily imply that all referees constantly perform outstandingly. The evaluations expressed in school grades and published by *Kicker* demonstrate that referee performance varies considerably across individuals and over time (see Frick, Gürtler, Prinz 2009 as well as Frick, Gürtler, Prinz, and Wiendl 2009).

Another interesting finding is that the number of matches a referee is assigned to over the course of his career is highly concentrated among a small minority of match officials: On the one hand, 20 out of 282 referees (7.0 percent) have been assigned to a single first division match in their entire career, whereas on the other hand, a small minority of 2.5 percent of the referees (7 out of 282) officiated more than 11 percent of the matches that have been played since 1963 (the respective Gini coefficient measuring the degree of concentration is rather high at 0.553).[13]

4. ESTIMATION TECHNIQUES

Statistical analysis of survival data in general and career length in particular is difficult insofar as there is no satisfactory way of handling right-censored data, that is, the referees for whom the event of being ejected from the pool is not observed within the time period of the study (t_4 in Figure 25.2). This problem, however, is less dramatic as more than 90 percent of the referees in my data set have already retired. At the same time, I also observe referees whose spells are left-censored (about 15 percent of all observations). These are the individuals who might have started their careers before the GBL was established in 1963–1964 (t_5 in Figure 25.2). Unfortunately, I am unable to distinguish between match officials who started their careers in 1963–1964 and those who had already been active in one of the predecessors of the GBL, that is, those who had already been active before 1963–1964. However, estimating the model with and without the referees with right- and/or left-censored spells leaves the findings virtually unchanged. This is not surprising, because the overwhelming majority of the match officials begins and ends their careers during the period of observation.

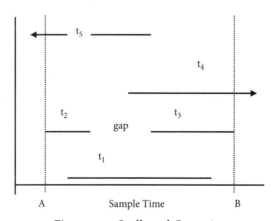

Figure 25.2 Spells and Censoring.
(*Notes*: A: Start of observation period (season 1963/64), B: End of observation period (season 2008/09), t1: Completed spell, t2, t3: Intermediate exit with subsequent re-entry, t4: Right-censored spell (no information on career length post 2008/09), t5: Left-censored spell (no information on career length before 1963/64)).

I first estimate a semi-parametric proportional hazard model (see Cox 1972), a well recognized and commonly used statistical technique for analyzing survival data. It is the most general regression model developed to investigate survival data, because it does not impose any assumption concerning the nature or the shape of the underlying survival distribution. The model assumes that the underlying hazard rate (rather than the survival time) is a function of the independent variables. The Cox model does not limit the pattern of the hazard rate like parametric models with a Weibull, Gompertz, exponential or log-logistic distribution and it further solves the problem of censored observations (Kiefer 1988).

In the Cox model, the conditional hazard function, given the vector z of covariate values at time t or the corresponding time interval, is assumed to be of the following form:

$$\lambda\,(t\,|\,z) = \lambda_0(t)\,\exp\,(\beta\,z) \tag{1}$$

where β is the vector of regression coefficients and $\lambda_0(t)$ denotes the baseline hazard function. The baseline hazard function corresponds to the probability for the respective referee leaving the league either voluntarily or involuntarily (or generally reaching an event) when all the explanatory variables are zero. The baseline hazard function is analogous to the intercept in ordinary regressions (since $\exp^0 = 1$). One additional feature of the model is that the exogenous variables can be time constant (such as nationality), but also—and more important—time varying (such as performance or age). The regression coefficients β (the covariates of interest) give the proportional change that can be expected in the hazard, related to changes in the independent variables.

Second, I estimate a Gompertz model, a parametric survival-time model that has, in the past, been extensively used by medical researchers analyzing mortality data. The Gompertz distribution has the following hazard and survivor function:

$$h(t) = \lambda\,\exp(\gamma t) \tag{2}$$

$$S(t) = \exp\,\{-\lambda\gamma^{-1}\,(e^{\gamma\lambda}-1)\} \tag{3}$$

This model is implemented by parameterizing $\lambda_j = \exp(x_j\,\beta)$, implying that $h_0 = \exp(\gamma t)$, where γ is an ancillary parameter to be estimated from the data. This distribution is particularly suitable for modeling data with monotone hazard rates that either increase or decrease exponentially with time. When γ is positive, the hazard function increases with time; when γ is negative, the hazard function decreases with time; and when γ is zero, the hazard function is equal to λ for all t, so the model reduces to an exponential.[14] Given that a number of parametric models are available, it is necessary to justify the selection of a particular one. When parametric models are nested, that is, when the same set of right-hand side variables is used in the estimations, the likelihood ratio or Wald test can be used to discriminate between them, because the best-fitting model is the one with the largest log-likelihood.[15] In the present context, the Gompertz model produces the best fit because its log-likelihood is far larger than the ones of the Weibull, the log normal, the log-logistic, the exponential, and the generalized gamma model.[16]

5. FINDINGS

The dependent variable in my estimations is career duration (in years) of individual referees in the GBL in the years 1963–1964 to 2008–2009 (46 consecutive seasons). My estimations are straightforward and few, if any of the variables warrant further explanation. I include as explanatory variables referee age at the start of the career (*age_start*) as well as the squared term of age at the start of the career, the number of matches per season (*m_p_s*), a nationality dummy (*foreigner,* equal to one if the referee is non-German) and a linear time trend (*trend*). Moreover, I include a set of interaction terms (i.e., multiplicative combinations of matches per season and age (*age_mps*), matches per season and nationality (*for_mps*) and matches per season and time trend (*tt_mps*). The means and standard deviations of the relevant variables are displayed in Table 25.1.

Although the test of the proportional hazards assumption clearly favors the Gompertz over the Cox-model, the estimated coefficients are surprisingly similar. In both cases, age at the beginning of the career seems to result in a higher hazard, and, therefore, a shorter survival time, controlling for other (potential) determinants of career length.

The hazard ratios reported correspond to a one-unit change in the corresponding variable.[17] This, in turn, implies that, in the linear specification, an additional year of age at the beginning of the career increases the risk of being kicked out of the referee pool by 8 percent (Cox model) and 11 percent (Gompertz model) per year, respectively (results not reported in Table 25.2). Including the squared term of age at the beginning of the career (see Table 25.2) changes the picture considerably, because it now turns out that the optimal age to enter the GBL, because it maximizes career length of a referee, is 27 in the Cox-model and 29 in the Gompertz model.[18] Moreover, older referees are assigned to a significantly higher number of matches, indicating particular returns to experience (and not as a special gift to those who have survived for a long time and are now approaching retirement).[19] Each additional match a referee is assigned to during a season reduces the risk of being ejected by about 45 percent. Perhaps surprisingly, that effect is strictly linear, as inclusion of a squared (and

Table 25.1 Variables, Means, and Standard Deviations

Variable	Mean	Std. Dev.	Min	Max
Career duration	6.27	4.65	1	20
Career matches	49.75	53.87	1	338
Matches per season	6.46	3.73	1	20
Age at start of career	35.36	4.62	23	47
Age at end of career	41.63	5.15	26	50
Foreigner	0.05	—	0	1
Linear time trend	16.55	12.25	1	46

Table 25.2 Estimation Results

Variable	Cox Model			Gompertz Model		
	Hazard Ratio	Robust Std. Err.	z	Hazard Ratio	Robust Std. Err.	Z
age_start	0.7409	0.1281	−1.74*	0.6664	0.1272	−2.13**
age_start2	1.0051	0.0023	2.20**	1.0069	0.0025	2.71***
m_p_s	0.5648	0.0810	−3.98***	0.5399	0.0891	−3.74***
foreigner	0.1080	0.0382	−6.29***	0.0784	0.0292	−6.83***
trend	1.0382	0.0118	3.31***	1.0481	0.0134	3.67***
age_mps	1.0096	0.0035	2.72***	1.0101	0.0041	2.46 **
for_mps	5.4904	1.9649	4.76***	7.3170	2.8754	5.06***
tt_mps	0.9994	0.0015	−0.42+	0.9989	0.0017	−0.59+
N of Subjects	282			282		
N of Failures	263			263		
Time at Risk	1,770			1,770		
Wald Chi2	244.9***			250.7***		
LL Base Model	−1,251.3			−376.2		
LL Full Model	−1,157.7			−241.5		
Test of PHA#	19.18***			—		

test of proportional hazard assumption.

+ not significant; * p < .10; ** p < .05; *** p < .01.

later on also a cubic) term proved to be statistically insignificant. However, because performance and the number of matches per season are closely correlated (see Frick, Gürtler, and Prinz 2009, Frick, Gürtler, Prinz, and Wiendl 2009), this implies that the best referees survive the longest—hardly a surprising result.[20]

The coefficient of the linear time trend seems to suggest that the risk of being ejected from the referee pool increases by about 4–5 percent per year, implying that referee careers are shorter today than they used to be in the early years of the GBL. This, however, is not true because two competing forces are at work here: On the one hand, being young at the start of the career fosters survival (recall that the optimal age to enter the market in terms of career length is somewhat around 28 years). On the other hand, in the 1960s, 1970s, and 1980s, those entering the pool were much older (35 years on average). Hence, the age effect dominates the trend effect that captures changes in the size and the composition of the referee pool.

The fact that we observe significantly longer careers in the second half of the observation period, i.e. since the early 1990s, is completely due to a small sub-group of referees surviving for a particularly long period. Thus, the distribution of career length has changed considerably over time: Although in the 1960s and 1970s and, to a lesser extent, in the 1980s, career duration in the population under study is normally distributed, we now observe a pronounced bimodal distribution, that is, today more than half of the match officials are replaced very quickly and the remaining referees manage to survive very long periods.[21] On the other hand, it seems plausible to assume that the rules applied to assign referees to matches have somewhat changed over time: Although in the early days of the GBL experience, in terms of age, was more important for survival, it is now clearly performance that counts. This, in turn, is not surprising, because the increasing remuneration not only makes it more attractive for referees to stay in the football business as long as possible, but it also increases the incentives for the GBL to more carefully select its referees (in the case of amateurs, mistakes and questionable decisions may be acceptable, in the case of [semi] professionals, however, this is clearly not acceptable any longer).

Figures 25.3–25.5 display the fitted survivor, hazard, and cumulative hazard functions resulting from the Gompertz-model. The plots show the survival experience of a match official with a covariate pattern equal to the average covariate pattern in the population under study. It appears that both the hazard as well as the cumulative hazard function have an exponential shape, that is, beyond a certain point the risk of being ejected from the pool of referees increases dramatically. This, in turn, explains why only about 20 percent of the individuals manage to survive for ten years or longer.

As already mentioned in the beginning, average career length of referees is significantly higher than career duration of players and head coaches. This is certainly due to the fact that the referees' job is physically less demanding than the players' job and that, therefore, aging is less of a problem for the match officials. Moreover, referees can better substitute declining physical abilities by experience. The on-average-rather-short careers of head coaches, in turn, are mostly due to the fact that, in many cases, promoted teams are relegated again after just one season. If these teams ever return to the first division (there are a number of "yoyo-teams") they have almost always hired a new head coach in the meantime. Thus, it is not surprising, that the distribution of career length of head coaches in the GBL exhibits an even more pronounced bimodal pattern than is the case for referees since the early 1990s.

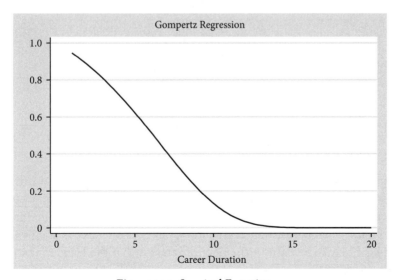

Figure 25.3 Survival Function.

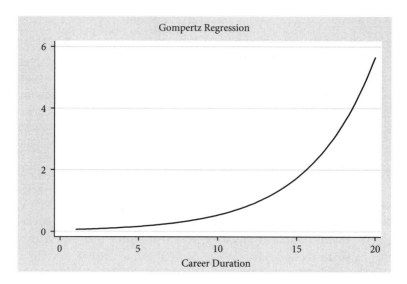

Figure 25.4 Hazard Function.

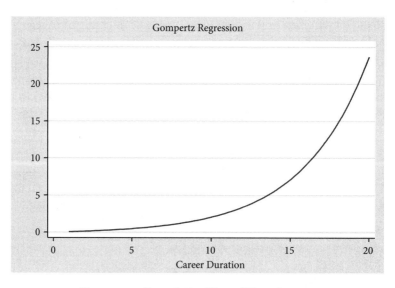

Figure 25.5 Cumulative Hazard Function.

6. SUMMARY AND IMPLICATIONS

This paper analyzes the determinants of career length of referees in the top-tier of German professional soccer, the GBL. Using data from the early 1960s until the most recent season (2008–2009) it appears that career duration is mainly determined by individual performance: The more matches a referee is assigned to, the longer he is likely to remain in the pool of referees that the league puts together before the start of the new season. Moreover, age at the beginning of the career and an increasing competitive pressure are also statistically significant. Referees who start young seem to survive longer but the increasing competitive pressure is detrimental to survival.

This study is the first to look at career duration of match officials in any of the leading European football leagues. Although the results are mostly as expected, it should be extended to the leagues in England, France, Italy, and Spain for a number of reasons: First, the institutional framework, including the selection of referees, varies considerably across the leagues. Second, and equally important, the remuneration of referees varies considerably, too. Although in some countries the referees are only remunerated according to the number of matches they have been assigned to (such as France), they also receive fixed up-front payments in other leagues (such as England, Italy, and Spain). Comparing the duration of individual careers in different institutional environments would, therefore, allow the researcher to better understand how selection and incentive effects interact. This, in turn, would allow designing tournament incentive systems that better align the interests of principals (here, football associations) and agents (here, referees).

NOTES

1 See, inter alia, Frick (2007a, 2007b), Frick, Pietzner, and Prinz (2007, 2009), Frick and Simmons (2008), Barros, Frick, and Passos (2009), Barros, Frick, and Prinz (2010), Goddard and Wilson (2009).
2 In the season 2008/2009 the 36 first and second division clubs in Germany generated aggregate revenues of more than €2 billion. Average player salaries as well as average head coach salaries peaked at €1.4 million per year (own calculations based on aggregate information provided by Deutsche Fussball-Liga 2010).
3 The assistants' role has changed considerably over the years. Initially, they were only responsible for the application of the "offside rule," while today they use modern communication technology ("headsets") that enable them to communicate verbally with the referee, pointing out fouls and other offenses the referee may not have registered.
4 Recently, FIFA has introduced what is called a "fourth man" whose job it is to control the activities on the two benches, that is, to monitor the teams' head coaches, support staff and substitute players.
5 Prior to 1996/1997 the size of that pool was considerably larger, ranging from 25 in 1995/1996 to 36 in 1989/90.
6 In the summer of 1963 the GBL started its inaugural season with 16 teams that had been admitted out of 46 applicants (for an overview see Frick 2006). Prior to the start of the third season (in the summer of 1965) the number of clubs was increased to 18 and following the reunification of East and West Germany, the GBL in 1991/92 expanded once again (now to 20 teams) to integrate the two top clubs from the former first division in East Germany. After that season, however, the size of the league was again reduced to the traditional number of clubs (n=18) by relegating four teams and promoting only two. Since each team plays each other club twice during a season—once at home and once on the opponent's ground—the number of matches

to be officiated was 256 in each of the first two seasons, 360 in 1991/92 and 306 in the remaining 43 years, resulting in 14,030 matches.

7 Using match data from the seasons 1995/1996–2004/2005 (n = 3,060 matches) published by "Kicker" soccer magazine Frick, Gürtler, and Prinz (2009) as well as Frick, Gürtler, Prinz, and Wiendl (2009) find that referees whose performance in a particular match is evaluated with grade 3,0 (acceptable; the mean) have to wait one week longer until their next match compared to referees whose last evaluation was 2,0 (good).

8 Initially, the age limit for referees was 50 years. Over the years this mandatory retirement age was gradually reduced to today's level of 47. Irrespective of their age, the referees' physical fitness is assessed at the start of each season.

9 The two assistants are paid half of what the referee receives. Moreover, about half of the referees in the pool are nominated by the DFB to officiate in international cup competitions, such as the Champions League, where considerable match fees are paid, too.

10 Compared to their colleagues in the other "Top 4" leagues in Europe, German referees are still "semiprofessionals" at best. Apart from their match fees, referees in England receive a fixed annual salary of €53,000, in Spain the respective amount is €50,484 and in Italy €32,400 (however, in the English "Premier League" as well as in the Spanish "Primera Division," the match fees are considerably lower; see Frick, Gürtler, and Prinz 2009: 315).

11 Of the 282 individuals in the sample 32 were relegated from the pool of referees once and returned again after one or more seasons. Another seven persons reappeared twice, that is they experienced two career interruptions. Thus, the number of spells is 328 while the number of persons is 282. Moreover, time at risk for the number of person-years is 1,770 (see Table 25.2) while it is 1,674 for the spell-years.

12 In both cases the Fleming-Harrington test for equality of the survivor function yields a statistically insignificant Chi^2-value (2.61 and 1.89). The Cox regression-based test and the Wilcoxon test deliver virtually identical results.

13 Moreover, in 13 out of 282 cases (4.6 percent) the number of matches per year is lower than one, indicating that these referees have been temporarily removed from the pool and have been nominated again one or more years later.

14 In both, the Cox- and the Gompertz-model presented below the robust variance estimator (Lin and Wei 1989) has been used because the same individuals appear repeatedly in the risk pool and the robust calculation tries to account for that "clustering."

15 When the models are not nested, that is when the sets of right-hand side variables are different, the "Akaike Information Criterion" (Akaike 1974) can (and should) be used to discriminate between alternative estimations.

16 The results of these estimations are, of course, available from the author upon request.

17 Recall that the empirical analysis is conducted at the person- and not at the person-year-level. This implies that in the findings reported below I cannot control for the impact of mandatory retirement on career length. I do, however, briefly report the results of the more detailed analyses. Since the findings are—apart from the impact of age—surprisingly similar to the ones discussed here I decided to present the results of the less complex estimation.

18 The detailed calculations are available from the author upon request. Only three referees in the sample started their careers at lower ages (at 23 and 26, respectively). In order to make it into the first division by the age of 26, a referee must have started his career at the age of 16 or 17 already. This, in turn, is unusually early, because

very young referees are said not to have enough "authority" to officiate a football match—be it in the first division or at a lower level of the league hierarchy.

19 Additional estimations with more disaggregated data (i.e. at the referee-year-level) reveal that the age at which a referee maximizes the annual number of matches he is assigned to is 37. More important, the mandatory retirement age adds a particular type of truncation that somewhat distorts the estimation with respect to age (i.e. an additional dummy for age 47 in results not reported here leads to statistical insignificance of the coefficient of age). Moreover, accumulated games refereed as my preferred measure of experience proved to be statistically insignificant while the dummy for returning referees (i.e. those who had to interrupt their careers due to poor performance) was negative and significant, indicating that they have a higher probability of being ejected again very quickly. The detailed results are available upon request.

20 The perhaps surprising results for referees of foreign nationality (their hazard risk is about 90 percent lower than that for Germans while it is increased more than five-fold for every match they officiate) are easy to explain: The foreigners (exclusively referees from Austria and Switzerland) were participants in a "guest program" of the DFB in the 1980s that was initiated to offer to the top referees from the two small football nations an opportunity to gain professional experience in front of large(r) crowds. Thus, their status was completely different in the sense that they did not have to qualify for the pool of referees but were invited to officiate one or two matches per season instead.

21 The respective kernel density plots are available from the author upon request. This change from a normal to a bimodal distribution of career lengths also explains why the survivor functions for the different decades are not significantly different from each other: Since the curve for the first and the last decade, for example, intersect once, the tests fail to find a significant difference.

REFERENCES

Akaike, H. 1974. A new look at the statistical model identification. IEEE Transaction and Automatic Control AC-19: 716–723.

Barros, C., B. Frick, and J. Passos. 2009. Coaching for survival: The hazards of head coach careers in the German Bundesliga. *Applied Economics,* 41: 3303–3311.

Barros, C., B. Frick, and J. Prinz. 2010. Analyzing head coach dismissals in the German Bundesliga with a mixed logit approach. *European Journal of Operational Research,* 200: 151–159.

Bender, T. 2003. Bundesliga-Lexikon: Das offizielle Nachschlagewerk, *Zumikon:* Sportverlag Europa.

Buraimo, B., D. Forrest, and R. Simmons. 2010. The twelfth man? Refereeing bias in English and German Soccer. *Journal of the Royal Statistical Society,* Series A, 173: 431–449.

Cox, D.R. 1972. Regression models and life-tables (with Discussion). *Journal of the Royal Statistical Society Series B,* 34: 187–220.

Deutsche Fußball-Liga. 2010. Bundesliga 2010: Die wirtschaftliche Situation im Lizenzfußball. Frankfurt.

Frick, B. 2006. Football in Germany. In *Handbook on the economics of sport,* eds. W. Andreff, and S. Szymanski, 486–496. Cheltenham: Edward Elgar.

Frick, B. 2007a. The soccer players' labour market. *Scottish Journal of Political Economy*, 54: 422–446.

Frick, B. 2007b. Salary determination and the pay-performance relationship in professional soccer: Evidence from Germany. In *Sports economics after fifty years: Essays in honour of Simon Rottenberg*, eds. P. Rodriguez, S. Késenne, and J. Garcia, 125–146. Oviedo: Ediciones de la Universidad de Oviedo.

Frick, B., O. Gürtler, and J. Prinz. 2009. Men in black: Monitoring and performance of German soccer referees. In *Football: Economics of a passion*, eds. H. Dietl, E. Franck, and H. Kempf, 309–321. Schorndorf: Hofmann.

Frick, B., O. Gürtler, J. Prinz, and A. Wiendl. 2009. Einkommens- oder Reputationsmaximierung? Eine empirische Untersuchung der Vergütung und Leistung von Bundesliga-Schiedsrichtern. *Die Betriebswirtschaft*, 69: 69–83.

Frick, B., G. Pietzner, and J. Prinz. 2007. Career duration in a competitive environment: The labor market for soccer players in Germany. *Eastern Economic Journal*, 33: 429–442.

Frick, B., G. Pietzner, and J. Prinz. 2009. Team performance and individual career duration: Evidence from the German Bundesliga. In *Myths and facts about football: The economics and psychology of the world's greatest sport*, eds. P. Andersson, P. Ayton, and C. Schmidt, 327–348. Cambridge: Cambridge Scholars Press.

Frick, B., and J. Prinz. 2006. Crisis? What crisis? The financial situation of professional soccer in Germany. *Journal of Sports Economics*, 7: 60–75.

Frick, B., and R. Simmons. 2008. The impact of managerial quality on organizational performance: Evidence from German soccer. *Managerial and Decision Economics*, 29: 593–600.

Goddard, J., and J.O.S. Wilson. 2009. Racial discrimination in English professional football: Evidence from an empirical analysis of players' career progression. *Cambridge Journal of Economics*, 33: 295–316.

Kahn, L. M. 2000. The sports business as a labor market laboratory. *Journal of Economic Perspectives*, 14: 75–94.

Kiefer, N. 1988. Economic duration data and hazard functions. *Journal of Economic Literature*, 26: 646–679.

Lin, D. Y., and L. J. Wei. 1989. The robust inference for the Cox Proportional Hazards Model. *Journal of the American Statistical Association*, 84: 1074–1078.

Rosen, S., and A. Sanderson. 2001. Labour markets in professional sports. *Economic Journal*, 111: F47–F68.

Simmons, R. 2009. Fan pressure and football outcomes. In *Myths and facts about football: The economics and psychology of the world's greatest sport*, eds. P. Andersson, P. Ayton, and C. Schmidt, 191–212. Cambridge: Cambridge Scholars Press.

INDEX

....

Arena Football League, 250
Arrow, Kenneth, 152
Ars Conjectandi (Bernoulli), 197
Arsenal, 68, 287
Asian Football Confederation (AFC), 450
Association for Intercollegiate Athletics for
       Women (AIAW), 405–6
Atkinson, G. S., 430
Atkinson, Scott E., 232–33
Atlanta Braves, 66, 73
attendance
   after hosting World Cup, 456–57
   March Madness and, 379–80
   NHL, 161–62, 162*f*
   NIT, 379–80, 390n1
   outcome uncertainty, 29
   success and, 16n11
   UOH research and, 29
   violence and, 163–66
auctions, all-pay, 6, 16n5
Automobile Racing Club of America
       (ARCA), 320
Auto-Regressive Conditional
       Heteroskedasticity (ARCH), 432

Baade, Robert A., 356–57, 378, 428, 453–55,
       472, 478, 480
Balsdon, Ed, 379
Baltimore Colts, 223–24, 241
Banerjee, Anurag N., 184–85
Barcelona, 68
Barclays Scottish Open, 306
Barnes, G. M., 419n1–420n1
Barney, J. B., 284
Barro, Robert, 339
Barros, C. B., 490
Base Ball Players' Fraternity, 101
"The Baseball Players' Labor Market"
       (Rottenberg), 117
basketball. *See also* March Madness; National
       Basketball Association; National
       Invitational Tournament
   in China, 152
   fixed-effects models, 415*t*, 416*t*
   global structure of leagues, 152
   men's coaches, NCAA, 412–14,
       412*t*, 413*t*
   NCAA, 360
   Olympic, 461
Bass, Ellen, 379
Bauman, A., 431

Baumann, Robert, 480
BCS. *See* Bowl Championship Series
Beane, Billy, 51–52, 73
Becker, Gary, 167, 285–86, 339
behavioral economics, 214–15
Belichick, Bill, 199
Bell, Bert, 224, 248
Bellman, Richard E., 200
Bellman equations, 200–201
Berkowitz, Steve, 351
Berlin Wall, 174n1
Berman, G., 428
Berman, S. L., 285, 293, 296
Bernard, A., 438
Bernoulli, Jakob, 197
Bernstein, L., 419n1
Berra, Yogi, 476
Berri, David, 143, 198, 202, 208–9, 214, 252,
       463
Berry, Robert C., 247
Bertsch, Shane, 303, 313
betting odds, 29
BHPS. *See* British Household Panel Survey
Big Five leagues, 289–90
   foreign players in, 291*t*
   globalization of, 290–91
   local talent in, 295*t*
   revenues, 289*t*
   salary caps in, 133
   television ratings, 72
Bird, Larry, 75n10, 129
Bird, P., 458
Blackmun, Harry, 104
blackout restrictions, 93, 225–26, 242
"blood lust" effect, 165, 169–72
Blue, Vida, 109
Bodvarsson, Orn B., 144–45
Bognanno, Michael L., 192, 302, 316
bonuses. *See* player bonuses
Borghesi, Richard, 252
Borland, Melvin V., 352
Boronico, Jess S., 207
Bosman, Jean Marc, 261, 278
Bosman ruling, 137, 259, 261–63, 290
   impact of, 263–66, 460
   youth development and, 293
Boston College, 360
Boston Red Sox, 63
Boulier, Bryan, 252, 378
Bourgheas, S., 279n2
Bowen, William G., 355, 357, 360, 365–67

ISC. *See* International Speedway
    Corporation
Italian Serie A, 289–90

Jaccard, J., 419n1
Jacksonville Jaguars, 231
Jasmand, S., 428
Jennings, Hugh, 100
Joe Robbie Stadium, 234
Johnston, Rick, 201, 214
Jones, John Colin Henry, 163–66
Jordan, Jeremy D., 207
Jordan, Michael, 72
Journal of Quantitative Analysis in Sports,
    217n5
Journal of Sports Economics, 18, 20, 25–26, 32
Jozsa, Frank P., 251

Kahane, Leo, 331
Kahn, Lawrence M., 110, 144–45, 339
Kamerschen, David R., 380
Kanazawa, Mark T., 145
Kasimati, E., 428
Kavetsos, G., 430, 432, 455
Keenan, Diane, 144–45
Keloharju, M., 302
Kennedy, Lesa France, 334n37
kernel density plots, 499n21
Késenne, Stefan, 123, 233, 263
Kesselring, R. G., 361
Kicker, 489
Kiis, Mike, 232
Killefer, Bill, 101–2
knock-out format, 4
Koch, James V., 144–45
Korr, Charles, 103
Koufax, Sandy, 95n16
Kovash, Kenneth, 201, 206–7, 209, 213
Krautmann, Anthony, 86–87, 143
Kuenn, Harvey, 103
Kuethe, Todd, 378
Kuhn, Bowie, 85, 104, 109
Kuper, S., 466
Kuypers, T., 260, 283

labor issues, in MLB, 88–90
labor markets
    features of sports, 260
    fixed-supply, 42
    in global era, 140–42
    human capital formation and, 288–95

international, 137–38
NBA, 143–45
regulations, 282
teams in global, 138–40
theories, 107–9
labor mobility, 137–38, 140–41
Ladies Professional Golf Association
    (LPGA), 303
Lahman, Sean, 199
Lajoie, Napoleon, 101
La Liga, 464
"Larry Bird" exception, 75n10
Larsen, A., 252
Las Vegas Motor Speedway, 326
Lauze, Michael A., 355
Lazear, Edward P., 150, 303
leagues. *See also* closed leagues; open leagues
    closed *v.* open, 4
    competitive balance defense and, 10
    cooperation within, 81–82
    expansions, 250–51
    global structure of, 152
    home-and-away, 7
    mixed with profit- and win-maximization,
        44, 47–49
    profit-maximization, 38
    quality of, 40
    restrictions on entry and, 90–91
    structures, 4–6
    win-maximization, 38
leakages, 476–77
Leeds, E. M., 466
Leeds, M., 428–29, 466
Leeds United, 68
left-censored (at zero) model, 209, 218n18
Lehn, Kenneth, 109–10, 143
leisure participation, 433, 434f, 434t
Lenz, Heinz Otto, 261–62
"Letter to a Friend on Sets in Court Tennis"
    (Bernoulli), 197
Levitt, Steven D., 201, 206–7, 209, 213
Lewis, Michael, 51, 215
Lima, Anthony, 95n27
Litan, Robert E., 357, 361, 422n26
Liverpool, 68
Lloyd, Earl, 140
Lockett, A., 285–86, 293, 296–97
Logit regression, 57, 310, 315t
Lombardi, Vince, 242
London Stock Exchange, 432
Long, James E., 365–66